The 'Lip

 The 'Egyptian Goatee'

 The 'Shaft Beard'

 The 'Full Beard'

We carry large & comprehensive stocks of all 4 kings.

Mark Bloxham
STAMPS LTD

W: www.philatelic.co.uk   T: +44 (0)1661 871953   E: mark@philatelic.co.uk

Stanley Gibbons Auctions

Seeking consignments for future auctions

If you are looking to sell your collection or have single quality items, then come to Stanley Gibbons Auctions where:

- Outstanding realisations and percentage of lots sold.
- Mailing list and client list second to none.
- We can also arrange special terms for single owner collections, providing a dedicated sale catalogue where appropriate.
- We are the only major central London philatelic auction house with a 15% Buyers premium.

Stanley Gibbons Auctions is perfect for sellers and buyers and for service is second to none.

Only 15% Buyer's Premium

Please contact Ryan Epps **repps@stanleygibbons.com**
or Steve Matthews **smatthews@stanleygibbons.com** or call **020 7836 8444**

Stanley Gibbons Limited
399 Strand, London, WC2R 0LX
+44 (0)20 7836 8444
www.stanleygibbons.com

GREAT BRITAIN SPECIALISED STAMP CATALOGUE

King Edward VII to King George VI

Volume 2

Page of die proofs for the 1913 Royal Cypher profile head issue from the H. A. Richardson Archive

Stanley Gibbons
Great Britain Specialised
Stamp Catalogue

Volume 2

King Edward VII to King George VI

14th Edition

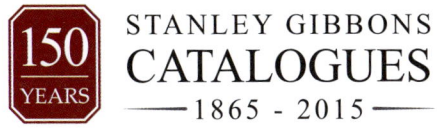

Stanley Gibbons Ltd · London and Ringwood

By Appointment to
Her Majesty The Queen
Philatelists
Stanley Gibbons Ltd
London

Published by Stanley Gibbons Ltd
Editorial, Publications Sales Offices
and Distribution Centre:
7 Parkside, Christchurch Road, Ringwood,
Hants BH24 3SH

© Stanley Gibbons Ltd 2015

Copyright Notice

The contents of this Catalogue, including the numbering system and illustrations, are fully protected by copyright. No part of this publication may be reproduced, stored in a retrieval system, or transmitted in any form or by any means, electronic, mechanical, photocopying, recording or otherwise, without the prior permission of Stanley Gibbons Limited. Requests for such permission should be addressed to the Catalogue Editor. This Catalogue is sold on condition that it is not, by way of trade or otherwise, lent, re-sold, hired out, circulated or otherwise disposed of other than in its complete, original and unaltered form and without a similar condition including this condition being imposed on the subsequent purchaser.

1st edition – February 1967
Reprinted – April 1967
2nd edition – July 1970
Reprinted – September 1970
3rd edition – March 1974
4th edition – May 1978
Reprinted – June 1979
5th edition – May 1980
6th edition – March 1984
7th edition – November 1986
8th edition – October 1989
9th edition – January 1993
10th edition – March 1996
11th edition – October 1999
12th edition – July 2005
13th edition – October 2009
14th edition – July 2015

British Library Cataloguing in
Publication Data.
A catalogue record for this book is available from the British Library.

Errors and omissions excepted. The colour
reproduction of stamps is only as accurate as
the printing process will allow.

ISBN-10: 0-85259-841-6
ISBN-13: 978-0-85259-841-2

Item No. 0286-15

Printed by Bell & Bain Ltd, Scotland

Contents

Preface xi
Introductory Notes xiii

The King Edward VII Issues (Section M)

General Notes 1
Section MA: Postage Issues (1902–13) 18
Section MB: Booklet Panes (1906–11) 64
Section MO: Departmental Official Issues (1902–04) 66

The King George V Issues (Section N)

General Notes on the Letterpress Issues 74
Section NA: The Downey Head Issue (1911–12) 80
Section NB: The Profile Head Issue, Wmk Royal Cypher (1912–22) 105
Section NC: The Profile Head Issue, Wmk Block Cypher (1924–26) 149
Section ND: Booklet Panes in Letterpress (1911–24) 166
Section NE: General Notes on the Photogravure Issues ... 176
The Photogravure Issue (1934–36) 178
Section NF: Booklet Panes in Photogravure (1935) 187
Section NG: General Notes on the Recess-printed High Values 192
The Recess-printed High Values (1913–34).... 197
Section NH: Commemorative Issues (1924–35) 209

The King Edward VIII Issue (Section P) 221
Section PB: Booklet Panes in Photogravure (1936) 228

The King George VI Issue (Section Q) 230
General Notes on the Photogravure Low Values 230
Section QA: Photogravure Low Values (1937–51) 231
Section QB: Booklet Panes in Photogravure (1937–54) 253
Section QC: Recess-printed "Arms" High Values (1939–48) 263
Section QD: Recess-printed "Festival" High Values (1951) 267
Section QE: Commemorative Issues (1937–51) 268

The Postage Due Stamps (Section R)
General Notes 275
Section RA: King George V (1914–31) 276
Section RB: King Edward VIII (1936–37) 281
Section RC: King George VI (1937–52) 282

Appendices
Appendix 1: Perforators 284
Appendix 2: Post Office Booklets of Stamps 291
Appendix 3: Booklet Pane Precancellations 319
Appendix 4: "Specimen" and "Cancelled" Overprints 321
Appendix 5: Protective Underprints 323
Appendix 6: Postage Rates 324
Appendix 7: Post Office Savings Bank Stamps 327
Appendix 8: Channel Islands. The German Occupation 1940 - 45 329
Appendix 9: Further Reading 334

Checklists
King Edward VII
Checklist of King Edward VII Issues 17
Checklist of King Edward VII Booklet Panes 64
King George V
Checklist of King George V Issues 78
Checklist of King George V Booklet Panes in Letterpress 166
Checklist of King George V Booklet Panes in Photogravure 187
King Edward VIII
Checklist of King Edward VIII Booklet Panes.. 228
King George VI
Checklist of King George VI Issues 230/1
Checklist of King George VI Booklet Panes 253

ITEMS SELECTED FROM CURRENT STOCK

Fine Stamps of Great Britain
Andrew Vaughan Philatelic

1910 7d Hentschel Half Tone Essay MB/3 Orange. A superb small format example

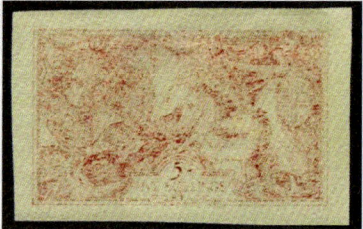

Sg 401 var 5/- Rough Plate Proof on Buff Paper in Carmine. A Fine 4 margin example.

Sg 404 £1 Green. A superb unmounted mint example

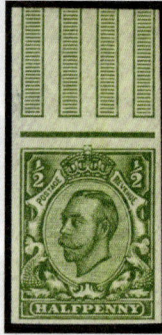

Sg 346b ½d Green IMPERF. A superb unmounted mint top marginal example

Sg 420c 1½d Red Brown "PRINTED ON THE GUM SIDE". A superb unmounted mint example

SG 322a ½d Green perf 14 superb used example

SG 381 wi 5d Brown inverted watermark. A superb unmounted mint example

Sg 285a 3d Grey on Lemon. A fine mounted mint example accompanied by a BPA certificate

Sg 361a 1d Scarlet Vermilion PRINTED ON BACK. A very fine unmounted mint example accompanied by a BPA certificate

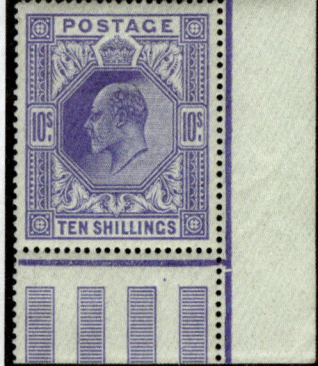

Sg 319 10/- Blue. A superb Post Office fresh unmounted mint corner marginal example with excellent

Sg 320 £1 Deep Green. A superb unmounted mint bottom margin example

Sg 474 Var 10d Turquoise Blue. A superb mounted mint strip of 5 with massive "DRY PRINT"

Andrew Vaughan Philatelics Limited
PO Box 6051 Tamworth
Staffordshire B78 3JB England

Tel: 01827 63367
Email: sales@stampsgb.co.uk
www.stampsgb.co.uk

Fine Stamps of Great Britain
Andrew Vaughan Philatelics

Thinking of selling your collection? WE PAY TOP PRICES!

- Full Mail Order Service
- Major Stamp Shows Attended
- Illustrated Monthly List On Request

Andrew Vaughan Philatelics Limited
PO Box 6051 Tamworth
Staffordshire B78 3JB England

Tel: 01827 63367
Email: sales@stampsgb.co.uk
www.stampsgb.co.uk

Embassy Philatelists

Est. 30 Years

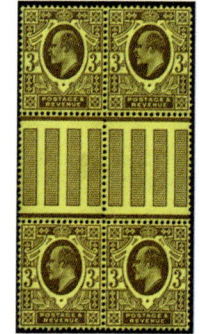

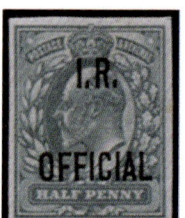

Imprimatur

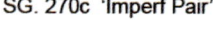

SG. 270c 'Imperf Pair'

**RETAIL LISTS & POSTAL AUCTIONS
PRODUCED MONTHLY
CATALOGUE SENT FREE ON REQUEST
1000'S OF ITEMS TO VIEW AND BUY
ON OUR WEBSITE**

www.embassystamps.co.uk

Email: info@embassystamps.co.uk
Tel: 02392 412 512

IF YOU BUY ONE G.B. BOOK THIS YEAR....
THEN TREAT YOURSELF TO A 'SEAHORSE-FEST'

WE HAVE TAKEN THE HIGHLIGHTS FROM THE TEN VOLUME SEAHORSE COLLECTION OF LEONARD LICHT AND CONDENSED IT INTO ONE BOOK FOR SPECIALIST AND NOVICE ALIKE TO ENJOY...

PRICE £25
(+ £7 p&p inland, £12 overseas)

PRICE £25
(+ £7 p&p inland, £12 overseas)

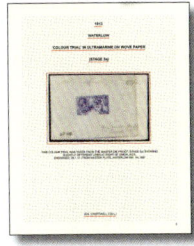 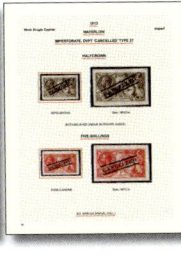 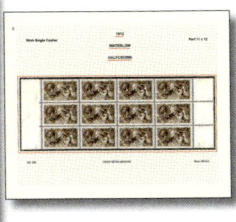 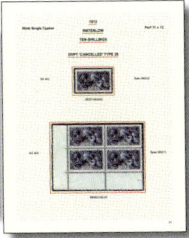 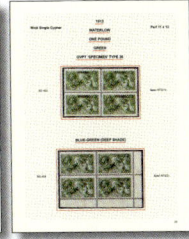

EBAY SHOP
Submit a 'best offer' today
http://stores.ebay.co.uk/
embassy-stamps

Embassy Philatelists Est. 30 Years
P.O. BOX 161, CHICHESTER, W.SUSSEX PO19 3SU
Tel: 02392 412 512   Fax: 02392 412 513
Email: info@embassystamps.co.uk
www.embassystamps.co.uk

BUYING
From single items to major collections, for a fast professional transaction call us today.

"EMAILS MAY HAVE KILLED THE ART OF LETTER WRITING.

BUT GOOD INVESTMENT NEWS IS STILL DELIVERED WITH STAMPS."

Invest in History

Whether you're looking to protect and grow your wealth, plan for retirement or create a legacy, rare stamps and coins could provide a safe haven investment option for you - they are tangible asset classes with a history of performance. Begin to build your portfolio from as little as £10,000.

Find out more at **sginvest.co.uk/4kings**
or call **0845 026 7170**

Est. 1856
STANLEY GIBBONS
Investment

The value of your investment can go down as well as up and you may not get back what you put in. Stamps and certain other collectibles are not designated investments for the purposes of the Financial Services and Markets Act 2000 (Regulated Activities) Order 2001 and as such are not subject to regulation by the Financial Conduct Authority (FCA) or otherwise. Past performance or experience does not necessarily give a guide for the future. Minimum investment £10,000. Stanley Gibbons Investment does not provide valuations; please visit www.stanleygibbons.com for information on valuations, and investment.stanleygibbons.com for full terms and conditions. Please note: Past performance does not necessarily give a guide for the future.

Preface

2015 is an important year for Stanley Gibbons Catalogues, for it was 150 years ago that Edward Stanley Gibbons published his first *Descriptive Price List and Catalogue of British, Colonial and Foreign Postage Stamps*, a long title for what was, in fact, a simplified listing of what he had in stock at the time.

It did not stay that way for long, though, as Gibbons and his successor as editor, Charles Phillips, gradually developed and expanded the listings, so that by the turn of the century it was already recognisable as the *Stanley Gibbons Stamp Catalogue* we have today.

As the hobby developed, however, the ways in which collectors followed it became more disparate and a 'one size fits all' catalogue was no longer suitable for everyone. Before the War the *Simplified Catalogue* was born and after it a need for a more specialised catalogue for Great Britain collectors was met in October 1963, when the first edition of Volume 1 of this work was published with great success, to be followed in February 1967 by the first edition of Volume 2.

Now 150 years on from that first *"Descriptive Price List and Catalogue"* we are pleased to bring you the 14th edition of Volume 2 of the *Great Britain Specialised Catalogue*. It might be supposed that after 48 years and 13 previous editions, there would be little new to add to it, but, in truth, while every catalogue, whether it includes new issues or not, contains a vast amount of new material, we cannot recall any specialised volume published in recent years which has contained quite so many improvements.

As a result, there are a great many contributors who we wish to thank. First, we must acknowledge the help of Douglas Muir RDP, whose research into the introduction of the first stamps of King George V was published in his 2010 book, *George V and the G.P.O., Stamps, Conflict and Creativity* and which he has now incorporated into sections N, NA and NB, correcting some long-held misconceptions concerning the sequence of events which led up to their issue.

Members of the Great Britain Philatelic Society have once again provided enormous amount of assistance. Past President Ian Harvey in most cases co-ordinating contributions. Ian himself has been responsible for the comprehensive listings of preparatory material for the introduction of stamp booklets, including the earlier trials which took place during Queen Victoria's reign and the essays and proofs of the "Four Kings"

period. He has also masterminded the improvements to the King George V controls and perforation types and added several new items, including the "wide" and "close" Harrison controls.

Elsewhere, The Postage Due listings have been substantially expanded to include original artwork, proofs and colour trials, as well as several new "cancelled" overprints, and the various essays for the King Edward VIII definitives are now illustrated and listed, while throughout the book there are new varieties, shades, controls, "specimen" overprints and much else besides. Thank you to all who contributed to this.

A full list of acknowledgements appears following the introductory notes, but we would particularly like to mention the contributions of Ross Candlish, Mike Jackson, Michael Sefi, Leslie Wilkinson and Anthony Zenios, while Bryan Kearsley has reviewed the "Seahorse" listings, his rewriting of which was such a key feature of the 13th edition.

The appearance on the market of material from a number of important collections of the period has allowed us not only to add several new items to the listings but has also provided the catalyst for perhaps the most obvious development to this volume; the addition of colour illustrations. We are grateful to the many collectors, dealers and auction houses who have assisted in this. The work is clearly on-going, however, and offers to advance the process for the next edition would be gratefully received.

Prices have, as always, been very carefully reviewed and updated in line with the current market. At the same time, a careful reassessment of the relative scarcities in popular areas such as shades, controls and booklets has resulted in some surprising increases as the true scarcity of some previously underappreciated items has been recognised.

Finally, we would like to thank our colleagues in both the Great Britain Specialist and in the Publications departments for their assistance and you, the catalogue user, for your patience in waiting for this volume, which has been so long in coming. We trust that you feel it has been worthwhile.

Hugh Jefferies
Vince Cordell

June 2015

WE SPECIALISE IN THE ISSUES OF
GREAT BRITAIN
1840–1970

PROOFS — ESSAYS — COLOUR TRIALS
CONTROLS — VARIETIES
STITCHED BOOKLETS — BOOKLET PANES
COIL LEADERS — ETC

Please send for our FREE illustrated price lists,
or visit www.candlishmccleery.com

WANTED

GREAT BRITAIN STAMPS — Mint or Used

We must buy, and cash is readily available should you wish to dispose of any of the following:
ISSUED STAMPS (on or off cover); PROOFS, ESSAYS, SPECIMEN and CANCELLED OVERPRINTS;
POSTMASTERS' and POST OFFICE NOTICES with or without stamps;
OLD POSTAL PAMPHLETS; BOOKLETS; COILS; ETC.

We also purchase collections of general or specialised Great Britain.

Please send details in the first place, and, if appropriate, arrangements can be made to value your collection. Alternatively, stamps can be sent by registered post and an offer made by return.

CANDLISHMcCLEERYLTD

PO BOX 2   HANLEY CASTLE   WORCESTER WR8 0ZF
TEL: 01684 311771   FAX: 01684 311778
EMAIL: websales@candlishmccleery.com

 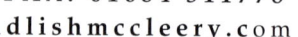

www.candlishmccleery.com

Introductory Notes

The aim of this catalogue is to classify in specialised form the stamps of Great Britain, to give distinguishing numbers to them and to quote prices which are current with Stanley Gibbons Ltd. at the time of going to press and at which they will supply if in stock.

Catalogue Numbers
All Specialised Catalogue numbers include a prefix letter or letters; shades normally have a number in brackets and subsequent varieties have letter identifications.

Essays, Die Proofs, Plate Proofs, Colour Trials, etc. do not have catalogue numbers which should therefore be described in full.

For each basic stamp a cross-reference is included to the S.G. catalogue number in the 2015 editions of the Stanley Gibbons *Commonwealth & British Empire Stamps Catalogue, 1840–1970* and the *Great Britain Concise Catalogue*.

Prices
Prices quoted in this catalogue are the selling prices of Stanley Gibbons Ltd. at the time the book went to press. They are for stamps in fine condition; in issues where condition varies prices may be higher for the superb and lower for the sub-standard. The unused prices for stamps of King Edward VII and King George V are for unmounted mint or lightly hinged examples. Unused prices for stamps of King Edward VIII and King George VI are for unmounted mint (though when not available unmounted, stamps are often supplied at a lower price).

Prices for used stamps refer to fine postally used examples. All prices are subject to change without prior notice and no guarantee is given to supply all stamps priced, since it is not possible to keep every catalogued item in stock.

If a variety exists in more than one shade it is priced for the commonest shade and will be worth correspondingly more in a scarcer shade. Except where otherwise stated, varieties are priced for single examples and extra examples required to make up positional blocks or booklet panes would be valued as normals.

Cylinder blocks containing varieties are indicated by an asterisk against the price (which includes the cost of the variety).

King Edward VII Controls are priced for unused lightly hinged corner pairs according to perforator type. Controls of the King George V Downey Head issues in Section NA are priced likewise, but all other Letterpress Controls, including the postage dues, are priced as unused singles, extra stamps being valued as normals, except in the case of non-standard perforation types, which are priced in strips of three. Controls and/or cylinder numbers of photogravure issues are priced for appropriate blocks according to circumstances, their size being stated in the lists.

Prices quoted for stamps "on cover" are for a single example of the stamp concerned on cover. Covers bearing either multiples of the stamp or other values used in conjunction with it will generally command a higher price.

The prices quoted for booklet panes are for lightly hinged panes with good perforations and complete with the binding margin. Prices for complete booklets are for those containing panes with average perforations as it is unusual for all panes to be well perforated.

Guarantee
All stamps supplied by Stanley Gibbons Ltd. are guaranteed originals in the following terms:

If not as described, and returned by the purchaser, we undertake to refund the price paid to us in the original transaction. If any stamp is certified as genuine by the Expert Committee of the Royal Philatelic Society, London, or by B.P.A. Expertising Ltd., the purchaser shall not be entitled to make any claim against us for any error, omission or mistake in such certificate.

Consumers' statutory rights are not affected by the above guarantee.

Expertisation
We do not give opinions as to the genuineness of stamps. Expert Committees exist for this purpose and enquiry can be made of the Royal Philatelic Society, 41 Devonshire Place, London W1N 1PE, or B.P.A. Expertising Ltd., P.O. Box 1141, Guildford, Surrey GU5 0WR. They do not undertake valuations under any circumstances and fees are payable for their services.

Correspondence
Letters should be addressed to the Catalogue Editor, Stanley Gibbons Ltd., 7 Parkside, Christchurch Road, Ringwood, Hants BH24 3SH, and return postage is appreciated when a reply is sought.

New information and unlisted items for consideration are welcomed.

Please note we do not identify stamps or number them by our Catalogue.

To order from this Catalogue
Always quote the Specialised Catalogue number, mentioning Volume 2, 14th Edition, and where necessary specify additionally the precise item wanted.

Detailed Introductory Notes
Before using the catalogue it is important to study the "General Notes" as these explain the technical background of the issues in question. They are to be found at the beginning of the relevant sections.

Exclusions
In dealing with varieties we record only those for which we can vouch, namely items we have seen and verified for ourselves.

Watermark Illustrations
The illustrations show watermarks as seen from the front of the stamp, except for the Multiple Cypher watermark described under the King George V Letterpress section. Here the watermark is illustrated as seen from the back of the stamp; the side usually chosen for inspection.

Quantities Sold
This information is based on figures published by the Post Office.

National Postal Museum Archive Material
During 1984 and 1985 surplus GB material from the National Postal Museum archives was included in three auction sales. The lots offered were mostly imprimaturs, which were handstamped on the reverse to indicate origin, and specimen overprints. This material is included in special entries, under

Introductory Note / Acknowledgements

headings clearly indicating their origin. Where items included in these sales had been previously listed a dagger is shown alongside the catalogue price.

Subject to the next paragraph, it should be emphasised that only items from lots which were sold at the sales of 26 April 1984, 19 February 1985 and 5 September 1985 are covered by the catalogue entries.

British Postal Museum & Archive Material

As a result of reorganisation in 2004, the NPM collections and archive were reconstututed into a charitable trust, the PBMA. In July 2013, in order to assist the funding of new premises, the BPMA auctioned further surplus GB imprimatur material from its archives. In this sale the imprimaturs did not recieve a handstamp indicating their origin. Where that sale was of duplicate material to the 1983/85 sales, that is indicated by an asterisk (*) in those listings. Otherwise, new items are described and listed separately.

Symbols and Abbreviations

†	(in price column)	does not exist
—	(in price column)	exists or may exist, but no market price is known (a blank conveys the same meaning)
I.	(above price column)	control imperforate selvedge (partially perf. margins are regarded as imperf.)
P.	(above price column)	control selvedge perforated through
*	(against price of a cylinder block)	price includes a listed variety
*	(against cylinder number)	an "abnormal" cylinder (see General Notes to Section ND)
from	(preceding price column)	several items listed, such as a number of different types, for which only the commonest is priced
Cyl	cylinder	
(F)	(after shade)	fluorescent under ultraviolet light (see Section M describing Inks and Shades)
(GBF)		"golden brown" flourescence, variety of (F)
mm.	millimetres	
M/S	manuscript	
No.	number	
NPM	The National Postal Museum, London (now the British Postal Museum & Archive)	
Pl.	plate	
R.	row (thus "R. 6/4" indicates the fourth stamp from the left in the sixth horizontal row from the top of a sheet of stamps)	

Note: Symbols —, ⌊, ⌴, ☐, in control and cylinder number listings for various photogravure issues refer to the shape of the bars bordering the control number.

Acknowledgements

We thank members of the Great Britain Philatelic Society who have once again generously assisted in helping us with the updating of this catalogue.

Particular thanks are due to Eric Abraham, Rowan Baker, Brian Bayford, Mike Board, Ross Candlish, Frank Compton, Garth Denman, Donald Farmborough, Derek Fulluck, John Garnsey, Mike Gatherer, John Gledhill, John Goodman, Trevor Harris, Ian Harvey, Mark Haycock, John Horsey, Mike Jackson, Allan Jones, David Kaiserman, Bryan Kearsley, Andrew Lajer, David Milstead, Philip Milton, Douglas Muir, Chris Owston, Paul Ramsay, Stephen Sayer, Michael Sefi, Tony Stanford, Alan Vaughan, Leslie Wilkinson, Richard Williams, David Wilson, Barrie Wright and Anthony Zenios.

Continuing thanks are due to the Great Britain Philatelic Society and Royal Philatelic Society for permission to use certain illustrations from their publications and to the Royal Mint Museum for the illustrations of Mackennal's South Africa medal and coin model in the introduction to the Profile Head issue. Many of the illustrations in the Seahorse section are taken from *Discovering Seahorses* by Bryan Kearsley and we would like to thank GB Philatelic Publications Ltd and the Author for permission to reproduce them.

STANLEY GIBBONS LTD

Hi, That's me Promoting Philately with Alan on the Alan Titchmarsh Show UK National ITV

When I was Knee-high to A Grasshopper a PUC £1 was £12... Look at it now...

Fortunately I remember it like Yesterday ...

It's one of my earliest philatelic memories. In my first year at senior school, having failed my 11+, and entered the 'B' stream (the 'B' stream learnt French, whereas the 'A' stream learned German) and being the second to last school-boy at senior school wearing short trousers, which is very 'character-forming' ... naturally (one might say) I was drawn to joining the School Stamp Club ...

I've written before about what I thought I was collecting – and what I was *actually* collecting ... so I won't bore you this time. Suffice it to say this is where I saw my 1st P U C £1, and as they say – I was 'hooked'. It's a cracking stamp – almost the 'bellwether', together with the 1d black and £5 orange of collecting GB stamps ...

... and so it seems appropriate on this 'KGV' themed page to mention that it was a used P U C £1 and the asking price (more than a year's pocket money) was £12. It goes without saying that almost 50 years ago I never ever collected a P U C £1 and nowadays a very fine used one is closer to £400 to £500 ... **BUT there is something that I can do about it for Y O U** ... if you are new to my Universal Philatelic Auctions I'll give you YOUR 1st £55 FREE ... so that you can spend it on a P U C £1 or any other of the typically more than 20,000 different lots from almost all countries of the world including up to 5,000 different lots of GB in each of my quarterly auctions.

It's easy to bid in U P A auctions. You've NO pernicious Buyer's Premiums adding up to 25% or more to the cost of your winnings ... and, furthermore, bidding at my auction U P A is RISK-FREE **as all lots are guaranteed**. If Y O U c o l l e c t Great Britain – You NEED a U P A catalogue – it's larger, with Massive Philatelic Choice, **300+ pages, up to 4,000 colour pictures PLUS It's FREE!**

£12 when I was in short trousers

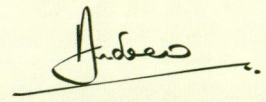

Just turn to the coupon page at the back of this catalogue and contact U P A Now – You've nothing to lose and £55 to gain (and usually we have up to 100 x 1d blacks on offer, up to 9 x £5 Orange and 5 to 10 x £1 P U C. I'm sorry they're not £12 but they're usually better value than retail and your 1st £55 spent is FREE. *Do it Now*

BB STAMPS LTD

Est. 1988

Comprehensive Great Britain Pricelists sent FREE on request.

PO Box 6277, Overton,
Hampshire, RG25 3RN, UK
Tel: 01256 773269
Fax: 01256 771708
Sales@bbstamps.co.uk

Current Price Lists are also available to download at our site in PDF format

www.bbstamps.co.uk

BB STAMPS LTD

Est. 1988

Free fully illustrated price lists sent on request.

PO Box 6277, Overton,
Hampshire, RG25 3RN, UK
Tel: 01256 773269 Fax: 01256 771708
www.bbstamps.co.uk E: Sales@bbstamps.co.uk

BB STAMPS LTD
Est. 1988

Free fully illustrated price lists sent on request.

PO Box 6277, Overton,
Hampshire, RG25 3RN, UK
Tel: 01256 773269 Fax: 01256 771708
www.bbstamps.co.uk E: Sales@bbstamps.co.uk

BB STAMPS LTD

Est. 1988

Free fully illustrated price lists sent on request.

PO Box 6277, Overton,
Hampshire, RG25 3RN, UK
Tel: 01256 773269 Fax: 01256 771708
www.bbstamps.co.uk E: Sales@bbstamps.co.uk

Great Britain illustrated Price List 1840 – 2015

Phone or write for your free copy of our latest 56 page list or visit our website

www.britishstamps.com

Swan Stamps
PO Box 501 Torquay, Devon TQ1 9FE
Phone: 01803 323430 email: steve@britishstamps.com

Give your collection the home it deserves

Frank Godden albums are a labour of love, with each individual album beautifully handmade to an unmistakable and unmatchable quality.

All leaves are now made to the internationally recognised standard for archival paper, the type that is used and recommended by all major museums.

Revered throughout the philatelic world for their supreme quality and craftsmanship, Frank Godden albums are built to last a lifetime and to offer you a lifetime of enjoyment.

If you are passionate about your collection, then Frank Godden provides the home it deserves.

Whether you are looking for the best quality albums, exhibition cases, protectors, leaves or interleaving, you can find whatever you are looking for at Stanley Gibbons, the new home of Frank Godden.

For more information, visit www.stanleygibbons.com/frankgodden

Stanley Gibbons Limited
7 Parkside, Christchurch Road, Ringwood, Hants, BH24 3SH
+44 (0)1425 472 363
www.stanleygibbons.com

IF YOU BUY ONE G.B. BOOK THIS YEAR....
THEN TREAT YOURSELF TO AN 'EDWARDIAN DELIGHT'

WE HAVE TAKEN THE HIGHLIGHTS FROM THE FIFTEEN VOLUME KING EDWARD VII COLLECTION OF LEONARD LICHT AND CONDENSED IT INTO ONE BOOK FOR SPECIALIST AND NOVICE ALIKE TO ENJOY...

PRICE £30
(+ £7 p&p inland, £12 overseas)

PRICE £30
(+ £7 p&p inland, £12 overseas)

PRE-ORDER NOW
DUE TO BE RELEASED AUGUST 2015

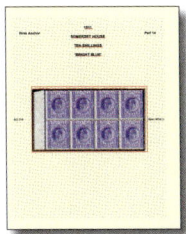 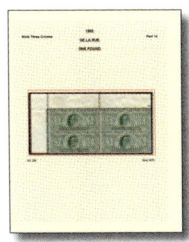   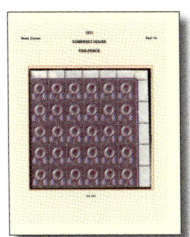

Embassy Philatelists
Est. 30 Years

P.O. BOX 161, CHICHESTER, W.SUSSEX PO19 3SU
Tel: 02392 412 512   *Fax:* 02392 412 513
Email: info@embassystamps.co.uk

www.embassystamps.co.uk

EBAY SHOP
Submit a 'best offer' today
http://stores.ebay.co.uk/embassy-stamps

BUYING
From single items to major collections, for a fast professional transaction call us today.

Mint G.B. Stamps Ltd

Unit 2 Lok 'n' Store, 1-4 Carousel Way, Riverside, Northampton, NN3 9HG
Tel: **01604 406371**   Mobile: **07851 576398**

The only retailer of just unmounted GB material from 1840-1970, if you want perfection you should be talking to us.

We specialise in shades/ listed and unlisted varieties/ watermark varieties and cylinder blocks and have comprehensive stocks of all basic SG listed items from single stamps to full sheets.

SG 175 – Blued paper

SG 108 – 6d Mauve

344a – No cross on crown

N11(6) – scarlet vermillion

SG 394 wi 10d R/c Inv

SG 405-413 De La Rue

N19(9) Intense

SG 264

SG 158 Plate 21

SG 161 Plate 17

www.mintgbstamps.co.uk
email: sales@mintgbstamps.co.uk

Six Great New Lists
from Trevor I. Harris AIEP
Member – The International Association of Expert Philatelists

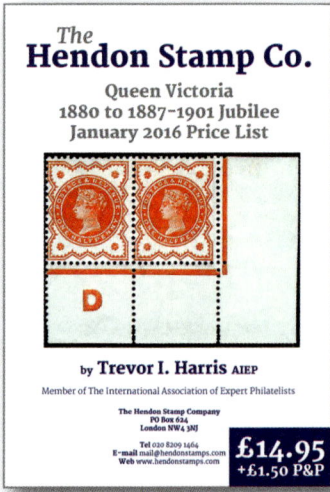

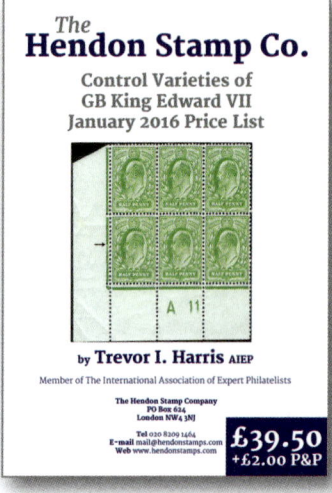
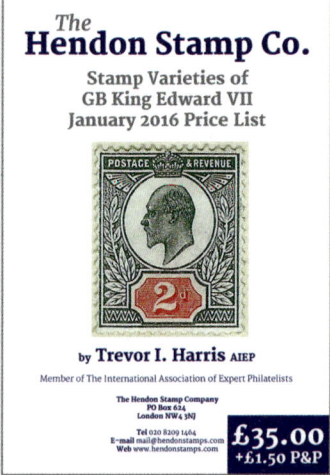
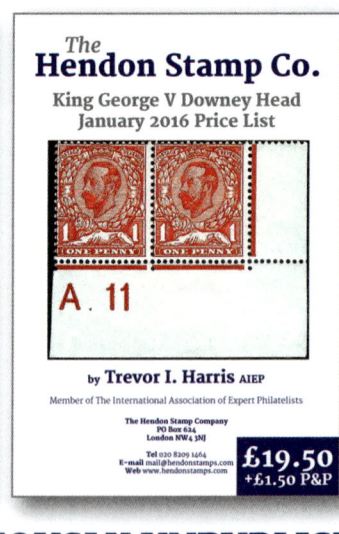
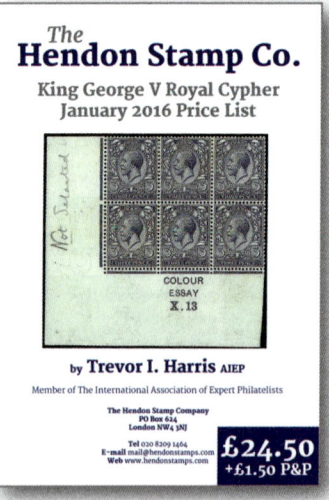

WITH MUCH PREVIOUSLY UNPUBLISHED INFORMATION

The Hendon Stamp Co.
PO Box 624, London NW4 3NJ
Tel: 020 8209 1464
E-mail: mail@hendonstamps.com
Website: www.hendonstamps.com

"It is our pleasure to help anyone with an interest in British stamps"

Ask about our expertisation service for GB 1855 - 1936

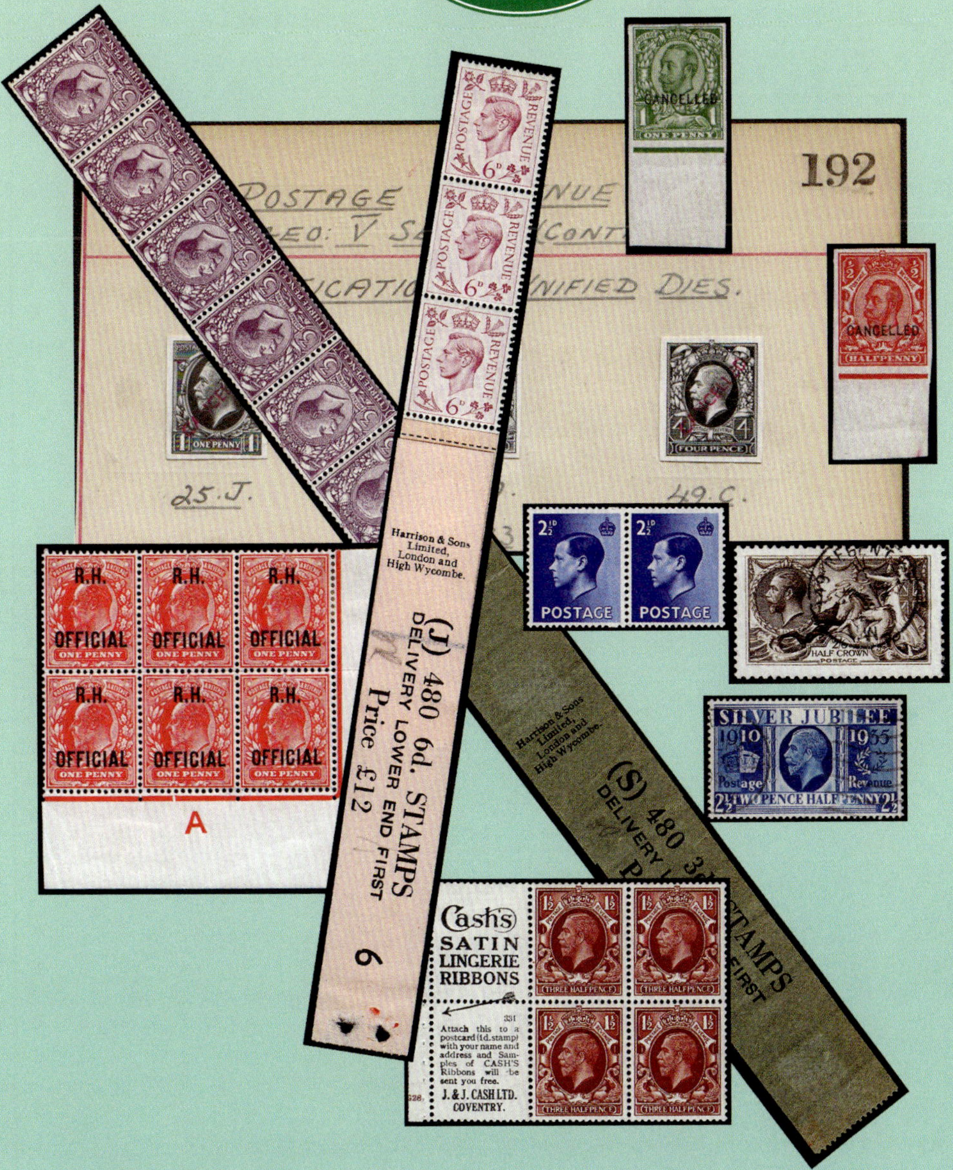

Join our mailing list now for free Quarterly and Specialised Lists featuring all aspects of British Philately from 1839 to 1951.

Andrew G Lajer Ltd
The Old Post Office, Davis Way, Hurst,
Reading, Berks, RG10 0TR UK.
T: + 44 (0) 1189 344151   F: +44 (0) 1189 344947
E: andrew.lajer@btinternet.com
www.andrewglajer.co.uk

PETER MOLLETT

SPECIALISTS IN THE FINEST STAMPS OF GREAT BRITAIN 1840 – 1952

QUEEN VICTORIA
EDWARD VII
GEORGE V
EDWARD VIII
GEORGE VI

Full-colour A4 booklets
regularly mailed to serious collectors.
Contact us to receive our next booklet.

- Wants lists welcomed
- Confidentiality assured
- Fine stamps and collections purchased
- Valuations for insurance and probate

P.O. BOX 1934 · RINGWOOD · HAMPSHIRE · BH24 2YZ
ENGLAND · U.K. · TELEPHONE & FAX: 01425 476666

General Notes **KING EDWARD VII** **M**

The King Edward VII Issues

Section M
General Notes

Printing Contracts. When King Edward VII came to the throne on 22 January 1901 the contract of 1899 between De La Rue and the Inland Revenue for printing stamps had nearly ten years still to run. Discussions about designs started immediately and De La Rue produced a series of paste-ups, incorporating the new King's head into the existing Queen Victoria designs. In the event only the ½d., 1d., 2½d. and 6d. values emerged with completely new designs, the remainder closely resembling their 1887 predecessors. From about 1908 it was decided to replace certain bicoloured values with monocoloured stamps and this process was being discussed when the King died on 6 May 1910.

When De La Rue's ten-year contract came up for renewal the Board of Inland Revenue suggested that savings in printing costs, caused by improved production methods, should be passed on to the Government. De La Rue, however, resisted this attempt to reduce the tender price and also refused to contemplate an alternative suggestion that the work be shared with Harrison & Sons. In these circumstances the Board rejected their tender for the further supply of postage stamps. De La Rue's chairman, Sir Thomas Andros De La Rue, died soon after. The new contractors, Harrison & Sons, took over from De La Rue on 1 January 1911. The new King George V stamps were not then ready and in April 1911 it became apparent that the stock of King Edward stamps would be insufficient. Arrangements were made for printings to be taken from the King Edward plates but Harrisons did not have the necessary machines for printing bicoloured stamps and could only print the monocoloured ones, so the remainder were printed at Somerset House. These are known as the King Edward VII Provisional Printings. They did not entirely cease until June 1913.

Paper contracts. At the time of the King's accession the contract for the supply of all paper for British postage stamps, dated 1897, was with R. D. Turner & Co. of Roughway Mill, Tonbridge, and still had four years to run. In 1904 it was renewed for a further period of seven years to October 1911. Although Turners did not get the subsequent paper contract for King George V stamps they continued to supply the Inland Revenue with Imperial Crown watermarked paper up to the end of the provisional printings.

Arrangement. Each value has been dealt with in turn, through changes of colour, perforation and printer, followed by the list of plate markings, printings, plating index and control and pricing schedules as appropriate. The preliminary Essays, Proofs and Colour Trials appear before the beginning of the list and Essays, Die Proofs and Colour Trials of the completed values are given under their respective values. Booklet panes follow in separate sections.

Historical sources. During the 1970s an immense amount of new and important historical material was, for the first time, opened to inspection. This includes the De La Rue archives (including the De La Rue/Inland Revenue correspondence), the British Library material from the Inland Revenue and the Inland Revenue files themselves. All these have provided a new understanding of the basic processes behind the issue of Edwardian stamps over the post office counter and have enabled a new look to be taken at old ideas and material.

On the ½d. and 1d. there is still much work to be done and the task of identifying the official plate numbers has yet to be achieved. In this edition, the tables describing the plate markings give the present position on these two values. Nevertheless the work on identifying the remaining values to the £1 with the official plate numbers, using archive and other material, has been completed. In this volume plate numbers are given for B(border), D(duty) and H(head) plates as appropriate to simplify plate descriptions and order of printing.

Invalidation. Stamps issued in the reign of King Edward VII were invalidated on 1 April 1930 from a Post Office notice dated 22 February, 1930. The stamps of Queen Victoria had, according to the *Post Office Guide*, been invalidated on 1 July 1915. Stamps issued in the reigns of King George V, King Edward VIII and King George VI were invalidated on 1 March 1972.

PAPER
Mill Sheets. All the paper emanating from Roughway Mill for the printing of postage stamps was in one size, i.e. in sheets of 22¾" × 22⅜", each sheet being known as a "mill sheet".

Two watermarks were used: Imperial Crown and Anchor.

The Anchor watermark was used only for the 2s.6d., 5s. and 10s. values and the mill sheet consisted of 224 Anchors comprising four panes each of seven horizontal rows of eight stamps.

The Crown watermark was arranged in two ways in the mill sheets. For all the remaining values, except the 9d., there were 480 crowns arranged as follows:

480 Crown Mill Sheet. In addition to the Crown watermarks each mill sheet incorporated a number of other features in the watermark. In the margins of each pane of 120 crowns was the word "POSTAGE" in double-lined capitals, repeated 12 times. In addition there was a watermark angle piece at each corner of each pane (16 in all) and another one in each corner of the mill sheet, so that each mill sheet had 20 watermark angle pieces. The four corner angles marked where the mill sheet had to be cut out of the continuous reel of paper in which it was made, such a reel being technically known as a "web". Occasionally, due to folds in the paper, these normally unseen watermark angle pieces can be found. There are also four small crosses and five large crosses in the watermark in the positions shown and indicated by capital letters outside the rectangle. Finally on every mill sheet of this paper there is a single-lined capital letter in the position shown in the middle between the 11th and 12th rows from the top. The letters D, E, F and G are known but their purpose is unknown.

320 Crown Mill Sheet. This was employed only for the 9d. value and has similar features to those of the 480-crown paper except that the word "POSTAGE" is different and there is no letter in the watermark. The letters indicating the panes are referred to in the listing of the 9d. value.

Post Office Sheets. The mill sheets were invariably guillotined by the printer into "Post Office sheets". These varied in size according to value. When printed, the mill sheet was cut down the central vertical line of three crosses giving two post office sheets of 240 crowns each for the ½d. to 7d. values. For the other values printed on 480-crown paper, i.e. the 10d.,

1

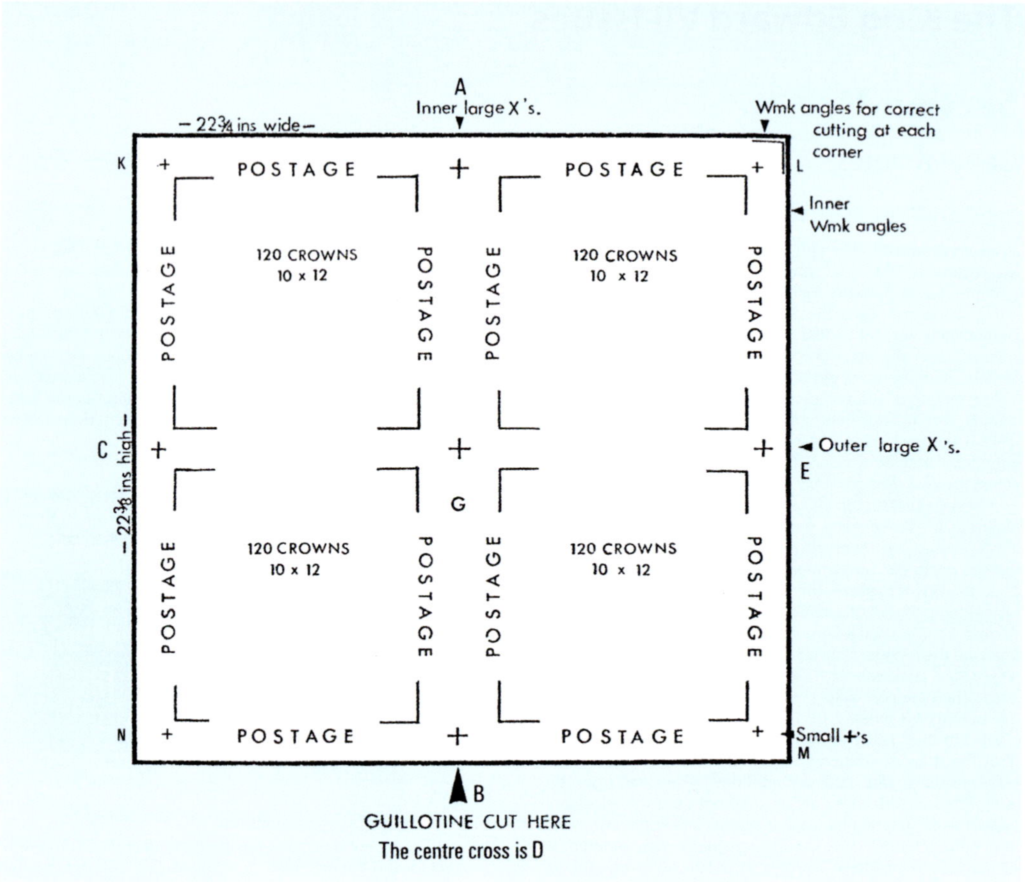

KING EDWARD VII *General Notes*

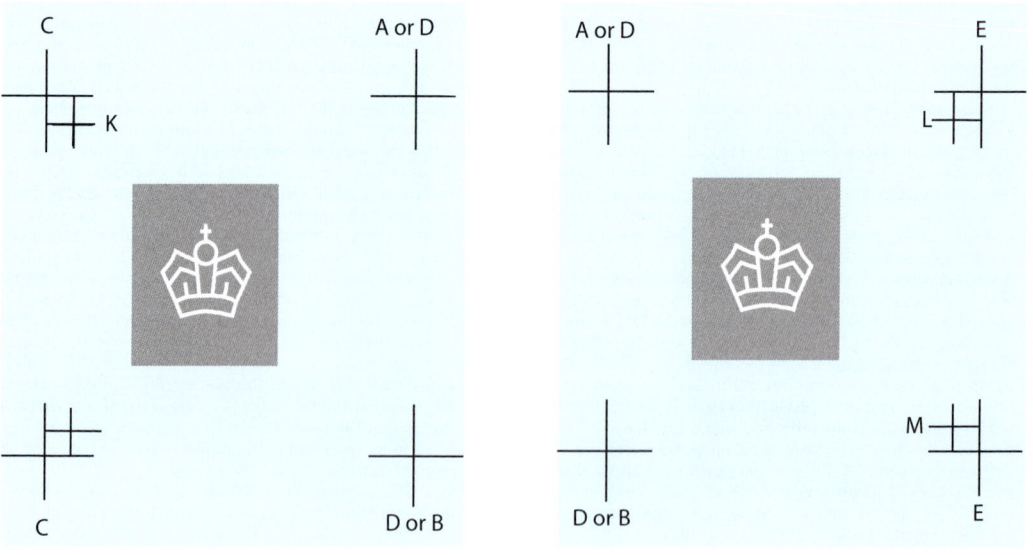

Diagram of 480 Crown Mill Sheet (Everything within the outer rectangle is part of the watermark except the references to the number of crowns)

Diagram X. Left Sheet Corner Crosses (Actual size)   Diagram Y. Right Sheet Corner Crosses (Actual size)

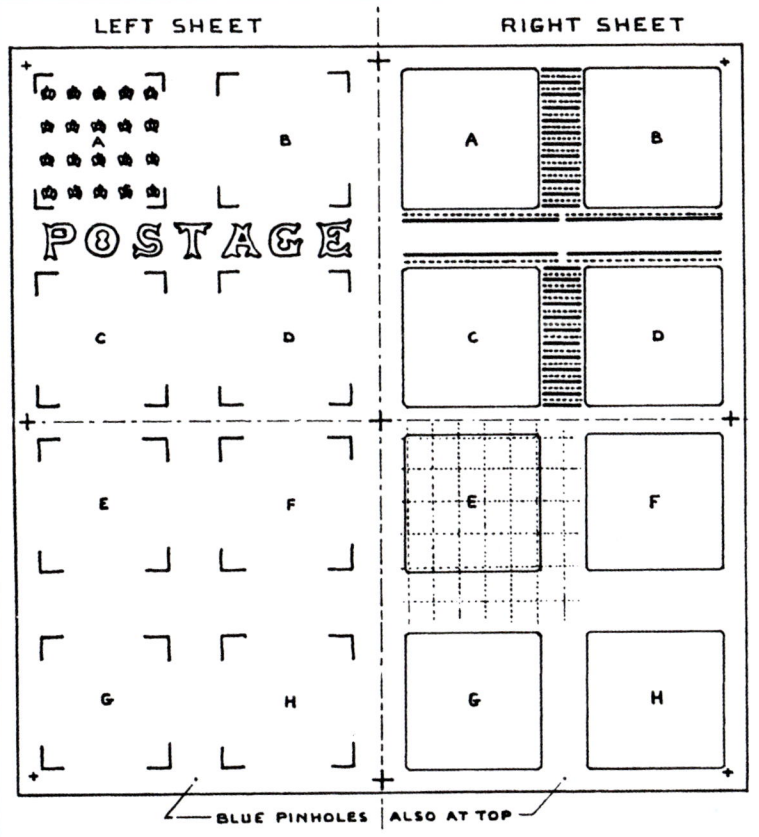

Diagram of 320 Crown Mill Sheet

1s. and £1, each 240-crown sheet was further sub-divided along the horizontal row of large crosses into post office sheets of 120. The 9d. value was only issued in post office sheets of one quarter of the mill sheet, i.e. with 80 crowns.

Recognising the Halves of the Mill Sheet. The plating of Edwardian stamps is greatly simplified by the ability of the collector to recognize from which half of the mill sheet, left or right, any piece has come. This can be done for any piece showing an undamaged corner selvedge, and any piece showing part of a letter in the watermark.

Examination of the 480-crown paper diagram shows that a cut along the line of crosses A, D and B (also called the "inner watermark crosses") leaves two halves, whose crosses are a mirror image of each other—that is if the sheet were folded exactly in half along the line A, D and B the watermark crosses on each half would fall exactly over each other. From this fact it is possible to assign each corner piece unequivocally to its correct half of the original mill sheet.

The essential details of the situation are shown in diagrams X and Y. The collector should place the crown of the corner stamp on his piece over the crown in each diagram in turn. He will find that in one or other case the watermark cross seen in the selvedge will fall close to or over one of the crosses on the diagram (i.e. large or small cross). The one that shows the closer fit will indicate from which side of the mill sheet his piece has come. To be more precise the diagrams show the positions of the crown relative to the inner corner angle pieces, but these are not always easily seen, hence the crown itself should be used.

The letters given to the corner crosses in the above diagrams relate to those in the diagram of the 480-crown mill sheet and a reference to this will show to which side of the mill sheet the corner piece belongs.

If the lines of the centre rectangle are taken to be the lines of the watermark angle pieces then the diagrams apply equally to both Imperial Crown watermark papers and also to the Anchor paper. Deciding the halves of the Anchor mill sheet is of no plating importance, hence the emphasis in the diagrams on the Imperial Crown paper.

The centre crosses A, D and B are hardly ever found complete. Being normally cut vertically, only a small part of the horizontal arm may show. Similarly as crosses C, D and E are often cut in a horizontal direction only a small short piece of one vertical arm may show. The centre cross D may not show at all. The large crosses C, D and E are shown both above and below the rectangle in the diagrams because they occur in the centre of the mill sheet and can therefore relate either to an upper or a lower pane. Crosses A, K and L can only relate to upper panes and B, M and N to lower panes.

With a little practice the collector will be able to assign practically all his corner pieces to left or right sheets but deciding whether they come from upper or lower panes is more difficult and sometimes impossible.

More detailed information about this and other facts regarding plate creation will be found in *Great Britain: The De La Rue Years 1878-1910, Vol. 1*, by W. A. Wiseman, FRPSL.

Other Aids to Plating from the Watermark. The watermark words "POSTAGE" in the 480-crown mill sheet can also be useful in plating and positioning studies. If the stamps are perfectly printed relative to the watermark the "T" of "POSTAGE" falls exactly over the perforation gutter between the 6th and

7th stamps in the top and bottom rows, and opposite the perforation gutter between the 5th and 6th rows on each side of each pane where it occurs. The first three stamps in any horizontal direction from any corner of any pane show no sign of "POSTAGE" unless the watermark is displaced, whereas in the vertical direction no sign of the word can be seen beside the first two stamps. Hence no corner block of four ever shows part of "POSTAGE".

Paper Quality. All the paper supplied was specified to be "animal tub-sized cream wove" of a certain weight per ream. The contracts had provision for checking the quality but in practice there was some variation. For example, some stamps are found on paper with distinct ribbing, giving the appearance of laid paper. The cause of this is not clear but it is not a different paper, being manufactured in the web like the rest.

Types of Paper. Three types of paper were supplied to the printers. **Ordinary paper** was supplied initially to De La Rue for printing all values. This was surfaced to varying degrees before printing, sometimes sufficiently for surface rubbing to occur after printing, this showing as smudging of the details of the impression. It was generally white in appearance but there is some variation and a few pieces show significant toning but not sufficient to affect the perceived shades to any appreciable degree.

Following a request from De La Rue in April 1905, the Inland Revenue gave approval for **chalk-surfaced paper** to be used in order to improve the appearance of the stamps and to make it more difficult for postmarks to be removed. The chalk coating was applied by De La Rue and the new paper was used for the 1½d., 2d., 3d., 4d. green and brown, 5d., 6d., 9d., 10d., 1s. and 2s.6d. values. The first value to appear was the 9d. in June 1905.

Initially the coating was applied thinly, but it was increased the following year in order to further enhance print quality. All ten values exist on the original (thin) coated paper and printings may be identified with a little experience.

Original coated paper feels little thicker than ordinary paper but responds to the silver test, whereas later chalk-surfaced papers feel distinctly thicker. Using a micrometer, mint original coated paper stamps measure ·0034 of an inch, compared with ·0032 for ordinary paper and between ·0039 and ·0042 for thick chalk-surfaced paper. Under long wave ultraviolet light, original coated paper is clearly brighter than ordinary, but less bright than the later papers. Dated cancellations on used examples will also assist identification, as initial printings on chalk-surfaced paper were all thin-coated; by late 1907 all values between 1½d. and 2s.6d., apart from the 2½d. were being printed on fully coated papers.

It should be noted that the colour of the chalk surfacing varies from brilliant white to distinctly yellowish, the majority being white or off–white and these variations do have a significant effect on the perceived shades. The more highly toned papers cause the green head plate ink to appear yellower and the purple one to appear darker than normal.

The actual surface of this paper also varies considerably. Sometimes it seems to be unstable to such an extent that it is impossible to find mint blocks of some chalk-surfaced paper printings which do not show very severe rubbing. The pale purple head plate shade of the 1½d. value is caused by such paper. The more highly toned paper usually shows much less rubbing than normal and pieces on brilliant white paper showing no signs of rubbing are very rare.

The "traditional" method of identifying chalk-surfaced papers has been that, when touched with a silver wire, a black mark is left on the paper, and the listings in this catalogue are based on that test. However, the test itself is now largely discredited for, although the mark can be removed by a soft rubber, some damage to the stamp will result from its use.

The difference between chalk-surfaced and ordinary papers is fairly clear: chalk-surfaced papers being smoother to the touch and showing a characteristic sheen when light is reflected off their surface. Under good magnification tiny bubbles or pock marks can be seen on the surface of the stamp and at the tips of the perforations the surfacing appears "broken". Traces of paper fibres are evident on the surface of ordinary paper and the ink shows a degree of absorption into it.

These characteristics are less pronounced on the original coated paper, nevertheless the notes given above should ensure accurate identification.

Post January 1911 paper. Identical paper manufactured by R. D. Turner was furnished to Harrisons and Somerset House for the provisional printings, and the same paper had been supplied previously to De La Rue. The reason for the difference in the quality of the printing is that ever since 1879 De La Rue had been plate-glazing the paper, whereas Harrison and Somerset House did not. At first, therefore, their printings displayed a coarser surface and uneven thickness. In the late summer of 1912 Harrison arranged for Samuel Jones to plate-glaze the paper at an additional cost and later Harrison supplied Somerset House with paper plate-glazed and ready for printing. Hence the later provisional printings are distinguishable by the better finish of the paper and clearer impressions.

PRINTING PROCESS.

All King Edward VII stamps were surface-printed. This process is also known as *letterpress*, while philatelists have traditionally referred to it as *typography*.

In letterpress the engraver cuts away from the soft steel die those parts of the design which are *not* to be printed. The ink roller is applied to the surface only of the electrotyped plate and the resulting impression has no depth of ink to it and feels flat under the fingertips compared with line-engraved stamps.

PLATES

Layout of Plates and Sheet Format. The layout of the crowns and other watermark features on the mill sheet decided essentially the layout of the plates themselves and to a large extent dictated printing techniques.

The illustration of the 480-crown paper shows that the crowns are set out in two pairs of two panes, each pane having 120 crowns in ten horizontal rows of 12. Between each vertical pair of panes a gap was left whose vertical dimension was exactly equal to that of a stamp. This gap is called the "interpane gutter". Obviously each crown watermark located the position of one stamp image on the plate, and hence each plate comprised two panes each containing 120 stamps (12×10), the upper and the lower. Around each pane was a coloured line, known as the "marginal rule", but the interpane gutter was treated differently in different values.

The monocoloured values (½d., 1d., 2½d., 3d., 4d. orange, 6d. and 7d.) had this space filled with 12 sets of four lined blocks or "pillars" and the marginal rule crossed the gutter at each end, while in the bicoloured values the gutter was blank and the marginal rule did not cross it at any point.

Marginal Continuous and Coextensive Rules

Interpane Gutter with Pillars and Continuous Rules

General Notes **KING EDWARD VII**

Blank Interpane Gutter, Coextensive and Short Bar Rules

These pillars and rules all formed part of the plate (see under "Plate Markings"). Thus every plate printed on the 480-crown paper comprised 240 stamp images, that is, it was 240-"set", except as indicated below for the 10d. and £1 values and for the 4d. value, where the brown duty plates were in fact 120-set.

In the £1 value each stamp covered three watermark crowns, so there were only 40 stamps (4×10) in each pane and 80 on the plate. The marginal rule was arranged as for the other monocoloured values, except that there were 11 vertical pillars in each section of the interpane gutter instead of four, there being four sections.

The 2s.6d., 5s. and 10s. values were arranged as the other monocoloured values except that there were eight sets of four pillars in the interpane gutter. Hence these plates were 112-set comprising two panes of 56 stamps (8×7).

Layout of 10d. Printers' Sheets
In the bicoloured values the 10d., which was printed on the 480-crown paper, was arranged in four panes each of four horizontal rows of 12. The head plates were made up as one unit of four such panes and were therefore 192-set. The duty plates were 48-set each, so that each pane comprised one plate. These were numbered from 1 upwards (see under "Plate Numbering") and it is likely that No. 1 was placed at the top, No. 2 second and so on, but this is not absolutely certain and it is conventional to give the four panes the letters W, X, Y and Z, as shown in the diagram.

The sheets were guillotined between X and Y panes to form post office sheets of 96 and the blank interpane gutter between these two was exactly the same as between the panes of any other bicoloured value. Between the W and X and Y and Z panes there are two rows of crowns over which no stamp images appear. To prevent fraudulent use of this watermarked paper the interpane margin was filled with long horizontal pillars (or "lined blocks" as they are called to distinguish them from those on monocoloured values) separated by short vertical lined blocks. There are two lines of blocks in the purple head plate ink and two in the red duty plate ink in each gutter, so that the crowns which do not have stamps on them are each covered by one head/duty pair. The lined blocks formed no part of either the head or duty plates.

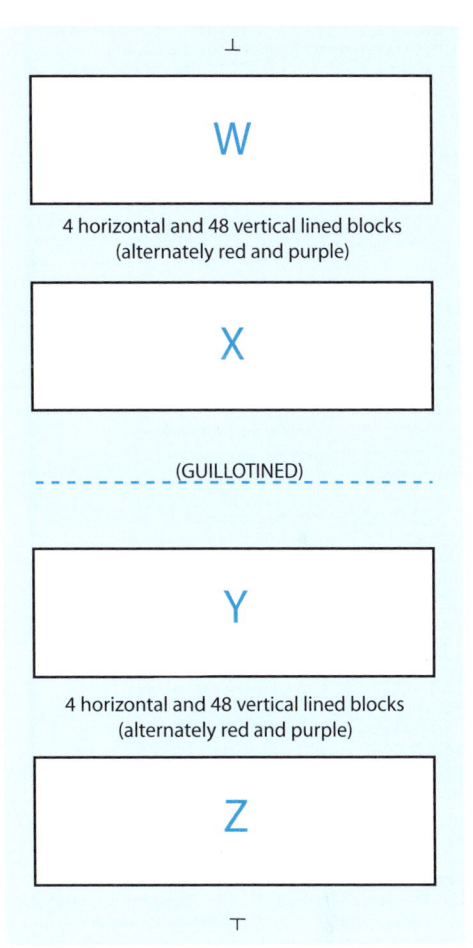

W

X

4 horizontal and 48 vertical lined blocks
(alternately red and purple)

-------- (GUILLOTINED) --------

Y

4 horizontal and 48 vertical lined blocks
(alternately red and purple)

Z

Layout for the 10d. printers' sheet

KING EDWARD VII *General Notes*

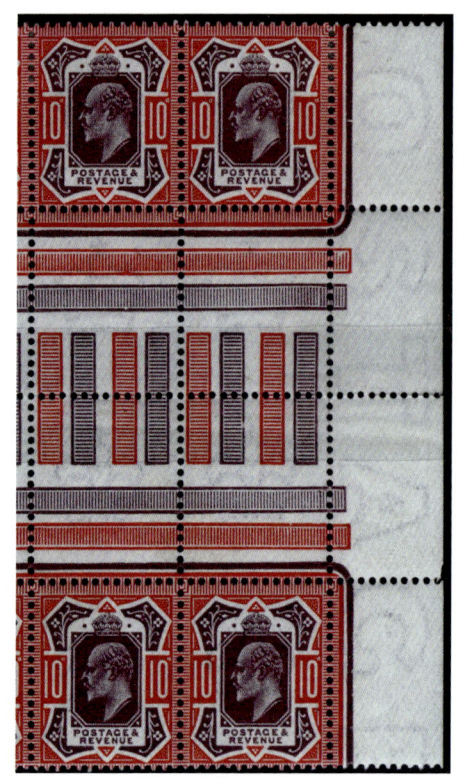

Interpane piece of the 10d. showing the continuous rules around each pane and the horizontal and vertical pillars or blocks between the panes

Layout of 9d. Printers' Sheets
The 9d. value, being printed on the 9d. paper, had head plates comprising eight panes of 20 stamps each (4 horizontal rows of 5 stamps), being 160-set. The duty plates were separate units, each plate being one pane in size, i.e. 20-set. Again, each duty plate had a number but the layout of these is obscure and it is conventional to give them letters as shown in the diagram.

The printers' sheets were guillotined between CD and EF panes to form post office sheets of 80 and the interpane gutter between these was blank. The positions of the interpane blocks are indicated in the diagram. They did not form part of the plate.

Plate Making. All plates used for printing King Edward VII stamps were made by De La Rue. They were mostly copper electrolyte plates, backed with solder and given an electrolytic coating of "steel" before use. They were made essentially in the same way as the master plates made by the Royal Mint and a full description of this process is given in *Great Britain: The De La Rue Years, Vol. 1* by W. A. Wiseman, FRPSL. However there was one major difference: the Royal Mint pressed the working plates from master plates while De La Rue generally made them from recently-struck leads.

A few De La Rue plates, especially the duty plates of the 4d., 9d. and 10d. values, were made from master plates. This meant one striking only of the necessary leads, but that for the 9d. duty plates took place in Victorian times. The only other strikings of duty plate leads for King Edward stamps were for the 1½d. value, for which one plate was made and used, and the 1s. value for which two plates were made but not used.

De La Rue Striking Books. Records of the striking of all leads were kept in special books, known as "Striking Books". The contents of numbers 5 and 6 referred to King Edward VII stamps and these survived the war but were broken up and put on the market in December 1975. Earlier books were badly damaged during the Second World War.

Each piece cut from these books is unique, usually giving the plate number and date of striking. Each entry refers to one "warrant", i.e. official instruction to make a plate or plates, hence the original books formed a record of every plate made, either individually or collectively, together with the striking of surplus leads for repair of plates but such a striking is not evidence of specific use. Each entry had a cut-down die proof attached recording the die from which the leads were taken.

The pieces cut from the Edwardian Striking Books are listed in abbreviated form and an illustration of one of these is shown under the ½d. value.

In addition to striking leads from the die for stamps, plate making from leads also involved the striking of leads for ancillary purposes, such as the marginal rules, pillars, etc.

Plate Numbering. 324 Great Britain plates were made by De La Rue bearing the head of King Edward VII. Of these 56 were fiscal plates. They were, however, all numbered in sequence from 1 to 324. This is called the "current number". In addition to this the successive plates for each value were numbered consecutively from 1 onwards and these are the true plate numbers. The combined numbers comprise the full plate number and are expressed thus: 4/264, the 4 being the plate number for that value and the 264 its current number.

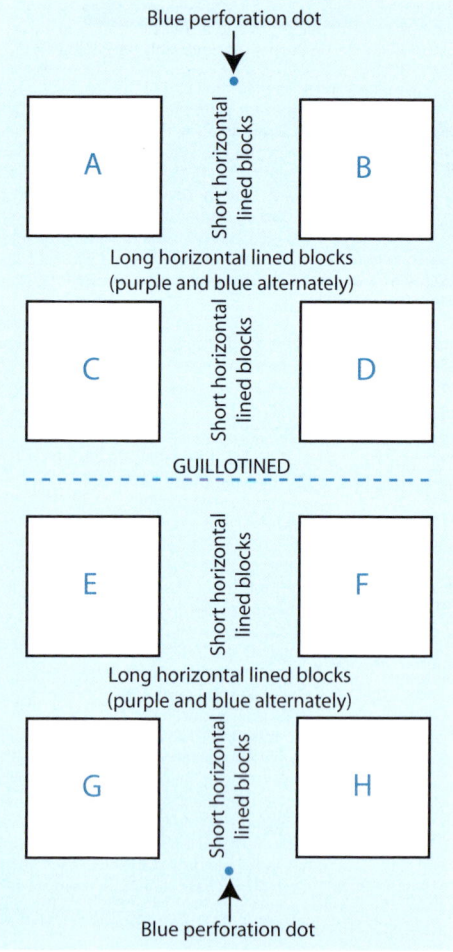

Layout for the 160–set printers' sheet for the 9d.value.

For the collector the interesting number is the plate number but the current number is also useful as it was allotted in the order in which the plates were actually made, with insignificant exceptions, and so helps to date them. Moreover both numbers are essential for anyone referring to official records.

General Notes **KING EDWARD VII**

Duty plates were given a single plate number, each value having its own series starting from 1. Thus every 20-set duty plate of the 9d. value had its own sequential number in the series of all the 20-set duty plates made from 1886 onwards. The 1½d., 2d., 5d. and 1s. were similar in that respect but the 4d. and 10d. had plate number series starting from 1901, independent of the Victorian series.

All these plate numbers, both head and duty, were incorporated into the non-printing margin of the plates, so that they could be read by the printers and others using them. Thus no plate numbers of King Edward stamps were ever printed on sheets of stamps but when registration and proof sheets were taken for record purposes, the Inspector certifying the sheets almost invariably recorded the plate number or numbers on the sheet. From this, and from many other clues, it has been possible to correlate various features on the plates, minor flaws, etc., with a given plate number and thus assign official plate numbers to plates which have hitherto been known under "philatelic" numbers.

Sheet markings. Various markings are found on the sheets as described below.

Registration Piece. Above and below the marginal rules of Nos. 6 and 7 at the top and bottom of the sheet there is a thin bar with a projection in the middle, upwards at top and downwards at bottom, sometimes referred to as a "T" mark. At the bottom and below this and at the top above it there is a coloured dot where the paper is invariably pierced by a needle. The dots were to ensure correct registration of the sheet in the perforating machine.

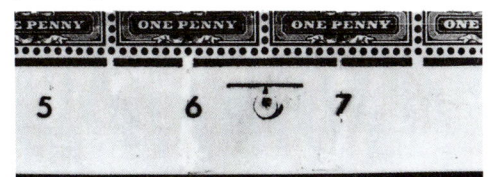

Die I Registration Piece

The "T" together with a short length of marginal rule, were all incorporated into a die used to strike leads, called a "registration (piece) die". A consequence of this was that the marginal rules in the area concerned required special treatment. In the 9d. value this registration die was replaced by a single tiny blue dot at top and bottom exactly between the A and B and G and H panes. For convenience this is called the "perforation dot".

Marginal Rules. The three types of marginal rule are to be seen in the two illustrations under "Layout of the Plates". They are:—
Continuous. The rule is virtually without any breaks.
Coextensive. The rule is divided into regular lengths, each about the width or height of the adjacent stamp.
Short bar. The rule is divided into short lengths, sometimes of a regular size, but bearing no relationship in size to the neighbouring stamp. They were almost invariably much shorter than coextensive rules.

Their purpose was to help protect the adjacent stamps from the impact of the printing rollers. They came from leads struck from an appropriate die, e.g. a separate one for the vertical and horizontal rules.

In the *continuous rule* plates the gaps between adjacent pieces of the rule were filled in by hand work which is often visible at the perforation gutters. This included joining in the short piece of rule formed by the registration piece die. In late 1902 this policy was abandoned because it was so time-consuming and thereafter the plates were made with coextensive rules. The short bar rules, and in a few cases the coextensive rules, were made by chopping up what had originally been continuous rule.

At first the *coextensive rule* was made from the existing dies (being left unjoined), including the registration piece die. For some reason this was not satisfactory and in 1904 a new registration piece die was introduced, known as Die II. This can be distinguished from Die I in having a tiny white dot in the rule below No. 6 in the bottom row and over No. 7 in the top row.

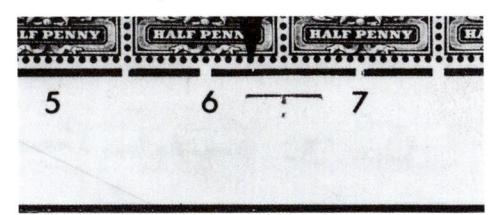

Die II Registration Piece

The 6/7 rule variety. In the Die I period there was some doubt about the best method of dealing with the rules over and under the 6th and 7th vertical columns. It was a consequence of using the registration piece die that when the leads were assembled in the chase prior to electroplating there were gaps in the middle under the middle of the 6th and 7th stamps in the bottom row and over the same stamps in the top row. In the bottom row the right-hand gap was about half the size of a normal gap between adjacent coextensive rules whilst in the top row it was the left-hand gap which was narrow (see illustration of the Die I registration piece).

These gaps could either be left as they were, filled in or a new gap opened out under the perforation gutter between the 6th and 7th columns and all these options were taken in the Die I period. Pieces with the gaps filled (with or without narrow gap under 6/7 gutter) are known as being the "6/7 rule" variety and are found on the ½d., 1d. and 6d. values, pieces with unfilled gaps being confined to the ½d. and 1d. There are no variations in the Die II registration piece.

Without gap under R. 6/7

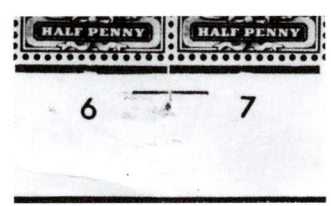

With new narrow gap under R. 6/7

Die I Registration Pieces with Gaps Filled (the 6/7 rule variety)

Exceptions. In the Edwardian stamps there were exceptions to the arrangements mentioned above. The 4d. green and brown head plate 4/250 with coextensive rules had a quite unique arrangement in this area of the plate, top and bottom. The plates of the 4d. orange and the 7d. values had no registration piece, and the rules were from new dies specially made for the purpose. Perforation dots are found under and over the 6/7 perforation gutters but how they were located on the plate is not known.

The marginal rules of the head and duty plates of the bicoloured stamps do not coincide at any point except in the 5d. value where they coincide horizontally near each pane (this was because the duty plates were used for the Victoria issues where the tablet positions are a little higher than on the Edward stamps and in consequence there is a correspondingly large gap at the bottom of each pane).

For the bicoloured stamps the rules were made from different dies, those close to the stamps being from "inner line" dies and those further away from "outer line" dies. The inner line dies included the registration piece die and represented something that was fixed to ensure correct perforation registration. The outer line dies included neither a registration piece nor a perforation dot. To ensure the correct registration of the head and duty plate printings it was necessary to have provision on the printing plates for some adjustment and this was done by making the outer line plates adjustable. As it was inconvenient to manoeuvre the whole plate the outer line plates became divided up into sections.

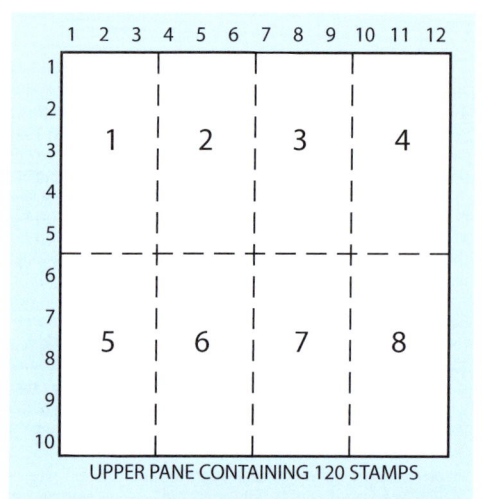

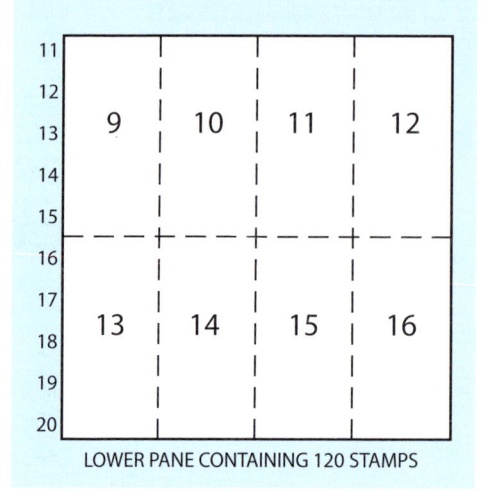

Diagram of Sections of Outer Line Plates

Mostly these sections comprised five horizontal rows of three stamps and there was thus 16 sections in each 240-set plate which are numbered as in the above illustration. Normally these sections would only be of academic interest, but Somerset House transferred some sections of one duty plate of the 2d. value on to another, thus providing an interesting field of study. Such partial substitutions were also made on the 9d. and 1s. where bits of both head and duty plates were moved about and added to as occasion demanded.

King George V plates began with the rules over and under the 6th and 7th stamps in the same state as they had been for the later King Edward VII plates. Later King George V plates were invariably made so that the rules in this area of the plates looked exactly the same as those in any other area. This was done by opening out a gap under the 6/7 column perforation gutter and closing those under and over the stamps themselves. The traces of this work can be found on the master plates in British Postal Museum and Archive. For further information on these matters see *The GB Journal* for January 1977, p. 14.

Controls. The letters date back only to 1882 (being first used for the 1881 1d. Lilac, Die II) and were used by De La Rue to assist in the financial control of the stocks of paper. Prior to the Edwardian period they were changed at irregular intervals but in the new reign they were at first changed annually in October. Towards the end of 1903 the Inland Revenue requested that a figure be added to the control letter to represent the year and that this figure be changed on 1 January in each year. Hence on 1 January 1904 the figure "4" was added to the current letter, which was "C". Thereafter the letters were changed annually at about the end of the first quarter so that each year date appears in combination with two different letters. In the listing of the controls in this catalogue the dates given refer to the first reported dates of issue, not those when the changes were made by the printers.

In the King Edward VII issues only the ½d. and 1d. values had Controls and these are listed and priced as *unused corner pairs*.

With Continuous Rule

With Coextensive Rule

Above are illustrated two typical ½d. Controls (D4 = 1904 and A11 = 1911). (The marginal rules have been fully described earlier in these notes.)

½d. value. The Controls were made up from type as required and were attached to the presses used by De La Rue. In the ½d. value Controls "A" and "B" are located under the 11th stamp in the bottom row but all the others are below the 2nd stamp. Control letters "A" (including the "A" in "A 11") and "B" are set in sans-serif capitals and the rest in serifed capitals.

1d. value. Controls appear under the 11th stamp in the bottom row and all letters are in sans-serif capitals.

The perforation types are fully illustrated and described in Appendix I. The few whole sheets of early Controls of both the ½d. and 1d. seen to date are Perf Types V4 or V4A.

Prices. The King Edward VII Control lists are set out according to the various perforation types. Prices are therefore for unused *corner pairs* with side and bottom selvedge intact. Controls in Section NA are also priced thus. Note that most other King George V letterpress Controls are priced for single unused examples with Control attached.

Plate markings. These are markings which are found on the marginal rules. They have been used by collectors for the purposes of identifying the different plates but they were never placed there by the printers for that purpose. As already explained the plates had their numbers engraved on them but outside the printing area.

The following diagrams show typical markings found on the marginal rules and are shown here for reference purposes in connection with both King George V stamps and King Edward VII issues, and some of them are only seen on the former

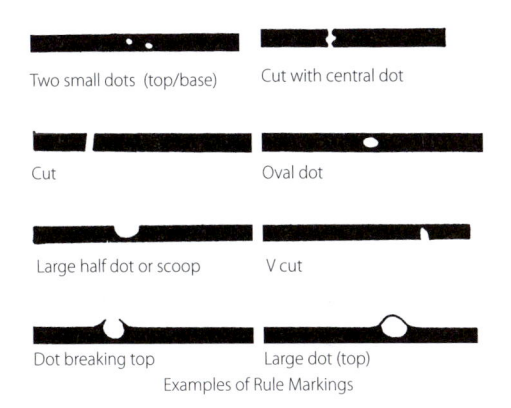

Two small dots (top/base)   Cut with central dot

Cut   Oval dot

Large half dot or scoop   V cut

Dot breaking top   Large dot (top)

Examples of Rule Markings

Descriptions in the Lists. Markings in the bottom marginal rule are given a position relative to the letters of the wording in the value tablet. Hence "Cut under (N)N of 7th" indicates a cut under the second N of PENNY of the 7th stamp in the row.

Markings in the vertical rules at the side are given a position in millimetres from the bottom of the rule. Thus "Cut 19th right side, 7 mm" indicates a cut on the right side of row 19 at a point 7 mm from the bottom of the rule. For greater accuracy the measurement is taken to the centre of the marking.

The marks found on the Edwardian issues can be divided between those employed by De La Rue and Harrisons and those placed there by Somerset House.

De La Rue and Harrison Markings. These generally take the form of straightforward cuts through the rule or half cuts. They are essentially linked to the side of the mill sheet upon which the plate was used. Thus plates found on left-hand halves have a cut or pair of cuts under odd numbered stamps in the bottom row, while those found on right-hand halves have them under even numbered stamps. In some instances this system was extended round the right-hand corner of the bottom row. Thus cuts right of the 20th row are found on right-hand sheets, right of the 19th row on left-hand sheets and right of the 18th row on right-hand sheets and so on.

The cuts appear to have indicated the position on the press from which the sheets were printed. Some plates started life without cuts. This happened when the plate was paired with another having a single cut, which gave the information required, thus obviating the need to make an additional mark or cut.

It is rare to find cuts filled up on De La Rue sheets, i.e. almost invisible ones, as generally when a plate was moved from one side of the press to the other, or to another machine requiring a different marking, the earlier cuts were left unchanged. Hence on some plates, especially in the ½d. and 1d. values, bottom rows can be found with a number of cuts under different stamps, some odd and some even, each one presumably representing a different position for the plate. Sorting these out in chronological order is quite a problem and the matter is confounded by the very occasional practice of moving a plate and not making a new mark. Thus it is possible to find sheets with left-hand sheet marks but which are in fact right-hand sheets, and vice versa.

Additional marks under the sixth and seventh stamps must not be confused with the normal gaps found on coextensive plates (see under "The 6/7 rule variety").

Somerset House Markings. These can be divided into four types which can be summarised as "date cuts", "ink dots", "guillotine dots" and "plate dots".

Date cuts. In 1911 it became the practice to mark the bottom marginal rule with two cuts under the 11th stamp to denote "1911" with a single cut under another stamp to indicate the month, e.g. a cut under the seventh for a printing made in July. In the 1½d. value a "V" mark was made instead of a cut. The first printing in 1912 of the 2d. value had two dots under the 12th stamp. On all other values two cuts were placed under the 12th stamp, all others (including De La Rue cuts) being filled up, sometimes so perfectly that it is often very difficult to locate the positions of the original ones. Printings in 1913 retained the old 1912 cuts.

Ink dots. From April 1912 a white dot was inserted right of the 20th, 19th or 18th rows of the 6d. value. An existing dot was completely removed before a new one was inserted and the change took place every time a different ink was used and they are therefore helpful in dating different printings. The 5d. value has a similar mark right of the 20th row which was placed there in 1913 but it is not known whether this has any connection with the ink.

Guillotine dots. Coloured dots in monocoloured stamps, and in the colour of the head plate ink in bicoloured stamps, were sometimes placed down the line of the centre mill sheet watermark crosses (A, D and B) to guide the guillotine cut between left and right halves. They are sometimes useful in recognising the left or right half of the mill sheet.

Plate dots. In the King George V issues Somerset House marked the plates with a white dot smaller than the ink dots to indicate the plate number for the particular value. This was placed in the marginal rule over the top row of each pane, the stamp number being determined by the plate. Thus a dot over the second stamp would indicate plate 2 of that value. This occurred in some values from the 1½d. upwards. In the case of later plates of the 6d. where these dots occur it is likely that they were put there for this purpose but not certain.

Scoops. So-called "scoops" occur on some King Edward VII and King George V plates but they happened through accident rather than intention. They are found on the outside of marginal rules in constant positions throughout the life of the plate and in varying degrees. They occur close to screws that fix the plates to the underplates. They are valuable for plate recognition.

Other Markings. Other markings are found mainly on King George V issues and some are illustrated. In most instances their purposes are not understood and some may have come about accidentally but they are helpful for plating purposes.

Plate varieties. A plate variety is a flaw on a stamp caused by an imperfection on the plate which has been transmitted to the stamp in the course of printing. Such a variety will be constant and will appear on every stamp printed from that position of the plate, sometimes in different states, unless it is discovered and subsequently corrected. There are other flaws which may be found on more than one copy which are not necessarily constant; they may be due to foreign matter adhering to the plate and therefore of a transient nature. They cannot be classed as plate flaws.

There are thousands of flaws on Edwardian and Georgian stamps and it is our policy to list only the more prominent ones whose positions have usually been established and we also quote the particular plate where this is known.

Substituted and displaced clichés. It is known that in early Victorian times De La Rue made repairs by cutting out old clichés and substituting new ones. However, records do not show whether this practice continued in the Edwardian period. Such a substitution may sometimes be revealed by the new cliché being slightly out of alignment but this was not always so.

It is now clear that the majority of the known examples of displaced clichés are due to other causes, such as deformation of the plate under stress, and they are in fact quite common. In view of this the varieties previously listed as "Substituted cliché" are now described as "Displaced cliché" and a few have been added.

Displaced Cliché at right

Pin (plug) repairs. When a small area of a plate was unsatisfactory one method of repairing it was by drilling out the offending area, putting a copper pin in the hole, knocking it flat and re-engraving that part of the design which was originally faulty. This is known as a "pin repair", a term used by the printers who employed this technique. Often this was done so well as to be unnoticeable but some obvious examples are known on the 1d. value where a typical one is illustrated. Other very similar varieties exhibiting small circles on the stamps exist but they are not necessarily pin repairs. An illustrated article by Dr. Michael Brooks about pin repairs was published in *The GB Journal*, Vol. 32, No. 2, May/June 1994.

Cliché location. When listing varieties where the plate number is known we quote this first "Pl." or, in the case of bicoloured stamps, "Pl. H" or "Pl. D" for head or duty plate. This is followed by the row number and the position in the row from the left, thus "R. 6/4" means the fourth stamp from the left in the sixth horizontal row from the top.

PRINTING

Layout, etc. The size and layout of the mill sheet governed the techniques of printing. Monocoloured low values were printed from two plates laid down side by side on to the undivided mill sheets. The 2s.6d. to £1 values were printed from a single plate on both sides of the mill sheet.

De La Rue printed the bicoloured values from two pairs of plates, one of each pair being a head plate and the other a duty plate. The duty plates, which received the nonfugitive ink, were printed first. However, Somerset House used only one pair of plates, i.e. 240-set instead of 480.

Before printing the paper was gummed and after printing the sheets were interleaved, stacked and left to dry for some days under Inland Revenue control.

Control of printing. Printing was controlled by the Inland Revenue at every stage, even when done at Somerset House. The first step was for the Accounts Branch to issue the printers with a "Warrant" in money terms in units of mill sheets. Thus a warrant for £200,000 in sheets of 480 at £4 per sheet of the 2d. value meant 100,000 sheets of 240. The printers were supplied with the precise quantity of paper needed and when invoicing for stamps supplied had to account for all paper wasted.

Printing of the ½d. and 1d. was continuous and warrants were issued for them, but for the other values it was usual for warrants to represent about one year's supply. They were numbered consecutively and dated. The number of printings of each value and their approximate dates are known. It is not, however, possible to identify every printing by shade or ink. In the tables of printings the numbers assigned to the printings bear no relationship to the warrant numbers.

Where we have included Printing Schedules, the dates given relate to the period during which the stamps were being printed. In the lists the dates for the introduction of the chalk-surfaced paper refer to the earliest recorded date of appearance to the nearest month and these are usually a month or two after printing. Thus for Spec. No. M29 5d., for instance, the fifth printing was the first on chalk-surfaced paper and took place during February/March 1906 and the first recorded use was in May 1906. Several dates hitherto accepted for the introduction of this paper have been shown not to accord with the published printing dates.

The above refers to De La Rue printings. Some of the Harrison printing dates are not known, but the Somerset House dates are included under "Printings".

Printing varieties. Some varieties are due to printing problems rather than plate making.

Watermark Varieties. It is extremely rare for a sheet to be printed on paper without watermark. Most stamps without watermark come from rows adjoining the selvedge and result from misplacement of the watermark. This accounts for stamps showing parts of the word "POSTAGE" in the watermark.

Most inverted watermarks come quite normally from booklet panes, being printed from special plates which have half the clichés inverted. Inverted and often misplaced watermarks from sheets, due to the more or less square sheets having been fed from the wrong way up, are quite rare.

Reversed watermarks occur more often in the King George V issues and result from the paper having been gummed on the wrong side. Similarly, watermarks may be found both inverted and reversed.

Recession Flaws. The pressure required for letterpress printing causes the paper to be slightly embossed, i.e. it is slightly raised at the back. In bicoloured printing, where the impressions of the head and duty plates come together there is a tendency for the head plate not to print properly in the area of the "embossing" caused by the duty plate. This produces what is known as a "recession flaw", which may vary from printing to printing but will remain constant within a printing. The best known examples of this type of flaw are the "no cross on crown" varieties of the 10d. value, where the cross can be found in all stages of recession (but not all cross on crown varieties are due to this cause). Other examples are known, including the loss of frame lines.

Double print (No. M26d)

Offsets and Double Prints. An "offset" (more accurately termed "setoff" but this is not used in philately) is simply a reverse impression on the back of a stamp taken from the sheet below in the stack due to the ink being still wet and the absence of an interleaving sheet. Such items are outside the scope of S.G. catalogues.

However, if the two sheets without interleaf are slightly shifted whilst the ink is still wet. the offset impression will make a faint non-coincident second impression on the face of the original sheet. This appears like a "double print".

It is important to distinguish between offset impressions, where the second impression is faint by comparison, and true double prints where the paper has passed through the press twice. These varieties are rarely found on Edwardian stamps but more often occur on Georgian stamps, especially the Downey Head issues.

INKS AND SHADES

A. De La Rue Printings. Research by M. R. Fox (see *The GB Journal* for March 1975, p. 44) has shown that in the King Edward VII period De La Rue always used the same composition of ink for the same value. Stamps were held by both De La Rue and the Inland Revenue as standards for colour matching of subsequent printings (see notes under "Specimens" in Appendix 4).

The inks for the monocoloured values and the duty plates of the bicoloured values were "singly fugitive", that is they were affected only by mineral solvents. The 6d. value and the head plates of the bicoloured values were printed in doubly fugitive inks, that is inks which were affected by both mineral and aqueous solvents. The latter were compounded mainly of vegetable dyes and were relatively unstable in that they could be affected by even the moisture in the air.

The green head plate ink was especially sensitive, and it is possible to detect what appears to be a slightly blue look in even well-preserved mint stamps. The vast majority of unused stamps today can be assumed to show much the same perceived shades as they did when they were printed. Naturally the same cannot be said for used examples as many have been carelessly soaked off paper, resulting in the ink going first blue and then pale yellow, depending upon the degree of exposure to water.

However, easily perceived shade variations are found in all De La Rue stamps of this period, sometimes even on the same sheet of stamps. In general, variation in depth of colour is of less importance than difference in tone. As already mentioned under "Types of Paper—Chalk-surfaced Paper" the toning of the paper does affect the perceived shades.

B. Somerset House Printings. It is known that Somerset House made numerous experiments with printing inks on the Provisional Issues but they have not yet been fully studied. We have therefore not attempted to make any alterations to our listing of these shades, although more perceived shades exist than are listed. Some footnotes relating to Somerset House shades will be found in the text and so do not need to be repeated here.

C. Harrison Printings. Harrison inks are virtually unknown but it is clear that different ones were tried in some values. It is not known if there was close liaison with Somerset House in these matters.

Fluorescent Inks. Under the influence of invisible ultraviolet rays some colouring matters give off visible light of various colours. In Edwardian times the compounds doing this were essentially artificial dyes derived from a chemical compound called "aniline". Hence inks that show fluorescence, especially when they give off orange or golden orange light, are called "aniline" shades. Though occasionally found in De La Rue printings, fluorescence is common in certain values printed by Harrison and Somerset House. Where they occur they are indicated by "(F)" after the shade description. It should be noted that many of these shades also exist from non-fluorescent ink printings, so the existence of fluorescence should not be taken as a determining factor in the identification of shades.

It soon became recognised that the dye used in the production of fluorescent inks was highly corrosive and was damaging the plates. It was therefore withdrawn in its concentrated form and mixed with non-fluorescent purple ink for printings of the 1½d., 6d. and 2s.6d. The resulting ink mix gives a reaction under ultraviolet light known as "golden brown" fluorescence. Where they occur, they are indicated by "(GBF)" after the shade description.

Collectors are warned not to look directly at the ultraviolet light when switched on. Follow the lamp manufacturer's instructions and for best results view the material in dark room conditions.

GUM.

The gum was invariably applied to the paper before printing. It varies in texture and colour, especially in De La Rue printings. There are no consistent differences between the gum used by De La Rue and that in the provisional printings except that the latter always have white gum and the former are sometimes darker; hence pieces with darker gum can be safely assigned to De La Rue issues.

The white gum of the paper used by Somerset House presented a problem in that it was sometimes difficult to see which side of the paper to print on. In August 1912 the 2s.6d. dull purple and 2s.6d. dark purple with golden brown fluorescence (M50(6) and (7)) were printed on paper with greenish tinted gum as a trial, and subsequent trials using greenish blue tinted gummed paper were carried out on the 1s., 2s.6d., 5s., 10s. and £1 values.

The trials were successful and from July 1913 all Somerset House printings were on paper with a bluish tinted gum. The values affected were the 5d., 6d., 7d., 9d., 10d., 1s., 2s.6d. and £1.

PERFORATION.

All De La Rue and Somerset House issues gauge 14 all round. Harrison issues gauged 14 to start with and were then changed to 15×14 to equalise the breaking force required to separate stamps along the horizontal and vertical gutters. For details about the various perforators see App++endix 1. They were designed to perforate half mill sheets.

BOOKLETS.

Booklets first appeared in 1904, although discussions on them had taken place in the previous reign. Special plates were made comprising 20 horizontal rows of 12 stamps with an interpane gutter between rows 10 and 11 to ensure that the crowns on the mill sheet would fit.

Each horizontal row had the first three stamps upright, the next three inverted, followed by a narrow vertical gutter (to allow for the binding margins) and then again three upright and three inverted stamps. This meant that half the stamps from booklets have the watermark inverted. The introduction of the central vertical gutter caused the crowns to be displaced left or right on all stamps and the outside stamps sometimes have part of the word "POSTAGE" in the watermark.

The first booklet issued contained 24 1d. stamps and sold at 2s.0½d. The next four booklets were sold at 2s. The first of these contained 12 1d. stamps and 23 ½d. stamps. In the next three issues the make-up changed to 18 1d. stamps and 11 ½d. stamps. This meant that one pane in the booklet comprised five stamps and the top left position was taken up by a St. Andrew's cross.

De La Rue made three 1d. plates and four ½d. plates and to provide for the panes of five ½d. stamps one pair of plates had the St. Andrew's cross in the first and seventh and the sixth and 12th positions in alternate rows.

The booklet panes are listed in sections after the sheet stamps and the complete booklets are listed and priced in Appendix 2.

COIL STAMPS.

Not many Edwardian coil stamps have been authenticated and no attempt has been made to list them. All were made up from ordinary sheets with joins on the back by the various promoters of the coin-operated dispensing machines. They were not made by the printers of the stamps in Edwardian times. Further information on this subject will be found in two articles by W. A. Wiseman published in *Gibbons Stamp Monthly* for January and February 1995. An experimental printing for coils was made using No. M6, see *The GB Journal*, Vol. 27 No. 5.

Apart from authenticated coil join pairs, single examples of coil stamps can sometimes be identified by a close examination of the perforations to check the method by which they were separated.

First in the field was Mrs. Kermode who conducted an official trial for the Post Office, installing machines at the House of Commons and at Threadneedle Street Branch Office in July 1906. The stamps were delivered sideways, separated by a knife and dispensed. The 1d. stamp No. M5 was employed and this would have *cuts through the perforations at both sides*. In 1907 the machine was modified to give vertical delivery and the stamps were pulled from the machine by the purchaser, thus showing *no cut marks*. These machines were supplied to the Post Office and commercial undertakings and were in use for many years. The 1d. stamps Nos. M5/7 were most commonly used with these machines but all values up to 1s. are known to have been issued from coil machines.

In 1907 experiments were made with the German Abel machine, later patented by the British Electric Automatic Machine Co. and known as the BEAM machine. This gave vertical delivery dispensing the stamps into a delivery box so that they show knife *cuts at top and bottom*. Nos. M5/7 were used. The machines were less successful and were withdrawn in 1914 with the advent of war with Germany.

Between November 1910 and January 1911 there was a short-lived experiment with the Rex machine which was adapted to affix the stamp on to the envelope. At first it employed whole sheets joined together and later half sheets which had been divided vertically. This produced a horizontal strip of stamps which were then issued singly after a three bladed knife had cut through the perforations on three sides. Thus stamps would show *cuts on all four sides* and only No. M5 was employed.

Finally, in 1910 there was an unsatisfactory experiment with the Kingsway machine which was designed to attract a revenue by displaying advertisements every time it was operated. This also used complete sheets joined together in a continuous roll. First it severed a horizontal strip of 12 stamps which was fed forward for cutting and dispensing stamps singly. The first marginal stamp might show pulled perforations on one side but the rest would have *cuts on all four sides*, and again No. M5 was used.

Distinguishing the provisional printings.
This is a difficult subject as there are no simple infallible tests that can be used. However, there are a few tests by which some stamps can easily be assigned but in other cases it is usually necessary to look at a combination of factors. We start by describing some general tests and then go on to deal with each value in turn.

PERFORATION Stamps perforated 15×14 were printed only by Harrison. It is worthwhile having the 2½d., 3d. and 4d. values in this perforation as their shades and appearance in most cases match the Harrison perf. 14 printings and they are therefore valuable reference material.

Except for the 6d. value all stamps on chalk-surfaced paper were printed by De La Rue.

Stamps perforated by the horizontal Type H1 comb machine can only be printed by De La Rue, whilst the ½d., 1d., 3d. and 4d. perf. 14 from the horizontal Type H2 machine must be Harrison printings and the £1 from the same machine must be printed by Somerset House. These can be identified by the selvedge by reference to the descriptions in Appendix 1.

In this connection it is possible to distinguish the use of vertical and horizontal comb perforators from single stamps without selvedge. Many perforators have imperfections such as uneven spacing of pins, pins out of alignment or of uneven size, etc. Place a ruler along one edge of the stamp and note any irregularities. Then transfer it to the opposite side and see if the same irregularities are repeated exactly. If this is so on the vertical sides then the stamp has been perforated by a vertical comb perforator. Similarly, repeated irregularities on the horizontal sides will reveal a horizontal comb perforator.

PAPER Differences in the quality of the paper affect the standard of printing and thus the general appearance of the stamps. The provisional printings are generally coarser because of the imperfections of the paper. In consequence under the glass the edges of the design are seen to be blurred with sudden changes of direction, whereas in the De La Rue products the edges are sharp and free flowing without changes of direction. This is a general characteristic which lasted until the introduction of the plate glazed paper towards the end of the Somerset House printings. However it does not apply to the 6d. value on chalky and other surfaced papers.

Plate-glazed paper. The process known as plate-glazing was employed to give the paper a very smooth finish prior to printing. The paper was passed through two smooth rollers set at different speeds. The end result was not always uniform and it is sometimes difficult to tell whether stamps are on the so-called plate-glazed paper. Under ultraviolet light they should react pale bluish violet as opposed to the drab of unsurfaced paper.

SHADES Study of the inks used can provide a valuable method of recognition of the two products. Somerset House tried many different inks and it is sometimes possible to follow their progressive use through different values as the same characteristics appear in different values at about the same time. The most important colours are the purples and greens used for the head plates and the reds and blues used for the duty plates, generally but not exclusively in the bicoloured values.

Purple inks. The early provisional purple inks show very red compared with the slate-purple of De La Rue. Later they became much closer to the De La Rue colour. During this period various purples appear which show a strong golden fluorescence under ultraviolet light. These fluorescent inks vary from reddish purple to the full deep slate-purple found in the early to middle 1912 printings of the 1½d. value. After this there was a reversion to redder purples, generally called plum, easily distinguishable from the De La Rue slate-purple and non fluorescent. The last Somerset House printings, especially of the 5d. and 9d. values, were in deep purple, darker even than the De La Rue slate-purple on chalky paper. The Harrison purple was redder than the De La Rue. For the 6d. value see below.

To summarise, reddish looking purples are Harrison or Somerset House printings, the dark purples are Somerset House but the slate-purples may be De La Rue or Somerset House.

Green inks. The early Somerset House greens are generally darker than those of the De La Rue. Later they began to get a closer match and it is sometimes difficult to distinguish them, especially in used condition. In the 2d. value some issues were made in an ink with a distinct olive appearance, far yellower than any De La Rue product.

To summarise, duller, darker greens and those with a clear olive look are Somerset House printings.

Red inks. The red provisional inks are much duller than the corresponding De La Rue ink, even when fairly close in shade. The early red printings were more scarlet than De La Rue but later they were more carmine. For example those 1s. values showing the dark green head plate and scarlet frame plate can never be muddled with De La Rue products but later printings are more difficult. The carmine ink used in later printings of the 2d. value suffused through the paper or failed to dry properly, hence it shows through the back, making it easily recognised. Such effects are never seen on De La Rue printings.

To summarise, the provisional reds are duller than the De La Rue ink and are often more scarlet in shade.

Blue inks. The De La Rue blue is unmistakable. It is a brilliant light ultramarine with a pale look about it compared with any provisional printing. The early provisional printings of the 9d. are in a bright blue but deeper and more violet than the De La Rue ultramarine. Later this gave way to a pale ink but it is still dull. After these the provisional blues became very dull, with a touch of grey in them. Later still they were displaced by brighter blues but duller than the early bright blue and the De La Rue ink.

To summarise, the De La Rue blue is a brilliant shade against which all the others appear dull except for the first bright blue.

Individual Values
½d. The green is generally darker, duller and bluer than De La Rue products but a wide range of provisional inks was used and some confusion may arise. See notes after No. M3.
1d. The provisional shades are generally duller. The rose-red shade has a distinct orange look to it, while the carmines generally look deeper and bluer but there are some confusing shades. Shades showing fluorescence can only be from provisional printings. See notes after No. M6.
1½d. The purple diagonal line in the S.E. corner is always thick on Somerset House printings due to a fresh make ready but

this is not an infallible guide as a few De La Rue stamps also show it thus. Normally De La Rue printings have this line thin. See notes after No. M10.

2d. Because a new duty plate was introduced in 1912 the duty tablets of later Somerset House printings have thick, even frame lines and well formed corners which are not rounded. Most of these can also be recognised by their ink (see under "Red inks" above).

2½d. The Harrison perf. 14 stamps always show a dull blue shade quite unlike any De La Rue product and they are nearly always poorly centred.

3d. The Harrison perf. 14 issues are on lemon paper whereas the De La Rue printings on ordinary paper are on orange-yellow. This is best seen from the back. Again, the Harrison printings are generally badly centred.

4d. The Harrison orange is bright, the only case where the provisional printing is consistently distinctly brighter than the De La Rue printings. The De La Rue stamps are deeper, duller and with a touch of grey or red in them.

5d. See notes about shades after No. M30. The majority of the unused stamps on the market are from Somerset House printings.

6d. This value is very complicated as there are De La Rue ordinary and chalk-surfaced papers and Somerset House ordinary, "Dickinson" coated and chalk-surfaced papers. The early provisional printings on ordinary paper were of a dull reddish purple which later became even darker. The "Dickinson" coated and chalk-surfaced papers produced very fine printings and the latter rarely shows rubbing, unlike the De La Rue chalky paper printings. The chalky provisional printings are easily confused but the provisional ink is darker (without being slate) than the De La Rue. The paper is always white. See further notes under Nos. M34 and M36.

7d. This is a very difficult value to assign with confidence and we cannot add anything to the notes which appear under No. M38.

9d. Owing to the mixture of blue and purple, none of the provisional printings can be confused with the ultramarine of De La Rue and the Somerset House purples are generally redder.

10d. The provisional purple ink begins reddish, usually with a scarlet duty plate. These scarlet inks are generally fluorescent and cannot be confused with De La Rue stamps which are basically carmine. The later slate-purple head and carmine duty plate inks cause more difficulty, especially when printed on plate glazed paper, but the inks are duller, especially the carmine.

1s. The early head and frame plate inks are quite different from the De La Rue inks while the later inks, being darker and duller than the De La Rue issues, should also present little problem.

2s.6d. The comments about the purple shades above generally apply to this value.

5s. This is the most difficult value of all in which to assign single stamps of the different printers. As stated in the notes after No. M52 the De La Rue ink tends to show through the back of the stamp but this is not a completely reliable guide.

10s. This is the only value in which a blue ink was used where the difference in shade between the two printers is not very great. However, the comments above about blue inks remain valid. The De La Rue ink is an ultramarine, a bright light colour, light in the sense of having a white look about it as it is not a pale colour. The Somerset House blues are duller, with a deeper violet or purple tone.

£1. This value is not easy to distinguish, even for experts. The De La Rue green is bluish whilst the Somerset House is a deeper, richer green.

Used Stamps
Used examples in good, clean, unrubbed condition and with dated postmarks can form the basis of a useful reference collection, the dates often assisting in the assignment to the printers.

STAMPS OVERPRINTED "SPECIMEN" OR "CANCELLED".
As with those of the Victorian issues they are listed in the basic lists after the varieties. Some overprint types are listed under National Postal Museum Archives as they were sold in the 1984/5 sales of Archive material and are only known from that source. The various types of overprint are illustrated in Appendix 4 where further information is given.

Imperforate Stamps From Registration Sheets. Imperforate single values from Post Office registration sheets are known. Not all values and printings are recorded in this form but those in private hands are listed.

ESSAYS, PROOFS AND COLOUR TRIALS
Essays. The earliest King Edward VII essays were paste-ups on the then current Queen Victoria stamps and they were followed by black and white photographic essays and some coloured ones for the new designs. Then came the abortive "Transvaal" essays and the "Canada" head essays. Essays in private hands from these groups are listed at the conclusion of these notes. Essays for the 2d. Tyrian plum and for the 1910 7d. value show a further advance in essay production as they were on highly glazed photographic paper in various colours. They are listed under their respective values.

Die proofs. De La Rue took proofs from their dies at various stages of making the die and they are known as "progressive die proofs". Die proofs of the head only are listed after the essays. Completed die proofs for the monocoloured values and the separate head and duty die proofs for the bicoloured values are listed under the values concerned.

They are normally on thin white glazed card cut to about 90×60 mm. As with the Victorian die proofs they frequently bear signatures, initials or instructions in manuscript and are generally handstamped "BEFORE HARDENING", "AFTER HARDENING" or "AFTER STRIKING" and dated.

These are followed by the pieces cut from the De La Rue Striking Books, information about which is given above under "PLATES". The dates written on these rarely include the year date and in a few cases where they do it may be incorrect due to reasons for which the books were kept originally. These dates relate to those on the "AFTER STRIKING" die proofs.

Plate proofs. These will be found listed after the Die Proofs.

Colour trials. The only colour trials made by De La Rue for the first issues were those for the 1d. value in 1901, for which a 20-set plate was made, and those ordered in December 1901 for the 2½d. owing to the decision not to print it in purple and blue.

The 1909 colour trials for the 1½d., 2d. and 4d. values were for two purposes: to decide whether the designs were satisfactory for printing in monocolour and to choose colours for the planned monocoloured series. It was decided that the 2d. design would not be suitable, hence the change of design for the abortive Tyrian plum and the need to make colour trials for this.

The 1910 colour trials for the 4d. were made following complaints that the selected orange colour was not satisfactory, but nothing came of these. Colour trials were also made for the 1910 7d. value.

Colour trials were also made for the 6d. value but the date of these and their purpose are not known.

All the colour trials are listed under the appropriate values after the die and plate proofs. The 1911 colour trials of Edward VII stamps made by Harrisons were for the King George V stamps and are listed there.

KING EDWARD VII *General Notes*

1901 "Paste up" of the Victorian "Jubilee" Issue

Series A

Series B

The ½d. to 1s. values (except 4½d.) and the 1d. lilac. The portrait of the Queen was cut from the design and a lithographed head (in appropriate colour) of King Edward VII substituted.

Series A ½d. to 1s. Cut down mounted on stamp size card with a three-quarter face likeness of King Edward VII facing left. 12 values exist..Each £11000
Ditto but affixed to card (77 × 100 mm.) and annotated "A" at top left. 12 cards exist...Each £14000

Series B As above, but with a quarter-face likeness facing left........................Each £11000
Ditto but affixed to card (77 × 100 mm.) and annotated "B" at top left. 12 cards exist...Each £14000

In addition, the frame and likeness of the 1d. lilac stamp exists in three other states.

Aa As in series A, but portrait reversed £11000
Bb As in series B, but portrait reversed...............£11000
C   Similar to A but portrait engraved instead of lithographed...£13000

On card 92×60 mm. dated "March 12 1901" (M/S)
    Series A, 1d. mounted on card ....
    As before but oval frame obliterated in ink ....

Transitional Essays. These show hand-painted alterations to the Victorian stamps. The values known are the 1½d., 2d., 3d., 4d., 5d., 9d., 10d. and 1s. They all had a crown superimposed above the Queen's head.

The portrait for the issued stamps was executed by Emil Füchs, an Austrian artist who also prepared a new design for the ½d., 1d., 2½d. and 6d. stamps. The remaining values of the issues were similar in design to their Victorian predecessors, but with the incorporation of the Crown above the head.

Photographic Essays. These were produced using a reduced "Canada Head" inserted in the frames of the Jubilee issue 2d., 4d., 9d. and 1s. values. They are listed following the "Canada Head" essays at the end of this section.

ESSAYS
1901 Essays of the Suggested Design for the ½d., 1d., 2½d. and 6d. Stamps

Frames and heads produced photographically or from temporary copper plates and pasted on card.

(1) Proof in black of the frame, inscribed "POSTAGE REVENUE". A photograph of the King's head inserted..£6000
(2) As above, but inscribed "POSTAGE & REVENUE". An engraved head inserted £6000
(3) As above, but printed in various colours. Red, green, purple on pink or purple on blue ....From £10000

De La Rue prepared official photographic copies, identically mounted, of the 2½d. and High Value essays, also certain 1d. essays. Since these are not "paste-ups", they are easily identifiable.

See under No. M16 for essays of the 2½d. value.

Essays for 2s.6d., 5s., 10s., £1 and £5
Artist's sunken sketches. Photographic, head and crown with backgrounds similar to the issued design hand painted in black and white ....Each from £24000

Enlarged bromide essays of the issued designs for all values, the bi-coloured stamps being made from composite paste-ups of the head and duty plates ....Each from £900

It was originally intended to have a £5 stamp, but no plate was made, and the value passed from currency. Die proofs from this will be found listed after the £1 value.

Die Proofs

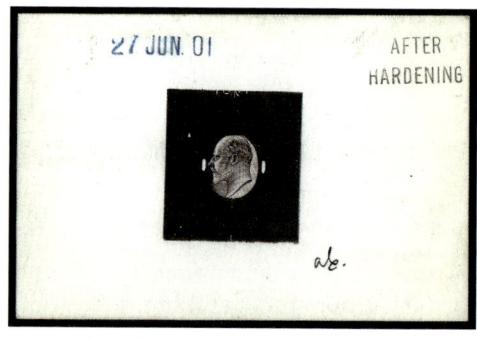

Large Head Boxed Uncleared Surround

Small Head Solid Background   Small Head Partly cleared by thin white contour line

The Approved Head
Large head
In black on white glazed card, used for ½d., 1d., 2½d., 6d., 7d., 2s.6d., 5s., 10s. and £1
With circular uncleared surround, stamped "6 JUN 01" and "BEFORE HARDENING"..£3000
As last but stamped "7 JUN 01" and "AFTER HARDENING" £3000
Similar but cut down to frame..£3000
With boxed uncleared surround, stamped "27 JUN 01" and "BEFORE HARDENING"..£3000
As last, but stamped "AFTER HARDENING" and endorsed "27/6/01" and initials in M/S £3000
As last initials "HB" and "TAC" but without date...................£3000
Stamped "4 Oct 01" and "AFTER HARDENING" and initialled in manuscript £3000
Stamped "2 Nov 01" and "BEFORE HARDENING" with head cleared..£3000
Head and oval frame complete, surround cleared, without marking..£4000
Ditto, but stamped "11 Dec 02" and "BEFORE HARDENING"..£4000

General Notes KING EDWARD VII

Small head on solid background
In black on white glazed card, used for the 1½d., 3d., 4d., 9d., 10d. and 1s. values
Without marking £3000
Stamped "1 AUG 01" and "BEFORE HARDENING"
and endorsed "Die" in M/S £3000
Stamped "4 SEP 01" and "BEFORE HARDENING"
and endorsed "Unified" in M/S £3000
Endorsed "After Hardening" in M/S £3000
Stamped "5 SEP 01" and "AFTER HARDENING" £3000

Small head partly cleared, with or without white contour line
As last and used for 2d. and 5d. values
Without marking £3000
Stamped "5 SEP 01" and "AFTER HARDENING" £3000

For similar die proofs sold from the De La Rue archive, see below.

The die proof of the "extra large size head", previously listed here, has been deleted as this was struck in connection with colonial stamps and is therefore outside the scope of this Catalogue.

Approved Frame with Value Tablet Blank
Die proof on white card
Without marking £3000
Stamped "AFTER HARDENING" and "1 AUG 01" £3000
The dies for the ½d., 1d. and 6d. were made from this master die, also the 2½d. value with modifications.

Head and Frame Without Value

Approved Head and Frame Without Value
Die proof of complete design except the value, for ½d., 1d. and 6d. values. In black on white glazed card
Endorsed in *reverse* "ORIGINAL DIE" (white letters on black uncleared surround) above and with
"P.6." below in M/S £6000
Stamped "1 AUG 01" and "BEFORE HARDENING" £5500
Stamped "1 AUG 01" and "AFTER HARDENING" £5500
Without markings (cleared borders) £5500
†See also below for two die proofs (approved head and frame without value), that were sold from the De La Rue archive.

Die Proofs from the De La Rue Archives
On card 92×60 mm unmounted with traces of gum or paper on the back

Large head
With circular uncleared surround, stamped "5 JUN 01" and "BEFORE HARDENING" and endorsed "Die & Punch" in M/S £4000
With boxed uncleared surround, stamped "27 JUN 01" and "BEFORE HARDENING" and endorsed "Original P.1" in M/S £4000
As last but stamped "2 JUL 01" and "BEFORE HARDENING" and endorsed "Original die. No. D.1." in M/S £4000
Small head on solid background
Stamped "31 JUL 01" and "BEFORE HARDENING"
and endorsed "Die" in M/S £3500
Stamped "1 AUG 01" and "BEFORE HARDENING"
and endorsed "Die" in M/S £3500
Stamped "5 SEP 01" and "AFTER HARDENING" and endorsed "Original P.20. Solid ground" £3500
Small head partly cleared with thin white contour line
Stamped "5 SEP 01" and "AFTER HARDENING" and endorsed "Original P.21. White ground" £3500
Approved head and frame without value
Stamped "1 AUG 01" and "BEFORE HARDENING"
and endorsed "Original die P.6." in M/S £3500
As above but without markings £3500

1911-12 Colour Trials
The Edward VII colour trials of 1911-12 will be found at the end of the General Notes to Section NA since they relate to the first Georgian stamps.

"Transvaal" Essays
Some months after the first Edwardian stamps were issued, further essays were prepared at the request of the King, who it is believed favoured the design of the Transvaal stamps to that of the ½d., 1d., 2½d. and 6d. of Great Britain.

Type 1   Type 2

Essays were prepared in October 1902 in the above Types.

Type 1. As illustrated
Type 2. As Type 1 but with thin line painted between the oval of the King's head and joined to the base of the crown in approximately the same colour as that of the frame.

Essays from the De La Rue Archives
Type 2, each mounted on card with manuscript "Cancelled"
In red numbered "2" £9000
In green numbered "5" £9000
In black and purple numbered "8" £9000

The remaining six essays were acquired by the National Postal Museum and comprise essays in black and red numbered "1", in carmine numbered "3", in black and green numbered "4", in black and blue numbered "6", in blue numbered "7" and in purple numbered "9".

It is believed that this set of nine essays represents all the colours that were used. Any others which have been recorded at various times result from inaccurate descriptions or colours that have faded.

Type 1
Die Proof on white glazed card
In black £7500
Printed from a plate and mounted on card. Perf. 14
In black and red, red, carmine, black and green, green, black and blue, black and purple, purple, black and orange .... From £8500
Examples are known to exist off card (*price from £6000*).

Type 2
Printed from a plate and mounted on card. Value tablets and crown touched in by hand with white paint. Perf. 14
In black and red, red, carmine, black and green, green, black and blue, blue, black and purple, purple .... From £8500
Examples are known to exist off card (*price from £6000*).
As above but pasted on card and numbered
No. 1 for 1d. Black and red £8500
No. 2 for 1d. Red £8500
No. 3 for 1d. Carmine £8500

15

1903 "Canada Head" Essays

Prepared by De La Rue using the head employed for the 1903 issue of Canada.

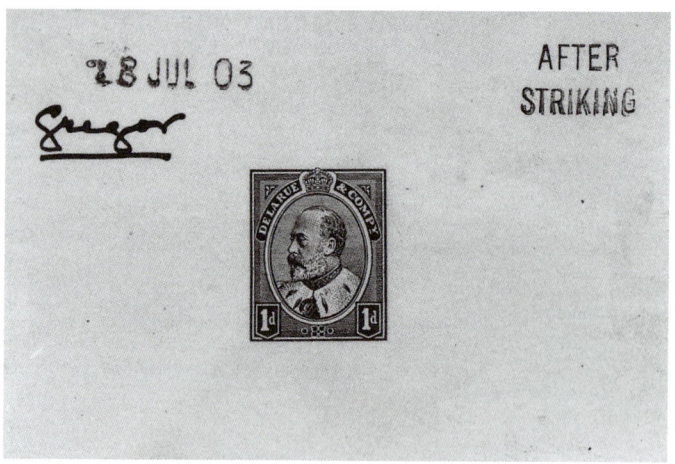

Die 1. Small Head

Die Proof. Die I in black on glazed card
Stamped "8 JUN 03" and endorsed "Turner" in M/S £5500
Stamped "10 JUN 03" and "AFTER STRIKING" and
endorsed "Gregor" in M/S £5500
Stamped "28 JUL 03" and "AFTER STRIKING" and
endorsed "Gregor" in ink... £5500
Stamped "28 JUL 03".. £5500
Updated but endorsed "Mr. T" in M/S........................... £5500

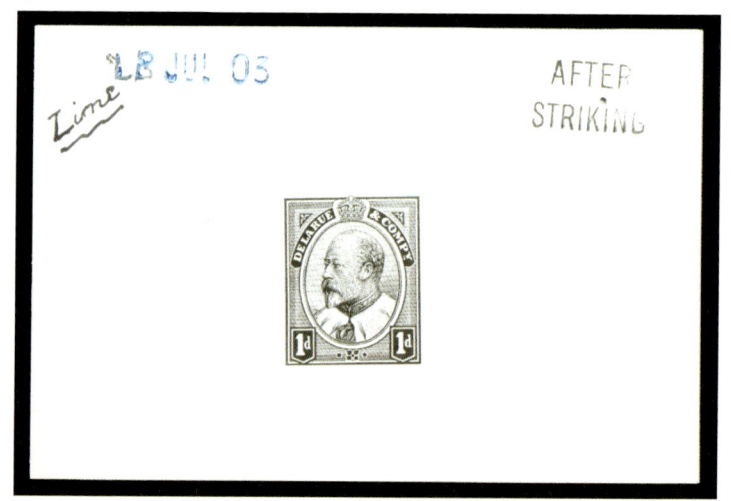

Die 2. Large Head. Heavily shaded

Die Proof. Die 2 in black on thick glazed card
Stamped "8 JUN 03" and endorsed "Turner" in M/S £6000
Stamped "27 JUL 03".. £6000
Stamped "28 JUL 03" and "AFTER STRIKING" with
"Zinc" in M/S £6000
Undated but endorsed "Mr. T" in M/S............................... £6000
Without markings £6000

Colour Trials
Die 2. Imperforate
On thick wove paper, plate glazed both sides
In ochre-brown, carmine-red, pale green, pale
orange ....From £3250

On thick proof card
In pale orange, ochre-brown, carmine-red, pale
green, pale blue .... From £3250
On thin wove paper. Wmk. Rosette. No gum
In pale orange, ochre-brown, carmine-red,
ultramarine, pale green... From £3250
On thin wove paper. No watermark. With gum
In pale orange, ochre-brown, carmine-red,
ultramarine, pale green... From £3250
On very thin high quality wove paper. No watermark or gum
In carmine-red, ultramarine, pale orange, pale
green, ochre-brown... £3250

Photographic Essays with Small Canada Head
The frames of the 2d., 4d., 9d. and 1s. values mounted on card, with the head of the King inserted. This head was a smaller version of that used for the 1903 issue of Canada.
Touched in by hand in white paint ....Each £7500

CHECKLIST OF KING EDWARD VII DEFINITIVES

Description	Spec. Cat. No.	S.G. Nos.	Page
De La Rue Printings on Ordinary Paper			
½d. blue-green	M1	215–16	19
½d. yellow-green	M2	217–18	20
1d.	M5	219–20	25
1½d.	M8	221–22	30
2d. green & red	M11	225–26	33
2d. Tyrian plum	M14	266a	37
2½d. purple on blue	M15	—	38
2½d. blue	M16	230–31	38
3d.	M19	232, 232b	41
4d. green & brown	M23	235–36	42
4d. orange	M25	239–41	44
5d.	M28	242	45
6d.	M31	245, 246	48
7d.	M37	249–49a	52
9d.	M39	250, 251	53
10d.	M42	254	55
1s.	M45	257	57
2s.6d.	M48	260	59
5s.	M51	263–64	61
10s.	M53	265	61
£1	M55	266	62
De La Rue Printings on Chalk-surfaced Paper			
1½d.	M9	233–24	30
2d.	M12	227–29	34
3d.	M20	232a, 232c–34	41
4d.	M24	236a, 238	42
5d.	M29	242a, 244	45
6d.	M32	245a, 248	48
9d.	M40	250a, 251a	53
10d.	M43	254b, 255–56	55
1s.	M46	257a, 259	57
2s.6d.	M49	261–62	59
Harrison Printings Perf 14			
½d.	M3	267–71	21
1d.	M6	272–75a	26
2½d.	M17	276	39
3d.	M21	277–77a	41
4d.	M26	278	44
Harrison Printings Perf 15×14			
½d.	M4	279–79a	22
1d.	M7	280–82	27
2½d.	M18	283–84	39
3d.	M22	285–85a	41
4d.	M27	286	45
Somerset House Printings			
1½d.	M10	287–89	31
2d.	M13	290–92	35
5d.	M30	293–94	46
6d. (ordinary paper)	M33	295, 297–300	48
6d. ("Dickinson" coated paper)	M34	301	49
6d. (chalk-surfaced paper)	M35, M36	296, 303	49
7d.	M38	305	52
9d.	M41	306–08	53
10d.	M44	309–11	56
1s.	M47	312–14	58
2s.6d.	M50	315–17	60
5s.	M52	318	61
10s.	M54	319	62
£1	M56	320	62

MA KING EDWARD VII Postage Issues (1902-13)

Section MA
Postage Issues (1902-13)

WATERMARKS. The ½d. to 1s. have watermark **W12** (Crown). The 2s.6d., 5s. and 10s. have watermark **W9** (Anchor). The £1 has three Crown watermarks on each stamp.

M1  M2  M3  M4  M5  M6  M7  M8  M9  M10  M11  M12  M13  M14  M15  M16  M17  M18

FUGITIVE INKS. As these stamps are printed in fugitive inks (*see* under "Inks and Shades" in the General Notes) the colours are particularly liable to suffer through immersion in water. Badly affected stamps are virtually worthless.

PRICES FOR STAMPS IN USED CONDITION
For well-centred, lightly used examples of stamps in Section MA, add the following percentages to the prices quoted.
De La Rue printings—3d. (M19/20) +**35**%, 4d. orange (M25) +**100**%, 6d. (M31/32) +**75**%, 7d. (M37) and 1s. (M45/46) +**25**%, all other values +**50**%.
Harrison printings—all values and perforations +**75**%.
Somerset House printings—1s. (M47) +**25**%, all other values +**50**%.

½d. Blue-green. M1 *Postage Issues (1902-13)* **KING EDWARD VII**

1902-11. ½d. Green, Type M1

1902 *(1 January).* **½d. Blue-green.** Perf. 14. De La Rue. Ordinary paper

M1 (=S.G.215/16)

		Unmtd mint	Mtd mint	Used
(1)	Dull blue-green	2·75	2·00	1·50
(2)	Blue-green	2·75	2·00	1·50
(3)	Deep blue-green	15·00	12·00	2·00
	Block of four	12·50	9·00	8·00
	Used on cover	†	†	2·50
a.	Watermark inverted	£3750	£2750	£2000
e.	Displaced cliché (Pl. 20, R 19/12 or R. 20/12) (horiz. pair with coextensive rule)		£375	
f.	Displaced cliché (Pl. 24, R. 20/12) (horiz. pair with continuous rule)		£375	
fa.	Displaced cliché (Pl. 24, R 20/2) (horiz pair with continuous rule)		£375	
g.	Diagonal scratch (Pl. 11, R. 19/6)		£190	
ga.	Right frame broken (Pl. 11, R. 19/1)		£190	
gb.	Top right corner broken (Pl. 11, R. 20/12)		£190	
h.	Bottom frame cut into (Pl. 33, R. 20/5)		£100	
i.	Split frame (Pl. 20, R. 11/8)		£250	
j.	Split left frame (several exist) *From*		£150	
k.	Left frame broken (Pl. 24c, R. 11/6)		£200	
l.	Gap in crown (Pl. 8, R. 20/11)		£190	
la.	Blob in bow (Pl. 8, R. 20/12) (late printings, control A)		£190	
m.	Minor frame breaks *From*		45·00	
s.	"Specimen", Type 15		£350	
t.	"Cancelled", Type 18		£1750	

Imperforate single from P.O. Registration Sheet..*Price unused* £20000

Nos. M1e/f are S. E. corner pairs and do not include the displaced clichés at R. 19/12. Add 100% for blocks showing two displaced clichés.

No. M1 was pre-released and exists on cover with No. M5(1d.), M16(2½d.) and M31(6d.) cancelled 31 December 1901.

An example is also known used at Weston-super-Mare on 23 December 1901.

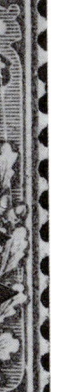

M1ga

M1g Extends up to R. 18/6

M1h, M2i

M1gb A minor constant break in the shading at left confirms this cliché which was later replaced during Control B

M1k, M2ha

M1l

M1i   M1j   M1la

Perforation 14 (Nos. M1 and M2).
Types: see Control List.

Die Proofs. In black on white glazed card
Without marking £3000

MA   KING EDWARD VII   Postage Issues (1902-13)   ½d. Yellow-green. M2

Without marking, endorsed "A. S. Roberts"	£3000
Without marking but initialled "EF" (E. Fuchs)	£3000
Cut down, endorsed "As approved by Mr. Fuchs"	£3000
Endorsed (M/S) "25/VI/1901 Emil Fuchs"	£3000
Endorsed (M/S) "21 Aug EF"	£3000
Endorsed "21 Aug or BEFORE HARDENING"	£3000
Endorsed "21 AUG 01 BEFORE HARDENING" and "Working Die No. 17" (M/S)	£3000
Endorsed "22 AUG 01 AFTER HARDENING"	£3000
Endorsed "22 AUG 01 AFTER HARDENING" and "Working Die No. 17" (M/S)	£3000
Endorsed (M/S) "Working Die No. 17 26-9-01"	£3000
Endorsed (M/S) "Jan 1907 After Striking"	£3000
Endorsed "AFTER STRIKING" with signatures dated: "7 JULY 03", "4 AUG. 04", "12 APR. 05", "15 APR. 05", "10 AUG. 05", "14 NOV. 05", "21 FEB. 06", "5 APR. 06", "20 JUN. 07", "3 APRIL 08", "23 JUN. 08", "23 DEC. 08", "3 MAR. 09", "2 APR. 10", "1 DEC. 10" ...... Each £3000	
In green on white glazed card: Partly engraved proof of value tablet and left half of frame	£18000

Die Proof from the De La Rue Archives
On card unmounted with traces of gum or paper on the back
Cut down (85×43 mm), endorsed "As approved by Mr. Fuchs" £3000

Pieces Cut from the Striking Books

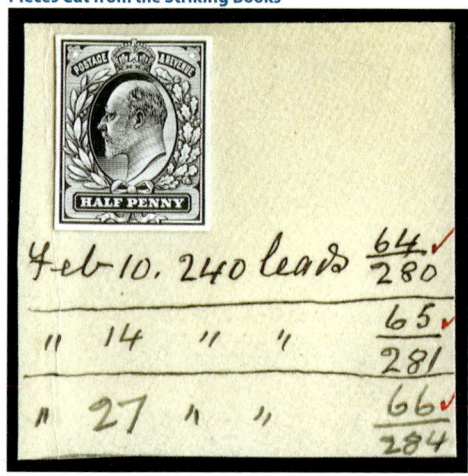

Typical Example showing Dates, Plates and Leads

Each piece is unique and the value of any one piece depends to some extent upon its condition. A full listing is beyond the scope of this Catalogue but we include one for each value and a few special items. For further information see General Notes under "De La Rue Striking Books".
    Struck on plain paper cut to size with various endorsements comprising dates, plates and/or number of leads

½d. value	From £2800
½d. and 1d. values on same piece	From £6250

Plate Proofs. No watermark, imperf.

Blue-green on yellowish paper	£140
Ditto, diagonally overprinted "CANCELLED"	£175
Blue-green on thick surfaced card	£140

NOTE. The change of colour was announced by a Post Office notice dated 22 November 1904. Postal staff working under artificial light were having difficulty sorting letters bearing the ½d. blue-green and 2½d. blue.

1904 *(26 November).* **½d. Yellow-green.** Perf. 14. De La Rue. Ordinary Paper

M2 (=S.G.217/18)

		Unmtd mint	Mtd mint	Used
(1)	Pale yellowish green	2·75	2·00	1·50
(2)	Yellowish green	2·75	2·00	1·50
	Block of four	12·50	9·00	8·00
	Used on cover	†	†	2·50
a.	Watermark inverted (ex. booklets) †	22·00	12·00	9·00
b.	Raised crown in watermark (corner block of 4) (Pl. 41b, 49b, 52c, 53a and 55, R. 19/2)		£425	
c.	No. M2 with St. Andrew's Cross attached (6.06)		£190	£200
ca.	Ditto watermark inverted		£190	£200
d.	Doubly printed. The bottom rows of one sheet with control H9 showed 13 stamps with partial or full doubling From		£37500	£27500
e.	Displaced cliché (Pl. 20, R. 19/12 or R. 20/12) corner pair		£375	
f.	Right frame broken (Pl. 18c, R. 10/12)		£150	
g.	Split left frame (Pl. ?, R. 1/5)		£150	
h.	Left frame broken (Pl. ?, R. 4/3)		£150	
ha.	Left frame broken (Pl. 24c, R. 11/6)		£150	
i.	Bottom frame broken (Pl. 33, R. 20/5)		£150	
j.	Minor frame breaks From		45·00	
k.	Left of crown broken (Pl. 63a, R. 20/5)		£150	
s.	"Specimen", Type 17		£400	
t.	"Specimen", Type 22		£275	
u.	"Cancelled", Type 20		£1800	

Imperforate *tête-bêche* pair from P.O. Registration Sheet........................... Unused *tête-bêche* pair £45000
†No. M2a. The prices are for booklet stamps. Inverted watermarks from sheets are worth much more but can only be differentiated by marginal examples or multiples differing from the booklet format of 3×2.
    Many cracks and breaks in the frame lines are known. We illustrate and catalogue five major examples.

20

½d. Yellow-green. M3 *Postage Issues (1902-13)* **KING EDWARD VII** **MA**

	Unmtd mint	Mtd mint	Used
i. Minor frame breaks *From*		60·00	
j. Vertical scratch below beard to stamp below (Pl. ?, R. 1/8)		£300	£225
k. Major bottom frame break and damage (Pl. 59b, R. 20/3)		£280	
l. Cross on Crown almost missing (Pl. 63b, R. 19/20 Nos. 1/3) *Each*		£280	
m. Left of Crown broken (Pl. 63b, R. 20/5)		£250	
n. Imperf. between stamp and right margin			
s. "Specimen", Type 22		£325	

†No. M3a watermark inverted—see note for No. M2a.

No. M3n came from an upper pane, bottom right corner, vertical strip of 3 with perforations misplaced.

The Harrison printings, with the exception of the two bright green shades, have a very flat appearance when compared with the De La Rue issues. There is less white in the design, and the shading extends well up to the sides of the Crown. The pale green shade (No. M3(5)) is the nearest approach to the De La Rue colour, but is bluer. The bright green shades are distinct; on No. (7) the design is rather spotted (Plate 64b).

In the Harrison printing the lines in the veining of the leaves and on the King's neck are noticeably strengthened.

M2f    M2g    M2h

M2k, M3m, M4m

Plate Proof. Imperf. without watermark
In issued colour on poor quality buff paper .... 50·00

1911 *(3 May).* **½d. Yellow-green.** Perf. 14. Harrison. Ordinary Paper

M3 (=S.G.267/71)

	Unmtd mint	Mtd mint	Used
(1) Dull yellow-green	3·75	2·75	1·50
(2) Dull green	4·25	3·00	1·50
(3) Deep dull green	17·00	11·00	6·00
(4) Deep dull yellow-green (very blotchy print)	75·00	40·00	40·00
(5) Pale bluish green	80·00	40·00	40·00
(6) Bright green (fine impression) (June 1911)	£450	£275	£170
(7) Deep bright green	£575	£325	£200
(8) Olive-green	£100	65·00	45·00
Block of four	20·00	16·00	8·00
Used on cover	†	†	4·00
a. Watermark inverted†	90·00	60·00	60·00
b. Watermark sideways	—	—	£35000
ba. Vertical strip of 6 showing "POSTAGE" watermark	£3750	—	—
c. No watermark		£35000	
d. Imperf. (pair)	—	£40000	†
e. With St. Andrew's Cross attached		£280	£300
f. Do. watermark inverted		£280	£300
g. Gash in crown (Pl. ?, R. 12/11)		£250	
h. Major frame breaks (Pl. 64b, R.18/10)		£250	
ha. Major frame break (Pl. 57b, R. 17/7)		£250	

M3/4g

M3/4h

M3ha    M3j (Extends to R. 2/8)

M3k    M3l

21

MA KING EDWARD VII   Postage Issues (1902-13)   ½d. Green. M4

For illustration of Nos. M3m, M4m, see No. M2k.

Perforation 14
Types: see Control List.

1911 (30 October). **½d. Green.** Perf. 15 × 14. Harrison. Ordinary Paper

M4 (=S.G.279/9a)

	Unmtd mint	Mtd mint	Used
(1) Dull green	65·00	40·00	45·00
(2) Deep dull green	80·00	40·00	45·00
(3) Deep dull green (very blotchy print)	£1100	£700	£400
(4) Pale bluish green	65·00	40·00	45·00
Block of four	£325	£200	£225
Used on cover	†	†	£100
g. Gash in Crown (Pl. ?, R. 12/11)		£280	£100
h. Major frame breaks (Pl. 64b, R. 18/10)		£280	
j. Left frame broken (Pl. 63b, R. 12/9)		£300	
m. Left of Crown broken (Pl. 63b, R. 20/5)		£220	

M4j

Perforations 15 × 14
Types V3 and V3A

Controls. Prices are for unused corner pairs

Printed by De La Rue

Control	Date	H1	H1A	V1 or V4	V2	V2A or V4A
(a) With continuous rule						
Blue-green						
A	Jan. 1902	8·00	9·50	£125	†	75·00
B	Dec. 1902	8·00	35·00	75·00	†	75·00
C	Oct. 1903	9·50	£160	9·50	†	50·00
C4	Feb. 1904	8·00	£125	9·50	†	32·00
D4	Apr. 1904	9·50	—	38·00	†	£125
Yellow-green						
D4	Nov.1904	75·00	†	60·00	†	£120
(b) With coextensive rule						
Blue-green						
B	Mid 1903	50·00	†	35·00	†	£160
C	Oct. 1903	11·00	£125	£125	†	30·00
C4	Jan. 1904	9·50	£160	9·50	†	9·50
D4	Apr. 1904	8·00	£160	8·00	†	27·00
Yellow-green						
D4	Nov. 1904	8·00	£125	8·00	†	—
D5	Mar. 1905	8·00	60·00	13·00	†	—
E5	Sep. 1905	8·00	£160	11·00	26·00	8·00
E6	June 1906	8·00	†	†	£160	8·00
F6	Aug. 1906	8·00	60·00	†	32·00	8·00
F7	July 1907	30·00	†	†	24·00	8·00
G7	Sep. 1907	9·50	†	†	8·00	8·00
G8	July 1908	9·50	£125	†	9·50	9·50
H8	Oct. 1908	8·00	35·00	†	8·00	8·00
H9	Aug. 1909	60·00	†	†	9·50	9·50
I9	Nov. 1909	9·50	†	†	8·00	8·00
I10	July 1910	8·00	£160	†	9·50	9·50
J10	Oct. 1910	8·00	†	†	8·00	8·00

The blue-green continuous rule printing with Control D4, perf. H1A exists from plates 23 and 25.
One example is known of Control F6 and several of Control E5 with Perf. Type V2(a).
A single example of Control I10 with bottom margin perforated through has been seen with "o" omitted.

Printed by Harrison
Perf. 14

Control	Date	H2	H2A	VI	V1A
A11	May 1911	12·00	12·00	32·00	£125

Control A 11 (Perf. Type H2A) is known with the watermark inverted.
Perf. 15 × 14

Control	Date	V3	V3A
A11	Oct. 1911	£150	£200

The H2 perforator is known in variations a, c, d and e and the H2A perforator in variations c, d and e. An exceptionally wide margin is needed to show the 14 holes of variation e.
Examples are known with perforator as Type V3 but having no extension hole in the bottom margin (price £1250).
A vertical post 5 mm. high, midway between two sheets and appearing 7½ mm. below their bottom stamps is occasionally seen on corner pieces of the Harrison printing perf. 14. This may have served a similar purpose to the guillotine dot of the De La Rue printings but seems only to have had limited use. It is known for a few control corner pieces from Plates 54 and 60b and on S.E. corner pieces from Plate 59b. The latter can be identified by a white spot which appears in the top left inner frame of R. 20/12. Reports of any sightings for other plates or values would be welcomed. (*Corner pair price £50 unused*).
The so-called "A 17" Control results from ink build up between the tops of "11" and is found on some pieces perf. 14 and perf. 15 × 14 from Plates 54 and 58c. (*Corner pair price from £75 unused*).

Plate Markings
A great deal of research on the Plates of the ½d. and 1d. values has been undertaken by the King Edward VII Study Circle of the Great Britain Philatelic Society, but more remains to be done. The findings to date are embodied in the information that follows. It is probable that a few more 1d. plates have yet to be identified.
In the plates with coextensive rule all are Die II except where Die I is stated. Further information about this and the "6/7" Rule will be found under "Marginal Rules" in the General Notes. See also under "Registration Piece".
To distinguish between left-hand sheets and right-hand sheets see under "Recognising the Two Halves of the Mill Sheet" in the General Notes.
Before this study can be completed much more material needs to be seen, preferably in the form of complete bottom strips. In the lists of Plate Markings a plate marking *preceded by a dagger* indicates that there remains some uncertainty about this item. The nature of the uncertainty is shown in the Control Schedules where a plate number *followed by an asterisk* means that the item has been reported previously but has not been confirmed during the present study but when *followed by a dagger* its existence has been deduced from an incomplete bottom row or side strip and awaits confirmation.
Anybody possessing such items is requested to submit them to the Editor for examination and this applies also to any marginal rule portions bearing cuts, etc. that do not agree with those listed—for instance a plate with a continuous rule of the 1d. with control A having a first cut under the 3rd stamp is one that the Study would very much like to see, and the same for the ½d. with cuts under 3rd or 6th.

½d. Green. M4 Postage Issues (1902-13) KING EDWARD VII

All the Plate Numbers are arbitrarily allocated philatelic numbers but it is hoped eventually to be able to correlate these with the official plate numbers.

The ½d. plate has now been added as Plate 71 with Continuous Rule, but no cuts have been seen, so more information is required. Corner pieces of this plate had been confused with those of Plate 9, as both have a prominent flaw in the marginal rule below R. 20/11 at the upper left. Both plates started with Control A, but whereas right-hand sheets were given for Plate 9, those of Plate 71 are left-hand. 71 is thought to have served as a master plate, with 9 a successful copy.

With Continuous Rule

Plate	Features
1a	2 cuts under FP of 3rd, damage starts in 12th rule
1b	Added cut under EN of 7th
1c	Added cut under PE of 2nd. Damage to 12th rule extends
1d	Added cut under FP of 6th
2a	2 large cuts under LFPE of 4th
†2b, c	Added cut under NN of 2nd and ¾ cut (base) under FP of 3rd
2d	Added cut under LF of 1st
3	Cut under P of 8th
4a	Cut under E of 5th
4b	Added cut under FP of 1st
4c	Added cut under PE of 2nd
4d	Side change with added cut likely for D4
5a	Cut under P of 4th, bottom rule temporarily damaged at right corner
5b	Added cut under P of 1st
6	Deleted. Now part of Plate 4
7	Deleted as being redundant
8a	Cut under PE of 1st
†8b, c	Added wide cut under PE of 8th and fine ½ cut (base) under FP of 4th
9a	Large cut under ENN of 8th. Distinctive rule flaw below 11th, as for Plate 71
9b	Added cut under P of 3rd
9c	Added cut under P of 1st
9d	Added cut under LF of 2nd
9e	Added 2 cuts under NY of 7th
9f	Added cut under FP of 4th
†10a	Cut under PE of 1st
10b	Added cut under FP of 2nd but only control triple seen for each state
11	Fine cut under P of 2nd
12	Deleted. Now part of Plate 24
13	Cut under P of 5th. Left B control, wide break under 11/12
14	Deleted. Now part of Plate 11
16	Deleted. Now part of Plate 65
18a	Cut under F of 4th
18b	Added cut under P of 7th
18c	Added cuts or breaks to right of R. 20 (12 mm.), and R. 18 (4 mm.). Rule below 12th becomes dropped
19	Cut under N(N) of 8th
21	Deleted. Now part of Plate 4
22	Deleted. Now part of Plate 2
†23	Cut under FP of 4th, 2 cuts under FPE of 5th
†24a	Cut under P of 7th
24b	Added two ¾ cuts (base) under LF of 6th. Rule below 12th dropped.
24c	Added 2 sloping cuts under ALF of 4th
24d	Added cut under FP of 3rd
†65a	3 cuts under 7th below F, N(N) and Y
65b	Added cut under EN of 2nd
65c	Added cut under 5th reported
66	Cut under PE of 3rd
67	Cut under PE of 6th
69a	Cut under 7th below P
69b	Added cuts under 7th below PE and N(N)
70	2 cuts under 6th, below L and P
71	Distinctive flaw below 11th as for 9a (only control strip of 3 seen and cut 5th probable)

With Coextensive Rule

Plate	Features
15	Die 1, 6/7 Rule. Cut under PE of 1st
20	Die 1, Cut under E of 3rd
25a	Die 1, 6/7 Rule. Large cut under AL of 1st
25b	Added cut under P of 8th
26a	Die 1, 6/7 Rule. Cut under F of 2nd
26b	Added cut under P of 1st (finer than P1. 15) repair gap under L of 11th
27	Die 1, 6/7 Rule. 2 sloping cuts under LF of 6th
28	Fine cut under P of 1st. Right of centre pillars, 2 plug-like breaks (16¼, 18½ mm.)
29	Cut under P of 2nd. From control E6 the right of rule under 1st damaged
30a	Thin cut under P of 3rd
30b	Added cut under FP of 4th
32	Cut under FP of 4th
33	1½ cuts under PE of 5th
34a	Cut under N(N) of 7th
†34b	Side change for control G8 strip of 3, no cut seen
35a	Cut under AL of 6th
†35b	Added ½ double cuts under L of 4th
†35c	Added ½ cut (base) under PE of 8th, ½ cut (base) under H and irregular cut or break under FP of 9th (with right control F6
36a	Cut under E of 8th. Poor alignment of rules and clichés, particularly under 4th and 9th
36b	Cut to right of 20th (3 mm.) and tiny cut base 12th (N)N
†36c	Added cuts under FP of 2nd, PE of 4th and ¼ cuts or nicks under and right of Y of 1st (with right control F 6)
36d	Added ¾ cut (base) under A of 1st
37a	Cut under FP of 10th
37b	Added ½ cut under P of 3rd, hollow rule under 2nd with control I 9
38a	Cut under NN of 9th
38b	Added cut under FP of 4th
38c	Added ¾ cut (base) under PE of 3rd
39	Slanting cut (left to right) under PE of 8th
40	Deleted. Now part of Plate 36
41a	No cuts; right-hand sheets, minute dot under H of 2nd
41b	Added ½ to full cut (base) under A of 2nd
42a	No cuts; right-hand sheets, 1 mm. registration piece gap under P and small dot under PE of 7th
42b	Added cut under P of 3rd
43a	No cuts; left-hand sheets, ¾ mm. registration piece gap under P of 7th, distinct scoop under AL of 9th; "flag" at top of S.E. corner "bit" Rule left of 19th dented (outer) (10½ mm.)
43b	Added cut under N(Y) of 7th
43c	Added cut under FP of 3rd
44	Deleted. Now part of Plate 47
45a	Cut under FP of 11th
45b	Added cut under PE of 5th
45c	Added 1½ cuts under PE of 1st
46a	Cut under P of 12th
46b	Added cut under P of 8th
46c	Added cut under F of 3rd
46d	Added cut under FP of 1st
47a	¾ cut (base) under H of 1st
47b	Added large cut under P of 5th
48	Deleted. Now part of Plate 42
49a	Cut under P of 4th
49b	Added cut under P of 3rd
49c	Return to right sheet but no new cut made
50	Deleted. Now part of Plate 37
51	Deleted. Now part of Plate 43

KING EDWARD VII Postage Issues (1902-13) ½d. Green. M4

Plate	Features
52a	No cuts; right-hand sheets, tapered rule below 2nd narrowing to right
52b	Added large semi-circular cut under PEN of 3rd
52c	Added cut, sometimes closed at base, under PE of 8th
52d	Added cut under E of 7th
53a	Irregular cut under A of 6th
53b	Added irregular cut under PE of 5th
53c	Return to right sheet, but no new cut made
54a	Cut, sometimes double, under PE of 1st
54b	Cut added rule 20 (10.7 mm.)
55	Cut under EN of 4th
56	Deleted. Now part of Plate 43
57a	Slanting cut, running down from left, under FP of 8th
57b	Added cut right side of 19th row (6 mm.)
58a	1½ cuts under HA of 1st. Faint flaw under FP of 11th
58b	Added cut under HA of 4th
58c	Added cut 18th right side (8 mm.)
59a	Cut under H of 2nd
59b	Added cut 17th right side (7¾ mm.)
60a	Heavily blurred cut E of 3rd
60b	Added cut 18th right side (11 mm.)
61	Cut under P of 5th.
61a	2 cuts, probably not intentional, added 19th right side (11¼, 14¼ mm.)
62	Deleted. Now part of Plate 54
63a	Cut under A of 6th
63b	Added cut 19th right side (10½ mm.)
64a	Cut under (N)N of 7th
64b	Added cut 20th right side (10½ mm.). Later a coloured line developed right of left corner "bit"
†68	No cuts; right-hand sheets, ¾ mm. registration piece gap under P of 7th (the S.W. corner "bit" is more to left and lower than that of Plate 42a)
17	59b
18	18c, 58b, 60b
19	24d, 57b, 61, 63b
20	18c, 36b, 36c, 36d, 64b

Centre pillars: 28

The corner "bits" can be of help in differentiating Plates 42, 43 and 68.

Index to Marginal Markings

Bottom Margin, stamp numbers

Stamp No.	Plates
1	2c, 4b, 4c, 5b, 8a, 8b, 9c, 9d, 9e, 9f, 10a, 10b, 15, 25a, 25b, 26b, 28, 34b, 36d, 45c, 46d, 47a, 47b, 54, 58a, 58b, 58c
2	1b/d, 2b, 2c, 4c, 9d, 9e, 9f, 10b, 11, 26a, 26b, 29, 36c, 36d, 41b, 59a, 59b, 65b, 65c
3	1a, 1b, 2b, 2c, 9b, 9c, 9d, 9e, 9f, 20, 24d, 30a, 30b, 37b, 38c, 42b, 43c, 46c, 46d, 49b, 52b, 52c, 52d, 60a, 60b, 66
4	2a, 2b, 2c, 5a, 5b, 8b, 9f, 18a, 18b, 18c, 23, 24c, 30b, 32, 35b, 35c, 36c, 36d, 38b, 38c, 49a, 49b, 55, 58b, 58c
5	4a, 4b, 4c, 13, 23, 33, 45b, 45c, 47b, 53b, 61
6	1b/d, 24b, 24d, 27, 35a, 35b, 35c, 53a, 53b, 63a, 63b, 67, 70
7	1b/d, 9e, 9f, 18b, 18c, 24a, 24c, 24d, 34a, 42a, 42b, 43b, 43c, 52d, 64a, 64b, 65a, 65b, 65c, 69a, 69b
8	3, 8b, 9a, 9b, 9c, 9d, 9e, 9f, 19, 25b, 35a, 36a, 36b, 36c, 36d, 39, 46b, 46c, 46d, 52c, 52d, 57a, 57b
9	35c, 38a, 38b, 38c
10	37a, 37b
11	9a, 26c, 45a, 45b, 45c, 58a, 58b, 58c, 71
12	36c, 36d, 46a, 46b, 46c, 46d

No cuts: 41a, 42a, 43a, 52a, 68
Basal scoop under NY of 4th: 8, 9, 13, (24), (28), (47), 60, (63)
Basal scoop under HAL of 9th: 9, 13, 28, (29), 30, 32, (34), (37), 38, 41, 43, 46, 47, (63), (68)
The scoops are sometimes very slight on the plates shown in brackets. Rule breaks and deliberate cuts are included in the table.

Control Schedule

As corner examples with full selvedge can be used to identify from which side of the mill sheet they come, Controls are recorded from both left and right sheets in the table which follows. See General Notes under "Recognising the Two Halves of the Mill Sheet".

As already stated an asterisk means that the plate with the particular control has been reported but not confirmed by the present study and a dagger indicates that its existence has been deduced from an incomplete bottom row or side strip and awaits confirmation.

Control	Plates with which it was used	
	Left Sheets	Right Sheets
A	1a, 4a, 5b, 8a, 13, 65a, 66, 69, 71†	2a, 3, 5, 8b, 9a, 11, 67
B	1a, 4b, 5b, 9b, 9c†, 10a†, 13, 15, 20†, 23, 24a, 65a, 66†, 71†	1b†, 2a†, 11, 18a, 19, 23†, 67, 70
C	9e†, 10a†, 15, 20, 23, 24a	1b, 2b, 9d†, 11†, 18a, 19, 26a†, 65b†
C 4	2c†, 9e†, 18b†, 20, 23, 24a†, 25a†, 26b, 65c†	1b†, 4c, 10b†, 18a, 19, 24b, 24c, 26a, 27
D 4 blue-grn	2c†, 4d†, 9e†, 18b, 20, 23, 24d, 25a, 26b†, 28, 30, 33, 34a	1b†, 2d†, 4c†, 9f, 18b, 19, 24c, 25b, 27, 29, 32
D 4 yell-grn	24d, 28, 30a, 33, 34	18c, 27, 29, 32, 35a, 36a
D 5	28, 30a, 33, 34a, 37b	29, 32, 35a, 36a, 37a
E 5	28, 30a*, 33, 34a, 37b	29, 30b, 32, 35, 36a, 36b, 38a
E 6	28, 33, 34a, 37b	29, 30b*, 32, 38a, 39
F 6	28, 33, 34a, 37b	29, 32, 35b, 35c†, 36c, 38a, 39, 41a
F 7	28, 33, 34a, 37b	35b†, 36c†, 38a, 39, 41a, 68
G 7	28, 33, 34a, 35c†, 37b, 39, 43a, 47a	35b†, 36c†, 38a, 41a, 42a, 43a, 68
G 8	28†, 36d†, 37b, 39†, 43a, 45a, 47	34b†, 38a, 41a, 42a, 46a, 68†
H 8	37b, 38c, 42b†, 43a, 45a, 45b, 47	37b, 38b, 41a, 41b, 42a, 46a, 46b, 49a, 52a, 68†
H 9	37b†, 38c, 42b, 43a, 45b, 47a, 52b	41b, 42b, 46b, 49a, 52a, 53a
I 9	37b†, 42b, 43a, 43b, 43c, 45c, 46c, 46d, 47a, 49b, 52b, 52d, 53a, 53b	41b, 46b, 49c, 52c, 53a, 55, 57a, 68†
I 10	43c, 45c, 46d, 47a†, 53b, 58a	41b, 49c, 55, 57a, 59a*
J 10	43c, 46d†, 47b, 54a, 58a, 60a, 61, 64a	41b, 49c, 53c, 55, 57a, 58b, 59a, 63a
A 11 (14)	57b, 59b, 63b	54b, 58c, 60b, 61, 64b
A 11 (15×14)	57b†, 59b, 63b	58c, 64b

Reported but unconfirmed are Controls F6 with plates 27 and 42a, also Control F7 with plate 42a.

●

Right Margin, row numbers

Row No.	Plates

1902-11. 1d. Red, Type M2

1902 (1 January). **1d. Red.** Perf. 14. De La Rue. Ordinary Paper

M5 (=S.G.219/20)

		Unmtd mint	Mtd mint	Used
(1)	Scarlet	2·75	2·00	1·50
(2)	Bright scarlet	2·75	2·00	1·50
(3)	Deep bright scarlet	8·00	6·00	2·25
(4)	Rose-carmine	40·00	30·00	20·00
	Block of four	12·50	10·00	8·00
	Used on cover	†	†	2·50
a.	Watermark inverted (ex. booklets)†	8·00	4·00	3·00
b.	Raised crown in watermark (R. 19/2) (corner block of 4)		£450	
c.	Imperf. (pair)	—	£35000	
d.	Imperf. margin at bottom of top pane*		£5750	
db.	Imperf. between stamp and right margin		£4000	
e.	Displaced cliché (Pl. 30c, R. 20(12) corner pair		£225	
f.	Displaced cliché (Pl. 51, R. 20/12) corner pair		£250	
g.	Pin repair, N.E. of value tablet and top frame break N.E. corner (Pl. 9, R. 12/12)		£280	
h.	Pin repair below ON of ONE		£280	
ha.	Pin repair below P of POSTAGE (Pl. 9, R. 20/12)		£280	
i.	Frame broken at right (Pl. 70a, R. 19/12)		£150	
j.	Flaw in E of ONE and P of PENNY (Pl. 58a, R 20/8)		£150	
k.	Spot under E of PENNY (Pl. 58a. R 20/10)		£150	
l.	Left frame thinned and vertical scratch (Pl. 9, R. 19/11, control E 5)		£150	
m.	Major plate crack (Pl. ?, R. 3 or 13/12)		£225	
ma.	Ditto. Continued (Pl. ?, R. 4 or 14/12)		£225	
n.	Spot under V of REVENUE (Pl. 50b, R. 20/11)		£150	
o.	Tail to E of REVENUE (Pl. 53a/c, R. 20/10)		£150	
oa.	Major plate crack (Pl. 53a, R. 20/12)		£275	
p.	No top to Crown (Pl. 85, R. 20/11)		£150	
q.	Minor frame breaks From		50·00	
r.	Cracked plate (various) From		50·00	
ra.	Inner frame broken at right (R. 1/3 of booklet pane with watermark upright		£225	
rb.	Plate crack below E to rule (Pl. 30, R. 20/12) *with bottom margin*			
s.	"Specimen", Type 15		£250††	
t.	"Specimen", Type 16		£350	
u.	"Specimen", Type 17		£400	
w.	"Specimen", Type 22		£275	
x.	"Cancelled", Type 20		£1800	

Imperforate *tête-bêche* pair from P.O. Registration Sheet.. Unused *tête-bêche* pair £45000

Deep shades of No. M5(4) which often have the appearance of being overinked are sometimes described as "blood-red".

†No. M5a. The prices are for booklet stamps. Inverted watermarks from sheets are worth much more but can only be differentiated by marginal examples or multiples differing from the booklet format of 3×2.

Numerous pin repairs are recorded in *The GB Journal*, Vol. 32, No. 2 May-June 1994. See also General Notes.

Many cracks and breaks in the frame lines are known on the 1d. value. We only list some of them. For further information see *Cracked Units on K.E. VII 1d.* by H. S. Doupé; published in 1962 by the G.B. Philatelic Society.

*No. M5d is from the top pane and shows imperforate between stamp and bottom (interpanneau) margin. The error was caused by a failure of the perforator when the sheet was fed from the top. After repair, the sheet was subsequently fed in from the bottom with the machine stopping after eleven beats omitting the one line of perforations. No. M5db was caused by a paper fold.

Nos. M5e/f are S.E. corner pairs and do not include the displaced clichés at R. 19/12. Add 100% for blocks showing two displaced clichés. See plate marking notes to distinguish the rules between plates 30 and 51 as both had coextensive rules.

††No. M5s exists from NPM archive sales.

No. M5 was pre-released and exists on cover with No. M1 (½d.), M16 (2½d.) and M31 (6d.) cancelled 31 December 1901. An example is also known used at Stratford, E London, on 30 December 1901.

M5g

M5j, M6ab, M6e, M7a

M5k, M6ac, M6f, M7b

M5n

M5p

KING EDWARD VII Postage Issues (1902-13) **1d. Red. M6**

1d. value without markings £6000
This was approved on 8 May 1901 by Emil Fuchs on behalf of the King subject to the laurel and oak being narrower to allow more space between the portrait and the frame.

Die Proofs in black on white glazed card:
Without marking £3000
Without marking but initialled (M/S) "EF" £3000
Endorsed (M/S) "As approved by Mr. Fuchs 19 Aug" £3000
Endorsed "BEFORE HARDENING 20 AUG 01" £3000
Endorsed "AFTER HARDENING 20 AUG 01" £3000
Endorsed "AFTER STRIKING" (various dates) £3000
Endorsed "Working Die No. 16" £3000

Die Proofs in scarlet on gummed paper. Watermark Crown
Four impressions struck as two vertical pairs £20000
These are believed to be unique.

Die Proofs from the De La Rue Archives
On card unmounted with traces of gum or paper on the back:
Essay in die proof form by F. W. Pearce with
approved frame but with beard and hair of
head plate not approved £6500
Complete die proof with uncleared surround,
without markings £3000
Cut down proof of frame plate (27×32 mm) £5000

Pieces cut from the Striking Books
See notes under the ½d. value.
Struck on plain paper cut to size with various endorsements comprising dates, plates and/or number of leads
1d value .... From £2800
See under ½d. value for pieces with ½d. and 1d. together.

Plate Proofs. All imperf. and without watermark
Pale or deep green on thin white card .... Each 80·00
Carmine on thin white paper £100
The above proofs are known with double, and
with triple impressions .... Each 80·00
Bright scarlet on poor quality buff paper .... 40·00
Bright scarlet on white wove paper .... 95·00

Colour Trials. Made from a special plate of 20 electros
1901. Watermark Crown, Imperf. or perf. 14
Dull purple, black on red, purple on red .... From £1750
1906. Watermark Crown. Imperf. or perf. 14. Trials for a suggested change of colour
Blue-geranium, cerise, deep carmine, carmine-red, carmine-lake, carmine-rose and dull rose .... From £1750

Edward VII 1d. Colour Trials of 1911. See under Section NA and description of the 1912 colour trials refer to Spec. No. N16 in Section NB.

1911 (3 May). **1d. Red.** Perf. 14. Harrison. Ordinary paper

M6 (=S.G.272/75a)

	Unmtd mint	Mtd mint	Used
(1) Rose-red	15·00	8·00	12·00
(2) Deep rose-red	15·00	8·00	12·00
(3) Intense rose-red	£375	£260	£160
(4) Pale rose-carmine	75·00	45·00	25·00
(5) Rose-carmine	85·00	55·00	30·00
(6) Deep rose-carmine	£600	£400	£275
(7) Aniline rose (F)	£300	£180	£140
(8) Aniline pink (F) (May 1911)	£1250	£750	£375
Block of four	60·00	40·00	60·00
Used on cover	†	†	18·00
a. No watermark (brick-red) (Pl. 58b)	75·00	50·00	
ab. As a. Flaw in E of ONE and P of PENNY (Pl. 58b)	£250		
ac. As a. Spot under E of PENNY (Pl. 58b)	£225		
b. Watermark inverted†	80·00	50·00	50·00
c. Bottom frame broken (Pl. 61b, R. 20/9)			£150

M5i

M5l Repaired with Control E 6 (possibly substituted cliché)

M5m/ma

M5o

M5ra, M6d

M5rb This variety was the original cliché replaced in Plate 30, see No. M5e

M5oa Later retouched

Perforation 14
Types: See Control List

Essays from the De La Rue Archives
Stamp size design with photographic centre and bromide frame on card:
Lettered "B" and stamped "19 APR 1901" £6000
With larger "&", lettered "A" and stamped "23 APR 1901". £6000
Stamp size photographic essay on card showing larger space between laurels and portrait:

1d. Red. M7 *Postage Issues (1902-13)* **KING EDWARD VII**

	Unmtd mint	Mtd mint	Used
d. Inner frame broken at right (R. 1/3 of booklet pane with watermark upright)		£200	
e. Flaw in E of ONE and P of PENNY (Pl. 58b, R. 20/8)		£150	
f. Spot under E of PENNY (Pl. 58b, R. 20/10)		£150	
s. "Specimen", Type 22		£325	
t. "Cancelled", Type 21 imperf.		£150	

Some of the rose-red shades show slight fluorescence.

Some shades of this value are difficult to classify. The best method of checking M6 Nos. (4), (5) and (6) is to use the identical perf. 15×14 shades for comparison purposes. The rose-red shades of Harrison are quite different from the scarlet of De La Rue, and little difficulty should be encountered here. M5 (4) is brighter than M6 (5). The latter has less white in the design, and the shading extends well up to the sides of the crown.

M6a occurs in shades of brick-red and was probably a trial printing. See also *The GB Journal*, Vol. 27 No 5 for an article describing the printing which was made in connection with an experiment for coils. For this printing the plate was cut and the upper pane placed below the lower one after removal of the Jubilee lines. Thus the two listed varieties from plate 58b, M6e and M6f, exist from this printing but in new positions.

Somerset House are also known to have prepared a trial printing of the 1d. in carmine-rose on thick unwatermarked paper.

†No. M6b watermark inverted—see note for No. M5a.

The plates which were used for the provisional printings, like those of the Halfpenny value, were probably resurfaced before use.

††No. M6s exists from NPM archive sales.

No. M6t shows the overprint set diagonally and exists misplaced.

M6/7c

Perforation 14
Types: See Control list

1911 (4 October). **1d. Red.** Perf. 15 × 14. Harrison. Ordinary Paper

M7 (=S.G.280/82)

	Unmtd mint	Mtd mint	Used
(1) Rose-red	80·00	45·00	25·00
(2) Deep rose-red	£125	75·00	30·00
(3) Intense rose-red	£600	£400	£275
(4) Pale rose carmine	45·00	30·00	15·00
(5) Rose-carmine	35·00	15·00	15·00
(6) Deep rose-carmine	45·00	25·00	15·00
(7) Carmine	£200	£125	40·00
Block of four	£175	75·00	75·00
Used on cover	†	†	30·00
a. Flaw in E of ONE and P of PENNY (Pl. 58b, R. 20/8)		£175	
b. Spot under E of PENNY (Pl. 58b, R. 20/10)		£175	
c. Bottom frame broken (Pl. 61b, R. 20/9)		£175	

Shade No. (1) may be found with extremely shiny gum.

Perforation 15 × 14
Types V3 and V3A

Controls. Prices are for unused corner pairs

Printed by De La Rue

			Perforation Type			
				V1		V2A or
Control	Date	H1	H1A	or V4	V2	V4A
(a) With continuous rule
A	Jan. 1902	11·00	28·00	9·50	†	11·00
B	Dec. 1902	11·00	30·00	8·00	†	11·00
C	Oct. 1903	11·00	24·00	9·50	†	24·00
C 4	Feb. 1904	11·00	28·00	8·00	†	38·00
D 4	Apr. 1904	27·00	£130	11·00	†	---
D 5	July 1905	50·00	†	50·00	†	---
(b) With coextensive rule
C	Oct. 1903	24·00	£130	38·00	†	35·00
C 4	Feb. 1904	11·00	£150	£120	†	---
D 4	Apr. 1904	11·00	£130	11·00	†	38·00
D 5	June 1905	11·00	£150	11·00	†	---
E 5	Aug. 1905	11·00	†	11·00	11·00	11·00
E 6	July 1906	11·00	£130	†	£130	11·00
F 6	Sept. 1906	11·00	£130	†	11·00	11·00
F 7	July 1907	11·00	£130	†	11·00	11·00
G 7	Oct. 1907	11·00	£150	†	11·00	11·00
G 8	July 1908	30·00	†	†	11·00	11·00
H 8	Oct. 1908	11·00	50·00	†	11·00	11·00
H 9	July 1909	11·00	60·00	†	11·00	18·00
I 9	Oct. 1909	11·00	£130	†	11·00	8·00
I 10	July 1910	35·00	£150	†	11·00	9·50
J 10	Sept. 1910	11·00	60·00	†	11·00	8·00

Corner pairs are known of Control E 5 with Type V2(a) showing bottom margin perforated through with only twelve pins. *Corner pair price £275 unused.*

The following control varieties are known:—

Control D 4 with imperf. bottom margin, Type H1 with the "4" almost omitted (above). *Unused single price £2500.*

Corner strip of three of Control F 7 perf. Type V2 with the "F 7" almost omitted. *Price unused £2500.*

One pair of Control G 7 from Plate 23 with the watermark inverted exists. *Price unused £6000.*

Examples occur where the control (e.g. I 9) is repeated under the 10th, 9th, 8th, 7th, etc., stamps, each impression fainter than its predecessor. Such examples are always perforated by the Type V2A perforator with right feed. The variety is caused by the comb head picking up the ink from the control, which had not properly dried, and at each descent of the comb a progressively fainter control became printed in the bottom margin. This variety has been seen with controls E 5, E 6 and G 7.

The scarce continuous rule, control D 4 with perf. Type V2A or V4A exists from plates 3, 7 and 14. C 4 with coextensive rule perf. Type V2A or V4A exists from plate 85.

KING EDWARD VII Postage Issues (1902-13) 1d. Red. M7

Printed by Harrison
Perf. 14

		Perforation Type			
Control	Date	H1	H2A	V1	V1A
A 11 (c)	Sept.1911	£200	†	†	†
A 11 (w)	May 1911	95·00	27·00	95·00	£100

Perf. 15 × 14

				V3	V3A
A 11 (c)	Oct. 1911			60·00	75·00

The H2 perforator is known in variations a, c, d and e and the H2A perforator in variations c, d and e.

(c) "close" and (w) "wide" refer to the space between the figures (1½ mm. and 2 mm. respectively).

An example of perforator as Type V3 is known but without extension hole in the bottom margin.

Plate Markings
See notes under "Plate Markings" of ½d. value.

With Continuous Rule

Plate	Features
†1a	Cut under PE of 10th
1b	Added cut under (P)E of 4th
1c	Added cut under PE of 8th
†2a	Cut under PE of 7th
2b	Probably added cut under an even numbered column
2c	Added slanting cut under NE of 11th
†3a	Crossed cuts under EP of 4th
3b	Added cut under P of 5th
3c	Added slanting cut under PE of 10th
4	¾ cut (base) under P of 10th
5	Cut under NE of 11th
6	Cut under EP of 12th
7	Cut under P of 12th
8	Deleted. Now part of Plate 14
†10	Cuts under E(N) and NN of 1st, N(N) of 5th and O and NE of 6th
†11a	Cut under(P)E of 5th
11b	Added cut under P of 2nd
11c	Added cut under EP of 11th
12	Deleted as being redundant
13	Cut sloping down, left to right, under (P)E of 4th
†14a	½ cut (base) under P of 9th, ½ cut (top) or damage under PE of 7th
14b	Added cuts under E(N) and N(Y) of 8th. Many rule breaks, including break or cut under (N)N of 10th. Rule below 12th drops during right control C 4
16a	Cut under PE of 8th
16b	Added cut under P of 4th
16c	Added cut slanting down from left to right under (E)N of 7th
17a	Cut under E(P) of 5th
17b	Added cut under P of 4th
†18a	Cut under NE of 6th
18b	Added cut under P of 9th
†19b	Cut under (P)E of 2nd, under PE of 8th and break under N(Y) of 10th
†20a	Cut under (P)E of 2nd
20b	Added cut under PE of 3rd
29	Deleted. Now part of Plate 2
32	Deleted. Now part of Plate 17
68a	Cut under P of 6th
68b	Added cuts under PE and N(N) of 5th
†69	Cut under E(N) of 7th
†70a	Cut sloping up left to right under (P)E of 6th, 2 pips (top) under N(E) of 8th
70b	Added cut under EP of 12th
72	Cut under P of 9th
73	Cut under P of 8th
†74a	Stamp 20/11, with control A, has disturbed shading over & RE
74b	Added ¾ cut (base) under P of 12th
75	Cut under (P)E of 8th differing from that on Plate 16
76	Cut under (P)E of 1st (Official Plate 1/1)
77	Cut under (N)E of 1st
†78a	Double cut under P of 10th
78b	Cut or cuts added, including under P of 11th leaning slightly forward

Plate	Features
†79	Thick and thin cuts under P and E of 1st. Basal nicks in rule below gutter 10/11 and ON of 11th
80a	Cut under (P)E of 7th
80b	Added cut under PE of 4th and ¾ cut (top) below gutter 9/10
81	Cut under PE of 2nd
†82	Cut under P of 4th, seen only on a strip of four of MO37, but although this overprint is believed to have the constant variety, upward projection from lowest inner oakleaf of control stamp, R. 20/11, confirmation of bottom strip required
†86	Cuts under PE of 2nd, (P)E of 4th and NN of 7th with right control C 4
87	Cut below (P)E of 4th but differing from Plate 13
88a	Cut sloping down, left to right, underP of 4th
88b	Added wide cut under (P)E of 3rd
88c	Probably added cut under an even numbered column

From control pieces with features not seen in the above plates it is thought that about another six plates may eventually be included. Each should have a cut or cuts that differ, perhaps only slightly, from the foregoing and any likely pieces should be submitted to the Editor.

With Coextensive Rule

Plate	Features
†9	Die I. ¾ flat-topped cut (base) under PE of 1st (Plate 49 cut has a pointed top). Control E 5 onwards have rule damage under P of 2nd
15	Deleted. Now part of Plate 30
21a	Cut under (P)E of 3rd (less curved right side and narrower base than Plate 37a)
21b	Added ¾ cut (top) under PE of 10th. This was formerly Plate 37 and items from control E 6 and later and previously listed as Plates 21a/b now belong to Plate 37
22a	¾ cut (base) under PE of 4th
22b	Added diamond-shaped cut under PE of 2nd
23a	Sloping cut under E(N) of 4th
23b	Added cut under P of 3rd
24a	Cut under PE of 5th
24b	Added wide ½ cut under NN of 2nd
25a	Cut under (N)E of 6th, burr shadow at right later
25b	Added ¾ cut (base) under PE of 12th
26a	Cut under (O)N of 6th, thin and regular
26b	Added cut under P of 11th; changes from left to right during control G 8
26c	Added ½ cut (base) under N(E) of 2nd; with control H 8 comes from left and right
27	Cut under N(N) of 7th
28a	Full and ¼ cut (base) under P of 8th
28b	Added diamond-shaped cut under P of 1st and full cut under NE of 6th
30a	Die I. Cut under P of 2nd; slanting crack under NE of 12th
30b	Added ½ cut (base) under EP of 10th
30c	Added cuts under O and (N)E of 6th
†31	1½ cuts under NE of 2nd; with none added for first change of side (information wanted about second change i.e. to H 8†)
33a	2 thick cuts under NE of 6th
33b	Added ½ cut (base) under P of 10th; short rule left of 11th
†34a	½ cut (top) under N(E) of 11th
34b	Added fine cut and dot under PEN of 9th (probably due to wear)
34c	Added cut 20th right side (5 mm.)
34d	Added cut 19th right side (8½ mm.)
35	½ cut (base) under EP of 2nd; change of side with control F 6
36	Cut under (P)E of 8th. Rule below 12th dropped from control E 5; change of side with control G 7
37a	Cut under (P)E of 3rd (more curved right side and wider base than Plate 21a)
37b	Added cut under (P)E of 2nd. Plate 37 contains controls E 6 to H 8 misplaced as Plate 21a/b, whilst the original E 5 item becomes Plate 21b

28

1d. Red. M7 Postage Issues (1902-13) KING EDWARD VII

Plate	Features
38a	Cut under PE of 2nd
38b	Added 2 double cuts under NN of 7th
39a	Dot under EP of 1st
39b	Added 2 irregular cuts under PEN of 4th
40a	Curved semi-double cut under PE of 2nd
40b	Added 2 cuts under EPE of 5th
41a	Thin "v" cut under (P)E of 5th. Side changed with no added cuts during control G 7
41b	Added ¾ cut under (P)E of 4th
42	Wide cut under (O)N of 6th
43a	½ cut (base) under Y of 7th
43b	Added cut or dot under P of 1st
†44a	Cut under P of 5th
44b	Added fine sloping cut under (P)E of 11th
†45	2 fine cuts under ON of 6th; right end of 10th probably broke away during right control G 8
†46a	2 ragged cuts under NE of 6th
46b	Added ½ cut (base), 1 cut and ½ cut (base) all under NEP of 5th
47a	Cut under NY of 7th
47b	Added cut under P of 5th
47c	Added 3 fractional sloping cuts (base) under EP of 2nd; 10th rule broken under Y and left section dropped
48a	1½ cuts under P of 8th
48b	Added 1½ cuts under (E)N of 7th
†49	½ cut with pointed top (base) under PE of 1st (Plate 9 had a flat-topped cut). A temporary change to right side with control I 10, so no additional cuts likely
50a	Cut under (N)E of 1st
50b	Added cut under EP of 4th
51a	½ cut under (P)E of 2nd and cut or break on 19th right side (11 mm.)
51b	Added ½ cut (base) under EP of 1st
52a	Ragged cut under PE of 3rd
†53a	Irregular cut under (P)E of 4th
53b	Added sloping cut under EN of 3rd and ¾ cut (base) under (O)N of 6th
53c	Added cuts under NN and NY of 7th
†54a	Irregular cut under PE of 5th
54b	Added cut under PE of 4th
54c	2 ½ cuts added (top) under (P)E of 8th
55	Deleted. Now part of Plate 53
†56	Irregular cut under N(N) of 5th. Changes to right side with control I 10 so further cuts likely
†57a	Cut with burr shadow to right under N(E) of 6th and dot at top left end of 12th rule; 5 cuts in centre rule to right of pillars (2.0, 6.7, 13.5, 17.5, 21.5 mm. up)
57b	Added 2 cuts under PEN of 5th and cut under EP of 8th
†58a	½ cut (top) under NY of 7th
58b	Added ½ cut (base) under N(N) of 1st and 2 cuts or breaks under EPE of 8th. Several flaw varieties
58c	Added cut 18th right side (11mm)
59	2 thick sloping cuts under ON of 6th. A proof on buff paper has fine cut or break under P of 11th, no examples seen on issued stamps
60	Small ½ cut (base) under PE of 2nd
†61a	½ cut (base) under P of 4th
61b	Added large cut under NN of 9th and cut 17th right side (8½ mm.). Some previous I 10 and J 10 control items now constitute Plate 84
†62a	Very fine cut (top) under EP of 5th
62b	Added big cut under PE of 11th. Cut 19th right side (12 mm.)
62c	Added cut 18th right side (11 mm.)
63a	½ cut (base) under (N)E of 3rd. Large cut under PE of 6th. Smaller cut under PE of 7th
63b	Added cut 17th right 12½ mm.)
63c	Added cut 20th right 9½ mm.)
64	Deleted. Now part of Plate 48
65	¾ cut (base) under EN of 7th
†66a	½ cut (base) under P of 8th (ragged)
66b	Added cut under EP of 10th (coarse and cut 18th right side (10½ mm.)
67	Deleted. Now part of Plate 44
†71	Die I, 6/7 Rule. Cut under P of 7th

Plate	Features
†84	½ cut (base) under EP of 4th (the similar ½ cut of Plate 61 is under P). Some I 10 and J 10 control items originally with Plate 61 belong to Plate 84. Left end of rule under 12th broken away during J 10
†85a	Die I, 6/7 Rule. Cut under PE of 6th
85b	Added cuts under EP and P of 8th

There are indications that one or two more coextensive rule plates could exist.

Index to Marginal Markings
Bottom Margin, stamp numbers

Stamp No.	Plates
1	9, 10, 28b, 39a, 39b, 43b, 49, 50a, 50b, 51b, 52b, 58b, 76, 77, 79
2	11b, 11c, 19b, 20a, 20b, 22b, 24b, 26c, 30a, 30b, 30c, 31, 35, 37b, 38a, 38b, 40a, 40b, 47c, 51a, 51b, 60, 81, 86
3	20b, 21a, 21b, 23b, 37a, 37b, 52a, 52b, 53b, 53c, 63a, 63b, 63c, 88b, 88c
4	1b, 1c, 3a, 3b, 3c, 13, 17b, 22a, 22b, 23a, 23b, 39b, 41b, 50b, 53a, 53b, 53c, 54b, 61a, 61b, 80b, 82, 84, 86, 87, 88a, 88b, 88c
5	3b, 3c, 10, 11a, 11b, 11c, 17a, 17b, 24a, 24b, 40b, 41a, 41b, 44a, 44b, 46b, 47b, 47c, 54a, 54b, 56, 57b, 62a, 62b, 62c, 68b
6	10, 18a, 18b, 25a, 25b, 26a, 26b, 26c, 28b, 30c, 33a, 33b, 42, 45, 46a, 46b, 53b, 53c, 57a, 57b, 59, 68a, 68b, 70a, 70b, 85a, 85b
7	2a, 2b, 2c, 14a, 14b, 16b, 27, 38b, 43a, 43b, 47b, 47c, 48b, 53c, 58a, 58b, 65, 69, 71, 80a, 80b, 86
8	1c, 14b, 16a, 16b, 19b, 28a, 28b, 36, 48a, 48b, 54b, 57b, 58b, 66a, 66b, 70a, 70b, 73, 75, 85b
9	14a, 14b, 18b, 34b, 34c, 34d, 61b, 72, 80b
10	1a, 1b, 1c, 3c, 4, 14b, 19, 21b, 30b, 30c, 33b, 45, 47c, 66b, 78a, 78b, 79, 80b
11	2c, 5, 11c, 26b, 26c, 33b, 34a, 34b, 34c, 44b, 62b, 62c, 78b, 79
12	6, 7, 25b, 30a, 30b, 30c, 57a, 57b, 70b, 74b

Basal scoop under NY of 4th: 17, 20, (24), (44), 46, 47, 82
Basal scoop under ONE of 9th: 2, (9), 10, 13, 20, (22), 24, 25, 28, 30, 31, (33), 35, 38, 39, 41, 42, 43, 44, 46, (48), 50, 54

The scoops are sometimes very slight on the plates shown in brackets. Rule breaks and deliberate cuts are included in the table.

Right Margin, row number

Row No.	Plates
Centre Pillars:	57a, 57b
17	61b, 63b, 63c
18	58c, 62c, 66b
19	34d, 51a, 51b, 62b, 62c
20	34c, 34d, 63c

Control Schedule
As corner examples with full selvedge can be used to identify from which side of the mill sheet they come, Controls are recorded from both left and right sheets in the table which follows. See General Notes under "Recognising the Two Halves of the Mill Sheet".

As already stated an asterisk means that the plate with the particular control has been reported but not confirmed by the present study and a dagger indicates that its existence has been deduced from an incomplete bottom row or side strip and awaits confirmation.

Control	Plates with which it was used	
	Left Sheets	Right Sheets
A	5, 11a, 11c†, 14a, 69, 72, 76, 77, 78b†, 79, 80a, 88b	1a†, 3a†, 4, 6, 7, 11b, 16a, 68a, 70a, 70b, 73, 74a†, 74b†, 75, 78a†, 80b, 81, 87, 88a

29

MA KING EDWARD VII Postage Issues (1902-13) 1½d. Purple and Green. M8

Control	Plates with which it was used	
	Left Sheets	Right Sheets
B	2a, 3b†, 11c†, 14a†, 17a†, 18b†, 68b, 79†, 86†, 87†	1a†, 1b, 1c, 3c†, 7, 10, 13†, 16a, 18a†, 19†, 20a†, 68a†, 82†, 86†, 87†, 88c†
C	2a†, 9, 16b†, 17a†, 18b*, 20b†	1c†, 3c*, 10, 13, 14b, 16a*, 19*, 30a
C 4	9, 11c, 16b†, 17a, 18b, 20b†, 71	2b†, 3c†, 7, 10†, 13†, 14b†, 19b, 30a, (79b†), 82†, 85a†, 85b†, 86
D 4	2c†, 9, 11c†, 17a†, 18b, 20b, 21a, 24a, 27, 71†	2b†, 3c, 7, 14b†, 17b, 22a, 22b, 23a, 25a, 26a, 28a, 30a, 31*, 85b
D 5	9, 18b, 21a, 24a, 27, 34a	7, 22b†, 23a, 25a, 28a, 30b, 33a, 35
E 5	9, 21a, 24a, 26b, 27, 34a, 37	21b, 23a, 25a, 25b, 28a, 30c†, 33a, 35, 36
E 6	9, 24a, 26b, 27, 28b, 33, 37a	23a, 25b, 28b†, 28c, 30c†, 33a, 35, 36, 38a, 42
F 6	9, 24a, 27, 35, 37a, 38b, 39a, 41a, 43a	23a, 24b, 36, 38a, 40a, 42
F 7	9†, 35, 37a, 38b, 39a, 41a, 43a	23a, 31*, 36, 38b, 40a, 42
G 7	35, 36, 37a, 39a, 40b, 41a, 42*, 43a, 44a	23a, 31, 36, 37b†, 38b, 40a, 40b, 41a, 42, 45, 46a†
G 8	23b, 26b, 31, 34a, 35, 36†, 39a, 43a†, 44a	25b, 26b, 31, 33a, 37b†, 41b, 42, 45, 46a, 48a
H 8	23b, 26b†, 26c†, 31, 34, 35, 39b, 43b, 44a, 47a, 49, 50a, 52a, 53b, 53c, 54a	25b, 26c, 31†, 33a, 37b, 39b, 41b*, 42†, 44, 45†, 46a, 48a, 50b, 51a, 53a
H 9	47a, 47b†, 49, 52a, 53c, 54a, 58a	46a, 48a, 50b, 51a, 53c, 57a
I 9	34a, 44a†, 46b, 47b, 49, 52a, 56, 58a	25b, 33a, 47c, 48a, 50b, 51a, 54†, 57a, 59
I 10	34a*, 49, 51a*, 52a, 58a, 62a	48a†, 49†, 50b†, 56†, 57b, 59, 60, 84
J 10	34b, 44b†, 48b, 49†, 51b, 52a, 52b, 54b, 58a, 62a, 63a, 65	25b, 33b, 48a, 49†, 54c, 56*, 58b†, 59, 60, 61a, 66a, 84
A 11 (w) (14)	62b, 63b	34c, 66b
A 11 (c) (14)	61b	58c†, 62c
A 11 (c) (15×14)	34c, 34d, 61b	58c†, 62c, 63c

1902-11. 1½d. Purple and Green, Type M3

1902-05. 1½d. Purple and Green. Perf. 14. De La Rue
A. 1902 (21 March). Ordinary Paper
M8 (=S.G.221/22)

		Unmtd mint	Mtd mint	Used
(1)	Dull purple and green	80·00	48·00	24·00
(2)	Slate-purple and green	95·00	50·00	24·00
	Block of four	£400	£240	£125
	Used on cover	†	†	50·00
a.	Watermark inverted	—	—	£900
b.	Damage in tablet (Pl. D4, R. 1/7)		£250	
ba.	State 2. Redrawn leaves and tablet retouched (Pl. D4, R. 1/7)		£350	
c.	Tablet repair (Pl. D4, R. 2/7)		£350	
d.	Retouch left of tablet and around large figure 1 (Pl. D4, R. 10/2)		£350	
e.	Deformed leaf (Pl. D4, R. 19/1)		£825	£425
f.	Frame broken at bottom (Pl. H1, R. 20/2)		£250	
g.	Frame broken at right (Pl. H1, R. 20/3)		£250	
s.	"Specimen", Type 15		£275	

Nos. M8d/e deformed leaf and left tablet retouch are the same varieties as K29e/f listed in Volume 1 and ascribed to Duty Plate 4 and Duty Plate 2.

M8b Damage in tablet (State 1)

M8ba Redrawn leaves and tablet retouched (State 2)

M8c Retouch repair between frame and figure "1

M8d

M8e   M8f   M8g

B. 1905 (July). Chalk-surfaced Paper
M9 (=S.G.223/24)

		Unmtd mint	Mtd mint	Used
(1)	Pale dull purple and green	75·00	45·00	24·00
(2)	Slate-purple and bluish green	75·00	45·00	24·00
(3)	Deep slate-purple and bluish green	95·00	55·00	40·00
	Block of four	£375	£225	£110
	Used on cover	†	†	45·00
c.	Frame broken at left (Pl. H5, R. 6/2)		£350	

1½d. Purple and Green. M10 *Postage Issues (1902-13)* **KING EDWARD VII** **MA**

		Unmtd mint	Mtd mint	Used
d.	Leaf and tablet repair (Pl. D6a, R. 20/9)		£425	
e.	Frame broken at top left		£225	
s.	"Specimen", Type 17		£700	
t.	"Cancelled", Type 18		£1800†	
u.	"Cancelled", Type 20		£2000	

Imperforate single from P.O. Registration Sheet...Price unused £20000
In the De La Rue printings, the uppermost line at the top of the fringe in the S.E. corner is usually faint.
†No. M9t exists from NPM archive sales.

M9c   M9e

No. M9c is a first state of No. M10c.

M9d, M10g

Perforation 14
Type H1 only

Die Proofs in black on white glazed card:
Head plate only
Without marking £3250
Endorsed "BEFORE HARDENING 20 NOV 01"........................ £3250
Endorsed "AFTER HARDENING 21 NOV 01", manuscript "1½" at lower left.................................. £3250
Endorsed "AFTER HARDENING 27 NOV 01" £3250
Endorsed "AFTER STRIKING 29 NOV 01"................................ £3250
Cut down and endorsed on back "Duplicate proof of Head die for 1½d. stamp registered 1 Feby 1902" in M/S £3250
Duty plate only
Endorsed "After Striking 19 APR 06".. £3250
  The date on this proof is not the striking date for Plate 7, nor any other plate.
Unfinished Die Proof of proposed monocoloured issue
With manuscript "Cancelled" and initials £6000

Die Proof from the De La Rue Archives
On card unmounted with traces of gum or paper on the back:
Head plate only, without markings £3250
Die for proposed monocoloured issue:
With uncleared surround, endorsed "Cancelled" in M/S .. £5500

Pieces Cut from the Striking Books
See notes under the ½d. value.
  Struck on plain paper cut to size with various endorsements comprising dates, plates and/or number of leads
1½d. head plates .... From £3000
1½d. duty plate 7 dated "Jan 11" (1904) £3000
1½d. duty plate with 2d. head plate and 6d. plate all together... £9750
Partly finished die for proposed monocoloured issue
Endorsed "This die partly finished/Chgd. 25 Aug 10"...... £12500

Colour Trials
Following the decision to print the 1½d., 2d. and 4d. values in one colour, Warrants were issued for the colour trials for two purposes, first to decide whether the existing designs were suitable for printing in monocolour and second to select which colours should be used. Nine Warrants were issued, three for each value, each on three different papers. These were for the normal white 480 crown paper, the yellow 480 crown paper used for the 3d. value and finally on three different papers tinted in colours not then in production and therefore without watermark. It is not known for certain how many colours were printed, but those actually submitted are known. De La Rue printed the purple inks in different depths and submitted what were the basic combinations several times over. 28 samples for each value were submitted to the Inland Revenue on 19 March 1909.
  The colour names given are descriptive of the actual colours submitted but have been simplified in some cases. The colour "Tyrian plum" is included as it was selected for the abortive 2d. monocoloured although existing examples of the colour trials bear little resemblance to the colour actually used for it. No names or descriptive notes were given to the trials.
  The tinted papers have white backs. As only three tinted colours were used other colours given in earlier editions are omitted. The colours may not have been consistent over the whole supply.
  All are perforated 14
On white paper. Watermark Crown
In carmine-lake, carmine, orange, orange-yellow,
    sage-green, dull blue-green, deep blue,
    violet, purple, Tyrian plum, brown, deep
    brown, olive-brown, slate .... From £9000
On yellow paper. Watermark Crown
In scarlet, green, four shades of purple .... From £9000
On tinted paper. No watermark
In three shades of purple on pink; two shades of
    purple on orange, black on orange; red on
    blue, purple on blue... From £7500
  On 16 March 1910 the deep brown shade was selected for the proposed new monocoloured stamp and work began on a new combined head and duty plate which was left unfinished owing to the death of the King.

1911 *(11 July).* **1½d. Purple and Green.** Perf. 14.
Somerset House. Ordinary. Paper

M10 (=S.G.287/89)

		Unmtd mint	Mtd mint	Used
(1)	Reddish purple and bright green	90·00	45·00	38·00
(2)	Reddish purple and yellow-green	90·00	45·00	35·00
(3)	Dull reddish purple and bright green (Jan. 1912)	55·00	30·00	25·00
(4)	Dull reddish purple and green (1912)	55·00	30·00	28·00

31

KING EDWARD VII Postage Issues (1902-13) 1½d. Purple and Green. M10

		Unmtd mint	Mtd mint	Used
(5)	Dull purple and green (Sept. 1911)	60·00	30·00	30·00
(6)	Deep plum and deep green	£350	£225	£125
(7)	Slate-purple and green (F) (Jan. 1912)	65·00	30·00	30·00
(8)	Pale slate-purple and green (F) (Feb. 1912)	60·00	30·00	30·00
(9)	Dark purple and green (GBF) (Feb. 1912)	£1250	£900	£300
(10)	Blackish purple and green (GBF) (Feb. 1912)	£1250	£900	£300
	Block of four	£275	£150	£125
	Used on cover	†	†	60·00
c.	Frame broken at left (Pl. H5, R. 6/4)	—	£350	
d.	Do. (Pl. ?, R. 8/4)	—	£350	
e.	Do. (Pl. ?, R. 9/4)	—	£350	
f.	Do. (Pl. ?, R. 10/4)	—	£350	
g.	Leaf and tablet repair (Pl. D6a, R. 20/9)	—	£200	
j.	Cracked plate	—	£200	
s.	"Specimen", Type 22	£1250	†	

In the Somerset House printings, the uppermost line at the top of the fringe in the S.E. corner is thick, and sometimes broken. Many stamps show damage to the circle round the medallion, and the frame lines are sometimes pitted, as though the plate had suffered corrosion.

With the exception of Nos. (7) and (8), all shades of purple appear redder when placed side by side with stamps from the De La Rue printings. Some of the above shades of purple are met with again on the 5d., 6d., 9d. and 10d. values.

† No. M10s exists from the NPM archive sales.

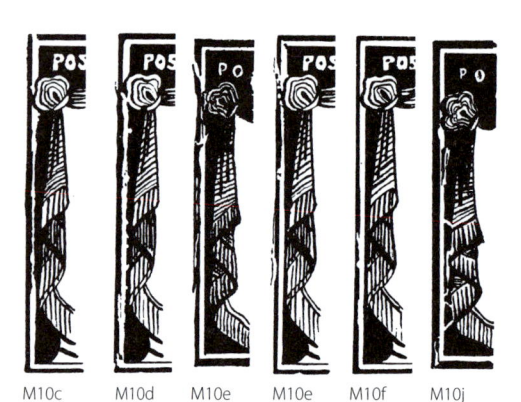

M10c   M10d   M10e   M10e Later state   M10f   M10j

No. M10c is a second state of No. M9c. No. M10g is illustrated under No. M9d.

Perforation 14
Types V1 V1A

Plate Descriptions

Official Pl. No.	S.G. Pl. No.	Features
Head Plates (Inner Line)		
1/60	H1	Continuous rules. Square corners at the interpane margin (all other bicoloured head plates with continuous rules have rounded corners). Cut under 2nd. Used only by De La Rue
2/64	H2	Continuous rules. Cut under 1st. Used only by De La Rue
3/66	H3	Continuous rules. No markings. Used only by De La Rue
4/249	H4	Coextensive rules. No markings in first state (see Printings). Used by De La Rue and Somerset House (see Printings for H4a,b)
5/263	H5	Coextensive rules. Tiny diagonal white line below middle of 2nd on most De La Rue printings. Used also by Somerset House (see Printings for H5a)
6/271	H6	Coextensive rules. Square dots at the interpane margin (all other bicoloured head plates with coextensive rules, except one, have curved corners). Cut preceded by nick under 2nd in De La Rue printings. Used also by Somerset House (see Printings for H6a,b,c)
Duty Plates (Outer Line)		
4	D4	Continuous rules at sides only. Used only by De La Rue
5	D5	Continuous rules at sides only. Used only by De La Rue
6	D6	Continuous rules all round but with breaks in horizontal rules every third stamp (a) upward bulge under 2nd about the 9th De La Rue printing. Also used by Somerset House
7	D7	Coextensive rules. Used only by Somerset House

These features identify the plates in their original states. Later states are indicated under the list of printings.

Printings
De La Rue

No. of Printing	Date	Left sheet	Right sheet	Notes
Ordinary Paper (No. M8)				
1	Feb./Aug. 1902	H2/D4	H1/D5	
2	Jan./Feb. 1903	H2/D4	H1/D5	
3	Nov./Dec. 1903	H2/D6	H1/D5	
4	July/Aug. 1904	H2/D6	H1/D5	
		H2/D6	H3/D5	
Chalk-surfaced Paper (No. M9)				
5	May/June 1905	H2/D6	H3/D5	
6	Dec. 1906/Feb. 1907	H4/D6	H3/D5	
7	Oct./Dec. 1907	H4a/D6	H5/D5	Cut preceded by nick under 1st in H4a
8	Dec. 1908/Feb. 1909	H4a/D6	H5/D5	
9	Dec. 1909/Jan. 1910	H4a/D6a	H6/D5	Upward dent under 2nd in D6a
10/12	1910	H4a/D6a	H6/D5	

The chalky paper used at about the time of the 7th and 8th printings had a very unstable top surface and stamps from these printings are heavily rubbed and found in the so-called "pale purple" shade.

The exact dates of the introduction of Plates H5 and H6 are uncertain.

Somerset House

No. of Printing	Date	Plates	Notes
Ordinary Paper (No. M10)			
1st	May 1911	H6a/D6a	H6a has added V cuts under 5th (denoting May) and two wide spaced cuts under 11th for 1911

2d. Green and Red. M11 *Postage Issues (1902-13)* **KING EDWARD VII**

No. of Printing	Date	Plates	Notes
2nd	Aug. 1911	H6b/D6a	H6b has marks under 2nd, V cuts under 5th and wide 1911 cuts all filled up. Cut under 8th (denoting August) and narrow date cuts under 11th added and purple dots over and under 12th stamp in top and bottom rows of each pane
3rd	Jan. 1912	H6c/D7	H6c cuts under 8th and 11th filled up. Cuts added under 12th to left of "1"
4th	Feb. 1912	H5a/D7	Diagonal line under 2nd removed; date cuts added under 12th under "1" and purple dots added as in H6b
5th	About Aug. 1912	H4b/D7	Cut and nick under 1st filled up; narrow thin date cuts under 12th to right of "1"; purple dots added as in H6b

The dates and numbers of printings after the 4th are at present obscure. The printings were on a substantial scale but probably not continuous.

At the time of the 4th printing a fluorescent head plate ink in slate-purple was used and H6c, which had been exposed to it, began to be badly corroded, with faults in the printing design appearing all over it. This plate was not used again and H5a was used with new inks, apparently until King George V stamps became available in sufficient numbers.

Price Schedule

Plate Combination Head/Duty	Left or Right sheet	Printing Usage	Recognisable Piece	Price per Pair
De La Rue				
(a) Ordinary Paper				
H1/D5	Right	1 to 4	S.W. corner	£115
H2/D4	Left	1, 2	Corner	£120
H2/D6	Left	3, 4	Pair with horiz. green cont. rule only	£160
H3/D5	Right	4	S.W. corner	£170
(b) Chalk-surfaced Paper				
H2/D6	Left	5	Pair with horiz. green & purple cont. rules	£135
H3/D5	Right	5, 6	Pair with horiz. purple cont. rule only	£200
H4/D6	Left	6 only	S.W. corner	£300
H4/D6	Left	6 to 12	Pair with horiz. green cont. rule and coext. purple rule	£115
H4a/D6	Left	7, 8	S.W. corner	£225
H5/D5	Right	7, 8	S.W. corner or interpane pair with curved corner pieces	£145
H4a/D6a	Left	9 to 12	S.W. corner	£195
H6/D5	Right	9 to 12	S.W. corner or interpane pair with square corner dots	£195
Somerset House				
H6a/D6a	—	1st	S.E. corner	£125
H6b/D6a	—	2nd	S.E. corner	90·00
H6c/D7	—	3rd	S.E. corner or interpane pair with square corner dots and green coext. rule	£140
H5a/D7	—	4th	S.E. corner	90·00
H4b/D7	—	5th	S.E. corner	£125

Prices are quoted for pairs, although single examples are sometimes adequate for identification.

Before attempting to identify recognisable pieces from De La Rue printings it is necessary first to establish whether an item comes from a left or right sheet, thus for H1/D5 "corner" means any corner of a right sheet and so on. For this purpose reference should be made to the General Notes under "PAPER. Recognising the Halves of the Mill Sheet".

See also in the General Notes under "PLATES", "SHEET MARKINGS" and "PLATE MARKINGS".

1902-11. 2d. Green and Red, Type M4

1902-10. 2d. Green and Red. Perf. 14. De La Rue

A. 1902 (25 March). Ordinary paper
M11 (=S.G.225/26)

		Unmtd mint	Mtd mint	Used
(1)	Yellowish green and carmine-red	£125	70·00	25·00
(2)	Pale greyish green and carmine-red (1904)	£125	70·00	25·00
(3)	Pale greyish green and scarlet-vermilion (1903)	£400	£280	£150
(4)	Grey-green and carmine-red (1904)	£125	70·00	35·00
(5)	Grey-green and scarlet-vermilion	£500	£300	£150
	Block of four	£625	£350	£125
	Used on cover	†	†	50·00
a.	Watermark inverted Shade (1)	£28000		
b.	Distorted tablet ("Rhombus", early state) (Pl. D3, R. 1/1)			£650
c.	Bottom right tablet corner raised (Pl. D4, R. 3/12)			£280
d.	Shading line below d thinned (Pl. D3, R. 10/2)			£225
e.	Displaced 2nd dot at upper right (Pl. H1, R. 6/6)			£275
f.	Scratch through O (Pl. H1, R. 18/2)			£350
g.	Irregular shading on right side of tablet (Pl. D3, R. 9/3)			£225
h.	Double frame break (Pl. D3, R. 6/4)			£275
s.	"Specimen", Type 16			£550

Imperforate single from P.O. Registration Sheet..Price unused £20000

M11b, M12b "Rhombus" early state

M11c, M12e

KING EDWARD VII — Postage Issues (1902-13) 2d. Green and Red. M12

M11d, M12g Later retouched on M12

M11g, M12n The irregular shading extends behind the value

M11h, Later retouched

M11e, M12h

M11f, M12i

		Unmtd mint	Mtd mint	Used
n.	Irregular shading on right side of tablet (Pl. D3, R. 9/3)		£200	
o.	Top shade line of tablet broken and joined to "2" (Pl. D4, R. 10/1)		£225	
s.	"Specimen", Type 17		£700†	
t.	"Cancelled", Type 18		£1800†	
u.	"Cancelled", Type 20		£2250	

†Nos. M12s and M12t exist from NPM sales.

M12c "Rhombus" later state

M12d, M13b Deformed tablet

M12f, M13d

M12o, M13h

B. 1906 (April). Chalk-surfaced paper
M12 (=S.G. 227/29)

		Unmtd mint	Mtd mint	Used
(1)	Pale grey-green and carmine-red	80·00	45·00	32·00
(2)	Dull blue-green and carmine (1907)	£180	90·00	50·00
(3)	Pale grey-green and scarlet (1909)	80·00	45·00	32·00
(4)	Grey-green and scarlet (1910)	80·00	45·00	30·00
	Block of four	£400	£225	£150
	Used on cover	†	†	65·00
a.	Watermark inverted		£20000	
b.	Distorted tablet ("Rhombus", early state) (Pl. D3, R. 1/1)		£700	
c.	As last, later state		£550	
d.	Deformed tablet (Pl. D4, R. 5/9)		£1000	
e.	Bottom right tablet corner raised (Pl. D4, R. 3/12)		£325	
f.	As last, retouched (bottom tablet corner still raised but no longer joined to lowest frame line)		£225	
g.	Shading line below d thinned (Pl. D3, R, 10/2)		£225	
h.	Displaced 2nd dot at upper right (Pl. H1, R. 6/6)		£325	
i.	Scratch beside O stronger (Pl. H1, R. 18/12)		£375	
j.	Lower left frame lines both broken ("Magnus" flaw) (Pl. H3, R. 8/3)		—	
k.	Flaws in oak leaves and frame break (Pl. H1, R. 15/11)			
l.	Large (Pl. H2, R. 6/8)		£600	
m.	3rd E of REVENUE shortened and flaw under it (Pl. H2, R, 5/8)		£325	

M12j

M12k

M12l

M12m

Perforation 14
Type H1 only

Die Proofs. In black on white glazed card (head plate only):
Without marking £3250
Endorsed "BEFORE HARDENING 19 DEC 01" £3250
Cut down and endorsed on back "Duplicate proof of Head die for 2d stamp registered 15 March 1902" (M/S) £3250
Endorsed "AFTER HARDENING 27 DEC 01" £3250
The Victorian die was used for the duty plate 5.

Pieces Cut from the Striking Books
See notes under the ½d. value
   Struck on plain paper cut to size with various endorsements comprising dates, plates and/or number of leads

2d. Green and Red. M13   *Postage Issues (1902-13)*   **KING EDWARD VII**   **MA**

2d. head plates .... *From* £3000
See under 1½d. value for piece which includes 2d. value.

Colour Trials
See the notes under "Colour Trials" for the 1½d. value.
The following were submitted to the Inland Revenue on 19th March 1909:—
All perforated 14
On white paper. Watermark Crown
In carmine-lake, carmine, orange, orange-yellow, sage-green, dull blue-green, deep blue, violet, purple, Tyrian plum, brown, deep brown, olive-brown, slate .... *From* £9000
On yellow paper. Watermark Crown
In scarlet, green, four shades of purple .... *From* £9000
On tinted paper. No watermark
In two shades of purple on pink, black on pink; two shades of purple on orange, red on blue, two shades of purple on blue .... *From* £9000
No colour was selected.

1911 *(8 August).* **2d. Green and Red.** Perf. 14. Somerset House. Ordinary Paper

M13 (=S.G.290/92)

		Unmtd mint	Mtd mint	Used
(1)	Deep dull green and red	60·00	28·00	22·00
(2)	Deep dull green and carmine	60·00	28·00	22·00
(3)	Deep dull green and bright carmine (Dec. 1911)	80·00	45·00	25·00
(4)	Grey-green and bright carmine (11 Mar. 1912)	55·00	28·00	28·00
	Block of four	£275	£140	£100
	Used on cover	†	†	55·00
a.	Top right corner damaged (Pl. D4, R. 1/3)		£250	
b.	Deformed tablet (Pl. D4, R. 5/9)		£925	£425
c.	Major bottom tablet frame break (Pl. D4, R. 13/7)		£250	
d.	Bottom right tablet corner raised (retouched state) (Pl. D4, R. 3/12)		£250	
e.	Frame damaged at bottom left (state 1) (Pl. H4, R. 2/5)		£275	
f.	As last, state 2		£275	
g.	Damage below POS (Pl. H4, R. 10/4)		£250	
h.	Top shade line of tablet broken and joined to "2" (Pl. D4, R. 10/1)		£250	
s.	"Specimen", Type 22		£325†	

The green shades are all deeper and duller than those of De La Rue. The carmine colour on Nos. (3) and (4) shows noticeably on the backs of the stamps.
Shade No (1) may be found with extremely thick shiny gum.
There are a very large number of minor flaws on the 2d. value (see The GB Journal, Vol. 15, October, November 1977, pp. 105, 126). Also articles in Gibbons Stamp Monthly, May, July, September, 1992.
†No. M13s exists from NPM archive sales.

M13a   M13c

M13e   M13f   M13g

Perforation 14
Types   V1   V1A

Plate Descriptions

Official Pl. No.	S.G. Pl. No.	Features
Head Plates (Inner Line)		
1/101	H1	Continuous rules. Cut under 2nd. Used only by De La Rue
2/104	H2	Continuous rules. No cuts. Used only by De La Rue
3/106	H3	Continuous rules. Cut under 1st. Used only by De La Rue
4/264	H4	Coextensive rules. No cuts. Used by De La Rue and Somerset House (see Printings for H4a,b,c)
5/278	H5	Coextensive rules. Used only by Somerset House
(Duty Plates) (Outer Line)		
3	D3	Short bar rules. Used by De La Rue and in part by Somerset House
4	D4	Short bar rules. Used by De La Rue and Somerset House
5	D5	Coextensive rules. Used only by Somerset House

Printings
De La Rue

		Plates		
No. of Printing	Date	Left sheet	Right sheet	Notes
Ordinary Paper (No. M11)				
1	Mar./Aug. 1902	H3/D4	H1/D3	Shade (1)
2	Feb./Mar. 1903	H3/D4	H1/D3	Shade (3)
3	Mar./Apr. 1904	H3/D4	H1/D3	Shades (2) and (4)
4	Nov./Dec. 1904	H3/D4	H1/D3	Shade (2)
Chalk-surfaced Paper (No. M12)				
5	Feb. 1906	H3/D4	H1/D3	Shade (1)
5 cont.	June/July 1906	H2/D4	H1/D3	Shade (1)
6	May/June 1907	H4/D4	H2/D3	Shade (2). Duty plates worn
7	Apr./May 1908	H4/D4	H2/D3	Shade (2). Duty plates repaired
8	Feb./May 1909	H4/D4	H2/D3	Shades (1) and (3)

Stanley Gibbons

Great Britain Department

BY APPOINTMENT TO
HER MAJESTY THE QUEEN
PHILATELISTS
STANLEY GIBBONS LTD
LONDON

Stanley Gibbons, a name synonymous with quality.

Ever since the birth of our hobby Stanley Gibbons has been at the forefront of GB philately and we invite collectors access to one of the finest GB stocks in the world by registering for our renowned free monthly brochure. Whatever your budget or collecting interests you will find a range of the highest quality material for the discerning collector.

To receive our monthly brochures or for further enquires please email gb@stanleygibbons.com or phone 020 7557 4424.

Est 1856
STANLEY GIBBONS

Proud PTS members

Stanley Gibbons
399 Strand, London, WC2R 0LX
+44 (0)20 7836 8444
www.stanleygibbons.com

2d Tyrian Plum. M14 *Postage Issues (1902-13)* KING EDWARD VII

No. of Printing	Date	Left sheet	Plates Right sheet	Notes
9	June/July 1910	H4/D4	H2/D3	Shades (1) (3) and (4)
10	Dec. 1910	H4/D4	H2/D3	Shades (1) (3) and (4)

Somerset House

No. of Printing	Date	Plates	Notes
Ordinary Paper (No. M13)			
1st	July 1911	H4a/D4	H4a has 2 cuts under 11th and 1 cut under 7th. Shade (1)
2nd	Aug. 1911	H4b/D4	H4b has added green dots over and under 12th in top and bottom rows of each pane. Shade (1)
3rd	Nov. 1911	H4c/D4, 3	H4c has added diagonal cut under 11th; parts of D3 substituted for D4. Shade (1) before substitution and shade (1) or (2) after
4th	Dec. 1911	H4c/D4, 3	More parts of D3 substituted for D4, especially sections 5 and 9. Shade (3)
5th	Jan. 1912	H5/D5	H5 has date dots under 12th. Shade (3)
6th	May 1912	H5/D5	New ink, shade (4)

The dates of the Somerset House printings are approximate.

Price Schedule

Plate Combination Head/Duty	Left or Right sheet	Printing Usage	Recognisable Piece	Price per Pair
De La Rue				
(a) Ordinary Paper				
H1/D3	Right	1 to 4	Corner	£125
H3/D4	Left	1 to 4	Corner	£125
(b) Chalk-surfaced Paper				
H1/D3	Right	5	S.W. corner	£240
H3/D4	Left	5	S.W. corner	£240
H2/D3	Left	5	S.W. corner	£325
H2/D3	Right	6 to 10	S.W. corner	£190
H4/D4	Left	6 to 10	Any pair with coextensive green rules	£110
Somerset House				
H4a/D4	—	1st	S.E. corner	£140
H4b/D4	—	2nd	S.E. corner	£100
H4c/D4, 3	—	3rd	S.E. corner, upper or lower pane	80·00
H4c/D4, 3	—	4th	Left interpane pair, no red side rules nor complete horiz. red rules	£175
H5/D5	—	5th, 6th	Any pair with coextensive red rules	75·00

Prices are quoted for pairs, although single examples are sometimes adequate for identification.

Before attempting to identify recognisable pieces see notes below the Price Schedule for the 1½d. value.

1910. 2d. Tyrian Plum, Type M5

1910 (May). **2d. Tyrian Plum.** Prepared for use but not issued. Perf. 14. De La Rue. Ordinary Paper

M14 (=S.G.266a)

	Unmtd mint	Mtd mint	Used
Tyrian plum	—	£115000	†
s. "Specimen", Type 17		£62000	

Although over 100,000 sheets were printed from the Tyrian plum plates and delivered to the Inland Revenue, release to post offices was delayed until current stocks of the bicoloured value had been used up. After the death of the King on 6 May 1910 it was decided not to proceed with this issue. Practically the whole of the stock was destroyed and very few unused examples survived but incredibly a miscellaneous lot purchased in 1993 contained one of these unused stamps.

One example is known on cover postmarked 5 May, and is in the Royal Philatelic Collection of H.M. Queen Elizabeth II.

Essays

Submitted to the Inland Revenue on 19 August 1909. On glazed card:

A rejected design with rectangular duty frame,
 in slate-purple or olive-green .... From £35000
A rejected design with an oval duty frame, in
 deep reddish brown, blue or bottle-green ..... From £35000
The accepted design in steel-blue or purple .... From £35000

Essays from the De La Rue Archives

Stamp size photographic essay on card pen-cancelled with cross: Design with oval duty frame in deep reddish
 brown, inscribed "Aug 19th 09" and "Dupl/
 Design subm. Blue" £25000

The other two designs described above with pen-cancelled cross were acquired by the National Postal Museum.

Die Proofs in black on white glazed card:

Endorsed "BEFORE HARDENING 1 DEC 09" £30000
Endorsed "AFTER HARDENING 2 DEC 09" £30000
On white glazed card:
Dull rose without marking £36000

For similar but printed on unwatermarked white paper see Colour Trials.

Piece Cut from the Striking Book

Struck on plain paper cut to size
2d. endorsed with Plates 6 to 10 with various
 dates from Dec 21 to Feb 25 further endorsed
 "Feb 25th 10" in red and "Feb 26, 20 leads"
 and cancelled by red ink line £40000

Colour Trials

On white wove paper watermarked Crown. Perf. 14
In orange, olive, sage-green, dull blue-green, pale
 blue, deep blue, violet, red-purple, purple,
 deep red-brown, pale red-brown, brown,
 deep brown, grey-brown, grey, black or
 yellow-ochre .... From £25000

Perforated colour trials on watermarked paper were also taken in the selected Tyrian plum colour but it is now considered that they cannot be positively distinguished from surviving examples from the supply which was printed.

On white paper without watermark. Imperf. with large margins, 3-10 mm.
In red-rose, green, Tyrian plum or pale brown ...... From £25000
On white paper watermarked Crown. Imperf.
In red-rose, green, mauve, Tyrian plum or deep
 orange-brown .... From £25000

The significance of the imperf. colour trials is not yet understood. The colours do not correspond with those of the perforated trials of 12 January 1910. Some may have arisen from the submission of the essays on 19 August 1909 but those with large margins probably derive from the Somerset House colour trials of 1911-12. The British Library has a *se-tenant* trial in brown of the Tyrian plum design with a 2d. King George V Downey head with "Cancelled", Type 24.

MA KING EDWARD VII Postage Issues (1902-13) 2½d. Purple on Blue. M15

1901. 2½d. Purple on Blue, Type M6

1901 (December). **2½d. Purple on Blue.** Perf. 14. De La Rue. Ordinary Paper

M15

	Unmtd mint	Mtd mint	Used
Purple on blue		£160000	†

The Registration sheet of this stamp was taken on 3 December 1901. Many thousands of sheets were printed and delivered to the Stamping Department, but were destroyed when the authorities changed their minds in favour of the adopted colour. Only a few examples have survived.

1902-11. 2½d. Blue, Type M6

1902 (1 January). **2½d. Blue.** Perf. 14. De La Rue. Ordinary Paper

M16 (=S.G.230/31)

	Unmtd mint	Mtd mint	Used
(1) Deep ultramarine	50·00	35·00	12·00
(2) Ultramarine	34·00	20·00	12·00
(3) Pale ultramarine	34·00	20·00	12·00
(4) Very deep bright ultramarine	£110	70·00	30·00
Block of four	£170	£100	60·00
Used on cover	†	†	25·00
a. Watermark inverted		—	£4200
c. Frame broken at right		—	
d. Minor frame breaks From		90·00	45·00
e. Retouched background (Pl. 1a, R. 11/12)		—	
f. Plate crack in wreath at left (Pl. 6, R. 19/1)		£250	£125
g. Line below 2 (Pl. ?, R. 1/7)		£250	£125
h. Malformed large 2 (Pl. ?, R. 2/4)		£400	£250
s. "Specimen", Type 15		£125	
t. "Specimen", Type 17		£900†	
u. "Cancelled", Type 20		£2000†	

The Registration sheet in the new colour was taken on 16 December 1901.

No. M16 was pre-released and exists on cover with No. M1 (½d.), M5 (1d.) and M31 (6d.) cancelled 31 December 1901.

†No. M16s exists from NPM archive sales.

M16c

M16e Shading at top right retouched and dent in frame of "REVENUE"

M16f, M18f

M16g    M16h

No. M16g had continuous rules (pl. 1 to 7) and No. M16h came from a plate with coextensive rules (pl. 11 or 12).

Perforation 14
Types H1 H1A

Essays

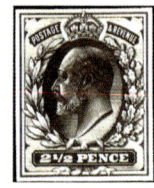

A    B

C    D

Composite essay with die proof head in photo surround partly touched up with black ink and mounted on card. Eight different essays were produced in July 1901 for the 2½d. stamp, differing in the design of the value tablets.

Mounted on card dated "July 10th 01" lettered "C", "E", "F" or "H" and "Dupl", £8500 *each*.

Essays from the De La Rue Archives
Photographic essays in stamp size on card:
Type A, inscribed "June 18th 01" and "Dupl" in
   design of the issued ½d... £8500
Type B, lettered "C"... £8500
Type C, lettered "F"... £8500
Type D, lettered "H".. £8500

2½d. Blue. M17 Postage Issues (1902-13) KING EDWARD VII

Types B to D were submitted to the Postmaster-General on 10 July 1901, together with four other designs which were acquired by the N.P.M. That lettered "B" was the accepted design which was endorsed "Approved/July 19th" and the others are lettered "D", "E" and "G".
Enlarged photographic bromides of the accepted designs .... Each £1100

Die Proofs in black on white glazed card:
Without marking £3250
Endorsed "28 AUG 01 BEFORE HARDENING".
Without marking but with (M/S) initials and date "7 SEPT 01" £3250
Endorsed "7 SEP. 01 AFTER HARDENING" £3250
Endorsed "BEFORE HARDENING 28 NOV 01" £3250
Endorsed "AFTER HARDENING 7 DEC 01" £3250
Endorsed "Working Die No. 19" £3250
Endorsed "Registered 3.12.1901" and "working Die No. 19" £3250

Pieces Cut from the Striking Books
See notes under the ½d. value.
Struck on plain paper cut to size with various endorsements comprising dates, and/or number of leads.
2½d. value .... From £3000

Plate Proofs
On thick white paper. No watermark, Imperf.
Ultramarine, violet-blue, deep ultramarine, steel blue .... Each £2100

Colour Trials
9 December 1901. Watermark Crown, Perf. 14.
In nine shades of blue comprising three shades of ultramarine (including issued colour), bright blue, milky blue, violet-blue, deep blue, greenish blue and pale dull blue .... From £2100
Imperforate in bright blue on gummed watermarked paper £3000

1911 (10 July). **2½d. Blue.** Perf. 14. Harrison. Ordinary Paper

M17 (=S.G.276)

	Unmtd mint	Mtd mint	Used
(1) Deep bright blue	£190	80·00	50·00
(2) Bright blue	£175	65·00	38·00
(3) Dull blue	£175	65·00	38·00
(4) Deep bright blue (very blotchy print)	£850	£700	£350
Block of four	£875	£325	£190
Used on cover	†	†	65·00
a. Watermark inverted	£2100	£1250	

Perforation 14
Types V1 V1A

1911 (14 October). **2½d. Blue.** Perf. 15×14. Harrison. Ordinary Paper

M18 (=S.G.283/84)

	Unmtd mint	Mtd mint	Used
(1) Deep bright blue	£100	50·00	30·00
(2) Bright blue	50·00	22·00	15·00
(3) Dull blue	50·00	22·00	15·00
Block of four	£250	£110	75·00
Used on cover	†	†	35·00
a. Watermark inverted	—	—	£2800
b. Imperf. between stamp and left margin		£6500	
f. Plate crack in wreath at left (Pl. 6, R. 19/1)		£250	£120

	Unmtd mint	Mtd mint	Used
g. Frame broken at right (Pl. ?, R. 19/12)		£400	£225
h. Frame broken at right		£425	£225
i. Frame broken at right (Pl. 2, R. 5/12)		£425	£225
j. Frame broken at right (Pl. ?, R. 5/12)		£425	£225
k. Frame broken at right		£425	£225
l. Frame broken at right (Pl. 6, R. 3/12)		£425	
m. Do. (Pl. 6, R. 4/12)		£425	
n. Do. (Pl. 6, R. 5/12)		£425	
o. Do. (Pl. 6, R. 6/12)		£425	
s. "Specimen", Type 22			
t. "Cancelled", Type 21 imperf.	£1750		

Shade No. (3) may be found with extremely thick shiny gum.
For illustration of No. M18f, see M16f.
No. M18t shows the overprint set diagonally and exists misplaced.

M18g  M18h  M18i

M18j  M18k  M18l

KING EDWARD VII Postage Issues (1902-13) 2½d. Blue. M18

M18m M18n M18o

The broken frame varieties g to o exist in progressive stages of wear.

Perforation 15 × 14
Types V3 V3A

Plate Descriptions

Official Pl. No	S.G. Pl. No	Features
1/19	1	Continuous rules. Cut preceded by nick under 2nd (a) For printing 7 only the plate changed sides with an added cut under ½ of 1st. Used only by De La Rue
2/21	2	Continuous rules. Thin cut between 2 and ½ of 1st. Used by De La Rue and Harrison
5/153	5	Continuous rules. Cut under 2 of 3rd. Used by De La Rue and Harrison, later with cut under 11th
6/155	6	Continuous rules. Cut under ½ of 4th. Used by De La Rue and Harrison
7/157	7	Continuous rules. Diagonal cut and nick under ½ of 1st. Only known used by De La Rue
11/210	11	Coextensive rules. No marking at first (a) later with thick cut under 2½ of 2nd. Used by De La Rue and Harrison
12/211	12	Coextensive rules. Thin cut under 2 of 1st. Used by De La Rue and Harrison

Plates 3/61 and 4/79 were made but not used as they were faulty. Plate 8/160 with continuous rules seems to have been satisfactory but there is no evidence of its use. Plates 9/189 and 10/190 were sent to Somerset House as reserves but never used.

Printings
De La Rue

No. of Printing	Date	Left sheet (Plates)	Right sheet (Plates)	Notes
1	Dec. 1901	2	1	In purple on blue (No. M15)
2	Dec. 1901/Feb. 1902	2	1	In ultramarine (No. M16)
3	Dec. 1902/Apr. 1903	2	1	
		5	6	
4	Nov. 1903/Feb. 1904	2	1	
		5	6	
5	Dec. 1904/Apr. 1905	7	1	
		5?	6?	
6	Sept./Oct. 1905	7	1	
		5?	6?	
7	Nov. 1906	1a	11	Plate 1 changed sides. Added vertical cut under ½ of 1st
		5?	6?	
		7	11a	Added cut under 2nd of Plate 11
8	Oct./Nov. 1907	7	11a	
		5?	6?	
9	Nov./Dec. 1908	7	11a	
		5?	6?	
10	May/Sept. 1910	12	11a	
		5?	6?	

It is believed that Plates 5 and 6 continued in use after the 4th printing but it is not known when they were discontinued.

Harrison
Too little is known about the Harrison printings to prepare a meaningful table of printings.

Price Schedule

Plate No.	Left or Right sheet	Printing Usage	Recognisable Piece	Price
De La Rue				
Perforation 14.		Types H1, H1A (No. M16)		
1	Right	2 to 6	S.W. corner pair	80·00
2	Left	2 to 4	S.W. corner pair	50·00
5*	Left	3, 4	S.W. corner strip of 3	
6*	Right	3, 4	S.W. corner strip of 4	
7	Left	5 to 9	S.W. corner pair	80·00
1a	Left	7	S.W. corner pair	
11 & 11a	Right	7 to 10	Any corner pair with coextensive rules	50·00
12	Left	10	Any corner pair with coextensive rules	95·00

*These plates could also exist for printings 5 to 10.
No plating pieces are known to exist of the initial printing in purple on blue.

Harrison

Perforation 14.		Types V1, V1A (No. M17)		
2	—	1st	S.W. corner pair	£160
5a	—	1st	S.E. corner with cut under ½ of 11th, S.W. corner strip of 3 or right interpane margin pair with cuts at right	£160
11a	—	1st	S.W. corner pair	£160
12	—	1st	S.W. corner pair	£160
Perforation 15 ×14.		Types V3, V3A (No. M18)		
2	—	2nd	S.W. corner pair	75·00
5a	—	2nd	S.E. corner with cut under ½ of 11th, S.W. corner strip of 3 or right interpane margin pair with cuts at right	60·00
6	—	2nd	S.W. corner strip of 4	£125
12	—	2nd	Any marginal pair with coextensive rules	60·00

It is not yet clear whether Harrisons consistently used plates in left and right positions, in the same manner that De La Rue did. Nor is it known at present whether Harrisons made any additional markings on Plates 2, 6, 11a or 12.

3d. Purple on Yellow. M19 *Postage Issues (1902-13)* **KING EDWARD VII** MA

Prices quoted are for pairs or strips, although single examples are sometimes adequate for identification.
Before attempting to identify recognisable pieces see notes below the Price Schedule for the 1½d. value.

1902-11. 3d. Purple on Yellow, Type M7

1902-06. 3d. Purple on Yellow. Perf. 14. De La Rue
A. 1902 (20 March). Ordinary Paper
M19 (=S.G.232, 32b)

		Unmtd mint	Mtd mint	Used
(1)	Dull purple on orange-yellow back, yellow front	95·00	50·00	18·00
(2)	Deep purple on orange-yellow back, yellow shades front	85·00	40·00	18·00
	Block of four	£425	£225	90·00
	Used on cover	†	†	35·00
a.	Watermark inverted			
s.	"Specimen", Type 15		£350	

Imperforate single from P.O. Registration
Sheet.. Price unused £15000

B. 1906 (March). Chalk-surfaced paper
M20 (=S.G.232a, 232c/34)

		Unmtd mint	Mtd mint	Used
(1)	Pale reddish purple on orange-yellow	£425	£225	80·00
(2)	Dull purple on orange-yellow	£425	£225	85·00
(3)	Dull reddish purple on lemon back, yellow front	£425	£225	85·00
(4)	Pale purple on lemon	85·00	45·00	20·00
(5)	Purple on lemon	85·00	45·00	20·00
	Block of four	£425	£225	£100
	Used on cover	†	†	60·00
b.	Broken scroll (Pl. 5, R. 20/2)		£275	
c.	Broken frame		£175	75·00
d.	Broken corner		£175	75·00
s.	"Specimen", Type 17		£700	
t.	"Cancelled", Type 20		£2000	

Perforation 14
Types   H1   H1A

Die Proofs in black on white glazed card:
Without marking £3250
Endorsed "BEFORE HARDENING 21 NOV 01" £3250
Endorsed "AFTER HARDENING 25 NOV 01" £3250
Cut down with "Duplicate proof of die registered
    1 Febr 1902" annotated on reverse in M/S £3250

Pieces Cut from the Striking Books
See notes under the ½d. value.
    Struck on plain paper cut to size with various endorsements comprising dates and number of leads
3d. value .... From £3000

1911 *(12 September).* **3d. Purple on Yellow.** Perf. 14. Harrison. Ordinary Paper

M21 (=S.G.277/7a)

		Unmtd mint	Mtd mint	Used
(1)	Purple on lemon	£225	£125	£225
(2)	Greyish purple on lemon	£240	£140	£250
(3)	Grey on lemon	£7000	£4500	
(4)	Dull reddish purple on lemon	£225	£125	£225
	Block of four	£1100	£625	£1250
	Used on cover	†	†	£550
b.	Broken scroll (Pl. 5, R. 20/2)		£400	
e.	Frame broken at right (Pl. 4, R. 9/12)		£450	
g.	Broken crown			
s.	"Specimen", Type 22		£300†	

†No. M21s exists from NPM archive sales.

Perforation 14
Types   H2(c)   H2A(c)
        H2(d)   H2A(d)
        V1   V1A

1911 *(18 September).* **3d. Purple on Yellow.** Perf. 15×14. Harrison. Ordinary Paper

M22 (=S.G.285/5a)

		Unmtd mint	Mtd mint	Used
(1)	Purple on lemon	70·00	45·00	15·00
(2)	Greyish purple on lemon	85·00	50·00	15·00
(3)	Grey on lemon	£4250	£3250	
(4)	Dull reddish purple on lemon	85·00	50·00	15·00
	Block of four	£350	£225	£175
	Used on cover	†	†	40·00
b.	Broken scroll (Pl. 5, R. 20/2)		£300	£175
e.	Frame broken at right (Pl. 4, R. 9/12)		£300	£175
f.	Frame broken at right (Pl. 5, R. 8/12)		£300	£175
g.	Broken crown		£300	£175

Varieties c and e both show progressive states of wear.
Variety g is from the 1st vertical row of the sheet.

M20/2b   M20c

M20d

41

MA KING EDWARD VII Postage Issues (1902-13) 4d. Green and Brown. M23

M21/2e   M22f   M21/2g

Perforation 15 × 14
Types   V3   V3A

Plate Descriptions

Official Pl. No.	S.G. Pl. No.	Features:
1/65	1	Continuous rules. Cut under 1st. Used by De La Rue and Harrison
2/67	2	Continuous rules. Cut under 2nd. Used only by De La Rue
3/69	3	Continuous rules. Cut under 3rd. Used only by De La Rue
4/71	4	Continuous rules. Cut under EN of 4th. Used by De La Rue and Harrison
5/78	5	Continuous rules. Cut under VE of 4th. Used by De La Rue and Harrison

Printings

No. of Printing	Date	Left Sheet (Plates)	Right Sheet (Plates)	Notes
De La Rue				
Ordinary Paper (No. M19)				
1	1902/6	1	2	No. M19 shades (1) and (2)
		3	4	
Chalk-surfaced Paper (No. M20)				
2	1906	1	2	No. M20 shades (1) to (5)
		3	4	
		3	5	
Harrison				
Ordinary Paper				
Perforation 14 (No. M22)				
1st	Sept. 1911	5	4	No. M21 shades (1) to (4)
Perforation 15 × 14 (No. 23)				
2nd	Sept. 1911	5	4	No. M22 shades (1) to (4)
		5	1	

Price Schedule

Plate No.	Left or Right Sheet	Printing Usage	Recognisable Piece	Price
De La Rue				
Perforation 14. Types H1, H1A				
(a) Ordinary Paper				
1	Left	1	S.W. corner pair	£110
2	Right	1	S.W. corner pair	£110
3	Left	1	S.W. corner strip of 3	£175
4	Right	1	S.W. corner strip of 4	£240
(b) Chalk-surfaced Paper				
1	Left	2	S.W. corner pair	£120
2	Right	2	S.W. corner pair	£120

Plate No.	Left or Right Sheet	Printing Usage	Recognisable Piece	Price
3	Left	2	S.W. corner strip of 3	£185
4	Right	2	S.W. corner strip of 4	£240
5	Right	2	S.W. corner strip of 4	£260
Harrison				
(a) Perforation 14. Types H2, H2A or V1, V1A				
4	Right	1st	S.W. corner strip of 4	£400
5	Left	1st	S.W. corner strip of 4	£400
(b) Perforation 15×14. Types V3, V3A				
1	Right	2nd	S.W. corner pair	£120
4	Right	2nd	S.W. corner strip of 4	£225
5	Left	2nd	S.W. corner strip of 4	£225

Prices quoted are for pairs or strips, although single examples are sometimes adequate for identification.

Before attempting to identify recognisable pieces see notes below the Price Schedule for 1½d. value.

1902-06. 4d. Green and Brown, Type M8

1902-06. 4d. Green and Brown. Perf. 14. De La Rue

A. 1902 (27 March). Ordinary paper
M23 (=S.G.235/36)

		Unmtd mint	Mtd mint	Used
(1)	Green and grey-brown	£125	70·00	35·00
(2)	Green and brown	£110	50·00	30·00
(3)	Green and chocolate-brown	£125	70·00	35·00
	Block of four	£625	£350	£175
	Used on cover	†	†	80·00
a.	Watermark inverted			£95·00
c.	Damaged 4 (S.W. corner) (Pl. ?, R. 3/8)		£225	
d.	Cracked plate		£275	
e.	Damaged d			
f.	Cracked plate (N.W. corner)			
s.	"Specimen", Type 16		£450†	

Imperforate single from P.O. Registration Sheet..Price unused £20000
†No. M23s exists from NPM archive sales.

B. 1906 (January). Chalk-surfaced paper
M24 (=S.G.236a, 238)

(1)	Green and chocolate-brown	75·00	40·00	20·00
(2)	Deep green and chocolate-brown	75·00	40·00	20·00
	Block of four	£375	£200	£100
	Used on cover	†	†	45·00
c.	Damaged 4 (S.W. corner) (Pl. ?, R. 3/8)		£225	
s.	"Cancelled", Type 18	£1800	†	

†No. M24s exists from NPM Archive sales.

M23/4c   M23d

4d. Green and Brown. M24 *Postage Issues (1902-13)* **KING EDWARD VII** **MA**

M23e   M23f

Perforation 14
Type   H1
A few sheets on chalky paper with Types V2 or V2A

Die Proofs in black on white glazed card. Head Plate only:
Without marking £3250
Endorsed "BEFORE HARDENING 28 NOV 01" £3250
Endorsed "AFTER HARDENING 28 NOV 01" £3250
Cut down and endorsed on back "Duplicate proof
   of Head die for 4d. stamp registered 29 March
   1902" (M/S) £3250
Endorsed "AFTER STRIKING 3 JAN 06" and initialled £3250
Endorsed "AFTER STRIKING 22 JAN 08" initialled
   "H. W." £3250

Pieces Cut from the Striking Books
For notes see under ½d. value.
   Struck on plain paper cut to size with various endorsements comprising dates, plate and/or number of leads
4d. head plates .... From £3000
4d. duty plate 4 dated "May 8" (1901) £3000

Plate Descriptions
Head Plates
The 240 set Outer Line Head Plates each comprise two panes of 120 (10 horizontal rows of 12) and were used only by De La Rue.
   In the case of Head Plates 1, 2, 3 and 4 each pane of 120 is made up of 12 sections (8 sections of 3 horizontal rows of 3 across the top and bottom of each pane plus 4 sections of 4 horizontal rows of 3 across the middle of each pane) the positions of which are marked in the case of the 3 continuous margin plates by breaks between the 3rd/4th and 7th/8th rows of stamps in each vertical rule, and by breaks between the 3rd/4th, 6th/7th, and 9th/10th stamps of each horizontal rule. These plates thus comprise 24 such sections—informally numbered 1 to 24 commencing from the NW corner of the upper pane.
   In the case of Head Plate 5 each pane of 120 (like the 1s. value) is made up of 6 sections of 20 stamps (5 horizontal rows of 4). The plate thus comprises 12 such sections informally numbered 1 to 12 commencing from the NW corner of the upper pane.

Official Pl No	S.G. Pl No	Features
1/77	H1	Continuous rules with all corners cut away. Cut under 2nd stamp bottom row lower pane (a) cut added in the rule under 11th stamp bottom row lower pane
2/82	H2	Continuous rules with all corners (except S.E. corner upper pane) cut away. Cut under 1st stamp and scoops in the top of the rules between the 10th/11th and 11th/12th stamps of the bottom row lower pane. Towards the end of the life of this plate the rule to the right of rows 19 and 20 disintegrated
3/84	H3	Continuous rules with all corners intact. No plate cut in the bottom row lower pane but a distinctive rule flaw (jagged hole closed at the top) under the 2nd stamp (a) cut added in the rule under the 10th stamp bottom row lower pane
4/250	H4	Coextensive rules. No plate cut but a small scoop under the rule of the 2nd stamp and a large scoop under the rule of the 4th stamp bottom row lower pane. There were also rule scoops to the left of rows 3 and 8 and to the right of rows 4, 7 and 14. Plate 4 has a unique arrangement of the registration rule pieces which show an extra rule break between the 6th and 7th stamps above the upper pane and below the lower pane, and there are also unusual rule breaks over the 5th and 8th stamps of the upper pane. (By contrast plate 5 has perfectly normal Die I registration pieces and no breaks over the 5th and 8th stamps) (a) cut added in the rule under 12th stamp bottom row lower pane
5/279	H5	Coextensive rules. Cut under 11th, very small scoop under the rule of the 2nd, and a full scoop under the rule of the 4th stamp bottom row lower pane. There were also rule scoops to the left of rows 2, 5, 12, 16 and 19, and to the right of rows 2, 9, 12 and 19

Duty Plates
With continuous rules the Inner Line Duty Plates comprise individual 120 set panes in 10 horizontal rows of 12 stamps. The records show that 12 such 120 set electros were made from, apparently, a master plate. The pairings of the Duty Plates with the appropriate Head Plate usage present difficulties, but the allocations which follow reflect the latest stage of research applied to the material available for examination.
   — D1 to D12   Continuous rules without plate cuts

Printings

No. of Printing	Date	Plates (480 set) Left Sheet	Right Sheet	Notes
De La Rue				
Ordinary Paper (No. M23)				
1 & 2	March 1902	H2/D3D4*	H1/D1D2	Shades (1) to (3)
3	Jan. 1904	H2/D3D6	H1/D1D5	
4	Sept. 1904	H2/D8D6	H1/D7D5	
		H3/D8D6	H1/D7D5	
Chalk-surfaced Paper (No. M24)				
5	Jan. 1906	H3/D8D6	H1/D7D5	Shades (1) and (2)
6	1906/07	H3a/D8D6	H1a/D7D5	Rule cut added to both Head Plates
		H3a/D7D5	H1a/D8D6	
7	late 1907	H4/D7D5	H1a/D8D6	
8	Aug. 1908	H5/D11D12	H4a/D9D10	Rule cut added to Head Plate 4

*In each case the first numbered Duty Plate comprised the upper pane of the plate and the second the lower pane.
   The plate and printing details are based on research by Michael Astley and Tony Wiseman. For more detailed information reference should be made to their original paper in *The Philatelic Journal of Great Britain* for December 1978, p. 95.

43

MA KING EDWARD VII   Postage Issues (1902-13)   4d. Orange. M25

Price Schedule

Plate Combination Head/Duty	Left or Right Sheet	Printing Usage	Recognisable Piece	Price per Pair
(a) Ordinary Paper				
H2/D3D4	Left	1 & 2	S.W. or S.E. corner pair	£200
H1/D1D2	Right	1 & 2	S.W. corner pair	£200
H2/D3D6	Left	3	S.W. or S.E. corner pair	£200
H1/D1D5	Right	3	S.W. corner pair	£200
H2/D8D6	Left	4	S.W. or S.E. corner pair	£200
H1/D7D5	Right	4	S.W. corner pair	£200
H3/D8D6	Left	4	S.W. corner pair	£200
(b) Chalk-surfaced Paper				
H3/D8D6	Left	5	S.W. corner pair	£150
H1/D7D5	Right	5	S.W. corner pair	£150
H3a/D8D6	Left	6	S.W. corner pair or S.E. corner strip of 3	£190
H1a/D7D5	Right	6	S.W. or S.E. corner pair	£150
H3a/D7D5	Left	6	S.W. corner pair or S.E. corner strip of 3	£190
H1a/D8D6	Right	6 & 7	S.W. or S.E. corner pair	£150
H4/D7D5	Left	7	S.W. corner pair	£150
H5/D11D12	Left	8	S.W. or S.E. corner pair	£150
H4a/D9D10	Right	8	S.W. or S.E. corner pair	£150

Prices quoted are for pairs, although single examples are sometimes adequate for identification.
Before attempting to identify recognisable pieces see note below the Price Schedule for 1½d. value.

1909-11. 4d. Orange, Type M8

1909 (1 November). **4d. Orange.** Perf. 14. De La Rue. Ordinary Paper

M25 (=S.G.239/41)

	Unmtd mint	Mtd mint	Used
(1) Brown-orange	£350	£180	£140
(2) Pale orange (Dec. 1909)	45·00	20·00	18·00
(3) Orange-red (Dec. 1909)	45·00	20·00	18·00
Block of four	£225	£100	90·00
Used on cover	†	†	40·00
s. "Specimen", Type 17		£700	
t. "Cancelled", Type 20		£2000	

Perforation 14
Type H1 only

Die Proofs in black on white glazed card:
Uncleared, without markings £4800
Endorsed "BEFORE HARDENING 30 AUG 09" £4800
Endorsed "AFTER HARDENING 2 SEP 09" £4800
Uncleared and cut down from working die and issued 1 Nov. 1909 and initialled £4800
Endorsed "BEFORE STRIKING" £4800
Endorsed "After striking 8 OCT 09" £4800

Die Proof from the De La Rue Archives
On card unmounted with traces of gum or paper on back: Cut down (56×40 mm.) with uncleared surround, initialled £4800

Piece Cut from the Striking Book
See notes under the ½d. value.
Struck on plain paper from the monocoloured die and cut to size
4d. plates 6 to 10 with Sept. and Oct. dates (1909) and "20 leads for repairs" £4200
4d. Die Proofs tend to have an irregular black surround to the design as they were flat when finished instead of being slightly raised. The same applies to the 7d. value.

Plate Proof.
In orange on poor quality buff paper .... 85·00
As above, double impression .... 95·00

Colour Trials
See the notes under "Colour Trials" for the 1½d. value.
The following were submitted to the Inland Revenue on 19 March 1909:
All perforated 14
On white paper. Watermark Crown
In carmine-lake, carmine, orange, orange-yellow, sage-green, dull blue-green, deep blue, violet, purple, Tyrian plum, brown, deep brown, olive, slate .... From £9000
On yellow paper. Watermark Crown
In scarlet, green, four shades of purple .... From £9000
On tinted paper. No watermark
In red on blue; two shades of purple on pink; two shades of purple on orange; two shades of purple on blue; black on pink; black on orange .... From £9000
Following complaints about the issued colour of the monocoloured 4d., the following colour trials were submitted on 12 April 1910:
On white paper. Watermark Crown
In yellow-orange, yellow, olive-yellow .... From £9000
On tinted paper. No watermark
In red on blue; purple on orange; deep purple on blue .... From £9000
The 1910 colour trials were printed from the monocoloured plate while those of 1909 were from the bicoloured plates which can be differentiated by the value circles which are larger, measuring about 6 mm. in diameter on the monocoloured plate compared with about 5½ mm.

1911 (12 July). **4d. Orange.** Perf. 14. Harrison. Ordinary Paper

M26 (=S.G.278)

	Unmtd mint	Mtd mint	Used
(1) Bright orange	£225	£120	55·00
(2) Deep bright orange	£250	£120	55·00
Block of four	£1100	£600	£350
Used on cover	†	†	£175
s. "Specimen", Type 22		£300†	

†No. M26s exists from NPM archive sales.

Perforation 14
Types   H2(c)   H2A(c)   V1   V1A
         H2(d)   H2A(d)

4d. Orange. M27 Postage Issues (1902-13) KING EDWARD VII

1911 (11 November). **4d. Orange.** Perf. 15×14. Harrison. Ordinary Paper

M27 (=S.G.286)

	Unmtd mint	Mtd mint	Used
(1) Bright orange	60·00	30·00	15·00
(2) Deep bright orange	75·00	40·00	18·00
(3) Very deep orange	£150	80·00	45·00
Block of four	£300	£150	75·00
Used on cover	†	†	65·00

Perforation 15 × 14
Types V3 V3A

Plate Descriptions

Official Pl. No.	S.G. Pl. No.	Features
6/301	6	Coextensive rules. No marking. Used by De La Rue and Harrison (a) added fine ½ cut under 2nd
7/302	7	Coextensive rules. No marking. Used by De La Rue and Harrison (a) added fine ½ cut under 1st
8/303	8	Coextensive rules. Fine ½ cut under 4th. Used by De La Rue and (reportedly)* by Harrison
9/304	—	This plate was not used
10/305	10	Coextensive rules. Fine ½ cut under 3rd. Used only by De La Rue

Printings
De La Rue

		Plates		
No. of Printing	Date	Left Sheet	Right Sheet	Notes
9 & 10	1909/11	7	6	No. M25 shades (1) to (3)
		7a	6a	Rule cut added to both plates
		10	8	

Harrison
Perforation 14

1st	July 1911	6a		No. M26 shades (1) and (2)
		7a		

Perforation 15 × 14

2nd	Nov. 1911	6a		No. M27 shades (1) to (3)
		7a		
		8*		

*Although the use by Harrison of plate 8 perforated 15×14 has long been recorded, several specialist collectors report that no piece has been seen by them. Accordingly the publishers would welcome confirmation of any existing plate cut strip of 4 with V3 perforation.

Price Schedule

Plate No.	Left or Right Sheet	Printing Usage	Recognisable Piece	Price
De La Rue				
Perforation 14. Type H1				
6	Right	9 & 10	S.W. corner pair	—
7	Left	9 & 10	S.W. corner pair	—
6a	Right	9 & 10	S.W. corner pair	55·00
7a	Left	9 & 10	S.W. corner pair	55·00
8	Right	9 & 10	S.W. corner strip of 4	£100
10	Left	9 & 10	S.W. corner strip of 3	80·00
Harrison				
Perforation 14. Types H2, H2A or V1, V1A				
6a	—	1st	S.W. corner pair	£240
7a	—	1st	S.W. corner pair	£240
Perforation 15 × 14. Types V3, V3A				
6a	—	2nd	S.W. corner pair	80·00
7a	—	2nd	S.W. corner pair	80·00
8	—	2nd	S.W. corner strip of 4	£150

Prices quoted are for pairs or strips, although single examples are sometimes adequate for identification.
Before attempting to identify recognisable pieces see notes below the Price Schedule for 1½d. value.

1902-11. 5d. Purple and Blue, Type M9

1902-06. 5d. Purple and Blue. Perf. 14. De La Rue

A. 1902 (14 May). **Ordinary paper**
M28 (=S.G.242)

	Unmtd mint	Mtd mint	Used
(1) Dull purple and ultramarine	£135	65·00	22·00
(2) Slate-purple and ultramarine	£135	65·00	22·00
Block of four	£625	£325	£110
Used on cover	†	†	50·00
b. Broken frame at right (Pl. H1, R. 15/8)		£325	
c. Damaged R.H. duty tablet (Pl. D3, R. 12/10)		£275	
d. Damaged L.H. duty tablet (Pl. D4, R. 11/4)		£225	
e. Thin VENUE (Pl. H2, R. 12/9)		£325	
f. Break over lion's tail (Pl. H2, R. 20/8)		£275	
g. Broken cross on Crown (Pl. H3, R. 1/12)		£550	
s. "Specimen", Type 16		£350	

Imperforate single from P.O. Registration Sheet.. Price unused £15000

B. 1906 (May). **Chalk-surfaced paper**

M29 (=S.G.242a, 244)

	Unmtd mint	Mtd mint	Used
(1) Dull purple and ultramarine	£115	55·00	22·00
(2) Slate purple and ultramarine	£115	55·00	22·00
Block of four	£575	£275	£110
Used on cover	†	†	40·00
a. Watermark inverted	£7500	£5000	
b. Broken cross on Crown (Pl. H3, R. 1/12)		£550	
c. Damaged R.H. duty tablet (Pl. D3, R. 12/10)		£325	
d. Damaged head plate		£375	
e. Damaged L.H. duty tablet		£275	
f. Damaged L.H. duty tablet (Pl. D4, R. 11/4)		£325	
g. Thin VENUE (Pl. H2, R. 12/9) (less marked)		£325	
h. Break over lion's tail (Pl. H2, R. 20/8)		£325	
i. Flaws on PO and A (Pl. H2, R. 11/1)		£375	
s. "Specimen", Type 17		£700	
t. "Cancelled", Type 19		£2250	
u. "Cancelled", Type 20		£2000	

The value tablets vary from pale to deep ultramarine.
† No. M29t exists from NPM archive sales.

KING EDWARD VII Postage Issues (1902-13) 5d. Purple and Blue. M30

1911 *(7 August).* **5d. Purple and Blue.** Perf. 14. Somerset House. Ordinary Paper

M30 (=S.G.293/4)

	Unmtd mint	Mtd mint	Used
(1) Dull reddish purple and cobalt blue	60·00	30·00	22·00
(2) Dull reddish purple and bright blue	60·00	30·00	22·00
(3) Deep dull reddish purple and bright blue	55·00	30·00	22·00
(4) Deep plum and cobalt-blue	60·00	30·00	25·00
(5) Plum and cobalt-blue (F) (Feb. 1912)	90·00	50·00	35·00
Block of four	£275	£140	£110
Used on cover	†	†	65·00
b. Broken cross on Crown (Pl. H3, R. 1/12)		£550	
c. Thin lion (Pl. H4, R. 7/3)		£150	
d. 2nd and 3rd harp strings broken (Pl. H4, R. 14/5)		£150	
e. 1st and 2nd harp strings broken (Pl. H4, R. 20/11)		£150	
f. Damaged shield (Pl. H4, R. 18/2)		£150	
g. Damaged R.H. duty tablet (Pl. D5, R. 20/12 et al.)		£150	
h. E of POSTAGE with top strokes joined (Pl. H4c, R. 1/1)		£150	
s. "Specimen", Type 22			

The value tablets became considerably worn and many minor varieties of breaks and missing lines may be found on both De La Rue and Somerset House printings. The two composite illustrations below show examples of typical breaks.

Damaged value tablets

The Somerset House printings are clearly distinguishable by colour. The purple shades all show a distinctive reddish hue when placed side by side with the De La Rue printings. The deep plum shade is the nearest approach to the De La Rue slate-purple colour, and difficulty is encountered with classification as this was a later printing with a fine impression. The cobalt-blue of the value tablet is, however, quite different from the ultramarine of the De La Rue printing.

M28/29c   M29e

M28b   M28d, 29f   M28e, M29g

M29d   M28f, M29h

M28g, M29/30b   M29i

Perforation 14
Types   H1   H1A

Die Proofs in black on white glazed card:
Head plate only
Without marking £3250
Endorsed "BEFORE HARDENING 20 DEC 01" £3250
Cut down and endorsed on back "Duplicate proof of Head die for 5d stamp registered 3 May 1902" (M/S) £3250
Endorsed "AFTER HARDENING" and (M/S) "27 Dec 01" £3250

Pieces Cut from the Striking Books
For notes see under ½d. value.
Struck on plain paper cut to size with various endorsements comprising dates, plates and/or numbers of leads
5d. head plates .... From £3000

Plate Proofs.
In issued colours on poor quality buff paper .... 80·00

M30c    M30d

5d. Purple and Blue. M30 Postage Issues (1902-13) KING EDWARD VII MA

M30e Several states

M30f

M30h

Perforation 14
Types   V1   V1A

Plate Descriptions

Official Pl. No.	S.G. Pl. No.	Features
Head Plates (Inner Line)		
1/111	H1	Continuous rules. Cut under 2nd. Used only by De La Rue
2/113	H2	Continuous rules. Cut under 1st. Used only by De La Rue
3/115	H3	Continuous rules. No marking. Used by De La Rue and Somerset House (see Printings for H3a)
4/248	H4	Coextensive rules. No cuts but square purple dots in interpane margin. Used by De La Rue and Somerset House (see Printings for H4a,b,c,d)
Duty Plates (Outer Line)		
3	D3	Short bar rules. Used only by De La Rue
4	D4	Short bar rules, especially short left and right of upper pane. Used only by De La Rue
5	D5	Continuous rules, with breaks in horiz. rules every 3rd stamp. Upward bulge under 2nd. Used by De La Rue and Somerset House
6	D6	Continuous rules, with breaks in horiz. rules every 3rd stamp. Used only by De La Rue

Printings
De La Rue

No. of Printing	Date	Plates Left Sheet	Plates Right Sheet	Notes
Ordinary Paper (No. M28)				
1	May/Aug. 1902	H2/D4	H1/D3	Head plate is in deeper purple in Printings 1 and 2 compared with 3 and 4
2	Apr./May 1903	H2/D4	H1/D3	
3	Feb./Mar. 1904	H2/D4	H1/D3	Plate H1 very worn
4	Feb./Mar. 1905	H2/D4	H3/D3	
Chalk-surfaced Paper (No. M29)				
5	Feb./Mar. 1906	H2/D4	H3/D3	
6	Apr./May 1907	H2/D4	H3/D3	Poor quality chalky paper
7	Mar./Apr. 1908	H2/D4	H3/D3	
8	June/Sept. 1910	H4/D4	H3/D3	
9	May/Sept. 1910	H3/D6	H2/D5	Plate H2 moved to right sheet and H3 to left sheet

The exact date of first use of Plate H4 is uncertain.

Somerset House

No. of Printing	Date	Plates	Notes
Ordinary Paper (No. M30)			
1st	July 1911	H3a/D5	H3a has added 2 cuts under 11th and 1 under 7th bottom pane and purple dots above and below 12th, both panes
2nd	Dec. 1911?	H4a/D5	H4a has 2 cuts under 11th, both panes and purple dots as H3a
3rd	Feb. 1912	H4b/D5	H4b has date cuts under 11th filled up, both panes and 2 cuts added under 12th bottom pane only
4th	Nov. 1912	H4c/D5	H4c has purple dots above and below 12th both panes removed
5th	1913	H4d/D5	H4d has white dot added to right of 12th, bottom pane

For the 4th printing the plate was repaired and the flaws on it were removed.

Shades (1) and (2) came from the 1st and 2nd printings. During the 3rd printing the ink was changed, was sometimes fluorescent and close to shade (4) but usually produced shade (3). The final printings were in shade (4).

Price Schedule

Plate Combination Head/Duty	Left or Right Sheet	Printing Usage	Recognisable Piece	Price per Pair
De La Rue				
(a) Ordinary Paper				
H1/D3	Right	1 to 3	S.W. corner pair, lower pane	£275
H2/D4	Left	1 to 4	Corner	£160
H3/D3	Right	4	S.W. corner pair, lower pane	£275
(b) Chalk-surfaced Paper				
H3/D3	Right	5 to 8	Corner pair with short bar blue rules	£225
H2/D4	Left	5 to 7	Corner pair with short bar blue rules and continuous purple rules	£200
H4/D4	Left	8	Pair with coextensive purple rules	£200
H2/D5	Right	9	Corner pair with continuous blue rules	£160
H3/D6	Left	9	Corner pair with continuous blue rules	£160
Somerset House				
H3a/D5	—	1st	S.E. corner of any pair with continuous purple rules	70·00
H4a/D5	—	2nd	S.E. corner	£120
H4b/D5	—	3rd	S.E. corner	£110
H4c/D5	—	4th	S.E. corner	80·00
H4d/D5	—	5th	S.E. corner	£120
H4/D5	—	2nd to 5th	Any pair with coextensive purple rules	70·00

Prices quotes are for pairs, although single examples are sometimes adequate for identification.

KING EDWARD VII — Postage Issues (1902-13) 6d. Purple. M31

Before attempting to identify recognisable pieces see notes below the Price Schedule for 1½d. value.

1902-13. 6d. Purple, Type M10

1902-05. 6d. Purple. Perf. 14. De La Rue

A. 1902 (1 January). Ordinary paper
M31 (=S.G.245, 246)

	Unmtd mint	Mtd mint	Used
(1) Pale dull purple	85·00	45·00	22·00
(2) Slate-purple	85·00	45·00	22·00
Block of four	£425	£225	£110
Used on cover	†	†	60·00
s. "Specimen", Type 15		£400†	

Imperforate single from P.O. Registration
Sheet .... Price unused £20000
†No. M31s exists from NPM archive sales.
No. M31 was pre-released and exists on cover with No. M1 (½d.), M5 (1d.) and M16 (2½d.) cancelled 31 December 1901.

B. 1906 (January). Chalk-surfaced paper
M32 (=S.G.245a, 248)

	Unmtd mint	Mtd mint	Used
(1) Pale dull purple	85·00	45·00	22·00
(2) Dull purple	85·00	45·00	22·00
(3) Slate-purple	85·00	45·00	22·00
Block of four	£425	£225	£110
Used on cover	†	†	75·00
a. Watermark inverted		—	£3500
b. Frame broken at right		—	£150
s. "Specimen", Type 17		£700	

Perforation 14
Types   H1   H1A

Die Proofs in black on white glazed card:
Without marking £3250
Endorsed "28 AUG 01 BEFORE HARDENING" £3250
Endorsed "7 SEP 01 AFTER HARDENING" £3250
Endorsed "29 APR. 04 AFTER STRIKING" £3250
Endorsed "Working Die No. 18" £3250
Endorsed "Registered 3.12.1901 AFTER
HARDENING Working Die No. 18" in M/S £3250

Pieces Cut from the Striking Books
See notes under the ½d. value.
   Struck on plain paper cut to size with various endorsements comprising dates, plates and/or number of leads
6d. value .... From £2600
   See under 1½d. value for piece which includes 6d. plate.

Plate Proofs
In grey-black on thick soft white paper ruled on
   both front and back within lines 10 mm. apart £225
In black on thin white card £160

Colour Trials
Watermark Crown. Imperf. on very thin paper
In buff, blue, dull purple, grey, slate, green,
   orange, carmine and bright rose .... From £9000
Chalky paper. No watermark
In deep red, red, purple, reddish purple, pale grey,
   grey, grey-black and black .... From £5800
   These were made on the selvedge of a British Colonial ½d. stamp on chalky paper. They show the green rule along the perforated edge either at top or bottom of the stamp; the other three sides are imperf.

1911-13. 6d. Purple. Perf. 14. Somerset House

A. 1911 (31 October). Ordinary paper, Fluorescent ink
M33 (=S.G.295, 297/300)

	Unmtd mint	Mtd mint	Used
(1) Royal purple (F) (31 Oct. 1911)	£110	50·00	90·00
(2) Reddish purple (F) (Nov. 1911)	60·00	30·00	28·00
(3) Very deep reddish purple (F) (Nov. 1911)	£120	55·00	45·00
(4) Dull purple (F)	60·00	30·00	22·00
(5) Dull lilac (F)	£300	£200	£140
(6) Dark purple (GBF) (May 1912)	£225	£125	95·00
(7) Blackish purple (GBF) (May 1912)	£225	£125	95·00
Block of four	£300	£150	£110
Used on cover	†	†	90·00
c. Frame broken at top right		—	£125
d. No cross on crown (Pl. 9, R. 11/11) (various shades)	£1800	£1200	
e. Flaw below N of PENCE (Pl. 9, R. 20/6)		£175	90·00
f. "J" flaw (Pl. 9, R. 10/12)		£175	90·00
s. "Specimen", Type 22		£400	

B. 1912 (March). Ordinary paper, non-fluorescent ink
M33A (=S.G.297/300)

	Unmtd mint	Mtd mint	Used
(1) Dull purple	60·00	30·00	22·00
(2) Dark purple	60·00	30·00	22·00
(3) Reddish purple (Oct. 1912)	60·00	30·00	25·00
(4) Pale dull purple (June 1913)	60·00	30·00	30·00
(5) Pale reddish purple (June 1913)	60·00	30·00	28·00
Block of four	£300	£150	£110
Used on cover	†	†	95·00
a. No watermark	£18000	†	†
ba. Frame broken at bottom right (Pl. 2a, R. 11/12)		£425	£225
bb. Frame repaired (Pl. 2b, R. 11/12)		£475	£225
c. Frame broken at top right		—	£175
d. No cross on crown (Pl. 9, R. 11/11) (various shades)	£1800	£1200	
e. Flaw below N of PENCE (Pl. 9, R. 20/6)		£175	90·00
f. "J" flaw (Pl. 9, R. 10/12)		£175	90·00
s. "Specimen", Type 22		£400	

   Shades (4) and (5) are mainly very fine impressions on thinner plate glazed but also exist on ordinary paper.

6d. Purple. M34 *Postage Issues (1902-13)* **KING EDWARD VII**

M32b  — M33Aba  — M33Abb

M33c, M33Ac  — M33f, M33Af, M36f

M33Ae, M36e

C. 1913 (March). "Dickinson" coated paper
M34 (=S.G.301)

(1) Dull purple	£425	£275	£190
(2) Dull reddish purple	£425	£275	£190
Block of four	£2200	£1400	£950
Used on cover	†	†	£425
s. "Specimen", Type 26			

This paper, although coated, does not respond to the silver point test. Its use was experimental and some experience is needed to identify it.

The surface has the smooth glossy appearance associated with chalk-surfaced paper and an aid to its identification is the dead white appearance of the back of the stamp. Possibly the paper was coated both sides. As the paper is rather thick the watermark is not immediately visible. Printings on this paper were from Plates 10 and 11.

No. M34s exists from NPM Archive sales.

D. 1911 (31 October). Chalk-surfaced paper
M35 (=S.G.296)

Bright magenta	£17500	£12500
s. "Specimen", Type 22		£5750

M36 (=S.G.303)

(1) Pale plum (July 1913)	£150	95·00	95·00
(2) Deep plum (July 1913)	60·00	30·00	75·00
Block of four	£300	£150	£375
Used on cover	†	†	£200
d. No cross on crown (Pl. 9, R. 11/11)		£1950	£1250
e. Flaw below N of PENCE (Pl. 9, R. 20/6)		£180	£250
f. "J" flaw (Pl. 9, R. 10/12)		£180	£250
s. "Specimen", Type 26			

The ink used for M35 reacted with the chalky surface of the paper and caused a variation in the colour, and the paper itself fluoresces bright lemon under long wave ultraviolet. It was withdrawn on the day after issue. Thereafter the 6d. stamps were issued on ordinary paper (M33) until the "Dickinson" coated paper was introduced in March 1913 (M34).

This was considered to be unsatisfactory and De La Rue were contracted to gum, plate-glaze and apply the chalk-surface coating to the paper which Somerset House used for M36. The gum is thick and yellowish. The impressions are very clear and normally lack the rubbed appearance of the earlier De La Rue printings.

No. M36s exists from NPM Archive sales.

Perforation 14
Type   V1   V1A

Plate Descriptions

Official Pl. No.	S.G. Pl. No.	Features
1/20	1	Continuous rules. Cut under P of 1st, and a purple dot both to the left and right of the interpane margin (a) added cut under P of 4th Used only by De La Rue
2/22	2	Continuous rules. Cut under P of 2nd (a) date cuts added under EN of 12th, purple dots added over and under the 12th stamp in the top and bottom rows of each pane, two circular scoops containing purple dots cutting into the last two pillars of the interpane margin, and a white dot in the margin rule to the right of the 19th row denoting (initially) ink MB 10394D/24816 (b) as before but the purple dots above and below the 12th stamps and in the circular scoops have been removed, the white dot to the right of the 19th row is filled, and a fresh white dot made in the rule to the right of the 18th row denoting (initially) ink MB 25598 Used by De La Rue and Somerset House—the only plate used by the latter whilst in continuous rule form
3/62	—	This plate was not used
4/80	—	This plate was not used
5/161	5	Continuous rules. Cut under XP of 3rd, and a purple dot both to the left and right of the interpane margin (a) added cut under P of 4th Used only by De La Rue
6/162	6	Continuous rules. Cut under PE of 1st Used only by De La Rue
7/163	7	Continuous rules. A ¾ cut (base) under P of 2nd, and a scoop in the rule below the 9th stamp. One printing is known on ordinary paper with a red dot added in the bottom margin under the 12th stamp (a) added ½ cut (base) under EN of 4th Used only by De La Rue

KING EDWARD VII   Postage Issues (1902-13) 6d. Purple. M36

Official Pl. No.	S.G. Pl. No.	Features
8/164	8	Continuous rules. Cut under P of 3rd, and scoops in the rules below the 4th and 9th stamps. (There is no purple dot adjoining either of the interpane margins) (a) added white dot under XP of 2nd (b) added cut (pyramidal) under PE of 2nd Used only by De La Rue
9/165	9	Continuous rules. A ¾ cut (base) under PE of 3rd. (There is no purple dot adjoining either of the interpane margins) Coextensive rules. (a) the plate was converted to one with coextensive rules by cutting up and dividing the original continuous rules—and believed unique in this respect. The cut under the 3rd stamp is filled and a fresh cut made under (P)E of 1st, date cuts added under (P)E of 12th, purple dots added over and under the 12th stamp in the top and bottom rows of each pane, two circular scoops containing purple dots made cutting into the last pillar (lower scoop touching the 4th pillar bar) of the interpane margin and above which the rule (below R. 10/12) received a ¾ cut (base)—probably accidental—under (C)E (The major differences between this plate in its coextensive form and all other plates of this value with coextensive rules are that the S.W. corner rule of the lower pane is joined to the vertical rule to the left of the 20th row; there is no white dot in the registration piece under R. 20/6 and 7; and the gaps between the registration piece and the adjoining rules are, unusually, of equal width) (b) as before but a white dot made in the margin rule to the right of the 20th row denoting (initially) ink MB 24655 (c) as before but the white dot in the rule to the right of the 20th row is filled and a fresh white dot made in the rule to the right of the 19th row denoting (initially) ink MB 10394D/24816 (d) as before but the purple dots above and below the 12th stamps and in the circular scoops, have been removed, the white dot to the right of the 19th row is filled, and a fresh white dot made in the rule to the right of the 18th row denoting (initially) ink MB 25598. The cut below R. 10/12 is now filled (e) the cut under (P)E of 1st is filled Used by De La Rue and Somerset House
10/191	10	Die I coextensive rules. Date cuts under and just to the left of P of 12th, also a white margin dot in the rule to the right of the 18th row denoting (initially) ink MB 25598. (This plate never received purple margin dots or interpane scoops but in comparison with plate 11, the rule to the right of the interpane gutter is relatively thin) Used only by Somerset House

Official Pl. No.	S.G. Pl. No.	Features
11/192	11	Die I coextensive rules. Date cuts under and just to the right of P of 12th, also a white margin dot in the rule to the right of the 18th row denoting (initially) ink MB 25598. There is a scoop in the rule below the 9th stamp. (This plate never received purple margin dots or interpane scoops but in comparison with plate 10, the rule to the right of the interpane gutter is relatively thick) Used only by Somerset House
12/226		This plate was a reserve at Somerset House and not used
13/227	13	Die II coextensive rules. Cuts under (P)E of 2nd and PE of 4th (a) Date cuts added under CE of 11th, purple dots added over and under the 12th stamps in the top and bottom rows of each pane, two circular scoops containing purple dots made cutting into the last two pillars of the interpane margin, and a purple dot to the right of the interpane margin (b) as before but the cut under the 4th stamp and the date cuts under the 11th are filled. Fresh date cuts made under EN of 12th which are far from clear and in many instances barely perceptible (c) as before but the date cuts re-made under P of 12th, and a white margin dot made in the rule to the right of the 20th row denoting (initially) ink MB 24655. (In the course of these printings the fillings of the original date cuts fell out giving rise to the variety "date cuts under both 11th and 12th stamps" (d) as before but the white dot in the rule to the right of the 20th row is filled and a fresh white dot made in the rule to the right of the 19th row denoting (initially) ink MB 19394D/24816 Used by De La Rue and Somerset House
14/299	14	Die II coextensive rules. Cut under X of 1st (a) date cuts added under EN of 11th, purple dots added over and under the 12th stamps in the top and bottom rows of each pane, two circular scoops containing purple dots made cutting into the last pillar (lower scoop touching the 3rd pillar bar) of the interpane margin, and there is now a purple dot to the left of the interpane margin Used by De La Rue and Somerset House
15/300	—	This plate was not used

Printings
De La Rue

		Plates		
No.of Printing	Date	Left Sheet	Right Sheet	Notes
Ordinary Paper (No. M31)				
1	1902/5	1	1a	Shades (1) and (2)
		6	2	
		8	7	
		(pairings unknown)		

6d. Purple. M36 *Postage Issues (1902-13)* **KING EDWARD VII** **MA**

No. of Printing	Date	Plates Left Sheet	Plates Right Sheet	Notes
Chalk-surfaced Paper (No. M32)				
2 & 3	1906/10	5	1a	Shades (1) (2) and (3)
		6	5a	
		8	7 & 7a	
		9	8a & 8b	
		14	13	
			(pairings unknown)	

Somerset House

No. of Printing	Date	Plates	Paper	Notes
Printings made during 1911 have date cuts under the 11th stamps				
1st	Oct. 1911	14a	13a	Chalky	No. M35 in bright magenta
		14a	13a	Ordinary	No. M33 shade (1) (F)
	Nov. 1911	14a	13a	Ordinary	No. M33 shades (2) (3) and (4) all (F)
Printings made during 1912/13 have date cuts under the 12th stamps				
2nd	March 1912	9a	13b	Ordinary	No. M33 (8) dull lilac (F) peculiar to this issue
3rd	May 1912	9b	13c	Ordinary	The plates have a white dot 20th row denoting ink MB 24655—in the shade of M33 A (1)
4th	May/June 1912	9c	13d	Ordinary	The plates have a white dot 19th row denoting ink
		9c	2a	Ordinary	MB 10394D/24816 believed to be M33A (2). Other shades occur including M33A (1)
5th	Oct. 1912	2b	9d	Ordinary	The plates have a white dot 18th row denoting ink MB 25598—in the shade of M33A (3)
6th	Nov. 1912	10	11	Ordinary	The new plates also have a white dot 18th row denoting ink MB25598. Other shades occur including M33A (1) and M33A (4) but not on plate-glazed paper

The 18th row white dots on plates 9, 10 and 11 remained for all later printings

7th	March 1913	11	10	Coated	No. M34 (1) and (2)
8th	June 1913	10	11		
		10	9d	Plate-glazed	Shades of M33A (4) and (5)
			11	9d	
9th	July 1913	11	9e	Chalky	No. M36 in deep plum

Price Schedule

Pl. No. and Sheet Side	Printing Usage	Date	Recognisable Piece	Price
De La Rue				
6t1 left	1	1902/05	S.W. strip of 4	£200
1a right	1		S.W. strip of 4	£200
2 right	1		S.W. corner pair H1 perf.	95·00
6 left	1		S.W. corner pair	95·00
7 right	1		S.W. corner pair	95·00
8 left	1		S.W. strip of 3	£150
1a right	2 & 3	1906/10	S.W. strip of 4	£220
5 left	2 & 3		S.W. strip of 4	£220
5a right	2 & 3		S.W. strip of 4	£220
6 left	2 & 3		S.W. corner pair	£110
7 right	2 & 3		S.W. strip of 4	£220
7a right	2 & 3		S.W. strip of 4	£220
8 left	2 & 3		S.W. strip of 3	£165
8a right	2 & 3		S.W. corner pair	—
8b right	2 & 3		S.W. corner pair	—
9 left	2 & 3		S.W. strip of 3 H1 perf.	—
13 right	2 & 3		S.W. strip of 4	£220
14 left	2 & 3		S.W. corner pair	£110
Somerset House				
13a right	1st	Oct. 1911	No. M35 S.E. corner pair	£26000
14a left	1st		No. M35 S.E. corner pair	—
13a right 14a left	1st		No. M33 (1) S.E. corner pair	£150
13a right 14a left	1st	Nov. 1911	No. M33 (2) & (4) S.E. corner pair	90·00
13a right 14a left	1st		No. M33 (3) S.E. corner pair	£120
9a left 13b right	2nd	March 1912	No. M33 (5) S.E. corner pair	—
9b left 13c right	3rd	May 1912	S.E. corner pair	—
9c left	4th	May/June 1912	S.E. corner block of 4	£150
13d right	4th		S.E. corner block of 4	£150
2a right	4th		S.E. corner block of 4	£150
2b left 9d right	5th	Oct. 1912	S.E. corner block of 6	£210
10 left 11 right	6th	Nov. 1912	S.E. corner pair	90·00
11 left 10 right	7th	March 1913	No. M34 corner pair	£550
10 left 11 right	7th		No. M34 corner pair	£550
10 left 9d right	8th	June 1913	M33A (4) and (5) S.E. corner pair	£100
11 left	8th		M33A (4) and (5) S.E. corner pair	£100
11 left 9e right	9th	July 1913	No. M36 S.E. corner pair	£100

Prices quoted are for pairs or strips, although single examples are sometimes adequate for identification.

Before attempting to identify recognisable pieces see notes below the Price Schedule for 1½d. value.

KING EDWARD VII Postage Issues (1902-13) 7d. Grey-Black. M37

1910-13. 7d. Grey-black, Type M11

1910 (4 May). **7d. Grey-Black.** Perf. 14. De La Rue. Ordinary Paper

M37 (=S.G.249/9a)

	Unmtd mint	Mtd mint	Used
(1) Grey-black	24·00	15·00	22·00
(2) Deep grey-black	£170	£110	£100
Block of four	£120	75·00	£110
Used on cover	†	†	£200
b. Raised crown in watermark (corner block of 4) (Pl. 1, R. 19/2)		£4000	
s. "Specimen", Type 17		£700	
t. "Cancelled", Type 20		£2000	
u. "Cancelled", Type 25		£2000	

Imperforate single from P.O. Registration
Sheet... Price unused £20000

Perforation 14
Type H1 only

Essays

1

2

3

4

Submitted 5 March 1909 on very highly glazed paper
Type 1 in slate £8500
Type 2 in carmine-lake £8500
Type 3 in brown £8500
Type 1 was selected but with larger value tablets as in Type 2.
Submitted 15 July 1909 on very highly glazed paper
Type 4 in grey-green £8500
Type 5 as Type 4 but with fringe added round
    design (card inscribed "5"). In grey-green £8500

Essays from the De La Rue Archives
Stamp-size photographic essays on card, pen-cancelled with cross:
Type 4 in grey-green £8500
Type 5, as Type 4 but with fringe added round
    design. In grey-green £8500
Types 1, 2 and 3 as described above pen-cancelled with cross were acquired by the N.P.M.

Die Proofs in black on white glazed card:
Endorsed "Die No. 86" £6750
Endorsed "BEFORE HARDENING 7 SEP 09" £6750
Endorsed "AFTER HARDENING 12 SEP 09" £6750
This die was faulty and defaced
Endorsed "Die No. 89" £6750
Endorsed "BEFORE HARDENING 7 DEC 09" £6750
Without marking but black surround whited out ... £6750
Endorsed "AFTER STRIKING 12 MAR 10" £6750
    As was the case for the 4d. orange, the 7d. Die Proofs tend to have an irregular black surround to the design as they were flat when finished instead of being slightly raised.

Die Proofs from the De La Rue Archives
On card unmounted with traces of gum or paper on the back: Cut down (83×47 mm.), with uncleared surround.
    Stamped "7 DEC 09" and "BEFORE HARDENING"......... £6750
As last but with surround painted out and without
    markings.. £6750

Piece Cut from the Striking Book
See notes under the ½d. value.
Struck on plain paper cut to size with various endorsements comprising dates, plates
1 to 3 and leads 7d. value... £6000

Colour Trials
Submitted on 24 February 1910 to the Inland Revenue
On white paper. Watermark Crown
In yellow-olive, olive, sage-green, dull blue-green,
    pale blue, deep blue, violet, slate-purple,
    purple, red-purple, deep red-brown, pale red-
    brown, brown, grey-brown, grey, black............ From £10000
    The grey colour was chosen from the colour trials, this having been selected from the essays. The grey-brown colour trial was submitted in duplicate.

1912 (1 August). **7d. Grey-black.** Perf. 14. Somerset House. Ordinary Paper

M38 (=S.G.305)

	Unmtd mint	Mtd mint	Used
(1) Deep slate-grey	£200	£120	50·00
(2) Slate-grey	30·00	15·00	22·00
(3) Pale grey (May 1913)	60·00	35·00	25·00
Block of four	£150	75·00	£120
Used on cover	†	†	£200
s. "Specimen", Type 26		£350	
t. "Cancelled", Type 25		£450	

M38(1) is on poorly surfaced paper which produced a coarse impression. The later printings, M38(2) and M38(3), are on finely calendered paper, and it is difficult to distinguish between these and the De La Rue printings.
    All the Somerset House issues show a trace of olive in the grey, some more so than others. The olive is always apparent to the keen eye and is even more noticeable under long wave ultraviolet.
    †Nos. M38s and M38t exist from NPM archive sales.

Perforation 14
Types V1 V1A

Plate Descriptions
Official   S.G.

Pl. No.	Pl. No.	Features
1/314	1	Coextensive rules. Cut under 2nd (a) date cuts added under & R of 12th and scoop in the interpane gutter cutting the pillars under and between the 6th and 7th stamps Used by De La Rue and Somerset House
2/315	2	Coextensive rules. Cut under 1st (a) date cuts added under RE of 12th Used by De La Rue and Somerset House
3/319	3	Coextensive rules. No cuts under 1st or 2nd, date cuts under & R of 12th Used only by Somerset House—plate not proofed until November 1912

9d. Purple and Blue. M39 *Postage Issues (1902-13)* KING EDWARD VII MA

Printings

No. of Printing	Date	Left Sheet	Plates Right Sheet	Notes
De La Rue				
Ordinary Paper (No. M37)				
1	1910	2	1	Shade (1) or rarely (2)
Somerset House				
Ordinary Paper (No. M38)				
1st	Aug. 1912	1a		Shade (1) rare on coarse unsurfaced paper
2nd	1912	1a		Shade (2)
3rd	Dec. 1912	2a		Shade (2)
4th	May 1913	3		Shade (3)

Price Schedule

Plate No.	Left or Right Sheet	Printing Usage	Recognisable Piece	Price per pair
De La Rue				
1	Right	1	S.W. corner pair lower pane H1 perf.	35·00
2	Left	1	S.W. corner pair lower pane H1 perf.	35·00
Somerset House				
With date cuts under 12th stamps lower pane only				
1a	—		1st S.E. corner pair	£270
1a	—		2nd S.E. corner pair	40·00
2a	—		3rd S.E. corner pair	40·00
3	—		4th S.E. corner pair	40·00

In the 1st Somerset House printing the impressions are very coarse.

Prices quoted are for pairs, although single examples are sometimes adequate for identification.

Before attempting to identify recognisable pieces see notes below the Price Schedule for the 1½d. value.

1902-13. 9d. Purple and Blue, Type M12

1902-05. 9d. Purple and Blue. Perf. 14. De La Rue

A. 1902 (7 April). Ordinary paper
M39 (=S.G.250, 251)

	Unmtd mint	Mtd mint	Used
(1) Dull purple and ultramarine	£250	£140	75·00
(2) Slate-purple and ultramarine	£250	£140	75·00
(3) Slate-purple and deep ultramarine	£250	£140	75·00
Block of four	£1250	£700	£375
Used on cover	†	†	£250
d. T in POSTAGE appears as "7" (Pl. H1, Pane B, R. 4/2)		£750	
s. "Specimen", Type 16		£450	
Imperforate single from P.O. Registration Sheet			Price unused £20000

B. 1905 (June). Chalk-surfaced paper
M40 (=S.G.250a, 251a)

	Unmtd mint	Mtd mint	Used
(1) Dull purple and ultramarine	£250	£140	75·00
(2) Slate-purple and pale ultramarine	£225	£140	75·00
(3) Slate-purple and ultramarine	£225	£140	75·00
(4) Slate-purple and deep ultramarine	£275	£175	90·00
Block of four	£1100	£700	£375
Used on cover	†	†	£250
a. Watermark inverted		—	£3500
b. Two breaks in S.W. frame (Pl. H2, Pane D, R. 1/5)		£425	£250
c. Left frame cracked (Pl. D (1), Pane B, R. 1/1)		£425	£250
d. T in POSTAGE appears as "7" (Pl. H1, Pane B, R. 4/2)		£425	
s. "Specimen", Type 17		£725	
t. "Cancelled", Type 18		£1800†	
u. "Cancelled", Type 20		£2000	

†No. M40t exists from NPM archive sales.

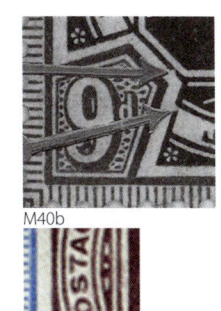

M40b

M40c and M41g   M40d

Perforation 14
Type H1 only

Die Proofs in black on white glazed card:
Head plate only
Without marking £3600
Endorsed "BEFORE HARDENING 28 NOV 01" £3600
Cut down and endorsed on back "Duplicate proof of Head die for for 9d stamp registered 5 April 1902" (M/S) £3600
Endorsed "BEFORE HARDENING 10 DEC 01" £3600
Endorsed "AFTER HARDENING 10 DEC 01" £3600

Piece Cut from the Striking Book
See notes under the ½d. value.
Struck on plain paper cut to size with various endorsements comprising dates, plates 1 to 3 and leads 9d. head plate £4000

1911 (24 July). **9d. Purple and Blue.** Perf. 14. Somerset House. Ordinary Paper

M41 (=S.G. 306/08)

	Unmtd mint	Mtd mint	Used
(1) Reddish purple and light blue	£200	95·00	75·00
(2) Deep dull reddish purple and deep bright blue (Sept. 1911)	£200	95·00	75·00
(3) Dull reddish purple and blue (Oct. 1911)	£125	60·00	60·00
(4) Slate-purple and cobalt-blue (F) (March 1912)	£300	£140	£110
(5) Deep plum and blue (July 1913)	£125	60·00	60·00
Block of four	£625	£300	£300

53

MA KING EDWARD VII Postage Issues (1902-13) 9d. Purple and Blue. M41

	Unmtd mint	Mtd mint	Used
Used on cover	†	†	£190
b. Irregular S.W. frame (Pl. H2, Pane G, R. 1/4)		£300	£180
c. Major frame breaks (Pl. H1, Pane G, R. 2/4)		£300	£180
d. Damaged S.E. corner (Pl. H2, Pane D, R. 1/2)		£300	£180
e. Damaged upper right corner (Pl. H2, Pane D, R. 2/2)		£300	
f. Break in base of upper right value tablet (Pl. D(3), Pane H, R. 1/1)		£300	
g. Left frame cracked (Pl. D(1), Pane B, R. 1/1)		£300	
s. "Specimen", Type 22		£450	

Shades in the 7th Somerset House printing vary from reddish purple, almost indistinguishable from (1) to plum (5). For illustration of No. M41g, see No. M40c.

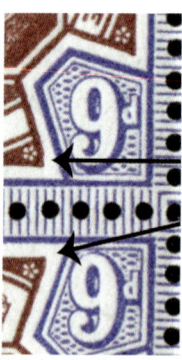

M41b

M41f

M41c

M41d and M41e

Perforation 14
Types   V1   V1A

Plate Descriptions

Official Pl. No.	S.G. Pl. No.	Features
Head Plates. All the Outer Line head plates have continuous marginal rules		
1/94	H1	Cut under 1st pane G and over 1st pane A. Used only by De La Rue except for panes substituted by Somerset House
2/96	H2	Cut under 2nd pane G and over 2nd pane A. Used by De La Rue and Somerset House (see Printings for H2a,b,c)
3/99	H3	Thin date cuts under 5th panes D and H. Used only by Somerset House

The registration sheet of Plate 1/94 has no De La Rue marks. It is possible that this plate and Plate 2/96 may exist in collectors' hands without markings and, if found, may be recognised by the side of the mill sheet from which they came.

Duty Plates

(1)	D(1)	Nick in left frame of 1st top row pane A and small crack left of 1st top and 4th rows pane B. Used by De La Rue and Somerset House
(2)	D(2)	No marking. Used only by De La Rue
(3)	D(3)	Used only by Somerset House

There were no complete Inner Line duty plates for the 9d. value. Each plate combination included eight duty plates for the eight panes of 20.

Plate (1) comprised official Plates 17, 19, 20, 23, 24, 25, 27 and 36 but their positions in the plate layout are not known. They did not vary and always appeared on left sheets when printed by De La Rue. However Plate 39 was used to substitute the B pane in the 6th Somerset House printing.

Plate (2) comprised official Plates 28 to 35 and are always found in the same but unknown positions on right sheets.

Plate (3) comprised official Plates 40 to 46 and 48. Except for Plate 48, all had been used for Queen Victoria printings and show flaws.

Printings
De La Rue

No. of Printing	Date	Plates Left Sheet	Right Sheet
Ordinary Paper (No. M39)			
1 to 3	1902–May 1904	H1/D(1)	H2/D(2)
Chalk-surfaced Paper (No. M40)			
4 to 7	1905–Nov. 1909	H1/D(1)	H2/D(2)

Somerset House

No. of Printing	Date	Plates	Notes
Ordinary Paper (No. M41)			
1st	June 1911	H2/D(1)	No added cuts. Only 1 ream of sheets printed
2nd	Aug. 1911?	H2a/D(1)	H2a has purple date dots added under 4th of panes D and H. Being inconsistent in position no definite guidance can be given to distinguish the two panes
3rd	Sep. 1911?	H2b/D(1)	H2b has date dots removed and 2 cuts added under 4th of panes D and H, those in H pane more to right and closer than those in D pane

54

10d. Purple and Red. M42 *Postage Issues (1902-13)* **KING EDWARD VII**

No. of Printing	Date	Plates	Notes
4th	Feb. 1912	H2c/D(1)	H2c has date cuts filled up and fine cuts added under 5th panes D and H, those in H pane being broader and more to right than those in D pane. S.E. corner of pane E severely damaged
5th	Aug. 1912	H2c, H1/D(1)	Pane A from H1 with cut over 1st unfilled substituted for pane E. F and G panes have substantial flaws. Head plate stack of short lined blocks between E and F panes were replaced inverted
6th	Oct. 1912	H2c, H1/D(1)	As 5th printing but pane G of H1 substituted for pane G of H2c and duty plate 39 substituted for pane B of D(1). Extremely rare printing
7th	Nov. 1912	H3/D(3)	Thin date cuts under 5th of panes D and H differing from those of printings 4 to 6 in being serrated. Head plate stacks of short lined blocks between C and D panes and G and H panes were inverted compared with earlier printings, while those of duty plates between E and F panes and G and H panes were also inverted

This is a complicated value and further guidance for distinguishing the printings is contained in an article by Michael Astley published in the February 1975 issue of *The GB Journal*.

Price Schedule

Plate Combination Head/Duty	Left or Right Sheet	Printing Usage	Recognisable Piece	Price per Pair
De La Rue				
Perforation 14. Type H1				
(a) Ordinary Paper				
H1/D(1)	Left	1 to 3	Corner of sheet	£225
H2/D(2)	Right	1 to 3	Corner of sheet	£250
(b) Chalk-surfaced Paper				
H1/D(1)	Left	4 to 7	Corner of sheet	£225
H2/D(2)	Right	4 to 7	Corner of sheet	£250
Somerset House				
H2/D(1)	—	1st	S.E. corner, panes D or H	£200
H2a/D(1)	—	2nd	S.E. corner, panes D or H	£160
H2b/D(1)	—	3rd	S.E. corner, panes D or H	£160
H2c/D(1)	—	4th	S.E. corner, panes D or H	£160
H2c, H1/D(1)	—	5th	N.W. corner, panes E or F	£160
H2c, H1/D(1)	—	6th	S.W. corner, pane G with cut under 1st, Single (pairs not known)	—
H3/D(3)	—	7th	S.E. corner, panes D or H, S.W. corner, pane G or N.W. corner, pane A	£150

With one exception prices quoted are for pairs, although single examples are sometimes adequate for identification.

Before attempting to identify recognisable pieces see notes below the Price Schedule for the 1½d. value and reference should be made to the lay-out of the plates for the 9d. value in the General Notes under "PLATES".

1902-12. 10d. Purple and Red, Type M13

1902-05. 10d. Purple and Red. Perf. 14. De La Rue

A. 1902 (3 July). Ordinary paper
M42 (=S.G.254)

	Unmtd mint	Mtd mint	Used
(1) Dull purple and carmine	£275	£150	75·00
(2) Slate-purple and carmine	£275	£150	75·00
(3) Slate-purple and carmine-pink	£550	£350	£125
Block of four	£1375	£750	£375
Used on cover	†	†	£225
b. No cross on Crown. Shade (1)	£775	£425	£300
g. Break in frame at back of head		£425	
s. "Specimen", Type 16		£500	
Imperforate single from P.O. Registration Sheet			Price unused £20000

A small printing of shade (2) from 1902 fluoresces bright "Cherry" red under long wave ultraviolet.

B. 1906 (August). Chalk-Surfaced Paper
M43 (=S.G.254b, 255/56)

	Unmtd mint	Mtd mint	Used
(1) Dull purple and carmine	£275	£140	75·00
(2) Slate-purple and carmine	£275	£140	75·00
(3) Slate-purple and deep carmine	£500	£350	£125
(4) Slate-purple and deep (glossy) carmine	£6500	£4500	£1500
(5) Dull purple and scarlet (Sept. 1910)	£260	£140	75·00
Block of four	£1300	£700	£375
Used on cover	†	†	£250
b. No cross on Crown. Shade (2)	£725	£450	£275
c. No cross on Crown. Shade (4)			
d. No cross on Crown. Shade (5)	£725	£450	£275
g. Break in frame at back of head		£425	£200
s. "Specimen", Type 17		£700	
t. "Cancelled", Type 18		£1800†	
u. "Cancelled", Type 20		£2000	

The glossy carmine colour of M43(4) gives the appearance of being enamelled.

M42b, M43b/d and M44k/l are "recession flaws" and were not the result of plate damage. When the frame was printed the paper around the inked part of the stamp was slightly depressed. As a result, when the head plate was applied it did not always come fully into contact with the paper where it was depressed and the Crown did not print. The variety may therefore be found in different sheet positions.

†No. M43t exists from NPM archive sales.

MA KING EDWARD VII Postage Issues (1902-13) 10d. Purple and Red. M44

Quoin flaw*    M42g, M43g

*Head plate flaws approximating to the above exist on Nos. M43/4. They were caused by overtightening quoins between the sub-electros. They are sometimes found in Rows 1 and 4 between stamps 4 and 5 and also 8 and 9.

Perforation 14
Type H1 only

Die Proofs in black on white glazed card:
Head plate only
Without marking £3600
Endorsed "BEFORE HARDENING 27 NOV 01" £3600
Cut down and endorsed on back "Duplicate proof
   of Head die for 10d. stamp registered 28 June
   1902" (M/S) £3600
Endorsed "AFTER HARDENING 28 NOV 01" £3600

Die Proof from the De La Rue Archives
On card unmounted with traces of gum or paper on the back:
Head plate only, without markings £3600

Pieces Cut from the Striking Books
See notes under the ½d. value.
   Struck on plain paper cut to size with various endorsements comprising dates, plates and/or leads
10d. head plate £3900
10d. duty plate £3900

Plate Proof in issued colours on poor quality buff paper ..£140

1911 (9 October). **10d. Purple and Red.** Perf. 14. Somerset House. Ordinary Paper

M44 (=S.G. 309/11)

		Unmtd mint	Mtd mint	Used
(1)	Dull reddish purple and scarlet	£425	£225	£110
(2)	Dull purple and scarlet	£200	95·00	75·00
(3)	Deep dull purple and scarlet	£175	95·00	75·00
(4)	Dull purple and deep scarlet	£500	£280	£200
(5)	Dull reddish purple and aniline pink (F)	£500	£280	£225
(6)	Dull reddish purple and carmine (May 1912)	£150	85·00	60·00
(7)	Deep dull purple and carmine	£150	85·00	60·00
(8)	Dark plum and carmine	£150	85·00	60·00
	Block of four	£750	£425	£300
	Used on cover	†	†	£225
h.	Repaired S.W. corner (shade 8) (Pl. D(1), Pane Y, R. 2/2)		—	£225

		Unmtd mint	Mtd mint	Used
i.	Mark after E of REVENUE (Pl. H2, R. 2/12)		£300	£200
j.	Cracked duty plate (Pl. D(1), Pane X, R. 4/12)		£400	
k.	No cross on Crown (shade 5)	£3800	£2800	
l.	No cross on Crown (shade 6)	£2800	£1800	
s.	"Specimen", Type 22		£375†	

†No. M44s exists from NPM archive sales.

M44h    M44j

M43i, M44i

No. M44h consists of a nick in the diagonal white line and only 9 dots instead of 12.

Perforation 14
Types   V1   V1A

Plate Descriptions
Head Plates
With continuous Outer Line marginal rules for each of the four panes of 48 except that each was made up of three sections of 16 (4×4) so that each horizontal head plate rule is broken after the fourth and eighth stamps.

Official Pl. No	S.G. Pl. No	Features
1/72	H1	Cut under 2nd, bottom row pane Z. Used only by De La Rue on right sheets
2/74	H2	Cut under 1st, bottom row pane Z. Used only by De La Rue on left sheets only and by Somerset House (see Printings for H2a,b)

Duty Plates
With continuous Inner Line, marginal rules for each of the four panes of 48. There were no complete duty plates for the 10d. value. Each combination included four duty plates for the panes of 48. Plate (1) comprises duty plates 1 to 4 and Plate (2) comprises duty plates 5 to 8. These were probably arranged in that order from the top downwards.

Official Pl. No	S.G. Pl. No	Features

1s. Green and Red. M45 *Postage Issues (1902-13)* **KING EDWARD VII** **MA**

(1) D(1) No marking. Used by De La Rue on right sheets and by Somerset House (see Printings for D(1a))
(2) D(2) No marking. Used only by De La Rue on left sheets

Head plate 3/76 was also made but never used and duty plates 9 to 12 (of which there is a proof in Royal Mail Heritage Services) were also made but never used.

Printings
De La Rue

No. of Printing	Date	Plates Left Sheet	Right Sheet	Notes
(a) Ordinary Paper (No. M42)				
1 to 4	June 1902– Apr. 1905	H2/D(2)	H1/D(1)	
(b) Chalk-surfaced Paper (No. M43)				
5 to 8	July 1906– Sep. 1909	H2/D(2)	H1/D(1)	Purple and carmine shades
9	Sept. 1910	H2/D(2)	H1/D(1)	Dull purple and scarlet

Somerset House

No. of Printing	Date	Plates	Notes
Ordinary Paper (No. M44)			
1st	Aug. 1911	H2a/D(1a)	Date cut added under 8th and 2 cuts under 11th of panes X and Z. The latter cuts are very similar for both panes but normally the right hand cut of pane Z is closed at the bottom by a very thin line of ink. Red dots under 12th of panes X and Z and over 12th of panes W and Y
2nd	May 1912	H2b/D(1a)	Cuts under 8th and 11th filled up and new cuts added under 12th of panes X and Z; those in the X pane being almost central and those in the Z pane are well to the left of centre

Price Schedule

Plate Combination Head/Duty	Left or Right Sheet	Printing Usage	Recognisable Piece	Price per Pair
De La Rue				
Perforation 14. Type H1				
(a) Ordinary paper				
H1/D(1)	Right		1 to 4 Corner of sheet	£275
H2/D(2)	Left		1 to 4 Corner of sheet	£275
(b) Chalk-surfaced Paper				
H1/D(1)	Right		5 to 8 Corner of sheet	£275
H2/D(2)	Left		5 to 8 Corner of sheet	£275
H1/D(1)	Right		9 Corner of sheet	£275
H2/D(2)	Left		9 Corner of sheet	£275
Somerset House				
Perforation 14. Types V1, V1A				
H2a/D(1a)	—		1st S.E. corner pair panes X or Z	£240
H2b/D(1a)	—		2nd S.E. corner pair panes X or Z	£240

Prices quoted are for pairs, although single examples are sometimes adequate for identification. Before attempting to identify recognisable pieces see notes below the Price Schedule for 1½d. value.

1902-12. 1s. Green and Red, Type M14

1902-05. 1s. Green and Red. Perf. 14. De La Rue

A. 1902 (24 March). Ordinary paper
M45 (=S.G.257)

	Unmtd mint	Mtd mint	Used
(1) Dull green and carmine	£220	£100	40·00
(2) Dull green and bright carmine	£220	£100	40·00
(3) Dull green and carmine-pink	£550	£375	£140
Block of four	£1100	£500	£200
Used on cover	†	†	£175
e. Frame broken at left (Pl. B3, R. 19/1)		£450	
f. Frame broken at left (Pl. B2, R. 12/1)		£500	
s. "Specimen", Type 16		£400	

Imperforate single from P.O. Registration Sheet..Price unused £15000

A small printing of shade (2) from 1902 fluoresces bright "Cherry" red under long wave ultraviolet.

B. 1905 (September). Chalk-surfaced paper
M46 (=S.G.257a, 259)

(1) Dull green and carmine	£220	£100	40·00
(2) Dull green and pale carmine	£300	£125	55·00
(3) Dull green and scarlet (Sept. 1910)	£230	£100	55·00
(4) Deep dull green and scarlet	£250	£125	55·00
Block of four	£1100	£500	£200
Used on cover	†	†	£200
d. "Full beard" to portrait		£7500	
e. Frame broken at left (Pl. B3, R. 19/1)		£475	
f. Frame broken at left (Pl. B2, R. 12/1)		£500	
g. Break in crown and damaged E (Pl. H2, R. 13/9)			
s. "Specimen", Type 17		£725	
t. "Cancelled", Type 18		£1800†	
u. "Cancelled", Type 20		£2000	

†No. M46t exists from NPM archive sales.

M45e, M46e   M45f, M46f

M46g, M47g

The frame break No. M45e also exists on the Queen Victoria 1 shilling No. K41 of 1900, Plate 1a, R. 19/1.

57

KING EDWARD VII Postage Issues (1902-13) 1s. Green and Red. M47

Perforation 14
Type H1 only

Die Proofs. In black on white glazed card.
Head and duty plate only:
Without marking (cleared) £3600
Without marking (uncleared) £3600
Endorsed "BEFORE HARDENING 4 DEC 01" £3600
Endorsed "AFTER HARDENING 10 DEC 01" £3600
As last but also endorsed "A.C. 10 Dec. 01" £3600
Cut down, with "Duplicate proof of Head die &
 duty die for 1/- stamp registered 25 Feb 1902"
 annotated on back in M/S £3600
Duty Plate only:
Endorsed "AFTER STRIKING 3 JUL. 07" endorsed
 "1/- Unified" and initialled in pencil £3600

Die Proof from the De La Rue Archives.
On card unmounted with traces of gum or paper on the back:
Head plate only with uncleared surround, without
 markings £3600

Pieces Cut from the Striking Books
See notes under the ½d. value.
 Struck on plain paper cut to size with various endorsements comprising dates, plates and/or leads
1s. head plate £3600
1s. duty plate £3600

1911 *(13 July).* **1s. Green and Red.** Perf. 14. Somerset House. Ordinary Paper

M47 (=S.G. 312/14)

	Unmtd mint	Mtd mint	Used
(1) Dark green and scarlet	£240	£120	60·00
(2) Deep green and scarlet (9 Oct. 1911)	£180	85·00	40·00
(3) Green and bright scarlet	£180	85·00	40·00
(4) Green and scarlet	£180	85·00	40·00
(5) Green and carmine (15 April 1912)	£140	60·00	40·00
Block of four	£800	£400	£200
Used on cover	†	†	£200
a. No watermark	£12000	£8000	
b. Watermark inverted	£240	£150	†
c. Watermark inverted and part of the word POSTAGE		£375	
ca. Block of 12 with complete word POSTAGE on six stamps, watermark inverted	£12000	—	—
d. Vertical scratch at back of ear (Pl. H2a) and bottom frame broken (Pl. B5, R. 20/11). No date cuts in marginal rule		£350	£175
da. Do. but with date cuts added (Pls. H2b/B5)		£325	
db. As da but frame break repaired (Pls. H2b/B5a)		£325	
dc. As db but date cuts removed (Pls. H2c or H2d/B5a or B5b)		£300	
g. Break in crown and damaged E (Pl. H2, R. 13/9)			
s. "Specimen", Type 22		£350	
t. "Specimen", Type 23			
u. "Specimen", Type 26		£350†	

Prices for M47d, M47da, M47db and M47dc are for singles with selvedge attached.

†No. M47u exists from NPM archive sales.
For illustration of No. M47g, see M46g.

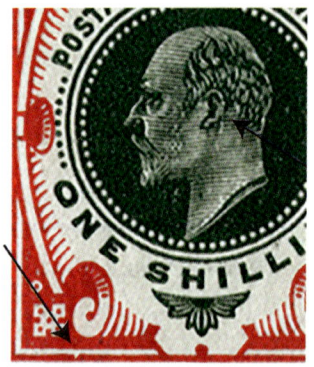

M47d, M47da

Perforation 14
Types V1 V1A

Plate Descriptions
Head (incorporating Duty) Plates
With continuous rules (cut away at the corners) the 240 set Outer Line Head Plates each comprise two panes of 120 stamps (10 horizontal rows of 12). Each pane of 120 is made up of 6 sections of 20 stamps (5 horizontal rows of 4) the positions of which are marked by a break in the mid-point of each vertical rule and by breaks between the 4th/5th and 8th/9th stamps of each horizontal rule. The plate thus comprised 12 such sections—informally numbered 1 to 12 commencing from the N.W. corner of the upper pane—and akin to the diagram in the introductory notes to the Edward VII issues which illustrates the 16 section layout of the 1½d., 2d. and 5d., Outer Line Plates. At least one substitution of a section is known for the 1s. value when section 10 (the S.W. corner lower pane) of Head Plate 1/86 was substituted in that same position in Head Plate 2/89 for the final issue. Other substitutions are probable but not yet proven due to the scarcity of the relevant material.

Official Pl. No	S.G. Pl. No	Features
1/86	H1	Cut under 2nd stamp bottom row lower pane. Used only by De La Rue
2/89	H2	Cut under 1st stamp bottom row lower pane, and a highly distinctive constant rule flaw under the 7th stamp bottom row lower pane
		(a) cut added in the rule under the 6th stamp of the lower pane
		(b) the cut under the 6th stamp is filled and wide date cuts added under the 11th stamps of the bottom rows of the upper and lower panes
2/89	H2	(c) the cut under the 1st stamp is filled, the date cuts under the 11th stamps are filled, and fresh narrow date cuts added under the 12th stamps of the bottom rows of the upper and lower panes
		(d) as before but the S.W. lower pane corner section of 20 stamps (5 rows of 4) is removed and the corresponding section from Head Plate 1/86 substituted—including its rule cut under the 2nd stamp of the bottom row. Used by De La Rue and Somerset House

Border Plates
With continuous rules the Inner Line "frame plates" comprise two panes each of 120 stamps in 10 rows of 12 for each 240 set plate. Some of the Border Plates are believed to have been used previously for the bi-coloured 1s. value of the Queen Victoria "Jubilee" issue.

2s.6d. Purple. M48 Postage Issues (1902-13) KING EDWARD VII

Official Pl. No	S.G. Pl. No	Features
2	B2	Rule corners cut away and a cut under the 2nd stamp bottom row lower pane. Used only by De La Rue.
3	B3	Rule corners cut away (apart from a thin semi-circular line on some printings joining the lower pane S.W. corner) and a cut under the 1st stamp bottom row lower pane. Used only by De La Rue
4	B4	Continuous rule corners with crack in the S.W. corner of the lower pane, no plate cut. Used only by De La Rue
5	B5	Continuous rule corners, no plate cut (a) red dots added in the margins above and below the 12th vertical rows of upper and lower panes (b) red dots of state (a) removed Used by De La Rue and Somerset House

Printings
De La Rue printed 480-set

		Plates		
No. of Printing	Date	Left Sheet	Right Sheet	Notes
Ordinary Paper (No. M45)				
1	1902/04	H2/B3	H1/B2	Shades (1) and (2)
Chalk-surfaced Paper (No. M46)				
2	1905/09	H2/B4	H1/B3	
		H2/B4	H1/B5	Shades (1) and (2)
3	1910	H2/B4	H1/B5	Shades (3) and (4)

Somerset House printed 240-set

No. of Printing	Date	Plates	Notes
Ordinary Paper (No. M47)			
Without date cuts			
1st	July 1911	H2a/B5	Shade (1)
With date cuts under the 11th stamps			
2nd	Oct 1911	H2b/B5	Shades (1) and (2)
3rd	late 1911	H2b/B5a	Shades (3) and (4)
With date cuts under the 12th stamps			
4th	Apr 1912	H2c/B5a	Shade (5)
5th	Oct 1912	H2d/B5b	Shade (5)

Price Schedule

Plate Combination Head/Border	Left or Right Sheet	Printing Usage	Colour	Recognisable Piece	Price
De La Rue					
(a) Ordinary Paper					
H1/B2	Right	1	Carmine	S.W. corner pair	£225
H2/B3	Left	1	Carmine	S.W. corner pair	£225
(b) Chalk-surfaced paper					
H1/B2	Right	2	Carmine	S.W. corner pair	£230
H2/B4	Left	2	Carmine	S.W. corner pair	£230
H1/B5	Right	2	Carmine	S.W. corner pair	£230
H1/B5	Right	3	Scarlet	S.W. corner pair	£240
H2/B4	Left	3	Scarlet	S.W. corner pair	£240

Somerset House
Ordinary Paper

Plate Combination	Left or Right Sheet	Printing Usage	Colour	Recognisable Piece	Top Pane	Bottom Pane
H2a/B5	—	1st	Scarlet	S.E. corner pair	—	—*
H2b/B5	—	2nd	Scarlet	S.E. corner pair	£220	£325*
H2b/B5a	—	3rd	Scarlet	S.E. corner pair	£220	£325*
H2c/B5a	—	4th	Carmine	S.E. corner pair	£175	£275*
H2d/B5b	—	5th	Carmine	S.E. corner pair	£175	£275*

*The five bottom pane pairs contain, respectively, and from 1st printing; M47d, M47da, M47db and M47dc in 4th and 5th printings.

Prices quoted are for pairs, although single examples are sometimes adequate for identification.

Before attempting to identify recognisable pieces see notes below the Price Schedule for 1½d. value.

1902-13. 2s.6d. Purple, Type M15

1902-05. 2s.6d. Purple. Perf. 14. De La Rue

A. 1902 (5 April). Ordinary paper
M48 (=S.G.260)

	Unmtd mint	Mtd mint	Used
(1) Lilac	£525	£280	£150
(2) Slate-purple	£525	£280	£150
Block of four	£2750	£1400	£750
Used on cover	†	†	£1250
b. Watermark inverted	£6750	£5000	£3500
s. "Specimen", Type 15		£425	
t. "Specimen", Type 16		£400	

Imperforate single from P.O. Registration Sheet...Price unused £28000

B. 1905 (7 October). Chalk-surfaced paper
M49 (=S.G.261/2)

(1) Pale dull purple	£675	£350	£180
(2) Dull purple	£600	£350	£180
(3) Slate-purple	£650	£350	£190
Block of four	£3000	£1750	£900
Used on cover	†	†	£1400
b. Watermark inverted	£11000	£7500	£4250
s. "Specimen", Type 17		£3250	

Perforation 14
Type H1 only

Essay from the De La Rue Archives. Photographic essay in stamp size on card:
In approved design, submitted to the Controller on 14 May 1901

Die Proofs. In black on white glazed card:
Without marking £4000
Endorsed "BEFORE HARDENING 8 NOV 01"........................... £4000
Endorsed "AFTER HARDENING 12 NOV 01"............................. £4000
As last but also endorsed in M/S "AC. 12 Nov. 01"................ £4000
Stamped "AFTER STRIKING 15 NOV 01" and
  endorsed in M/S "AC. 15 Nov 01"
Cut down, with "Duplicate proof of die registered
  27 Decr. 190." Annotated on reverse in M/S.................. £4000

KING EDWARD VII
Postage Issues (1902-13) 2s.6d. Purple. M50

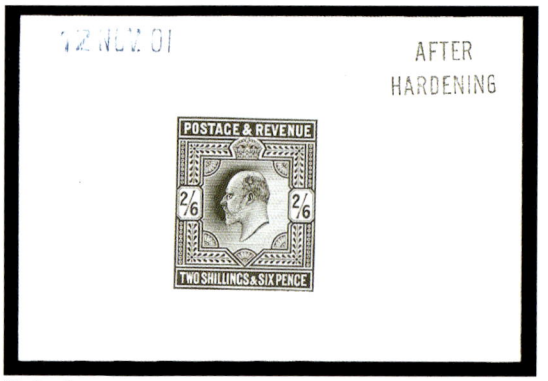

Die Proof

Die Proofs from the De La Rue Archives. On card unmounted with traces of gum or paper on the back:

Cut down (86×54 mm.) with head in oval and
 partially uncleared surround to head and
 background £5500
Cut down (68×51 mm.) with solid dark ground
 in front of head, lettered "A." and annotated
 "CANCELLED" in M/S £5500
Cut down (68×51 mm.) with lightened
 background, lettered "B." and annotated
 "CANCELLED" in M/S £5500

Piece Cut from the Striking Book
See notes under the ½d. value.
Struck on plain paper cut to size with various
 endorsements comprising dates, plates 1 and 2 and leads
2s.6d. value £5000

Plate Proof in issued colour on poor quality buff
paper £175
As above, double impression £190

1911 *(15 September)*. **2s.6d. Purple.** Perf. 14. Somerset House. Ordinary Paper

M50 (=S.G.315/17)

	Unmtd mint	Mtd mint	Used
(1) Dull greyish purple (F)	£1750	£950	£450
(2) Dull reddish purple (Oct. 1911)	£625	£300	£200
(3) Dark purple	£675	£325	£200
(4) Pale dull reddish purple (18 Mar. 1913)	£625	£300	£200
(6) Dark purple (GBF)	£900	£450	£240
(7) Blackish purple (GBF)	£900	£450	£240
Block of four	£3200	£1500	£1100
Used on cover	†	†	£1700
b. Watermark inverted	†	†	—
s. "Specimen", Type 22		£425†	
t. "Cancelled", Type 24	£3500†		

†Nos. M50s and M50t exist from NPM archive sales.
Note that there is no shade (5).

Perforation 14
Types V1 V1A

Plate Descriptions

Official Pl. No.	S.G. Pl. No.	Features

The 112 set plate comprises two panes each of 56 stamps (7 horizontal rows of 8).

1/51	1	No marking
		(a) coloured dots added in the margins above and below the last vertical rows in each pane. Cuts added under the 7th stamp bottom row of both panes, those in the lower pane being thicker and broader
		(b) cuts under 7th stamps filled up and cuts added under 8th stamp bottom row of both panes
		(c) added white dot in the marginal rule at right of corner stamp both panes

Printings and Price Schedule

					Price Top pane	Price Bottom pane
Series	Date	Plate	Paper	Position		
De La Rue						
1	1902	1	Ordinary	S.E. corner pair	£700	£700
2	1905	1	Chalky	S.E. corner pair	£750	£750
Somerset House						
With 1911 date cuts under 7th stamp
1st	1911	1a	Ordinary	S.E. corner pair		
			Dull greyish purple (F)		£2000	£2000
			Dull reddish purple		£700	£700
With 1912 date cuts under 8th stamp
2nd	1912	1b	Ordinary	S.E. corner pair	£700	£700
3rd	1913	1c	Plate glazed	S.E. corner pair	£700	£700

5s Red. M51 *Postage Issues (1902-13)* **KING EDWARD VII** **MA**

1902-12. 5s. Red, Type M16

1902 (5 April). **5s Red.** Perf. 14. De La Rue. Ordinary Paper

M51 (=S.G.263/4)

	Unmtd mint	Mtd mint	Used
(1) Bright carmine	£850	£450	£220
(2) Deep bright carmine	£900	£450	£220
Block of four	£4250	£2250	£1100
Used on cover	†	†	£950
a. Watermark inverted		£6500	£5500
s. "Specimen", Type 16		£400	
t. "Specimen", Type 17		£3250	

Imperforate single from P.O. Registration
Sheet..*Price unused* £28000
A small printing of both shades from 1902 fluoresces bright "Cherry" red under ultraviolet light.

Perforation 14
Type H1 only

Essay from the De La Rue Archives. Photographic essay in stamp size on card:
In approved design, submitted to the Controller
on 14 May 1901.. £6500

Die Proofs in black on white glazed card:
Without marking £4250
Endorsed "BEFORE HARDENING 22 NOV 01"..................... £4250
Endorsed "AFTER HARDENING 25 NOV 01" £4250
With initials and (M/S) "25.11.01".. £4250

Piece Cut from the Striking Books
See notes under ½d. value.
Struck on plain paper cut to size with various endorsements comprising dates, plates 1 and 2 and leads
5s. value £6000

Plate Proof in issued colour on poor quality buff
paper £180

1912 (29 February). **Red.** Perf. 14. Somerset House. Ordinary Paper

M52 (=S.G.318)

	Unmtd mint	Mtd mint	Used
(1) Carmine-red	£875	£425	£200
(2) Carmine	£875	£425	£200
Block of four	£4400	£2100	£1000
Used on cover	†	†	£1750
s. "Specimen", Type 26		—†	

†No. M52s exists from NPM archive sales.
An aid to identification in this difficult value is the back of the stamp. The ink used by De La Rue had a permeating quality which gives the appearance of an offset of the design on the back. No. (2) is the later printing with fine impression. A small printing of No. (1) exists in fluorescent ink and is extemely rare.

Perforation 14
Types V1 V1A

Plate Descriptions

Official S.G. Pl.
Pl. No. No. Features

The 112 set plate comprises two panes each of 56 stamps (7 horizontal rows of 8).

1/68   1   No marking
(a) added small carmine dots in the margins above and below the last vertical rows of both panes. Date cuts added under the 7th stamp in the bottom row of both panes. Top pane cuts very fine and small, lower pane cuts thicker and broader
(b) date cuts in state (a) filled up and cuts made under the 8th stamp in the bottom row of both panes

Printings and Price Schedule

				Price Top pane	Bottom pane
Series	Date	Plate	Position		
De La Rue					
1	1902/10	1	S.E. corner pair	£1000	£1000
Somerset House					
With 1911 date cuts under 7th stamp					
1st	Feb. 1912	1a	S.E. corner pair	£1100	£1100
With 1912 date cuts under 8th stamp					
2nd	Oct. 1912	1b	S.E. corner pair	£1100	£1100

1902-12. 10s. Blue, Type M17

1902 (5 April). **10s. Blue.** Perf. 14. De La Rue. Ordinary Paper

M53 (=S.G.265)

	Unmtd mint	Mtd mint	Used
(1) Ultramarine	£2000	£1000	£500
(2) Deep ultramarine	£2100	£1100	£525
Block of four	£10000	£5000	£2500
a. Watermark inverted	—	—	£40000
s. "Specimen", Type 16		£500	
t. "Specimen", Type 17		£2800	

Imperforate single from P.O. Registration
Sheet..*Price unused* £30000

Perforation 14
Type H1 only

Essay from the De La Rue Archives. Photographic essay in stamp size on card:
In approved design, submitted to the Controller
on 14 May 1901.. £6500

Die Proofs in black on white glazed card:
Without marking £4500
Endorsed "BEFORE HARDENING 22 NOV 01"..................... £4500
Endorsed "AFTER HARDENING 25 NOV 01" £4500
Endorsed "AFTER STRIKING" and in M/S "AC.
4 DEC 01"... £4500
As last but additional M/S "HW. 25.11.01"............................. £4500

Piece Cut from the Striking Book
See notes under ½d. value.
Struck on plain paper cut to size with various endorsements comprising dates, plates 1 and 2 and leads
10s. value £6000

Plate Proof in issued colour on poor quality buff
paper £1100

61

KING EDWARD VII — Postage Issues (1902-13) 10s. Blue. M54

1912 *(14 January).* **10s. Blue.** Perf. 14. Somerset House. Ordinary Paper

M54 (=S.G.319)

	Unmtd mint	Mtd mint	Used
(1) Bright blue	£2100	£1100	£625
(2) Blue	£2100	£1100	£625
(3) Deep blue	£2300	£1200	£775
Block of four	£10800	£5500	£3100

Perforation 14
Types V1 V1A

Plate Descriptions

Official Pl. No.	S.G. Pl. No.	Features
		The 112 set plate comprises two panes each of 56 stamps (7 horizontal rows of 8).
1/73	1	No marking (a) blue dots added in the margins above and below the last vertical row in each pane. Upper pane with very fine cuts added under the gutter between the 7th and 8th stamps, in the bottom row (sometimes almost entirely removed during perforation). Lower pane cuts are larger and appear under the corner square of the 7th stamp bottom row (b) cuts in state (a) filled up and cuts made under the last stamp in the bottom row of both panes

Printings and Price Schedule

				Price	
Series	Date	Plate	Position	Top pane	Bottom pane
De La Rue					
1	1902/10	1	S.E. corner pair	£2100	£2100
Somerset House					
With 1911 date cuts under 7th stamp					
1st	Jan. 1912	1a	S.E. corner pair	—	—
With 1912 date cuts under 8th stamp					
2nd	July 1912	1b	S.E. corner pair	£2250	£2250

1902-11. £1 Green, Type M18

1902 *(16 July).* **£1 Green.** Perf. 14. De La Rue. Ordinary Paper

M55 (=S.G.266)

	Unmtd mint	Mtd mint	Used
(1) Dull blue-green	£3500	£2000	£825
Block of four	£19500	£10000	£5500
a. Watermark inverted		£110000	£24000
s. "Specimen", Type 16		£1400	
t. "Specimen", Type 17		£3800	
u. Large "cancelled" in violet and black manuscript cross		£3000	
Imperforate single from P.O. Registration Sheet .... Price unused £30000			
Single unused and used examples are known of No. M55a.			

Perforation 14
Type H1 only

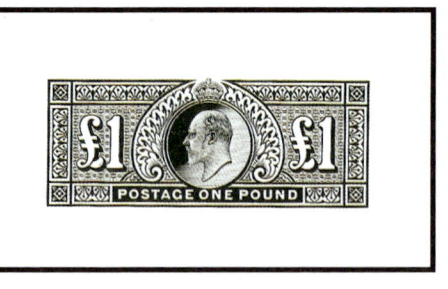

Essays from the De La Rue Archives. Photographic essays in stamp size on card:
With "POSTAGE ONE POUND" in an arc below the King's head submitted to the Controller on 14 May 1901 .... £9000
In approved design, submitted to the Controller on 23 May 1901 .... £9000

Die Proofs in black on white glazed card:
Without marking £4800
Endorsed "BEFORE HARDENING 16 DEC 01" £4800
Endorsed "AFTER HARDENING 19 DEC 01" £4800
As last but additional M/S "AC. 19 DEC 01" £4800
Endorsed "AFTER HARDENING 13 MAR 02" £4800

Piece Cut from the Striking Book
For notes see under ½d. value.
Struck on plain paper cut to size with various endorsements comprising dates, plates 1 and 2 and leads
£1 value £6000

1911 *(3 September).* **£1 Green.** Perf. 14. Somerset House. Ordinary Paper

M56 (=S.G.320)

	Unmtd mint	Mtd mint	Used
(1) Deep green	£3000	£2000	£750
Block of four	£16000	£10000	£4500
s. "Specimen", Type 22		£2200	

Perforation 14
Types H2 (f or g) H2A (f or g)

Plate Descriptions

Official Pl. No.	S.G. Pl. No.	Features
		The 80 set plate comprises two panes of 40 stamps (10 horizontal rows of 4).
1/106	1	No marking (a) date cuts added under the 4th stamp bottom row of both panes (b) cuts in state (a) filled up and a white dot made in the rules above and below the last stamp in the 4th vertical rows of both panes

Somerset House did not add marginal dots for this value.

Printings and Price Schedule

				Price	
Series	Date	Plate	Position	Top pane	Bottom pane
De La Rue					
1	1902/10	1	S.E. corner single	£2250	£2250
Somerset House					
With 1911 date cuts under 4th stamp					
1st	Sept. 1911	1a	S.E. corner single	£2250	£2250
With 1912 date dot under 4th stamp					
2nd	April 1912	1b	S.E. or N.E. corner single	£2250	£2250

£1 GREEN, THE "LOWDEN" FORGERY
Produced by photo lithography and line-perforated, and usually found affixed to brown paper with a forged Channel Islands postmark. The watermark was impressed on the surface of the paper, therefore it washes off when the brown paper is soaked off. The stamp is a good imitation of the Somerset House shade, but the impression is coarser than that of the original and the lines of shading are faint and broken. *Price* £1250.

For further information see the article by Harry Dagnall published in *The GB Journal*, Vol. 31, No. 1 March–April 1993.

£5 (Unissued)

Essay from the De La Rue Archives.
Photographic essay in stamp size on card
submitted to the Controller on 14 May 1901 .... £25000

Die Proofs in black on white glazed card:
Endorsed "BEFORE HARDENING 11 MAR 02" £18000
Endorsed "AFTER HARDENING 13 MAR 1902" £18000
As last but initialled "GKR" in lower left corner £18000
Cut down (66×42½ mm.) and endorsed in M/S
   "Proof of Die prepared but not registered as it
   was resolved to discontinue the £5 stamp/1902" £18000

Piece Cut from the Striking Book
For notes see under ½d. value.
Struck on plain paper cut to size in design similar to 1882 issue but with King Edward VII portrait surmounted by Crown
£5 value endorsed in red "After this die was made
   the G.P.O. decided not to issue a £5 Duty/
   Charged Mar 12th 02" and ruled through in
   red and stamped "13 MAR 02" £30000

Section MB

Booklet Panes in Letterpress (1904-11)

CHECKLIST OF KING EDWARD VII BOOKLET PANES

Spec. Cat. Nos.	Description	From Booklets Nos.	Page
MB1, MB1a	6×½d. De La Rue	BA2–5	64
MB2, MB2a	5×½d. De La Rue and one green cross	BA2–5	64
MB3, MB3a	6×½d. Harrison	BA6	65
MB4, MB4a	5×½d. Harrison and one green cross	BA6	65
MB5, MB5a	6×1d. De La Rue	BA1–5	65
MB6, MB6a	6×1d. Harrison	BA6	65

BOOKLET PANE PRICES. Prices quoted are for lightly mounted examples with good perforations all round and with binding margin attached in the most common shade. Panes in scarcer shades are all worth more, having regard to the shade prices in section MA. Panes showing some degree of trimming will be worth less than the published prices in this Catalogue. Unmounted mint panes are worth more and the following percentages may be added to the basic panes.
De La Rue printings- (MB1/a, MB2/a, MB5/a) **+40%**
Harrison printings- (MB3/a, MB4/a, MB6/a) **+25%**

The booklet pane perforators are described in Appendix 1. As issued panes are collected by reference to the different selvedge perforations, issued panes are listed accordingly. Since Specimen and pre-cancelled panes are much scarcer, no perforation distinction is made in the listing.

½d. Booklet Panes of six. De La Rue

MB1/a, MB3/a

From Booklets BA2/5

	Perf. type	
	E	P
A. Watermark upright		
MB1 (containing No. M2×6) (6.06)	£275	£275
s. "Specimen", Type 17	£2400	
t. "Specimen", Type 22	£2000	
u. Cancelled St. Andrew's Cross, Type A	£525	
v. Cancelled "E.C.'A", Type B	£600	
w. Cancelled "E.C.'U", Type C	£600	
x. Cancelled "E.C.K", Type D	£600	
B. Watermark inverted		
MB1a (containing No. M2a×6) (6.06)	£275	£275
as. "Specimen", Type 17	£2400	
at. "Specimen", Type 22	£2000	
au. Cancelled St. Andrew's Cross, Type A	£525	
av. Cancelled "E.C.'A", Type B	£600	
aw. Cancelled "E.C.'U", Type C	£600	
ax. Cancelled "E.C.K", Type D	£600	

½d. Booklet Panes of five with one Green St. Andrew's Cross. De La Rue

MB2/a, MB4/a

From Booklets BA2/5

	Perf. type	
	E	P
A. Watermark upright		
MB2 (containing No. M2×5) (6.06)	£700	£700
s. "Specimen", Type 17	£2600	
t. "Specimen", Type 22	£2400	
u. Cancelled St. Andrew's Cross, Type A	£700	
v. Cancelled "E.C.'A", Type B	£800	
w. Cancelled "E.C.'U", Type C	£800	
x. Cancelled "E.C.K", Type D	£800	
y. Cancelled "London Chief Office, E.C.", Type E		
B. Watermark inverted		
MB2a (containing No. M2a×5) (6.06)	£700	£700
as. "Specimen", Type 17	£2600	
at. "Specimen", Type 22	£2400	
au. Cancelled St. Andrew's Cross, Type A	£700	
av. Cancelled "E.C.'A", Type B	£800	
aw. Cancelled "E.C.'U", Type C	£800	
ax. Cancelled "E.C.K", Type D	£800	

Type E has not been recorded on panes with watermark inverted.

Die Proof. In black on white glazed card
St. Andrew's Cross dated "24 JAN. 06"....................... £8500

½d. Booklet Panes MB3 *Departmental Official Issues (1902-04)* **KING EDWARD VII** **MB**

½d. Booklet Panes of six. Harrison
From Booklet BA6

	Perf type
	E
A. Watermark upright	
MB3 (containing No. M3×6) (6.11)	£325
s. "SPECIMEN", Type 22*	£1800
t. Cancelled "London Chief Office, E.C.", Type E	£750
B. Watermark inverted	
MB3a (containing No. M3a×6) (6.11)	£325
as. "Specimen", Type 22	£2000
at. Cancelled "London Chief Office, E.C.", Type E	£750

* Including that from the National Postal Museum archives.

½d. Booklet Panes of five with One Green St. Andrew's Cross. Harrison
From Booklet BA6

	Perf type
	E
A. Watermark upright	
MB4 (containing No. M3×5 plus label) (6.11)	£800
t. Cancelled "London Chief Office, E.C.", Type E	£900
B. Watermark inverted	
MB4a (containing No. M3a×5 plus label) (6.11)	£800
as. "Specimen", Type 22*	£2300
at. Cancelled "London Chief Office, E.C.", Type E	£800

* Including that from the National Postal Museum archives.

1d. Booklet Panes of Six. De La Rue

MB5/a, MB6/a

MB5/b, MB6b

From Booklets BA1/5

	Perf. type	
	E	P
A. Watermark upright		
MB5 (containing No. M5×6) (16.3.04)	£250	£250
b. Nos. 3 and 6 on pane showing displaced clichés	£1200	
c. Inner frame broken (R. 1/3 - see M5ra)	£300	
s. "Specimen", Type 17	£2400	
t. "Specimen", Type 22	£1800	
u. Cancelled St. Andrew's Cross, Type A	£475	
v. Cancelled "E.C.'A", Type B	£500	
w. Cancelled "E.C.'U", Type C	£500	
x. Cancelled "E.C.K", Type D	£500	
y. Cancelled "London Chief Office, E.C.", Type E	£1000	
B. Watermark inverted		
MB5a (containing No. M5a×6) (16.3.04)	£250	£250
as. "Specimen", Type 17	£2400	
asa. "Specimen", Type 16*	£2100	
at. "Specimen", Type 22	£1800	
au. Cancelled St. Andrew's Cross, Type A	£475	
av. Cancelled "E.C.'A", Type B	£500	
aw. Cancelled "E.C.'U", Type C	£500	
ax. Cancelled "E.C.K", Type D	£500	

* Including that from the National Postal Museum archives.

1d. Booklet Panes of Six. Harrison
From Booklet BA6

	Perf type
	E
A. Watermark upright	
MB6 (containing No. M6×6) (6.11)	£250
b. Nos. 3 and 6 on pane showing displaced clichés From	£1000
c. Inner frame broken (R. 1/3 - see M6d)	£350
t. Cancelled "London Chief Office, E.C.", Type E	£600
B. Watermark inverted	
MB6a (containing No. M6b×6) (6.11)	£250
ap. With plate mark	£400
as. "Specimen", Type 22*	£1750
at. Cancelled "London Chief Office, E.C.", Type E	£600

* Including that from the National Postal Museum archives.

National Postal Museum Archives
On 26 April 1984 Christie's Robson Lowe auctioned, inter alia, booklets BA5(6) and BA6 and booklet panes MB3s, MB4as and MB6as on behalf of the NPM. In error, the auction house described all the specimen overprints as Type 15, whereas they are Type 22 (Type 15 not having been used in any booklets). Accordingly, this error is corrected by deletion of all previous references to Specimen Type 15 booklet panes deriving from the archives. Instead it is noted that a few of the booklet panes overprinted Specimen Type 22 derive from this source.

Section MO

Departmental Official Issues (1902-04)

Introduction. These stamps are overprinted with the name of a Department and in most cases the word "OFFICIAL". They were for the sole use of essentially autonomous Government Departments. The only stamps which had general use were those overprinted "Government Parcels" which were supplied to, and used by, all Departments.

Certain offices in London, Edinburgh and Dublin were designated Department Head Offices. They enjoyed essentially free use of letter post by right and did not have to use postage stamps on outgoing mail with most incoming mail similarly allowed to pass free. Since there was no weight limit on letter post the heavy packets caused the Post Office severe problems over many years. When Parcel Post was introduced in 1883 this was mitigated by the free issue of Government Parcels overprints. All Government Offices received them free whether Head Office, or "Local". Mail from Head Offices had to be certified externally on each item that it was on Departmental business. At first this was done by manuscript, handstamped or even printed facsimile signatures, but those were phased-out from the 1850's until, by 1900, practically all Departments used handstamped "cachets", certifying or franking stamps. Some of the larger Departments had branch offices outside the three capital cities which had to purchase postage stamps for their mail with cash from post offices.

In 1882 the Inland Revenue was allowed to have its own "I.R. OFFICIAL" overprinted stamps subject only to quarterly returns of the numbers and value of those used. This meant a loss of P.O. cash receipts and set a precedent which effectively blocked the use of overprints by other Departments for many years. In 1896 the Army and the Office of Works (a very small Department) were allowed to use their own stamps, but only on cash payment at the time of issue from Somerset House to the using Department. This prevented a direct loss of cash flow and set a new precedent which was followed in 1902 and 1903 by the Board of Education and the Navy.

None of these Departmental overprints were supposed to be sold, or otherwise made available, to the public in unused condition. The Inland Revenue and the Army did, however, employ non-civil servants to carry out some of their business and the definition of who was entitled to obtain official stamps by Act was impossible. No civil servant who released unused Departmental overprints to the public was deemed to be guilty of any legal offence. So there was a traffic in such overprints, especially those widely used like the Government Parcels stamps. In addition certain philatelists probably received regular supplies of the Inland Revenue overprints. No other mechanism can account for the numbers of such stamps as the mint £1 Official on Orbs paper (SG O12) around today. This practice came to the knowledge of the then Chairman of the Board of Inland Revenue and in 1896 he formulated specific regulations for his staff which were intended to prevent the trade. The effect of these measures was to drive it underground where it continued, although on a reduced scale. In 1903 a series of events led to this trade being terminated. In September of that year W. Richards, a senior Inland Revenue employee, and A. B. Creeke, the well-known philatelist, were convicted of a technical offence in connection with the supply of I.R. Official overprints and imprisoned.

Events in the Inland Revenue did not necessarily reflect the situation in other Departments since they were all effectively autonomous. The Treasury was concerned by the premium over face value of unused overprints offered by stamp dealers and they wished to rectify the situation. A Committee was set up and it recommended the immediate withdrawal of all Departmental overprints. The official date was 13 May 1904, but because so many are dated 14 May, that day is generally regarded by collectors as the last day of general authorised usage. For purely administrative reasons some usage after 13 May was tolerated. This tolerance ended in mid-July; any examples used after then must be regarded with the utmost suspicion.

Direct revenue to the Post Office substantially increased in spite of an incentive to all Departments in the form of a 25% discount on purchases of postage stamps. In the meantime, the Inland Revenue had secured use of printed "Official Paid" franks, later Official/crown/paid "logos". Gradually more Inland Revenue local offices began to use them and direct revenue was again lost by local post offices. New social legislation—Labour Exchanges, National Insurance and so on—produced a whole new series of local offices with enormous demands on the post. They were authorised to use the same system of franks and from then on nothing could stop their spread to all Departments who wished to use them.

By 1914 a virtually uniform official mail existed across all Departments at great loss of direct revenue to the Post Office. This system of official mail lasted until very recent times, when its inefficiencies were at last realised. Now, Government mail is little if any different from that of any other large user. Proper postage budgets are needed and the Post Office is fully reimbursed for its services.

All the stamps listed were printed and overprinted by Thomas De La Rue on ordinary paper. Types **L1**, **L6a** and **L10** were derived from die-struck leads and the other overprints were probably printed from electros developed by repeating rows of hand-set type. All stamps were perforated 14. The ½d. to 1s. have watermark **W12** (Crown); 2s.6d., 5s., and 10s. have watermark **W9** (Anchor). The £1 has three Crown watermarks on each stamp.

> **Warning.** Many of the Official stamps may be found with forged overprints and collectors should be on their guard when buying. Some of the forgeries are easy to detect but to determine the genuineness of the overprint requires the use of modern highly sophisticated equipment. It is therefore recommended that these stamps should be purchased only when supported by R.P.S. or B.P.A. certificates dated subsequent to 1973.

Inland Revenue — Departmental Official Issues (1902-04) — KING EDWARD VII — MO

INLAND REVENUE

These stamps were used by revenue officials in the provinces, mail to and from Head Office passing without a stamp. The London office used these stamps only for foreign mail. A Post Office Circular dated 26 September 1882, contained the following notice: "The Postmaster-General has approved of the use, on and after 1st October next, of stamps overprinted I.R. Official, for denoting the Postage and Registration Fees on letters transmitted by certain officers of Inland Revenue, stationed outside the metropolis…"

Many of the dates of issue are from Wright and Creeke or from the contemporary philatelic press. Unlike the postage stamps these issues for Departments were not generally available to the public.

6d. No. MO4. Eight unused examples are known and only one of these is in private hands. However in the British Postal Museum & Archive there is a perforated sheet of No. MO4 but it lacks a block of six, leaving 234 stamps. Instructions were issued within the Inland Revenue Department that used examples of No. MO4 were to be so heavily cancelled that they would be worthless to collectors with the result that practically all used examples of this stamp, which are in any case very rare indeed, are of very poor quality.

I.R. OFFICIAL L1
I. R. OFFICIAL L2

1902-04. Stamps of 1902 Overprinted with Type L1 (½d. to 1s.) or Type L2 (5s., 10s., £1)

MO1 (=S.G.O20)

	Mtd mint	Used
½d. blue-green, M1 (4.2.02)	32·00	4·50
Block of four	£175	30·00
Used on cover	†	£150
s. "Specimen", Type 15	£425†	
Imperforate single from P.O. Registration Sheet	Price unused £20000	

MO2 (=S.G.O21)

1d. scarlet, M5 (4.2.02)	22·00	3·00
Block of four	£110	25·00
Used on cover	†	95·00
s. "Specimen", Type 15	£425†	
Imperforate single from P.O. Registration Sheet	Price unused £20000	

MO3 (=S.G.O22)

2½d. ultramarine, M16 (19.2.02)	£1000	£280
Block of four	£6400	£1400
s. "Specimen", Type 15	£580	
t. "Specimen", Type 16	£580†	

MO4 (=S.G.O23)

6d. pale dull purple, M31 (14.3.04)	£475000	£200000
s. "Specimen", Type 16	£45000	
t. "Cancelled", Type 18		

MO5 (=S.G.O24)

1s. dull green and carmine, M45 (29.4.02)	£3750	£900
Block of four	£19250	£4500
s. "Specimen", Type 16	£1200†	

MO6 (=S.G.O25)

5s. bright carmine, M51 (29.4.02)	£45000	£11000
a. Raised stop after "R"	£50000	£13000
s. "Specimen", Type 16	£8500†	
t. "Cancelled", Type 18	£10000	

MO7 (=S.G.O26)

10s. ultramarine, M53 (29.4.02)	£100000	£48000
a. Raised stop after "R"	£125000	£48000
s. "Specimen", Type 16	£24000†	
t. "Cancelled", Type 18		

MO8 (=S.G.O27)

£1 dull blue-green, M55 (29.4.02)	£62500	£25000
s. "Specimen", Type 16	£16000†	
t. "Cancelled", Type 18	£18000	

†Nos. MO1s, MO2s, MO3t, MO4t, MO5s, MO6s/t, MO7s/t and MO8s/t exist from NPM archive sales.

Controls

½d. Continuous	A	£300
½d. Continuous	B	£300
1d. Continuous	A	£250
1d. Continuous	B	£250

Plates used

½d. A control plate 65 (left), 3 (right), B control 13 (left), 67 (right)

1d. A control plate 5 and 17 (left), 6 and 68a (right), B control 3b (left), 10 (right)

GOVERNMENT PARCELS

Government Parcels overprints were created by the Post Office to encourage all Departments to send parcels by parcel post and not letter post which for many of them was free. In consequence these stamps also were provided free. They were originally intended to be used on parcels between 3 lbs (pounds) and 7 lbs, but by the reign of King Edward VII these limits were ignored, although they were never formally changed.

These overprints had no connection with the calculation of the proportion of money raised by parcel post due to the Railways. That was found by "sampling" which automatically took into account the proportion of Government parcels.

Use ceased on 14 May 1904 when surplus stocks were called in. Fine used examples are difficult to find as the majority of those used were cancelled with the normal heavy rubber parcel post marks.

Control
1d. Continuous A £750

S	VT	RCE	PA
Var. a	Var. b	Var. c	Var. d
(R. 19/8)	(R. 15/12)	(R. 20/3)	(R. 20/8)

Variety a is also found on the 9d. (MO12), R. 2/1 every pane.

GOVT
PARCELS
L3

1902. Stamps of 1902 Overprinted with Type L3

MO9 (=S.G.O74)

	Mtd mint	Used
1d. scarlet, M5 (30.10.02)	75·00	22·00
Block of four	£375	£110
a. Open top loop to "S"	£175	
b. Thin "VT"	£175	
c. Large "C"	£175	
d. "PA" close	£175	
s. "Specimen", Type 16	£350†	

MO10 (=S.G.O75)

2d. yellowish green and carmine-red, M11 (29.4.02)	£225	60·00
Block of four	£1200	£325
a. Open top loop to "S"	£500	
b. Thin "VT"	£500	
c. Large "C"	£500	
d. "PA" close	£500	
s. "Specimen", Type 16	£350†	

MO11 (=S.G.O76)

6d. pale dull purple, M31 (19.2.02)	£275	60·00
Block of four	£1400	£325
a. Open top loop to "S"	£550	
b. Thin "VT"	£550	
c. Large "C"	£550	
d. "PA" close	£550	
e. Overprint double, one albino	£35000	
s. "Specimen", Type 15	£350	
t. "Specimen", Type 16	£425	

MO12 (=S.G.O77)

9d. dull purple and ultramarine, M39 (28.8.02)	£650	£175
Block of four	£3900	£1000
a. Open top loop to "S"	£1500	
s. "Specimen", Type 16	£500†	

MO13 (=S.G.O78)

1s. dull green and carmine, M45 (17.12.02)	£1350	£300
Block of four	£7000	£1600
s. "Specimen", Type 16	£550†	

†Nos. MO9s, MO10s, MO12s and MO13s exist from NPM archive sales.

Office of Works — Departmental Official Issues (1902-04) — KING EDWARD VII — MO

OFFICE OF WORKS.

"O.W. Official" overprints on the 1887 ½d. and the 1881 1d. were first issued on 24 March 1896 with King Edward VII ½d. and 1d. stamps being overprinted in February 1902. Overprints were issued to Head and Branch (local) offices in London and to Branch (local) offices at Birmingham, Bristol, Edinburgh, Glasgow, Leeds, Liverpool and Manchester. About 95% of all genuine used overprints (of the ½d. and 1d.) bear postmarks from those cities. Used examples from other places, including Southampton, are less common and many bear forged overprints. No genuine example showing Covent Garden c.d.s. has yet been seen.

The overprints on stamps of value 2d. and upwards were created later in 1902, the 2d. for registration fees and the rest for overseas mail. Since the King Edward VII 5d. and 10d. stamps had not been created when requests for those values came in, the overprints were made on the corresponding Queen Victoria stamps.

PRICES FOR STAMPS IN USED CONDITION. For well-centred lightly used examples of Nos. MO14/18, add **25%** to each of the used prices.

Controls
½d. Continuous	A	£2250
½d. Continuous	B	£2250
1d. Continuous	A	£2250
1d. Continuous	B	£2250

Plates used
½d. A and B plate 67, 1d. A plates 11 (left) and 75 (right), B plates U109 (left)* 87 (right)

*U109 is a rare plate which has not yet been assigned a plate number by researchers. It may be a state of an already known plate or it may be a totally new one.

O. W.
OFFICIAL
L4

1902-03. Stamps of 1902 Overprinted with Type L4

MO14 (=S.G.O36)

	Mtd mint	Used
½d. blue-green, M1 (–.2.02)	£575	£180
Block of four	£3000	£1100
Used on cover	†	£2000
s. "Specimen", Type 15	£425†	

MO15 (=S.G.O37)

1d. scarlet, M5 (11.2.02)	£575	£180
Block of four	£3000	£1100
Used on cover	†	£425
s. "Specimen", Type 15	£425†	

MO16 (=S.G.O38)

2d. yellowish green and carmine-red, M11 (27.4.02)	£2000	£450
Block of four	£12000	†
Used on cover	†	£3250
a. "C.W." for "O.W."	£4000	£1750
s. "Specimen", Type 16	£850	

MO17 (=S.G.O39)

2½d. ultramarine, M16 (29.4.02)	£3400	£675
Block of four		
Used on cover	†	£4250
a. "C.W." for "O.W."	£4750	£1800
s. "Specimen", Type 16	£900	

MO18 (=S.G.O40)

10d. dull purple and carmine, M42 (28.5.03)	£47500	£7000
Block of four	£225000	†
s. "Specimen", Type 16	£8000	
t. "Cancelled", Type 18	£10000	

†Nos. MO14s and MO15s exist from NPM archive sales.

C.W.
MO16a, MO17a
(R. 10/3 and 20/3)

MO KING EDWARD VII Departmental Official Issues (1902-04) Army

ARMY

"Army Official" overprints were first issued on 1 September 1896 for use by District and Station Paymasters nationwide including Cox and Co, the Army Agents, who were Paymasters to the Household Division. In due course usage spread to other Army establishments. A considerable trade developed in mint Army Official stamps which was largely suppressed by mid-1902.

ARMY **ARMY**

OFFICIAL **OFFICIAL**
L5   L6a

1902. Stamps of 1902 Overprinted with Type L5

MO19 (=S.G.O48)

	Mtd mint	Used
½d. blue-green, M1 (11.2.02)	5·50	2·25
Block of four	28·00	20·00
Used on cover	†	£100
e. Long left leg to "A" and dot below "R" in "ARMY"	£100	60·00
f. Very short left leg to "A" in "ARMY"	£100	60·00
g. Stop between legs of "R"	£100	60·00
h. Splayed "Y"	£100	60·00
j. Long top to second "F"	£100	60·00
m. Tall "L"	£100	60·00
q. "C" for "O"	£200	
r. Short "Y"	£100	
s. "Specimen", Type 15	£350†	

MO20 (=S.G.O49)

	Mtd mint	Used
1d. scarlet, M5 (11.2.02)	5·50	2·25
Block of four	28·00	20·00
Used on cover	†	£100
a. "ARMY" omitted	†	—
e. Long left leg to "A" and dot below "R" in "ARMY"	£100	60·00
f. Very short left leg to "A" in "ARMY"	£100	60·00
g. Stop between legs of "R"	£100	60·00
h. Splayed "Y"	£100	60·00
j. Long top to second "F"	£100	60·00
m. Tall "L"	£100	60·00
p. Shaved top to "ARM"	£100	60·00
q. "C" for "O"	£200	
r. Short "Y"	£100	
s. "Specimen", Type 15	£350†	

MO21 (=S.G.O50)

	Mtd mint	Used
6d. pale dull purple, M31 (23.8.02)	£175	80·00
Block of four	£950	£500
f. Very short left leg to "A" in "ARMY"	£350	£200
h. Splayed "Y"	£350	£200
j. Long top to second "F"	£350	£200
m. Tall "L"	£350	£200
s. "Specimen", Type 16	£425†	

†Nos. MO19s, MO20s and MO21s exist from NPM archive sales.

AR **ARM** **Y** **FF**
Var. e Var. f Var. h Var. j
(R. 14/4) (R. 14/4) (R. 2/3) (R. 20/11)

L **ARM** **CF** **ARMY**
Var. m Var. p Var. q Var. r
(R. 10/2) (R. 4/12) (R. 10/10) (R. 10/11)

King Edward VII stamps were overprinted from a plate known as "forme 2" which by 1903 had become very worn. Forme 2 was made up of stereos consisting of rows of six overprints, some of which show reducing spacing between "ARMY" and "OFFICIAL" going from left to right. This can result in obvious mis-alignment between the overprints on the stamps in column 6 and 7. A new plate, known as "forme 4", made from a die was created and used to overprint the 6d. in 1903, but overprints were withdrawn before it could be used for the two low values.

During February 1902 "forme 2" was overhauled and a number of varieties, including variety e (R. 14/4), were removed from it. Some sheets of the ½d. had, however, already been overprinted. The forme was corrected to variety f, although the dot below the left leg of the "R" was not completely removed, distinguishing later printings of R. 14/4 from other "Short 'A's". Varieties j and m were on the original plate, but were not removed. Variety p arose later, as did many others. Variety q, C for O (R. 10/10), occurred during the 17th overprinting in September 1902 and was reported in the 31 July 1903 issue of the *Stanley Gibbons Monthly Journal*. It was corrected for the 18th, and last, overprinting from "forme 2". Variety r is L 36i/38i on the Queen Victoria stamps ("short" Y—actually tall ARM), and also occurs on all three "forme 2" King Edward VII overprints.

Controls
½d. Continuous	A	£180
½d. Continuous	B	£250
1d. Continuous	A	£180
1d. Continuous	B	£250

Plates used
½d. A control—4(R*), 5(L* and R), 65(L), 66(L), 67(R), 69(L). B control—2a(R), 9(L).

1d. A control—1(R), 2a(R), 5(L), 6(R), 7(R), 11(L and R), 14(L), 16(R), 68(R), 69(L), 70(R), 73(R), 79(L), 80(L and R), 81(R), 88a(L). B control—11(R).

*R = right sheet, L = left sheet.

1903. (December). Stamp of 1902. Overprinted with Type L6a

MO22 (=S.G.O52)

	Mtd mint	Used
6d. pale dull purple, M31 (–.12.03)	£3000	£1600
Block of four	£15000	

Die Proof. In black on white glazed card:
Type L6a endorsed "23 Mar 03" £9000

BOARD OF EDUCATION

First issued in the reign of King Edward VII, stamps overprinted for the Board of Education were available on 19 February 1902. Since the 5d. and 1s. showing King Edward VII were not ready, stamps bearing Queen Victoria's portrait were used. These two stamps are listed in Volume 1 of this Catalogue.

BOARD OF EDUCATION
L7

1902-04. Stamps of 1902. Overprinted with Type L7

MO23 (=S.G.O83)

		Mtd mint	Used
½d.	blue-green, M1 (19.2.02)	£180	40·00
	Block of four	£1000	£280
	Used on cover	†	£550
s.	"Specimen", Type 15	£375	

MO24 (=S.G.O84)

		Mtd mint	Used
1d.	scarlet, M5 (19.2.02)	£180	40·00
	Block of four	£1000	£280
	Used on cover	†	£550
s.	"Specimen", Type 15	£375	

MO25 (=S.G.O85)

		Mtd mint	Used
2½d.	ultramarine, M16 (19.2.02)	£4900	£450
	Block of four	£25000	
s.	"Specimen", Type 15	£1100	

MO26 (=S.G.O86)

		Mtd mint	Used
5d.	dull purple and ultramarine, M28 (6.2.04)	£35000	£10000
s.	"Specimen", Type 16	£7000	
t.	"Cancelled", Type 18	£8500	

MO27 (=S.G.O87)

		Mtd mint
1s.	dull green and carmine, M45 (23.12.02)	£200000
s.	"Specimen", Type 16	£38000
t.	"Cancelled", Type 18	£75000

Controls

½d. Continuous	A	£1500
1d. Continuous	A	£1800

ROYAL HOUSEHOLD

Only the ½d. and 1d. King Edward VII issues were overprinted in 1902. These were for the use of Heads of the Royal Households in the various Royal Palaces. They were overprinted in black by De La Rue.

R.H.

OFFICIAL
L8

1902. Stamps of 1902. Overprinted with Type L8

MO28 (=S.G.O91)

		Mtd mint	Used
½d.	blue-green, M1 (29.4.02)	£375	£200
	Block of four	£2000	
	Used on cover	†	£1100
s.	"Specimen", Type 16	£750	

MO29 (=S.G.O92)

		Mtd mint	Used
1d.	scarlet, M5 (19.2.02)	£325	£175
	Block of four	£1800	
	Used on cover	†	£1000
s.	"Specimen", Type 15	£750†	

†No. MO29s exists from NPM archive sales.

Controls

½d. Continuous	A	£2000
1d. Continuous	A	£2000

MO KING EDWARD VII — Departmental Official Issues (1902-04) Admiralty

ADMIRALTY

These were for use in the various Admiralty Departments throughout the country and they were overprinted in black by De La Rue. The first overprint was made in 1903 (Type **L9**) but soon after it was found that this electro was damaged and it was remade using a thicker type in a slightly narrower setting (Type **L10**).

ADMIRALTY   ADMIRALTY

OFFICIAL   OFFICIAL
L9   **L10** (with different "M")

1903 (1 April). Stamps of 1902. Overprinted with Type L9

MO30 (=S.G.O101)

	Mtd mint	Used
½d. blue-green, M1 (1.4.03)	30·00	15·00
Block of four	£150	75·00
Used on cover	†	—
s. "Specimen", Type 16	£400	

MO31 (=S.G.O102)

1d. scarlet, M5 (1.4.03)	20·00	8·00
Block of four	£100	40·00
Used on cover	†	£325
s. "Specimen", Type 16	£400	

MO32 (=S.G.O103)

1½d. dull purple and green, M8 (1.4.03)	£325	£150
Block of four	£2000	£1000
s. "Specimen", Type 16	£500	

MO33 (=S.G.O104)

2d. yellowish green and carmine-red, M11 (1.4.03)	£350	£160
a. pale greyish green and scarlet-vermilion		
Block of four	£2200	£1200
s. "Specimen", Type 16	£500†	

MO34 (=S.G.O105)

2½d. ultramarine, M16 (1.4.03)	£475	£150
Block of four	£3000	£1200
s. "Specimen", Type 16	£500	

MO35 (=S.G.O106)

3d. dull purple on orange-yellow, M19 (1.4.03)	£425	£160
Block of four	£2800	£1250
s. "Specimen", Type 16	£500	

†No. MO33s exists from NPM archive sales.

Controls
½d. Continuous   A*
½d. Continuous   B   £500
1d. Continuous   A*
1d. Continuous   B   £500

*The existence of these Controls has been previously reported but has not been confirmed during recent research. The Editor would be grateful to receive any evidence of their existence.

1903-04. Stamps of 1902. Overprinted with Type L10

MO36 (=S.G.O107)

	Mtd mint	Used
½d. blue-green, M1 (–.9.03)	60·00	25·00
Block of four	£280	£125
Used on cover	†	£550
s. "Specimen", Type 16	£400	

MO37 (=S.G.O108)

1d. scarlet, M5 (–.12.03)	60·00	25·00
Block of four	£280	£125
Used on cover	†	£160
s. "Specimen", Type 16	£400	

MO38 (=S.G.O109)

1½d. dull purple and green, M8 (–.2.04)	£1200	£650
Block of four	£8500	£3800

MO39 (=S.G.O110)

2d. yellowish green and carmine-red, M11 (–.3.04)	£2700	£900
Block of four	£13500	£4500
s. "Specimen", Type 16	£750†	

MO40 (=S.G.O111)

2½d. ultramarine, M16 (–.3.04)	£2900	£950
Block of four	£15000	
s. "Specimen", Type 16	£750	

MO41 (=S.G.O112)

3d. dull purple on orange-yellow, M19 (–.12.03)	£2600	£400
Block of four	£13500	£2000
s. "Specimen", Type 16	£750†	

†Nos. MO39s, MO40s and MO41s exist from NPM archive sales.

Controls
½d. Continuous   B   £600
1d. Continuous   B   £600

Die Proof. In black on white glazed card:
Type L10 endorsed "27 MAR 03" £9000

BOARD OF TRADE

This Department was the first to use official stamps. Instead of overprinting current stamps they were perforated with a "Crown" over the letters "B.T.". Unfortunately, insufficient information or records exist to make a complete listing but all values from ½d. to 1s. were so perforated. Collectors should be warned that no less than ten different forgeries have been recorded of this "perforated" variety.

●―――

STATIONERY OFFICE

Following the Board of Trade's practice in perforating current postage stamps for departmental mail, the Stationery Office perforated their supplies of postage stamps with a "Crown" over the letters "S.O.". Similarly no official records have been SEEN TO GIVE COMPLETE DETAILS.

●―――

"C.A." OVERPRINTS

In 1903 the 1d. Scarlet was overprinted in black with the letters "C.A." (4·5 mm. high, 10·5 mm. long); later the 6d. Dull Purple also appeared with this overprint. A cover is also known bearing a 1d. Downey Head Die 1B stamp bearing this overprint and post-marked "11 JAN 12". It had been generally assumed that these initials referred to the Crown Agents but they denied ever having issued stamps with this overprint. It is now established that the overprints were made at Australia House as receipt stamps and refer to "Commonwealth of Australia".

No. M5 1d. scarlet oveprinted "C.A." *price £190 unused*.
For other overprints see Appendix 5 in this Catalogue.

●―――

The King George V Issues

Section N

General Notes on the Letterpress Issues

King George V acceded to the throne on 6 May 1910, an appropriate day for the philatelist king. His accession coincided with a complete change in contracts for stamp printing. There was also a new and energetic Postmaster General, Herbert Samuel, who had decided ideas about the designs required and when the stamps should be available.

Because of over-charging in the past De La Rue lost the stamp printing contract. This meant not only new printers but also new suppliers of engraved dies and printing plates. Printers appointed were Harrison & Sons Ltd in a new factory at Hayes, and the Royal Mint were asked to create both the stamp dies and the printing plates. Lack of experience in both these fields, combined with pressure from the PMG, resulted in the poor printing of the first stamps issued and ultimately in the change from a three-quarter portrait (the "Downey Head") to profile portraits by the Australian sculptor Bertram Mackennal who had been chosen to model the King's head for coins and medals.

Arrangement. The letterpress issues of King George V are arranged as follows:

The Downey Head Issue (1911–12)	Section **NA**
The Profile Head Issue, Wmk. Royal Cypher (1912–22)	Section **NB**
The Profile Head Issue, Wmk. Block Cypher (1924–26)	Section **NC**
Postal Union Congress Commemoratives, ½d., 1d., 1½d., 2½d. (1929)	in Section **NF**

Printers. Harrison & Sons held the contract for printing the letterpress stamps until 1924, and from 1924 until 1933 these stamps were printed by Waterlow and Sons.

Harrison & Sons, who regained the contract in 1934, were to have produced a new set of stamps by the photogravure process. They were, however, unable to get this process under way in time to supply the new stamps before the existing stock of letterpress stamps would have become exhausted. In consequence Harrison made provisional printings by letterpress, aided in the initial stages by Waterlows.

Preliminary printings of most values were made at Somerset House during 1912–13, and the government printers also were solely responsible for supplies of the 6d. value from 1913 to 1933.

Plates and Printing. The plates were produced by the Royal Mint, the first plates being steel-faced but later they were nickel-faced to combat wear.

Almost every plate, at some time during its use, carried a marking made in the marginal rule. It is believed that these marks were made by the operators for their own guidance for various purposes and to serve to identify individual plates. They consist of cuts and dots made in the marginal rules and examples of these are shown in the General Notes on the King Edward VII issues under "Plate Markings". Reference should be made to these notes in order to follow the descriptions used for the King George V issues.

The research work initiated by the late Lt.-Col. Stanton is chronicled as an appendix to *The Postage Stamps of Great Britain*, Part IV, published by the Royal Philatelic Society London. Over the years, new discoveries entailed much regrouping and re-numbering and the listing of several "new" plates, arbitarily numbered in the order of their discovery.

With the 12th edition of this catalogue, following extensive research by Mr Tony Lawrence, we were finally able to allocate the "official" numbers to the majority of these plates on all values other than the 1d. It will be noted that in some cases, markings previously allocated to separate plates have proved to have come from a single unit. For this reason, and for the convenience of collectors, we have retained the "philatelic" numbers that have become accepted over the years.

SHEET FORMAT
Harrison 1911 contract. Each sheet consisted of 240 stamps arranged in two panes of 120; the panes contained ten horizontal rows of 12 stamps, and were separated horizontally from one another by an interpane gutter containing "pillars" as illustrated in the General Notes on the King Edward VII issues, under "Plates".

The ½d. and 1d. plates of 1911–12 (Dies 1 and 2) and a few 2d. Die 1 plates had marginal rules as for the King Edward VII ½d. and 1d.; that, is coextensive, with breaks at top above the sixth and seventh stamps and at bottom below the sixth and seventh stamps, with no break between them.

The issues of 1912–22 had coextensive lines all round the panes.

Waterlow 1924 contract. Each plate contained 240 stamps in 20 rows of 12, with no divisions between the halves. There was an arrow in each side margin between the tenth and 11th rows.

When Waterlows took over the contract in 1924 they used several of the Harrison plates modified so as to conform with the new layout. The interpane gutter was removed, and the two halves of the plate brought together.

Somerset House 6d. Until 1924 the arrangement was the same as for the Harrison 1911 contract. In 1925 this was changed to conform with the arrangement used by Waterlows.

Advertisement Pane

Booklet Panes. The arrangement is the same as that given for King Edward VII. For the advertisement panes, a special plate was made having two vertical blanks on the binding edge of each pane. The advertisements were printed at a separate operation.
Paper. The Crown watermark paper continued to be made by R. D. Turner & Co. Paper with the Simple Cypher watermark was made by William Joynson and that with the Multiple Cypher watermark by Basted Mills. All these papers were gummed by Samuel Jones and from about the end of 1912 they were plate-glazed as well, which greatly improved the quality of the printing. Reference should be made to the General Notes on the King Edward VII issues under "Types of Paper: Post January 1911 paper".

This good standard of paper continued in use up to 1916. During and after the War period from 1917 to about 1921 the quality varied and, as a result of poorer calendry, the printings assumed a coarser and duller appearance. In 1922 the general appearance of the stamps returned to the earlier high standards.

In 1911 an experimental printing of the 1d. stamp was made on chalk-surfaced paper. Chalk-surfaced paper was used for the 6d. value up to 1925 and again in 1936, for a short period in the Harrison printings.

Postal Notice announcing George V stamps to be issued on Coronation Day (illustration greatly reduced).

No. 7.

INTRODUCTION OF
GEORGE V. POSTAGE STAMPS

SALE OF LETTER CARDS, THIN POST-CARDS AND BOOKS OF STAMPS AT FACE VALUE.

REDUCTION IN PRICES OF EMBOSSED ENVELOPES & WRAPPERS

Halfpenny and Penny adhesive Postage Stamps of new design bearing the effigy of His Majesty King George, and registered letter envelopes and thin post-cards bearing impressed stamps with the same effigy, will be placed on sale on the 22nd of June, the day of His Majesty's Coronation, at all Post Offices open on that day. At other Post Offices they will first be sold on the 23rd of June, or, at Offices which are closed on that day also, on the 24th of June. New adhesive stamps of other denominations and other articles of stationery bearing impressed stamps of new design will be issued as soon as possible afterwards.

Adhesive postage stamps and stamped stationery of the present issue will also be on sale at Post Offices until the remaining stocks are exhausted. All Edward VII. postage stamps and all stamps of previous issues which are at present available in payment of postage will still be available.

The following reductions in the prices of the principal articles of stamped stationery, WHICH WILL APPLY TO ARTICLES BOTH OF THE PRESENT AND THE NEW ISSUES, will take effect on Coronation Day:—

POST-CARDS.—Thin post-cards bearing ½d. stamp—½d. each. (Stout post-cards will continue to be sold at 6d. a packet of 11, or ¾d. for a single card).

LETTER CARDS bearing 1d. stamp—1d. each.

BOOKS OF STAMPS.—Books containing eighteen 1d. and twelve ½d. stamps of George V. design will be issued at an early date—price 2s. each. Pending their issue the present books, containing eighteen 1d. and eleven ½d. stamps of Edward VII. design, will, on and after the 22nd of June, be sold for 1s. 11½d. instead of 2s. as at present.

EMBOSSED ENVELOPES.—
   Court size (bearing 1d. stamp)—1s. a packet of 11.
   Commercial size (bearing 1d. stamp)—2s. a packet of 23.
   Foolscap size (bearing ½d. stamp)—1s. a packet of 21.
   Commercial size (bearing ½d. stamp)—1s. a packet of 22.

NEWSPAPER WRAPPERS. (Bearing ½d. stamp)—1s. a packet of 22. (Bearing 1d. stamp)—2s. a packet of 23.

All cards, envelopes and wrappers are sold in any quantities less than a complete packet at proportionate prices. Full tables of these prices will appear in the Post Office Guide issued on the 1st of July.

GENERAL POST OFFICE,
20th June, 1911.

By Command of the Postmaster General.

[1126]   Printed for His Majesty's Stationery Office by W. P. Griffith & Sons Ld., Prujean Square, Old Bailey, E.C.   6/11

KING GEORGE V — General Notes on the Letterpress Issues

Watermarks. The watermarks used for the letterpress issues of King George V are as follows *and are shown as seen from the front of the stamp*:

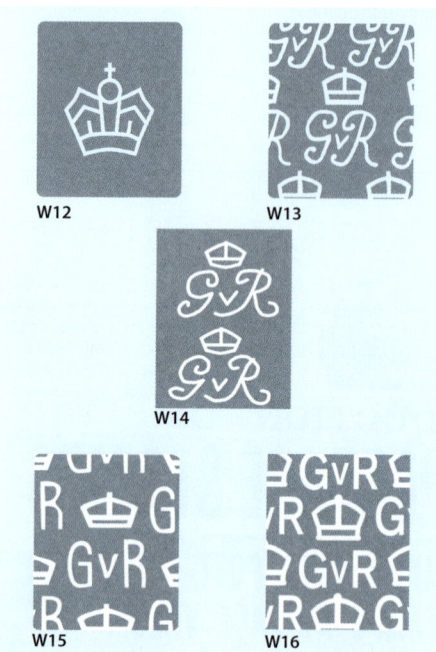

W12

W13

W14

W15

W16

Wmk W12. The Crown watermark used for the King Edward VII issues. The marginal watermarks also remain unchanged (*see* under "Recognising the Halves of the Mill Sheet" and diagram of 480-Crown Mill Sheet in the General Notes on the King Edward VII issues).

Wmk W13. The Multiple Cypher watermark, used for a short time with the ½d. and 1d. Downey Head Die 2 issues. In 1913, stocks of this paper were used for making up vertical rolls of ½d. and 1d. stamps (N15 and N17). Subsequently a sheet or part sheet of each value was found; blocks of four are known of both values.

Wmk W14. The Simple Cypher watermark. This is found with the three variations illustrated below.

Type I was used for the issues of 1912–13.

Type II was formerly thought to have been first introduced for the Profile Head stamps but has now been recorded on the ½d. of the Downey Head issue (N5) with Control B 13. It was in general use until 1917 and reappeared as the general watermark in the later issues from 1922 to 1924, but was also used occasionally between 1918 and 1921.

Type III was in general use from 1917 to 1922 and occasionally afterwards.

It seems probable that Types II and III are associated with the quality of paper. For example, the 8d. stamp on ordinary yellow paper is always Type II and the poorer quality granite paper, which appeared in 1917, is always Type III.

W14 Type I   **W14** Type II   **W14** Type III

The best method of collecting these watermark types is to obtain specimens from either the top or bottom margin of the sheet. The watermarks can then be seen more clearly.

It is not practical to quote prices for these watermark types but in Section NB details are given in footnotes of those known to exist.

In watermark **W14**, "POSTAGE" appears in the margins on both sides of each pane, as in the King Edward VII issues. Occasionally sheets were incorrectly fed into the printing press, resulting in the word "POSTAGE" appearing on five stamps of the first or the 12th vertical rows. The remaining five stamps were either without watermark or showed a line.

Where they occur, these misplaced watermarks are listed and priced either as single stamps showing letters from "POSTAGE" or as vertical strips sufficient to show the complete "POSTAGE" watermark. Note that to qualify as the listed variety, *no trace of the Simple Cypher watermark should be present on the stamp*.

Broken dandy roll varieties also occur on **W14** and prices quoted for these are for unused single stamps in the cheapest shade and with watermark upright.

Wmk W15. The Block Cypher watermark, used solely by Waterlow and Harrison (1934 contract).

Wmk W16. A variant of **W15** used with an experimental paper by Waterlow in 1924–25.

"Royal Cypher" Watermark. This term is used for convenience in the heading to Section NB and is taken to embrace both the Simple Cypher watermark (**W14**) and the Multiple Cypher watermark (**W13**).

Watermark Varieties. The following six illustrations show watermark varieties *as seen from the back of the stamp* and taking **W13** as an example:

Upright   Inverted

Reversed   Inverted and Reversed

Sideways   Sideways-inverted

Note that the watermarks on booklet stamps appeared upright or inverted in equal quantities. The prices quoted in this catalogue for N2a, N3b, N8a, N9a, N10b, N14c, N16b, N18b, N19b, N20b, N33a, N34b and N35c are for booklet stamps. The same stamps *from sheets* with watermark inverted command a substantial premium over these prices, but as evidence of their origin they need to have sheet margins attached or to be in a block or strip larger than 3×2 or of a different shape.

No Watermark. The 1½d. and 5d. 1912–22, and ½d., 2d. and 2½d., 1924–26, are from *whole* sheets completely without watermark. Similar varieties due to *watermark misplacement* are listed as "Without watermark".

Double Watermark. The ½d. (B. 13) and 2½d. are known. In comparison with the first, the second watermark is very faint. The variety is caused by pressure applied to two sheets of

76

watermarked paper in the glazing process. See Nos. N14 and N21.

Perforation.
All stamps in this section are comb-perforated 15×14 on the Grover machines, *unless otherwise stated*.

Shades.
The series of stamps issued during the years 1912–23 is notable for the wide range of colours and shades.

The stamps issued in these years are treated as one issue, although ideally they should be separated into three groups.
 (a) Issues of 1912–14
 (b) The war period 1915–19
 (c) Issues of 1920–24

The collection sorted in this manner reveals that the shades in groups (a) and (c) are fairly constant, and those in group (b) show great contrasts. However, for practical purposes the series has to be treated as one unit, as the colours of the three periods overlap and sharp lines of division cannot be drawn. The chief reason for the startling variations from the normal in group (b) is the fact that the World War of 1914–18 interrupted the supply of aniline dyes from Germany.

Early in 1916 experiments were carried out with British dyes, and printings of the ½d. and 1d. stamps are known in various shades of green and red overprinted "cancelled".

The compilation of the check-list has been a job of the utmost difficulty, particularly with the naming of the colours. In general we have adhered to the terms most familiar to philatelists, and wherever possible have described the colours in such a manner as to make them self-evident. We have not attempted to list every known shade and some of those given should be regarded as covering a range of intensity.

The controls give an indication of the time of printing. The figure refers to the year, although this was sometimes an accounting year rather than a calendar year. The letters changed part-way through the year, sometimes there were three in one year but more usually two.

Due to the length of time this issue was at press, it is only possible to list the shades in colour groups. The rarer shades, because of their brief appearances, are more precise and distinctive, but the basic shades that traversed the span of 12 years will show minor variations of hue in the published descriptions.

Wherever possible, a rough indication of the year or years when the shade was in use has been noted. This has been made possible by a study of the controls, which indicate the year the plate was at press. Where no dates are given, it must be taken that the colour group is generally spread over the entire issue.

Fugitive Inks. Experiments with fugitive inks seem to have been made during 1919 and 1920. Many of the values change their appearance when immersed in water, and used specimens of a diffused hue are usually from these printings. The ½d. olive-green of 1916 was highly fugitive, and produces a bright yellow-green after immersion in water.

Varnish Ink. Printings in a heavy thick glossy ink are known on some ½d., 1d., 5d. and 1s. values. These varieties are listed as "varnish ink", and are probably caused by inadequate mixing of the pigments by the printer. Other values in "varnish ink" are known, but until more information is known they are not listed here.

Provisional Printings.
These are the printings made by Waterlow and Harrison just prior to the issue of the photogravure stamps. For further information see *King George V. A Study of the Provisional Issues of 1934 and 1935* by J. B. B. Stanton and K. G. Rushworth.

Coil Stamps.
The experiments in the use of coil machines for selling stamps took place in the reign of King Edward VII and information about these is given in the General Notes there. By 1912 many machines had been installed using coils made up from sheets by their promoters. In 1912 the Post Office began issuing rolls of stamps manufactured by the printers. At first they were all made up from sheets with joins on the back at every tenth stamp in the case of vertical delivery rolls and every 12th stamp for horizontal delivery rolls. As pairs with coil joins can easily be identified they are listed under the basic stamps.

In the Profile Head issue there was one experiment in making continuous rolls of the 1d. with the Simple Cypher watermark but in 1924 it was more common for the stamps with the Block Cypher watermark to be in continuous rolls. As these are more difficult to identify they are not individually listed. However, we record details of all the coils issued, stating their code identification (as printed on the leader), the earliest known date of issue, number of stamps, total face value and method of delivery.

The price of the roll was stated on the coil leader and at first it was the practice to make a handling charge for rolls sold over the counter: 1d. for coils of 500 and 2d. for coils of 1000, but the charge varied from time to time so that sometimes a coil was reissued at a different price. Moreover, those used in the Kermode post office machines did not have any premium expressed and were generally labelled "KERMODE". From 1 September 1927 the charges were dropped and all coils were sold at face value. As this information is only of interest to specialists who collect coil leaders we record only the actual face value of the rolls, not the prices at which they were sold.

All the letterpress coils normally have the watermark upright but if sheets with inverted or reversed watermarks happened to be used in coil manufacture, inverted and reversed watermarks may be found on coil stamps but no attempt has been made to list these. Similarly, plate varieties which occur on sheets may be found on coil stamps.

There are no precise dates of issue for coil stamps as a rule, particularly in the case of the early issues. It is assumed that in each case the first coil stamps were released about the same time as the relative sheet stamps (except where otherwise stated), and approximate dates are given for later issues. Prices given for coil leaders are for one or more stamps attached to the leader. Wembley leaders are wrappers only.

Further information about stamps produced in rolls will be found in *King George V Stamps Issued in Rolls* by Leslie Wilkinson, published in 1998.

Controls. The system of controls was now extended to all values from ½d. to 1s. As before, the control was screwed into the plate flange before printing, and removed when printing had ceased. The Somerset House controls all had a stop after the letter which enable these printings to be distinguished.

The controls are listed and priced after their respective values in the catalogue.

Position. The control appears below the second stamp in the bottom row, except for the 1d. value where it is beneath the 11th stamp.

Prices. Control pieces in Section NA are classified according to the perforation type. Therefore, as in the King Edward VII issues, they are priced for unused *corner pairs* with side and bottom selvedge intact.

Controls in Sections NB and NC (and Controls of the 1929 P.U.C. low values) are classified according to Perforation Type as described in Appendix 1 where the appearance of the four sheet margins is described.

For controls with perforation Type 2(E) and Type 2A(P), generally the most common, prices quoted are for *single* unused examples with Control attached. For corner pairs or strips of these the "normal" prices for the additional stamps must be added.

For controls with other perforation types, usually more scarce, prices are quoted for *corner strips of three*.

L 18	D 25
Letters and figures with serifs. Used from L 18 onwards	Small thick letters and figures, with serifs. Used with Block Cypher wmk

KING GEORGE V — General Notes on the Letterpress Issues

Left: Harrison control with imperforate bottom margin *Centre*: Somerset House control with single extension hole. *Right*: Somerset House control with bottom margin perforated through

CHECKLIST OF KING GEORGE V ISSUES

Description	Spec. Cat. Nos.	S.G. Nos.	Page
LETTERPRESS ISSUES			
1911–12 Downey Head Issues			
½d. Die 1A	N1	321–23	91
½d. Die 1B	N2, N3	324–26, 334–35	93, 94
½d. Die 2	N4	338–40	94
	N5, N6	344, 346–8	95
1d. Die 1A	N7	327–28	97
1d. Die 1B	N8	329–33	99
	N9, N10	332/3, 336–7	101
1d. Die 2	N11	341–3	101
	N12, N13	345, 349–50	103
1912–22 Profile Head Issues, Wmk Simple Cypher			
½d.	N14	351–56	111
1d.	N16	357–61	117
1d. experimental ptg.	N17A	—	123
1½d.	N18	362–65	123
2d. Die I	N19	366–69	127
2d. Die II	N20	370	130
2½d.	N21	371–73a	131
3d.	N22	374–77	133
4d.	N23	378–80	135
5d.	N25	381–83	137
6d.	N26	384–86	139
7d.	N27	387–89	140
8d.	N28	390–91	143
9d. agate	N29	392–93	144
9d. olive-green	N30	393a–93b	146
10d.	N31	394	146
1s.	N32	395–96	147
RECESS-PRINTED			
1913–34 "Seahorse" High Values			
2s.6d. Waterlow	N63	399–400	198
2s.6d. De La Rue	N64	405–408	199
2s.6d. B.W.	N65	413a–415a	199
2s.6d. re-engraved die	N73	450	208
5s. Waterlow	N66	401	204
5s. De La Rue	N67	409–410	204
5s. B.W.	N68	416	205
5s. re-engraved die	N74	451	208
10s. Waterlow	N69	402	205
10s. De La Rue	N70	411–413	205
10s. B.W.	N71	417	206
10s. re-engraved die	N75	452	208
£1	N72	403–404	207
LETTERPRESS ISSUES			
1913 Profile Head Issue, Wmk Multiple Cypher			
½d.	N15	397	117
1d.	N17	398	123
1924–26 Profile Head Issue, Wmk Block Cypher			
½d.	N33	418	149
1d.	N34	419	151
1½d.	N35	420	153
2d. Die II	N36	421	157
2½d.	N37	422	158
3d.	N38	423	159
4d.	N39	424	160
5d.	N40	425	160
6d. chalky paper	N41	426	161
6d. ord. paper	N42	426a	162
9d.	N43	427	162
10d.	N44	428	163
1s.	N45	429	164
RECESS-PRINTED			
1924 British Empire Exhibition			
1d.	NCom1	430	209
1½d.	NCom2	431	209
1925 British Empire Exhibition			
1d.	NCom3	432	210
1½d.	NCom4	433	210
LETTERPRESS ISSUES			
1929 Postal Union Congress			
½d.	NCom5	434	210
1d.	NCom6	435	210
1½d.	NCom7	436	210
2½d.	NCom8	437	211
£1 (Recess)	NCom9	438	215
PHOTOGRAVURE ISSUES			
1934–36 Photogravure Issue			
½d. intermediate format	N46	—	179
½d. small format	N47	439	179
1d. large format	N48	—	180
1d. intermediate format	N49	—	180
1d. small format	N50	440	180
1½d. large format	N51	—	181
1½d. intermediate format	N52	—	182
1½d. small format	N53	441	182
2d. intermediate format	N54	—	183
2d. small format	N55	442	183
2½d.	N56	443	183
3d.	N57	444	184
4d.	N58	445	184
5d.	N59	446	185
6d. (unissued)	—	—	178
9d.	N60	447	185
10d.	N61	448	185
1s.	N62	449	185
1935 Silver Jubilee Issue			
½d.	NCom10	453	216
1d.	NCom11	454	216
1½d.	NCom12	455	216
2½d. blue	NCom13	456	217
2½d. Prussian blue	NCom14	456a	217

The Downey Head Issue (1911–12) **KING GEORGE V**

The original three-quarter profile Downey photograph, subsequently cropped and retouched to show the head only, and the full profile portrait supplied to the Royal Mint, similarly cropped and retouched

The Downey Head
In June 1910, official photographs were taken of the new king by W. & D. Downey, photographers of royalty for over 40 years. These photographs were mainly for use as origination by the Royal Mint for coins and medals but were also suggested by the King as the basis for the stamps. The King (and Queen Mary) preferred "those showing both eyes" as reported in a letter to the Post Office. This would be the three-quarter profile, originally with full-dress military uniform, though probably here cropped and retouched to show the head only. Slightly later, it was also submitted to the Mint and Mackennal for coins and medals but was useless in that regard as it was not a true profile. Another photograph, this time a full profile, was then supplied to the Mint, clearly taken at the same time and thus then used for coins. These photographs were to prove crucial to the story of the first stamps of King George V.

The three-quarter profile photograph had to be translated into an engraved head die suitable for letterpress or surface printing. Before, this had been accomplished by skilled and experienced, in-house engravers at De La Rue. Now, the Mint had to find one. Their own engravers had no experience of letterpress postage stamp dies, being more used to embossed punches. The engraver they employed was John Augustus Charles Harrison, no connection with the printing firm. Born in 1872, he came from an engraving family, joining the staff of Waterlow Brothers & Layton at about the age of 17. By about 1900 he had become free-lance, specialising in heraldic book-plates and illustrations. His experience was largely in engraving in intaglio, or recess, and not for letterpress. The only known contemporary photograph shows him working at home at a desk by a window with a paper screen filter to provide an even light.

Harrison recorded his progress with the engraving of the head die by taking proofs at different stages, both at home and at the Royal Mint. The first documentary mention of his work on the effigy comes on 14 November 1910 when the Inland Revenue forwarded "two impressions taken from the steel die which has been engraved by the Royal Mint from the photograph of His Majesty King George V". This was the final version of stage 1 of the engraving of the die (1c) with the surround uncleared. Harrison now cleared the die, cutting away the metal from the surround, and made various improvements - stage 2, and as such it was approved by the King on 27 December. (see section on Dies and Printing Plates)

The engraver J.A.C. Harrison at work

Section NA

The Downey Head Issue (1911–12)

Frame Designs

Quite separately, designs were sought by Samuel for the frames. Invitations to artists were sent on 1 July to G. W. Eve, A. Garth Jones and C. W. Sherborn with a submission date of 30 July. At least one design had to include a lion couchant as a symbol of empire. All agreed to provide designs and each submitted three. Virtually all of these are in the collections of the British Postal Museum & Archive. None was immediately attractive but nevertheless Samuel submitted them to the King, with a preference for those by Eve. The King did "not care very much for any of them" and suggested instead that Mackennal be approached for designs. Despite this he later said that he liked both of Eve's "Wreath" and "Pillar" designs and, slightly amended, these were approved for values of 4d and above at the end of October. As submitted, these had images of the King's head in profile.

After some hesitation Mackennal agreed to supply designs for the frames and initially did so on 14 September providing six designs, one of which was larger and intended for the high values. Two designs featured the necessary lion couchant and all this artwork, bar the original large design for what became the Seahorses, is now held in the BPMA collections. Two of these original designs as submitted have pencil profile heads sketched in.

There followed a long exchange of letters and amended designs between Mackennal, Samuel and the King, often between Mackennal and the King direct. Eventually, two new designs were approved – the Nautilus or Dolphin frame, and Mackennal's Wreath frame. All the stages of these designs reside in the Royal Philatelic Collection. The approved three-quarter "Downey" head now had to be inserted into these frames and each of the values engraved.

Miscellaneous Essays

During this period a few other quite separate essays were also prepared. As early as 26 May, but after they had been informed that their contract was to end, De La Rue submitted two essays (½d in green and 1d in red) of their own design with a full-face portrait. Although originally engraved these had been produced photographically by the Printex process. They pointed out that the crowns were in the corners of the stamps as the King had "informed our Chairman some years ago that he did not like the crown suspended over the head". Nothing more was to come of these, though two versions of the 1d exist.

De La Rue essays

½d. design in green	£3800
Two 1d. designs in carmine	Each £2800

In September, the Royal Mint prepared a series of stamp-sized mock-ups incorporating versions of the country name. At the same time engraved, recess essays were prepared of frames (but without any country name) to illustrate security work. Later, one had the approved "Downey" head inserted.

Perkins Bacon also produced Printex essays in different sizes and colours with a nearly full-face portrait of the King. These could date from the same period in 1910 but are described as from October and November 1911 in the Royal Philatelic Collection. None of these played any part in the production process of the issued stamps.

Type A   Type B (shown actual size)

As type A, large format original essay, details touched in with black ink and Chinese white (76x93mm)	£3800
Type A on wove paper in carmine-pink (there were 32 in the sheet)	Each £300
Type B on glazed paper in red, green, blue, violet or black	From £2800
As Type B but head in blue and frame in apple-green	£2800
As Type B but stamp size toned photographic proof	£2800
As Type B but stamp size, produced by the Printex method, mounted on card. In sepia or blue on bluish paper	£2800

Colour trials

When the first trials for colour were produced in December 1910 no stamp die had yet been engraved. As a result zinc blocks were prepared by Carl Hentschel & Co. Ltd of the two designs by then approved, the "Pillar" and "Wreath" designs by George Eve. The "Pillar" design had a 7d value, the "Wreath" a 3d value and both had the three-quarter Downey profile photograph inserted. These half-tone "advance proofs" were printed at Somerset House in a total of 48 inks manufactured by Mander Brothers, Slater & Palmer and Winstone & Sons Ltd. For the 3d "Wreath" design there were two versions, one with a white background to the King's head, one with a solid. Not every version was proofed for all three manufacturers and yellow paper was used for two proofs intended for the final 3d denomination, so there were a total of 126 different proofs submitted on 13 December (Table 1).

Table 1

Colour	Print Number	7d Rate On Sheet No.	3d Rate White margin round the Head On Sheet No.	Solid Colour round the Head On Sheet No.
Winstone & Sons				
1d. red	W 1			
10d. Red	W 2			
1s. Red	W 3			
2d. Red	W 4	086	0117	0101
2½d. Blue	W 5	&	&	&
5d. Blue	W 6	087	0118	0102
9d. Blue	W 7			
Blue	W 8			
5d. Mauve	W 9			
9d. Mauve	W 10			
1½d. Purple	W 11	091	0121	0105
10d. Purple	W 12	&	&	&
Deep Green	W 13	092	0122	0106
Mid Green	W 14			
Pale Green	W 15			
2d. Green	W 16			
Dark Brown	W 17			
3d. for printing on yellow paper	W 18			
Light Brown	W 19	093	0125	0109
4d. Orange	W 20	&	&	&
1s. Green	W 21	094	0126	0110
1½d. Green	W 22			
½d. Green	W 23			
Blue	W 24			
6d. Purple	W 25	097 &	0129 &	0113 &
7d. Slate Grey On Yellow paper	W 26	098	0130	0114
3d. Brown	W 18		0133 & 0134	0137 & 0138
Mander Bros				
3d. Rose Pink	M/B 1			
Red	M/B 2			
Orange	M/B 3	073		081
Brown	M/B 4	&		&
Dark Green	M/B 5	074		082
Light Green	M/B 6			
Grey 21545	M/B 7			
L. Blue 21546	M/B 8			
D. Blue 21547	M/B 9	0196	0192	200
Violet 21548	M/B 10	&	&	&
Buff 21549	M/B 11	0197	0193	201
Mauve 21641	M/B 12			
Slater & Palmer				
4d. Orange	S/P 1			
1d. Red	S/P 2			
½d. Green	S/P 3	0173	0165	

Colour	Print Number	7d Rate On Sheet No.	3d Rate White margin round the Head On Sheet No.	Solid Colour round the Head On Sheet No.
3d. Brown	S/P 4		&	&
2½d. Blue	S/P 5	0174	0166	
7d. Grey	S/P 6			
Fine Bronze	S/P 7	0185 &	181 &	
ditto	S/P 8	0186	182	

These were not satisfactory. Some images were printed too large, some too small. Also the colour of a stamp is affected by the design and so a final selection was to be postponed until the dies up to 2½d. had been approved.

On white unwatermarked paper unless otherwise stated

Small Format
3d. In various colours on white or yellow paper ......From £350
7d. In various colours .... From £350

Large Format
3d. In various colours on white, also purple on yellow paper.. From £350
In black on white paper with Crown watermark........ £1250
7d. In various colours .... From £350
In black...£400

Some of the essays are known in multiple pieces comprising two or three different values on the same piece and these are rare, especially the ½d. to 3d. values.

NA KING GEORGE V *The Downey Head Issue (1911–12)*

Table 2

Value	Colour Designation	Supplier	Number
½d.	Green	Winstone & Sons	W/23
	Green	Slater Palmer	SP/36
	Green	Winstone & Sons	W/35
	Light Green	Winstone & Sons	W/44
1½d.	Violet Grey	Mander Brothers	MB/73
	Dark Brown	Mander Brothers	MB/48 No. 21691
	Claret	Mander Brothers	MB/86 No. 22027
	Violet	Mander Brothers	MB/87 No. 22032
	Dark Brown	Winstone & Sons	W/41 No. 39
	Deep Red	Mander Brothers	MB/77 No. 22021
	Bright Purple	Winstone & Sons	W/64 No. 46
	Bright Purple	Winstone & Sons	W/66 No. 48
	Violet Grey	Mander Brothers	MB/73 No. 21867
	Bartollozzi Brown (14.2.11)	Mander Brothers	MB/90 No. 22186
	Tyrian Purple	Winstone & Sons	W/93 No. 56
	Dutch Brown	Mander Brothers	MB/91 No. 22208
	Magenta	Mander Brothers	MB/95 No. 22236
2d.	Mid Cadmium Yellow (10.1.11)	Slater Palmer	SP/86
	Yellow	Winstone & Sons	W/90 L.P. No. 49
	Yellow Stamp	Mander Brothers	MB/72 No. 21768
	Special Deep Cadmium Yellow (10.1.11)	Slater Palmer	SP/87
	Special Ruby Brown	Slater Palmer	SP/84 No. 155
	Special Stamp Brown	Slater Palmer	SP/83 No. 128
	Special Stamp Brown	Slater Palmer	SP/81 No. 164
	Dark Brown	Winstone & Sons	W/17 No. 35
	Light Brown	Winstone & Sons	W/19 No. 34
	Bartollozzi Brown	Mander Brothers	MB/90 No. 22186
	Tyrian Purple	Winstone & Sons	W/93 No. 56
	Dutch Brown	Mander Brothers	MB/91 No. 22208
	Magenta	Mander Brothers	MB/95 No. 22236
	Light Brown/ yellow	Winstone & Sons	W/19
	Special Stamp Brown/ yellow	Slater Palmer	SP/81
	Blue Stamp	Mander Brothers	MB/61 No. 21869
	Purple Stamp	Mander Brothers	MB/70 No. 21731
	Blue Violet Stamp	Mander Brothers	MB/69 No. 21860
	Bright Purple	Winstone & Sons	W/64 No. 46
	Bright Purple	Winstone & Sons	W/65 No. 47
	Bright Purple	Winstone & Sons	W/66 No. 48
	Blue Stamp/ yellow	Mander Brothers	MB/61 No. 21869
	Purple Stamp/ yellow	Mander Brothers	MB/70 No. 21731
	Bright Purple/ yellow	Winstone & Sons	W/66 No. 48
	Bartollozzi Brown/ yellow	Mander Brothers	MB/90 No. 22186
	Tyrian Purple/ yellow	Winstone & Sons	W/93 No. 56
2½d.	Blue	Slater Palmer	SP/10
	Blue	Mander Brothers	MB/79
	Royal Blue	Mander Brothers	MB/66
	Steel Blue	Mander Brothers	MB/80
3d.	Mid Cadmium Yellow	Slater Palmer	SP/86
	Yellow	Winstone & Sons	W/90
	Yellow Stamp	Mander Brothers	MB/72
	Special Deep Cadmium Yellow	Slater Palmer	SP/87
	Blue Stamp	Mander Brothers	MB/61 No. 21869
	[Blue Violet Stamp]	Mander Brothers	MB/69
	[Purple Stamp]	Mander Brothers	MB/70
	[Bright Purple]	Winstone & Sons	W/64
	[Bright Purple]	Winstone & Sons	W/66
	[Bright Purple]	Winstone & Sons	W/65
	Special Stamp Brown	Slater Palmer	SP/81
	Special Ruby Brown Stamp	Slater Palmer	SP/84
	Special Stamp Brown	Slater Palmer	SP/83
	Light Brown	Winstone & Sons	W/19 No. 34
	Dark Brown	Winstone & Sons	W/17 No. 35
	Bright Purple/ yellow	Winstone & Sons	W/66
	Purple Stamp/ yellow	Mander Brothers	MB/70
	Blue Stamp/ yellow	Mander Brothers	MB/61
	Light Brown/ yellow	Winstone & Sons	W/19
	Special Stamp Brown/ yellow	Slater Palmer	SP/81
	Dutch Brown	Mander Brothers	MB/91 No. 22208

W/44.

MB/86

MB/95

MB/72

W/93

MB/80

W/19

The Downey Head Issue (1911–12) KING GEORGE V

Value	Colour Designation	Supplier	Number
4d.	Special Stamp Orange	Slater Palmer	SP/88
	Grey Stamp	Mander Brothers	MB/89 No. 2
	Special Stamp Maroon	Slater Palmer	SP/60
	Green	Winstone & Sons	W/56 No. 26
	Special Stamp Green	Slater Palmer	SP/40
	Special Ruby Black	Slater Palmer	SP/92
	Vermilion	Slater Palmer	SP/23
	Amber	Winstone & Sons	W/91
	Deep Red Stamp	Mander Brothers	MB/77
	Brown Stamp	Mander Brothers	MB/84
	Grey Green	Mander Brothers	MB/46
	Mauve Stamp	Mander Brothers	MB/12
	Red Stamp	Mander Brothers	MB/49
	Olive Brown Stamp	Mander Brothers	MB/75
5d.	Special Stamp Orange	Slater Palmer	SP/88
	Grey Stamp	Mander Brothers	MB/89
	Special Stamp Maroon	Slater Palmer	SP/60
	Green	Winstone & Sons	W/56 No. 26
	Special Stamp Green	Slater Palmer	SP/40
	Special Ruby Black	Slater Palmer	SP/92
	Deep Red Stamp	Mander Brothers	MB/77
	Amber	Winstone & Sons	W/91
	Vermilion	Slater Palmer	SP/23
	Mauve Stamp	Mander Brothers	MB/12
	Grey Green	Mander Brothers	MB/46
	Brown Stamp	Mander Brothers	MB/84
	Red Stamp	Mander Brothers	MB/49
	Olive Brown Stamp	Mander Brothers	MB/75
	Sage Green	Mander Brothers	MB/82
6d.	Mauve	Mander Brothers	MB/12 No. 216[41]
	Vermilion C	Slater Palmer	SP/23
	Pearl Green	Mander Brothers	MB/92
	Grey Green	Mander Brothers	MB/46
	Brown	Mander Brothers	MB/84
	Deep Red	Mander Brothers	MB/77 No. 22
	Red	Mander Brothers	MB/49
	Olive Brown	Mander Brothers	MB/75
	Payne Grey	Mander Brothers	MB/94
	Orange	Slater Palmer	SP/88
	Grey	Mander Brothers	MB/89
	Maroon	Slater Palmer	SP/60
	Ruby black	Slater Palmer	SP/92
	Green	Slater Palmer	SP/40
	Green	Winstone & Sons	W/56
7d.	Pearl Green	Mander Brothers	MB/92 No. 2
	Vermilion	Slater Palmer	SP/23
	Mauve	Mander Brothers	MB/12
	Deep Red	Mander Brothers	MB/77
	Brown	Mander Brothers	MB/84 No. 22
	Grey Green	Mander Brothers	MB/46
	Orange	Slater Palmer	SP/88
	Grey	Mander Brothers	MB/89
	Maroon	Slater Palmer	SP/60
	Ruby Black	Slater Palmer	SP/92
	Green	Slater Palmer	SP/40
	Green	Winstone & Sons	W/56
	Red	Mander Brothers	MB/49
	Olive Brown	Mander Brothers	MB/75
	Payne Grey	Mander Brothers	MB/94
8d.	Vermilion C	Slater Palmer	SP/23
	Red	Mander Brothers	MB/49
	Olive Brown	Mander Brothers	MB/75 No. 21804
	Mauve	Mander Brothers	MB/12
	Grey Green	Mander Brothers	MB/46 No. 20836
	Brown	Mander Brothers	MB/84
	Maroon	Slater Palmer	SP/60
	Orange	Slater Palmer	SP/88
	Ruby Black	Slater Palmer	SP/92 No. 160[?]
	Deep Red	Mander Brothers	MB/77
	Green	Winstone & Sons	W/56
	Green	Slater Palmer	SP/40

SP/92

SP/60

MB/92

SP/88

MB/12

KING GEORGE V — The Downey Head Issue (1911–12)

Value	Colour Designation	Supplier	Number
8d.	Pearl Green	Mander Brothers	MB/92
	Payne Grey	Mander Brothers	MB/94
9d.	Vermilion C	Slater Palmer	SP/23
	Red	Mander Brothers	MB/49
	Olive Brown	Mander Brothers	MB/75
	Mauve	Mander Brothers	MB/12 No. 21641
	Grey Green	Mander Brothers	MB/46
	Brown	Mander Brothers	MB/84
	Maroon	Slater Palmer	SP/60
	Orange	Slater Palmer	SP/88
	Ruby Black	Slater Palmer	SP/92
	Deep Red	Mander Brothers	MB/77
	Green	Winstone & Sons	W/56 No. 26
	Green	Slater Palmer	SP/40 No. 154
	Payne Grey	Mander Brothers	MB/94
	Pearl Green	Mander Brothers	MB/92
10d.	Red Brown	Mander Brothers	MB/34
	Olive Brown	Mander Brothers	MB/75
	Vermilion	Slater Palmer	SP/23
	Brown	Mander Brothers	MB/84
	Grey Green	Mander Brothers	MB/46
	Mauve	Mander Brothers	MB/12
	Payne Grey	Mander Brothers	MB/94
	Maroon	Slater Palmer	SP/60 No.170
	Orange	Slater Palmer	SP/88
	Ruby Black	Slater Palmer	SP/92
	Deep Red	Mander Brothers	MB/77
	Green	Winstone & Sons	W/56
	Green	Slater Palmer	SP/40
	Pearl Green	Mander Brothers	MB/92
1s.	Vermilion	Slater Palmer	SP/23
	Olive Brown	Mander Brothers	MB/75
	Red Brown	Mander Brothers	MB/34
	Mauve	Mander Brothers	MB/12
	Grey Green	Mander Brothers	MB/46
	Brown	Mander Brothers	MB/84
	Ruby Black	Slater Palmer	SP/92
	Orange	Slater Palmer	SP/88
	Maroon	Slater Palmer	SP/60
	Green	Slater Palmer	SP/40
	Green	Winstone & Sons	W/56
	Deep Red	Mander Brothers	MB/77
	Pearl Green	Mander Brothers	MB/92
	Payne Grey	Mander Brothers	MB/94

MB/46

MB/75

SP/40

SP/23

The Downey Head Issue (1911–12) **KING GEORGE V** **NA**

First Proof

New line blocks were now made by Hentschel in January 1911 with the stage 2 Downey Head. There were six values to 3d. and black proofs were taken, but both artist and Royal Mint stressed that these should not be shown to the King. The size of the numerals was too thick. Further blocks, also proofed in black, had thinner values.

All six values together as a block, in black (on piece) ...£25000
Single example...£3500

Second Proof

A. All six values printed together as block of six in
   black (on piece)...£25000
Single example...£3500

W/44     MB/86

MB/45    MB/80    W/19

The revised Hentschel blocks were then used for further "advance proof" colour trials in February 1911, together with versions of the two designs by Eve accepted for the higher values with a much smaller Downey head. From 14 to 18 February 177 different proofs were supplied in values up to 1s, inks all coming from the same three manufacturers. All were on pages marked ""Essays for colour only, not for design" (Table 2).

B. On white unwatermarked paper unless otherwise stated
½d.   In various shades of green .... From £1350
1d.   In various shades of red .... From £1350
1½d. In various colours .... From £1350
2d.   In various colours on white or tinted
       paper... From £1350
2½d. In various shades of blue and one in
       green.. From £1350
3d.   In various colours on white or tinted
       paper..From £1350
    For details of the frame bromide used for the 1d. and 2½d. values see Section NB.

SP/88    SP/92    SP/60

MB/92    SP/88    MB/46

SP/40    SP/23

On white unwatermarked paper unless otherwise stated
4d.   In various colours ....From £950
5d.   In various colours ....From £950
6d.   In various colours ....From £950
7d.   In various colours on white or coloured paper From £950
8d.   In various colours ....From £950
       In black on various green papers ....From £950
       In various colours with shading around
       head removed ....From £950
9d.   In various colours ....From £950
       In black on various shades of yellow paper.......From £950
       In red with shading around head removed.................£950
10d. In various colours ....From £950
       In black on various coloured papers .... From £1000
1s.   In various colours ....From £950
       In black on various coloured papers .... From £1000

On 2 March the Inland Revenue at Somerset House printed more colour proofs based on the colours of suggested foreign stamps, some in combination with existing values of the Edward VII series (Table 3). This was followed through March by yet more essays (Table 4) including several on tinted papers made by Jones or Spicer, some 40 more being sent on 25 March. Various preliminary selections were made by the Post Office from these proofs, known as Colour Schemes A to D.

85

KING GEORGE V — The Downey Head Issue (1911–12)

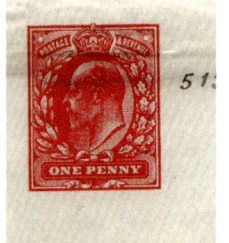

Table 3 March 1911 Hentschel + Edward VII essays –

Value	Colour Designation	Supplier	Number
½d. Edward VII + ½d. Downey Hentschel	Green	Stamping Dept.	SD/11
1d. Edward VII + 1d. Downey Hentschel	Red	Stamping Dept	SD/1
2½d. Edward VII + 2½d. Downey Hentschel	Blue	Winstone & Sons	W/5
3d. Edward VII + 3d. Downey Hentschel	Brown	Slater Palmer	SP/4
4d. Edward VII + 4d. Downey Hentschel	Orange No. 16	Winstone & Sons	W/20
6d. Edward VII + 6d. Downey Hentschel	Deep Purple	Mander Bros	MB/39
7d. Edward VII + 7d. Downey Hentschel	Grey	Slater Palmer	SP/6
Colour Scheme A			
½d. Edward VII + ½d. Downey Hentschel	[green]	Stamping Dept.	S.D./3, 5138, Also overprinted CANCELLED, 5135
1d. Edward VII + 1d. Downey Hentschel	[red]	Stamping Dept	S.D./2, 5133, Also overprinted CANCELLED, 5130
1½d. Downey Hentschel	[purple]	Stamping Dept	S.D./4, 5142, Also overprinted CANCELLED, 5140
2d. Edward VII Tyrian Plum die + 2d. Downey Hentschel	[brown]	Stamping Dept	S.D./5, 5147, Also overprinted CANCELLED, 5145
2½d. Edward VII + 2½d. Downey Hentschel	[blue]	Stamping Dept	S.D./6, 5151, Also overprinted CANCELLED, 5150
3d. Edward VII + 3d. Downey Hentschel	[yellow]	Stamping Dept	S.D./7, 5158, Also overprinted CANCELLED, 5155
4d. Edward VII + 4d. Downey Hentschel	[sage green]	Stamping Dept	S.D./8, 5165, Also overprinted CANCELLED, 5160
5d. Downey Hentschel	[orange]	Stamping Dept	S.D./9, 5169, Also overprinted CANCELLED, 5167
6d. Edward VII + 6d. Downey Hentschel	[purple]	Stamping Dept	S.D./15, 5199, Also overprinted CANCELLED, 5128
7d. Edward VII + 7d. Downey Hentschel	[pale blue]	Stamping Dept	S.D./10, 5175, Also overprinted CANCELLED, 5172
8d. Downey Hentschel	[green]		S.D./11, Also overprinted CANCELLED, 5177
9d. Downey Hentschel	[ruby brown]		S.D./12, Also overprinted CANCELLED 5182
10d. Downey Hentschel	[pale grey]	Stamping Dept	S.D./13, 5190, Also overprinted CANCELLED, 5187
1s. Downey Hentschel	[black]	Stamping Dept	S.D./14, 5194 Also overprinted CANCELLED 5192

Edwardian trials in Edwardian colours .... From £5750
Edwardian trials in proposed Georgian colours .... From £5750
Se-tenant pairs of King Edward VII and King George V in Edwardian colours (spaced 30 mm. apart) .... From £20000
Se-tenant pairs of King Edward VII and King George V in proposed Georgian colours (spaced 12 mm. apart) .... From £20000

The colour makers' reference numbers were as follows:
King Edward colours: ½d. SD11, 1d. SD1, 2½d. W5, 3d. SP4 (on yellow paper), 4d. W20, 6d. MB39, 7d. SP6.
Proposed Georgian colours: ½d. SD3, 1d. SD2, 2½d. SD6, 3d. SD7, 4d. SD8, 6d. SD15, 7d. SD10.

1912 King Edward VII 1d. Watermark Simple Cypher W14
(a) Imperforate and with part gum from King George V colour trial sheet margin (approx. 45×33 mm.)
In scarlet-vermilion .... —
In carmine-lake ("Blue Geranium") .... —
In rose-red .... —
(b) Perf. 15×14. With part gum
In scarlet .... —
For notes and illustration see below Spec. No. N16, Section NB.

86

Table 4 2 March 1911 Hentschel dies

Value	Colour Designation	Supplier	Number
½d.	Green	Winstone & Sons	W/22
	Green	Stamping Dept.	S.D./3
1d.	Red	Mander Brothers	M.B./101
	Red	Stamping Dept.	S.D./2
1½d.	Dutch Brown	Mander Brothers	M.B./91
	Magenta	Mander Brothers	M.B./95
	Magenta	Stamping Dept.	S.D./12
2d.	Magenta	Mander Brothers	M.B./95
	Brown	Stamping Dept.	S.D./5
2½d.	Blue	Mander Brothers	M.B./66
	Deep Blue	Stamping Dept.	S.D./6
3d.	Yellow	Stamping Dept.	S.D./16
	Orange	Stamping Dept.	S.D./16
	Grey	Stamping Dept.	S.D./18
4d.	Bartolozzi Brown	Mander Brothers	M.B./90
	Dutch Brown	Mander Brothers	M.B./91
	Orange	Stamping Dept.	S.D./16
5d.	Sage Green	Stamping Dept.	S.D./17
	Pale Blue	Stamping Dept.	S.D./10
6d.	Purple	Mander Brothers	M.B./39
	Purple	Mander Brothers	M.B./13
7d.	Payne's Grey	Mander Brothers	M.B./94
	Grey	Slater Palmer	S.P./6
	Bright Sage Green*	Stamping Dept.	S.D./19
	Mauve*	Mander Brothers	M.B./106
	Magenta*	Mander Brothers	M.B./95
	[Verdant Green]*	Slater Palmer	S.P./93
	Bistre Brown*	Mander Brothers	M.B./108
	Black*	Winstone & Sons	W/98
	Bright Sage Green on blue*	Stamping Dept.	S.D./19
	Turquoise on yellow*	Huber	H/5
	Turquoise on blue*	Huber	H/5
	Brown on green*	Stamping Dept.	S.D./5
	[Art Purple] on blue*	Slater Palmer	S.P./95
	[Art Purple] on rose*	Slater Palmer	S.P./95
	Dutch Brown	Mander Brothers	M.B./91
8d.	Violet	Mander Brothers	M.B./97
	Maroon	Stamping Dept.	S.D./12
	[Black] on Green No.1	[Winstone & Sons]	[W/98?]
	[Black] on Green No.2	[Winstone & Sons]	[W/98?]
	[Black] on Green No.3	[Winstone & Sons]	[W/98?]
	[Black] on Green No.4	[Winstone & Sons]	[W/98?]
	[Black] on Green No.5	[Winstone & Sons]	[W/98?]
9d.	Maroon	Slater Palmer	S.P./60
	Black/yellow	Winstone & Sons	W/98
	[Black] / Lemon	Winstone & Sons	W/98
	[Black] / Crown Watermarked Yellow	Winstone & Sons	W/98
	[Black] / Amber	Winstone & Sons	W/98
	[Black] / Golden Yellow	Winstone & Sons	W/98
	[Black]/ Lemon	[Winstone & Sons]	[W/98]
	[Black]/ Yellow	[Winstone & Sons]	[W/98]
	[Black]/ Deep Canary	[Winstone & Sons]	[W/98]
	[Black]/ Amber	[Winstone & Sons]	[W/98]
	[Black]/ Golden Yellow	[Winstone & Sons]	[W/98]
10d.	Pearl Green	Mander Brothers	M.B./92
	Black/ blue	Winstone & Sons	W/98
	[Black] / V.W. Mauve	Winstone & Sons	W/98
	[Black] / Violet	Winstone & Sons	W/98
	[Black] / Blue	Winstone & Sons	W/98
	[Black] / Blue [darker]	Winstone & Sons	W/98
	[Black]/ Mauve	[Winstone & Sons]	[W/98]
	[Black]/ Violet	[Winstone & Sons]	[W/98]
	[Black]/ Blue No. 1	[Winstone & Sons]	[W/98]
	[Black]/ Blue No. 2	[Winstone & Sons]	[W/98]
	[Black]/ Blue No. 3	[Winstone & Sons]	[W/98]

Value	Colour Designation	Supplier	Number
1s.	Ruby Black	Slater Palmer	S.P./92
	Black/ rose	Winstone & Sons	W/98
	[Black] / Pale Pink	Winstone & Sons	W/98
	[Black] / Rose	Winstone & Sons	W/98
	[Black] / Cerise	Winstone & Sons	W/98
	[Black] / Red	Winstone & Sons	W/98
	Bright Sage Green*	Stamping Dept.	S.D./19
	Mauve*	Mander Brothers	M.B./106
	Magenta*	Mander Brothers	M.B./95
	[Verdant Green?]*	Slater Palmer	S.P./93
	Bistre Brown*	Mander Brothers	M.B./108
	Black*	Winstone & Sons	W/98
	Bright Sage Green on blue*	Stamping Dept.	S.D./19
	Turquoise on yellow*	Huber	H/5
	Turquoise on blue*	Huber	H/5
	Brown on green*	Stamping Dept.	S.D./5
	[Art Purple?] on blue*	Slater Palmer	S.P./95
	[Art Purple?] on rose*	Slater Palmer	S.P./95
	[Black] on pale pink	[Winstone & Sons]	[W/98]
	[Black] on rose	[Winstone & Sons]	[W/98]
	[Black] on Cerise No. 1	[Winstone & Sons]	[W/98]
	[Black] on Cerise No. 2	[Winstone & Sons]	[W/98]
	[Black] on Red	[Winstone & Sons]	[W/98]

* 7d and 1s printed together 25 March 1911
? = presumed

SP/95

SP/60

KING GEORGE V — The Downey Head Issue (1911–12)

Dies and Printing Plates

All dies in the production process of the letterpress low values, and all printing plates, were made for, or by, the Royal Mint. While the Inland Revenue concentrated on producing colour trials from December 1910 through to March 1911, work continued on the creation of the dies for the lower values, and, when available, these were also utilised to proof the appropriate inks for those particular denominations.

There were some 18 or 20 stages from the engraver beginning his work to the finished working die used to create the printing plate. Based on the Downey photograph J.A.C. Harrison produced a very careful black and white line drawing much larger than the final engraved effigy. This line drawing was photographed down to the correct size on to a glass plate. The next stage was to transfer the image to a polished, softened steel block. Harrison engraved the die using a lightly etched design as a guide. This design was now reversed in relation to the original photograph and the engraver's sketch. The die is negative, in relief. To achieve this, the engraver cut away those parts of the design which are not required to print, as in a wood engraving.

With the engraving of the head complete, the die was hardened and it thus became the master head die, with the image in reverse. It was placed in a transfer press where, under great pressure, impressions were taken on to a softened steel transfer roller. These impressions were exact replicas of the die but with the image now right-reading and the non-printing parts of the design standing up in relief. The roller was then hardened in turn and eight head dies were produced, each with one impression. These were to become master dies for the various groups of stamp designs. Harrison then etched and engraved the respective frame designs around these heads, the designs still being in reverse. The last stages were another roller from the finished master die for each value to create the dies from which leads were struck to make up the forme from which the master plate was made.

At all the various stages proofs, or pulls, were taken to see that no imperfections had crept in. Many of these die proofs were taken at the Royal Mint, but Harrison worked at home, and he also took a number of intermediate pulls there to check his own progress.

Downey Head Dies

J. A. C. Harrison's first engraved head die is known in four primary stages, one intermediate and the accepted final stage.

Stage 1a. Circular clearing around design. Shading of circumference of design in solid colour and showing blurred lines of colour; moustache partly shaded; lobe of ear in solid colour; parting of hair light and distinct.

Stage 1b. Circle of solid colour replaced by even shading except at lower left; moustache more detailed with fine lines of shading; ear lobe shaded; hair parting slightly darkened.

Stage 1c. Circumference now completely shaded through; ear lobe more detailed; tiny line breaks to give white highlight at tip of King's nose. Proofed at the Royal Mint and submitted to the King. There are different versions of this stage showing various attempts to perfect the highlights on the nose.

Stage 1d. As stage 1c, but outer circle mostly cleared; shading on nose restored, added detail to moustache and beard reshaped. Proofed in November 1910.

Stage 1a

Stage 1b

Stage 1c

Stage 1d

The Downey Head Issue (1911–12) KING GEORGE V

Stage 2

Stage 2a. Die now part cleared into square. As stage 1d. except for a slight highlight on bridge of King's nose. Used by Hentschel & Co. to insert in Mackennal's sketch die frame and used for making blocks to print the colour essays.

Stage 2b. As Stage 2a with head completely cleared in a 13½ mm. circle of shading. Proofed in January 1911 at the Royal Mint and accepted for making working dies.

Die Proofs
Stage 1a. On fine wove paper
In black, dull blue-green or red .... From £3000
Stage 1b. On fine wove paper
In black, dull green or dull red .... From £2500
Stage 1c. On fine wove paper or glazed card
In black, deep blue, purple or bright red .... From £2500
Stage 1d. On fine wove paper
In black
Stage 2. On fine wove paper or glazed card
In black, blue, green or red .... From £2500
  Proofs are known of other heads prepared for use on Postal Stationery, Postal Orders and Savings Bank stamps.
.... (Price from £750.)

Perkins, Bacon Die Proofs

Perkins, Bacon produced a die from a three-quarter face head. The first proof illustrated was letterpress and shows an uncleared oval shaded frame. It also exists partly cleared in a thick black oval. The second illustration is a negative version of this so that the wells print out in recess or intaglio form. This may have been intended for a dummy stamp. (*Price from £1100.*)

W. & D. Downey Die Proof

(a)    (b)

Upset that the court photograph was partly blamed for the poor likeness of the King on the Die 1A stamps, W. & D. Downey themselves commissioned an engraver to produce a die from their photograph.

A photographic proof of Downey's large King's head (b) was affixed to the firm's publicity card. In vertical format; this has the W. & D. Downey imprint, coat-of-arms and their Ebury Street address at foot. Two other publicity cards exist which were probably prepared at the same time. These show the original issue (Die 1a), improved issue (Die 2) and a paste-up of Die 1a frame with W. & D. Downey cleared head as (b) which is annotated "Head Engraved by us" in blue-green for the ½d. and carmine for the 1d.

Uncleared proof in red (a) £3750
Cleared proof in green (b) £3750
Cleared proof in carmine (b) £3750

KING GEORGE V — The Downey Head Issue (1911–12)

Plate making
Printing plates were created in a complicated process involving master plates and working plates. To make the master printing plate of any particular value the leads struck from the final dies were firmly locked in a shallow metal box or chase, arranged for sheet stamps in two panes of 120 images with a gutter in between. This was then put into an electrolytic depositing bath which created a copper skin or shell. As it was thin and flexible it needed to be backed with molten type metal to give it the necessary rigidity. The backing was then planed and slabbed to give a perfectly flat surface on the front printing surface. After proofing in black, and any imperfections corrected, this then became the master plate from which all working plates derived. Any different format of sheet layout (for such things as booklets and rolls) would require a separate master plate.

The working plates which actually printed the stamps were created in a similar way to the master plate. First, however, a black wax mould was taken from the master plate. This was then placed in the depositing bath and then backed as before. Initially the working plates were of copper with a slight steel finish. Soon, however, they had a nickel face for greater durability. This meant being placed in two baths, one after the other, for both nickel and copper. After 1929 there was a further chromium facing. In total, some 1150 working plates were made for all George V stamps, postage and fiscal.

Printing
Harrison & Sons Ltd were new to postage stamp printing. After visiting the principal stamp printing works on the continent they purchased three rotary machines to calendar the paper to make it smooth and four fast-running Miehle printing machines, high class commercial machines, as used by the French Government. The combination of these machines and Harrison's inexperience resulted in poor quality printing. De La Rue had printed on slower Wharfedale presses and the Inland Revenue, in charge of stamp printing for the Post Office, required Harrisons to change to production on Wharfedale presses with plate-glazed paper rather than calendered. When the ½d and 1d stamps were first issued on Coronation Day, 22 June 1911, the King was reported to have declared: "Make me look like a stuffed monkey!".

Proofs of unissued values
While attempts were made throughout 1911 to improve the dies of the ½d. and 1d. stamps (dies 1b and a re-engraved die 2) work also continued on the dies for other low values. These were the 1½d. from the master Dolphin die; the 2½d. from the master Lion die; and the 2d. and 3d. from the master die of Mackennal's Wreath design. Various improvements in the original dies were incorporated into these. Master plates were made by the Mint for all values up to 3d. Working plates were made for the 1½d., 2d. and 2½d. and sheets of the 2d. and 2½d. were printed in various shades of brown and blue in September and October.

From August to October 1911 dies were engraved for values from 4d. to 7d. utilising Eve's Wreath frame and the Downey Head and proofs were taken from these. Problems arose with the size of the existing head in Eve's frame and the King was very disappointed with the results so far. Thus, work was stopped on all "Downey Head" values above 1d. on 15 November, though the re-engraved versions of the ½d. and 1d. were registered and issued to post offices from 30 December.

Engraver's Dies for the Unissued Values

Fig. 19    Fig. 20    Fig. 21

Fig. 22    Fig. 23    Fig. 23a

Fig. 23b    Fig. 24    Fig. 24a

Fig. 25    Fig. 26

Engraved at the Royal Mint by H. P. Hugill (4d.) or J. A. C. Harrison (others)

Fig. 19 was produced from the original ½d./1½d. master die with the value engraved later. Fig. 22 was produced from the original 1d./2½d. master die with the value engraved later. Figs. 20, 21 and 23b are Mackennal's wreath design. Figs. 24/25 are Eve's wreath design. Fig. 26 is Eve's pillar design which was initially for the 8d. to 1s. values.

The early Royal Mint engravings had the Die 1 Downey Head. This head was rolled out on to pieces of die steel which then had the appropriate frames engraved around them. The head was also reworked on each value. These amended heads have hitherto been described as "Die 2" although, technically they are all reworked versions of Die 1 and are now described as such. Naturally, although the Die 1 heads are all the same, the reworked vary from value to value.

1½d. Fig. 19. Die proofs
    Die 1 head, uncleared. On thick glazed paper in grey-black £4750
    Reworked head. On card in brown, yellow-brown, orange, chocolate-brown, turquoise-green, purple or violet .... From £5000
    As above but on thin wove paper in red-brown, chocolate-brown or magenta .... From £5000

2d. Fig. 20 (without value). Master die for 2d.
    Die 1 head, uncleared (numbered "6C" above design)*
    On paper without watermark in black or pink ... From £4750
    On paper watermarked Crown in rose-red, ochre-brown or slate-grey .... From £5000

2d. Fig. 21 (with value)
    Die proof (Die 1 Head) uncleared, on white glazed card in black £4750
    Die proof (Reworked head) fully cleared, on wove paper in black £4750
    Die proof (Reworked head), fully cleared, on proof paper in light brown, annotated "proof from the mint July 1911" £5000
    Colour trials from printing plate. Reworked head. Wmk. Crown. Perf. 15×14, in bistre £7000

2½d. Fig. 22
    Die 1 or Reworked head. Four stages, differing in the lettering of the value.
    On thin card in black .... From £5750

½d. Green, Type N1. *The Downey Head Issue (1911–12)* KING GEORGE V NA

1911-12 ½d. Green

Colour trials from printing plate. Reworked head. Wmk. Crown. Perf. 15×14, in indigo-blue....... £7000

3d. Fig. 20 (without value). Master die for 3d. Die 1 head, uncleared (numbered "7C" above design)* On paper watermarked Crown in slate-blue............. £5000

3d. Fig. 23. Shaded background to head with upper corners shaded. Reworked head Uncleared die proofs on thick white paper in red or black.. From £4750
Cleared die proof on thick white glazed paper in black.. £4750
Plate proofs cut close on card in pale red-brown or yellowish-brown............................. £1800
Plate proofs on gummed paper in pale violet, orange or claret ....
Uncleared die proof on thick white paper in black. As Fig 23 but with solid colour behind figures in value tablet £4750

3d. Fig. 23a. White background to head with upper corners shaded. Reworked head Cut down die proofs used as colour trials on thick white paper in rose, orange, green, grey, pale purple, blue geranium (carmine-lake) or brown... From £4000
Uncleared die proof on proof paper in rose-red...... £5750

3d. Fig. 23b. Shaded background to head with upper corners solid. Reworked head Uncleared die proofs on thick white paper in various colours including green, red-brown, bistre-brown, orange, rose-red, yellow and slate-grey.. From £4000
Plate proofs cut close on paper watermarked Crown (upright or sideways), in various colours including orange, pale brown, chocolate-brown, grey-green, pale violet, maroon, blue geranium (carmine-lake) and grey .... From £4000

4d. Fig. 24. Reworked head on solid background Uncleared die proof on proof paper in black............ £5250

4d. Fig. 24a. Reworked head with shaded background Uncleared die proof on proof paper in black............ £5250
As last but in orange £5500
Cleared on paper watermarked Crown in bright orange.. £5500

5d. Fig. 25. Reworked head Uncleared die proof on card in black........................... £4750
As last but in light blue...................................... £4750
Die proofs used as colour trials on white proof paper in various colours, including light blue .... From £4750
On paper watermarked Crown in light blue............. £4750

8d. Fig. 26 (without value) Uncleared die proofs on paper watermarked Crown with gum in black or purple.................. From £4750
As last but in grey-black..................................

*Complete die proofs containing the die number above are worth at least twice the prices quoted.

N1 Dies 1A and 1B

Ornament above P of HALFPENNY has two thin lines of colour; beard is undefined

N2 Die 2

Ornament has one thick line; beard well defined

Die 1A  Die 1B

Die 1A. The three upper scales on the body of the right-hand dolphin form a triangle. The centre jewel of the cross inside the crown is suggested by a comma.
Die 1B. The three upper scales are incomplete. The centre jewel is suggested by a crescent.

1911 (22 June). **½d. Green, Type N1.** Wmk. Crown. Die 1A

N1 (=S.G.321/23)

	Unmtd mint	Mtd mint	Used
(1) Green	8·00	4·00	4·00
(2) Pale green	10·00	5·00	4·00
(3) Deep green	45·00	25·00	10·00
(4) Bluish green	£400	£300	£180
(5) Yellow-green	50·00	30·00	4·00
a. Watermark inverted	£20000	—	£2000
b. Error. Perforation 14 (8.11)		£20000	£1000
ba. Do. On cover			£1400
c. White blob right of left ½ (Pl. 7, R. 20/2 Control A 11)			£250
d. White spot at top of forehead (Pl. 7, R. 19/3)			£250
e. White spot under ear (Pl. ?, R. 20/3)			£250
s. "Specimen", Type 22			£800

No. N1 is known pre-released at Todmorden on 21 June 2011.

N1c  N1d

N1e

91

NA KING GEORGE V The Downey Head Issue (1911–12) ½d. Green, Type N1.

Controls. Prices are for unused corner pairs.

Control	Perf. Type				
	1A	2	2A	2(c)	3
Perf. 15×14					
A 11 (w)	35·00	45·00	£125	£150	£275
Perf. 14	V1A				
A 11 (c)	—				

Control A 11 (w) V1A. One known.

An example of Control A 11(c), perf 15×14, was reported but confirmation is required for listing.

The perf. 14 stamps were perforated on an old machine used by Harrison to perforate King Edward VII stamps and giving Type V1A. One single Control example is known from official plate No. 5/5. For further information on this error see articles published in the December 1994, March 1995, and February 1998 issues of *Gibbons Stamp Monthly*.

Die Proofs of the Accepted Design

Without value with reversed "2" above design
On thick card in green £3750
Ditto, in rose-pink or deep red-brown .... Each £2500
On proof paper in bright pink or deep carmine .... Each £2200
On proof paper with small dot after "2", in pink £2200

28 March 1911. Finished die with reversed "5A" above design
On thin card in dull green £3500
On paper watermarked Imperial Crown in pale
    yellowish green £3500
Ditto, but in lake-brown (intended for 1½d. value) £5750

4 April 1911. After hardening
Cut close with uncleared borders on proof paper
    in three different shades of green including
    issued colour .... Each £3500
Ditto, on paper watermarked Imperial Crown in
    pale green £4750
Ditto, on calendered gummed paper,
    watermarked Imperial Crown in dull green,
    mounted on card annotated on reverse
    "4.4.1911 stamped paper, calendered,
    gummed and watermarked" £5750

Plate Proofs
Imperf. on thick paper in black £2500
Perf. 14 on thick paper in bluish green .... —

Imprimatur
Die 1A Imperforate. Wmk. Crown on gummed
    paper in issued colour £7000
It is believed that there is only one example of the imprimatur in private hands.

Colour Essays. See under General Notes.

Bromides

a b c

d e

Bromides of Mackennal's sketch for ½d value.
a. Enlarged bromide of completed die with
    uncleared value tablets (76×92mm) £2200
b. Enlarged bromide of "HALFPENNY" lettering
    designed by G.W. Eve £525
c. Reduced bromide (29×35mm) with vignette
    void, "½" at upper left and "HALFPENNY"
    added by G.W. Eve, but upper right corner void £1600
d. As above, but "1½" added at upper right, with
    additional "THREE HALFPENCE" tablet below £2000
e. Enlarged bromide for the unissued 1½d value £2500

Plate Markings
The listing of these ½d. Die 1A plates has been revised according to recent research. Seven plates were put to press, and our numbering follows the official numbers.

Plate	Marking
2	No marking. (Official plate 2/2) (left sheet)
4	No marking. (Official plate 4/4) (right sheet)
5	Dot (breaking left) R.18 right side, 13.5 mm.; slight scoop (outer) R.12 right side. (Official plate 5/5) (right sheet)
6	Half dot (inner) R.17 right side, 13.5 mm. (Official plate. 6/6) (left sheet)
7a	Scoop (outer) R.2 right side, 14 mm. (Official plate 7/7) (right sheet)
7b	Added cut R.20 right side, 11 mm. (right sheet)
7c	Added cut R.18 right side, 10.5 mm. (right sheet)
8	Cut R.19 right side, 11.5 mm. (Official plate 8/8) (left and right sheets—plate changed sides in press)
9	Cut R.19 right side, 8.75 mm. (Official plate 9/9) (left sheet)

Control Schedule
Control A 11 (w) was used with all these plates. Confirmation is required of the use of Control A 11 (c) on this issue.

½d. Green, Type N1 *The Downey Head Issue (1911–12)*   KING GEORGE V

1911 ½d. Green, Type N1. Crown but Die 1B

N2 (=S.G.324/26)

	Unmtd mint	Mtd mint	Used
(1) Bright green	13·00	8·00	1·50
(2) Pale bright green	15·00	10·00	1·50
(3) Yellow-green	18·00	12·00	1·50
(4) Bright yellow-green	70·00	40·00	12·00
(5) Green	13·00	8·00	2·00
(6) Deep green	60·00	35·00	10·00
(7) Very deep green	£650	£450	£160
(8) Bluish green	£260	£160	£100
a. Watermark inverted (ex booklet panes)	35·00	20·00	7·00
b. Watermark sideways	—		£5500
c. Cracked plate (Pl. 3, R. 20/2)			£300
d. Gash in Crown (R. 1/1 of booklet pane NB1)			£400
e. Varnish ink. Shade (6)			£3000
f. Broken left frame by dolphin's tail (Pl. 7, R. 19/1)			£275
g. Blob above E of POSTAGE and white flaw in corner (Pl. 8, R. 19/2)			£275
h. White spot right of left "½" (Pl. 10b, R. 20/3)			£275
j. Indent below Y (R. 1/1 of booklet pane NB1a)			£350
s. "Specimen", Type 22			£350

Imperforate tête-bêche pair from P.O. Registration Sheet...*Unused tête-bêche pair* £20000

	Perf. Type					
Control	1	1A	2	2A	2(c)	3
A 11 (w)	£200	75·00	50·00	£100	£150	£300
A 11 (c)	£125	50·00	50·00	£100	†	£300

(c) "close" and (w) "wide" refer to the space between the figures at foot (1.5 mm. and 2 mm. respectively).

The following watermark variety is known:
Wmk inverted: A 11 (w) Perf. Type 2 .... £7500

Die Proof
On thick paper in green £5000

Plate Proofs
On thick paper in black £2400
Imperf. trial on paper watermarked Multiple Cypher, with gum, in green from Control A 11 (c).........£600

Plate Markings
Two minute nicks either side, R.19 left side, 8 mm. is a master plate flaw.

Plate	Marking
1a	Cut R.20 left side, 12.75 mm., cut R.20 right side, 11.75 mm.; minute dot at left under R.20/3
1b	Added cut R.18 right side, 10.5mm.; cut R.19 right side, 17.5 mm.
1c	Added cut R.17 left side, 13.5 mm.; cut R.17 right side, 14 mm.
2	Cut R.18 left side, 14.5 mm.; cut R.20 left side, 12.25 mm.; cut R.20 right side, 12.5 mm.
3	Cut R.17 left side, 11.5 mm.
4	Cut R.20 right side, 8.25 mm.
5a	Cut R.17 right side, 10.25 mm. R. 20/3 rule bulges up under FP
5b	Added cut under PE of R.12/12
5c	Added double cut R.17 left side
6	Cut R.17 left side, 12.5 mm.; cut R.17 right side, 14.25mm.; cut R.19 right side, 13 mm.; slight depression (inner) R.20 left side, 12.5–5 mm.
7	Cut under FP of R.20/11; cut R.20 right side, 10.75 mm.
8a	No marking
8b	Added cut R.18 left side, 11.75 mm.; slight depression (inner) R.20 left side, 2.5 mm.
9a	Cut R.19 left side, 13 mm.; cut R.20 left side, 12 mm.; cut R.19 right side, 12.5 mm.; cut right side, 12.5 mm.
9b	Added cut R.18 left side, 14.5 mm.
10a	Cut under P of R20/11
10b	Added cut R.19 left side, 10.5 mm.; cut R.19 right side, 12 mm.
11a	Cut under FP of R.20/12. Rule under R.20/2 thinner at right
11b	Added cut R.17 right side
12	Cut under HA of R.20/12; cut R.20 right side, 12.5 mm.
13	Cut R.18 left side, 14.5 mm.
14	Oval cut R.18 right side, 10.5 mm.
15	Cut R.20 right side, 11.5 mm.; cut R.19 right side, 17.5 mm.; oval cut R.18 right side, 10.5 mm.
16	Cut R.20 right side, 10 mm.
17	Notch at right below R.20/2
18	Cut R.17 left side; double cut R.18 left side; cut R.20 left side.
19	Cut R.18 right side, 10.5 mm.; cut R.20 right side, 8.5 mm.
20	Cut R.17 right side, 10.5 mm.; cut R.20 right side, 10 mm.

N2c

N2d   N2f   N2g

N2h   N2j

Controls. Prices are for unused corner pairs.

NA KING GEORGE V The Downey Head Issue (1911–12) ½d. Green, Type N1.

Index to Plate Markings
Bottom Margin, Stamp Numbers

Stamp No.	Plate
2	11a, 11b, 17
3	1a, 1b, 5a, 5b, 5c
11	7, 10a, 10b, 11a, 11b
12	5a, 5b, 11a, 11b, 12

Left Margin, Row Numbers

Row No.	Plate
17	1b, 3, 5c, 6, 18
18	2, 8b, 9b, 13, 18
19	9a, 9b, 10b
20	1a, 1b, 2, 6, 8b, 9a, 9b, 18

Right Margin, Row Numbers

Row No.	Plate
17	1c, 5a, 5b, 5c, 6, 11b, 20
18	1b, 1c, 14, 15, 19
19	1b, 1c, 6, 9a, 9b, 10b, 15
20	1a, 1b, 2, 4, 7, 9a, 9b, 12, 15, 16, 19, 20

No Marking 8a

Control Schedule
Control A11 was used with all plates.

1912 (28 September). **½d. Green, Type N1.** but Wmk. Simple Cypher (Booklets only). Die 1B

N3 (=S.G.334/35)

	Unmtd mint	Mtd mint	Used
(1) Green	90·00	45·00	40·00
(2) Pale green	90·00	45·00	40·00
(3) Deep green	£200	£120	65·00
a. Without watermark			
b. Watermark inverted	90·00	45·00	40·00
c. Watermark reversed	£1500	£1100	£800
d. Watermark inverted and reversed	£1600	£1100	£800
e. Varnish ink. Shade (3)		£3500	
f. White flaw after Y (R. 2/2 of booklet pane, with wmk upright)			£300
g. Diagonal scratch below PE of PENNY (R. 1/2 of booklet pane with wmk upright)			£300
s. "Specimen", Type 22	£300		
t. "Specimen", Type 26			

Imperforate tête-bêche pair from P.O. Registration Sheet... Unused tête-bêche pair £20000

N3f

1912 (1 January). **½d. Green, Type N2.** Wmk. Crown. Die 2

N4 (=S.G.338/40)

	Unmtd mint	Mtd mint	Used
(1) Green	15·00	8·00	4·00
(2) Pale green	35·00	25·00	8·00
(3) Deep green	28·00	15·00	8·00
(4) Myrtle-green	£250	£150	40·00
(5) Bluish green	£200	£130	40·00
(6) Yellow-green	15·00	8·00	4·00
(7) Bright yellow-green	70·00	40·00	10·00
a. Watermark inverted	£1600	£1100	£650
b. No cross on Crown. Shade (6)	£190	£110	55·00
c. No cross on Crown and broken frame		£160	65·00
d. No cross on Crown. Shade (5)		£280	
da. Do. with broken frame		£350	
e. Part double printing (lower portion)*		£1500	
f. White spot in oval below E of POSTAGE (Pl. 10a, R. 1/11)		£225	95·00
g. Coil join (vert. pair) (8.12)			
h. Printed double, one albino			
k. White scales (Pl. 20, R. 1/3)		£225	
s. "Specimen", Type 26		£325	

A similar variety to No. N4c occurs in N5 attributed to plate wear.

*In No. N4e a small part of the sheet has made extra contact with the plate and the variety can be described as a "kiss" print.

N4f, N5i

N4k, N5k, N6k

Plates. 19 Plates were used.
Controls. Prices are for unused corner pairs.

	Perf. Type				
Control	1	1A	2	2A	3
B. 12	†	†	†	£15000	†
B 11	†	†	50·00	85·00	—
B 12 (c)	—	£125	35·00	35·00	£250
B 12 (w)	†	†	50·00	50·00	†
None*	†	†	£175	†	†

*The missing control is an error and the price is for a corner pair.

(c) "close" and (w) "wide" refer to the space between the "B" and the serif of the "1" (4.5 mm. and 6 mm. respectively).

Control B. 12 Perf. Type 2A was used at Somerset House.

Coils
Vertical delivery made up from sheets with joins every tenth stamp

Code No.	Issued	Number in roll	Face value		
C	Aug. 1912	1000	£2.1.8	Top delivery	£500
D	Aug. 1912	1000	£2.1.8	Bottom delivery	£700
G	Aug. 1912	500	£1.0.10	Top delivery	£500
H	Aug. 1912	500	£1.0.10	Bottom delivery	£500

½d. Green, Type N2 *The Downey Head Issue (1911–12)* **KING GEORGE V** **NA**

Die Proofs
Transitional stages leading to Die 2 frame

All the following have revised impressions of Die I after amendments on rollers and are on thin card.

Stage 1

Stage 2

Stage 1. Die 1A frame
Two lines of colour in background of dolphins; one line of colour in dolphins' foreheads; two lines in central ornament with lines of shading at sides; "H" of "HALFPENNY" open at top and bottom
In emerald-green.. £6500

Stage 2. Proofed 6 August 1911
As Stage 1 but background of dolphins solid and no shading at sides of central ornament; "H" solid at top and bottom
In light chestnut on thin card £6500
In grey-black on thin card £5750

Stage 3

Stage 4

Stage 3. Proofed 6 October 1911
As Stage 2 but foreheads of dolphins cut away and solid line at left of central ornament
In green on proof paper.. £6500

Stage 4. Die 1B frame. Proofed 20 October 1911
As Stage 3 but some lines of shading added to dolphins' foreheads
In green on proof paper.. £6500

Stage 5

Stage 5. The accepted Die 2. Proofed 28 October 1911
As Stage 4 but shading added in dolphins' heads and above them as well as at sides of central ornament
In grey-black... £5500
Do. Cut to stamp size, mounted on card with typewritten annotation below; "Die used for making leads for master plate 7th Dec 1911".............. £4250

The Stage 3 die was used for the colour trials that follow and working dies were prepared from it for striking leads.

Plate Proofs
On thick paper, in black or green.................................. *From* £2000
In green on paper, Wmk. Crown (upright or sideways) £2500

Colour Trials
No watermark. Imperf.
In various colours from the accepted die.................. *From* £2500
Watermark Crown (upright or sideways). Imperf. With gum
In green, cerise, azure, deep claret, and bluish green from the accepted die .... *From* £2500

Colour Trials in Reversed Colours
Imperforate on gummed wmk. Crown paper, overprinted "Cancelled", Type 24
½d. in scarlet and 1d. in green................................... *Pair* £20000*
* Believed to be unique in private hands. A corner marginal block of each value in the reversed colours without overprint reside in the Royal Philatelic Collection. The 1d. block has B 12 control and they are believed to Have been printed by Harrisons on 30 January 1912.

1912 *(August).* **½d. Green, Type N2**. but Wmk. Simple Cypher. Die 2

N5 (=S.G.344)

	Unmtd mint	Mtd mint	Used
(1) Green	14·00	7·00	3·00
(2) Pale green	15·00	8·00	3·00
(3) Deep green	18·00	10·00	4·00
(4) Yellow-green	20·00	12·00	4·00
a. Without watermark	£1500	£750	
b. Watermark inverted	£550	£350	£225
c. Watermark reversed	£550	£350	£225
d. Watermark inverted and reversed	15·00	8·00	4·50
e. No cross on Crown. Shade (1)	£300	£200	£125
ed. Do. watermark inverted and reversed		£250	

NA KING GEORGE V — The Downey Head Issue (1911–12) ½d. Green, Type N2.

	Unmtd mint	Mtd mint	Used
f. No cross on Crown and broken frame*		£250	
g. Coil join (vert. pair)			
h. Wmk. "POSTAGE", (vert. block of 10 (2 3 5))		£650	
i. White spot in oval below E of POSTAGE (Pl. 10a, R. 1/11)		£225	95·00
k. White scales (Pl. 20, R. 1/3)		£225	85·00
s. "Specimen", Type 26**		£550	
t. "Cancelled", Type 24†		£300	

*Examples of No. N5f vary in appearance due to faulty make-ready. The cross on the crown and most of the frame at left is omitted.

No. N5h is similar to No. N6j but may be distinguished by the Cypher watermark.

For illustration of No. N5i see No. N4f and No. N5k see No. N4k.

** No. N5s came from control B 12(w).
† No. N5t exists from NPM archive sales.

N5f, N6ha

Plates. 18 Plates were used.
Controls. Prices are for unused corner pairs.

	Perf. Type	
Control	2	2A
B 12 (c)	35·00	30·00
B 12 (w)	30·00	30·00
B 13	30·00	30·00

(c) "close" and (w) "wide" refer to the space between the "B" and the serif of the "1" (4.5 mm. and 6 mm. respectively).

The following watermark varieties are known:
Wmk inverted, Type I: B 12 (c) Type 2; B 13 Type 2A
Wmk reversed, Type I: B 12 (w) Type 2; B 13 Type 2A
Wmk inverted and reversed, Type I: B 12 (c) Type 2; B 12 (w) Types 2 and 2A; B 13 Types 2 and 2A
Wmk upright, Type II: B 13 Types 2 and 2A

Coils
Vertical delivery made up from sheets with joins every tenth stamp

Code No.	Issued	Number in roll	Face value		
C	Aug. 1912	1000	£2.1.8	Top delivery	£500
D	Aug. 1912	1000	£2.1.8	Bottom delivery	£700
G	Aug. 1912	500	£1.0.10	Top delivery	£500
H	Aug. 1912	500	£1.0.10	Bottom delivery	£500

1912 (October). **½d. Green, Type N2.** but Wmk. Multiple Cypher. Die 2

N6 (=S.G.346/8)

	Unmtd mint	Mtd mint	Used
(1) Green	20·00	12·00	8·00
(2) Pale green	25·00	15·00	8·00
(3) Deep green	40·00	25·00	10·00
(4) Yellow-green	20·00	15·00	8·00
a. Watermark inverted	20·00	12·00	20·00
b. Watermark reversed	22·00	15·00	20·00

	Unmtd mint	Mtd mint	Used
c. Watermark inverted and reversed	£150	£100	£100
d. Watermark sideways	†	†	£4000
e. Crown missing in watermark		£200	
f. Imperforate	£250	£175	
g. Printed on gummed side	—	—	†
h. No cross on Crown. Shade (1)	£280	£175	£125
ha. No cross on Crown and broken frame			
i. Coil join (vert. pair)			
j. Wmk. "POSTAGE", (vert. block of 10 (2×5))		£650	
k. White scales (Pl. 20, R. 1/3)		£225	85·00
l. Dark blob on Y (coil stamp with join at bottom)		£350	
m. White spot in oval below "E" of "POSTAGE" (Pl. 10a, R. 1/11)	£275	£150	85·00

An additional marginal rule has been seen at the bottom of a right-hand corner pair from Plate 13 (see notes after Controls of No. N8).
A single example of No. N6g is known.
For illustrations No. N6ha, see N5f, and No. N6k, see N4k.

N6l

This may not be a plate flaw but a number of examples are known

Plates. Ten Plates were used.
Controls. Prices are for unused corner pairs.

	Perf. Type	
Control	2	2A
B. 12	£3000	£3000
B 12 (c)	45·00	45·00
B 12 (w)	60·00	45·00

(c) "close" and (w) "wide" refer to the space between the "B" and the serif of the "1" (4.5 mm. and 6 mm. respectively).
Control B. 12 was used for Somerset House printings.

The following watermark varieties are known:
Wmk inverted: B 12 (c) Types 2 and 2A; B 12 (w) Types 2 and 2A
Wmk reversed: B 12 (c) Types 2 and 2A; B 12 (w) Types 2 and 2A
Wmk inverted and reversed: B 12 (c) Type 2

Coils
Vertical delivery made up from sheets with joins every tenth stamp

Code No.	Issued	Number in roll	Face value		
C	Oct. 1912	1000	£2.1.8	Top delivery	£500
D	Oct. 1912	1000	£2.1.8	Bottom delivery	£700
G	Oct. 1912	500	£1.0.10	Top delivery	£500
H	Oct. 1912	500	£1.0.10	Bottom delivery	£500

Plate Markings

Plate	Marking
1a	Small dot under P of R.20/5
1b	Added dot under E of R.20/12
2	Small dot under LF of R.20/6; gap under R.20/7 narrower
3	Big double dot under (N)N of R.20/7
4	Pear dot under FP of R.20/8; rule broken under E of R.20.10 in later printings with B12(c) Crown wmk.

1911-12. 1d. Red

N3 Dies 1A and 1B Lion unshaded

N4 Die 2 Lion shaded

Die 1A

Die 1B

Die 1A. The second line of shading on the ribbon to the right of the crown extends right across the wreath. The line nearest to the crown on the right-hand ribbon shows as a short line at the bottom of the ribbon.
Die 1B. The second line of shading is broken in the middle. The first line is little more than a dot.

1911 *(22 June).* **1d. Red, Type N3.** Wmk. Crown. Die 1A

N7 (=S.G.327/8)

	Unmtd mint	Mtd mint	Used
(1) Carmine-red	10·00	4·50	2·50
(2) Pale carmine-red	15·00	6·00	2·50
(3) Deep carmine-red	75·00	40·00	15·00
(4) Carmine	25·00	14·00	6·00
(5) Pale carmine	25·00	14·00	3·00
(6) Rose-pink	£200	£120	35·00
b. Without watermark		£3500	
c. watermark inverted	£2200	£1500	£1250
d. Watermark sideways	†	†	£17000
f. No cross on Crown. Shade (5)	£1250	£850	£500
g. Varnish ink. Shade (3)		£3500	
h. White fleur-de-lis (Pl. 4, R. 16/1)		£350	
i. Flaw between E and P (Pl. 9, R. 20/11)		£325	
j. Gash under crown (Pl. 13b/13c, R. 19/11)		£225	
k. Pale area by lion's paws (Pl. 13b, R. 20/11)		£225	
s. "Specimen", Type 22		£550	

For the experimental printing previously listed as No. N7a (Pl. 1a), see under Paper Trial below.

A single example is known of No. N7d with part "Brentwood" cancellation.

The 1d., perf. 14, formerly listed as No. N7e is now considered to be of proof status — see below.

The flaw N7i may be connected with the marking in the marginal rule.

Under long-wave ultraviolet, Somerset House printings generally fluorescent dark plum and Harrison printings fluoresce pink.

Plate	Marking
5	Small dot under FP of R.20/9; tiny dot (top) 0.5 mm. from left under R.20/6
6	Small dot under P of R.20/10; base of R.20 left side completely bevelled off
7	Small dot under F of R.20/11
8	Small dot (base) under FP of R.20/12 (sometimes showing as a ½ dot (base))
9	Minute dot R.20 left side, 6 mm.
10a	Big dot under F of R.20/5
10b	Added fine "V" cut R.20 left side, 5 mm. (Sometimes showing as a diagonal line)
11	Big dot under HA of R.20/6; fine 'X' cut in R.20 left side, 5.5 mm.
12a	Big dot under AL of R.20/7
12b	Added horizontal 'V' cut in R.20 left side 6.5 mm.
13	Big oval dot (top) under FP of R.20/8 two fine diagonal cuts R.20 left side 5 mm. forming and open 'V'
14	Small dot under PE of R.20/9, 20th left side partly bevelled off
15	Minute nick under NY of R.20/9 dot (base) under PE of R.20/11
16a	Dot under FP of R.20/1, horizontal dash under HALFP of R.20/2. Dot under NN of R.20/12
16b	Added cut under A of R.20/12
17	½ cut (base) and dot under N(N)Y of R.20/12
18	Long dot under HA of R.20/12 S.E corner missing below R.20/8
19	R.20 left side bent
20	¾ cut (base) under PE of R.20/9
21	½ cut (base) under N(N) of R. 20/9
22	Small dot (top) under F of R.20/12 fine diagonal ½ cut R.19/1
23	Dot under PE of R.20/12
24	No marking

Index to Plate Markings
Bottom Margin, Stamp Numbers

Stamp No.	Plate
1	16a, 16b
2	16a, 16b
5	1a, 1b, 10a, 10b
6	2, 5, 11
7	2, 3, 12a, 12b
8	4, 13, 18
9	5, 14, 15, 20, 21
10	4, 6, 21
11	7, 15
12	1b, 8, 16a, 16b, 17, 18, 22, 23

Left Margin, Row Numbers

Row No.	Plate
19	22
20	6, 9, 10b, 11, 12b, 13, 14, 19

No Marking: Plate 24

Control Schedule
All Wmk. Crown unless marked (s) Simple Cypher or (m) Multiple Cypher

Control	Plate with which it was used
B 11	1a, 2, 3, 4, 5, 6, 7, 8, 22
B 12(c)	1a, 2, 3, 4, 5, 6, 7, 8, 10a, 10b, 11, 12, 13, 14, 15, 16a, 17, 18
B 12(w)	10b, 12, 13, 16a
B 12(c)(s)	4, 11, 12, 13, 15, 16b, 18
B 12(w)(s)	8, 10b, 11, 12, 13, 17, 19, 20, 21, 22, 23
B. 12(m)	9
B 12(c)(m)	11, 12, 13, 15, 16a, 16b, 18
B 12(w)(m)	10b, 12, 13
B 13(s)	1b, 4, 5, 8, 13, 16b, 17, 19, 20, 21, 22, 23, 24
None	17

Somerset House control B. 12(m) was used with a plate other than Plate 9 which has not yet been identified.

NA KING GEORGE V *The Downey Head Issue (1911–12)* **1d. Red, Type N3.**

N7h

N7i

N7j

N7k
This flaw is variable in appearance

Controls. Prices are for unused corner pairs.

Control	Perf. Type				
	1	1A	2	2A	2(c)
A. 11	£350	£250	£200	£250	†
A 11 (w)	†	60·00	60·00	£100	£125
A 11 (c)	†	†	£200	£250	—

(c) "close" and (w) "wide" refer to the space between the figures at foot (1.5 mm. and 2 mm. respectively).
Control A. 11 was used for Somerset House printings.
Control A 11 (w) may exist with Perf. Type 3.

Die Proofs

Early Stage   Completed Die
The very first Die engraved by J. A. C. Harrison

The design differs from the issued Die 1A stamps and is very similar to the Hentschel essays for colour only.
Cleared die proofs on card
Early stage of engraving, outline of lion and part
    of wreath only. In black...................................... £7250
Completed die. In red £7250
  The die was discarded in favour of the following transitional stages leading to Die 1A. All have a Die 1 head (as Downey Head Stage 2b).

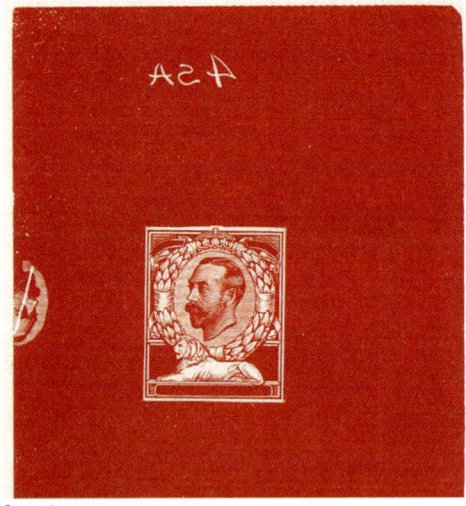

Stage 1

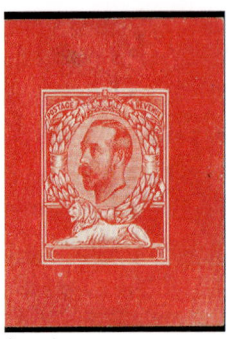

Stage 2   *Stage 5*

Fig. A   *Fig. B*

Fig. C

Stage 1. Proofed 23 February 1911
No inscription or value. Ribbon at right with fourth line of shading broken (Fig. A)
In scarlet on proof paper with "4SA" engraved in
    reverse.. £3500

Stage 2. Proofed 2 March 1911
As Stage 1 but with "POSTAGE" and "REVENUE" added and lighter shading around lion
In pale rose-red on thick glazed card engraved
    "B.1" in reverse.. £4750

98

Stage 3. Proofed 3 March 1911
As Stage 2 but fourth line of shading now completed (Fig. B)
In pale rose-red on thick glazed paper................................... £3500
Stage 4. Proofed 23 March 1911
As Stage 3 but additional colour at bottom right of Crown leaving only one lower line of shading in upper right part of ribbon instead of two lines (Fig. C)
In pale rose-red on thick glazed card.. £3500
Stage 5. Proofed 31 March 1911. The accepted Die 1A
As Stage 4 but value added and shading deepened, especially on the lion, but finer lines of shading removed. Uncleared
In deep grey on proof card engraved "6 B" in reverse £4750
In scarlet on paper watermarked Crown pasted
   on thick card, proofed early April 1911
   (usually cut close to margins) £3750

Stamps of Proof Status

1d. Carmine

Carmine. Watermark Crown. Four examples are known which were first illustrated and described in *The British Philatelist* in 1915, one of the four is now in the Royal Philatelic Collection. These stamps have a plum flourescence under ultraviolet
....£25000

Perf 14 with normal top
Pale carmine-red. Watermark Crown......................................£18000

Imperf with thickened top frame line
Carmine. No Watermark... £2800

Imperf with normal top
Carmine. Watermark Crown... £2800

Very few of these stamps exist and, as the reason for their preparation is unknown, they are described as 'of proof status'. No used examples are known. There appears to be no connection between these perforated stamps and the ½d. perf 14 of August 1911.

Paper Trial
This was an experimental printing to see if thick chalk-surfaced paper without watermark was practical for this value. The plate used was 1a. Perf. 15×14. With gum
In carmine on thick chalk-surfaced paper................................. £280
Ditto with Control A. 11 (Somerset House).....................*single* —

Further trials were made on Austrian type enamelled paper but using Die 2. Those that exist in private hands are listed under "Paper Trials" above No. N12.

Colour Essays. See under General Notes.

Plate Markings

Plate	Marking
1	Dot R.19 right side, 11 mm.; cut under EP of R.20/2; cut under NN of R.20/7
2a	Cut under P of R.20/1
2b	Added cut R.20 right, 13.5 mm.
3a	Dot R.20 right side, 12.75 mm.; fine diagonal cut through R.19 left side, 18 mm.; rule broken under EP of R.20/11 in later printings
3b	Added cut under (P)E of R.20/9; dot R.20 right side enlarged
4a	Small 'U' mark under (N)E of R.20/3
4b	Added ½ dot (inner) R.19 right side, 10.25mm.; dot R.19 left side, 12.5 mm.; small nick (lower) under (N) E of R.20/9
4c	Added cut under (P)E of R.20/11
6	Dot R.17 right side, 9.5 mm.; rule broken under NN of R.20/2 in later printings
9	½ dot (outer) R.20 right side, 10 mm.; small dot (breaking inner) R.20 left side, 8.75 mm.; rule broken under (N)E of R.20/11 in later printings
10	Cut R.19 right side, 10.5 mm.; left of R.20/11 rule cut away
13a	Dot R.18 right side, 10.5 mm.; small nick (outer) R.20 right side, 13 mm.
13b	Added dot R.18 left side, 12.5 mm.
13c	Added cut under (P)E of R.20/10

Plates 5, 7, 8, 11 and 12, previously listed here are now recognised to have been parts of other plates in this list and have been deleted.

Index to Plate Markings
Bottom Margin, Stamp Numbers

Stamp No.	Plate
1	2a, 2b
2	1, 6
3	4a, 4b, 4c
7	1
9	3b, 4b, 4c
10	13c
11	3a, 3b, 4c, 9, 10

Left Margin, Row Numbers

Row No.	Plate
18	13b, 13c
19	3a, 3b, 4b, 4c
20	9

Right Margin, Row Numbers

Row No.	Plate
17	6
18	13a, 13b, 13c
19	1, 4b, 4c, 10
20	2b, 3a, 3b, 9, 13a, 13b, 13c

Control Schedule
Control A. 11 was used with Plates 1 and 2a, A 11 (w) with all plates (including Plates 1 and 2a) and A 11 (c) with Plates 2b, 13b and 13c.

●━━━

1911. 1d. Red, Type N3. Crown but Die 1B

N8 (=S.G.329/31)

	Unmtd mint	Mtd mint	Used
(1) Carmine	15·00	10·00	3·00
(2) Pale carmine	15·00	10·00	4·00
(3) Deep carmine	75·00	45·00	6·00
(4) Bright carmine	30·00	18·00	3·00
(5) Deep bright carmine	£110	70·00	15·00
(6) Carmine-red	20·00	15·00	3·00
(7) Pale carmine-red	25·00	15·00	3·00
(8) Rose-pink	£225	£125	45·00
a. Watermark inverted (ex booklet panes)	35·00	20·00	7·50
ab. Without watermark		£2000	
b. No cross on Crown. Shade (5)	£1100	£800	£500
c. Varnish ink. Shade (1)		£3500	
d. White spot left of O, and white dot above T of POSTAGE (Pl. 14, R. 20/11 control A 11 (c))		£200	
e. Frame break over EP (Pl. 3b/3c, R. 19/11)		£200	
f. Small white spot on forehead (Pl. 4, R. 20/11)		£200	

KING GEORGE V The Downey Head Issue (1911–12) 1d. Red, Type N3.

	Unmtd mint	Mtd mint	Used
g. Scratch to right of left figure "1" (Pl. 6a/6b, R. 20/11)		£200	
h. Broken ribbon under last E of REVENUE (Pl. 16, R. 20/10)		£200	
i. White scratch to left of lion's face (Pl. 16, R. 20/11)		£125	
j. Broken left frame (R. 1/2 of booklet pane)		£350	
k. Pale lion (Pl. 12, R. 19/12)		£250	
l. Open top to leaf (R. 2/3 of booklet pane, No. NB3)		£400	
m. White dot to left of lion's paws (Pl. 10b, R. 20/1)		£250	
n. Frame break above "E" of "ONE" (Pl. 10b, R. 20/7)		£250	
s. "Specimen", Type 22		£550	

Imperforate *tête-bêche* pair from P.O. Registration Sheet.............................. *Unused tête-bêche pair* £20000

Under long-wave ultraviolet, Somerset House printings generally fluoresce dark plum and Harrison fluoresce pink.

N8d

N8e

N8f   N8g

N8h   N8i

N8j   N8k

N8l, N9g, N10g

Controls. Prices are for unused corner pairs.

	Perf. Type				
Control	1	1A	2	2A	2(c)	3
A. 11	†	†	40·00	50·00	†	†
A 11 (w)	†	†	£250	£450	—	†
A 11 (c)	£300	£125	40·00	50·00	£125	£150

(c) "close" and (w) "wide" refer to the spaces between the figures (1.5 mm. and 2 mm. respectively).

Control A. 11 was used for Somerset House printings.

Additional marginal rules are known below the control A. 11 for Plates 9a and 15 printed by Somerset House. They exist as one, two or three rules, the latter at the very bottom of widely trimmed sheets. It is believed that three rules were normally printed, the number showing depending upon the width of the trim. They were used to prevent the fraudulent use of unwatermarked paper. Other stamps are reported to have been treated in this way.

Die Proofs
In carmine or rose-red on thick paper. Uncleared
   and cut close.. Each £4250
Cleared proof in carmine-pink on paper with
   Crown watermark. Two impressions 17 mm.
   apart on one piece... £9000
As last in carmine, but single impression from
   working die 68×67 mm. £4500

Plate Proofs. Imperforate. From master Die 1B
In carmine or rose-red, cleared and on ordinary
   proof paper £4250
In carmine on chalk-surfaced paper. No
   watermark, with gum.. £280
In pale carmine on thin proof paper. No
   watermark or gum.. —
In black on thick paper. No watermark or gum £4750
In carmine on gummed R. D. Turner (plate glazed)
   paper. Crown watermark...................................... £4750
The plate proof on chalk-surfaced paper fluoresces bright lemon under long-wave ultraviolet; but those in pale carmine or black do not.

Two horizontal pairs, which probably formed a block, are known on the R. D. Turner paper. The left-hand examples are creased. A single is known of the black plate proof with rule in the top margin.

Plate Markings
Minute nick, R.19 right side, 8.5 mm. is a master plate flaw.

Plate	Marking
1	No marking
2	Cut R.20 right side, 9 mm.
3a	No marking
3b	Added cut R.20 right side, 11.5 mm.
3c	Added cut R.17 right side, 11 mm.

Red, Type N3 *The Downey Head Issue (1911–12)* **KING GEORGE V** **NA**

Plate	Marking
4	Cut R.20 right side, 14.5 mm.; cut R.17 right side, 12 mm. and fine cut, 20 mm.; damage (outer) to R.15 right side, 5 mm.
5	Cut R.20 right side, 13.5 mm.; right below R.20/12 thicker at base
6a	No marking
6b	Added ½ dot (outer) R.20 right side, 12 mm.
7	Cut under PE of R.20/12; cut R.20 right side, 10 mm.; damage under NY of R.20/11; fine cut R.20 left side, 10.5 mm.
8a	½ cut (base) under (N)E of R.20/11; cut R.19 right side, 13.75 mm.; large break R.18 left side, 13.5 mm.; very fine cut R.19 left side, 17 mm.
8b	Added cut R.20 right side, 11.75 mm.
9a	Minute nick at top 1 mm. from left under R.20/11; scoops in 3rd and 4th pillars below R.10/12 in inter-pane gutter
9b	Nick has disappeared; added cut R.19 right side, 15.75 mm.
10a	No marking
10b	Added cut R.19 right side, 11.5 mm.
11	Cut R.19 right side, 9 mm.
12	Cut R.19 right side, 8 mm.
13	Deleted. Now part of Plate 15
14	Cut R.17 right side, 9 mm.; below R.20/12 split at right
15a	Minute dot under (P)E of R.20/9
15b	Dot has disappeared; added cut R.18 right side, 14.5 mm.
16	Cut R.17 left side, 16 mm.

Index to Plate Markings

Bottom Margin, Stamp Numbers

Stamp No.	Plate
9	15a,
11	7, 8a, 8b, 9a
12	5, 7, 9a, 9b, 14

Left Margin, Row Numbers

Row No.	Plate
17	16
18	8a. 8b
19	8a, 8b
20	7

Right Margin, Row Numbers

Row No.	Plate
15	4
17	3c, 4, 14
18	15b
19	8a, 8b, 9b, 10b, 11, 12
20	2, 3b, 3c, 4, 5, 6b, 7, 8b

No Marking: Plates 1, 3a, 6a, 10a

Control Schedule

Control A. 11 was used with Plates 3, 9a and 15a, A 11 (c) with all the rest and A 11 (w) with at least Plates 7 and 8a.

●━━━

1912 *(April).* **Red, Type N3**. Wmk. Crown but Scarlet (Booklets only). Die 1B

N9 (=S.G.332/3)

	Unmtd mint	Mtd mint	Used
(1) Scarlet	75·00	45·00	18·00
(2) Pale scarlet	£110	65·00	20·00
(3) Bright scarlet	75·00	45·00	18·00
(4) Aniline scarlet	£375	£240	£110
a. Watermark inverted	75·00	45·00	18·00
f. White flaw above right value (R. 2/1 of booklet pane. No. NB4a)			£375
g. Open top to leaf, (R. 2/3 of booklet pane, No. NB4)		£375	
s. "Specimen", Type 22		£750	

For note on the aniline scarlet No. N9(4), see below No. N11.
For illustration of No. N9g, see N8l.

N9/N10f
●━━━

1912 *(28 September).* **1d. Red, Type N3**. but Wmk. Simple Cypher (Booklets only). Die 1B

N10 (=S.G.336/7)

	Unmtd mint	Mtd mint	Used
(1) Scarlet	40·00	30·00	30·00
(2) Pale scarlet	40·00	30·00	30·00
(3) Bright scarlet	40·00	30·00	30·00
(4) Deep bright scarlet	£160	£110	50·00
a. Without watermark		£2750	
b. Watermark inverted	40·00	30·00	30·00
c. Watermark reversed	£1600	£1100	£800
d. Wmk. Inverted and reversed	—	—	£850
e. Varnish ink. Shade (3)		£3500	
f. White flaw above right value (R. 2/1 of booklet pane, No. NB5a)		£375	
g. Open top to leaf, (R. 2/3 of booklet pane, No. NB5)		£375	
s. "Specimen", Type 22		£325	
t. "Specimen", Type 26		£550	

Imperforate *tête-bêche* pair from P.O. Registration Sheet..*Unused tête-bêche pair* £20000

For illustration of No. N10f, see No. N9f and for No. N10g, see No. N8l.
●━━━

1912 *(1 January).* **1d. Scarlet, Type N4**. Wmk. Crown. Die 2

N11 (=S.G.341/3)

	Unmtd mint	Mtd mint	Used
(1) Scarlet	10·00	5·00	2·00
(2) Bright scarlet	10·00	5·00	2·00
(3) Deep bright scarlet	18·00	10·00	4·00
(4) Very deep bright scarlet	£275	£175	75·00
(5) Aniline scarlet	£275	£175	£100
(6) Scarlet-vermilion	£1700	£950	£350
a. Watermark inverted	£650	£425	£400
ab. Without watermark	£4500	£3500	—
b. No cross on Crown. Shade (2)	£150	80·00	55·00
ba. Do. wmk. inverted		£700	
c. No cross on Crown and broken frame		£180	
d. No cross on Crown. Shade (5)	£2000	£1400	
da. Do. with broken frame		£1700	

101

KING GEORGE V — The Downey Head Issue (1911–12) 1d. Scarlet, Type N4

	Unmtd mint	Mtd mint	Used
e. Coloured blot on O of ONE (Pl. 5b, R. 20/10)		£250	
f. Printed double, one albino	£350	£250	
g. Coil join (vert. pair) (8.12)			
h. Wmk. "POSTAGE" (inverted), strip of 4 from top row		£750	
j. Varnish ink			
s. "Cancelled", Type 24		£350	
t. "Cancelled", Type 25		£600	

Our prices for the aniline scarlet 1d., Nos. N9 (4) and N11 (5), are for specimens in which the colour is suffused on the surface of the stamp and shows through clearly on the back. The correct aniline reaction is a bright golden emission on both sides of the stamp. Specimens without these characteristics, but which show orange "aniline" reactions under long-wave ultraviolet are relatively common.

No. N11ab came from a sheet with an inverted watermark. Examples can only be distinguished from No. N12a by attached selvedge showing the inverted Crown.

Shade (6) is known with control B 11.

N11e
Examples of this variety also show a disturbance to the left of "1" above the variety

Controls. Prices are for unused corner pairs

Control	1	1A	2	2A	3
B. 11	†	†	60·00	75·00	†
B 11	£150	£100	25·00	50·00	£250
B. 12	†	†	45·00	65·00	†
B 12 (c)	†	£100	30·00	25·00	£200
B 12 (w)	†	†	25·00	25·00	†

(c) "close" and (w) "wide" refer to the space between "B" and the serif of "1" (4.5 mm. and 6 mm. respectively).

The inverted watermark occurs with control B 12 (c) but confirmation of perforation types is needed.

Controls B. 11 and B. 12 were used for Somerset House printings.

Coils
Vertical delivery made up from sheets with joins every tenth stamp

Code No.	Issued	Number in roll	Face value		
A	Aug. 1912	1000	£4.3.4	Top delivery	£500
B	Aug. 1912	1000	£4.3.4	Bottom delivery	£500
E	Aug. 1912	500	£2.1.8	Top delivery	£500
F	Aug. 1912	500	£2.1.8	Bottom delivery	£500

Die Proofs
The following have revised impressions of Die I after amendments on rollers.

Stage 1a

Stage 1b

Stage 1a. Proofed 6 October 1911
More lines of shading on lion's back but white patches left on fore paws and haunches
In dull grey on proof paper, uncleared £4750
In pale orange on proof paper, uncleared £5750
Stage 1b. The accepted Die 2. Proofed about 30 October 1911
Lion almost completely shaded
In grey-black, blue-geranium or carmine on proof paper, uncleared £5750
In blue or blue-geranium, cleared and cut down on Crown watermarked (sideways) paper, with gum £4750

Colour Trials
From Stage 1b (accepted Die 2)
Taken at various stages of completion of the die and showing minor differences of detail to right-hand ribbon and shading of leaves to wreath (previously known as the amended or modified die)
Imperf. No watermark
In issued colour, carmine or royal scarlet .... From £2750
In yellow £4750
Taken between 20 October and 29 November 1911
Watermark Crown (upright). Imperf. With gum
In blue £3750
In pink, carmine or royal scarlet .... From £2750
As above and pale blue-green, but watermark sideways .... From £2750
From plates used for printing
Watermark Crown (upright only). Perf. 14·8×14. With gum
In vermilion, carmine, brownish carmine, royal scarlet, brilliant scarlet, blood-red, rose-carmine, magenta-rose or violet-rose .... From £1500

Paper Trials. No watermark. Imperf.
On Austrian enamelled paper
(a) Carmine £225
(b) Scarlet (fluorescent) £275
On wove paper
(a) In carmine on John Dickinson extra superfine very white paper £140
(b) In carmine. John Allen special finish very thin paper £140
(c) Ditto plate glazed on face only £140
(d) Ditto but plate glazed both sides £140
(e) In scarlet. John Allen. Special Finish paper £140
(f) Ditto with machine finish underside £140
(fa) Ditto but showing part "Indiana Vellum" watermark ... £140
(g) As (e) but thinner paper £140
(h) As (e) on gummed paper £140

Specialists recognise two types of (g). In one the grain angle of the paper measured from the vertical is 32° and in the other it is 56°. The same applies to (c) at 56° and (d) at 32°.

1d. Scarlet, Type N4 — The Downey Head Issue (1911–12) — KING GEORGE V

1912 (August). **1d. Scarlet, Type N4.** but Wmk. Simple Cypher. Die 2

N12 (=S.G.345)

	Unmtd mint	Mtd mint	Used
(1) Scarlet	15·00	8·00	4·50
(2) Bright scarlet	15·00	8·00	4·50
(3) Deep bright scarlet	80·00	50·00	20·00
a. Without watermark	£1500	£1200	£950
b. Watermark inverted	28·00	18·00	25·00
c. Watermark reversed	£200	£125	£125
d. Watermark inverted and reversed	20·00	12·00	20·00
e. No cross on Crown. Shade (1)	£175	£100	50·00
eb. Do. watermark inverted		£220	
ec. Do. watermark reversed		£250	
ed. Do. watermark inverted and reversed		£220	
f. Ditto with machine finish underside		£200	35·00
g. No cross on Crown and broken frame		£150	75·00
h. Watermark "POSTAGE" (vert. strip of 5)		£750	
i. Coil join (vert. pair)			
s. "Cancelled", Type 24		£400	

No. N12h was from a sheet on which the watermark was inverted.

Controls. Prices are for unused corner pairs

	Perf. Type	
Control	2	2A
B 12 (w)	25·00	45·00
B 13	40·00	25·00

The notes below the Controls of N8 about additional marginal rules also apply to the above and one additional marginal rule is known to exist with Controls B 12 (w) (Plates 12, 13 and 16a) and B 13 (Plates 15 and 16b).

The following watermark varieties are known:
Wmk inverted: B 12 (w) (perf. Types need confirmation)
Wmk reversed: B 12 (w) Types 2 and 2A
Wmk inverted and reversed: B 12 (w) Types 2 and 2A

Coils

Vertical delivery made up from sheets with joins every tenth stamp

Code No.	Issued	Number in roll	Face value		
A	Aug. 1912	1000	£4.3.4	Top delivery	£500
B	Aug. 1912	1000	£4.3.4	Bottom delivery	£500
E	Aug. 1912	500	£2.1.8	Top delivery	£500
F	Aug. 1912	500	£2.1.8	Bottom delivery	£500

1912 (October). **1d. Scarlet, Type N4.** but Wmk. Multiple Cypher. Die 2

N13 (=S.G.349/50)

	Unmtd mint	Mtd mint	Used
(1) Scarlet	25·00	18·00	10·00
(2) Bright scarlet	25·00	18·00	10·00
(3) Deep bright scarlet	£180	£110	20·00
a. Watermark inverted	40·00	22·00	28·00
b. Watermark reversed	40·00	22·00	28·00
c. Watermark inverted and reversed	£1600	£1000	£650
d. Watermark sideways	£325	£190	£220
e. Imperforate	£225	£150	

	Unmtd mint	Mtd mint	Used
f. No cross on Crown. Shade (1)	£225	£150	60·00
fa. Do. watermark inverted		£200	
fb. Do. watermark reversed		£200	
fd. Do. watermark sideways	£1200	£750	
g. No cross on Crown and broken frame		£200	90·00
h. Crown missing in watermark		£200	
i. Coil join (vert. pair)			

Controls. Prices are for unused corner pairs

	Perf. Type	
Control	2	2A
B. 12	£3500	£3500
B 12 (w)	35·00	45·00
B 12 (w) wmk sideways	£3000	£2000

Control B. 12 was used for Somerset House printings.

The following watermark varieties are known:
Wmk inverted: B 12 (w) Types 2 and 2A
Wmk reversed: B 12 (w) Types 2 and 2A
Wmk inverted and reversed: B 12 (w) (perf. Types need confirmation)

Coils

Vertical delivery made up from sheets with joins every tenth stamp

Code No.	Issued	Number in roll	Face value		
A	Oct. 1912	1000	£4.3.4	Top delivery	£500
B	Oct. 1912	1000	£4.3.4	Bottom delivery	£500
E	Oct. 1912	500	£2.1.8	Top delivery	£500
F	Oct. 1912	500	£2.1.8	Bottom delivery	£500

Plate Markings

Minute dot at left under R.20/1 is a master plate flaw.

Plate	Marking
1a	No marking
1b	Added dot under EP of R.20/5
1c	Added cut under right serif of P of R.20/11
2a	Break R.19 right side, 13.5 mm.
2b	Added dot under NE of R.20/6
3a	No marking
3b	Added dot under NN of R.20/7
4a	Scoop (base) under right of R.20/8; disturbance (base) under left of R.20/11; also small dash just below rule of R.20/11 under (N)E; S.W. corner off R.20 left side
4b	Added dot under N(E) of R.20/8
5a	Small dash just below rule of R.20/11 under EN; rule under base of R.20/11 extends to right
5b	Added dot under P(E) of R.20/9
6a	Dot above R.1/1 in top row
6b	Added dot under PE of R.20/1; added dot under EP of R.20/10
7a	Small shreds break in of (base) of 11th under (P)E and at right
7b	Added dot under E(P) of R.20/11
8a	Nick above R.1/2 in top row; minute dot R.19 right side, 15 mm.
8b	Dot has disappeared; added dot under EP of R.20/12
9a	Dash under PE of R.20/11
9b	Added dot under EP of R.20/11
10a	Dash under PE of R.20/12; R.20/11 rule thin and irregular
10b	Added dot under (N)E of R.20/12
11	Cut under PE of R.20/9

KING GEORGE V — The Downey Head Issue (1911–12) 1d. Scarlet, Type N4.

Plate	Marking
12	½ cut under PE of R.20/10
13	Cut under P of R.20/11
14	Cut under (P)E of R.20/12; ½ dot (outer) 17th left side, 20 mm.
15	Small dot R.19 right side, 9.25 mm.; minute dot under PE of R.10/11
16a	Two small dots R.20 right side, 10.5, 16 mm.; rule broken under EP of R.20/11 in later printings on Crown paper; minute dot to right of rule under R.20/2
16b	Added dot under P of R.20/12
17	Dot under P of R.20/9
18	Dot under PE of R.20/10
19a	Small patch of pale colour between R.20/11 and R.20/12 rules
19b	Added ½ dot under (P)E of R.20/11

Index to Marginal Markings
Top Margin, Stamp Numbers

Stamp No.	Plate
1	6a, 6b
2	8a, 8b

Bottom Margin, Stamp Numbers

1	6b
2	16a
5	1b, 1c
6	2b
7	3b
8	4a, 4b
9	5b, 11, 17
10	6b, 12, 18
11	1c, 4a, 4b, 5a, 5b, 7a, 7b, 9a, 9b, 10a, 10b, 13, 15, 16a, 16b, 19a, 19b
12	8b, 10a, 10b, 14, 16b, 19a, 19b

Left Margin, Row Numbers

Row No.	Plate
16	14
20	4a, 4b

Right Margin, Row Numbers

19	2a, 2b, 8a, 15
20	16a, 16b

No Markings: Plates 1a, 3a

Control Schedule
All Wmk. Crown unless marked (s) Simple Cypher or (m) Multiple Cypher

Control	Plate with which it was used
B. 11	6a, 8a
B 11	1a, 1b, 2b, 3a, 3b, 4a, 4b, 5a, 5b, 6b, 7a, 7b, 8b
B. 12	2a, 6a, 8a
B 12 (c)	1c, 2b, 3b, 4b, 5b, 6b, 7b, 8b, 9a, 9b, 10a, 10b, 19a, 19b
B 12 (w)	11, 12, 13, 14, 15, 16a
B 12 (s)	11, 12, 13, 16a
B 12 (m)	11, 12, 13, 16a
B 13 (s)	11, 12, 15, 16b, 17, 18

Section NB

The Profile Head Issue, Wmk Royal Cypher (1912–22)

INTRODUCTION.

By November 1911, when the King expressed his dissatisfaction with the three-quarter profile "Downey Head", work had already stopped on producing dies for values higher than those already issued. The King suggested that a full profile would be preferable and supplied a die proof of the engraving by De La Rue for Colonial and South African stamps. This had been based originally on Mackennal's work for the Royal Mint for coins and medals.

Mackennal's South Africa medal

The first effigy that Mackennal had created was for the medal to be given to those who had helped to create the new Union of South Africa. Medals were required for the inauguration in November 1910 of the united South African parliament. Mackennal based his plaster model on one of the full profile photographs taken by W. & D. Downey in June. The final version, dated 27 September, was in many ways the basis for all subsequent effigies. His model for the coinage followed on 15 November.

The coin model

When work on the coinage model was complete at the Mint in January 1911 Mackennal turned his attention to an embossed die for registered envelopes. As before, he created a plaster model of the head, this time based on his work for the coinage but with different depths of relief. The embossed die for the head was ready by 16 March in time for registered envelopes to be available on Coronation Day, 22 June.

Mackennal continued working on medals at the Mint - first Coronation medals, and then naval and military medals, with the King in appropriate uniform for each. The latter can most easily be distinguished by the epaulettes on the King's uniform on the naval medal, which are lacking on that of the military.

Thus, when the crisis came with the Downey three-quarter profile in November 1911 all these profile heads were available for possible use as replacements.

The first step was to insert profile photographs into the existing frames. Reduced stamp-size photographs were therefore produced incorporating a photograph of the die of the Colonial head, a profile Downey photograph and a photograph of the plaster model of the Coinage head, all in different sizes. On 21 December 1911 it was decided to proceed with the engraving of the Coinage head at a size to fit the existing frames by Mackennal – the Dolphins and Wreath frames, but not the Lion design.

An Alternative Design

Medal head approved

Mackennal had always hated the Lion design. It had been forced upon him by Herbert Samuel, the Postmaster General, but, despite a great deal of amendment, he had never found it satisfactory. With the demise of the three-quarter profile "Downey" head Mackennal took the opportunity to create a totally new frame design for the 1d. and 2½d. values to replace it. As before, he submitted this directly to the King, bypassing the PMG. This design featured a frame of oak and laurel leaves and Mackennal produced it in the form of a sculptured model. He submitted a photograph of it to the King who approved it on 21 February 1912, immediately after his return from India. However, the effigy of the King used by Mackennal in the new design was a larger version based on his model of the naval and military medals, and not the Coinage Head, and Mackennal was insistent that this Medal Head be used for this particular design. The King agreed and that the Coinage Head could be used for the other values. Thus, two different profile heads were approved for use in the different frames of values up to 4d.

Master dies were then prepared from April to July 1912 for the 1d. and 2½d. Oak and Laurel Leaves design, the 1½d. Dolphins design, and the 2d. and 3d. Wreath design, all by Mackennal. The 4d., now also in Mackennal's Wreath design, followed in December and the new ½d. was ready by the same time. Colour trials for the 4d. took place in November and December using, first, the 2d. die followed by the 4d.

2d. pearl green

4d. bronze

Table 5. 18 November 1912. Colour trials for 4d. using 2d. die/ 10 December 1912 4d. die

Value	Colour	Number	Notes
2d.	Grenate Lake	E.90	
	Magenta	E.92	Provisionally selected for 5d. 24 June 1912
	Grey	E.94	
	Buff Lake	E.96	
	Cerise Lake	E.98	
	Maroon	E.100	
	Dahlia Claret	E.101	
	Azure Blue	E.102	Provisionally selected for 4d. 24 June 1912
	Brilliant Rhone Blue	E.103	
	Turquoise Blue (yellow shade)	E.104	
	Turquoise Blue	E.105	
	Raw Umber	E.106	Provisionally selected for 7d. 24 June 1912
	Brown	E.107	
	Dutch Brown	E.108	
	Sage	E.109	
	Pearl Green	E.110	
	Turquoise Green	E.112	
	Pale Bronze Green	E.113	
	Deep Bronze Green	E.114	
4d.	Grey	E.94	
	Deep Bronze Green	E.114	
	Pearl Green	E.110	Approved by the King 14 December 1912

Printex Colour Trials

Turning to the frame designs by George Eve, colour trials were produced using the Printex or Motley process. This process was first used on an experimental basis to print sheets of stamps in July 1912 to help speed up the production of the other values. Quality was not good enough but it was used for colour trials at the beginning of 1913.

The Motley, or Printex, process was photographic. After a careful, enlarged line drawing was produced in reverse a master photograph was created on glass, positive and reversed. By placing this in a form of step-and-repeat printing machine, a reversed multi-negative was produced. From this a copper plate with a light-sensitised surface was etched after exposure to light through the multi-negative. The British patents for the photographic printing frames were registered in the joint names of Alfred Henry Motley (hence the name), Clark Aubert Miller and Herbert Morris Pilkington. Later it was produced by the Printex Company. It was used to produce the mock "Ideal" 1d stamp design printed at the Jubilee International Stamp Exhibition, held under the auspices of the Junior Philatelic Society (Fred Melville) at the Royal Horticultural Halls in London from 14 to 19 October, 1912.

Printex artwork

In January 1913, a series of colour trials were made by the Printex method using both the Wreath and Pillar designs in blocks of four. The Wreath design had a 7d. value with alternative backgrounds to the King's Coinage Head – one tinted, the other solid. Line versions also exist in the Royal Philatelic Collection. At the end of the month further trials were made with Pillar design in the 8d. value with the Medal Head of the King. This time there were four different surrounds to the King's head (plain line, graduated line, solid and half solid). The King, when asked, preferred the graduated line surround.

8d. half solid

The Profile Head Issue **KING GEORGE V** **NB**

Table 6 Printex colour trials/ Coinage Head 7d., Medal Head 8d., blocks of 4 January 1913

Value	Colour	Number	Notes
7d.	Bistre Brown	E.191	Tinted surround
	Grey	E.192	Tinted surround
	Gloriosa Blue	E.189	Tinted surround
	Tyrian Red	E.194	Tinted surround
	Maroon	E.196	Tinted surround
	Tyrian Red	E.198	Solid surround
	Maroon	E.199	Solid surround
	Bistre Brown	E. 200	Solid surround
	Grey	E. 201	Solid surround
	Gloriosa Blue	E. 202	Solid surround
	Black*	-	Line surround
	Magenta*	-	Line surround
8d.	black	-	Line surround
	Tyrian red	-	Line surround
	agate lake	-	Line surround
	maroon	-	Line surround
	black	-	Graduated surround
	maroon	-	Graduated surround
	agate lake	-	Graduated surround
	Tyrian red	-	Graduated surround
	black	-	Half-solid surround
	Tyrian red	-	Half solid surround
	maroon	-	Half solid surround
	agate lake	-	Half solid surround
	black	-	Solid surround
	agate lake	-	Solid surround
	Tyrian red	-	Solid surround
	maroon	-	Solid surround
	magenta	-	Solid surround

*In The Royal Philatelic Collection

A Third Profile Head

A smaller head of the King was required for Eve's frames for the 5d. to 1s. stamps. Initially, this was to be the Coinage Head. However, Mackennal insisted that the King preferred the head as on the new penny stamp – i.e. the Medal Head. As a result a smaller version of this was created and came to be known as Medal Head II. Frames were amended by Eve to accommodate this and master dies produced for each value. From the master dies of the 5d. Pillars design and the 9d. Wreath design special nickel plates of four were produced to create yet another series of colour trials in June 1913. Over 30 different shades were provided for each of the two designs. A few of these were on tinted papers.

Table 7 June 1913 Special nickel plate from master colour die essays

Value	Colour	Number	Notes
5d.	Azure blue	E. 6	M.B. D/11060D. Selected for 10d. Duty 4/7/13 Provisional for 8d. Duty 17/6/13 Also overprinted CANCELLED
	Umber	E. 11	Provisionally selected for the 7d. MB 11062/D Selected for 1s. Duty Also overprinted CANCELLED
	Magenta	E. 92	Provisionally selected for 5d. Also overprinted CANCELLED
	Grey	E. 94	As on Colour Scheme D. Colour used for 7d. Edward VII. Also overprinted CANCELLED

Value	Colour	Number	Notes
5d.	Crimson Lake	E. 123	Also overprinted CANCELLED
	Agate Lake	E. 129	Also overprinted CANCELLED
	Agate	E. 130	M.B. 24792 Selected for 9d. Duty 11/6/13 Also overprinted CANCELLED
	Sepia Brown	E. 142	Also overprinted CANCELLED
	Dutch Brown	E. 146	As on Colour Scheme D. Also overprinted CANCELLED
	Brown	E. 149	Overprinted CANCELLED
	Deep Bronze Green	E. 167	M.B. 27531 Selected for 7d. Duty 16/7/13 Also overprinted CANCELLED
	Turquoise Green	E. 169	Also overprinted CANCELLED
	Green	E. 203	Also overprinted CANCELLED
	Grey	E. 204	Also overprinted CANCELLED
	Claret	E. 205	Also overprinted CANCELLED
	Green	E. 206	Selected for 7d. Duty 17/6/13 and countermanded Also overprinted CANCELLED
	Phototype Brown	E. 207	Also overprinted CANCELLED
	Salmon Red No. 2	E. 208	21/12/14
	Salmon Red No. 1	E. 209	21/12/14
	Japanese Blue	E. 211	Also overprinted CANCELLED
	Cypress Green	E. 212	Also overprinted CANCELLED
	Bistre Green	E. 214	Also overprinted CANCELLED
	Fawn	E. 215	M.B. 11020/D Selected for 5d. Duty 17/6/13 Also overprinted CANCELLED
	Blue Green	E. 216	Also overprinted CANCELLED
	Grenat	E. 217	Also overprinted CANCELLED
	Dutch Brown	E. 218	Also overprinted CANCELLED
	Ru Ochre	E. 219	Also overprinted CANCELLED
	Rose Veyron	E. 220	Also overprinted CANCELLED
	Rose	E. 221	Also overprinted CANCELLED
	Purple	E. 222	Official Purple used for 6d. Unified stamp MB 25598 Superseded Also overprinted CANCELLED
	Blue	E. 224	Also overprinted CANCELLED
	Light Blue	E. 225	Also overprinted CANCELLED
	Black on Yellow tinted paper	E. 226	Overprinted CANCELLED

KING GEORGE V — The Profile Head Issue

Value	Colour	Number	Notes
5d.	Black on Lemon tinted paper	E. 227	Dense Black Special for Stamps MB 10949?D Selected for 10d. Duty 17/6/13 altered to 8d. Duty 4/7/13 Also Overprinted CANCELLED
	Black on Buff tinted paper	E. 228	Overprinted CANCELLED
	Black on Light Green tinted paper	E. 229	Also overprinted CANCELLED
	Black on Dark Green tinted paper	E. 230	Also overprinted CANCELLED
	Black on Rose tinted paper	E. 231	Also overprinted CANCELLED
9d.	Azure Blue	E. 6	
	Umber	E. 11	Provisionally selected for the 7d.
	Magenta	E. 92	Provisionally selected for the 5d.
	Grey	E. 94	As on Colour Scheme D. Colour used for 7d. Edward VII.
	Crimson Lake	E. 123	
	Agate Lake	E. 129	
	Agate	E. 130	
	Sepia Brown	E. 142	
	Dutch Brown	E. 146	As on Colour Scheme D
	Brown	E. 149	
	Deep Bronze Green	E. 167	
	Turquoise Green	E. 169	
	Grey	E. 204	
	Claret	E. 205	
	Green	E. 206	
	Phototype Brown	E. 207	
	Salmon Red No. 2	E 208	
	Japanese Blue	E. 211	
	Cypress Green	E. 212	
	Bistre Green	E. 214	
	Fawn	E. 215	
	Blue Green	E. 216	
	Grenat	E. 217	
	Dutch Brown	E. 218	
	Ru Ochre	E. 219	
	Rose Veyron	E. 220	
	Rose	E. 221	
	Purple	E. 222	Official Purple used for 6d. Unified stamp
	Blue	E. 224	
	Light Blue	E. 225	
	Green [Light]	-	
	Black on Yellow tinted paper	E. 226	
	Black on Lemon tinted paper	E. 227	Overprinted CANCELLED
	Black on Buff tinted paper	E. 228	
	Black on Light Green tinted paper	E. 229	
	Black on Dark Green tinted paper	E. 230	Overprinted CANCELLED
	Black on Rose tinted paper	E. 231	

Colours finally accepted were (in the given terminology): 5d. fawn (215), 6d. purple (222), 7d. deep bronze green (167), 8d. black on lemon tinted paper (227), 9d. agate (130), 10d. azure blue (6) and 1s. umber (11).

Die Proofs
In various states, uncleared
In blue on proof paper £4750
In shades of red or pink, green or black on proof paper .... From £3250
In black on card £2600
In final accepted state, uncleared
(a) On proof paper
In scarlet, green or black .... From £3250
(b) On thin card
In scarlet, green or black .... From £3250
(c) On paper watermarked Imperial Crown
In scarlet, green or black .... From £4750

These proofs are sometimes found cut down and inserted in cardboard bevelled frames which are usually dated 28 February 1912 (*Prices from £3000*).

Bromides
Mid-1912. Bromides of coinage heads in different sizes from Mackennal's bas-relief plaque for insertion into frames to give different percentage widths overall. No initials in truncation.
(a) Head image 30·7 mm. wide=41·4% of total width of frame for 1d. and 2d. values .... *Each £2600*
(b) Head image 29·5 mm. wide=39·4% of total width of frame for 1d. and 2d. values .... *Each £2600*
November 1912. Reproduced from Harrison's line sketch illustrated on previous page and dated "2.11.12".
36·1 mm. wide=47·4% of total width of frame £3750
A coinage head bromide, inscribed "47·4", was later discovered combined with a Downey Head frame for the 1d. and unissued 2½d. values.
(a) Frame (75 × 90 mm.) of the 1d. and 2½d. Downey Head with coinage head inserted ....
(b) A similar bromide essay reduced to stamp size but without "Twopence Halfpenny" value tablet inscribed "47·4" in M/S ....
(c) Head image 29 mm. wide, inscribed "photo of medallion used for ½d. and 1½ d. stamp" and initialled by J.A.C Harrison £2600

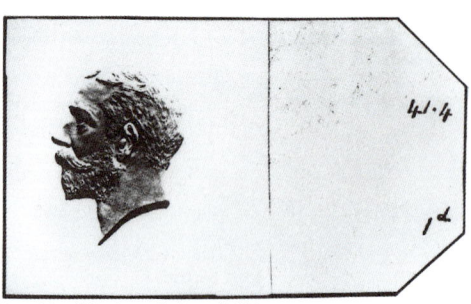

Bromide of Mackennal's Bas-relief Plaque

MEDAL HEAD DIES
The "large" medal as used in the 1d./2½d. master design

Medal Head

Mackennal sculptured the design in clay and included the already adopted full profile medal head. A photograph was sent to the King and this was approved on 21 February 1912. The head used was small and had the initials B M Sc in the truncation.

Bromide (120 × 164 mm.) mounted in sunken frame inscribed "Appd. G.R.S(?)" and dated in pencil on reverse "8.3.12" £3750
Bromide (91×30mm) inscribed "Appd.G.R.S" at base and "alternative size for effigy only 6.3.12" at top £3750
Bromide reduced to stamp size and mounted on thick brown card, annotated in manuscript "45.7".....

Soon afterwards it was decided to use a larger version of the head for the 1d. and 2½d. values. Mackennal sculptured the design in clay and included the new full profile medal head.

J. A. C. Harrison's Sketch

J. A. C. Harrison produced a pen and ink sketch of the head and from this engraved the die ready for proofing early in April 1912.

Die Proofs
Stage 1a. Proofed by J. A. C. Harrison in early April 1912. Uncleared and without background shading. Undated
In black on proof paper.. £5250
Stage 1ab. As last, but with background partially shaded.
In black on proof paper.. £5250
Stage 1b. As last, but with background shading to head in an oval
In black on proof paper.. £5250
Stage 2. As last, with basic outline of frame engraved around head
In black on proof paper.. £5250
Stage 3. As last, with more of the frame engraved, including POSTAGE
In rose-pink or scarlet on proof paper .... From £6000

Stage 1a

Stage 2

KING GEORGE V *The Profile Head Issue*

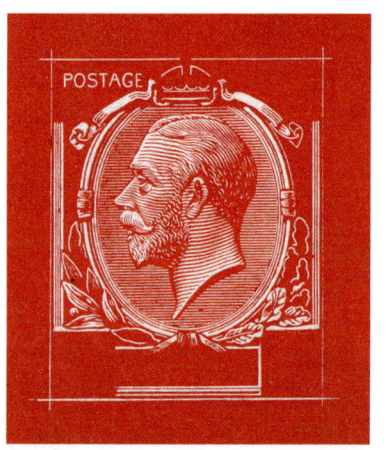

Stage 3

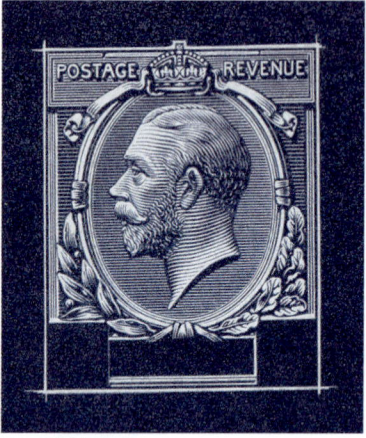

Stage 4b. Master Die

Master Die for 1d. and 2½d. values.
Stage 4a. As Stage 4b but thin frame lines as shown in Stage 3. Undated
In black on proof paper £5750
Stage 4b. On proof paper, dated 15 May 1912
In brown-carmine, pale rose-red or deep
  rose-red .... Each £3250
In deep turquoise-blue, dull royal blue or
  slate-blue .... Each £7500
In black £2400
In red on gummed Crown watermarked paper £8500

Stage 4c.

Stage 4c (as 4b but with uncreased details at
  sides and around value tablets) in blue on
  gummed Multiple Cypher watermarked paper £10000
  This die was proofed at the Royal Mint on 16 May 1912 and a roller impression was taken up. On 22 May the Royal Mint proofed a die which was rolled out from this roller. This secondary die was sent to Harrison for him to engrave the figures and words for the 1d. value. On 16 July 1912 an identical master die was sent to Harrison for him to engrave the 2½d. on. The smaller version of the head was used for the 5d. to 1s. values.
  For stage 5 (completed die) see under N16 and N21.
Die proof of the smaller head in black on proof
  paper .... From £2750

Bromide
November 1912. Large bromide (120 × 165 mm.) reproduced from Harrison's sketch of April 1912 and dated "2.11.12".
34·5 mm. wide=46% of total width of frame £2750

Die Proofs from the H.A. Richardson Archive
Cleared stamp-size proofs in black on white glazed card overprinted "CANCELLED" in red. Mounted on manila paper and dated .... Each from £5000

PRINTERS
The stamps in Section NB were printed by Harrison & Sons, except for the 6d. printed at Somerset House by the Stamping Department of the Board of Inland Revenue, where printings of other values were also made (distinguishable only by the stop Controls).

SHEET FORMAT.
Each sheet consisted of 240 stamps arranged in two panes of 120; the panes contained ten horizontal rows of 12 stamps, and

½d. Green, Type N6. Royal Cypher   *The Profile Head Issue*   **KING GEORGE V**   **NB**

were separated horizontally by an interpane gutter containing "pillars" as illustrated in the General Notes on the King Edward VII issues under "Plates". The issues of 1912–22 had coextensive rules all round the panes.

PERFORATION.
Types 2 or 2A were used throughout the issue (see Appendix 1). In addition, the variety without the single extension hole in the bottom margin, Type 2(c), is known on the ½d., 1d., 1½d., 2d., 2½d., 4d., 6d., 7d. and 1s. values and Type 3 on the 1d., Type 3A on the 2d. and both Types 3 and 3A on the 6d. values

Imperforate stamps. Imperforate stamps of this issue exist but may be wartime colour trials.

CONTROLS.
Prices quoted are for single unused mounted examples with Control attached. The priced lists are sub-divided into Controls with imperforate selvedge (2(E)) and those with the selvedge perforated through (2A(P)). Partially perforated margins are regarded as imperforate.

Position. The Control appears below the 2nd stamp in the bottom row (R. 20/2), except for the 1d. value where it is beneath the 11th stamp

Additional plate and control information. For some time collectors have been aware that the King George V plate information for the ½d. to 1s. values within this section has been incomplete. To address this, a study has been undertaken of the black proof sheets held at the British Library and the "official" numbers from those sheets have been incorporated into the listings. For the convenience of collectors these numbers will continue to be cross-referenced to the established "SG" plate numbers given in earlier editions of this catalogue. Plate allocations for varieties continue to refer to "SG" plate numbers.

Plate Markings. The lists have been updated to include all the newly recorded markings and the plates to which they belong.

Existing — indicates those markings shown on the black plate proofs prior to the plate first being put to press.

Added — indicates those markings, deliberately or accidentally added during the life of the plate.

Control Schedules. These lists have also been amended to include all updated and new information. It should be pointed out that from the put to press dates it is possible to establish the first control used with each plate. A number of these have not been seen and hence not recorded in the past. One explanation is that they may have been printed prior to markings being added to the plate. As most collectors of controls are aware, there are a considerable number of control pieces that cannot be attributed to the existing list of plates. Most of these are devoid of markings. These pieces may well be those early missing controls.

1913 (16 January). **½d. Green, Type N6.** Wmk. Simple Cypher

N14 (=S.G.351/56)

	Unmtd mint	Mtd mint	Used
(1) Green	3·00	1·00	1·00
(2) Deep green	10·00	5·00	2·00
(3) Pale green	8·00	6·00	1·00
(4) Very pale green (1919)	£300	£200	75·00
(5) Very deep green (1919)	£550	£400	£125
(6) Bright green	3·00	1·00	1·00
(7) Deep bright green	15·00	10·00	2·00
(8) Yellow-green	10·00	6·00	3·00
(9) Dull yellow- ("apple") green (1915)	25·00	18·00	12·00
(10) Very yellow- ("Cyprus") green (1914)	£13000	£9000	†
(11) Bright yellow-green	75·00	50·00	10·00
(12) Olive-green (1915)	£200	£125	45·00
(13) Pale olive-green (1916)	£150	£100	35·00
(14) Blue-green (1913 & 1918)	60·00	40·00	25·00
(15) Deep blue- ("Myrtle") green	£300	£225	65·00
(16) Deep myrtle-green	£950	£800	£250
(17) Cobalt-green (1922)	40·00	25·00	6·00
(18) Deep cobalt-green (1922)	£400	£300	60·00
a. Partial double print	—	£25000	†
aa. Gummed both sides	£27500	—	†
b. Without watermark	£200	£150	£150
c. Watermark inverted	4·00	3·00	1·50
d. Watermark reversed	80·00	55·00	55·00
e. Watermark inverted and reversed	6·00	4·00	3·50
ea. Watermark double			
f. "New Moon", flaw (R. 2/3 of booklet pane)		£450	£350
fa. Ditto, watermark inverted		£450	£350
g. Cracked plate (R. 9 or 19/1 and vert. coil)		£300	
h. "Ruffled Hair" (Pl. 28, R. 20/1)		£650	
i. Broken left frame (R. 1/1 of booklet pane No. NB6a)		£300	
ia. White spot on tablet (R. 2/2 of booklet pane No. NB6a)		£225	
j. Stop after "HALFPENNY" (Pl. 16c, R. 19/3)		£150	
k. Coloured mark on right dolphin's eye (R. 43, R. 20/2)		95·00	
ka. Blob over eye (Pl. 43a, R. 19/1)		£300	
l. White spot in hair (Pl. 53a, R. 19/3)		£200	
m. Deformed "E" in "HALFPENNY" (Pl. 49b, R.20/2)		£200	
ma. Damage to serif of "E" (Pl. 4, R. 18/1)		£125	
o. White spot above right dolphin's mouth (Pl. 46b, R. 20/3)		90·00	
p. Broken line below "LF" (Pl. 72, R. 10/7)		£175	
r. Printed double, one albino (4 mm. to right of printed impression) with C 13 control Strip of 3		£5000	
ra. Coil join (vert. pair)			
rb. Coil join (horiz. pair) (9.20)			
s. "Specimen", Type 23		£150	

N5   N6   N7

N8   N9

KING GEORGE V The Profile Head Issue ½d. Green, Type N6. Royal Cypher

	Unmtd mint	Mtd mint	Used
t. "Specimen", Type 26	£175		
u. Do. Imperf.	90·00		
v. "Cancelled", Type 24	80·00		
w. "Cancelled", Type 28	£225		

Imperforate *tête-bêche* pair from P.O. Registration
Sheet.. *Unused tête-bêche pair* £20000
N14 (1) is known printed on uncalendered paper.

The variety "solid shading to left of "HALFPENNY" has been deleted. It was almost certainly the result of overinking.

Shade (10) is fluorescent under long-wave ultraviolet with the reaction quite unlike any other shade in this group, whilst shades (12) and (13) are highly fugitive.

Six specimens are known of variety a showing partial double prints in the lower portions of the stamp (control G 15).

No. N14aa was gummed on both sides and then printed over the gum.

Variety No. N14ea was from a B. 13 printing.

Variety h is only found with control I 16 on part of the printing. Printings with the J 17 control being from the rechromed plate.

Variety j. is found on late printings with control G 15 and all printings with control H 16.

Variety ka is not fully constant but a number of examples are known.

No. N14r shows the (unprinted) albino impression on the gummed side particularly on the control margin.

No. N14v is usually from cancelled booklet panes (with upright or inverted watermarks) used in 1917 booklet stitching trials.

For variety v in grey-green see "Colour Trials". No. N14w is probably a colour trial printed as an experiment in 1916.

N14j

N14k

N14ka

N14l
Repaired with control M18

N14m

N14g, N15g

N14f

N14h

N14ma

N14o

N14i

N14ia

N14p

Watermark Varieties. The following have been recorded:
Wmk upright: Types I, II, III
Wmk inverted: Types I, II, III
Wmk reversed: Types I, II, III
Wmk inverted and reversed: Types I, II, III

112

½d. Green, Type N6. Royal Cypher *The Profile Head Issue* **KING GEORGE V** **NB**

Misplaced Watermarks
ya. Single stamp showing letters from "POSTAGE" .... 12·00
yb. Vertical strip sufficient to show complete "POSTAGE" watermark £190
yc. Vertical strip sufficient to show complete "POSTAGE" watermark double, with selvedge attached, the selvedge having the "POSTAGE" watermark inverted £4250

Broken Dandy Roll Varieties
za. Missing Crown .... 50·00
zb. Missing G .... 30·00
zc. Missing v .... 30·00
zd. Missing R .... 35·00
ze. Missing Gv .... 30·00
zf. Missing vR .... 35·00
zg. Missing Crown vR .... 35·00
zi. Missing left side to R .... 30·00
zj. Missing tail to R ("GvP") .... 20·00
zk. Long tail to G .... 30·00

Controls. Prices are for unused singles.
Somerset House Printings:

Control	Perf. Type 2(E.)	2A(P.)
B. 13	4·00	£500

Watermark varieties known:
Wmk upright, Type I; wmk inverted, Type I; wmk reversed, Type I; wmk inverted and reversed, Type I; wmk upright, Type II; Type I wmk double

Harrison Printings:

Control	Perf. Type 2(E.)	2A(P.)
C 13	2·00	2·00
C 14	8·00	8·00
D 14	2·00	2·00
E 14	2·00	2·00
F 15	2·00	2·00
G 15	2·50	2·50
H 16	2·00	3·00
I 16	2·00	2·00
J 17	2·00	2·00
K 17	15·00	15·00
K 18	8·00	8·00
L 18	8·00	8·00
M 18	10·00	10·00
M 19	3·00	3·00
N 19	2·50	2·50
O 19	8·00	8·00
O 20	5·00	5·00
P 20	2·00	2·00
Q 20	9·00	9·00
Q 21 (c)	5·00	5·00
Q 21 (w)	5·00	5·00
R 21	3·00	3·00
S 21	20·00	20·00
S 22	17·00	17·00
T 22	6·00	6·00
U 22	5·00	5·00
U 23	3·00	3·00
V 23	2·00	2·00
W 23	15·00	15·00
W 24	£275	£275

(c) "close" and (w) "wide" refer to the space between "Q" and "2" (5.75 mm and 7 mm respectively)

Variety Type 2(c) (I/I) strips of three

C 13	£125
D 14	—
G 15	—
J 17	—
U 23	—

Watermark varieties known:
Wmk upright, Type I: C 13, D 14.
Wmk upright, Type II: C 13, C 14, D 14, E 14, F 15, G 15, H 16, I 16, J 17, K 17, K 18, N 19, O 19, O 20, P 20, Q 21(c), Q 21(w), R 21, T 22, U 22, U 23, V 23, W 23, W 24.
Wmk inverted, Type II: C 13, C 14, E 14, F 15, G 15, H 16, I 16, U 23, V 23, W 23, W 24.
Wmk reversed, Type II: C 13, C 14, F 15, G 15, H 16.
Wmk inverted and reversed, Type II: C 13, C 14, D 14, E 14, F 15, G 15, H 16, I 16, U 23, V 23.
Wmk upright, Type III: J 17, K 17, K 18, L 18, M 18, M 19, N 19, O 19, O 20, P 20, Q 20, Q 21(c), Q 21(w), R 21, S 21, S 22, T 22, U 22, U 23, V 23, W 23.
Wmk inverted, Type III: J 17, K 17, K 18, L 18, M 18, M 19, N 19, O 19, O 20, P 20, Q 20, Q 21, R 21, S 21, T 22.
Wmk reversed, Type III: J 17, K 17, L 18, M 19, P 20, S 21 T 22.
Wmk inverted and reversed, Type III: J 17, K 17, K 18, L 18, M 18, M 19, N 19, O 19, O 20, P 20, Q 20, Q 21, R 21, S 22, T 22, U 22.

Coils
Vertical delivery made up from sheets with joins every tenth stamp

Code No.	Issued	Number in roll	Face value		
C	1913	1000	£2.1.8	Top delivery	£250
D	1913	1000	£2.1.8	Bottom delivery	£250
G	1913	500	£1.0.10	Top delivery	£250
H	1913	500	£1.0.10	Bottom delivery	£250
KERMODE	Mid 1920	1000	£2.1.8	Top delivery	£175

Sideways delivery made up from sheets with joins every 12th stamp

P	Sept. 1920	480	£1.0.0	Left side delivery	£250

Die Proofs
Approved die, uncleared (Sept. 1912)
In green on proof paper £6500
As last but cut close £4750
In green on paper watermarked Simple Cypher (cut close only) £4750
In black on card £6000
Cleared for working purposes (Nov. 1912)
In black on card £6000

Colour Trials

1916 Trials
Perforated 15×14. Watermark Simple Cypher in grey-green overprinted "Cancelled" Type 24 .... £600

The colour trial listed here was one of three shades from ink supplied by British Dyes Ltd which exist perforated and overprinted "Cancelled", Type 24. The other two are close to issued shades and so are not listed separately. Neither was accepted and they only exist with the "Cancelled" overprint. These trial stamps "Cancelled" Type 24 should not be confused with issued stamps, listed as N14v.

1923 Fastness Trials
Imperforate colour fastness trials on gummed watermarked paper with printer's reference number on reverse in manuscript.
In green (shades), blue-green or yellow-green £3000
These stamps are from the same sheet and five reference series are known; 1468, 2188, 2222, O and 5, followed by 'No.', with numbers 1 to 5. It is believed that the shades arise from the tests carried out on the stamps.

NB KING GEORGE V The Profile Head Issue ½d. Green, Type N6. Royal Cypher

Plate Markings

Official Plate	SG Plate	Markings
79a	1a	Existing minute dot under H of R. 20/2; added dot above R. 1/1 and R. 1/11
79b	1ab*	Dot above R. 1/1 and R. 1/11 filled in
79c	1b	Added cut under N(N) of R. 20/1
80a	2a	Existing indents in rule base under PE of R. 20/1 and LFP of R. 20/12; added dot above R. 1/2, 9.25 mm. and R. 11/2, 9.25 mm.
80b	2b	Dots above R. 1/2 and R. 11/2 filled in; added large dot bulging (sometimes breaking) base under FP of R. 20/3
80c	2c	Added dot under E of R. 20/3
81a	3a	Existing nick outer R. 2 right side, 9 mm; dot added above R. 1/3 and R. 11/3
81b	3ab*	Dots above R. 1/3 and R. 11/3 filled in
91a	3b	Added small dot R. 17 left side, 11 mm.
91b	3c	Added large cut under P of R. 20/1
82a	4a	Existing small dot breaking outer R. 17 right side, 16.3 mm; added dot above R. 1/4 and R. 11/4; see Pl 32a/b
85a	4ab*	Added dot above R. 1/6 and R. 11/6
85b	4b	Dots above R. 1/6 and R. 11/6 filled in; added sloping cut (base) under FP of R. 20/4
85c	4c*	Added small dot R. 18 left side, 12.5 mm
89	5	Dot (top) under H of R. 20/1
87a	6a	Existing indent (top) under EN of R. 20/3; added dot (top) under PE of R. 20/1; ½ cut (top) to left of H of R. 20/6
87b	6b	Added dot under N (N) of R. 20/1
90a	7a	Existing ½ cut (base) under LF of R. 20/1; added small dot R. 20 left side, 13.75 mm.
90b	7b	Added dot under PE of R. 20/2
88	8	Added ½ cut (top) under LF of R. 20/2
84a	9*	Added dot above R. 1/5 and R. 11/5
84b	9a	Dots above R. 1/5 and R. 11/5 filled in; added irregular cut under E of R. 20/3
84c	9b	Added ½ nick R. 20 left side (slanting down to outer edge), 22-21.5 mm.
84d	9c	Added two dots R. 20 left side, 10, 12 mm.
92a	10a	Added small dot R. 19 left side, 10.5 mm.
92b	10b	Added small dot under A of R. 20/1
86a	11a	Existing R. 11 right side rule, lower end, bevelled outer; cut within rule at left below R. 20/9
86b	11b	Added cut R. 20 left side, 12.75 mm.
93a	12a	Existing scoop (top) out of rule above R. 1/1, 2-10 mm; dash within rule right end below R. 20/2
93b	12b	Added dot under PE of R. 20/3
93c	12c	Added sloping cut under FP of R. 20/3
94a	13a	Added dot under FP of R. 20/1
94b	13b	Added dot under PE of R. 20/1
94c	13c	Added dot (inner) R. 20 left side, 9.75 mm.
94d	13d	Added dot under PE of R. 20/2
96a	14a	Added dot under P of R. 20/2
96b	14b	Added dot (top) under EN of R. 20/2
96c	14c	Added dot under LF of R. 20/3; added dot at left above R. 1/1; added nick R. 18 left side, 6.5 mm added ½ dot (outer) R. 18 left side 12.5 mm ½ dot (inner) R. 1 left side, 11 mm (uncertain when added).
96d	14d	Added ½ dot (top) under P of R. 20/3; added ½ dot (inner) R.18 left side, 10 mm. ½ dot (inner) R. 1 left side, 11½ mm (uncertain when added)
N.M.	15	Added dot under PE of R. 20/1
99a	16a	Added dot under PE of R. 20/2
99b	16b	Added two dots R. 19 left side, 11, 14 mm.
99c	16c	Added cut under N (N) of R. 20/1
N.M.	17	Added dot (top) under P of R. 20/3
N.M.	18	Added dot under FP of R. 20/4
N.M.	19	Added three dots (left dot minute) under LFPE of R. 20/2
N.M.	20a	Added three dots (centre dot minute) under LFP of R. 20/3
N.M.	20b	Added dot under A of R. 20/1

Official Plate	SG Plate	Markings
108a	21a	Existing minute dot outer R. 3 left side, 15.75 mm; 2 dots (top/base) under FPE of R. 20/4
110a	21ab*	Existing ½ dot (outer) R. 19 left; two ½ dots upper under FP and PE of R. 20/4
110b	21b	Added cut under LF of R. 20/3
95a	22*	No markings
95b	22a	Added nick (top) under FP of R. 20/4; added dot (top) under PE of R. 20/4
95c	22b	Added dot (base) under FP of R. 20/4
95d	22c*	Added three sloping cuts R. 19 left side, 7.5 to 9 mm.
112a	23a	Added dot (top) under H of R. 20/1
112b	23ab*	Nick, base, left end of rule under R. 20/9, 1.5-2 mm.
112c	23b	Added cut under HA of R. 20/4
N.M.	24	Added dot under H of R. 20/2
114	25	Added dot under H of R. 20/3
115	26	Master plate flaw nick outer R. 17 left side, 14 mm. added dot under H of R. 20/4
116	27	Added two dots under NN of R. 20/1
111a	28a	Added two small dots under PEN of R. 20/2
111b	28b	Added dot under P of R. 20/1
N.M.	29	Added two dots under AL of R. 20/3
N.M.	30	Added two dots under HAL of R. 20/4
119a	31a	Added double ½ cut (top/base) under HA of R. 20/2
119b	31b	Added dot covering base of above cut
82b	32a	Dots above R. 1/4 and R. 11/4 filled in; added tiny dot under P of R. 20/1
82c	32b	Added fine double cut under PE of R. 20/3; See Pl 4a
125	33	Existing outer R. 3 right side chipped; Added tiny dot under PE of R. 20/3
120a	34a	Added cut under PE of R. 20/1
120b	34b	Added dot under NN of R. 20/9
N.M.	35	Added cut under E of R. 20/2
121a	36a	Existing nick R. 19 right side outer 9.2 mm; added cut under P of R. 20/3
121b	36b	Added three dots under HALF P of R. 20/3
122	37	Existing underside indent in rule under EN of R. 20/4 and nick R. 20 right side outer, 5.7 mm; Added cut under F of R. 20/4
129a	38a	Added four dots from left to under right of F of R. 20/4
129b	38b	Added dot (breaking base) under PE of R. 20/1; added dot R. 20 left side, 11.5 mm; added two dots R. 17 left side, 7 and 11.3 mm.
	39	Withdrawn
N.M.	40	Added small, slightly ovoid dot (central) under PE of R. 20/1
N.M.	41	Added dot, barely bulging top, under P of R. 20/2; right of rule under R. 20/3 has small downward projection
N.M.	42	Added dot (breaking base) under FP of R. 20/1; scoop (outer) R. 2 left side
135a	43a	Existing very fine ¼ cut base under (N)N of R. 20/3; coloured mark on right dolphin's eye of R. 20/2
135b	43b	Added ½ dot (top) under E of R. 20/10
134a	44a	No details of markings
134b	44b	Added small oval dot (bulging and during later stages with Control K18, breaking base) under right serif of P of R. 20/2
141a	45a	Existing nick outer R. 6 right side, 1.5 mm; nick outer R. 15 right side, 10.5 mm; nick top above R. 1/9, 6.75 mm; ½ dot above R. 1/1, 9.5 mm; added large dot R. 19 right side, 7.5 mm
141b	45b	Added small dot R. 20 left side, 11.5 mm.
138a	46a	Master plate flaw nick R. 17 left side, 14 mm; added cut under N(N) of R. 20/1
138b	46b	Added cut R. 20 right side, 11.5 mm; large dot (breaking outer) R. 18 right side, 11 mm.
N.M.	47	Added dot (central) under right serif of P of R. 20/2; added two dots R. 19 left side, both breaking outer, 4.5, 8.5 mm.

½d. Green, Type N6. Royal Cypher The Profile Head Issue KING GEORGE V NB

Official Plate	SG Plate	Markings
158	48	Existing dot above R. 1/6, 3.1 mm; minute ½ dot upper under LF of R. 20/2; minute ½ dot (base) under N(N) of R. 20/2; added oval dot breaking base under PE of R. 20/1; added two minute dots under A, N(N) of R. 20/5. Base of R. 20 left side damaged (outer). Small dot R.18 left side, 22 mm.
137a	49a	Added dot (breaking top) under PE of R. 20/9
	49b	Added small, slightly ovoid dot (base) under right serif of P of R. 20/2
N.M.	50	Added nearly round dot (bulging—later breaking base) under right serif of P of R. 20/2
139a	51a	Added large dot R. 17 right side, 8.75 mm.
139b	51b	Added dot under PE of R. 20/1
142a	52a	Existing key flaw small nick top of rule below left leg of N(N) R. 20/2; bottom third of R. 18 left side rule thinner; nick outer R. 17 left side, 14 mm; nick outer R. 8 left side, 19.2 mm. Added large dot under E of R. 20/9
142b	52b	Added small dot R. 20 left side, 14 mm.
146	53	Flaw white spot in hair R. 19/3
146a	53a	Added small dot R. 17 right side, 4.5 mm.
146b	53b	Added slanting cut R. 19 right side, 4 mm.
N.M.	54a	Added dot R. 19 left side, 10 mm.
N.M.	54b	Added dot (top) under FP of R. 20/2
N.M.	54c	Added dot under E of R. 20/2
151	55	Added dot (base) under F of R. 20/1
N.M.	56	Added small dot (central) R. 18 right side, 11.5 mm; added small dot (inner) R. 17 right side, 10 mm.
136a	57a	Added large dot (later breaking inner) R. 17 right side, 11 mm.
136b	57b	Added ½ dot (top) under N(N) of R. 20/9
N.M.	58	Base of R. 20 right side bevelled off; added dot R. 17 right side, 9.5 mm.
147a	59a*	Scoop R. 19 left side outer, 8-11 mm, with vertical dash to right of it
147b	59b*	Added dot R. 18 right side, 10 mm.
N.M.	60a	Added dot under F of R. 20/10
N.M.	60b	Added four dots under AL, FP, and two joined under E of R. 20/3
150a	61a	Existing nick outer R. 19 right side, 14.5 mm; added dot bulging/breaking outer R. 19 left side, 6.5 mm.
150b	61b	Added dot (top) under FP of R. 20/9
150c	61c	Added four dots from left end to left of F of R. 20/4
140a	63*	No details of plate markings
140b	63a	Not known when added: Large dot (breaking outer) R. 18 right side, 10 mm; dot (breaking inner) R. 3 right side, 11.5 mm.
140c	63b	Added small dot (central) R. 17 right side, 10 mm.
N.M.	64	Added three dots breaking inner R. 19 right side, 6, 8, 11 mm. (Waterlow Pl 52)
145a	65*	Existing dot R. 14 left side, 13.5 mm. no further details when plate markings added
145b	65a	Added small double dot R. 18 right side, 11.75 mm.
145c	65b	Added dot, breaking base, under PE of R. 20/10
145d	65c	Added dot R. 19 left side, 9 mm.
154a	66a	Existing nick outer R. 14 left side, 10 mm; added dot (central) R. 19 left side, 9.5 mm.; added dot (breaking inner) R. 2 left side, 11.5-12 mm.
154b	66b	Added two fine cuts R. 19 left side, 11.5-13.3 mm.
N.M.	67	Added small dot inner R. 18 right side, 11 mm.
153	68	Added small dot above R. 1/11, 0.75 mm; added dot R. 1 left side, 12 mm; added dot inner R. 20 left side, 11.5 mm.
N.M.	69	Added two cuts R. 19 left side, 7, 9.5 mm.
N.M.	70	Added ½ dot (base) under P and nick under NY both of R. 20/4
164	71	Added large oval dot breaking top and bottom under PE of R. 20/2; R. 20 left side thins towards base
163	72	Existing nick left (lower) end of rule under R. 20/4; existing R. 19 right side bevelled lower outer; added oval dot under FP of R. 20/3
	73	No marking
160	74	Existing nick inner R. 17 right side, 11.75 mm; added oval dot (widely breaking top) to right of P of R. 20/2
N.M.	75	Added large oval dot either bulging or just breaking top, under PE of R. 20/2
N.M.	76	Added small dot (outer) R. 18 left side, 11 mm. Damage to frame line under PE, R.20/5
N.M.	77	Added two large dots R. 19 left side, 11, 13.5 mm.
N.M.	78	Added five cuts under HALF of R. 20/12; minute fine nick (outer) R. 19 left side, 8.25 mm. (Waterlow Plate 34)
N.M.	79	Base of R. 20/2 rule cut away from under ENNY to right end; added four large dots R. 19 right side (Waterlow Plate 6)
N.M.	80	Added large dot (central) R. 19 left side, 9.5 mm. (Waterlow Plate 7)
N.M.	81	Added ½ cut and ½ dot (outer) R. 19 left side, 11, 13.5 mm; added cut R. 18 left side, 13.5 mm.
N.M.	82	Added small dot (outer) R. 20 left side, 11.5 mm.
N.M.	83	Added two small cuts under NN of R. 20/11 (Waterlow Plate 16)

N.M.	—	Not matched
Existing	—	Markings on the black plate proof prior to the plate being first put to press
Added	—	Markings deliberately or accidentally made during the life of the plate
*	—	New plate allocation
†	—	Plate renumbered
R	—	row

Index to Marginal Markings
Top Margin

Stamp No.	Plate
R. 1/1	1a, 12a, 12b, 12c, 14c, 14d, 45a, 45b
R. 1/2	2a
R. 1/3	3a
R. 1/4	4a
R. 1/5	9
R. 1/6	4ab, 48
R. 1/9	45a, 45b
R. 1/11	68

Bottom Margin

Stamp No.	Plate
R. 20/1	1b, 2a, 2b, 2c, 3c, 5, 6a, 6b, 7a, 7b, 10b, 13a, 13b, 13c, 13d, 15, 16c, 20b, 23a, 23ab, 23b, 27, 28b, 32a, 32b, 34a, 34b, 38b, 40, 42, 46a, 46b, 48, 51b, 55
R. 20/2	1a, 1b, 7b, 8, 12a, 12b, 12c, 13d, 14a, 14b, 14c, 14d, 16a, 16b, 16c, 19, 24, 28a, 28b, 31a, 31b, 35, 41, 44b, 47, 48, 49b, 50, 52a, 52b, 54b, 54c, 71, 74, 75, 79
R. 20/3	2b, 2c, 6a, 6b, 9a, 9b, 9c, 12b, 12c, 14c, 14d, 17, 20a, 21b, 25, 29, 32b, 33, 36a, 36b, 41, 43a, 43b, 60b, 72
R. 20/4	4b, 4c*, 18, 21a, 21ab, 21b, 22a, 22b, 22c, 23b, 26, 30, 37, 38a, 38b, 61c, 70, 72
R. 20/5	48, 76
R. 20/6	6a, 6b
R. 20/9	11a, 11b, 23ab, 23b, 34b, 49a, 49b, 52a, 52b, 57b, 61b, 61c
R. 20/10	43b, 60a, 60b, 65b, 65c
R. 20/11	83
R. 20/1	2a, 2b, 2c, 78

NB KING GEORGE V   *The Profile Head Issue* ½d. Green, Type N6. Royal Cypher

Left Margin, Row Numbers

Row No.	Plate
1	14d, 68,
2	42, 66a, 66b
3	21a, 21ab, 21b
8	52a, 52b
14	65, 65a, 65b, 65c, 66a, 66b
17	3b, 3c, 26, 38b, 46a, 46b, 52a, 52b
18	4c, 14c, 14d, 76, 81,158
19	10a, 10b, 16b, 16c, 22c, 47, 54a, 54b, 54c, 59a, 59b, 61a, 61b, 61c, 65c, 66a, 66b, 69, 77, 78, 80, 81
20	7a, 7b, 9b, 9c, 11b, 13c, 13d, 38b, 45b, 48, 52b, 68, 71, 82

Right Margin, Row Numbers

Row No.	Plate
2	3a, 3ab
3	33, 63a, 63b
6	45a, 45b
11	11a, 11b
15	45a, 45b
17	4a, 51a, 51b, 53a, 53b, 56, 57a, 57b, 58, 63b, 74
18	46b, 56, 59b, 63a, 63b, 65a, 65b, 65c, 67
19	36a, 36b, 45a, 45b, 53b, 59b, 61a, 61b, 61c, 64, 72, 79
20	37, 46b, 58

No Markings 22, 73
Details of markings unknown 44a, 63, 65

Control Schedule

Control	Plate with which used
B. 13	1a, 2a, 3a, 4a, 4ab, 9
C 13	1ab, 1b, 2b, 3b, 3c, 4b, 4c, 5, 6a, 7a, 8, 9a, 9b, 10a, 11a
C 14	1b, 2b, 3c, 4c, 5, 6a, 7a, 8, 9b, 10a, 11a, 11b, 12a
D 14	1b, 2b, 3c, 4c, 5, 7a, 7b, 8, 10a, 11b, 12a, 12b, 13a, 14a, 22
E 14	2c, 6b, 9c, 12b, 12c, 13a, 13b, 13c, 13d, 14a, 14b, 15, 16a, 16b, 17, 18, 19, 20a, 21a, 22a, 22b
F 15	6b, 10b, 13d, 14b, 14c, 15, 16b, 17, 18, 19, 20a, 21a, 22b, 23a, 24, 25, 26, 27
G 15	6b, 10b, 14d, 16b, 16c, 19, 20a, 21a, 21ab, 21b, 22c, 23ab,23b, 24, 25, 26, 27, 28a, 29, 30, 31a
H 16	3ab, 16c, 23b, 25, 27, 28a, 29, 30, 31a, 32a, 32b, 33, 34a, 35, 36a, 37
I 16	27, 28a, 30, 31a, 32b, 33, 34a, 35, 36b, 37, 38a
J 17	28a, 28b, 29, 31a, 31b, 32b, 33, 34b, 35, 36b, 38a, 38b, 40, 41, 42, 43a, 44, 45a, 46a, 46b, 47, 49a, 50, 51a, 57a, 63
K 17	42, 43a, 43b, 44b, 45a, 46b, 49b, 50, 51a, 52a
K 18	42, 43b, 44b, 45a, 46b, 49b, 50, 51a, 52a, 57a
L 18	43b, 45a, 45b, 46b, 52a, 53a, 54a, 57a, 63a, 65a
M 18	42, 43b, 44b, 45a, 46b, 51a, 52a, 53, 53a, 54a, 63a, 65a
M 19	42, 46b, 49b, 51b, 52a, 52b, 53b, 54a, 54b, 55, 56, 57b, 59a, 60a, 61a, 61b, 63a, 65b
N 19	42, 51b, 52b, 53b, 54b, 54c, 55, 56, 59b, 60b, 61c, 63b, 65c
O 19	55, 56, 58, 59b, 61c, 65c, 66a, 68
O 20	59b, 66a, 67
P 20	55, 56, 59b, 61c, 65c, 66a, 66b, 67, 68, 69
Q 20	55, 61c, 65c, 68, 69
Q 21	48, 55, 58, 61c, 65c, 66b, 68, 69, 70, 71, 72, 74, 76
R 21	48, 68, 70, 71, 72, 74, 75, 76
S 21	68, 70, 71, 72, 76
S 22	68, 70, 71, 72
T 22	48, 66b, 68, 70, 71, 72, 73, 74, 75
U 22	48, 58, 66b, 68, 70, 71, 72, 74, 75, 77
U 23	48, 64, 66b, 68, 70, 71, 72, 73, 74, 75, 76, 77, 78, 79, 80, 81, 83
V 23	71, 73, 74,76, 77, 78, 79, 80, 81, 82, 83
W 23	78, 81, 83
W 24	78, 81
?	20b

Plate Conversions

SG Plate	Official Plate
1a, ab, b	79
2a, b, c	80
3a, ab	81
3b, c	91
4a	82
4ab, b, c	85
5	89
6a, b	87
7a, b	90
8	88
9, 9a, b, c	84
10a, b	92
11a, b	86
12a, b, c	93
13a, b, c, d	94
14a, b, c, d	96
15	N.M.
16a, b, c	99
17	N.M.
18 and 19	N.M.
20a, b	N.M.
21a	108
21ab, b	110
22, a, b, c	95
23a, ab, b	112
24	N.M.
25	114
26	115
27	116
28a, b	111
29	N.M.
30	N.M.
31a, b	119
32a, b	82
33	125
34a, b	120
35	N.M.
36a, b	121
37	122
38a, b	129
39	—
40	N.M.

SG Plate	Official Plate
41	N.M.
42	N.M.
43a, b	135
44, a, b	134
45a, b	141
46a, b	138
47	N.M.
48	158
49a, b	137
50	N.M.
51a, b	139
52a, b	142
53, a, b	146
54a, b, c	N.M.
55	151
56	N.M.
57a, b	136
58	N.M.
59a, b	147
60a, b	N.M.
61a, b, c	150
63, a, b	140
64	N.M.
65, a, b, c	145
66a, b	154
67	N.M.
68	153
69	N.M.
70	N.M.
71	164
72	163
73	—
74	160
75	N.M.
76	N.M.
77	N.M.
78	N.M.
79	N.M.
80	N.M.
81	N.M.
82	N.M.
83	N.M.

Official Plate	SG Plate
79	1a, ab, b
80	2a, b, c
81	3a, ab
82	4a, 32a, b
83	N.M.
84	9, 9a, b, c
85	4ab, b, c
86	11a, b
87	6a, b
88	8
89	5
90	7a, b
91	3b, c
92	10a, b
93	12a, b, c
94	13a, b, c, d
95	22, a, b, c
96	14a, b, c, d
97	Not sent
98	N.M.
99	16a, b, c
100	N.M.
101	Dud
102	Dud
103	Dud
104	Dud
105	Dud
106	N.M.
107	N.M.
108	21a
109	N.M.
110	21ab, b
111	28a, b
112	23a, ab, b

Official Plate	SG Plate
113	N.M.
114	25
115	26
116	27
117	N.M.
118	N.M.
119	31a, b
120	34a, b
121	36a, b
122	37
123	Dud
124	Dud
125	33
126	Dud
127	Dud
128	Dud
129	38a, b
130	N.M.
131	N.M.
132	N.M.
133	No Entry
134	44a, b
135	43a, b
136	57a, b
137	49a, b
138	46a, b
139	51a, b
140	63, a, b
141	45a, b
142	52a, b
143	N.M.
144	N.M.
145	65, a, b, c
146	53, 53a, b

½d. Green, Type N6. Royal Cypher *The Profile Head Issue* **KING GEORGE V** **NB**

Official Plate	SG Plate
147	59a, b
148	N.M.
149	N.M.
150	61a, b, c
151	55
152	N.M.
153	68
154	66a, b
155	N.M.
156	No Entry
157	N.M.
158	48
159	No Entry
160	74

Official Plate	SG Plate
161	No Entry
162	N.M.
163	72
164	71
165	N.M.
166	N.M.
167	N.M.
168	N.M.
169	N.M.
170	N.M.
171	N.M.
172	May not have been used

1913 *(August)*. **½d. Green, Type N6.** Wmk. Multiple Cypher

N15 (=S.G.397)

	Unmtd mint	Mtd mint	Used
(1) Bright green	£250	£150	£180
(2) Green	£250	£150	£180
a. Watermark sideways	†	†	£18000
b. Block of four	£2000	£1500	
c. Watermark inverted	£1200	£900	
d. Crown missing in watermark		£550	
e. Coil join (vert. pair)		£350	
g. Cracked plate (see N14g)		£300	

Imperforate single from P.O. Registration Sheet..*Price unused* £9000

Originally issued in vertical rolls of 500 stamps. Subsequently sheets or part sheets were found, so that horizontal pairs, blocks and three control pieces are known.

Control. Wmk. Multiple Cypher (block of six)

	Perf. Type	
Control	2 (I/E.)	2A (P./P.)
C 13	£18000	†

Coil
Vertical delivery made up from sheets with joins every tenth stamp

Code No.	Issued	Number in roll	Face value		
G	Aug. 1913	500	£1.0.10	Top delivery	£400

1912 *(8 October)*. **1d. Red, Type N5.** Wmk. Simple Cypher

N16 (=S.G.357/61)

	Unmtd mint	Mtd mint	Used
(1) Bright scarlet	3·00	1·00	1·00
(2) Deep bright scarlet	30·00	20·00	5·00
(3) Scarlet	2·00	1·00	1·00
(4) Deep scarlet	15·00	9·00	1·00
(5) Brick-red	7·00	5·00	1·00
(6) Deep brick-red	£140	90·00	30·00
(7) Vermilion	9·00	5·00	2·50
(8) Pale red	22·00	15·00	2·50
(9) Pale rose-red	30·00	20·00	5·00
(10) Pink	£375	£300	
(10a) Carmine	£175	£125	—
(11) Carmine-red	20·00	11·00	5·00
(12) Bright carmine-red	30·00	20·00	5·00
(13) Deep carmine-red	£550	£400	£100
(14) Scarlet-vermilion (1913 & 1918)	£180	£125	50·00
(15) Orange-vermilion (1917-19)	£225	£150	50·00
(16) Deep orange-vermilion (1918)	£550	£375	£100
a. Without watermark	£250	£125	£150
b. Watermark inverted	4·00	2·00	1·00
c. Watermark reversed	£125	85·00	85·00
d. Watermark inverted and reversed	6·00	3·00	3·00
e. Tête-bêche (pair)	—	£80000	†
f. Printed on the back*	£450	£300	†
fb. Printed double, one albino with C 13 control Strip of 3		£5500	
g. Varnish ink (controls C 13, G 15)		£3000	
h. Q for O (Control E 14, R. 1/4)	£240	£175	£175
i. Q for O (Control T 22, R. 4/11)†	£450	£350	£190
j. Reversed Q for O (Pl. 96, Control T 22, R. 15/9)	£400	£300	£240
k. Inverted Q for O (Pl. 114b, Control V 23, R. 20/3)	£500	£375	£240
ka. Inverted and reversed Q for O and spot in centre (R. 2/3 of booklet pane with wmk upright)		£350	
l. Broken frame (Pl. 17, R. 19/12)		£300	
m. Broken corner (Pl. 43, R. 19/10)		£300	
n. Spot under eye (Pl. ?, R. 20/12)		£250	
na. White spot on King's eyebrow (Pl. 104, R. 20/10)			
o. Ragged beard (Pl. ?, R. 1/12)		£350	
p. Large blob over ear (transient flaw) (Pl. 67a, Control J 17, R. 19/11)		£400	
q. Two white dots below "POSTAGE" (Pl. 33, R. 19/11)		£300	
r. Coil join (vert. pair)			
ra. Coil join (horiz. pair) (9.20)			
s. "Specimen", Type 23		£200	
t. "Specimen", Type 26		£250	
u. Do. Imperf.		90·00	
w. "Cancelled", Type 24		80·00	
x. Do. Imperf.		90·00	

Imperforate tête-bêche pair from P.O. Registration Sheet...*Unused tête-bêche pair* £20000

*The impression on variety f is set sideways, and is very pale. No. N16fb is similar to the same variety listed under N14r.

†There are two versions of variety i as illustrated but it is not known if they occur in different positions or whether one is a second state of the other.

Shade (10) shows a distinctive fluorescence under long-wave ultraviolet.

N16i   N16i   N16j

N16h   N16k   N16ka

117

KING GEORGE V The Profile Head Issue 1d. Red, Type N5. Royal Cypher

N16l  N16m
N16n  N16na 
N16o  N16p 
N16q 

zh. Missing Crown GvR .... 70·00
zi. Missing left side to R .... —
zj. Missing tail to R ("GvP") .... 20·00
zk. Long tail to G .... 35·00

Controls. Prices are for unused singles.
Harrison Printings:

	Perf. Type	
Control	2 (E)	2A (P)
C 12	3·00	3·00
C 13	2·00	2·00
C 14	6·00	6·00
D 14	2·00	2·00
E 14	2·00	2·00
F 15	2·00	2·00
G 15	3·00	3·00
H 16	2·00	2·00
I 16	2·00	2·00
J 17	2·00	2·00
K 17	4·00	4·00
K 18	3·00	3·00
L 18	5·00	5·00
M 18	15·00	15·00
M only ("18" omitted)	£14000	†
M 19	10·00	10·00
N 19	2·00	2·00
O 19	10·00	10·00
O 20	15·00	15·00
P 20	2.50	2.50
Q 20	5·00	5·00
Q 21 (c)	20·00	20·00
Q 21 (w)	20·00	20·00
R 21	10·00	10·00
S 21	15·00	15·00
S 22	10·00	10·00
T 22	5·00	5·00
U 22	20·00	12·00
U 23	15·00	12·00
V 23	2·00	2·00
W 23	8·00	5·00
W 24	40·00	40·00

(c) "close" and (w) "wide" refer to the space between "Q" and "2" (5.75 mm and 7 mm respectively).

Variety Type 2(c) (I/I)
strips of three

D 14	£150
J 17	—
N 19	—
T 22	—

Variety Type 3(P/E)
strip of three

G 15	—

Only a single strip of the control G 15 is known in perf Type 3 format and currently, there is no evidence that Harrison used a Type 3 perforator on any other Royal Cypher issues.

Watermark varieties known:
Wmk upright, Type I: C 12, C 13.
Wmk inverted, Type I: C 12.
Wmk reversed, Type I: C 12.
Wmk inverted and reversed, Type I: C 12.
Wmk upright, Type II: C 13, C 14, D 14, E 14, F 15, G 15, H 16, I 16, J 17, K 17, K 18, N 19, O 19, O 20, P 20, Q 21(c), R 21, S 22, T 22, U 22, U 23, V 23, W 23, W 24.
Wmk inverted, Type II: C 13, D 14, E 14, F 15, G 15, I 16, M 19, U 23, V 23, W 23, W 24.
Wmk reversed, Type II: D 14, G 15, H 16, I 16.
Wmk inverted and reversed, Type II: C 13, C 14, D 14, E 14, F 15, G 15, H 16, I 16, U 23, V 23, W 23, W 24.

Watermark Varieties. The following have been recorded:
Wmk upright: Types I, II, III
Wmk inverted: Types I, II, III
Wmk reversed: Types I, II, III
Wmk inverted and reversed: Types I, II, III

Misplaced Watermarks
ya. Single stamp showing letters from "POSTAGE" .... 15·00
yb. Vertical strip sufficient to show complete "POSTAGE" watermark £190
yc. Vertical strip sufficient to show complete "POSTAGE" watermark, with selvedge attached, the selvedge having the "POSTAGE" watermark inverted.

Broken Dandy Roll Varieties
za. Missing Crown .... 55·00
zb. Missing G .... 30·00
zc. Missing v .... 30·00
zd. Missing R .... 35·00
zf. Missing vR .... 35·00
zg. Missing Crown vR .... 35·00

1d. Red, Type N5. Royal Cypher *The Profile Head Issue* **KING GEORGE V**

Wmk upright, Type III: J 17, K 17, K 18, L 18, M 18, M only, M 19, N 19, O 19, O 20, P 20, Q 20, Q 21(c), Q 21(w), R 21, S 21, S 22, T 22, U 22, U 23, V 23, W 23, W 24.
Wmk inverted, Type III: J 17, K 17, K 18, L 18, N 19, O 20, P 20, Q 20, Q 21, R 21, S 21, S 22, T 22.
Wmk reversed, Type III: K 17, L 18, M 19, P 20, Q 20, R 21, S 21, T 22.
Wmk inverted and reversed, Type III: J 17, K 17, K 18, L 18, M 18, M 19, N 19, O 19, O 20, P 20, Q 20, Q 21, R 21, S 22, T 22.

Coils
Vertical delivery made up from sheets with joins every tenth stamp

Code No.	Issued	Number in roll	Face value		
A	1913	1000	£4.3.4	Top delivery	£400
B	1913	1000	£4.3.4	Bottom delivery	£400
E	1913	500	£2.1.8	Top delivery	£300
F	1913	500	£2.1.8	Bottom delivery	£300
KERMODE	Mid-1920	1000	£4.3.4	Top delivery	£200

Experimental coils from continuous reels with vertical delivery
| E | 1923 | 500 | £2.1.8 | Top delivery | — |

Sideways delivery made up from sheets with joins every 12th stamp
| O | Sept. 1920 | 480 | £2.0.0 | Left side delivery | £150 |

In 1915 1d. stamps were printed on paper of better quality, known as "currency" paper made by William Joynson & Son. This was an imperforate printing and the watermark employed was Simple Cypher. It is understood that plate 28a was used, but there was no control number. The paper needed more ink than normal, to give a good print, and the sheets were eventually perforated, made into coils and sold through automatic vending machines.
Imperforate remainders... £1000
Imperforate, "cancelled", Type 24, bottom right corner pair without control .... —

Bromides

Bromide of Eve's "Lion couchant" design

Stamp-size bromide of Eve's "Lion Couchant"
 design with varying degrees of shading £1600
Stamp-size bromides of completed frame (1d. or 2½d.) produced to allow comparison of different portrait sizes .... *From* £1600

Die Proofs

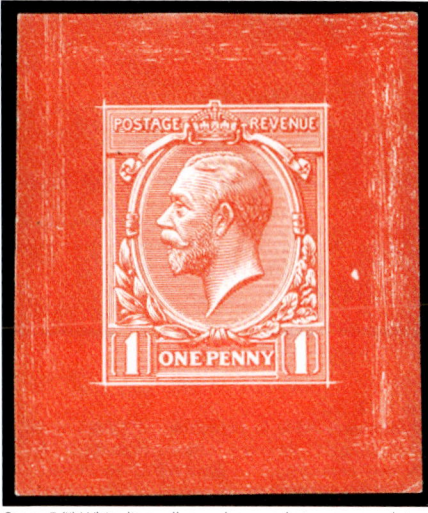

Stage 5 (ii) White lines all round, crossed at corners and stepped at left opposite the King's nose.

Stage 5. Completed by 30 May 1912 but subsequently slightly amended and hardened for working purposes about the end of June. On proof paper, card or watermarked paper. Uncleared with white guide lines
(i) In black on proof paper. Thin white lines all round ....
(ii) In deep rose-red, bright scarlet, ultramarine
      or black (*illustrated*) .... *From* £5500
(iii) In red on gummed Crown watermarked
      paper (upright).. £5500
(iv) In red on gummed Crown watermarked
      paper (sideways)... £8000
(v) In red on gummed Multiple Cypher
      watermarked paper (inverted) £8500
(vi) In black on proof paper. Left-hand line thicker
      and without step..

Colour Trials
In die proof form, cleared with "stepped" frame at left corrected.
(i) In red on gummed Multiple Cypher
      watermarked paper.. £3250
(ii) In red, geranium pink or geranium blue on
      gummed Simple Cypher watermarked paper............. £8000
(iii) In red on gummed "NHI" (National Health
      Insurance" watermarked paper...................... £7000
(iv) In red on gummed Crown watermarked paper.......... £3250
    (i) and (iii) are known with two impressions on a single piece.
In die proof form but cut close to margins, so imperf
On thick paper or thin card
In four shades of red including geranium blue,
      also in blue .... *From* £2750
On paper watermarked Imperial Crown (vertical or sideways).
In four shades of red including geranium blue,
      also in blue .... *From* £3000

NB KING GEORGE V The Profile Head Issue 1d. Red, Type N5. Royal Cypher

1912 Colour Trial

Trials in 1912

Colour trials were made in eight different shades of red on paper with Simple Cypher watermark, perforated 15× 14.

They were printed from 1d. plate No. 1/199, 240-set, with Control C/X 8/12 in the bottom margin, together with a 1d. stamp of King Edward VII which was left imperforate. See Section NA, under King Edward VII Colour Trials.

As with the colour essays of the 1911 issue some were marked with the colour makers' reference numbers as shown below. The colours in the second column are as we would describe them.

Inscribed	Shade
A M/B Scarlet 25568	Pale scarlet-vermilion
B M/B Scarlet 25569	Scarlet-vermilion
C S.P Scarlet I	Deep scarlet-vermilion
D M/B Scarlet 25612	Scarlet
E M/B Scarlet 25602	Bright scarlet
F S.E. Scarlet 3181	Rose-red (present colour)
G Scarlet 1182	Deep rose-red
H Blue Geranium	Carmine-lake

The colour makers were Mander Bros. (A, B, D, E); Slater & Palmer (C) and Shackell Edwards & Co. (F, G, H).

As far as is known only two sheets of each were prepared, one of which is in the Royal Philatelic Collection.

In carmine-lake ("Blue Geranium") £500
In the other seven shades .... From £425
Block of 12 (6 × 2) from right of sheet similar to
    that illustrated ....

Trials in 1916 and 1918

Perforated 15 × 14. Watermark Simple Cypher
In brown-red (1916) overprinted "Cancelled", Type 24 .... £525

In 1916 experiments were carried out using inks supplied by British Dyes Ltd; described as Monolite Fast Scarlet, Monolite Red and Monolite Fast Red (Paranitraniline Red). The latter is brown-red and is listed above but the others were close to issued shades and so are not listed separately.

In 1918 experiments were carried out using inks supplied by Mander Bros in shades of scarlet. These stamps, "Cancelled" Type 24, are close to issued shades so are not listed separately. These trial stamps should not be confused with issued stamps listed as No. N16w.

1d. Advertisement Trials

About 1922 the Post Office prepared trial advertisements on the back of the issued 1d. stamps with "Specimen" overprint.

Different advertisements were used on the same sheet and we illustrate one of these. The project was not proceeded with and so the stamps were never issued.
Overprinted "Specimen" Type 23 No. N16s.
(a) "Route Cablegrams" £400
(b) "The P. O. Savings Bank" £400
(c) "Instal the Telephone" £500

Sheet format was 12 × 20 comprising the quantities of 132(a), 76(b) and 32(c). The layout of the three advertisements differs between the upper and lower panes.

Plate Markings

Plate	Marking
1	No marking
2a	Dot under left serif of P of R. 20/1
2b	Added ½ dot (inner) and dot R. 20 left side, 8 mm.
3a	Dot under E(N) of R. 20/2
3b	Added two dots under O(N)E of R. 20/3
3c	Added dot and ½ dot (outer) R. 20 left side, 10·5 mm.
4a	Small dot under P of R. 20/3
4b	Added minute dot at left, under R. 20/3. Dash with indentation adjacent R.15 right side, 5mm.
5a	Dot under P of R. 20/4; tiny nick under NN of R. 20/11
5b	Added dot under N(N) of R. 20/4. Notch to rule under R. 20/10
5c	Added dot under N(E) of R. 20/1
6a	Dot under PE of R. 20/1
6b	Added dot under N(E) of R. 20/1 Dot R. 18 right side, 10 mm. Rule under R. 20/11 thin
7	Dot under P of R. 20/3 ½ dot (inner) R. 17 left side, 12·5 mm. Dot R. 17 right side, 10 mm. Nick left base of R. 20/12. Rule under R. 20/11 thin.
8a	Slanting internal cut under PE of R. 20/1
8b	Added small dot under (P)E of R. 20/5
8c	Added ½ dot (inner) and dot bulging (inner) R. 20 left side, 8·5, 7 mm.
9	Dot R. 20 left side, 13·5 mm.
10a	2 large dots under (O)N, E(N) of R. 20/2
10b	Added long dot under EP of R. 20/2
11a	Dot (breaking right) R. 18 right side, 10 mm.
11b	Added small dot R. 18 right side, 4·75 mm., the original dot now bulging right
12	Dot (central) R. 18 right side, 12 mm.
13	Long dot (breaking right) R. 19 left side, 8 mm.
14a	Dot R. 19 left side, 12 mm. Two internal cuts to left of O and under O of R. 20/2
14b	Added two internal cuts under NE and P of R. 20/2
15	Dot R. 17 right side, 8·75 mm.
16	Small dot R. 20 left side, 7·75 mm. Dot R. 18 right side, 11 mm. Top R. 19 left side bevelled.
17	Triangular dot under E(N) of R. 20/2
18	Triangular dot under P of R. 20/3

1d. Red, Type N5. Royal Cypher *The Profile Head Issue* KING GEORGE V

Plate	Marking
19	Irregular dot, which is large and sometimes plain, but at other times hardly visible (top) under EN of R. 20/4. Small dot above R. 1/11 upper pane.
20	Small dot R. 18 right side, 11 mm. Rule thinner at top.
21	Dot R. 18 right side, 7·5 mm.
22	Dot (bulging right) R. 17 right side, 11 mm.
23	½ cut (base) and ½ dot (top) under (N)N of R. 20/1
24	2 small dots under ONE of R. 20/2
25	Two small dots at left and under PE of R. 20/4
26	Dot breaking left R. 18 right side, 11·75 mm.
27	Small dot R. 18 right side, 12 mm.
28	Dot (right) R. 18 right side, 11 mm.
29a	Dot (left) R. 20 left side, 12·5 mm. Tiny nick (inner) R. 20 right side 19·5 mm.
29b	Added cut to left of O below R. 20/1. Added large dot to left of O below R. 20/4
30	Flat oval dot under EN of R. 20/1
31	Dot (breaking base) under EP of R. 20/2
32a	¾ dot (base) left of O of R. 20/3
32b	Added large dot R. 20 left side, 10 mm.
33	Dot under O of R. 20/4. Dot R. 18 right side, 12·25 mm. Base of R. 20/10 damaged at right
34	Dot R. 18 right side, 8·5 mm.
35	Minute nick under NY of R. 20/11. Dot R. 17 right side, 10 mm. (Smaller and more regular than Pl. 7)
36	Curved dot under PEN of R. 20/1 (breaking base)
37a	Dot R. 20 left side, 8·75 mm. Right end of rule under R. 20/3 damaged
37b	Added slanting ¾ cut (base) under PE of R. 20/3
37c	Added wide ¾ cut (base) under PEN of R. 20/2
38a	Curved dot under PE of R. 20/3
38b	Added dot R. 19 left side, 11 mm.
39a	Curved dot under E(P) of R. 20/3
39b	Added curved dot under PE of R. 20/4
40a	Dot under (N)E of R. 20/3; dot under P of R. 20/7. Dot R. 18 left side, 13 mm. Dot R. 19 left side, 11 mm. (breaking inner)
40b	Added dot R. 17 left side, 11·25 mm.
41	Dot under N(E) of R. 20/4. Dot under P of R. 20/8 ½ dot (inner) R. 17 left side, 12 mm.
42a	Dot under P of R. 20/6
42b	Added dot under EN of R. 20/1 and under EN of R. 20/2
43	Horizontal gash (base) under PE of R. 20/1
44	Dot under P of R. 20/1. Dot under P of R. 20/5. Dot R. 20 left side, 10·5 mm. Dot R. 17 left side, 14 mm.
45	Large dot breaking base under EN of R. 20/2. Dot R. 20 left side, 10 mm. Dot R. 19 left side, 12·5 mm.
46a	Curved dot under NE of R. 20/3
46b	Added large irregular curved dot under EPE of R. 20/1
47	Small dot under P of R. 20/2
48	Curved dot under N(N) of R. 20/2. Dot under NE of R. 20/3 which later became larger oval dot (breaking base)
49	Dot under NE of R. 20/2; minute dot under ON of R. 20/12. X cut R. 20 left side, 12–14 mm.
50	Large ½ dot (base) under PE of R. 20/2. Dot R. 19 left side, 10 mm.
51	½ dot (top) under PE of R. 20/3
52	Dot under PE of R. 20/1
53a	Large dot (breaking top) under EP of R. 20/3. Long dot R. 19 right side, 11 mm. Cut R. 15 left side, 12·5 mm. Rules at sides thick
53b	Added large dot (breaking base) under EN of R. 20/1
54	Indent (base) under ON of R. 20/5. Dot (breaking inner) R. 19 left side, 10 mm.
55	Dot R. 20 left side, 11·5 mm. The rule is 23 mm. high (see Plate 119)
56a	Small oval dot under PE of R. 20/1. Base (outer) R. 20 left side rounded
56b	Added dot (top) under (N)E of R. 20/3
57	Dash under EN and dot under (N)N of R. 20/1. Dot and irregular ½ cut (base) under EP of R. 20/2. Dot (base) under NE of R. 20/3. Four cuts R. 19 right side, 9·5–11 mm.
58	Large dot (breaking top) under PEN of R. 20/2
59	Oval cut under EP of R. 20/2. Nick (base) at right end of R. 20/10

Plate	Marking
60	Dot under P of R. 20/2. Two oval cuts under PE of R. 20/3
61a	Dot and oval dot under EPE of R. 20/2. Large dot (breaking top) under NE of R. 20/4
61b	Added large dot (top) under N(N) of R. 20/4
62	Irregular dot with spur breaking base under E(P) of R. 20/4
63	Dot under EP and dash to the right of Y of R. 20/4. Nick (outer) R. 20 left side, 10 mm. Dot R. 17 left side, 15·25 mm. Base R. 20 left side bevelled. ½ dot (top) above to right of rule
64	Inverted V cut (base) under (P)E of R. 20/2
65a	Indent (base) under NN of R. 20/11
65b	Added diagonal cut with internal nick below it R. 18 right side, 10 mm., 9·5 mm.
66	X cut R. 17 right side, 14·5 mm. X cut and straight cut R. 18 right side, 13·5, 12·5 mm.
67a	Two dots over two cuts R. 19 right side, 9, 13 mm. Rule under R. 20/11 thinner. Dot (top) under P of R. 20/3
67b	Added X cut R. 17 right side, 10 mm. X cut R. 18 right side, 10·5 mm.
68a	Dot (breaking base) under P of R. 20/1
68b	Added half dot (breaking base) under NE of R. 20/2
68c	Added three dots under PE, NN to right of Y of R. 20/11
69a	Dot (base) under PE of R. 20/1
69b	Added dot R. 20 left side, 13·75 mm.
70a	Dot under EN of R. 20/2
70b	Added two irregular dots breaking top and base under (P)E of R. 20/3
71	½ dot (top) under PE of R. 20/10. Small dot R. 18 right side, 6 mm.
72	Nick (base) at right end of R. 20/11
73a	Dot R. 18 right side, 9·5 mm.
73b	Added dot under (N)N of R. 20/1. Added ½ dot (inner) R. 20 left side, 9·25 mm.
74	Dot (base) under EP of R. 20/2. Dot (central) R. 19 left side, 14 mm.
75a	Dot central joined by small ½ cut bottom of rule to left of O of R. 20/9. Dot (sometimes breaking base) to left of P of R. 20/10. Two dots, left of O and under (N)E of R. 20/2
75b	Added slanting ½ cut R. 18 right side (inner)
76	Diagonal cut R. 19 right side, 14-13 mm. Thin tapering cut, 13 mm. (forming a rudimentary V)
77a	Dot under (P)E of R. 20/1. ½ dot (inner) R. 20 left side, 11·75 mm. Dot R. 19 left side, 11·5 mm.
77b	Added dot (outer) R. 19 left side, 13·25 mm.
78	Cut at right of R. 20/1
79	Dot under EP of R. 20/1
80a	Dot under EN of R. 20/2. Dot R. 19 left side, 10·5 mm.
80b	Added four dots under EN, NY of R. 20/11
81	Dot under (N)E of R. 20/10
82	Dot (top) under EP of R. 20/2
83	Dot R. 20 left side breaking outer, 10·5 mm. Rule R. 20 left side bevelled at base. Tiny nick (base) under EP of R. 20/4. Nick below N(N) of R. 20/6
84	½ dot (base) at extreme left of R. 20/11
85	Dot R. 19 left side, 10·5 mm.
86	Cut under (P)E of R. 20/2. Two tall dots R. 2 left side, 10, 14·5 mm.
87a	Dot (breaking inner) R. 20 right side, 12 mm.
87b	Added dot under PE of R. 20/10
88a	Dot R. 17 right side, 3 mm.
88b	Added dot R. 19 left side, 7 mm.
89	Dot (inner) R. 18 right side, 9·75 mm.
90	Tall dot R. 17 right side, 12·5 mm.
91	Dot R. 18 right side, 9·5 mm. Minute nick R. 19 right side, 12.75mm.
92	Three cuts R. 20 right side, 8, 12·5, 17 mm. Small dot R. 17 right side, 5·5 mm. Minute dot R. 20 left side, 6·5 mm.
93	Four half cuts (outer) R. 20 right side, 5, 8·75, 12·25, 15·5 mm. Dot R. 18 right side, 10.5mm.
94	Tiny dot (inner) R. 20 left side, 12 mm.
95	Large dot (breaking left) R. 18 right side, 11·5 mm.
96	Left of R. 20/12 thinner. Dot R. 17 right side, 9mm.

NB KING GEORGE V The Profile Head Issue 1d. Red, Type N5. Royal Cypher

Plate	Marking
97a	½ dot (base) under (P)E of R. 20/1
97b	Added dot joined to tiny dot, R. 20 left side, 9·5 mm.
98	Vacant
99	Tall dot R. 20 right side, 12 mm. (Waterlow Plate 3)
100	Dot R. 20 left side, 13·5 mm.; two small cuts left of O and under O of R. 20/3
101	Fine tall dot R. 19 left side, 8·25 mm. Notch at end of R. 20/12 (Waterlow Plate 5)
102	Thick irregular cut R. 19 right side, 14·25–13 mm., thin tapering cut, 13 mm. (Rather similar to Plate 76, but the upper cut is thicker and longer)
103	Dot R. 18 right side, 10 mm.; fine diagonal cut R. 19 right side with outer part of rule indented, 10 mm.
104	Thin X cut over diagonal cut R. 17 right side, 7 mm. Internal crescent cut R. 20 left side, 11 mm.
105	Dot breaking top under right serif of P of R. 20/9
106	Dot inner right side of R. 8 right side, 10·5 mm. Large oval ½ dot (top) under PE of R. 20/9. Dot breaking inner R.18 right side, 11.5mm
107	Dot (base) under EP of R. 20/9
108	Dot (base) under P of R. 20/9 (bulging base). Rules at sides, particularly the left, very irregular
109	Cut R. 15 left side, 12·5 mm. Rules at sides thinner than Plate 53
110	Cut R. 16 left side, 12 mm.
111	Tiny dot under PE of R. 20/3. Rule R. 19 left side very thick. Rule R. 20 left side tapers slightly at base
112	Small dot (inner) R. 18 left side, 11 mm. Small dot under P of R. 20/2. Dot under PE of R. 20/3. Nick (inner) R. 18 right side, 21 mm.
113	Minute nick R. 19 right side, 16 mm. Tall dot (breaking left) R. 18 right side, 12 mm.
114a	Cut with central dot under O of R. 20/3. Tiny dot above R. 1/5
114b	Added two cuts with central dots, R. 20 left side, 13, 17·5 mm. (Waterlow Plate 1)
115	Small dot R. 18 right side, 16 mm.
116	Dot R. 18 right side, 10 mm.
117	Dot R. 17 right side, 12 mm.; dot R. 18 right side, 14 mm. ½ dot (top) above R. 1/1 to left of rule
118	Tiny ½ dot (outer) R. 20 right side, 5·5 mm. Large irregular dot R. 19 left side, 10·75 mm. (Waterlow Plate 4)
119	Dot (breaking inner) R. 20 left side, 11·5 mm. The rule is 22·75 mm. high (to distinguish from plate 55)
120	Minute nick (outer) R. 20 left side, 2·5 mm. (Waterlow Plate 6)
121	Small dot R. 20 left side, 11·75 mm. Rule damaged R. 15 right side. Tiny dot above R. 1/3
122	Small dot under PE of R. 20/8 (seen on control R. 21)
123	2 intersecting dots (cut and ½ dot breaking line) R. 18 right side, 12 mm.
124	Dot R. 17 right side, 10 mm.
125	Semi-circular cut-out with adjacent crescent R. 19 right side, 4 mm.
126	Dot R. 18 right side, 22.5mm.
127	Internal downward sloping dash R. 19 right side, 10mm.
128	Dot R. 18 right side, 10mm.

Index to Marginal Markings
Top Margin, Stamp Numbers

Stamp No.	Plate
1	63, 117
3	121
5	114a, 114b
11	19

Bottom Margin, Stamp Numbers

Stamp No.	Plate
1	2a, 2b, 5c, 6a, 6b, 8a, 8b, 8c, 23, 29b, 30, 36, 42b, 43, 44, 46b, 52, 53b, 56a, 56b, 57, 68a, 68b, 68c, 69a, 69b, 73b, 77a, 77b, 78, 79, 97a, 97b
2	3a, 3b, 10a, 10b, 14a, 14b, 17, 24, 31, 37c, 42b, 45, 47, 48, 49, 50, 57, 58, 59, 60, 61a, 61b, 64, 68b, 68c, 70a, 70b, 74, 75a, 75b, 80a, 80b, 82, 86, 112
3	3b, 4a, 4b, 7, 18, 32a, 32b, 37a, 37b, 37c, 38a, 38b, 39a, 39b, 40a, 40b, 46a, 46b, 48, 51, 53a, 53b, 56b, 57, 60, 67a, 67b, 70b, 100, 111, 112, 114a, 114b
4	5a, 5b, 5c, 19, 25, 29b, 33, 39b, 41, 61a, 61b, 62, 63, 83
5	8b, 8c, 44, 54
6	42a, 42b, 83
7	40a, 40b
8	41
9	75a, 105, 106, 107, 108
10	33, 59, 71, 75a, 75b, 81, 87b
11	6b, 7, 35, 65a, 65b, 67a, 67b, 68c, 72, 80b, 84
12	7, 49, 96

Left Margin, Row Numbers

Row No.	Plate
2	86
15	53a, 53b, 109
16	110
17	7, 40b, 41, 44, 63
18	40a, 40b, 112
19	13, 14a, 14b, 16, 38b, 40a, 40b, 45, 50, 54, 74, 77b, 80a, 80b, 85, 88b, 91b, 101, 111, 118
20	2b, 3c, 8c, 9, 16, 29a, 29b, 32b, 37a, 37b, 37c, 44, 45, 49, 55, 56a, 56b, 63, 69b, 73b, 77a, 77b, 83, 92, 94, 97b, 100, 104, 111, 114b, 119, 120, 121

Right Margin, Row Numbers

Row No.	Plate
15	4b, 121
17	7, 15, 22, 35, 66, 67b, 88a, 88b, 90, 92, 96, 104, 117, 124
18	6b, 11a, 11b, 12, 16, 20, 21, 26, 27, 28, 33, 34, 65b, 66, 67b, 71, 73a, 73b, 75b, 89, 91a, 93, 95, 96, 103, 106, 112, 113, 115, 116, 117, 123, 126, 128
19	53a, 53b, 57, 67a, 67b, 76, 91, 102, 103, 113, 127
20	87a, 87b, 92, 93, 99, 118

No Marking: Plate 1

Control Schedule
Control Plates with which it was used

C 12	1, 2a, 3a, 4a, 5a, 6a, 6b, 7
C 13	1, 2a, 2b, 3a, 3b, 3c, 4a, 4b, 5a, 5b, 5c, 6b, 7, 8a, 8b, 8c, 9, 10a, 11a, 11b, 12, 15, 16, 25
C 14	4b, 5c, 8c, 12, 13, 14a, 15, 16, 19, 43
D 14	9, 12, 13, 14a, 15, 16, 17, 18, 19, 20, 21, 22, 25, 43
E 14	10b, 12, 14b, 15, 16, 17, 18, 19, 22, 23, 24, 25, 26, 27, 28, 29a, 37a
F 15	16, 29b, 30, 31, 32a, 33, 34, 35, 37a, 52
G 15	27, 29b, 32b, 33, 35, 36, 37a, 37b, 37c, 38a, 39a, 39b, 40a, 41, 42a, 42b, 43, 44, 52, 55, 64
H 16	30, 31, 36, 37c, 38a, 39b, 40a, 40b, 41, 42b, 44, 45, 46a, 55, 110, 125
I 16	38a, 38b, 40b, 41, 46b, 47, 48, 49, 50, 51, 53a, 54, 55, 109, 125
J 17	49, 51, 53a, 53b, 55, 56a, 56b, 57, 58, 59, 60, 61a, 61b, 62, 63, 65a, 65b, 66, 67a, 67b, 69a, 72, 73a, 76, 102, 104, 111
K 17	49, 63, 65a, 66, 67b, 68a, 69b, 70a, 71, 72, 73a, 74, 76, 104, 105, 112
K 18	63, 65a, 65b, 68b, 70b, 71, 72, 74, 75a, 76, 77a, 80a, 104, 105, 107
L 18	70b, 74, 75a, 76, 77a, 103, 104, 105, 107,127
M 18	69b, 70b, 71, 74, 103, 104
M 19	70b, 71, 73a, 77b, 78, 80a, 105
N 19	68c, 73b, 75a, 78, 79, 80a, 80b, 81, 82, 84, 108,127
O 19	75a, 78, 79
O 20	75b, 90, 113, 119
P 20	68a, 68c, 73b, 80b, 85, 87a, 88a, 89, 95
Q 20	85, 87a, 113
Q 21	87a, 88b, 113
R 21	72, 75b, 87a, 87b, 89, 113, 122
S 21	75b, 87b, 96, 106, 122
S 22	83, 86, 87b, 91, 94, 96, 97b, 114a
T 22	86, 87b, 91, 92, 93, 94, 96, 106
U 22	87b, 91, 92, 93, 94, 97b, 116

1d. Red, Type N5, Royal Cypher *The Profile Head Issue* **KING GEORGE V** **NB**

Control	Plates with which it was used
U 23	91, 92, 93, 97b
V 23	92, 93, 101, 114b, 115, 117, 118, 121
W 23	83, 86, 99, 101, 115, 118,123
W 24	99, 101, 117, 120, 123, 124
?	97a, 100

1913 (August). 1d. Red, Type N5, Wmk. Multiple Cypher

N17 (=S.G.398)

	Unmtd mint	Mtd mint	Used
(1) Scarlet	£350	£225	£225
(2) Dull scarlet	£350	£225	£225
(3) Bright scarlet			
a. Block of four	£3000	£2000	
c. Watermark inverted	£1600	£1100	
d. Crown missing in watermark		£500	
e. Coil join (vert. pair)		£600	

Shade (3) reacts golden red under long-wave ultraviolet light.

Imperforate single from P.O. Registration Sheet..Price unused £9000

Originally issued in vertical rolls of 500 stamps. Subsequently sheets or part sheets were found, so that horizontal pairs, blocks and three control pieces are known.

Control. Wmk. Multiple Cypher (block of six)

	Perf. Type
Control	2 (I/E).
C 13	£18000

Coil

Vertical delivery made up from sheets with joins every tenth stamp

Code No.	Issued	Number in roll	Face value		
E	Aug. 1913	500	£2.1.8	Top delivery	£450

1922. 1d. Red. Type N5. Wmk. Simple Cypher. Somerset House Experimental Printing

N17A

	Unmtd mint	Mtd mint	Used
Pale scarlet	£875	£525	£525
b. Coil join (vert. pair)		£1700	
s. "Specimen", Type 30		£1000	

This was probably from a 1921 experimental coil printing made by Somerset House on Simple Cypher watermarked paper. It is distinguishable from No. N16 in pale red by its very coarse impression, whilst the paper is also rougher and of a different texture. Possibly it had not been plate-glazed.

The wording on the coil leaders has been reset and lacks Harrison's name. The leader and tail joins were crudely made using coarse white paper but more often brown or red paper, quite different from the Harrison joins. The trailers were invariably blank but some of the Harrison trailers were stamped with "JOINED BY . . ." and "DATE . . ." for record purposes and the paper was usually yellow.

Coil Trial

Unwatermarked from pane of 90 (9 × 10)180 - set at Somerset House

No watermark. Imperforate in pale scarlet £1000

Coil

Vertical delivery printed in continuous reels

Code No.	Issued	Number in roll	Face value		
E	1922	500	£2.1.8	Top delivery	£2000

1912 (15 October). 1½d. Red-brown, Type N6. Wmk. Simple Cypher

N18 (=S.G.362/65)

	Unmtd mint	Mtd mint	Used
(1) Red-brown	10·00	6·00	1·50
(2) Pale red-brown	20·00	14·00	2·50
(3) Deep red-brown	9·00	5·00	1·50
(4) Very deep red-brown (1922)	£450	£300	90·00
(5) Chocolate-brown	20·00	11·00	2·00
(6) Deep chocolate-brown (1918-19)	£140	90·00	10·00
(7) Chocolate (1919)	£450	£300	90·00
(8) Brown (1918)	£600	£400	£150
(9) Pale brown (1918)	£750	£450	£150
(10) Yellow-brown (1916-18)	30·00	20·00	16·00
(11) Deep yellow-brown (1916)	£125	75·00	10·00
(12) Bright yellow-brown (1920-21)	25·00	18·00	8·00
(13) Chestnut	5·00	3·00	1·00
(14) Bright chestnut (1922-23)	£125	75·00	15·00
(15) Orange-brown (1919-20)	10·00	6·00	1·00
(16) Bright orange-brown (1920)	£100	60·00	15·00
a. No watermark	£350	£240	£240
b. Watermark inverted	9·00	5·00	2·00
c. Watermark reversed	70·00	50·00	50·00
d. Watermark inverted and reversed	15·00	8·00	8·00
e. PENCF variety (Pl. 12, R. 15/12)	£400	£300	£250
f. PENCF variety (Pl. 29, R. 15/12)	£175	£125	£110
fa. D. Wmk. Inverted and reversed		£1700	
g. PENCE repaired (Pl. 12, R. 15/12)		£625	
h. PENCE repaired (Pl. 29, R. 15/12)		£475	
ha. Do. No watermark			
i. Blurred beard (Pl. ?, R. ?/12)		£750	
j. Gash behind head (Pl. ?, R. 19/2)		£300	
k. White spot top right corner (vert. coil)		£450	
l. CE damaged (Pl. ?, R. ?/12)		£250	
m. Final E of PENCE damaged (Pl. ?, R. ?/10)		£250	
n. Top frame damaged (Pl. 15b, Control N 19, R 20/2)		£275	
o. Break in shading at left (Pl. 16a, b, R. 20/2)		75·00	
p. Frame break at bottom below second E (Pl. 45, R. 20/2)		85·00	
r. Coil join (vert. pair) (8.18)			
ra. Coil join (horiz. pair) (5.20)			
s. "Specimen", Type 23		£125	
t. "Specimen", Type 26		£300	
u. "Cancelled", Type 24		£500	

Imperforate tête-bêche pair from P.O. Registration Sheet..Unused tête-bêche pair £20000

NB KING GEORGE V   The Profile Head Issue   1½d. Red-brown, Type N6.   Royal Cypher

N18e/f

N18p

N18g/h "Pence" repaired

The PENCF variety and corrected versions from philatelic plate 12a (thin rule) and plate 29 (thick rule)

These are the philatelic plate numbers not the official plates which were 14/585 and 15/586. The error was found and repaired by the printer on 18 March 1921 and exists only on these two plates.

N18i

N18j

N18k

Nos. N18i/j were not fully constant, nevertheless a number of examples are known

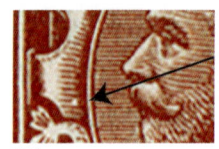

N18l

N18m

N18n

N18o

Watermark Varieties. The following have been recorded:
Wmk upright: Types I, II, III
Wmk inverted: Types II, III
Wmk reversed: Types II, III
Wmk inverted and reversed: Types I, II, III
  No. N18a came from a sheet without watermark.

Misplaced Watermarks
ya. Single stamp showing letters from "POSTAGE" .... 15·00
yb. Vertical strip sufficient to show complete
       "POSTAGE" watermark £275
yc. Vertical strip sufficient to show complete
       "POSTAGE" watermark with selvedge
       attached, the selvedge showing "POSTAGE"
       watermark inverted ....

Broken Dandy Roll Varieties
za. Missing Crown .... 55·00
zb. Missing G .... 25·00
zc. Missing v .... 25·00
zd. Missing R .... 25·00
ze. Missing Gv .... 25·00
zf. Missing vR .... 25·00
zg. Missing Crown vR .... 25·00
zj. Missing tail to R ("GvP") .... 20·00
zk. Long tail to G .... 55·00

Controls. Prices are for unused singles.
Somerset House Printings:

	Perf. Type	
Control	2(E.)	2A(P.)
A. 12 (w)	10·00	£225
A. 12 (c)	10·00	£2500

(w) "wide and (c) "close" refer to the spacing between the "A" and the serif of the "1" (4 mm. and 1.75 mm. respectively). A. 12 (w) was the first control used.

Watermark varieties known:
Wmk upright, Type I: A. 12 (w), A. 12 (c).
Wmk inverted and reversed, Type I: A. 12 (w), A. 12 (c).

Harrison Printings:

	Perf. Type	
Control	2(E)	2A(P)
C 13	10·00	10·00
D 14	10·00	10·00
F 15	20·00	20·00
G 15	15·00	20·00
H 16	10·00	25·00
J 17	10·00	20·00
K 18	15·00	30·00
18 only (K omitted)	£3000	£2400
L 18	6·00	6·00
M 18	10·00	10·00
M 19	8·00	8·00
19 only (M omitted)	†	£15000
N 19	6·00	6·00
O 19	7·00	7·00
O 20	6·00	6·00
Q 20	20·00	20·00
Q 21 (c)	20·00	20·00
Q 21 (w)	20·00	20·00
T 22	6·00	6·00
U 22	6·00	6·00
U 23	6·00	6·00

1½d. Red-brown, Type N6. Royal Cypher *The Profile Head Issue* **KING GEORGE V** NB

Control	Perf. Type 2(E)	2A(P)
V 23	6·00	6·00
W 23	6·00	6·00
W 24	£300	£275

(c) close and (w) "wide" refer to the space between "Q" and "2" (5.75 mm and 7 mm respectively).

Variety Type 2 (c) (I/I)
strips of three
C 13	—
J 17	£125
N 19	—

Watermark varieties known:
Wmk upright, Type I: C 13.
Wmk upright, Type II: C 13, D 14, F 15, G 15, H 16, J 17, K 18, L 18, N 19, O 19, O 20, Q 21(c), Q 21(w), T 22, U 22, U 23, V 23, W 23, W 24.
Wmk inverted, Type II: U 22, U 23, V 23.
Wmk reversed, Type II: U 22, U 23, W 23.
Wmk inverted and reversed, Type II: C 13, D 14, F 15, G 15, U 22, U 23, V 23, W 23.
Wmk upright, Type III: J 17, K 18, 18 only, L 18, M 18, M 19, 19 only, N 19, O 19, O 20, Q 20, Q 21(c), Q 21(w), T 22, U 22, U 23, V 23, W 23.
Wmk inverted, Type III: L 18, M 18, M 19, N 19, O 19, O 20, Q 21, T 22.
Wmk reversed, Type III: L 18, N 19, Q 21, T 22.
Wmk inverted and reversed, Type III: L 18, M 18, M 19, N 19, O 19, O 20, Q 20, Q 21, T 22.

Coils
Vertical delivery made up from sheets with joins every tenth stamp

Code No.	Issued	Number in roll	Face value		
J	Aug. 1918	1000	£6.5.4	Top delivery	£400
K	Aug. 1918	1000	£6.5.4	Bottom delivery	£400
L	Aug. 1918	500	£3.2.8	Top delivery	£400
M	Aug. 1918	500	£3.2.8	Bottom delivery	£400

Sideways delivery made up from sheets with joins every 12th stamp
| N | May 1920 | 480 | £3.0.0 | Right side delivery | — |
| N | Late 1920 | 480 | £3.0.0 | Left side delivery | £400 |

Die Proofs
Finished die in black on white glazed card £5750
Finished die in brown on wove paper £7500
Finished die in red or brown on paper, Wmk.
  W. 14 .... From £7500

Plate Markings

Official Plate	SG Plate	Markings
1a	1a	Added dots above R. 1/1 and R. 11/1. R. 17 left side base outer bevelled and small dot R. 12 left side, 5.5 mm.
1b	1b/25	Dots above R. 1/1 and R. 11/1 filled in and added cut R. 19 left side, 5.5 mm. (same Plate as 25)
2a	2a	Added dots above R. 1/2 and R. 11/2; scoop under THR of R. 20/10. R. 1 right side split at top
2b	2b	Dots above R. 1/2 and R. 11/2 filled in
2c	2c	Added minute dot under L of R. 20/1
2d	2d	Added very fine cut above R. 1/1. Added dot R. 20 right side, 11.5 mm.
3a	3a	Dots above R. 1/3 and R. 11/3, small dot R. 14 left, 14.3 mm.
3b	3b	Dots above R. 1/3 and R. 11/3 filled in
3c	3c	Added minute dot under L of R. 20/2. Large internal cut R. 18 right side, 5-10 mm.
3d	3d	Added very fine cut above R. 1/2, 7.8 mm.
3e	3e	Added dot R. 19 right side, 8.5 mm.
4a	4a	Dots above R. 1/4 and R. 11/4
4b	4b/5a	Dots above R. 1/4 and R. 11/4 filled in
4b	5a	Dot (base) to left of T of R. 20/1
4c	5b	Added ½ dot (inner) R. 19 left side, 6.25 mm.
5a	6a	Added large dot (breaking base) to left of T of R. 20/2
5b	6b	Added fine ½ cut (base) under P of R. 20/2. Added dot under AL of R. 20/9
6	7	Added dot (top) left of T of R. 20/3. Added nick (outer) R. 3 left side, 21 mm.
7a	8a	Dot (base) to left of T of R. 20/4
7b	8ab*	Added fine cut (base) under FP of R. 20/2
7c	8b	Added ½ cut (outer) R. 19 left side, 9.5 mm.
N.M.	9	Large dot (bulging top) under T of R. 20/1
9a	10a	Existing ½ dot outer R. 13 right side, 15 mm. 2 dots R. 19 left side, 8.5, 9 mm. lower dot breaking outer
9b	10b	Added tiny nick (base) under H of R. 20/2
8	11	Dot R. 20 left side, 11.5 mm. Crack (outer) R. 11 right side
15a	12a	Existing minute dot under F of R. 20/12. Plate flaw F for E R. 15/12; added two cuts R. 20 left side, 5.5, 7 mm.
15b	12b	Added dot under A of R. 20/9
16a	13a	Existing nick top above R. 1/4, 6.1 mm. Nick/dot (base) under F of R. 20/11. Two cuts R. 19 left side, 7, 8 mm. Rules R. 18-20 left side irregular.
16b	13b	Added nick (base) under HA of R. 20/2
N.M.	14a	Cut R. 20 left side, 10 mm. Fine cut under H of R. 20/1
N.M.	14b	Cut under H filled in
20a	15a	Existing ½ cut R. 17 left side, (outer) 7.5 mm. and nick (inner) R. 20 left side, 13.5 mm.
20b	15b	Added dot under AL of R. 20/2
N.M.	16a	Dot R. 17 left side, 11.5 mm.
N.M.	16b	Added small dot under A of R. 20/3 and cut R. 18 right side, 10.5 mm.
N.M.	17	Large dot (breaking base) under H(A) of R. 20/1
23	18	Added large oval dot under L of R. 20/2 (breaking base) and tall oval dot R. 19 left side, 11.5 mm., usually breaking right, sometimes left as well
22	19	Added nick (inner) R. 19 left side, 10.5 mm.
24a	20a	Existing cut outer R. 1 right side, 7 mm and ½ dot outer R. 2 right side. Added cut R. 20 left side, 6.5 mm.
24b	20b	Added ½ cut under TH of R. 20/1
28	21	Existing fine ½ cut (base) under L of R. 20/2. Large ½ dot (base) under L of R. 20/11
N.M.	22	Double dot under A of R. 20/10
N.M.	23	No marking
25a	24aa*	Existing dot R. 2 (outer) right side. Added double dot under AL of R. 20/9, 9, 9.5 mm.
25b	24a	Added dot (outer) R. 19 left, 6.5 mm.
25c	24b	Added nick under EN of R. 20/2
1b	25	Added cut R. 19 left side, 5.5 mm. (Same Plate as 1a, b)
N.M.	26	Oval (blurred) cut R. 20 left side, 15 mm.
N.M.	27	Small dot (outer) R. 19 left side, 6.75 mm. Note Rule at R. 19 left measures 22.75 mm. See Plate 24. On late printings from U 23, the rule under R. 20/1 is broken at bottom left
N.M.	28	Small dot under A of R. 20/4
14	29	Existing small dot R. 18 left 1.5 mm. (Also F for E flaw, R. 15/12). Added ½ dot (outer) R. 20 right side, 21 mm. Two cuts outer R. 4 right side, 5.5 and 6.5 mm.
13	30	No marking on lower pane. ½ cut outer R. 3 right side, 10 mm.
N.M.	31	½ dot (inner) R. 19 left side, 12 mm. Nick under NC of R. 20/4
38	32	Existing ½ dot base above R. 1/1, 11-12 mm; dot above R. 1/1, 10.5 mm. R. 16 right side 18 mm and nick base under F of R. 20/9. Added dot R. 17 left side, 11 mm. and ½ dot (outer) R. 20 left side, 8-9 mm.

125

NB   KING GEORGE V   The Profile Head Issue   1½d. Red-brown, Type N6. Royal Cypher

Official Plate	SG Plate	Markings
39	33	Existing ½ dot (outer) R. 20 left side, 10.5 mm. Nick outer R. 13 right, 11.5 mm. Nick outer R. 15 left side, 4 mm.
N.M.	34	Dot (inner) R. 20 left side, 13 mm.
N.M.	35	Small dot R. 20 left side, 9 mm.
N.M.	36	Oval cut R. 17 right side, 9.5 mm.
N.M.	37	Small nick (base) to left of T of R. 20/2
N.M.	38	Tall dot R. 19 left side, 10.5 mm.
N.M.	39	Dot (outer) R. 20 left side, 11.5 mm. ½ dot (outer) R. 19 left side, 10 mm.
N.M.	40	Two cuts R. 18 right side, 8.75, 10.5 mm.
N.M.	41	½ dot (outer) R. 20 left side, 5 mm. (Waterlow Plate 10)
N.M.	42	Outer side of R. 20 left side damaged, 4-5 mm.
N.M.	43	Small ½ dot (base) under A of R. 20/4. Nick (outer) 7 mm. and tiny dot 11 mm., both R. 17 left side. (Waterlow Plate 11)
N.M.	44a	Small dot (inner) R. 18 left side, 9.25 mm.
N.M.	44b	Added dot under H of R. 20/10. Added tiny dots under HR and (E)E of R. 20/11
N.M.	45	Small ½ dot (inner) R. 20 right side, 12 mm. Tiny dot below EE of R. 20/12
N.M.	46	Dot (outer) at foot of R. 1 right side. Small dot R. 18 right side, 12.5 mm. Dot (outer) R. 20 right side, 7 mm.
N.M.	47	Small nick R. 13 left side, 9 mm. Small ½ dot (outer) R. 15 left side, 15 mm. Dot R. 19 right side, ½ mm., also internal nick, 10 mm. Tiny dot under A of R. 20/10.

> N.M. — Not matched
> Existing — Markings on the black plate proof prior to the plate being first put to press
> Added — Markings deliberately or accidentally made during the life of the plate
> * — New plate allocation
> † — Plate re numbered
> R — row

Index to Marginal Markings

Top Margin, Stamp Numbers

Stamp No.	Plate
1	1a, 2d, 32
2	2a, 3d, 3e
3	3a
4	4a, 13a, 13b

Bottom Margin, Stamp Numbers

Stamp No.	Plate
1	2c, 2d, 4b, 5a, 5b, 9, 14a, 17, 20b, 27
2	3c, 3d, 3e, 6a, 6b, 8ab, 8b, 10b, 13b, 15b, 18, 21, 24b, 37
3	7, 16b
4	8a, 8ab, 8b, 28, 31, 43
9	6b, 12b, 24a, 24b, 32
10	2a, 2b, 2c, 2d, 22, 44b, 47
11	13a, 13b, 21, 44b
12	12a, 12b, 45

Left Margin, Row Numbers

Row No.	Plate
3	7
12	1a, 1b/25
13	47
14	3a, 3b, 3c, 3d, 3e
15	33, 47
17	1a, 1b/25, 15a, 15b, 16a, 16b, 32, 43
18	13a, 13b, 29, 44a, 44b
19	1b/25, 5b, 8b, 10a, 10b, 13a, 13b, 18, 19, 24a, 24b, 27, 31, 38, 39
20	11, 12a, 12b, 13a, 13b, 14a, 14b, 15a, 15b, 20a, 20b, 26, 32, 33, 34, 35, 39, 41, 42

Row No.	Plate

Right Margin, Row Numbers

Row No.	Plate
1	2a, 2b, 2c, 2d, 20a, 20b, 46
2	20a, 20b, 24aa*, 24a, 24b
3	30
4	29
11	11
13	10a, 10b, 33
16	32
17	36
18	3c, 3d, 3e, 16b, 40, 46
19	3e, 24b, 47
20	2d, 29, 45, 46

No Marking: Plate 23

Control Schedule

Control	Plates with which it was used
A. 12w	1a, 2a
A. 12c	1a, 2a, 3a, 4a
C 13	2b, 3b
D 14	2b, 3b
F 15	2c, 3c
G 15	2c, 3c
H 16	2c, 3d
J 17	2c, 2d, 3e
K 18	2c*, 2d, 3e, 4b/5a, 6a, 7, 8a, 10a, 11
(K) 18	2c
L 18	2d, 3e, 5a, 6a, 7, 8a, 8ab, 8b, 9, 10a, 11, 12a, 13a, 16a, 29, 30, 44a
M 18	5a, 6b, 9, 13a, 14a, 15a, 16a, 19, 23, 29, 44a
M 19	5a, 5b, 6b, 7, 8b, 9, 10b, 11, 13a, 14b, 15a, 15b, 16a, 16b, 28, 29, 44b
(M) 19	14b
N 19	7, 8b, 10b, 11, 13a, 13b, 14b, 15b, 17, 18, 19, 20a, 21, 24aa*, 25, 28, 29, 30
O 19	1b, 12a, 17, 18, 20a, 21, 24aa*, 24a, 25, 26
O 20	17, 18, 21, 22, 24a, 26
Q 20	18, 20a, 21, 25, 40
Q 21	12b, 18, 19, 20a, 21, 24a, 24b, 26, 29
T 22	8b, 12b, 17, 18, 20a, 22, 24b, 25, 26, 27, 29, 31, 32, 33, 34, 35, 36
U 22	20a, 25, 27, 31, 32, 33, 34
U 23	18, 20a, 20b, 25, 27, 28, 31, 32, 33, 34, 39
V 23	17, 18, 20b, 35, 37, 38, 39, 40, 41, 42, 43, 45, 47
W 23	37, 38, 39, 40, 41, 42, 43, 45, 46
W 24	38, 39

* The K of K 18 is wide and appears at an angle on plate 2c.

2d. Orange, Type N7. Royal Cypher — The Profile Head Issue — KING GEORGE V — NB

Plate Conversions

SG Plate	Official Plate	Official Plate	SG Plate
1	1	1	1 and 25
2	2	2	2
3	3	3	3
4	4	4	4 and 5
5	4	5	6
6	5	6	7
7	6	7	8
8	7	8	11
9	N.M.	9	10
10	9	10	N.M.
11	8	11	N.M.
12	15	12	N.M.
13	16	13	30
14	N.M.	14	29
15	20	15	12
16	N.M.	16	13
17	N.M.	19	N.M.
18	23	20	15
19	22	21	N.M.
20	24	22	19
21	28	23	18
22	N.M.	24	20
23	N.M.	25	24
24	25	26	N.M.
25	1	27	N.M.
26	N.M.	28	21
27	N.M.	29	N.M.
28	N.M.	30	N.M.
29	14	31	N.M.
30	13	32	N.M.
31	N.M.	33	N.M.
32	38	34	N.M.
33	39	35	N.M.
34	N.M.	36	N.M.
35	N.M.	37	N.M.
36	N.M.	38	32
37	N.M.	39	33
38	N.M.	40	N.M.
39	N.M.	41	N.M.
40	N.M.	42	N.M.
41	N.M.	43	N.M.
42	N.M.	44	N.M.
43	N.M.	45	N.M.
44	N.M.	46*	N.M.
45	N.M.	47	N.M.
46	N.M.	48*	N.M.
47	N.M.	49	N.M.
		50	N.M.
		51	N.M.

Notes.
N.M. = not matched.
* Official plates 46 and 48 have no entries against them in the records. Therefore it is not certain if they were put to press.

DIE I

Inner frame-line at top and sides close to solid of background. *Four* complete lines of shading between top of head and oval frame-line. White line round "TWOPENCE" thin.

DIE II

Inner frame-line farther from solid of background. *Three* lines between top of head and oval. White line round "TWOPENCE" thicker.

1912 *(20 August)*. **2d. Orange, Type N7.** Wmk. Simple Cypher. Die I

N19 (=S.G.366/69)

	Unmtd mint	Mtd mint	Used
(1) Orange-yellow (1912)	14·00	8·00	3·00
(2) Reddish orange (Nov. 1913)	10·00	6·00	3·00
(3) Deep reddish orange (1916)	£160	£100	30·00
(4) Pale orange	15·00	10·00	1·50
(5) Orange	8·00	4·00	3·00
(6) Brown-orange (1921)	95·00	50·00	20·00
(7) Bright orange	8·00	5·00	3·00
(8) Deep bright orange	25·00	18·00	1·50
(9) Intense bright orange	£1750	£1150	£475
a. Without watermark	£350	£200	£150
b. Watermark inverted	22·00	12·00	12·00
c. Watermark reversed	25·00	15·00	12·00
d. Watermark inverted and reversed	18·00	10·00	10·00
e. Frame line double. Shade (1)		£225	
f. Broken frame at left (Pl. 14, R. 19/1)		£300	
g. Damaged left value tablet (Pl. ?, R. 1/4)		£775	
h. Coil join (vert. pair) (7.20)			
i. Coil join (horiz. pair) (9.20)			
s. "Specimen", Type 26		£250	
t. "Cancelled", Type 24		£475	

Imperforate (single) from P.O. Registration Sheet £7500

Shade (9) is a printing in fugitive ink, highly suffused, and showing through to the back of the stamp. Shade (8) is also known printed in fugitive ink.

Variety e occurs between the 6th and 7th stamps on some rows of the sheet.

The change of colour from orange-yellow to reddish orange in 1913 was deliberate.

NB KING GEORGE V The Profile Head Issue 2d. Orange, Type N7. Royal Cypher

N19e  N19f  N19g

Watermark Varieties. The following have been recorded:
Wmk upright: Type I (orange-yellow); Type I (reddish orange); Types II, III (orange)
Wmk inverted: Type I (orange-yellow); Types II, III (orange)
Wmk reversed: Type I (orange-yellow); Type II (orange)
Wmk inverted and reversed: Type I (orange-yellow); Type I (reddish-orange); Types II, III (orange)

Misplaced Watermarks
ya. Single stamp showing letters from "POSTAGE" .... 17·00
yb. Vertical strip sufficient to show complete "POSTAGE" watermark £300
yc. Vertical strip sufficient to show complete "POSTAGE" watermark double, with selvedge attached, the selvedge having the "POSTAGE" watermark inverted .... —

Broken Dandy Roll Varieties
za. Missing Crown .... 55·00
zb. Missing G .... 30·00
zc. Missing v .... 30·00
zd. Missing R .... 30·00
ze. Missing Gv .... 30·00
zf. Missing vR .... 55·00
zg. Missing Crown vR .... 35·00
zh. Missing Crown GvR £125
zj. Missing tail to R ("GvP") .... 18·00
zk. Long tail to G .... 35·00

Controls.
Somerset House Printings:
Prices for strips of three

Control	Perf. Type 2 (I/E)	2A (P./P.)
C. 13	20·00	20·00
Variety Type 2 (c) (I/I)		
C. 13	25·00	
Variety Type 3A (I/P)		
C. 13	25·00	

Wmk upright, Type I/E, or inverted and reversed, Type I/E.

Harrison Printings:
Prices for unused singles

Control	Perf. Type 2 (E)	2A (P.)
no control*	55·00	55·00
C 14	7·00	7·00
D 14	6·00	6·00
F 15	8·00	15·00
G 15	8·00	10·00
H 16	7·00	£475
I 16	7·00	60·00
J 17	7·00	10·00
K 17	15·00	35·00
L 18	7·00	10·00
M 19	15·00	25·00
N 19	8·00	15·00
O 19	15·00	£150
O 20	7·00	7·00
P 20	6·00	6·00
Q 20	6·00	6·00
Q 21 (c)	6·00	6·00

Control	Perf. Type 2 (E)	2A (P.)
Q 21 (w)	6·00	6·00
R 21	6·00	6·00
S 21	11·00	11·00
S 22	9·00	9·00
T 22	30·00	35·00

*The prices quoted are for bottom left-hand corner pairs with selvedge attached and originate from the 1912 printing.
(c) "close" and (w) "wide" refer to the space between "Q" and "2" (5.75 mm and 7 mm respectively).

Variety Type 2 (c) (I/I)
Strip of three
Q21   —

Watermark varieties known:
Wmk upright, Type I: no control.
Wmk inverted, Type I: no control.
Wmk reversed, Type I: no control.
Wmk inverted and reversed, Type I: no control.
Wmk upright, Type II: C 14, D 14, F 15, G 15, H 16, I 16, J 17, K 17, N 19, O 19, O 20, P 20, Q 21 (c), Q 21 (w), R 21, T 22.
Wmk inverted, Type II: H 16, I 16, R 21.
Wmk reversed, Type II: G 15, I 16.
Wmk inverted and reversed, Type II: G 15, H 16, I 16.
Wmk upright, Type III: J 17, K 17, L 18, M 19, N 19, O 19, O 20, P 20, Q 20, Q 21 (c), Q 21 (w), R 21, S 21, S 22, T 22.
Wmk inverted, Type III: K 17, M 19, N 19, O 20, P 20, Q 20, Q 21, S 21.
Wmk reversed, Type III: P 20.
Wmk inverted and reversed, Type III: L 18, M 19, N 19, O 19, O 20, P 20, Q 20, Q 21, R 21, S 21, T 22.

Coils
Vertical delivery made up from sheets with joins every tenth stamp

Code No.	Issued	Number in roll	Face value		
Q	July 1920	1000	£8.6.8	Bottom delivery	£550
R	July 1920	500	£4.3.4	Top delivery	£550
R	July 1920	500	£4.3.4	Bottom delivery	£550
KERMODE	Mid 1920	1000	£8.6.8	Top delivery	£650

Sideways delivery made up from sheets with joins every 12th stamp

| T | Sept. 1920 | 480 | £4.0.0 | Left side delivery | £550 |

Die Proofs
Head placed too high in frame with solid background, uncleared
In black on white glazed card £6500
In black on white glazed card, dated 30.5.12 .... £6500
Head in normal position with horizontal background shading, uncleared
In black on white glazed card, dated on reverse "19.6.12" £6500
Cleared in black on white glazed card (cut to stamp size), ... £3250

Plate Proofs
Special plate of four on surfaced paper in black or orange .... Per block from £12000

Colour Trials
Imperf. On gummed paper
In cadmium orange, bright green, magenta or the issued colour .... From £2800

Plate Markings
This value departed from the normal usage in the setting of the marginal rules. The SG Plate No. settings are:
A All rules fully co-extensive; rule under 6th vertical row very long (20 mm.). (Plates 1, 2, 3, 4 and 5.)

2d. Orange, Type N7. Royal Cypher *The Profile Head Issue* **KING GEORGE V** **NB**

B Cuts above and below 6th and 7th vertical rows; no cuts between 6th and 7th rows. (Plates 7, 10, 13, 16 and 19.)
C As Setting B but cuts have been filled in. (Plates 9 and 18.)
D As Setting A, but rule under 6th vertical row measures 19.5 mm. (Plates 8, 11 and 21.)
E As Setting D, but rule under 6th vertical row measures 19 mm. This setting shows signs of having cuts above and below 6th and 7th vertical rows filled in. (Plate 20.)

The settings of the remaining plates (6, 12, 14, 15 and 17) are not known.

Official Plate	SG Plate	Markings
3a	1	No Marking (same as plate 4)
6a	2a	Dot above R. 1/6 and R. 11/6. Dash under E of R. 20/2
6b	2b	Dash under E less evident, but traces showing at bottom of rule
6c	2c	Added tall oval dot R. 19 left side, 12 mm. Later this dot breaks left and right edges of rule
1	3	Added dot above R. 1/8 in upper pane only. Cut under PE of R. 20/1
3b	4	Added cut under WO of R. 20/2
2a	5a	Dots above R. 1/2 and R. 11/2. R. 20 left side shows bulge in the centre and a progressive thickening towards the base
2b	5b	Dots above R. 1/2 and R. 11/2 filled in
N.M.	6	Large dot R. 20 left side bulging rule at right, 12 mm.
15	7	Existing ½ dot outer R. 8 right side 13.75 mm and R. 2 left side top outer bevelled
15a	7a	Added dot R. 19 left side, 11 mm.
15b	7b	R. 19 dot now breaking right side of rule. Added dot R. 19 left side (breaking outer), 8.5 mm. Added dot to right of R. 1/4
N.M.	8a	Fine dot R. 20 left side, 13 mm.
N.M.	8b	R. 18 left side damaged slightly at left; added dot R. 20 left side, 14 mm.
21a	9a	Existing nick (inner) R. 20 left side, 2.2 mm. Added dot R. 17 right side, 9.5 mm.
21b	9b	Added oblique dot R. 20 left side, 14 mm.
N.M.	10	Dot R. 18 right side, 8 mm.
13	11	Existing R. 6 left side bevelled inner. Added dot R. 17 right side, 11.5 mm. ½ dot (outer) R. 18 left side, 11.5 mm.
N.M.	12	Outer base of R. 19 left side bevelled off. Nick (outer) 20th left side, 10 mm.
10	13	Added tall dot R. 19 left side, 11.5-12 mm, usually breaking rule at left and bulging rule slightly at right
N.M.	14	Scoop (outer) R. 19 left side, 8.5-11 mm. Outer frame of R. 19/1 broken opposite left value tablet (This is same Plate as 21a, b)
N.M.	15	Large dot R. 17 left side, 13 mm. Elongated dot R. 19 left side, 11 mm.
17	16	Existing nick (base) under W of R. 20/1. Nick (outer) R. 19 left side, 2 mm. Part dot inner R. 9 right side, 7 mm and dot above R. 1/5, 0.7 mm. Dot R. 17 left side, 12 mm.
24a	17a	Existing small dots R. 5 and R. 7 right side, both 21 mm. Added oval cut R. 20 left side, 11.5 mm.
24b	17b	Added three tiny dots R. 1 right side
7a	18a	Existing ½ dot (outer) R. 18 right side, 18 mm.
7b	18b	Added ½ dot (inner) R. 20 left side, 8 mm.
23a	19a	Added round dot breaking inner R. 18 right, 11.2 mm.
23b	19b	Added tall oval dot R. 19 left side, breaking left and right 14.5 mm. Added dot R. 20 right side, 10 mm.
12	20	Existing R. 5 left side bevelled outer. Added dot R. 17 left side, 13.5 mm.

Official Plate	SG Plate	Markings
N.M.	21a	Dot R. 18 left side, (breaking right), 12 mm.
N.M.	21b	Added scoop outer R. 19 left side, 8.5-11 mm. (This is same plate as 14)
4	22	No Markings.
9	N.M.	Existing R. 17 left side, base (outer) bevelled, right end base rule broken above R. 1/6

Official plates 11, 14, 16, 19 and 22 have not been matched yet.

Index to Marginal Markings
Top Margin, Stamp Numbers

Stamp No.	Plate
1	7b
2	5a
4	7b
5	16
6	2a, 2b, 2c
8	3

Bottom Margin, Stamp Numbers

1	3, 16
2	2a, 2b, 2c, 4

Left Margin, Row Numbers

Row No.	Plate
2	7, 7a, 7b
5	20
16	11
17	15, 16, 20, official pl. 9
18	8b, 11, 21a, 21b
19	2c, 7a, 7b, 12, 13, 14, 15, 16, 19b, 21b
20	5a, 5b, 6, 8a, 8b, 9a, 9b, 12, 17a, 17b, 18b

Right Margin, Row Numbers

1	17b
5	17a, 17b
7	17a, 17b
8	7, 7a, 7b
9	16
17	9a, 9b, 11
18	10, 18a, 18b, 19a, 19b
20	19b

No Marking: Plate 1, 22

Control Schedule

Control	Plates with which it was used
None	1, 3, 4
C.13	2a, 5a
C 14	3, 4
D 14	3, 4, 22
F 15	3, 4
G 15	3, 4
H 16	3, 4
I 16	3, 4
J 17	3, 4, 5b
K 17	3, 4, 5b
L 18	3
M 19	3, 5b
N 19	3, 4, 5b
O 19	3, 4, 5b
O 20	2a, 4, 5b, 6, 7, 11, 13, 18a, 20
P 20	2a, 2b, 3, 4, 5b, 6, 7a, 7b, 8a, 8b, 9a, 11, 12, 13, 20, 21a
Q 20	2b, 3, 5b, 6, 7b, 8b, 9a, 13, 21a,
Q 21	2b, 6, 7b, 8b, 9b, 11, 12, 13, 14, 15, 16, 18b, 19a, 21b
R 21	2b, 2c, 8b, 9b, 10, 11, 12, 15, 16, 17a, 17b, 18a, 19a, 19b
S 21	2c, 7b, 8b, 12, 16, 17a, 18b, 19b
S 22	6, 9b, 12, 16, 17a, 18b, 19b
T 22	9b, 12, 15, 16, 17b, 18b, 19b

NB **KING GEORGE V** *The Profile Head Issue* **2d. Orange, Type N7. Royal Cypher**

Plate Conversions

SG Plate	Official Plate	Official Plate	SG Plate
1	3. (part)	1	3
2a,b,c	6	2	5a, b
3	1	3	1 and 4
4	3 (part)	4	22
5a, b	2	6	2a. b, c
6	N.M.	7	18a, b
7a, b	15	9	N.M.
8a, b	N.M.	10	13
9a, b	21	11	N.M.
10	N.M.	12	20
11	13	13	11
12	N.M.	14	N.M.
13	10	15	7a, b
14/21a, b	N.M.	16	N.M.
15	N.M.	17	16
16	17	18*	
17a, b	24	19	N.M.
18a, b	7	20*	
19	23		
20	12	21	9a, b
21 (part of 14)	N.M.	22	N.M.
		23	19
22	4	24	17a, b

Note:
N.M. = not matched.
* There are no entries in the records against official plate 18. Plate 20, though sent to Harrisons, has no recorded put to press date. Therefore it is not certain if this plate was used.

1921 *(September).* **2d. Orange, Type N7.** Die II

N20 (=S.G.370)

(1) Orange	8·00	5·00	3·50
(2) Pale orange	12·00	8·00	3.50
(3) Deep orange	40·00	20·00	4·00
(4) Bright orange	15·00	10·00	2·00
a. Without watermark	£3500	£2500	
b. Watermark inverted	60·00	40·00	40·00
c. Watermark inverted and reversed	£200	£140	£130
d. Frame break below "N" (Pl. 3, R. 20/2)			75·00
s. "Specimen", Type 15			£800
t. "Specimen", Type 23			£950

No. N20 is known with so-called varnish ink but as stated in the General Notes we defer listing.

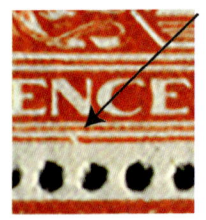

N20d

Watermark Varieties. The following have been recorded:
Wmk upright: Types II, III
Wmk inverted: Types II, III
Wmk inverted and reversed: Types II, III

Misplaced Watermarks
ya. Single stamp showing letters from "POSTAGE" .... 60·00
yb. Vertical strip sufficient to show complete "POSTAGE" watermark £550

Broken Dandy Roll Varieties
za. Missing Crown .... 60·00
zc. Missing v. .... 35·00

Controls. Prices are for unused singles.
Harrison Printings:

	Perf. Type	
Control	I.	P.
S 21	80·00	35·00
S 22	12·00	12·00
T 22	35·00	12·00
U 22	12·00	10·00
U 23	10·00	10·00
V 23	20·00	10·00
W 23	10·00	10·00
W 24	£300	£300

Watermark varieties known:
Wmk upright, Type II: T 22, U 22, U 23, V 23, W 23, W 24.
Wmk inverted, Type II: W 23, W 24.
Wmk inverted and reversed, Type II: W 23, W 24.
Wmk upright, Type III: S 21, S 22, T 22, U 22, U 23, V 23, W 23.
Wmk inverted, Type III: S 22.
Wmk inverted and reversed, Type III: S 21, S 22, T 22, U 23.

Imprimatur from the National Postal Museum Archives
Imperforate, watermark Type W14
Watermark upright £7500

Plate Markings

Official Plate	SG Plate	Markings
45	1	Oval dot R. 19 left side, sometimes breaking rule at left and right, 13 mm. Nick outer frame R. 18 right side, 12 mm.
49	2	Dot (outer) R. 20 left side, 14.25 mm. ½ dot (base) under P of R. 20/1
N.M.	3	Lower part of R. 20 left side slightly tapered. Dot (top) under OP of R. 20/9. Dot (breaking inner) R. 17 right side, 12.5 mm. (Waterlow Plate 17)
N.M.	4	Dot R. 20 left side, 13 mm. (Waterlow Plate 4)
N.M.	5	Dot R. 19 left side, 12.5 mm. Scratch R. 20 left side (not always visible) (Waterlow Plate 5)
N.M.	6	Dot under P of R. 20/10; dot (central) R. 18 right side, 13 mm. (Waterlow Plate 18)

Control Schedule

Plate	Controls employed
1	S 21, S 22, T 22, U 22, U 23, V 23
2	S 21, S 22, T 22, U 22, U 23
3	S 21, S 22, T 22, V 23, W 23, W 24
4	T 22, U 23, V 23, W 23, W 24
5	T 22, U 23, V 23, W 23, W 24
6	S 22, T 22

2½d. Blue, Type N5. Royal Cypher *The Profile Head Issue* **KING GEORGE V** **NB**

Eve's Wreath Design

Bromide with head void and value tablets cleared.

Bromide with bas-relief head added.

Stamp-size proof on thin, soft card (62×75mm)	£2250
Bromides of above (29×35mm) with varying degrees of shading to background	From £1400
Proof (80x150mm) with vignette void and value tablets uncleared, endorsed "2d+3d" at top	£5000
Stamp-size bromide similar to above but with value tablets cleared (30x37mm)	£1700
Similar to above but with Mackennal's bas-relief plaque head added	£2000
Similar to above with "2" in left-hand tablet, "3" in right-hand tablet and both values written in full at foot	£2000

1912 *(18 October).* **2½d. Blue, Type N5.** Wmk. Simple Cypher

N21 (=S.G.371/73a)

	Unmtd mint	Mtd mint	Used
(1) Cobalt-blue (1912-14)	22·00	12·00	4·00
(2) Cobalt-violet-blue (1912)	50·00	30·00	8·00
(3) French blue (1913-16)	£100	70·00	6·00
(4) Bright blue (1914-17)	22·00	12·00	4·00
(5) Deep bright blue (1915-22)	£350	£225	75·00
(6) Milky blue (1917)	75·00	45·00	5·00
(7) Pale milky blue (1917)	£1800	£1250	£350
(8) Powder blue (1918)	55·00	30·00	5·00
(9) Violet-blue (1918)	45·00	25·00	5·00
(10) Blue	22·00	12·00	4·00
(11) Pale blue (1917-19)	25·00	15·00	4·00
(12) Deep blue (1920-22)	28·00	15·00	4·00
(13) Dull blue (1920)	22·00	15·00	4·00
(14) Indigo-blue (1920)	£5000	£3500	£2500
(15) Indigo-blue (toned paper) (1920)	£7000	£5000	
(16) Royal blue (1920)	£425	£300	
(17) Dull Prussian blue (Dec. 1920)	£1850	£1500	£850
(18) Dull Prussian blue (toned paper) (1921)	£10000	£6000	
(19) Ultramarine (1919-23)	30·00	20·00	4·00
a. Without watermark	£3000	£2500	
b. Watermark inverted	£120	85·00	75·00
c. Watermark reversed	95·00	65·00	65·00
d. Watermark inverted and reversed	45·00	28·00	28·00
e. Watermark double. (Shades 1 and 2)			
s. "Specimen", Type 15		£950	
t. "Specimen", Type 23		£120	
u. "Specimen", Type 26		£375	
v. Imperf. optd. "Cancelled", Type 24		£225	
w. "Cancelled", Type 24		£800	

Shade (7) is from a worn printing of Plate 1 (Control J 17).

Shades (14), (15) and (16) are printed in fugitive ink; used examples in the correct shades are consequently very rare. Most printings of shade (12) Controls O 20 and P 20 are also fugitive.

Shades (14) and (15) are from Control O 20 and should not be confused with shades (17) and (18) which exist from Controls O 20 and R 21.

Shade (18) is slightly deeper than (17) and both are unlike the Prussian blue shade of the 2½d. Jubilee issue.

No. N21e was from a A. 12 printing.

Watermark Varieties. The following have been recorded:
Wmk upright: Types I, II, III
Wmk inverted: Types I, II, III
Wmk reversed: Types II, III
Wmk inverted and reversed: Types I, II, III

Misplaced Watermarks
ya.	Single stamp showing letters from "POSTAGE"	50·00
yb.	Vertical strip sufficient to show complete "POSTAGE" watermark	£850
yc.	Vertical strip sufficient to show complete "POSTAGE" watermark double, with selvedge attached, the selvedge having the "POSTAGE" watermark inverted	£4500

Broken Dandy Roll Varieties
za.	Missing Crown	60·00
zb.	Missing G	35·00
zc.	Missing v	32·00
zd.	Missing R	35·00
ze.	Missing Gv	35·00
zf.	Missing vR	40·00
zg.	Missing Crown vR	35·00
zi.	Missing left side to R	35·00
zj.	Missing tail to R ("GvP")	32·00
zk.	Long tail to G	35·00

Controls. Prices are for unused singles.
Somerset House Printings:

	Perf. Type	
Control	2 (E.)	2A (P.)
A. 12	20·00	£950
J. 17	£850	†

Watermark varieties known:
Wmk double, Type I: A. 12.
Wmk upright, Type I: A. 12.
Wmk inverted, Type I: A. 12.
Wmk inverted and reversed, Type I: A. 12.
Wmk upright, Type II: J. 17.

Harrison Printings:

	Perf. Type	
Control	2 (E.)	2A (P.)
C 13	15·00	15·00
C 14	15·00	15·00
D 14	75·00	75·00
E 14	15·00	15·00
G 15	15·00	15·00
H 16	15·00	15·00
I 16	15·00	35·00
J 17	15·00	25·00
K 17	20·00	£1200
L 18	18·00	18·00
M 18	25·00	25·00
M 19	25·00	25·00
N 19	15·00	15·00
O 19	15·00	15·00
O 20	20·00	15·00
P 20(w)	15·00	15·00
Q 21	35·00	35·00
R 21	25·00	25·00
S 21	25·00	25·00
S 22	75·00	85·00

NB KING GEORGE V — The Profile Head Issue — 2½d. Blue, Type N5. Royal Cypher

Control	Perf. Type 2 (E.)	Perf. Type 2A (P.)
T 22	20·00	20·00
U 23	20·00	20·00
V 23	20·00	20·00

Variety Type 2 (c) (I/I)
Strip of three
C 14 .... £200

Watermark varieties known:
Wmk upright, Type I: C 13
Wmk inverted, Type I: C 13
Wmk inverted and reversed, Type I: C 13
Wmk upright, Type II: C 13, C 14, D 14, E 14, G 15, H 16, I 16, J 17, K 17, L 18, M 18, O 20, R 21, U 23, V 23.
Wmk inverted, Type II: C 14, J 17, N 19.
Wmk reversed, Type II: G 15.
Wmk inverted and reversed, Type II: C 13, C 14, G 15, H 16.
Wmk upright, Type III: J 17, K 17, L 18, M 18, M 19, N 19, O 19, O 20, P 20, Q 21, R 21, S 21, S 22, T 22.
Wmk inverted, Type III: L 18, O 19, O 20, Q 21, R 21.
Wmk inverted and reversed, Type III: J 17, L 18, M 18, M 19, N 19, O 19, O 20, P 20, R 21, T 22.

Die Proofs
The transfer die for the 2½d. was taken from the same roller as the 1d. die and Harrison completed engraving the figures and words of value on 30 July 1912. The die was proofed at the Royal Mint on 20 August 1912.
Uncleared in blue on thick paper £8500
Uncleared in blue on gummed Royal Cypher
    watermarked paper £11000
Uncleared in blue on gummed "NHI" (National
    Health Insurance) watermarked paper £13000

Colour Trials
Imperf. on gummed watermarked paper in
    cobalt-violet-blue £4750

Plate Markings

Official Plate	SG Plate	Markings
1		This is the only plate without the Master plate flaw small coloured mark above E of REV, R. 20/1
1a	1a	Added dots above R. 1/1 and R. 11/1
1b	1b	Dots above R. 1/1 and R. 11/1 filled in
2a	2a	Added dots above R. 1/2 and R. 11/2
2b	2b	Dots above R. 1/2 and R. 11/2 filled in. R. 11 right side nick outer, 19 to 20 mm.
	3b	R. 20 left side tends to bend inwards at base. R. 19 right side outer damaged,12-14 mm.
3	6	Existing nick inner R. 20 left side, 5.5 mm. Existing nick outer R. 14 left side, 5.5 mm. Existing R. 12 left side bevelled top outer. Existing small ½ dot base under F of R. 20/12
4a	3a	Existing tiny dot R. 12 left side, 12.5 mm. Added dots above R. 1/4 and R. 11/4
4b	3ab	Dots above R. 1/4 and R. 11/4 filled in R. 20 right side, waist with minute dot, 13.5 mm.
	5	R. 20/1 rule left end only part prints leaving two white patches, these slowly disappear through control H 16. R. 20/2 small rule flaw develops top right end under 2
5a	12	Existing both R. 4 and R. 12 right side (outer) bevelled at base.
	4a	Added dots above R. 1/5 and R. 11/5
5b	4b	Dots above R. 1/5 and R. 11/5 filled in
6	13*	No details of markings
9	2c	Added oval dot under P of R. 20/1
10a	1c	Existing nick, outer R. 3 left side, 13 mm.
10b	1d	Added oval dot under P of R. 20/2
12	8a	R. 1 left side bevelled at top
13a	8ab*	Rule under R. 20/7 thins at right
	8ac*	No further details of markings
13b	8b	Added circular dot under P of R. 20/1 (Waterlow Plate 6)
14	7a	Existing nick top of rule under Y of R. 20/1
15a	9a	Rule under R. 20/11 base left end slightly bevelled. Scoop outer R. 2 right side, 11.5-15 mm.
15b	9b	Added ½ dot base under FP of R. 20/2
16	7b	Existing nick under PE of R. 20/7. Existing R. 20 left side base bevelled outer
17a	11a	Existing nick top under PE of R. 20/12
17b	11b	Added cut under F of R. 20/2 (Waterlow Plate 4)
18	10	Existing nick bottom of rule above R. 1/9, 8 mm. Added cut under (P)E of R. 20/1. (Provisional printing, Plate 15)

* = New Plate allocation

Control Schedule

Official Plate	SG Plate	Controls used
1a	1a	A. 12
1b	1b	C 13
2a	2a	A. 12
2b	2b/3b	C 13

Two sets of plate markings are same state.

3	6	C 14, G 15
4a	3a	A. 12
4b	3ab*/5	C 14, D 14, E 14, G 15, H 16, I 16
5a	12/4a	A. 12
5b	4b	C 14, G 15, H 16, I 16
		B 13*, G 15**
6	13*	B 13*, G 15**
9	2c	I 16, J 17
10a	1c	I 16
10b	1d	I 16, J 17
12	8a	J 17**, K 17, M 19, N 19
13a	8ab*	J. 17 Somerset Hse. ptg.
	8ac*	M 19**, N 19
13b	8b	N 19, O 19, P 20, Q 21, R 21, S 22, T 22
14	7a	K 17, L 18, M 18
15a	9a	M 18, N 19
15b	9b	N 19, O 20, Q 21, R 21
16	7b	O 19, O 20, Q 21
17a	11a	R 21
17b	11b	S 21, S 22, T 22, U 23, V 23
18	10	S 21, S 22, T 22, U 23, V 23

* = New plate allocation
** = These controls are known to exist as the plates were first put to press during the relevant control periods but have not been positively identified.

3d. Violet, Type N7. Royal Cypher — The Profile Head Issue — KING GEORGE V — NB

Plate Conversions

SG Plate	Official Plate	Official Plate	SG Plate
1a, b	1	1	1a, b
1c, d	10	2	2a, b, and 3b
2a, b	2 (part of)	3	6
2c	9	4	3a, ab* and 5
3a, ab	4 (part of)	5	4a, b and 12
3b	2 (part of)	6	13*
4a, b	5 (part of)	9	2c
5	4 (part of)	10	1c, d
6	3	12	8a
7a	14	13	8ab*, ac*, b
7b	16	14	7a
8a	12	15	9a, b
8ab*, ac*, b	13	16	7b
9a, b	15	17	11a, b
10	18	18	10
11a, b	17		
12	5 (part of)		
13*	6		

1912 (9 October). **3d. Violet, Type N7.** Wmk. Simple Cypher

N22 (=S.G.374/77)

	Unmtd mint	Mtd mint	Used
(1) Reddish violet (1912-13)	35·00	20·00	5·00
(2) Dull reddish violet (1912-13)	22·00	12·00	3·00
(3) Violet	15·00	8·00	3·00
(4) Pale violet (1917-18)	17·00	10·00	3·00
(5) Very pale violet (1916)	£400	£300	£100
(6) Bright violet	12·00	8·00	1·50
(7) Bluish violet (Nov. 1913)	15·00	9·00	3·00
(8) Lavender-violet	45·00	30·00	2·00
(9) Dull violet (1920)	12·00	8·00	1·50
(10) Very deep violet (1922-23)	£200	£130	75·00
(11) Heliotrope (1919)	60·00	40·00	10·00
(12) Brownish violet (1921)	£100	60·00	5·00
a. Without watermark	£600	£400	£225
b. Watermark inverted	£160	95·00	£110
c. Watermark reversed	£800	£450	£450
d. Watermark inverted and reversed	40·00	30·00	30·00
da Watermark double			
e. Frame broken (Pl. 4, R. 20/2)		80·00	
f. Extension to E (Pls. 13a, b, R. 19/2)		£150	
s. "Specimen", Type 15		£950	
t. "Specimen", Type 23		£250	
u. "Cancelled", Type 24		£750	
v. "Specimen", Type 26		£300	

Shade (11) heliotrope has a decidedly pinkish tone. The change of colour from reddish to bluish violet was deliberate.
Imperforate (single) from P.O. registration sheet.............. £7500

N22e   N22f

Watermark Varieties. The following have been recorded:
Wmk upright: Types I, II (reddish violet); Type I (violet); Types I, II, III (bluish violet)
Wmk inverted: Type II (reddish violet); Type I (violet); Types II, III (bluish violet)
Wmk reversed: Types I, II, III

Wmk inverted and reversed: Types II, III

Misplaced Watermarks
- ya. Single stamp showing letters from "POSTAGE"..............55·00
- yb. Vertical strip sufficient to show complete "POSTAGE" watermark..........................£500

Broken Dandy Roll Varieties
- za. Missing Crown..60·00
- zb. Missing G..40·00
- zc. Missing v..35·00
- zd. Missing R.. —
- ze. Missing Gv.. —
- zf. Missing vR..40·00
- zg. Missing Crown vR.......................................40·00
- zi. Missing left side to R...................................40·00
- zj. Missing tail to R ("GvP")...............................35·00
- zh. Long tail to G..45·00

Controls. Prices are for unused singles.
Somerset House Printings in reddish violet:

	Perf. Type	
Control	2 (E.)	2A (P.)
A. 12 (w)	30·00	£350
A. 12 (c)	40·00	65·00
B. 13	35·00	£100

(w) "wide" and (c) "close" refer to the spacing between "A" and "1" (4 mm. and 1.25mm. respectively).

Watermark varieties known:
Wmk upright, Type I: A. 12 (w), A. 12 (c), B. 13.
Wmk inverted, Type I: B. 13.
Wmk reversed, Type I: A. 12 (w)
Wmk inverted and reversed, Type I: A. 12 (w), B. 13.

Somerset House Printings in bluish violet:

	Perf. Type	
Control	2 (E.)	2A (P.)
C. 13	20·00	£100

Wmk upright, Type II only.

Harrison Printings in reddish violet:

	Perf. Type	
Control	2 (E.)	2A (P.)
C 13	25·00	25·00

Wmk upright, Types I or II.

Harrison Printings in bluish violet shades:

	Perf. Type	
Control	2 (E.)	2A (P.)
C 13	8·00	8·00
D 14	8·00	8·00
E 14	8·00	8·00
F 15	8·00	8·00
G 15	35·00	25·00
H 16	25·00	£100
I 16	8·00	8·00
J 17	10·00	15·00
L 18	8·00	8·00
M 18	8·00	8·00
N 19	8·00	8·00
O 20	8·00	8·00
P 20	8·00	8·00
Q 21	12·00	12·00
R 21	8·00	8·00
S 21	70·00	50·00
S 22	8·00	8·00
T 22	15·00	15·00
U 22	8·00	8·00
U 23	8·00	8·00
V 23	10·00	15·00

133

KING GEORGE V The Profile Head Issue   **3d. Violet, Type N7. Royal Cypher**

	Perf. Type	
Control	2 (E.)	2A (P.)
W 23	20·00	20·00

Watermark varieties known:
Wmk upright, Type I: E 14.
Wmk upright, Type II: C 13, D 14, E 14, F 15, G 15, H 16, I 16, J 17, N 19, O 20, R 21, U 22, U 23, V 23, W 23.
Wmk inverted, Type II: G 15, U 22, U 23, V 23.
Wmk reversed, Type II: I 16.
Wmk inverted and reversed, Type II: C 13, E 14, F 15, G 15, I 16, U 22.
Wmk upright, Type III: J 17, L 18, M 18, N 19, O 20, P 20, Q 21, R 21, S 21, S 22, T 22, U 23, V 12, W 23.
Wmk inverted, Type III: L 18, N 19.
Wmk reversed, Type III: Q 21.
Wmk inverted and reversed, Type III: J 17, L 18, O 20, Q 21, R 21, S 22.

Eve's Pillar Design.

Bromides of Eve's Pillar Design.

Stamp-size hand-drawn essay on thin card (80×84mm).
Bromides of above with varying degrees of shading to background (29×35mm)................................£1400

Colour Trial
Imperforate on gummed watermarked paper in bluish violet.. £4750

Produced from a 240-set plate under special control X. 13 watermarked Simple Cypher, perf. 15 × 14 and known only in a control block of six
In shade of violet not selected ....*Control block of six* £40000
One example recorded and endorsed "Not Selected" in manuscript.

Die Proofs
Uncleared in black on white glazed card............................. £8750

Plate Markings

Official Plate	SG Plate	Markings
1a	1a	Existing dot above R. 1/1, 2 mm. Added dot above R. 1/1, 9.5 mm. Added dot above R. 11/1, 9.3 mm.
1b	1b	Dots above R. 1/1 and R. 11/1 filled in
1c	1c	Added dot above R. 1/1, 17.5 mm. Added dot above R. 11/1, 17.7 mm.
2a	2a	Existing ½ dot top right end under R. 20/5. Added dot above R. 1/2, 9.5 mm. Added dot above R. 11/2, 9.4 mm.
2b	2b	Dots above R. 1/2 and R. 11/ 2 filled in
2c	2bb*	Internal nick R. 19 right side, 10.2 mm.
2d	2c	Added cut R. 20 left side, 12.5 mm.
3a	3a	Added dot above R. 1/3, 9.5 mm. Added dot above R. 11/3, 9.7 mm.
3b	3b	Dots above R. 1/3 and R. 11/3 filled in
4a	4a	Added dot above R. 1/4, 9.2 mm. Added dot above R. 11/4, 9.2 mm.
4b	4b	Dots above R. 1/4 and R. 11/4 filled in
6	4c	Existing dot breaking inner R. 2 left side 15.5 mm. Added dot above R. 1/6, 9.4 mm. Added dot above R. 11/6, 9.0 mm.
7a	12aa*	Existing nick (outer) R. 12 right, 15.7 mm.
7b	12a	Rule broken away bottom right R. 20/2 and added cut above R. 1/11, 10 mm.
7c	12b	Horizontal dash under PE of R. 20/2 and Rule broken away bottom left under R. 20/3
8a	13a	Added cut above R. 1/12, 7.5 mm.
8b	13b	Added large ½ dot base under E P R. 20/1
9	5	Existing minute dot under EN of R. 20/11 and Added diamond shaped cut under EP of R. 20/2
10a	6a	Existing nick (outer) R. 1 right, 13 mm.
10b	6b	Added cut under E(E) of R. 20/1
11a	7a	Existing gap in top of cross R. 20/3 and ½ dot (outer) R. 14 right, 3 mm.
11b	7b	Added cut under EP of R. 20/2
12	11	Existing R. 17 right side outer bevelled at base and base of rule scooped out under REE P of R. 20/8
13a	8a	Base R. 20 right side bevelled
13b	8b	Added nick outer R. 19 left side, 5.75 mm.
14	9	Added ½ dot inner R. 20 left side, 12.8 mm. (Waterlow Plate 4, Harrison prov. ptg. Plate 4)
15	10	Added dot R. 19 left side, 13 mm. (Waterlow Plate 3)

* = New plate allocation

Control Schedule

Official Plate	SG Plate	Controls used
1a	1a	A. 12(c), B. 13
1b	1b	C 13
1c	1c	C. 13, F 15, H 16
2a	2a	A. 12(w), A. 12(c), B. 13
2b	2b	C 13
2c	2bb*	D 14, E 14
2d	2c	E 14, F 15, H 16, I 16
3a	3a	A. 12(w), A. 12(c)
3b	3b	C 13, F 15
4a	4a	A. 12(c)

4d. Grey-green, Type N7. Royal Cypher — The Profile Head Issue — KING GEORGE V — NB

Official Plate	SG Plate	Controls used
4b	4b, c	C 13, F 15, G 15
6	4c	C. 13 F 15, G 15
7a	12aa*	I 16, J 17
7b	12a	J 17, L 18
7c	12b	M 18, N 19, Q 21
8a	13a	I 16, L 18, M 18
8b	13b	M 18, N 19, O 20, P 20
9	5	M 18, N 19, O 20, P 20, Q 21, T 22, U 23, V 23
10a	6a	Q 21, R 21
10b	6b	R 21
11a	7a	Q 21, R 21
11b	7b	R 21
12	11	S 21, S 22, T 22, U 22, U 23
13a	8a	S 21, S 22, T 22
13b	8b	U 22
14	9	U 23, V 23, W 23
15	10	U 23, V 23, W 23

* = New plate allocation
(w) = wide
(c) = close

An additional C13 control position has been identified but not matched with a plate.

1913 (15 January). **4d. Grey-green, Type N7.** Wmk. Simple Cypher

N23 (=S.G.378/80)

	Unmtd mint	Mtd mint	Used
(1) Grey-green	25·00	15·00	2·00
(2) Pale grey-green	40·00	25·00	5·00
(3) Deep grey-green	75·00	45·00	25·00
(4) Slate-green	25·00	15·00	2·00
(5) Pale slate-green	40·00	30·00	2·00
(6) Bluish grey-green (1919)	35·00	25·00	4·00
(7) Deep slate-green (1921)	£250	£175	75·00
a. Without watermark	£475	£350	£275
b. Watermark inverted	50·00	30·00	30·00
c. Watermark reversed	£500	£300	£300
d. Watermark inverted and reversed	£110	80·00	80·00
e. Break above O of FOUR (Pl. 1, R. 19/2)		85·00	
f. Cracked plate (Pl. 2, R. 19/1)		85·00	
g. Breaks in bottom frame (R. 10/11)		£425	
h. Frame breaks at foot (Pl. ?, R. 5/12)		£425	
i. Flaw on lower left inner frame (Pl?, R. 2/5)		£150	
j. Blob on nose		£400	
s. "Specimen", Type 15		£950	
t. "Specimen", Type 23		£125	
u. "Cancelled", Type 24		£700	
v. "Specimen", Type 26		£150	

Eve's wreath design had been intended for the 4d., but after trials the Mackennal wreath design was selected.

Variety e, from Plate 1c first occurs during the F 15 control period.

Variety f is first seen with control I 16 and repaired 25.9.21 with control Q 21.

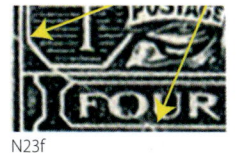

N23e   N23f

N23g   N23i

N23h   N23j
Progressive flaw as seen on Control I 16

Watermark Varieties. The following have been recorded:
Wmk upright: Types I, II, III
Wmk inverted: Types I, II, III
Wmk reversed: Type II
Wmk inverted and reversed: Types I, II, III

Misplaced Watermarks
ya. Single stamp showing letters from "POSTAGE" .... 55·00
yb. Vertical strip sufficient to show complete "POSTAGE" watermark £500

Broken Dandy Roll Varieties
za. Missing Crown .... 60·00
zb. Missing G .... 55·00
zc. Missing v .... 35·00
zd. Missing R .... —
ze. Missing Gv .... 55·00
zf. Missing vR .... 55·00
zg. Missing Crown vR .... 55·00
zi. Missing left side to R .... 55·00
zj. Missing tail to R ("GvP") .... 35·00
zk. Long tail to G .... 55·00

Controls. Prices are for unused singles.
Somerset House Printings:

	Perf. Type	
Control	2 (E.)	2A (P.)
B. 13	18·00	75·00

Watermark varieties known: wmk upright, Type I; wmk inverted, Type I, wmk inverted and reversed, Type I.

Harrison Printings:

	Perf. Type	
Control	2 (E.)	2A (P.)
C 13	20·00	20·00
D 14	22·00	22·00
F 15	20·00	20·00
G 15	20·00	20·00
H 16	20·00	£125
I 16	20·00	20·00
J 17	20·00	20·00
K 17	22·00	£2200
K 18	20·00	20·00
M 18	20·00	20·00
N 19	22·00	22·00
O 20	22·00	22·00
Q 21 (c)	£125	£125
R 21	22·00	22·00
S 21	£175	£120

KING GEORGE V — The Profile Head Issue — 4d. Grey-green, Type N7. Royal Cypher

Control	Perf. Type 2 (E.)	2A (P.)
S 22	30·00	60·00
T 22	20·00	20·00
U 22	£125	£125
U 23	80·00	25·00
V 23	22·00	22·00

Variety Type 2 (c) (I/I)
Strip of three
J 17 .... £200

Watermark varieties known:
Wmk upright, Type I: C 13.
Wmk upright, Type II: C 13, D 14, F 15, G 15, H 16, I 16, J 17, K 17, K 18, O 20, R 21, U 22, U 23, V 23.
Wmk inverted, Type II: G 15.
Wmk reversed, Type II: C 13.
Wmk inverted and reversed, Type II: C 13, G 15, I 16, U 22.
Wmk upright, Type III: J 17, K 17, K 18, M 18, N 19, O 20, Q 21, R 21, S 21, S 22, T 22, U 23.
Wmk inverted, Type III: K 17, M 18.
Wmk reversed, Type III: J 17.
Wmk inverted and reversed, Type III: J 17, K 17, M 18, R 21.

Bromides of Eve's Wreath Design

Fig. 26a 21·5 mm.

Fig. 26b 22·3 mm.

Eve's original design in sunken frame, dated 7 May 1912
Original had coinage head pasted in. Value and
 lettering weak. 21·5 mm. high............................. £1150
Similar to above but not in sunken frame, dated on reverse 16 May 1912
Lettering better defined. Lines of shading behind
 head slope down from left to right, 22·3 mm.
 high £875
Large master design (78 × 94 mm.) inscribed
 on face "4d. The First Essay. 8:VI:12" with
 Harrison's accepted coinage head inserted. Value omitted.
Large master design (71 × 89mm) with Mackennal's
 bas-relief plaque head inscribed "47.4" and "4d" £3000
Lines of shading behind head slope down from
 right to left.. £1800

Similar to Fig. 26a but only 22 mm. high
Mounted on card with M/S noting "Mr. Eve's
 emendations". Lines of shading behind
 head horizontal..
Lines of shading behind head horizontal............................. £1100
As above but not on card £500
On card with M/S "Make plate and submit to
 Board with colour scheme—F.G. 13 June 1912" £1600
As above but lines of shading to head slope down
 from right to left. Dated on reverse 10 June 1912 ....£750
As Fig. 26b on pale blue card with typed note
 "Design for 4d. Postage Stamp amended by
 Mr. Eve to correspond with the amended 5d.
 design. (Motley Process)."
Lines of shading behind head horizontal and
 graduated from top to bottom £1600
As Fig. 27c, stamp-size bromide with image
 reversed, mounted on card, various
 endorsements and dated "18.6.12" £2800

Trials of Eve's Wreath Design

Fig. 27a 22·8 mm.  Fig. 27b 22·5 mm.

Fig. 27c 22 mm.  Fig. 28 22·5 mm.

Figs. 27a/c by Miller and Motley using their Printex machine and used as trials for colour. Large coinage head. Shading at sides of design extends down to P of POSTAGE and last E of REVENUE. The measurements are taken between top and bottom frame lines.
(a) Fig. 27a 22·8 mm. high. Left-hand ribbon above R of FOUR
 has an ornament in it
Uncleared die proof with reversed "K"* above design
In black on thin card (but only 22 mm. high)....................... £3000
In purple-brown on thin card £3000
In various colours on thick white ungummed paper taken
 from plate of four impressions .... *Block of four from* £6250
As last but single examples .... *From* £1500
In black on thin glazed card .... Block of four £2800
As last but single example £650
(b) Fig. 27b. 22·5 mm. Solid colour in left-hand
 ribbon above R of FOUR
In blue on gummed paper watermarked Crown
 taken from plate of four impressions (June
 1912).. *Block of four* £7250
As last but single example £1750
(c) Fig. 27c. As (b) but only 22 mm. high
In various colours on white gummed paper
 without watermark...................................... *From* £1500
In blue on pink, brown on pink, orange on blue or
 claret on blue... *From* £1600
 Fig. 28 produced from a die engraved at the Royal Mint by J. A. C. Harrison's assistant, Mr. Lewis. Large coinage head. Heavy shading at sides of the design extends only to the A of POSTAGE and first E of REVENUE. 22·5 mm. high.
Uncleared die proof in pale blue on gummed
 paper watermarked Simple Cypher, upright
 or sideways. Uncut.. £3750
As last but cut close to margin .... *From* £1600

136

5d. Brown, Type N8. Royal Cypher — *The Profile Head Issue* — KING GEORGE V — NB

Uncleared die proof in red-brown	£3500
Cleared die proof in black on card dated "16.9.12"	£3000
Cleared die proof in black on card dated "3.10.12"	£3000
Cleared die proof in black on card dated "8.10.12"	£3000
Cleared die proof in black on card dated "Recd 9.10.12"	£3000
Cleared die proof in pale blue on paper dated "16.12.12"	£3500
Cleared die proof in blue on card dated "14.12.12"	£3500

Complete die proofs containing the die number above are worth at least twice the prices quoted.

For illustration of typical block of four from a special plate see under the 7d. value.

Die Proofs

Uncleared in black on white glazed card	£6500
From cleared working die on gummed paper in grey, pearl-grey and bronze-green on official card dated "10 Dec. 1912"	£9000

Plate Proofs

In pale ultramarine on thick paper	£1600
In grey-green on thin gummed paper	£1600
In pale grey-green on gummed watermarked paper	£5500

Colour trial

Perforated in bluish grey-green on gummed watermarked paper (Somerset House printing, control "B.13")	£3500

Plate Markings

Official Plate	SG Plate	Markings
1a	1a	Added dot above R. 1/1, 9.75 mm. Added dot above R. 11/1, 10.25 mm. Tiny white dot in left frame R. 19/1, 10.75 mm.
1b	1b	Dots above R. 1/1 and R. 11/1 filled in
1c	1c	Added small dot under RP of R. 20/1
1d	1d	Dot under RP of R. 20/1 enlarged
1e	1e	Rule under R. 20/3 bevelled lower left end
2a	2a	Added dot above R. 1/2, 9.3 mm. Added dot above R. 11/2, 9.5 mm.
2b	2b (part)	Dots above R. 1/2 and R. 11/2 filled in
3a	2b (part)	No details on markings
3b	2c	Added small dot under RP of R. 20/2
3c	2d	Dot under RP of R. 20/2 enlarged (Harrison prov. ptg. Plate 8)
4a	3a	Split R. 19 left side outer, 8-9 mm.
4b	3b	Added dot under RP of R. 20/1 (N.B. Rule under R. 20/3 not bevelled) (Waterlow Plate 4)

Control Schedule

Official Plate	SG Plate	Controls used
1a	1a	B. 13
1b	1b	C 13, D 14
1c	1c	F 15, G 15
1d	1d	G 15, H 16, I 16
1e	1e	I 16, J 17, K 17, K 18, O 20, Q 21, R 21, S 21, S 22, T 22, U 22
2a	2a	B. 13
2b	2b (part)	C 13
3a	2b (part)	C 13, D 14
3b	2c	F 15, G 15
3c	2d	G 15, H 16, I 16, J 17, K 18, M 18, N 19, O 20, Q 21, R 21, S 21, S 22, T 22, U 22, U 23, V 23
4a	3a	I 16, J 17, M 18
4b	3b	N 19, Q 21, R 21, S 21, U 23, V 23

1913 *(30 June).* **5d. Brown, Type N8.** Wmk. Simple Cypher

N25 (=S.G.381/83)

	Unmtd mint	Mtd mint	Used
(1) Brown	25·00	15·00	5·00
(2) Reddish brown	90·00	60·00	10·00
(3) Yellow-brown	25·00	15·00	5·00
(4) Ochre-brown (1916)	£250	£175	50·00
(5) Ginger-brown (1917)	45·00	30·00	10·00
(6) Bistre-brown	£250	£185	75·00
a. No watermark	£2000	£1200	
aa Do. "U23" control block of six	£30000	†	†
b. Watermark inverted	£1500	£1100	£1100
c. Watermark inverted and reversed	£500	£400	£400
d. Watermark reversed	†	†	—
e. Varnish ink (Control H 16)	£3000	£2000	
f. Lower left frame break (Pl. ?, R. 20/1 control B. 13)		£250	
g. White blotch near "V" of "REVENUE" (Pl. 1c, R. 20/2)		£200	
s. "Specimen", Type 15		£950	
t. "Specimen", Type 23		£325	
u. "Specimen", Type 26		£250	
v. "Cancelled", Type 24		£800	

Imperforate (single) from P.O. Registration sheet £7500

N25f   N25g

Watermark Varieties. The following have been recorded:
Wmk upright: Types I, II, III
Wmk inverted: Types II, III
Wmk inverted and reversed: Types II, III
No. N 25a came from a sheet without watermark.

Misplaced Watermarks

ya. Single stamp showing letters from "POSTAGE"	80·00
yb. Vertical strip sufficient to show complete "POSTAGE" watermark	£900

Broken Dandy Roll Varieties

za. Missing Crown	60·00
zb. Missing G	50·00
zc. Missing v	40·00
zd. Missing R	—
zf. Missing vR	45·00
zg. Missing Crown vR	45·00
zi. Missing left side to R	45·00
zj. Missing tail to R ("GvP")	40·00
zk. Long tail to G	45·00

Controls. Prices are for unused singles.
Somerset House Printings:

	Perf. Type	
Control	2 (E.)	2A (P.)
B.13	18·00	25·00

Watermark varieties known: Types I or II, upright only.

137

NB KING GEORGE V The Profile Head Issue 5d. Brown, Type N8. Royal Cypher

Harrison Printings:

Control	Perf. Type 2 (E.)	2A (P.)
C 14	18·00	18·00
D 14	18·00	18·00
F 15	18·00	18·00
G 15	18·00	18·00
H 16	18·00	25·00
I 16	25·00	25·00
J 17	18·00	18·00
K 17	18·00	80·00
L 18	18·00	18·00
N 19	18·00	18·00
O 19	25·00	25·00
Q 21 (w)	30·00	35·00
R 21	35·00	75·00
S 21	25·00	35·00
S 22	18·00	£500
T 22	18·00	18·00
U 23	18·00	18·00
V 23	18·00	£175

Watermark varieties known:
Wmk upright, Type II: C 14, D 14, F 15, G 15, H 16, I 16, J 17, K 17, N 19, O 19, Q 21, R 21, U 23, V 23.
Wmk inverted, Type II: H 16.
Wmk inverted and reversed, Type II: D 14.
Wmk upright, Type III: J 17, K 17, L 18, N 19, O 19, Q 21, S 21, S 22, T 22, U 23.
Wmk inverted, Type III: L 18, N 19.
Wmk inverted and reversed, Type III: N 19

Fig. 28a 23 mm.    Fig. 28a 22·5 mm.

Fig. 28b 22·5 mm.    Fig. 28c 22·25 mm.

Bromides of Eve's Wreath Design
There is no evidence of any engraved die with this design used for this value.
Fig. 28a. Shading at sides extends down to P of POSTAGE and last E of REVENUE.
Large coinage head (12 mm.). Even horizontal lines of shading to background
Dated "27.6.12". 23 mm. high £1750
Dated "2.7.12". 22·5 mm. high £1750
As Fig. 28a on pale blue card with typed note
"Embodying Mr. Eve's latest emendations (Motley Process)"..
Fig. 28b. Shading at sides extends only to E of POSTAGE and R of REVENUE.
With coinage head and inside of Crown in solid colour. Image completely reversed. Even lines to background of head, Undated £2000
With medal head and inside of Crown shaded.
A bromide of Eve's artwork 22·5 mm. high.
Graduated lines to background of head
Dated "22.11.1912" £2000
Dated "28.11.1912" £2000
As last but 23 mm. high and endorsed "Photograph taken at The Mint 29 Nov 1912 of Eve's Sketch for an amended Design for 5d. and other Rates"........ £1750

Bromides of Eve's Pillar Design
Fig. 28c. With medal head. 22·25 mm. high. Graduated shading to background
Dated "29.4.13". 22·25 mm. high £1750
Dated "29.4.13". 22·75 mm. high £1750
The last bromide was sent to Harrison who made his own engraving sketch from an enlargement.

Die Proofs from Eve's Pillar Design
Without value in black. Master die for 5d. to 8d.................. £6500
Fully cleared in black on thin white glazed card,
  endorsed "2.5.13" in manuscript.. £6500
Fully cleared in black on white glazed card,
  endorsed "6 May 13" in manuscript.................................. £6500
Fully cleared in black on white glazed card,
  endorsed "8.5.13" in manuscript.. £6500
Fully cleared in black on white glazed card,
  endorsed "13.5.13"... £6500
Fully cleared in black on gummed sideways watermarked paper, endorsed "2.5.13" in manuscript

Plate Proof
In an imperforate block of four on Stamping Dept. card, dated "6 Jun. 1913" with a swatch of colour underneath and used for colour trials
In ochre or green on paper watermarked Simple Cypher (upright).. Block of four £28000
As last but single examples .... From £6750

Plate Markings

Official Plate	SG Plate	Markings
1a	1a	Added dot above R. 1/1, 9.9 mm. Added dot above R. 11/1, 9.2 mm.
1b	1b	Dots above R. 1/1 and R. 11/1 filled in
1c	1c	Added 1½ sloping cuts under EN of R. 20/1
2a	2a	Existing minute dot left end under R. 20/6. Added dot above R. 1/2, 9.5 mm. Added dot above R. 11/2
2b	2b	Dots above R. 1/2 and R. 11/2 filled in
2c	2c	Added sloping cut under P of R. 20/2
3a	3	Tiny internal cut R. 19 right side, 14 mm. (Waterlow Plate 1a)
4a	4*	No Markings

* = New plate allocation

Control Schedule

Official Plate	SG Plate	Controls used
1a	1a	B. 13
1b	1b	C 14, D 14, F 15, G 15, H 16
1c	1c	H 16, I 16, J 17, K 17, L 18, N 19, O 19, Q 21, R 21
2a	2a	B. 13
2b	2b	C 14, D 14, F 15, G 15, H 16
2c	2c	H 16, I 16, J 17, K 17, L 18, Q 21, S 21, S 22
3a	3	Q 21, R 21, S 21, T 22**, U 23**, V 23
4a	4*	S 22**, T 22**, U 23**, V 23

* = New plate allocation
** For controls S 22, T 22 and U 23 it is very difficult to distinguish the difference between plates 3 and 4 as it requires a minimum of a bottom row with rule 19th. right attached. Therefore, from unproven material seen at this time the above looks the most likely case. Help is needed with large pieces of these three controls.

6d. Purple, Type N8. Royal Cypher — The Profile Head Issue — KING GEORGE V — NB

1913 *(1 August).* **6d. Purple, Type N8.** Wmk. Simple Cypher. Chalk-Surfaced Paper

N26 (=S.G.384/86)

	Unmtd mint	Mtd mint	Used
(1) Dull purple (1913)	45·00	25·00	10·00
(2) Slate-purple (1913)	£200	£125	75·00
(3) Reddish purple	30·00	15·00	7·00
(4) Pale reddish purple	35·00	20·00	2·00
(5) Deep reddish purple	85·00	50·00	5·00
(6) Purple	30·00	20·00	2·00
(7) Rosy mauve	30·00	15·00	2·00
(8) Plum	30·00	20·00	2·00
a. Without watermark	£3500	£2000	£1000
b. Watermark inverted	85·00	50·00	50·00
c. Watermark reversed	£5250	£4250	
d. Watermark inverted and reversed	£150	£100	£100
e. Perforation 14 (10.20)	£150	90·00	£110
eb. Watermark inverted			
ed. Watermark inverted and reversed			
ee. Broken frame below "X P" of "SIX PENCE" (R. 16/9)	£1200		
s. "Specimen", Type 15		£950	
t. "Specimen", Type 23		£200	
u. "Specimen", Type 26		£250	
v. "Cancelled", Type 24		£350	
w. "Cancelled", Type 28		£700	

Imperforate (single) from P.O. registration sheet £8000

N26ee

Watermark Varieties. The following have been recorded:
Perf 15 × 14:
Wmk upright: Types II, III
Wmk inverted: Types II, III
Wmk reversed: Types II, III
Wmk inverted and reversed, Types II, III
Perf 14:
Wmk upright: Types II, III
Wmk inverted: Type III
Wmk inverted and reversed: Type III

Misplaced Watermarks
ya. Single stamp showing letters from "POSTAGE" .... 85·00
yb. Vertical strip sufficient to show complete "POSTAGE" watermark £950

Broken Dandy Roll Varieties
za. Missing Crown .... 65·00
zab. Do. Perf 14 .... £250
zc. Missing v .... 35·00
zd. Missing R .... 40·00
zda. Do. Perf 14 .... —
zf. Missing vR .... 40·00
zg. Missing Crown vR .... 40·00
zi. Missing left side to R .... 45·00
zj. Missing tail to R ("GvP") .... 35·00
zka. Long tail to G (perf 14) .... —

Controls. Prices are for unused singles.
Somerset House Printings, Perf 15 × 14:

	Perf. Type	
Control	2 (E.)	2A (P.)
C. 13 (dull purple)	30·00	40·00
C. 13 (reddish purple)	22·00	25·00
D. 14	18·00	†
E. 14	18·00	18·00
F. 15	30·00	£1200
G. 15	18·00	†
H. 16	18·00	†
I. 16	18·00	†
J. 17	18·00	†
K. 17	18·00	†
L. 18	18·00	75·00
L 18 [no stop]	25·00	†
M. 18	20·00	£2000
N. 19	18·00	£250
O. 19	18·00	†
P. 20	18·00	†
Q. 20	18·00	†
R. 21	18·00	†
S. 21	18·00	£225
T. 22	20·00	—
U. 22	18·00	†
V. 23	18·00	†
W. 23	18·00	†

Variety Type 2(c) (I/I)
Strip of three
C. 13 Reddish purple	£120
W. 23	80·00
A. 24 Plum	£100
B. 24 Plum	£180

Variety Type 3 (P/E)
Strip of three
| C. 13 Dull purple | £180 |
| C. 13 Reddish purple | £180 |

Variety Type 3A (I/P)
Strip of three
| C. 13 Dull purple | £250 |

A. 24 and B. 24 are always Type 2(c)

Watermark varieties known:
Wmk upright, Type II: C. 13 (both shades); D. 14, E. 14, F. 15, G. 15, H. 16, I. 16, J. 17, O. 19, P. 20, Q. 20, S. 21, V. 23, W. 23, A. 24, B. 24.
Wmk inverted, Type II: C. 13 (reddish purple), E. 14, H. 16, W. 23, A. 24.
Wmk reversed, Type II: D. 14.
Wmk inverted and reversed, Type II: D. 14, E. 14.
Wmk upright, Type III: J. 17, K. 17, L. 18 (with and without stop), M. 18, N. 19, O. 19, P. 20, Q. 20, R. 21, S. 21, T. 22, U. 22, V. 23, A. 24, B. 24.
Wmk inverted, Type III: L. 18, M. 18, N. 19, O. 19, P. 20, Q. 20, R. 21, S. 21, U. 21, U. 22, V. 23.
Wmk reversed, Type III: O. 19.
Wmk inverted and reversed, Type III: K. 17, N. 19, O. 19, P. 20, T. 22, U. 22.

Somerset House Printings, Perf 14:

	Perf. Type
Control	2 (E.)
Q. 20	£125
R. 21	£175

Watermark varieties known:
Wmk upright, Type II: Q. 20, R. 21.
Wmk upright, Type III: Q. 20, R. 21.
Wmk inverted, Type III: R. 21.
Wmk inverted and reversed, Type III: R. 21.

139

KING GEORGE V — The Profile Head Issue — 7d. Olive, Type N8. Royal Cypher

Bromides

Bromides of Eve's wreath design.

Bromide proof (29×35mm) with value "6" lightly drawn in upper corners, lines of shading behind head sloping down, right to left........................ £1650
As above but with value figures completed and "SIX PENCE" added... £1650

Die Proof
Uncleared in black on white glazed card dated "28.5.1913"... £6500
Uncleared in black on white glazed card, undated............ £6000

Plate Markings
Plates with interpane margin.
  Plate markings such as those used by Harrisons and Waterlows were not used at Somerset House, and plating can only be accomplished by the study of fortuitous marks. It seems that the 6d. stamps were printed in pairs of plates and these were marked above the top rows of the panes with a dot above the 1st or 2nd stamps to signify the position in the press.

Official Plate	SG Plate	Markings
1	1	Added dots above R. 1/1, 9.25 mm. and R. 11/1, 9 mm.
2	2	Added dots above R. 1/2, 9.25 mm. and R. 11/2, 9 mm.
3a	3a	Added dots above R. 1/1, 9 mm. and R. 11/1 9.6 mm.
3b	3b	Added small dot under (P)E of R. 20/2
4	4	Existing base outer R. 17 right side bevelled. Existing R. 20/3 small coloured mark between inner and outer right frames 9.3 mm.
5a	5	No markings
5(-)*	5	Not sure when dots added above R. 1/1 and R. 11/1
5b	5	Dot above R. 1/1, 9.2 mm. and R. 11/1, 9.5 mm.
6	7	No markings
7a	6	Existing projection under X of R. 20/1
7(-)*	6	Not sure when dot added above R. 1/2
7b	6	Dot above R. 1/2, 5 mm.

Plate 6 was also used with the Block Cypher watermark.

Control Schedule

Official Plate	SG Plate	Controls used.
1	1	C. 13, D. 14, E. 14, F. 15, G. 15, H. 16
2	2	C. 13, D. 14, E. 14, F. 15, G. 15, H. 16
3a	3a	I. 16, J. 17, K. 17, L. 18
3b	3b	L. 18, M. 18, N. 19, O. 19, P. 20, Q. 20
4	4	I. 16, L. 18, Q. 20, R. 21, S. 21
5a	5	L. 18
5*(-)	5	M. 18, N. 19, O. 19, P. 20
5b	5	Q. 20
6	7	Q. 20, R. 21, S. 21, T. 22, U. 22, V. 23, W. 23, A. 24, B. 24
7a	6	S. 21
7*(-)	6	T. 22, U. 22, V. 23, W. 23, A. 24
7b	6	B. 24

Note:–* It is not certain when dots were added so for now we show (-). When established the controls will be reallocated to (a) or (b).
  Plate 6 was also used with the Block Cypher watermark.

1913 (1 August). 7d. Olive, Type N8. Wmk. Simple Cypher
N27 (=S.G.387/89)

	Unmtd mint	Mtd mint	Used
(1) Olive	35·00	20·00	10·00
(2) Olive-grey	40·00	22·00	9·00
(3) Bronze-green (1915)	£120	70·00	25·00
(4) Sage-green (1917)	£120	70·00	18·00
a. Without watermark	£950	£650	£400
b. Watermark inverted	85·00	50·00	55·00
c. Watermark inverted and reversed	£5750	£4750	
d. Watermark reversed	†	†	—
e. Frame break top right (Pl. ?, R6?/12)			
s. "Specimen", Type 26		£200†	
t. "Cancelled", Type 24		£275	

†No. N27s exists from NPM archive sales.
Imperforate (single) from P.O. registration sheet................ £7500

Watermark varieties. The following have been recorded:
Wmk upright: Types I, II, III
Wmk inverted: Type III

Misplaced Watermarks
ya. Single stamp showing letters from "POSTAGE"............. 95·00
yb. Vertical strip sufficient to show complete "POSTAGE" watermark.. £1400

Broken Dandy Roll Varieties
za. Missing Crown..£135
zc. Missing v..50·00
zj. Missing tail to R ("GvP") ....50·00

Controls. Prices are for unused singles.
Somerset House Printings:

	Perf. Type	
Control	2 (E.)	2A (P.)
C. 13	50·00	—

Wmk upright, Types I and II only.

Harrison Printings:

	Perf. Type	
Control	2 (E.)	2A (P.)
C 13	30·00	30·00
D 14	25·00	25·00
F 15	40·00	40·00
G 15	25·00	25·00
H 16	25·00	25·00
J 17	30·00	30·00
L 18	30·00	£250

Variety Type 2 (c) (I/I)
Strip of three
J 17   £175

Watermark varieties known:
Wmk upright, Type II: C 13, D 14, F 15, G 15, H 16, J 17.
Wmk upright, Type III: J 17, L 18.
Wmk inverted, Type III: H 16, J 17, L 18.

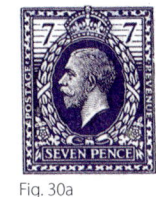

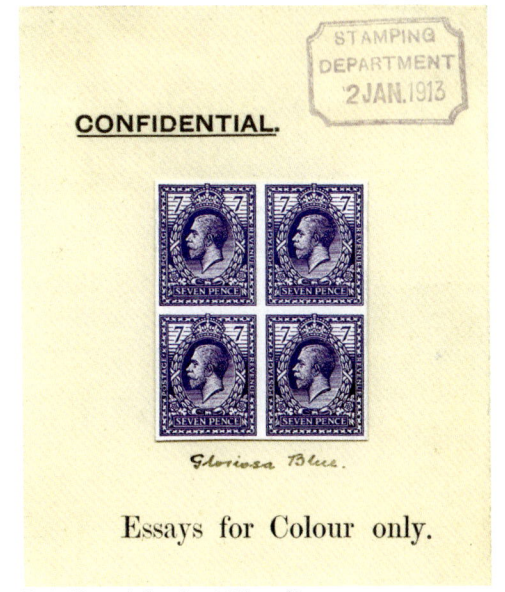

7d. Olive, Type N8. Royal Cypher *The Profile Head Issue* **KING GEORGE V** **NB**

Fig. 29

Fig. 29a

Fig. 30a

Fig. 30b

Fig. 30c

Typical Example from Special Plate of Four

Trials of Eve's Wreath Design
There is no evidence of any engraved die with this design used for this value.
Trials by Miller and Motley using their Printex machine
Fig. 29. Large coinage head (12 mm.). Shading at sides extends down to P of POSTAGE and last E of REVENUE. Frame 22·5 mm. high
In black on card taken from plate of four
 impressions .... Block of four £2500
As last but single example £550
In bistre-brown, turquoise or magenta on
 gummed paper without watermark .... From £1900
In bistre-brown or magenta on gummed paper
 without watermark and overprinted "ESSAY"... From £1900
Fig. 29a. Smaller coinage head (10½ mm.). Shading at sides extends down to P of POSTAGE and last E of REVENUE. Frame 22 mm. high
In black on light brown card with pencil
 manuscript by Seymour Bennett and dated
 "22 October 1912"... £1400
Figs. 30a/c. Smaller coinage head (10½ mm.) Shading at sides extends only to E of POSTAGE and R of REVENUE. Three different types of background shading to the head. Frame 22 mm. high

(a) Fig. 30a. With background of solid colour
In black on card taken from plate of four
 impressions .... Block of four £2500
As last but single example £550
In bistre-brown, grey, maroon, Tyrian red (dated
 "3 Jan. 1913"), gloriosa-blue or bright
 yellow-green (lime) on thick paper without
 watermark and ungummed except for lime
 shade, taken from plate of four
 impressions .... Block of four from £7750
As last but single example .... From £1850
In bistre-brown, grey, maroon or Tyrian red in
 blocks of four mounted on Stamping Dept.
 card dated "3 Jan 1913".. £8750
(b) Fig. 30b. With background of solid colour from 8 to 12 o'clock
In black on card taken from plate of four
 impressions .... Block of four £2500
As last but single example £550
In bright yellow-green (lime) on thick gummed
 paper without watermark..£1850
In black on light brown card £650
In Tyrian red on gummed paper without
 watermark... Block of four £7750
As last but single example £1850
In bistre-brown, grey, gloriosa blue or Tyrian red
 on thin glazed card without watermark Block of four £7750
As last but single example £1850
(c) Fig. 30c. With background evenly shaded with horizontal lines
In black on card taken from plate of four
 impressions .... Block of four £2500
As last but single example £550
In black on light brown card and endorsed by
 Seymour Bennett "An Essay by the Printex
 Process for a new Design for 7d. A copy
 handed to me 29 Oct 1912 to Mr. Eve" and signed... £1800
In sepia on card with background to head hand-
 inked to produce solid colour as Fig. 30a..................... £1850

Die Proofs
Uncleared in black on white glazed card dated
 "5.6.1913".. £7000
Do. Undated £6500

Plate Markings

Official Plate	SG Plate	Markings
1	1a	Existing dot above R. 1/5. Added dot above R. 1/1. Added dot above R. 11/1
2a	1b	No markings
2b	1c	Added small dot under (VE)N of R. 20/1. Thin ½ cut above R.1/1
3a	2a	No details of the plate markings
3b	2b	Added small dot under NP of R. 20/2

Control Schedule

Official Plate	SG Plate	Controls used
1	1a	C. 13
2a	1b	C 13, D 14
2b	1c	F 15, G 15, H 16, J 17, L 18
3a	2a	C 13, D 14
3b	2b	F 15, G 15, H 16.

Stanley Gibbons

Great Britain Department

BY APPOINTMENT TO
HER MAJESTY THE QUEEN
PHILATELISTS
STANLEY GIBBONS LTD
LONDON

Stanley Gibbons, a name synonymous with quality.

Ever since the birth of our hobby Stanley Gibbons has been at the forefront of GB philately and we invite collectors access to one of the finest GB stocks in the world by registering for our renowned free monthly brochure. Whatever your budget or collecting interests you will find a range of the highest quality material for the discerning collector.

To receive our monthly brochures or for further enquires please email gb@stanleygibbons.com or phone 020 7557 4424.

STANLEY GIBBONS
Est 1856

Proud PTS members

Stanley Gibbons
399 Strand, London, WC2R 0LX
+44 (0)20 7836 8444
www.stanleygibbons.com

8d. Black on Yellow, Type N8. Royal Cypher — The Profile Head Issue — KING GEORGE V — NB

1913 (1 August). **8d. Black on Yellow, Type N8.** Wmk. Simple Cypher

N28 (=S.G.390/91)

	Unmtd mint	Mtd mint	Used
(1) Black on yellow paper	55·00	32·00	11·00
(2) Black on yellow-buff (granite) paper (May 1917)	60·00	40·00	15·00
a. Without watermark	£3500	£2500	
b. Watermark inverted	£220	£150	£150
c. Watermark reversed	£350	£240	£240
d. Watermark inverted and reversed	£6750	£5250	
e. Frame broken lower right side (R. 20/10)		£300	£150
f. Frame broken (R. 1–10?/12)		£350	£175
s. "Specimen", Type 26		£250†	
t. "Cancelled", Type 24			£375

The granite paper is of poorer quality and shows hairs and other particles in the texture.
†No. N28s exists from NPM archive sales.

N28e   N28f

Watermark Varieties. The following have been recorded:
Wmk upright: Types II, III
Wmk inverted: Type II
Wmk reversed: Type II
Wmk inverted and reversed: Type II

Misplaced Watermarks
ya. Single stamp showing letters from "POSTAGE" £100
yb. Vertical strip sufficient to show complete "POSTAGE" watermark £1650

Broken Dandy Roll Varieties
zc. Missing v £100
zi. Missing left side to R £100
zj. Missing tail to R ("GvP") .... 90·00

Controls. Prices are for unused singles.
Somerset House Printings:

	Perf. Type
Control	2(E.)
C. 13	45·00

Wmk upright, Type II only.
Control C. 13 with a faked bottom perf. margin exists.

Harrison Printings:

	Perf. Type	
Control	2 (E.)	2A (P.)
D 14	50·00	45·00
F 15	40·00	40·00
G 15	40·00	40·00
H 16	40·00	40·00
I 16	50·00	50·00
J 17	42·00	42·00
K 18	£500	55·00

Watermark varieties known:
Wmk upright, Type II: D 14, F 15, G 15, H 16, I 16, J 17.
Wmk inverted, Type II: F 15.
Wmk reversed, Type II: G 15, H 16.
Wmk inverted and reversed, Type II: D 14.
Wmk upright, Type III (granite paper): J 17, K 18.

As Fig. 31 but graduated shading

Bromides of Eve's Pillar Design
Bromides with large margins of Eve's original artwork for 8d. value with medal head and graduated background shading, mounted on card
Dated "22.11.12" £1000
Also dated "22.11.12" but with Chinese white additions to numerals—intended by Eve as a master die for 8d. to 1s. values £1100
As Fig. 31 but with graduated shading around head
With large margins £1100
As last but reduced to ¾ size and mounted on brown card £550
As last but with clear background to head £550
As Fig. 31 but with graduated shading around head and "POSTAGE & REVENUE" straight. Mounted on card and endorsed "Motley process/Bromide print from mint" £1400
Large master design (75·5 × 92 mm.) for Figs. 33a etc. with medal head. Background to head completely clear. Six copies made and distributed in accordance with the instructions given on the reverse by Seymour Bennett
Dated "18 Jan. 1913" £1400
As above but with background to head painted in as Fig. 33a £1400
As above but with background to head painted in as Fig. 33b £1400
As above but with background to head painted in as Fig. 33d £1400
Subsequently it was decided to change the position of the "A" in "POSTAGE" and "V" in "REVENUE":—
With the top of the letters almost level with "GE" and "ENU" respectively
Dated "1.1.13" and initialled "E.W.". (Eve) £1100
With the letters angled differently and slightly lower
Large master design (73×89mm) of Eve's original artwork dated "30.12.12" with modified letters and highlights in Chinese white £1400
Completed bromide of above £1000
Dated "9.4.13" with M/S "Design Approved by Sir Matthew Nathan" and G.P.O. file No. A ER/9413 .... £1100
Dated "12.4.13" and initialled by Eve with M/S recommendation for adoption of "A" and "Vz" etc. £1100
Enlarged photograph (74 × 90 mm.) made at the G.P.O., dated "9.4.13" ....

Fig. 31 22·5 mm.   Fig. 32 22·5 mm.   Fig. 32 Optd. "ESSAY"

143

NB KING GEORGE V   *The Profile Head Issue*   9d. Agate, Type N9.   Royal Cypher

Fig. 33a 22 mm.    Fig. 33b 22 mm.    Fig. 33c 22 mm.

Fig. 33c Optd "ESSAY"    Fig. 33d 22 mm.

Trials of Eve's Pillar Design
Trials from an engraved die
Fig. 31. Large coinage head (12 mm.). Crown has shading inside it. Frame 22·5 mm. high
Uncleared die proof in black on proof paper,
 dated "13.9.12".. £4000
Uncleared die proof in brown on proof paper,
 dated "18.9.12".. £4000
Cleared die proof in black on proof paper £4000
Cleared die proof in black on proof paper, dated
 "8.10.12" and endorsed "New Design"................... £4000

Trials by Miller and Motley using their Printex machine
Fig. 32. Coinage head (11 mm.). Crown has solid colour inside it. Even shading to head. Frame 22·5 mm. high
In black on card taken from a plate of four
 impressions .... Block of four £2500
As last but single example £550
In various colours on thin card .... From £1850
In black on lemon on thick gummed paper £1850
In red-brown on white gummed paper £1850
Overprinted "ESSAY" in various colours on
 gummed white paper .... From £1850
Overprinted "ESSAY" in black on salmon, black on
 lemon or black on verdant green on gummed
 white paper without watermark £1850
Figs. 33a/d. Medal head (11½ mm.). Crown has shading inside it. Frame 22 mm. high.
 Four different types of background shading to the head
(a) Fig. 33a. With background of solid colour
In black on card taken from a plate of four
 impressions .... Block of four £2500
As last but single example £550
In magenta, red-brown, brown-orange or agate
 on gummed paper with Simple Cypher
 watermark, on Stamping Dept. card dated
 "29 Jan 1913", annotated "Essay for general
 character of design only"................. Block of four from £8000
As last but single example .... From £1850
In black on light brown card (16 × 19·5 mm.) £825
(b) Fig 33b. With background of solid colour from 8 to 12 o'clock
In black on card taken from a plate of four
 impressions .... Block of four £2500
As last but single example £550
In red-brown, orange-brown or agate on
 gummed paper with Simple Cypher
 watermark .... Block of four from £8000
As last but single example .... From £1850
(c) Fig. 33c. With background of graduated shading
In black on card taken from a plate of four
 impressions on Stamping Dept. card, dated
 "6 Feb. 1913" .... Block of four £2500
As last but single example £550

In red-brown, orange-brown or agate on
 gummed paper with Simple Cypher
 watermark....................... Block of four £8000
As last but single example £1850
Overprinted "ESSAY" in sage-green, magenta,
 red-brown, orange-brown or bistre on white
 gummed paper without watermark .... From £1850
Overprinted "ESSAY" in pale blue-grey on thick card........ £1850
In black on light brown card (16 × 19·5 mm.) £825
(d) Fig. 33d. With background evenly shaded with horizontal lines
In black on card taken from a plate of four
 impressions ....Block of four £2500
As last but single example £550
As last but annotated in pencil "Fine Lines
 Surround, 19 Mch. 1913" ....Block of four £2700
In agate, red-brown or orange-brown on
 gummed paper with Simple Cypher watermark........ £1850
 For illustration of typical block of four from a special plate see under the 7d. value.

Die Proofs
Uncleared in black on white glazed card with
 pencil-drawn frame around uncleared
 surround and annotated in manuscript
 "square up to pencil lines", dated "8/5"........................... £7000
Uncleared in black on white glazed card dated
 "5.6.1913".. £7000
Uncleared in black on white glazed card undated............ £6500

Imprimatur from the National Postal Museum Archives
Imperforate, watermark Type W14
Watermark upright £7500

Plate Markings

Official Plate	SG Plate	Markings
1a	1a	Added dots above R. 1/1 and R. 11/1
1b	1b	Dots above R. 1/1 and R. 11/1 filled in. No additional markings
2	2*	Existing nick (inner) R. 20 right side, 19.7 mm.
3	3*	No details of plate markings

 * = New plate allocation

Control Schedule

Official Plate	SG Plate	Controls used
1a	1a	C. 13
1b	1b	D 14, J 17
2	2*	D 14
3	3*	J 17

 * = New plate allocation

1913 *(30 June).* **9d. Agate, Type N9.** Wmk. Simple Cypher
N29 (=S.G.392/93)

	Unmtd mint	Mtd mint	Used
(1) Agate	30·00	15·00	6·00
(2) Pale agate	45·00	25·00	6·00
(3) Deep agate	45·00	25·00	6·00
(4) Very deep agate	£950	£700	£300
a. Without watermark	£1500	£950	
b. Watermark inverted	£240	£175	£175
c. Watermark inverted and reversed	£240	£175	£175
d. Printed double, one albino with F 15 control (Strip of three)		£6750	
e. Frame broken at left (each side of O of POSTAGE (R. 3/1)		£425	£250

9d. Agate, Type N9. Royal Cypher *The Profile Head Issue* **KING GEORGE V** NB

	Unmtd mint	Mtd mint	Used
s. "Specimen", Type 26	£425		
t. "Cancelled", Type 24		£1100	

No. N29d shows the albino impression on the gummed side particularly on the control margin. See also No. N14r.

N29e, N30e

Watermark Varieties. The following have been recorded:
Wmk upright: Types II, III
Wmk inverted: Types II, III
Wmk inverted and reversed: Types II, III

Misplaced Watermarks
ya. Single stamp showing letters from "POSTAGE" ....85·00
yb. Vertical strip sufficient to show complete
     "POSTAGE" watermark..£1200

Broken Dandy Roll Varieties
za. Missing Crown..£100
zb. Missing G..70·00
zc. Missing v...70·00
zd. Missing vR..70·00
zh. Missing Crown GvR...£175
zj. Missing tail to R ("GvP")...60·00
zk. Long tail to G .... —

Controls. Prices are for unused singles.
Somerset House Printings:

	Perf. Type
Control	2 (E.)
B. 13	25·00

Wmk upright or inverted, Type II only.
Control B. 13 with a faked bottom perf. margin exists.

Harrison Printings:

	Perf. Type	
Control	2 (E.)	2A (P.)
E 14	†	25·00
F 15	25·00	75·00
G 15	25·00	25·00
H 16	35·00	25·00
I 16	25·00	85·00
J 17	25·00	25·00
K 17	28·00	25·00
K 18	60·00	28·00
L 18	25·00	25·00
N 19	25·00	25·00
O 19	25·00	25·00
O 20	25·00	25·00
P 20	25·00	25·00
Q 20	35·00	£100
R 21	25·00	25·00
S 21	25·00	25·00
S 22	25·00	50·00

Watermark varieties known:
Wmk upright, Type II: E 14, F 15, G 15, H 16, I 16, J 17, O 20, R 21.
Wmk inverted, Type II: F 15.
Wmk inverted and reversed, Type II: G 15.
Wmk upright, Type III: J 17, K 17, K 18, L 18, N 19, O 19, O 20, P 20, Q 20, R 21, S 21, S 22.
Wmk inverted, Type III: L 18, O 19, P 20, Q 20.
Wmk inverted and reversed, Type III: J 17, O 19, P 20, Q 20, S 21, S 22.

Die Proofs
In black on white glazed card (27×27mm) undated £6000
In black on white glazed card, fully cleared,
     endorsed "2.5.1913" in M/S... £6500
In black on white glazed card, fully cleared,
     endorsed "7.5.1913" in M/S... £6500
In black on gummed paper watermarked Simple
     Cypher (sideways), fully cleared, endorsed
     "2.5.1913" in M/S.. £6500

Plate Proof
In black on poor quality buff paper..£325

Imprimatur from the National Postal Museum Archives
Imperforate, watermark Type W 14
Watermark upright £7500

Plate Markings

Official Plate	SG Plate	Markings
1	1a	Added dots above R. 1/1 and R. 11/1
2a	2a	Added dots above R. 1/2 and R. 11/2
2b	2aa*	Small nick outer R. 19 right side, 12-12.5 mm.
2c	2b	Added tiny nick outer R. 19 left side, 12.8 mm.
5a	1b, c, d	Existing minute dot under PE of R. 20/3. Flaw in base of rule under CE R. 20/1 (see below)
5b	1e	Added nick top outer R. 20 left side
5c	1f	Added dot top under EN of R. 20/1
6	3aa*	No markings known
6a	3a	Small internal nick R. 19 left side, 11-12 mm.
	3a/b	Added small cut under N(I) of R. 20/4.**
6b	3b	Added ½ dot under P of R. 20/2

* = New state of plate allocation
Note:- **This cut was added some time between control periods L 18 and R 21
SG Plate 1b/d. Flaw below R. 20/1 exists as a tiny dot with control F15 and develops until J17 after which it is transient and not repaired as previously listed. This also applies to R. 20/3 where the minute dot was not filled and is seen with most later controls.

Control Schedule

Official Plate	SG Plate	Controls used
1	1a	B. 13
2a	2a	B. 13, L 18, N 19, O 19, O 20
2b	2aa*	P 20, Q 20
2c	2b	R 21, S 21, S 22
5a	1b, c, d	E 14, F 15, G 15, H 16, I 16, J 17, K 17, K 18
5b	1e	L 18, N 19
5c	1f	N 19, O 20, S 21
6	3aa*	K 17
6a	3a	K 18, L 18
	3a/b	N 19
6b	3b	N 19, O 19, O 20, P 20, Q 20, R 21, S 21, S 22

* = New state of plate allocation

145

NB KING GEORGE V The Profile Head Issue 9d. Olive-green Type N9. Royal Cypher

1922 (September). **9d. Olive-green Type N9.** Wmk. Simple Cypher

N30 (=S.G.393a/b)

(1) Olive-green	£225	£110	30·00	
(2) Pale olive-green	£250	£120	40·00	
(3) Deep olive-green	£300	£150	60·00	
a. Watermark inverted	£1200	£900	£750	
b. Watermark inverted and reversed	£1500	£1100	£950	
e. Frame broken at left each side of O of POSTAGE (R. 3/1)		£600		
ea. Ditto. Wmk inverted				
f. Frame broken at right (R. 6?/12)				
s. "Specimen", Type 15		£750		
t. "Specimen", Type 23	£1000			

N30f

Watermark Varieties. The following have been recorded:
Wmk upright: Types II, III
Wmk inverted: Type II
Wmk inverted and reversed: Type II

Broken Dandy Roll Variety
z. Missing v £225

Controls. Prices are for unused singles.
Harrison Printings:

	Perf. Type	
Control	2 (E.)	2A (P.)
T 22	£130	£130
U 23	£130	£130
V 23	£150	£150

Watermark varieties known:
Wmk upright, Type II: U 23, V 23.
Wmk inverted, Type II: U 23.
Wmk inverted and reversed, Type II: U 23.
Wmk upright, Type III: T 22, U 23.

Colour Trials
Imperf on gummed paper from a special plate of four impressions, produced at the Royal Mint.
Block of four in bronze-green or dull turquoise-blue, mounted on Stamping Dept. card endorsed "Essay for colour only" and dated "27.7.22" £28000
As above but in turquoise-green with one stamp removed and endorsed "for HM" (His Majesty) in pencil £22000
Block of four in agate on gummed watermarked paper £17000

Imprimatur from the National Postal Museum Archives
Imperforate, watermark Type W 14
Watermark upright £7500

Plate Markings
Plates 1f, 2b and 3b as used for 9d. Agate, see No. N29.

Control Schedule

Official Plate	SG Plate	Controls employed
5c	1f	T 22, U 23
2c	2b	T 22, U 23, V 23
6b	3b	T 22, U 23, V 23

●————————————————

1913 (1 August). **10d. Turquoise-blue, Type N9.** Wmk. Simple Cypher

N31 (=S.G.394/a)

	Unmtd mint	Mtd mint	Used
(1) Bright turquoise-blue	60·00	35·00	20·00
(2) Turquoise-blue	40·00	22·00	20·00
(3) Deep turquoise-blue	£150	90·00	30·00
(4) Greenish blue	45·00	25·00	20·00
(5) Pale greenish blue	45·00	25·00	20·00
a. Watermark inverted	£4000	£3000	£1900
b. Watermark inverted and reversed	£475	£325	£275
c. Frame broken by E of POSTAGE (R. 9/?)	£700	£500	£300
s. "Specimen", Type 15		£950	
t. "Specimen", Type 23		£650	
u. "Cancelled", Type 24		£425	
v. "Specimen", Type 26		£425	

No. N31 is known with so-called varnish ink but as stated in the General Notes we defer listing.
Imperforate (single) from P.O. registration sheet £8000

N31c

Watermark Varieties. The following have been recorded:
Wmk upright: Types I, II, III
Wmk inverted: Types II, III
Wmk inverted and reversed: Types II, III

Misplaced Watermarks
ya. Single stamp showing letters from "POSTAGE" £110
yb. Vertical strip sufficient to show complete "POSTAGE" watermark £1750

Broken Dandy Roll Varieties
za. Missing Crown £110
zc. Missing v .... 70·00
zg. Missing Crown vR .... 70·00
zj. Missing tail to R ("GvP") .... 70·00

Controls. Prices are for unused singles.
Somerset House Printings:

	Perf. Type	
Control	2 (E.)	2A (P.)
C. 13	25·00	£2000

Wmk upright or inverted and reversed, Type II only.
Control C. 13 with perf. margin should have certificate of provenance.

Harrison Printings:

	Perf. Type	
Control	2 (E.)	2A (P.)
D 14	35·00	35·00
F 15	35·00	35·00

146

1s. Bistre-brown, Type N9. Royal Cypher *The Profile Head Issue* **KING GEORGE V**   NB

	Perf. Type	
Control	2 (E.)	2A (P.)
G 15	35·00	35·00
H 16	28·00	75·00
I 16	28·00	50·00
J 17	28·00	28·00
K 18	95·00	28·00
M 19	28·00	85·00
O 19	28·00	28·00
Q 21 (c.)	—	75·00
Q 21 (w.)	35·00	—
S 21	28·00	28·00
S 22	40·00	£175
T 22	80·00	£100
U 23	40·00	40·00

Watermark varieties known:
Wmk upright, Type I: F 15.
Wmk upright, Type II: D 14, F 15, G 15, H 16, I 16, J 17, K 18, U 23.
Wmk inverted, Type II: H 16.
Wmk upright, Type III: J 17, K 18, M 19, O 19, Q 21, S 21, S 22, T 22.
Wmk inverted, Type III: M 19.
Wmk inverted and reversed, Type III: O 19, Q 21.

Die Proof
Uncleared in approved design
In black on white glazed card dated "7.6.13" £8750

Colour trial
Imperforate on gummed watermarked paper in
  turquoise-blue £5500

Plate Markings

Official Plate	SG Plate	Markings
1	1a	Added dots above R. 1/1 and R. 11/1
2(a)	1b	Added two minute dots under PE of R. 20/1; Base of rule R. 20 left side bends inwards
2(b)	1c	Added large dot under P of R. 20/2 (Waterlow plate 1c) (Harrison Provisional printing Plate 1c)
3(a)	2a	Existing R. 16 right side bevelled at base
3(b)	2b	Added large dot under PE of R. 20/1 (Waterlow plate 2b) (Harrison Provisional printing Plate 2b)

Control Schedule

Official Plate	SG Plate	Controls used
1	1a	C. 13
2(a)	1b	D 14, F 15, G 15, H 16, I 16, J 17, K 18, M 19
2(b)	1c	M 19, Q 21, S 21, S 22
3(a)	2a	D 14, G 15, K 18, M 19
3(b)	2b	M 19, O 19, Q 21, S 21, S 22, T 22, U 23

1913 (1 August). **1s. Bistre-brown, Type N9.** Wmk. Simple Cypher

N32 (=S.G.395/96)

	Unmtd mint	Mtd mint	Used
(1) Bistre	40·00	20·00	4·00
(2) Pale bistre-brown	35·00	20·00	4·00
(3) Deep bistre-brown	70·00	40·00	4·00
(4) Buff-brown	45·00	25·00	4·00
(5) Pale buff-brown	45·00	25·00	4·00
(6) Fawn-brown (1916-17)	£250	£150	75·00
(7) Bistre-brown	55·00	35·00	12·00
(8) Pale bistre	45·00	25·00	4·00
(9) Olive-brown (1920)	£120	80·00	18·00
(10) Deep bronze-brown (1920)	£1350	£1000	
(11) Yellow-brown (1920)	£1100	£850	—
a. Without watermark	£3000	£2000	
b. Watermark inverted	£350	£250	£200
c. Watermark inverted and reversed	£120	70·00	70·00
d. Varnish ink (Controls G 15, I 16, R 21)		£2500	
s. "Specimen", Type 15		£950	
t. "Specimen", Type 23		£650	
u. "Cancelled", Type 24		£375	
v. "Specimen", Type 26		£375	
w. "Specimen", Type 31 in violet or black		£475	

Shade (10) is from a part sheet on which the impressions were centred low and to the right.
   Shade (1) Bistre was originally described as Olive-bistre and was numbered as (7). Shade (8) was previously described as Pale olive-bistre (now Pale bistre).
   Shade (11) originates from control Q20.
imperforate (single) from P.O. registration sheet £8000

Watermark Varieties. The following have been recorded:
Wmk upright: Types II, III
Wmk inverted: Type III
Wmk inverted and reversed: Types II, III

Misplaced Watermarks
ya. Single stamp showing letters from "POSTAGE" .... 80·00
yb. Vertical strip sufficient to show complete "POSTAGE" watermark £1250

Broken Dandy Roll Varieties
za. Missing Crown £110
zc. Missing v .... 60·00
zd. Missing R .... 60·00
ze. Missing Gv .... —
zf. Missing vR .... 60·00
zi. Missing left side to R .... 60·00
zj. Missing tail to R ("GvP") .... 55·00
zk. Long tail to G .... 60·00

Controls. Prices are for unused singles.
Somerset House Printings:

	Perf. Type	
Control	2 (E.)	2A (P.)
C. 13	30·00	85·00

Wmk upright, Type II only.

Harrison Printings:

	Perf. Type	
Control	2 (E.)	2A (P.)
D 14	25·00	25·00
E 14	£1000	£1000
F 15	25·00	25·00
G 15	35·00	25·00
H 16	25·00	50·00
I 16	25·00	40·00
J 17	25·00	40·00

KING GEORGE V

The Profile Head Issue   **1s. Bistre-brown, Type N9. Royal Cypher**

Control	Perf. Type 2 (E.)	Perf. Type 2A (P.)
K 17	25·00	£150
L 18	25·00	25·00
M 19	28·00	25·00
N 19	40·00	40·00
O 19	25·00	25·00
O 20	28·00	25·00
P 20	40·00	40·00
Q 20	25·00	25·00
R 21	25·00	25·00
S 21	25·00	25·00
S 22	25·00	25·00
T 22	25·00	25·00
U 22	40·00	50·00
U 23	30·00	30·00
V 23	35·00	35·00

Variety Type 2 (c) (I/I)
Strip of three
J 17   £225

Watermark varieties known:
Wmk upright, Type II: D 14, E 14, F 15, G 15, H 16, I 16, J 17, K 17, O 20, R 21, U 22, U 23, V 23.
Wmk inverted and reversed, Type II: D 14, F 15, G 15, I 16, U 22.
Wmk upright, Type III: J 17, K 17, L 18, M 19, N 19, O 19, O 20, P 20, Q 20, R 21, S 21, S 22, T 22, U 23.
Wmk inverted, Type III: J 17, K 17, O 19, P 20, Q 20, R 21, S 21.
Wmk inverted and reversed, Type III: L 18, N 19, O 19, P 20, Q 20, S 21.

Official Plate	SG Plate	Markings
6	4	Existing large cut R. 19 left side, 19 mm. Existing nick outer R. 20 right side, 8 mm. (Waterlow Plate 2)
N.M.	6	No markings

* = New SG Plate 7. Note this may be as previously listed as SG Plate 2a or plate 6, but unconfirmed at time of going to press.

Control Schedule

Official Plate	SG Plate	Controls used
1a	1a	C. 13
1b	5a	I 16, J 17, K 17, L 18
1c	5b	M 19
1d	5c	M 19, N 19, O 19, O 20, P 20, Q 20, R 21, V 23
2	1b	D 14, E 14, F 15, G 15, H 16, I 16, J 17, M 19, O 19, O 20
3a	2b	D 14, E 14, F 15, G 15, H 16, I 16, J 17, M 19
3b	2c	M 19, N 19, O 19, O 20
4	7*	O 20, R 21
5	3	O 20, P 20, Q 20, R 21, S 21, S 22, T 22, U 22, U 23, V 23
6	4	R 21, S 21, S 22, T 22, U 22, U 23, V 23
N.M.	6	T22, V 23

* = New plate allocation as described above

Die Proof
Uncleared in approved design
In black on white glazed card dated "12th June 1913."..... £7500

Colour Trial
Imperforate on gummed watermarked paper in bistre... £5500

Plate Markings

Official Plate	SG Plate	Markings
1a	1a	Added dots above R. 1/1 and R. 11/1. Small internal slanting mark R. 19 left side, 3.4-4 mm.
1b	5a	Dots above R. 1/1 and R. 11/1 filled in. Tiny nick inner R. 19 left side, 14 mm.
1c	5b	Added dash left below R. 20/2
1d	5c	Added cut under S of R. 20/1. Added nick base right end below R. 20/4 (Waterlow Plate 5)
2	1b	Developing nick base outer R. 20 left side
3a	2b	Existing nick outer R. 19 right side, 10.5 mm.
3b	2c	Added cut under S of R. 20/2
4	7*	Added nick outer R. 19 right side, 14.5 mm. (Waterlow Plate 3)
5	3	Existing nick outer right frame, opposite V of REV of R. 20/1. Added upward nick outer R. 19 left side, 4 mm.

Section NC

The Profile Head Issue, Wmk Block Cypher (1924-26)

WATERMARK. All the stamps in this section have watermark **W15**, except for the varieties on experimental **W16** paper listed under the 1d. and 1½d.

PERFORATION. This is normally Type 2 (E), left feed, and much less frequently Type 2A, right feed, from the same perforator comb. Periodically, probably as additional perforators at times of high production, particularly from 1924 to 1926, Waterlow and Somerset House used Type 2(c) and Type 3A, both left feed. On the change of contract in 1934, Harrison used Type 4, left feed, regularly (and, presumably, Type 4A, right feed, which would be indistinguishable from Type 2A on the same controls on some values). Illustrations of all perforators are contained in Appendix I.

Type 2 A (P)
- ½d. A 24, B 24, C 25, E 26, H 27, L 29, V 34
- 1d. A 24, B 24, C 25, V 34
- 1½d. B 24, C 25, F 26, I 28, N 30, V 34
- 2d. B 24, I 28, R 32, V 34
- 2½d. G 27, V 34, W 35
- 3d. G 27
- 4d. X 35
- 6d. C. 25, E. 26, M. 30, W 35, X 35, B 37, D 38
- 9d. X 35

Variety Type 2 (c)
- ½d. B 24, E 26, H 27
- 1d. B 24, E 26, P 31
- 1½d. B 24, E 26, H 27, P 31
- 2d. B 24, P 31
- 2½d. E 26, P 31
- 3d. B 24
- 4d. B 24, E 26
- 6d. B 24, C 25
- 9d. P 31

Type 3 A
- ½d. A 24, C 25, E 26, F 26, G 27, H 27, L 29, O 31, V 34
- 1d. A 24, B 24, L 29, V 34
- ½d. A 24, H 27, K 29
- 2d. B 24,
- 3d. G 27,
- 5d. A 24,
- 6d. E. 26, I. 28, J. 28, M. 30
- 9d. A 24
- 10d. A 24
- 1s. A 24

Type 4
- ½d. U 34, V 34
- 1d. U 34, V 34
- 1½d. U 34, V 34
- 2d. U 34, V 34
- 2½d. V 34
- 3d. V 34
- 4d. V 34
- 5d. V 34
- 6d. V34, W 35
- 9d. V 34
- 1s. V 34

CONTROLS. The notes given on controls in Section NB apply here. The perforation type is identified by the four margins of the sheet, not merely the control piece. For perforator Types 2 and 2A, the price lists refer to single unused examples with control attached. However, as a single example of the same control from perforator Type 3A would be indistinguishable from Type 2A, those with Type 3A are listed as a variety in control strips of three and priced accordingly. In the Type 2A list, the existence of Type 3A as well is noted by * beside the price. Where Type 3A only exists, that is noted by * instead of a price

in the Type 2A list. Also, perforation Types 2(c) and 4 are treated as varieties and are listed and priced in control strips of three.

1924 *(February*).* **½d. Green, Type N6.** Wmk. Block Cypher

N33 (=S.G.418)

		Unmtd mint	Mtd mint	Used
(1)	Green	2·00	1·00	1·00
(2)	Pale green	2·50	1·20	1·00
(3)	Deep green	4·00	2·75	1·00
(4)	Bright green	2·00	1·00	1·00
(5)	Deep bright green	10·00	6·00	2·00
(6)	Yellow-green	35·00	20·00	8·00
a.	Watermark inverted	7·00	3·50	1·00
b.	Watermark sideways (5.24)	18·00	9·00	3·25
c.	Watermark sideways-inverted	£600	£450	
d.	Doubly printed	£16000	£12000	
e.	Imperf. between right side and margin		£8000	
f.	Coil join (horiz. pair)			
g.	No watermark with Control D 25 (pair)		£12500	
ga.	No watermark (single)	£6000	—	
s.	"Specimen", Type 15		£1000	
t.	"Specimen", Type 23		90·00	
ta.	Ditto opt double one albino			
tb.	"Specimen", Type 29			
u.	"Specimen", Type 30		£120	
ua.	"Specimen", Type 32		£2200	
v.	"Cancelled", Type 24		£550	
w.	"Cancelled", Type 28		£110	
wa.	"Cancelled", The 28P		90·00	
x.	"Cancelled", Type 33P		90·00	
y.	"Cancelled", Type 33		£250	
z.	"Specimen", Type 32 and "Cancelled", Type 24		£2200	

*Issued first in 3s. Booklet BB24 edition No. 55 in February. Sheets were first reported in May.

No. N33g is a control pair. Single examples, No. N33ga, differ from N14b in shade.

N33d An example of a double print, each varies slightly

NC KING GEORGE V The Profile Head Issue ½d. Green, Type N6. Block Cypher

Controls. Prices are for unused singles.
Waterlow Printings:

Control	Perf. Type 2(E)	Perf. Type 2A(P)
A 24	3·00	40·00*
B 24	3·00	£100
C 25	4·00	£175*
D 25	3·00	†
E 26	3·00	£350*
F 26	3·00	*
G 27	3·00	*
H 27	3·00	£125*
I 28	3·00	†
J 28	3·00	†
K 29	4·00	†
L 29	4·00	£350*
M 30	3·00	†
N 30	3·00	†
O 31	3·00	*
P 31	3·00	†
Q 32	3·00	†
R 32	3·00	†
S 33	3·00	†
T 33	3·00	†
U 34	£500	†

*See perf Type 3A below

Strips of three
Variety Type 2 (c) (I/I)

B 24	£100
E 26	—
H 27	—

Variety Type 3A (I/P)

A 24	—
C 25	—
E 26	—
F 26	£225
G 27	£150
H 27	£125
L 29	—
O 31	£2000

Watermark varieties known:
Wmk inverted: A 24, B 24, C 25, D 25, E 26, F 26, G 27, H 27, I 28, J 28, K 29, L 29, M 30, N 30, O 31, Q 32, R 32, T 33.
No watermark as a pair with Control D 25, one known.

Harrison Printings:

Control	Perf. Type 2 (E)	Perf. Type 2A (P)
U 34‡	4·00	†
U 34 [streaky gum]	50·00	†
V 34	4·00	60·00*
V 34 [streaky gum]	50·00	£100

‡Known doubly printed, see N33d.
* See perf. Type 3A below
Watermark varieties known:
Wmk inverted: U 34, V 34 (E).

Strips of three
Variety Type 3A (I/P)

V 34	—

Variety Type 4 (I/2E)

U 34	25·00
V 34	20·00
V 34 [streaky gum]	75·00

Coils
Vertical delivery printed in continuous reels

Code No.	Issued	Number in roll	Face value		
D	1924	960	£2.0.0	Bottom delivery	£250
G	1924	480	£1.0.0	Top delivery	£175
KERMODE	1924	960	£2.0.0	Top delivery	£100
KERMODE	Aug. 1927	1920	£4.0.0	Bottom delivery	£100
W	1928	960	£2.0.0	Bottom delivery	£125
Y	1928	1920	£4.0.0	Bottom delivery	£100

Sideways delivery made up from sheets with joins every 12th stamp

| P | 1924 | 480 | £1.0.0 | Left side delivery | — |

Sideways delivery printed in continuous reels with watermark sideways (Crown pointing to left)

| P | May 1924 | 480 | £1.0.0 | Left side delivery | £100 |

Imprimaturs from the National Postal Museum Archives
Imperforate, watermark Type W15
Watermark upright (pair) £8500
Watermark sideways (pair) £8500
Tête-bêche pair £20000

Plate Markings

Plate	Marking
1	Large dot (top) under N(N) of 3rd
2	Dot (base) under EN of 1st
3	Minute dot (inner) 20th left side, 10½ mm. Vertical dash 16th left side, 16 mm.
4	Tiny dot 19th left side, 8 mm.
5	(a) Dot (base) under PE of 2nd (b) Projection below rule under L of 1st; ½ dot (outer) 19th left side, 13 mm.
6	Base of 2nd rule cut away from under ENNY to right end; 4 large dots 19th right side (as Harrison Plate 79)
7	Large dot (central) 19th left side, 9½ mm. (as Harrison Plate 80)
8	½ dot (top) under E of 3rd. Tiny half dot 18th left side 1½ mm.
9	Dot (breaking outer) 18th left side, 12 mm.
10	½ dot (top) under F of 4th
11	½ dot and ½ cut (top) under E of 2nd
12	½ dot (top) under PE of 3rd; rule 19th left side damaged (top)
13	Split at right end of rule under 2nd. Dot (inner) 19th left side, 7½ mm.
14	2 large dots under PEN of 3rd
15	Dot (outer) 20th left side, 6½ mm.
16	2 small cuts under NN of 11th (as Harrison Plate 83) with small ½ cut (base) under L of 1st
17	2 dots 19th left side, 10½ mm., 13½ mm.
18	Dot under F of 2nd. Dot breaking top under L of 4th
19	Large dot (outer) 20th left side, 11mm. Indent (base) under 11th
20	Dot (base) under FP of 1st
21	Dot under P of 3rd
22	Small dot 20th left side, 11½ mm.
23	Large dot 19th left side, 12 mm. Tiny dots under F of 7th and A of 12th
24	Nick at left of rule below 3rd
25	Minute dot at base of 20th left side
26	Indistinct dot 19th left side, 16 mm. Dot (top) under FP of 11th
27	Nick at right of 2nd. Two dots 20th right side, 1 mm. and 21½ mm.
28	Dot (central) above 3rd top row. Minute dot 20th left side, 7½ mm.
29	½ dot (outer) 19th left side, 11 mm. Gash below 8th
30	Indents (base) under H and L of 1st

1d. Red, Type N5. Block Cypher *The Profile Head Issue* **KING GEORGE V** **NC**

Plate	Marking
31	Left end of rule below 1st very thick and curves upwards. Top of 20th left bevelled (outer)
32	Cut at top of 1st left side with dot half way down. Dot above 4th top row
33	Very fine cut 19th left side, 13 mm.
34	Five cuts under HALF of 12th; Minute fine nick (outer) 19th left side, 8¼ mm. (as Harrison Plate 78)
35	Rule 19th right side has projection at base. Two internal cuts under F of 12th
36	Dot 19th left side, 13¼ mm.
37	Nick bottom left corner below 9th. Dot 20th right side, 2½ mm.
38	Dot extreme right of rule under 11th
39	Tiny dot 19th right side, 18½ mm.
40	Small dot at top of both 19th and 20th rules at right side
41	Small dot 18th left side, 13 mm.
42	Dot and small dot 3rd left side. Scoop (outer) 4th right side
43	Dot 4th left side. 2 tiny dots 1st right side
44	Tiny dot above 1st top row. Dot (to right) above 3rd top row. Dot (top) 4th right side
45	Large and small dots 3rd left side, 11½ mm. 4th right side damaged
46	Tiny dot under LF of 3rd
47	Dot (breaking top) under P(E) and nick under (N)N of 3rd
48	No marking
49	Small vertical nick at top of 20th right side
50	20th left side ragged and thickens at base. 7th rule thins at left
51	Minute dot 20th right side, 8 mm.
52	3 dots breaking inner 19th right side, 5½, 7½, 10½ mm. (as Harrison Plate 64)
53	Tiny half dot (outer) 17th left side, 8 mm.
54	Small dot 17th left side, 13¼ mm.
55	Dot under FP of 4th

Index to Marginal Markings

Top Margin, Stamp Numbers

Stamp No.	Plate
1	44
3	28, 44
4	32

Bottom Margin, Stamp Numbers

1	2, 5, 16, 20, 30, 31
2	5, 6, 11, 13, 18, 27
3	1, 8, 12, 14, 21, 24, 46, 47
4	10, 18, 55
7	23, 50
8	29, 37
11	16, 19, 26, 38
12	23, 34, 35

Left Margin, Row Numbers

Row No.	Plate
1	32
3	42, 45
4	43
16	3
17	53, 54
18	8, 9, 41
19	4, 5, 7, 12, 13, 17, 23, 26, 29, 33, 34, 36
20	3, 15, 19, 22, 25, 28, 31, 50

Right Margin, Row Numbers

1	43
4	42, 44, 45
19	6, 39, 40, 52
20	27, 37, 40, 49, 51

No Marking: Plate 48

Control Schedule

Waterlow Printings, 1924–33

Control	Plates with which it was used
A 24	1, 2, 3, 4, 5, 10, 41, 46, 54
B 24	1, 3, 5, 6, 7, 9, 10, 35, 41, 54
C 25	1, 2, 3, 5, 6, 7, 8, 9, 10
D 25	1, 2, 4, 5, 6, 8, 9, 11, 12, 17, 35, 52
E 26	4, 5, 6, 8, 11, 13, 17, 34
F 26	4, 11, 12, 13, 14, 15, 16, 17, 22, 45, 53
G 27	8, 11, 12, 13, 14, 15, 16, 17, 43, 53
H 27	4, 12, 13, 14, 15, 42
I 28	8, 10, 11, 12, 13, 18, 19, 20, 21, 43, 53
J 28	8, 10, 18, 19, 20, 21, 22, 23
K 29	8, 10, 18, 19, 20, 21, 22, 23, 36, 47, 55
L 29	10, 18, 19, 20, 21, 22, 23, 25, 36
M 30	23, 24, 25, 26, 36
N 30	19, 22, 23, 24, 25, 26, 28, 44
O 31	24, 25, 26, 27, 28
P 31	24, 26, 27, 28, 37
Q 32	24, 25, 27, 29, 37, 38
R 32	27, 29, 39
S 33	27, 29
T 33	27, 29, 40

Waterlow Provisional Printing, 1934

U 34	32, 48, 49

Harrison Provisional Printing, 1934

U 34	30, 31, 49, 50
V 34	30, 31, 32, 33, 48, 50, 51

1924 *(February*).* **1d. Red, Type N5.** Wmk. Block Cypher

N34 (=S.G.419)

	Unmtd mint	Mtd mint	Used
(1) Scarlet	2·00	1·00	1·00
(2) Pale scarlet	2·00	1·00	1·00
(3) Scarlet-vermilion	3·00	2·00	1·00
(4) Deep scarlet-vermilion	80·00	40·00	10·00
a. Experimental paper, Watermark Type W. 16 (10.24)	40·00	22·00	
b. Watermark inverted	7·00	4·00	1·50
c. Watermark sideways (1924)	40·00	20·00	15·00
d. Inverted Q for O in ONE (Pl. 1, R. 20/3)	£850	£500	
e. Damaged and uneven top frame. No Cross on Crown		£550	
f. Gash in Crown (Pl. 7, R. 20/12)		£275	
g. Left pillar with worn shading (Pl. ?, Control F 26, R. 20/7)		£180	
h. Partial double print, one inverted		—	
i. Broken oval and shading lines in front of neck (Pl. ?, Control B 24, R. 8/11, watermark Type W.16)			
s. "Specimen", Type 15		£1000	
t. "Specimen", Type 23		90·00	
u. Imperf. opt. "Specimen", Type 23		90·00	
ua. Do. Wmk. sideways		£250	
ub. "Specimen", Type 29			
v. "Specimen", Type 30		£120	
va. "Specimen", Type 32		£2200	
w. "Cancelled", Type 24		£550	
x. "Cancelled", Type 28		£110	

151

NC KING GEORGE V *The Profile Head Issue* 1d. Red, Type N5. Block Cypher

	Unmtd mint	Mtd mint	Used
xa. "Cancelled", Type 28P		75·00	
y. "Cancelled", Type 33P		75·00	
z. "Cancelled", Type 33			£200
za. "Specimen", Type 32 and "Cancelled", Type 24			£2200

*Issued first in 3s. Booklet BB24 edition No. 55 in February. Sheets are believed to have been issued in April.

No. N34h exists from the top right corner of a sheet with an inverted triangular part impression extending diagonally across the normal impression from "P" of "POSTAGE" to "Y" of "PENNY" with rules horiz. top and right side.
For illustration of N34d see N16k.

N34e

N34f N34g

N34i

Controls. Prices are for unused singles.
Waterlow Printings:

	Perf. Type	
Control	2 (E)	2A (P)
A 24	3·00	45·00*
B 24	3·00	£100
C 25	3·00	35·00
D 25	£100	†
E 26	3·00	†
F 26	3·00	†
G 27	3·00	†
H 27	3·00	†
I 28	3·00	†
J 28	3·00	†
K 29	4·00	†
L 29	3·00	*
M 30	3·00	†
N 30	3·00	†
O 31	3·00	—
P 31	3·00	†
Q 32	3·00	†
R 32	12·00	†
S 33	3·00	†
T 33	3·00	†
U 34	£650	†

*See perf Type 3A below

Strips of three
Variety Type 2 (c) (I/I)

B 24	£150
E 26	—

P 31	—
Variety Type 3A (I/P)	
A 24	—
B 24	—
L 29	£500

Watermark varieties known:
Wmk inverted: A 24, B 24, C 25, D 25, E 26, F 26, G 27, H 27, I 28, J 28, K 29, L 29, M 30, O 31, Q 32, T 33.

Waterlow printing, experimental wmk **W16**:

	Perf. Type
Control	2 (E)
B 24	£300

Harrison Printings:

	Perf. Type	
Control	2 (E)	2A (P)
U 34	7·00	†
U 34 [streaky gum]	50·00	†
V 34	7·00	£150*
V 34 [streaky gum]	50·00	£180

*See perf Type 3A below

Strips of three
Variety Type 3A (I/P)

V 34	—

Variety Type 4 (I/2E)

U 34	35·00
V 34	20·00
V 34 [streaky gum]	75·00

Watermark variety known:
Wmk inverted: U 34.

Coils
Vertical delivery printed in continuous reels

Code No.	Issued	Number in roll	Face value		
B	1924	960	£4.0.0	Bottom delivery	£250
E	1924	480	£2.0.0	Top delivery	£175
KERMODE	1924	960	£4.0.0	Top delivery	£100
KERMODE	1924	1000	£4.3.4	Top delivery	£125
KERMODE	Aug. 1927	1920	£8.0.0	Bottom delivery	£125
X	1928	960	£4.0.0	Bottom delivery	£100
Z	1928	1920	£8.0.0	Bottom delivery	£125

Sideways delivery printed in continuous reels with watermark sideways

O	1924	480	£2.0.0	Left side delivery	£100

Imprimaturs from the National Postal Museum Archives
Imperforate, watermark Type W15
Watermark upright (pair) £8500
Watermark sideways (pair) £8500

Plate Markings

Plate	Marking
1	As for Harrison Plate 114b
2	Small dot at right of 11th
3	Dot (inner) 20th right side, 12 mm. Irregular dot 11–12 mm. 20th left side. Nick (base) under (N)N of 4th. Damage to left base of rule under 11th (Harrison Plate 99)
4	Dot 19th left side, 10¾ mm. Tiny half dot (outer) 20th right side, 5½ mm. (Harrison Plate 118)
5	Dot 19th left side, 8¼ mm. (Harrison Plate 101)
6	½ cut (outer) 18th left side, 7½ mm. Nick 20th left side (outer), 2½ mm. Small ½ cut base under left of 9th. Large double dot breaking both sides, 18th right side, 12 mm. (Harrison Plate 120)
7	Large ½ dot (breaking inner) 19th left side, 13 mm. Indent (base) under (N)N of 8th
8	Dot 17th right side, 11 mm.

1½d. Red-Brown, Type N6. Block Cypher — The Profile Head Issue — KING GEORGE V — NC

Plate	Marking
9	Dot 17th right side, 7½ mm. Rule 15th left side damaged (centre). Cut 20th left side 14½ mm. Nick (top) 6th under P
10	Dot 20th left side, 12 mm. Tiny dot 17th right side, 7½ mm.
11	Rule 19th left side damaged (outer). Minute dot 17th right side, 14 mm.
12	Dot 17th left side, 10½ mm.
13	Dot under EP of 1st
14	Dot 18th left side, 12½ mm. Rule 19th left bevelled at base
15	20th left side severely damaged at left and broken near base
16	Left at 10th broken away at base
17	Horizontal dash at left of 11th
18	Nick 3rd right side, 6½ mm. Small nick at left base of 6th. No other marking on sheet
19	Dot 4th left side, 11½ mm. 20th left side irregular. 12th right side bevelled at base
20	Cut 4th left side, 11 mm. Tiny nick 20th left side, 17½ mm. Scoop 6th right side
21	Minute dot to right of Y of 2nd. No other marking on sheet
22	Tiny dot and double dot 1st left side, 20½, 11 mm. ½ dot at right end of 3rd. Dot over 4th and ½ dot at right of 5th all top row
23	Nick at left of 11th
24	Base of 20th right side bent in
25	As for Harrison Plate 117
26	Two dots 20th left side, 16 and 17½ mm.; two nicks 19th left side, 12 and 15½ mm.; crescent shaped cut (breaking inner) 1st left side, 19½ and 21 mm.; dot above centre 1st top row
27	Dot breaking outer under PE of 1st
28	R. 20/2 dot breaking base between ON and dot breaking top beneath Y. Control unknown
29	Dot central above 1st. Crescent shaped cut breaking inner 1st left side, 21 and 22 mm. and dot 2nd left side, 10½ mm.

Index to Marginal Markings

Stamp No.   Plate

Top Row, Stamp Numbers

1	25, 26, 29
4	22
5	1, 22

Bottom Row, Stamp Numbers

1	13, 27
2	21
3	1, 22
4	3
6	9, 18
8	7
9	6
10	16
11	2, 3, 17, 23
12	19

Left Margin, Row Numbers

Row No.	Plate
1	22, 26, 29
2	29
4	19, 20
15	9
17	12
18	6, 14
19	4, 5, 7, 11, 14, 26
20	1, 3, 6, 9, 10, 15, 19, 20, 26

Right Margin, Row Numbers

3	18
6	20
12	19

Row No.	Plate
17	8, 9, 10, 11, 25
18	6, 25
20	3, 4, 24

Control Schedule

Waterlow Printings, 1924–33

Plate	Controls
1	C 25, E 26
2	F 26, G 27
3	F 26, G 27
4	F 26, G 27, H 27
5	C 25
6	C 25, D 25, E 26
7	C 25, E 26
8	F 26, H 28
9	B 24, C 25
10	A 24, B 24, C 25
11	B 24
12	B 24, C 25, H 27
13	F 26, G 27
14	A 24, B 24
15	M 30
16	K 29, L 29, M 30, N 30
17	Q 32, R 32, S 33, T 33
18	K 29
19	L 29, M 30
20	M 30
21	J 28
22	?
25	C 25

Waterlow Provisional Printing, 1934

24	U 34

Harrison Provisional Printings, 1934–35

23	U 34, V 34
26	U 34, V 34
27	V 34

1924 (February*). **1½d. Red-Brown, Type N6.** Wmk. Block Cypher

N35 (=S.G.420)

	Unmtd mint	Mtd mint	Used
(1) Red-brown	2·00	1·00	1·00
(2) Deep red-brown	6·00	4·00	1·00
(3) Pale red-brown	35·00	25·00	6·00
(4) Chestnut (1924)	6·00	3·00	1·00
(5) Bright chestnut (1926-7)	10·00	6·00	1·00
(6) Orange-brown (1925)	10·00	6·00	1·00
(7) Chocolate-brown (1924)	15·00	10·00	2·00
(8) Yellow-brown (1932-34)	2·00	1·00	1·00
(9) Deep yellow-brown (1934)	22·00	12·00	1·00
(10) Bright yellow-brown (1934)	15·00	10·00	1·00
a. Tête-bêche (pair)	£750	£500	£800
aa. Do. with gutter margin	£800	£550	£850
b. Experimental paper, Watermark Type W16 (10.24)	£160	£120	£120
ba. Do. with wmk. inverted	£850	£750	£350
c. Watermark inverted	3·50	2·00	1·00
d. Watermark sideways (8.24)	20·00	10·00	3·50
da. Wmk. sideways-inverted		£900	
e. Printed on the gummed side	£1200	£750	†
f. Imperf. between right side and margin		£1800	

153

KING GEORGE V   The Profile Head Issue   1½d. Red-Brown, Type N6. Block Cypher

	Unmtd mint	Mtd mint	Used
fa. Imperf. between left side and margin		£3750	
g. Varnish ink (Controls L 29, U 34)		£3500	
h. Double impression	—	—	†
i. Coil join (horiz. pair)			
j. Frame broken at left (R. ?/11)		£800	
k. Blob on King's nose (from horiz. coil)		£400	
ka. Spot on King's nose (from horiz coil)		£300	
l. Missing top to final E in HALFPENCE (R. ?/10)		£675	
m. Frame damage (R. 2/1 of Booklet pane of 6)		£525	
n. White spot on dolphin (Pl. 34a, 34b, R. 20/3)		£110	
o. Broken white frame below first E (vert coil)		£375	
p. Coloured mark on fin and white spot behind head of left dolphin (Pl. 3, R. 20/3)		70·00	
q. Frame missing top left and top marginal rule (R. 1/?)		£750	
r. Frame missing at right		£750	
s. "Specimen", Type 15		£1000	
t. "Specimen", Type 23		90·00	
ta. "Specimen", Type 29			
u. "Specimen", Type 30		£120	
ua. "Specimen", Type 32		£2200	
v. "Cancelled", Type 24		£550	
w. "Cancelled", Type 28		£110	
wa. "Cancelled", Type 28P		75·00	
x. "Cancelled", Type 33P		75·00	
y. "Cancelled", Type 33		£200	
ya. Do. Watermark sideways		£950	
z. "Specimen", Type 32 and "Cancelled", Type 24		£2200	

*Issued first in 3s. Booklet No. BB24 edition No. 55 in February. Sheets were reported to have been issued on 4 April.
Variety e. One sheet known to exist from Control U 34.
Variety k comes from the Waterlow printings made into continuous coils (Wmk. sideways) on every 13th stamp and is scarce. Variety ka. is from the same position but is assumed to be a later state and is less scarce.
Variety N35n exists from the two states of plate 34a/b. Bottom marginal examples from plate 34b show a white dot in the rule below HA, plate 34a does not. Non-marginal examples of the variety are identical.

Controls. Prices are for unused singles.
Somerset House Emergency Printing (during General Strike):

	Perf. Type
Control	2 (E)
E.26	£1600

Waterlow Printings:

	Perf. Type	
Control	2 (E)	2A (P)
A 24	3·00	*
B 24	3·00	£250
C 25	3·00	£3000
D 25	3·00	†
E 26	3·00	†
F 26	3·00	£175

1½d. Red-Brown, Type N6. Block Cypher *The Profile Head Issue* **KING GEORGE V** **NC**

Control	Perf. Type 2 (E)	2A (P)
G 27	3·00	†
H 27	3·00	*
I 28	3·00	£225
J 28	3·00	†
K 29	4·00	*
L 29	3·00	†
M 30	3·00	†
N 30	3·00	£2000
O 31	3·00	†
P 31	3·00	†
Q 32	3·00	†
R 32	10·00	†
S 33	3·00	†
T 33	3·00	†
U 34	£600	†

*See perf. Type 3A below

Strips of three
Variety Type 2 (c) (I/2E)

B 24	£150
E 26	—
H 27	—
P 31	—

Variety Type 3A (I/P)

A 24	30·00
H 27	£225
K 29	£450

Watermark varieties known:
Wmk inverted: A 24, B 24, C 25, D 25, E 26, F 26, G 27, H 27, I 28, J 28, K 29, M 30, N 30, O 31, P 31, Q 32, T 33.

Waterlow Printings on experimental **W16** paper:

Control	Perf. Type 2 (E)
A 24	£400
B 24	£600
D 25	£400

Watermark variety known:
Wmk inverted: D 25.

Harrison Printings:

Control	Perf. Type 2 (E)	2A (P)
U 34	5·00	†
U 34 [streaky gum]‡	50·00	†
V 34	6·00	—
V 34 [streaky gum]	50·00	—

‡ Known printed on the gum.

Strips of three
Variety Type 2 (c) (I/2E)

U 34	30·00
V 34	30·00
V 34 [streaky gum]	75·00

Coils
Vertical delivery printed in continuous reels

Code No.	Issued	Number in roll	Face value		
K	June 1924	950	£6.0.0	Bottom delivery	£225
L	June 1924	480	£3.0.0	Top delivery	£225

Sideways delivery made up from sheets with joins every 12th stamp

| N | 1924 | 480 | £3.0.0 | Left side delivery | £325 |

Sideways delivery printed in continuous reels with watermark sideways

| N | Aug. 1924 | 480 | £3.0.0 | Left side delivery | £200 |

Imprimaturs from the National Postal Museum Archives
Imperforate, watermark Type W15
Watermark upright (pair) £8500
Watermark sideways (pair) £8500

Plate Markings

Plate	Marking
1	Dot (base) under PE of 1st
2	Small dot (base) under HA of 2nd
3	Small dot (base) under AL of 3rd. Small dot 18th left side, 16½ mm
4	Small dot 20th left side, 14½ mm.
5	Small dot 19th left side, 16 mm.
6	½ dot (outer) and full dot 18th left side, 21, 10 mm.
7	19th outer left side scooped out 4–6 mm. Dot 18th right side, 13 mm.
8a	Dot under F of 4th. Dot 20th right side
8b	Added nick outer 19th left side, 18½ mm
9	Dot and ½ dot (inner) 19th left side, 9½, 10½ mm. Scoop outer 16th left side, 18 mm.
10	½ dot (outer) 20th left side, 5 mm. 19th left side badly scored (outer) (Harrison Plate 41)
11	½ dot (base) under A of 4th (Harrison Plate 43)
12	Line under 1st bevelled at left. Nick (outer) base of 20th right side. Large dot 4th left side
13	Dot 20th left side, 11 mm.
14	Oval dot 19th left side, 8 mm.
15	19th left side bulges in middle. 20th left side thins at base
16	Large dot 1st left side, 12 mm. Dot at left over 1st top row. Base of 20th left side bent inwards. Nick to left side, 18 mm, ½ dot bottom under T of 9th
17	Dot 20th left side, 10 mm.
18	Fine dot (inner) 20th left side, 11 mm.
19	Nick (outer) 19th left side, 14 mm. Dot 1st left side, 11 mm.
20a	Large dot (top) under LF of 1st
20b	Added fine dot under EN of 3rd
21a	Dot (top) under AL of 2nd
21b	Added dot 20th left side, 10 mm.
21c	Added minute dot under A of 1st
22a	½ dot (inner) 15th left side, 13 mm. Notch (base) to right of (C)E of 2nd. Base of 19th left side bevelled 1–2 mm.
22b	Added minute dot under L of 1st
23a	Minute dot under EH of 2nd
23b	Second dot under 1st
24	Tiny dot under F of 3rd
25	Tiny dot under L of 4th
26	Large and small dot 20th left side. Both 6½ mm.
27	Dot 19th left side, 8 mm. Small nick (base) under FP of 3rd
28	Two minute dots under HA of 1st (usually visible). Two minute dots under NC of 2nd
29	Double nick at left of 2nd
30	Scratch under NC of 3rd
31a	Double notch (base) under EN of 2nd
31b	Added notch (base) under FP of 2nd
32	Vertical score 20th left side
33	½ dot (base) under HA of 3rd
34a	19th left side damaged (outer), 8–10 mm.
34b	Small dot (top) under HA of 3rd added. 19th left damaged (outer), 8–10 mm.
35	Oval dot under EE of 3rd
36	Dot (base) under HR of 3rd
37	2 dots, top and bottom, 20th left side, 19½, 3 mm.
38	2 dots, top and bottom, 19th left side, 21, 3 mm, tiny dot 20th left side, 22½ mm.
39	No marking, 20th left side thick and irregular
40	2 dots top and bottom, 20th left side, 21, 2 mm.
41	2 dots top and bottom, 19th left side, 20½, ½ mm. Cut 18th left side, 11 mm.
42	Base of 20th left side bends inwards
43	Small dot 20th right side, 6½ mm.
44	Internal cut 17th left side, 7½ mm.
45	2 internal cuts 15th right side at top
46	20th left side tapers from 8 mm. to base
47a	Internal score 19th left side, 17–19 mm.
47b	Added dot 19th left side, 16½ mm.
48	Tiny nick under base of N of 3rd

NC KING GEORGE V The Profile Head Issue 1½d. Red-Brown, Type N6. Block Cypher

Plate	Marking
49	Small dot under C of 1st
50	Small dot 17th right side, 14½ mm.
51	Dot 16th left side, 10 mm.
52	Deleted. Now part of Plate 34
53	Dot over 1st in upper row. Dot 1st left side, 11 mm.
54	Tiny dots under E(E) of 12th and 20th right side (inner), 12 mm.
55	Dot 17th left side, 10½ mm. Minute dot under HA of 11th. Two dots 19th right side, 7, 9¼ mm. (an example is known without the dots on 19th right side.
56	Tiny dot 15th left side, 16 mm. Scoop (outer) 16th left side, 16–20 mm.
57	Dot 2nd left side, 16 mm. Dot under HA of 9th
58a	Dot 3rd left side, 13 mm. Notch 14th left side 6–7 mm.
58b	Added dot under F of 10th
59	Small dot 20th right side, 10½ mm.
60	Base of 20th left side rounded at left
61	Dot (outer) 1st left side 10½ mm. Dot central above 2nd top row, control unknown
62	Dot 18th left side.
63	Dot 17th left side.

Index to Marginal Markings

Stamp No.	Plate

Top Row, Stamp Numbers

1	16, 53

Bottom Row, Stamp Numbers

1	1, 12, 20a, 20b, 21c, 22b, 23b, 28, 49
2	2, 21a, 21b, 21c, 22a, 22b, 23a, 28, 29, 31a, 31b
3	3, 20b, 24, 27, 30, 33, 34b, 35, 36, 48
4	8a, 8b, 11, 25
9	16, 57
10	58b
11	55
12	54

Left Margin, Row Numbers

Row No.	Plate
1	16, 19, 53
2	57
3	58a
4	12
15	22a, 56
16	51, 56
17	44, 55, 63
18	3, 6, 41, 62
19	5, 7, 8b, 9, 10, 14, 15, 19, 22a, 22b, 27, 34a, 34b, 38, 41, 47a, 47b
20	4, 10, 13, 15, 16, 17, 18, 21b, 21c, 26, 32, 37, 39, 40, 42, 46

Right Margin, Row Numbers

15	45
17	50
18	7
19	55
20	8, 12, 43, 54, 59

Control Schedule

Waterlow Printings, 1924–33

Control	Plates employed
A 24	1, 2, 3, 4, 5, 6, 8a, 44, 48
B 24	1, 2, 3, 4, 6, 7, 8a, 28, 43, 44, 48, 50, 55, 59
C 25	1, 2, 3, 7, 8a, 8b, 9, 10, 11, 43, 54
D 25	1, 2, 3, 7, 8b, 9, 10, 11, 43, 54, 55
E 26	1, 8b, 11, 12, 13, 14, 15, 19, 56
F 26	3, 10, 12, 13, 14, 16, 43, 45, 48, 56, 58a
G 27	12, 13, 14, 16, 58
H 27	13, 15, 17, 18
I 28	13, 15, 17, 18, 19, 57, 58b
J 28	18, 19, 20a, 21a, 22a, 47a, 51, 62
K 29	20a, 21a, 22a, 47a, 62
L 29	20a, 20b, 21a, 21b, 22a, 22b, 23a, 23b, 24, 25, 47a, 47b, 62
M 30	19, 20b, 22b, 24, 25, 26, 27, 28, 47b
N 30	26, 27, 28, 29, 30, 62, 63
O 31	21b, 21c, 27, 28, 29, 31a, 32, 62

Control	Plates employed
P 31	29, 31a, 31b, 32, 46
Q 32	28, 29, 31b, 32
R 32	28, 29, 32, 34a, 60
S 33	33, 34a, 34b, 35, 36, 37, 49, 60
T 33	34b, 35, 36, 37, 38, 39, 40, 41
?	53

Somerset House Printing, 1926

E. 26	15

This printing was made during the General Strike of 1926 with a dot in the control. The dot has been seen in two positions suggesting that either the control was moved between printing or more than plate 15 was used.

Waterlow Provisional Printings, 1934

U 34	38, 39

Harrison Provisional Printings, 1934

U 34	38, 39, 40, 41, 42
V 34	38, 39, 40, 42

2d. Orange, Type N7. Block Cypher — The Profile Head Issue — KING GEORGE V — NC

1924 (July). **2d. Orange, Type N7.** Wmk. Block Cypher. Die II
N36 (=S.G.421)

	Unmtd mint	Mtd mint	Used
(1) Orange	4·00	2·50	2·50
(2) Deep orange	15·00	10·00	2·50
(3) Yellow-orange	7·00	4·00	2·50
(4) Deep yellow-orange	50·00	30·00	10·00
(5) Pale yellow-orange	20·00	13·00	2·50
a. No watermark	£2250	£1800	
b. Watermark inverted	90·00	55·00	55·00
c. Watermark sideways (7.26)	£210	£120	£120
ca. Triple frame break (sideways coil)		£275	
cb. Frame break below W in TWO (sideways coil)		£275	
d. Partial double print	—	£35000	†
e. Coil join (vert. pair)			
f. Coil join (horiz. pair)			
s. "Specimen", Type 23		£100	
sa. Ditto, opt double, one albino			
sb. Ditto, opt treble, two albino			
sc. Imperf. optd. "Specimen", Type 23. Wmk sideways		£250	
t. "Specimen", Type 32		£2250	
u. "Specimen", Type 32 and "Cancelled", Type 24		£2250	

Variety a. Two sheets of 240 were found from Control C 25.
Nos. N36ca/cb are from sideways coils and repeated every 13th stamp.
No. N36d is known with a partial double print involving a vertical strip of three from the top left corner of the sheet.

N36ca

Controls. Prices are for unused singles.
Waterlow Printings:

	Perf. Type	
Control	2 (E)	2A (P)
A 24	25·00	†
B 24	4·00	£250*
C 25	4·00	†
D 25	4·00	†
E 26	4·00	†
F 26	4·00	†
G 27	4·00	†
H 27	8·00	†
I 28	5·00	£150
J 28	10·00	†
K 29	5·00	†
L 29	6·00	†
M 30	8·00	†
N 30	5·00	†
O 31	12·00	†
P 31	4·00	†
Q 32	4·00	†
R 32	5·00	£300
S 33	40·00	†
T 33	5·00	†
U 34	—	†

*See perf. Type 3A below

Strips of three
Variety Type 2 (c) (I/I)
B 24	£225
P 31	—

Variety Type 3A (I/P)
B 24	—

Watermark varieties known:
Wmk inverted: A 24, B 24, C 25, D 25, E 26, F 26, G 27, H 27, I 28, J 28, K 29, M 30, P 31, R 32.
No wmk: C 25.

Harrison Printings:

	Perf. Type	
Control	2 (E)	2A (P)
U 34	9·00	†
U 34 [streaky gum]	50·00	†
V 34	8·00	—
V 34 [streaky gum]	75·00	—

Strips of three
Variety Type 4 (I/2E)

U 34	50·00
V 34	50·00

Coils
Vertical delivery made up from sheets with joins every 20th stamp

Code No.	Issued	Number in roll	Face value		
Q	1924	960	£8.0.0	Bottom delivery	£300
R	1924	480	£4.0.0	Top delivery	£300

Sideways delivery made up from sheets with joins every 12th stamp
T	1924	480	£4.0.0	Left side delivery	—

Sideways delivery printed in continuous reels with watermark sideways
T	July 1926	480	£4.0.0	Left side delivery	£425

Imprimaturs from the National Postal Museum Archives
Imperforate, watermark Type W15
Watermark upright (pair) £8500
Watermark sideways (pair) £8500

Plate Markings

Plate	Marking
1	Base of 20th left side rounded off
2	Left of rule under 1st pointed below; base of rule under 12th irregular and bevelled at left; large dot 18th right side, 11 mm.
3	Minute dot 20th left side, 11½ mm.; rule under 1st slightly scooped out under OP
4	Dot 20th left side, 13 mm. (Harrison Plate 4)
5	Dot 19th left side, 13 mm. (Harrison Plate 5)
6	Dot 19th left side breaking right, 9 mm. Base of rules under 1st, 2nd and 3rd very irregular
7	Lower portion of 19th left side shows internal damage; ½ dot (inner) 20th left side, 11 mm., with minute dot to left of it
8	Flaw in base of 19th left side; dot with offshoot dot above and to right of it 20th left side, 13 mm.; nick to left of 1st at base
9	Dot 19th left side, 11¾ mm.; minute dot (base) under P of 2nd
10	Large dot (breaking top) under P of 1st
11	½ dot (top) under P of 2nd
12	Dot 19th left side, 11½ mm. Nicks (base) at left and right of 2nd
13	Dot 20th left side, 12 mm.
14a	Dot 19th left side, 11 mm.; indent base under and to right of E of 2nd
14b	Added dot 19th left side, 13 mm.
15	No marking
16	Indent (base) under C of 1st

KING GEORGE V — The Profile Head Issue — 2½d. Blue, Type N5. Block Cypher

Plate	Marking
17	Dot (top) under OP of 9th; dot (breaking inner) 17th right side, 12½ mm. (Harrison Plate 3)
18	Dot under P of 10th; dot (central) 18th right side, 13 mm.; rule under 2nd appears thinner than those under 1st and 3rd. (Harrison Plate 6)

Index to Marginal Markings

Stamp No.	Plate
Bottom Row, Stamp Numbers	
1	2, 3, 6, 8, 10, 16
2	5b, 6, 9, 11, 12, 14a, 14b, 18
3	6
9	17
10	18
12	2

Left Margin, Row Numbers

Row No.	Plate
19	5a, 5b, 6, 7, 8, 9, 12, 14a, 14b
20	1, 3, 4, 7, 8, 13

Right Margin, Row Numbers

17	17
18	2, 18

No Marking: Plate 15

Control Schedule
Waterlow Printings, 1924–33

Plate	Controls
1	A 24, B 24, C 25, I 28
2	A 24, B 24, F 26, L 29, M 30, N 30, P 31, Q 32, R 32
3	B 24, C 25, D 25, F 26, H 27, I 28, K 29, L 29
4	B 24, C 25, D 25, E 26
5	B 24, C 25, D 25, E 26, I 28, J 28
6	F 26, G 27, H 27, I 28, J 28
7	F 26, G 27, H 27, K 29, L 29, M 30
8	J 28, K 29, L 29
9	J 28, K 29, L 29
10	M 30, N 30, O 31, P 31
11	M 30, N 30, O 31, P 31, Q 32, R 32
12	N 30, Q 32, R 32, S 33, T 33, U 34
13	N 30, O 31, R 32, T 33, U 34
14a	O 31
14b	O 31, Q 32, R 32, S 33, T 33
17	E 26
18	D 25

Harrison Provisional Printings, 1934

12	U 34
14b	U 34
15	U 34, V 34
16	V 34

1924 (10 October). **2½d. Blue, Type N5.** Wmk. Block Cypher

N37 (=S.G.422)

	Unmtd mint	Mtd mint	Used
(1) Blue	10·00	5·00	3·00
(2) Pale blue (1924)	18·00	10·00	5·00
(3) Bright blue	15·00	10·00	3·00
(4) Ultramarine	35·00	25·00	5·00
a. No watermark	£3800	£2800	
b. Watermark inverted	£140	90·00	90·00
c. Error. Watermark sideways	†	†	£18000
e. Coil join (vert. pair) (9.29)			
f. Coil join (horiz. pair) (2.35)			
s. "Specimen", Type 23		£550	
t. "Specimen", Type 32		£2250	
u. "Specimen", Type 32 and "Cancelled", Type 24		£2250	

Variety N37a. Two sheets known to exist from Control B 24. One used example of No. N37c has been reported.
An example of No. N37 has been seen with the "v" in the watermark omitted.

Controls. Prices are for unused singles.
Waterlow Printings:

	Perf. Type	
Control	2 (E)	2A (P)
B 24	8·00	†
C 25	9·00	†
D 25	15·00	†
E 26	8·00	†
G 27	8·00	£500
H 27	40·00	†
I 28	12·00	†
K 29	8·00	†
M 30	8·00	†
N 30	8·00	†
O 31	£2000	†
Q 32	12·00	†
R 32	10·00	†
S 33	30·00	†
T 33	25·00	†

Strips of three
Variety Type 2 (c) (I/I)

E 26	£225
P 31	—

Watermark varieties known:
Wmk inverted: B 24, C 25, D 25, E 26, G 27, I 28, M 30.
No wmk: B 24.

Harrison Printings:

	Perf. Type	
Control	2 (E)	2A (P)
V 34	20·00	†
V 34 [streaky gum]	95·00	†
W 35	20·00	£275

Strip of three
Variety Type 4 (I/2E)

V 34	£100

Watermark varieties known:
Wmk inverted: V 34.

Coils
Vertical delivery made up from sheets with joins every 20th stamp

Code No.	Issued	Number in roll	Face value		
F	Sep. 1929	960	£10.0.0	Bottom delivery	£1500

Sideways delivery made up from sheets with joins every 12th stamp

| M | Feb. 1935 | 480 | £5·00 | Left side delivery | £1750 |

Imprimatur from the National Postal Museum Archives
Imperforate, watermark Type W15
Watermark upright (pair) £8500

Plate Markings

Plate	Marking
1a	Tiny dot 19th right side; nick (base) to right of 8th
1b	Added dot 19th left side (inner), 12 mm.
2	20th left side very thick and irregular rule under 1st curves slightly upwards towards left end. Large dot 2nd left side
3	Dot (inner) 20th left side, 13½ mm.
4	Cut under F of 2nd. (Harrison Plate 11b)
5	Large dot (outer) 19th left side, 11½ mm.
6	Circular dot under P of 1st. (Harrison Plate 8b)
7	Dot 20th left side, 10½ mm.
8	Small dot 19th left side, 11 mm.
9	20th left side bends in at base; rule under 1st splays out at left end; minute dot under Y of 2nd
10	Dot 20th left side, 7 mm.; minute dot at right of 2nd
11	Scratch in rule under Y of 1st
12	Dot 19th left side, 10½ mm.
13	Base of 20th left side has an inward projection
14	No marking

3d. Violet, Type N7. Block Cypher   The Profile Head Issue   KING GEORGE V   NC

Plate	Marking
15	Cut under (P)E of 1st. (Harrison Plate 10)

Control Schedule
Waterlow Printings, 1924–33

Plate	Controls employed
1a	B 24, C 25
1b	D 25, E 26
2	M 30, N 30, O 31, Q 32, R 32, S 33
3	D 25, E 26, G 27
4	E 26, G 27, I 28
5	E 26, G 27, H 27, I 28
6	G 27, H 27
7	I 28
8	I 28
9	Q 32, R 32, S 33
10	K 29
11	T 33
12	K 29
13	Q 32, T 33
14	I 28, M 30, N 30

Harrison Provisional Printings, 1934–35

Plate	Controls employed
11	V 34
13	V 34, W 35
15	V 34, W 35

1924 (10 October). **3d. Violet, Type N7.** Wmk. Block Cypher

N38 (=S.G.423)

	Unmtd mint	Mtd mint	Used
(1) Violet	20·00	10·00	2·50
(2) Pale violet (1924–25)	30·00	20·00	2·50
(3) Pale dull reddish violet (1924–25)	40·00	30·00	2·75
(4) Deep violet	25·00	15·00	3·75
(5) Bright violet	30·00	20·00	6·00
(6) Deep brownish violet	90·00	60·00	20·00
a. Watermark inverted	£140	90·00	70·00
b. Coil join (vert. pair) (9.32)			
c. Coil join (horiz. pair) (2.35)			
d. Right 3 broken (Pl. 5, R. 20/2)		60·00	
s. "Specimen", Type 23		£750	
t. "Specimen", Type 32		£2250	
u. "Specimen", Type 32 and "Cancelled", Type 24		£2250	
v. "Cancelled", Type 33		£550	

N38d This variety also exists with watermark inverted.

Controls. Prices are for unused singles.
Waterlow Printings:

	Perf. Type	
Control	2 (E)	2A (P)
B 24	14·00	†
C 25	25·00	†
D 25	14·00	†
E 26	16·00	†
G 27	14·00	£400*
I 28	16·00	†
K 29	50·00	†
M 30	16·00	†
N 30	20·00	†
P 31	15·00	†

	Perf. Type	
Control	2 (E)	2A (P)
R 32	15·00	†
S 33	45·00	†
T 33	30·00	†

*See perf. Type 3A below:

Strips of three
Variety Type 2 (c) (I/I)
B 24	£175
P 31	—

Variety Type 3A (I/P)
G 27	—

Watermark varieties known:
Wmk inverted: B 24, C 25, D 25, E 26, G 27, I 28.

Harrison Printings:

	Perf. Type
Control	2 (E)
V 34	24·00

Strip of three
Variety Type 4 (I/2E)
V 34	75·00

Coils
Vertical delivery made up from sheets with joins every 20th stamp

Code No.	Issued	Number in roll	Face value		
C	Sep. 1932	960	£12.0.0	Bottom delivery	£1500

Sideways delivery made up from sheets with joins every 12th stamp
| S | Feb. 1935 | 480 | £6.0.0 | Left side delivery | £1750 |

Imprimatur from the National Postal Museum Archives
Imperforate, watermark Type W15
Watermark upright (pair) £8500

Plate Markings

Plate	Marking
1a	Tiny nick (base) to right of 2nd bottom row
1b	Added cut 20th left side, 10 mm.
2	20th left side heavy and irregular
3	Dot 19th left side, 13 mm. (Harrison Plate 10)
4	½ dot (inner) 20th left side, 12¾mm. (Harrison Plate 9)
5	Tiny dot 20th left side, 11 mm.
6	Tiny dot (inner) 19th left side, 9 mm.
7	No marking. 20th left side irregular
8	No marking. 20th left side sharply defined

Control Schedule
Waterlow Printings, 1924–33

Plate	Controls employed
1a	B 24
1b	B 24, C 25, D 25
2	B 24, C 25
3	D 25, E 25, E 26, G 27, R 32
4	E 26, G 27, I 28, K 29, M 30, P 31, R 32
5	E 26, G 27, I 28, K 29, M 30, N 30, P 31, R 32, S 33, T 33
6	I 28, K 29, M 30, N 30, P 31
7	M 30, N 30, P 31, R 32, S 33, T 33
8	S 33, T 33

Harrison Printings:

Plate	Controls employed
3	V 34
4	V 34

159

KING GEORGE V — The Profile Head Issue — 4d. Grey-Green, Type N7. Block Cypher

1924 (23 October). **4d. Grey-Green, Type N7.** Wmk. Block Cypher

N39 (=S.G.424)

	Unmtd mint	Mtd mint	Used
(1) Deep grey-green	30·00	20·00	2·50
(2) Grey-green	28·00	12·00	2·50
(3) Very deep grey-green (1934–35)	75·00	45·00	15·00
a. Watermark inverted	£240	£150	£150
b. Printed on the gummed side	£6000	£4000	†
s. "Specimen", Type 23		£650	
t. "Specimen", Type 32		£2250	
u. "Cancelled", Type 28		£650	
v. "Specimen", Type 32 and "Cancelled", Type 24		£2250	
w. "Cancelled", Type 33		£650	

Controls. Prices are for unused singles.
Waterlow Printings:

	Perf. Type
Control	2 (E)
B 24	17·00
C 25	17·00
E 26	35·00
G 27	17·00
I 28	17·00
K 29	30·00
M 30	17·00
O 31	17·00
Q 32	17·00
R 32	30·00
T 33	17·00

Strips of three
Variety Type 2(c) (I/I)

B 24	£100
E 26	—

Watermark varieties known:
Wmk inverted: B 24, C 25, E 26, G 27, I 28, M 30, O 31.

Harrison Printings:

	Perf. Type	
Control	2 (E)	2A (P)
V 34	24·00	†
W 35	75·00	†
X 35	24·00	—

Strip of three
Variety Type 4 (I/2E)

V 34	75·00

Imprimatur from the National Postal Museum Archives
Imperforate, watermark Type W 15
Watermark upright (pair) £8500

Plate Markings

Plate	Marking
1a	2 diagonal cuts 20th right side, 4, 7 mm. Base of 2nd bottom row bevelled at right
1b	Base of 2nd repaired
2a	Base of 20th left side splays out to left. ½ dot (outer) 4th left side, 12½ mm.
2b	Added tiny dot under P of 11th bottom row
3	2 cuts 20th left side 17, 18½ mm.
4	Dot under RP of 1st bottom row (Harrison Plate 4)
5	Dot at top of 19th left side
6	No marking
7	No marking. 20th left side irregular. Rule under 1st, 2nd and 3rd bottom row thinner than Plate 6
8	Dot under RP of 2nd bottom row (Harrison Plate 2d)

Control Schedule
Waterlow Printings, 1924–33

Plate	Controls employed
1a	B 24, C 25, E 26
1b	G 27, I 28, K 29, Q 32, R 32, T 33
2a	B 24, C 25, E 26, G 27
2b	K 29, M 30, O 31
3	E 26, G 27, I 28, K 29, M 30, O 31
4	Q 32
5	O 31, Q 32, R 32, T 33
6	R 32

Harrison Provisional Printings, 1934–35

5	V 34, W 35
6	V 34
7	V 34, X 35
8	X 35

1924 (17 October). **5d. Brown, Type N8.** Wmk. Block Cypher

N40 (=S.G.425)

	Unmtd mint	Mtd mint	Used
(1) Brown	40·00	20·00	3·00
(2) Deep brown	65·00	40·00	3·00
(3) Reddish brown (1927–28)	£100	70·00	6·00
(4) Bright ochre-brown	40·00	20·00	3·00
(5) Deep bright ochre-brown (1934)	£100	60·00	20·00
a. Watermark inverted	£210	£150	£150
s. "Specimen", Type 23		£140	
t. "Specimen", Type 26		£950	
u. "Specimen", Type 32		£2250	
v. "Specimen", Type 32 and "Cancelled", Type 24		£2250	
w. "Cancelled", Type 33		£700	

Controls. Prices are for unused singles.
Waterlow Printings:

	Perf. Type
Control	2 (E)
A 24	30·00
C 25	28·00
F 26	28·00
H 27	£100
I 28	35·00
K 29	28·00
L 29	28·00
M 30	£100
O 31	28·00
Q 32	45·00
S 33	35·00
T 33	£450
U 34	£550

Strip of three
Variety Type 3A (I/P)

A 24	£120

Watermark varieties known:
Wmk inverted: A 24, C 25, F 26, I 28, S 33.

Harrison Printings:

	Perf. Type
Control	2 (E)
U 34	£650
V 34	35·00
X 35	35·00

Strip of three
Variety Type 4 (I/2E)

V 34	75·00

6d. Purple, Type N8. Block Cypher The Profile Head Issue KING GEORGE V NC

Imprimatur from the National Postal Museum Archives
Imperforate, watermark Type W15
Watermark upright £8500

Plate Markings

Plate	Marking
1a	No marking. Tiny diagonal internal cut, 14 mm. 19th right side. (Harrison Plate 3)
1b	Added dot 19th left side, 10 mm.
2a	Base of 20th left side slightly bent inwards
2b	Added dot 20th left side, 14 mm.

Control Schedule
Waterlow Printings, 1924–33

Plate	Controls employed
1a	A 24, C 25
1b	C 25, F 26, H 27, I 28, K 29, L 29, M 30, O 31, Q 32, S 33, T 33
2a	C 25
2b	C 25, F 26, H 27, I 28, K 29, L 29, M 30, O 31, Q 32, S 33, T 33

Waterlow Provisional Printing, 1934
| 2b | U 34 |

Harrison Provisional Printings, 1934–35
| 1b | U 34, V 34, X 35 |
| 2b | U 34, V 34, X 35 |

●━━━

1924 *(September)* and **1936. 6d. Purple, Type N8.**
Chalk-Surfaced Paper. Wmk. Block Cypher

N41 (=S.G.426)

	Unmtd mint	Mtd mint	Used
Somerset House Printings (1924/5)			
(1) Plum	50·00	35·00	6·00
(2) Rosy mauve	40·00	20·00	3·00
Harrison Printings (1936)			
(3) Reddish purple	20·00	12·00	2·50
(4) Deep reddish purple	30·00	18·00	2·75
a. Watermark inverted	90·00	60·00	60·00
b. Watermark inverted and reversed	£700	£450	£400
s. "Specimen", Type 30			

Controls. Prices are for unused singles.
Somerset House Printings:

	Perf. Type	
Control	2(E)	2A (P)
B. 24	35·00	†
C. 25	35·00	—
D. 25	35·00	†

Strips of three
Variety Type 2 (c) (I/I)
| B 24 | £100 |
| C 25 | — |

Watermark varieties known:
Wmk inverted: B. 24, C. 25, D. 25.
Wmk inverted and reversed: B. 24, C. 25.

Harrison Printings:

	Perf. Type
Control	2 (E)
Y 36	£150
Z 36	20·00

Watermark varieties known:
Wmk inverted: Z 36.

Imprimatur from the National Postal Museum Archives
Imperforate, watermark Type W15
Watermark upright (pair)... £8000

Plate Markings
Somerset House Printings, 1924–25
Plates with interpane margin.

Plate markings such as those used by Harrison and Waterlow were not used at Somerset House, and plating can only be accomplished by the study of fortuitous marks. It seems that the 6d. stamps were printed in pairs of plates and these were marked above the top rows of the panes with a dot above the 1st or 2nd stamps to signify the position in the press.

Plate	Marking
6	Dot above 2nd in upper pane (to left of rule). Small projection under X of 1st
8	Scoop above 1st top row. Minute dot under EN of 2nd, with irregular rule, progressively to obscure dot
9	Rule under 1st thin at left and thick at right. Rules under 2nd and 3rd irregular
10	No marking. Thin rules
11	Nick under N of 2nd
12	Scoop (base) to left of 2nd
13	Protrusion top of 1st under C
14	Two small diagonal nicks under PE, C of 2nd
15	Minute dot under P of 2nd
16	Tiny nick under to left of S of 2nd; rule under 1st thinner at left
17	Nick (top) under I of 1st
18	No markings. Thick rules

Plate 6 was also used with the Simple Cypher watermark.
Harrison Printings, 1936
19a	No marking
19b	Rule under 3rd shows progressive wear to right (base). Finally showing nick under N
20	19th and 20th left sides bevelled at their adjacent ends
21	2 cuts 1st left side
22	Rules 19th and 20th left side thin
23	Cut 1st left side; shallow nick (base) under CE of 1st; horizontal mark in 2nd under E(N)

Index to Plate Markings
Top Margin, Stamp Numbers

Stamp No.	Plate
1	8
2	6

Bottom Margin, Stamp Numbers
1	6, 9, 13, 16, 17, 23
2	8, 9, 11, 12, 14, 15, 16, 23
3	9, 19b

Left Margin, Row Numbers

Row No.	Plate
1	21, 23
19	20, 22
20	20, 22

No Markings: Plates 10 (thin rules), 18 (thick rules), 19a

Controls
Somerset House Printings, 1924–25

Plate	Controls employed
6	B. 24
8	C. 25, D. 25

Harrison Printings, 1936
16	Y 36
19a	Y 36
19b	Y 36
19b	Z 36

●━━━

161

KING GEORGE V — The Profile Head Issue — 6d. Purple, Type N8. Block Cypher

1926 (June) and **1934–38**. **6d. Purple, Type N8.** As last, but Ordinary Paper. Wmk. Block Cypher

N42 (=S.G.426a)

	Unmtd mint	Mtd mint	Used
Somerset House Printings (1926–33)			
(1) Rosy mauve	15·00	10·00	2·00
(2) Pale rosy mauve (1927–28)	20·00	12·00	3·00
(3) Reddish purple (1932–33)	12·00	8·00	2·00
Harrison Printings (1934–38)			
(4) Deep reddish purple (1934–36)	15·00	9·00	2·00
(5) Purple (1935–38)	8·00	4·00	1·50
(6) Deep purple (1935–38)	30·00	20·00	4·00
a. Watermark inverted	£140	90·00	90·00
b. Imperf. between stamp and left margin		£3750	
s. "Specimen", Type 23		£425	
t. "Specimen", Type 26		£800	
u. "Specimen", Type 32		£2250	
w. "Specimen", Type 26 and "Cancelled", Type 24		£2250	
x. "Cancelled", Type 33 (Somerset House)		£475	

No. N42b is a Somerset House printing. It was caused by a top left corner sheet fold.
No. N42w is a Somerset House printing, shade (2).

Controls. Prices are for unused singles.
Somerset House Printings:

	Perf. Type	
Control	2 (E)	2A (P)
D. 25	£400	†
E. 26	15·00	£600*
F. 26	15·00	†
G. 27	15·00	†
H. 27	15·00	†
I. 28	25·00	*
J. 28	15·00	*
K. 29	10·00	†
L. 29	10·00	†
M. 30	12·00	£900*
N. 30	20·00	†
O. 31	20·00	†
P. 31	15·00	†
Q. 32	12·00	†
R. 32	25·00	†
S. 33	30·00	—
T. 33	8·00	†

* See perf. type 3A below:

Strips of three
Variety Type 3A (I/P)

E. 26	—
I. 28	75·00
J. 28	75·00
M. 30	—

Watermark varieties known:
Wmk inverted: E. 26, F. 26, G. 27, H. 27, I. 28, J. 28, K. 29, L. 29, M. 30, N. 30.

Harrison Printings:

	Perf. Type	
Control	2 (E)	2A (P)
V34	15·00	†
W35	30·00	40·00
X35	10·00	60·00
Y36	10·00	†
Z36	8·00	†
A37	25·00	†
B37	£125	£450
C38	20·00	†
D38	25·00	£125

Strips of three
Variety Type 4 (I/2E)

| V 34 | £100 |
| W 35 | £100 |

Watermark varieties known:
Wmk inverted: V 34, W 35, X 35, Y 36, Z 36, A 37, B 37, C 38, D 38.

Imprimatur from the National Postal Museum Archives
Imperforate, watermark Type W15
Watermark upright (pair) £8000

Control Schedule
Somerset House Printings, 1926–33

Plate	Controls employed
8	D. 25, E. 26, F. 26, G. 27, H. 27
9	G. 27, H. 27, I. 28, J. 28, K. 29, M. 30, P. 31
10	E. 26, F. 26, G. 27, I. 28, L. 29
11	E. 26, J. 28, K. 29
12	K. 29, L. 29, M. 30, N. 30
13	K. 29, L. 29, M. 30, N. 30, R. 32
14	N. 30, O. 31, P. 31
15	O. 31, T. 33
16	R. 32, S. 33, T. 33
17	S. 33, T. 33
18	Q. 32, S. 33, T. 33

Harrison Printings, 1934–38

16	V 34, W 35, X 35, Y 36, Z 36
19a	V 34, W 35
19b	X 35, Y 36, Z 36, A37
20	X 35, Y 36, Z 36, A 37
21	X 35, Z 36, A 37, B 37, C 38, D 38
22	Z 36, A 37, C 38
23	Z 36, A 37, B 37, C 38, D 38

1924 (11 November). **9d. Olive-Green, Type N9.** Wmk. Block Cypher

N43 (=S.G.427)

	Unmtd mint	Mtd mint	Used
(1) Olive-green	40·00	12·00	3·50
(2) Pale olive-green	42·00	20·00	3·50
(3) Deep olive-green	45·00	25·00	3·50
(4) Olive-yellow-green (1933)	75·00	50·00	22·00
a. Watermark inverted	£175	£120	£120
s. "Specimen", Type 23		£140	
t. "Specimen", Type 26		£800	
u. "Specimen", Type 32		£2250	
v. "Specimen", Type 32 and "Cancelled", Type 24		£2250	

Controls. Prices are for unused singles
Waterlow Printings:

	Perf. Type
Control	2 (E)
A 24	20·00
C 25	20·00
F 26	20·00
I 28	22·00
J 28	24·00
L 29	20·00
N 30	28·00
P 31	20·00
R 32	20·00
T 33	90·00

Strips of three
Variety Type 2 (c) (I/I)
P 31 £225
Variety Type 3A (I/P)
A 24 50·00

10d. Turquoise, Type N9. Block Cypher — The Profile Head Issue — KING GEORGE V — NC

Watermark varieties known:
Wmk inverted: A 24, C 25, F 26, I 28, J 28, P 31.

Harrison Printings:

Control	Perf. Type 2 (E)	2A (P)
V 34	30·00	†
W 35	45·00	†
X 35	25·00	60·00

Strip of three
Variety Type 4 (I/2E)

V 34	£120

Imprimatur from the National Postal Museum Archives
Imperforate, watermark Type W15
Watermark upright (pair) £10000

Plate Markings

Plate	Marking
1	Irregular cuts 19th left side, 11 mm.
2	Sloping internal cut 20th left side, 13 mm. After re-chroming in 1926, this cut got progressively smaller, finally showing as a tiny dot. Two small dots above 1st and small dot 1st left side 11 mm.
3	Minute dot 19th left side, 11 mm.
4	No marking. Thick rules at left
5	No marking. Thin rules at left
6	Small dot central 18th left side, 12 mm.

Control Schedule

Plate	Controls employed
Waterlow Printings, 1924–33	
1	A 24, C 25, F 26, I 28, J 28, L 29, N 30, P 31, R 32, T 33
2	A 24, C 25, F 26, I 28, J 28, L 29, N 30, P 31, R 32, T 33
6	C 25
Harrison Provisional Printings, 1934–35	
1	V 34, W 35
2	V 34, W 35, X 35
3	V 34, W 35
4	W 35, X 35
5	X 35

●—————

1924 *(28 November).* **10d. Turquoise, Type N9.** Wmk. Block Cypher

N44 (=S.G.428)

	Unmtd mint	Mtd mint	Used
(1) Turquoise-blue	85·00	40·00	40·00
(2) Deep greenish blue	£100	50·00	40·00
(3) Dull greenish blue	70·00	40·00	40·00
(4) Deep dull greenish blue (1935)	£100	60·00	45·00
a. Watermark inverted	£3750	£2750	£2000
b. Frame breaks, at top right and at right (R. 16/4)		£850	
ba. Frame break at bottom left (R. 16/5)		£800	
s. "Specimen", Type 23		£750	
t. Do. Imperf.		£180	
u. "Specimen", Type 32		£2250	
v. "Specimen", Type 32 and "Cancelled", Type 24		£2250	

N44b/ba

Controls. Prices are for unused singles.
Waterlow Printings:

Control	Perf. Type 2 (E)
A 24	£350
D 25	£100
F 26	80·00
G 27	75·00
J 28	75·00
L 29	90·00
O 31	£120
Q 32	£120
S 33	£150
U 34	£400

Strip of three
Variety Type 3A (I/P)

A 24	£120

Watermark varieties known:
Wmk inverted: D 25, F 26.

163

KING GEORGE V — 1911-24. Booklet panes in Letterpress — 1s. Bistre-Brown, Type N9. Block Cypher

Harrison Printings:

Control	Perf. Type 2 (E)
U 34	£500
V 34	£300
W 35	70·00

Imprimatur from the National Postal Museum Archives
Imperforate, watermark Type W15
Watermark upright (pair) £10000

Plate Markings

Plate	Marking
1c	Base of 20th left side bends inwards. Two minute dots under PE of 1st. Large dot under P of 2nd
2b	Base of 16th right side bevelled. Large dot under PE of 1st
3	Dot and minute dot 1st left side, 18, 22½ mm.

Plates 1c and 2b were also used with the Simple Cypher watermark.

Control Schedule

Plate	Controls employed

Waterlow Printings, 1924–33
- 1c   A 24, D 25, F 26, G 27, J 28, L 29, O 31, Q 32, S 33
- 2b   A 24, D 25, F 26, G 27, J 28, L 29, O 31, Q 32, S 33
- 3   G 27

Waterlow Provisional Printing, 1934
- 1c   U 34

Harrison Provisional Printings, 1934-35
- 1c   V 34
- 2b   U 34, V 34, W 35
- 3   W 35

1924 (October*). **1s. Bistre-Brown, Type N9.** Wmk. Block Cypher

N45 (=S.G.429)

	Unmtd mint	Mtd mint	Used
(1) Bistre-brown	50·00	22·00	3·00
(2) Buff-brown	70·00	40·00	3·00
(3) Pale buff-brown (1924–25)	75·00	42·00	4·00
(4) Fawn-brown	75·00	42·00	4·00
(5) Deep fawn-brown (1935)	£250	£150	30·00
a. Watermark inverted	£600	£375	£375
s. "Specimen", Type 23		£550	
t. Do. Imperf.		£180	
u. "Specimen", Type 32		£2250	
v. "Specimen", Type 32 and "Cancelled", Type 24		£2250	
w. "Specimen", Type 31 in violet or black		£475	

* The exact date of issue is unknown but the earliest date seen by us is 16.10.24.

Controls. Prices are for unused singles.
Waterlow Printings:

Control	Perf. Type 2 (E)
A 24	35·00
B 24	£175
D 25	45·00
F 26	35·00
H 27	50·00
I 28	35·00
J 28	65·00
K 29	£150
L 29	35·00
N 30	35·00
P 31	35·00
R 32	45·00
S 33	£175
U 34	£550

Strip of three
Variety Type 3A (I/P)

A 24	£150

Watermark varieties known:
Wmk inverted: A 24, D 25, F 26, I 28, J 28, L 29.

Harrison Printings:

Control	Perf. Type 2 (E)	2A (P)
U 34	50·00	†
V 34	45·00	£225
W 35	65·00	†
X 35	65·00	†

Strip of three
Variety Type 4 (I/2E)

V 34	£100

Imprimatur from the National Postal Museum Archives
Imperforate, watermark Type W15
Watermark upright (pair) £10000

Plate Markings

Plate	Marking
1	No marking
2	Cut 19th left side, 18½ mm. (Harrison Plate 4)
3a	Dot 20th left side, 12½ mm.
3b	Added large dot 20th left side
4a	½ dot (inner) 19th left side, 13 mm.; small nicks at each end of rule under 2nd
4b	Added dot (outer) 19th left side, 6 mm.
5	Cut under S of 1st. (Harrison Plate 5c)

Control Schedule

Plate	Controls employed
Waterlow Printings, 1924–33	
1	A 24, B 24, D 25
2	A 24, B 24, D 25
3a	F 26, H 27, I 28, J 28, K 29, L 29, N 30, P 31, R 32
3b	R 32, S 33
4a	F 26, H 27, I 28, J 28, K 29, L 29, N 30, P 31, R 32, S 33
4b	S 33

Waterlow Provisional Printing, 1934
3b	U 34
4b	U 34

Harrison Provisional Printings, 1934–35
3b	U 34, V 34, W 35, X 35
4b	U 34, V 34
5	W 35, X 35

Section ND

1911-24. Booklet panes in Letterpress

Checklist of King George V Booklet Panes in Letterpress

Spec. Cat. Nos.	Description	From Booklets Nos.	Page
I. Downey Head Issue			
NB1, NB1a	6 × ½d. Die 1B, wmk Crown	BB1–2	167
NB2, NB2a	6 × ½d. Die 1B, wmk Simple Cypher	BB3–5	167
NB3, NB3a	6 × 1d. carmine Die 1B, wmk Crown	BB1	167
NB4, NB4a	6 × 1d. scarlet Die 1B wmk Crown	BB2	167
NB4b, NB4c	6 × 1d. aniline scarlet Die 1B, wmk Crown	BB2	168
NB5, NB5a	6 × 1d. scarlet Die 1B	BB3–5	168
II. Profile Head Issue, Wmk Simple Cypher			
NB6, NB6a	6 × ½d.	BB6–11, BB18–19, BB18–19, BB22, BB31–32	168
NB7, NB7a	6 × 1d.	BB6–11, BB18–19, BB22, BB30–32	169
NB8, NB8a	6 × 1½d.	BB11, BB18–19, BB22–23, BB31–32	169
NB9, NB9a	4 × 1½d. and two printed labels	BB11	170
NB10, NB10a	6 × 2d. Die I	BB20 (part), BB30–31, BB32 (part)	170
NB11, NB11a	6 × 2d. Die II	BB20 (part), BB21, BB32 (part)	170
III. Profile Head Issue, Wmk Block Cypher			
NB12, NB12a	6 × ½d.	BB12, BB14, BB24, BB26, BB33–35	171
NB13, NB13a	6 × 1d.	BB12, BB14, BB24, BB26, BB33–35	172
NB14, NB14a	6 × 1½d.	BB12, BB14, BB24, BB26, BB33–35	172
NB15, NB15a	4 × 1½d. and two printed labels	BB12, BB14, BB33–35	173

BOOKLET PANE PRICES. Prices quoted are for lightly mounted examples with good perforations all round and with binding margin attached in the most common shade. Panes in scarcer shades are all worth more having regard to the shade prices in sections NA, NB and NC. Panes showing some degree of trimming will be worth less than the published prices in this Catalogue. Unmounted mint panes are worth more and the following percentages may be added to the basic panes.

Nos. NB9, NB9a, + **15%**, Nos. NB15, NB15a, + **40%**. Non-advertisement panes of 6 + **30%**.

The booklet pane perforators are described in Appendix 1. As issued panes are collected according to the different selvedge perforations, issued panes are listed accordingly. For the specimen and pre-cancelled panes, being much scarcer, no perforation distinction is made in the listing.

I. Downey Head Issue

½d. Booklet Panes of Six. Harrison

NB1/a, NB2/a

6 × ½d. Green. Die 1B. Watermark Crown
From Booklets BB1/2

	Perf Type		
	E	I	P
A. Watermark upright			
NB1 (containing No. N2 × 6) (8.11)	£250	£375	£375
b. Gash in crown (R.1/1– see N2d)	£400		
s. "Specimen", Type 22	£3000		
t. Cancelled "London Chief Office, E.C.", Type E	£300		
u. Cancelled "London (Chief Office) E.C.", Type F	£400		
v. Cancelled "London, E.C.", Type G	£300		
B. Watermark inverted			
NB1a (containing No. N2a × 6) (8.11)	£250	£375	£375
ab. Indent below Y (R.1/1— see N2j)	£400		
ap. With plate mark	£500		
as. "Specimen", Type 22	£3000		
at. Cancelled "London Chief Office, E.C.", Type E	£300		
au. Cancelled "London (Chief Office) E.C.", Type F	£400		
av. Cancelled "London, E.C.", Type G	£300		

6 × ½d. Green. Die 1B. Watermark Simple Cypher
From Booklets BB3/5

	Perf Type
	E
A. Watermark upright	
NB2 (containing No. N3 × 6) (9.12)	£375
b. White flaw after Y (R.2/2 – see N3f)	£450
s. "Specimen", Type 22	£3000
t. Cancelled "London E.C.", Type H	£325
u. "Specimen", Type 26	£4000
v. Cancelled "London E.C.", Type I	£400
B. Watermark inverted	
NB2a (containing No. N3b × 6) (9.12)	£375
ap. With plate mark	£650
as. "Specimen", Type 22	£3000
at. Cancelled "London E.C.", Type H	£325
au. "Specimen", Type 26	£4000
av. Cancelled "London E.C." Type I	£400

1d. Booklet Panes of Six. Harrison

NB3/a, NB4/c, NB5/a

6 × 1d. Carmine. Die 1B. Watermark Crown
From Booklets BB1

	Perf Type		
	E	I	P
A. Watermark upright			
NB3 (containing No. N8 × 6) (8.11)	£250	£375	£375
b. Broken left frame (R. 1/2 — see N8j)	£550		
c. Open top to leaf (R. 2/3 — see N8l)	£500		
p. With plate mark	£500		
s. Cancelled "London Chief Office, E.C.", Type E	£300		
t. "Specimen", Type 22	£3000		
B. Watermark inverted			
NB3a (containing No. N8a × 6) (8.11)	£250	£375	£375
ap. With plate mark	£500		
as. Cancelled "London Chief Office, E.C.", Type E	£300		
at. "Specimen", Type 22	£3000		

6 × 1d. Scarlet. Die 1B. Watermark Crown
From Booklet BB2

	Perf Type
	E
A. Watermark upright	
NB4 (containing No. N9 × 6) (4.12)	£400
d. Open top to leaf (R. 2/3 – see N9l)	£550
s. "Specimen", Type 22	£5000
t. Cancelled "London (Chief Office) E.C.", Type F	£425
u. Cancelled "London E.C.", Type G	£425
B. Watermark inverted	
NB4a (containing No. N9a × 6) (4.12)	£400
ab. White flaw above right value (R. 2/1 — see N9f)	£550
as. "Specimen", Type 22	£5000
at. Cancelled "London (Chief Office) E.C.", Type F	£425
au. Cancelled "London, E.C.", Type G	£425

ND KING GEORGE V 1911-24. Booklet panes in Letterpress 6 × 1d. Aniline Scarlet. Royal Cypher

6 × 1d. Aniline Scarlet. Die 1B. Watermark Crown

	Perf Type
	E
A. Watermark upright	
NB4b (containing No. N9(4) × 6)	£1500
u. Cancelled "London E.C.", Type G	£800
B. Watermark inverted	
NB4c (containing No. N9a(4) × 6)	£1500
u. Cancelled "London E.C.", Type G	£800

6 × 1d. Scarlet. Die 1B. Watermark Simple Cypher
From Booklets BB3/5

	Perf Type
	E
A. Watermark upright	
NB5 (containing No. N10 × 6) (9.12)	£275
c. Open top to leaf (R. 2/3 — see N10g)	£450
s. "Specimen", Type 22	£2400
t. Cancelled "London, E.C.", Type H	£350
u. "Specimen", Type 26	£3500
v. Cancelled "London E.C.", Type I	£400
B. Watermark inverted	
NB5a (containing No. N10b × 6) (9.12)	£275
ab. White flaw above right value (R. 2/1 — see N10f)	£450
as. "Specimen", Type 22	£2400
at. Cancelled "London, E.C.", Type H	£350
au. "Specimen", Type 26	£3500
av. Cancelled "London E.C." Type I	£400

II. Profile Head Issue, Wmk. Simple Cypher

For these panes with Block Cypher watermark see Nos. NB12/15

½d. Booklet Panes of Six. Harrison

NB6/a, NB12/a

6 × ½d. Green. Watermark Simple Cypher
From Booklets BB6/11, BB18/19, BB22 and BB31/32

	Perf Type		
	E	I	P
A. Watermark upright			
NB6 (containing No. N14 × 6) (4.13)	£120	£150	£120
a. "New Moon" flaw (R. 2/3 — see N14f)	£2750		
t. "Cancelled", Type 24	£550		
u. Cancelled "London E.C.", Type H	£400		
v. Cancelled "London E.C.", Type I	£200		
w. "Specimen", Type 26	£1600		
y. Cancelled "London E.C.", Type G	£600		
B. Watermark inverted			
NB6a (containing No. N14c × 6) (4.13)	£120	£150	£120
ab. Broken left frame (R. 1/1 — see N14i)	£400		
ac. White spot on tablet (R. 2/2 — see N14ia)	£300		
ad. "New Moon" flaw (R. 2/3 — see N14fa)	£3000		
ap. With plate mark	£300		
as. "Specimen", Type 23	£1800		
at. "Cancelled", Type 24	£550		
au. Cancelled "London E.C.", Type H	£400		
av. Cancelled "London E.C.", Type I	£200		
ax. "Cancelled "London (Chief Office) E.C.", Type F	£800		
ay. Cancelled "London E.C.", Type G	£600		

Booklet panes with E perf selvedges are stapled, coming from booklets issued up to July 1917 (to Series 1, Edition No. 64) and stitched thereafter up to February 1919 (from Series 1 Edition No.62 to series 2, Edition No. 6.) Panes with I and P selvedges are always stitched.

Imprimatur from the National Postal Museum Archives
Booklet pane of six. Imperforate, watermark Type W14
 Two panes as No. NB6 arranged horizontally *tête-bêche* with marginal pillars at right

168

1d. Booklet Panes of Six. Harrison

NB7/a, NB13/a

6 × 1d. Scarlet. Watermark Simple Cypher
From Booklets BB6/11, BB18/19, BB22 and BB30/32

	Perf Type		
	E	I	P
A. Watermark upright			
NB7 (containing No. N16 × 6) (4.13)	£120	£150	£120
c. Inverted and reversed Q for O and spot in centre (R. 2/3–see N16ka)	£400		
p. With plate mark	£300		
s. "Specimen", Type 23	£1800		
t. "Cancelled", Type 24	£500		
u. Cancelled "London E.C.", Type H	£400		
v. Cancelled "London, E.C.", Type I	£200		
w. "Specimen", Type 26	£2000		
x. Cancelled "London (Chief Office) E.C.", Type F	£800		
y. Cancelled "London E.C.", Type G	£500		
B. Watermark inverted			
NB7a (containing No. N16b × 6) (4.13)	£120	£150	£120
ap. With plate mark	£300		
at. "Cancelled", Type 24	£500		
au. Cancelled "London E.C.", Type H	£400		
av. Cancelled "London E.C.", Type I	£200		
aw. "Specimen", Type 26	£2000		
ax. Cancelled "London (Chief Office) E.C.", Type F	£800		
ay. Cancelled "London E.C.", Type G	£500		

Booklet panes with E perf selvedges are stapled, coming from booklets issued up to July 1917 (to Series 1, Edition No. 64) and stitched thereafter up to February 1919 (from Series 1, Edition No.62 to Series 2, Edition No. 6.) Panes with I and P selvedges are always stitched.

Imprimatur from the National Postal Museum Archives
Booklet pane of six. Imperforate, watermark Type W14
    Two panes as No. NB7 arranged horizontally *tête-bêche* with marginal pillars at right

1½d. Booklet Panes of Six. Harrison

NB8/a, NB14/a

6 × 1½d. Red-brown. Watermark Simple Cypher
From Booklets BB11, BB18/19, BB22/23 and BB31/32

	Perf Type		
	E	I	P
A. Watermark upright			
NB8 (containing No. N18 × 6) (10.18)	£350	£225	£150
u. Cancelled "London E.C.", Type H	£400		
v. Cancelled "London E.C.", Type I	£200		
B. Watermark inverted			
NB8a (containing No. N18b × 6) (10.18)	£350	£225	£150
ap. With plate mark	£425		
as. "Specimen", Type 23	£1800		
au. Cancelled "London E.C.", Type H	£400		
av. Cancelled "London E.C.", Type I	£200		

Imprimatur from the National Postal Museum Archives
Booklet pane of six. Imperforate, watermark Type W14
    Two panes as No. NB8 arranged horizontally *tête-bêche* with marginal pillars at right

ND KING GEORGE V 1911-24. Booklet panes in Letterpress 4 × 1½d. Red-brown. Block Cypher

1½d. Booklet Panes with Advertising Labels. Harrison

NB9/a, NB15/a

4 × 1½d. Red-brown. with two labels printed in black.
Watermark Simple Cypher
From Booklet BB11

	Perf Type	
	I	P
A. Watermark upright		
NB9 (containing No. N18 × 4) (2.24)	£700	£600
s. "Specimen", Type 23	£1800	
u. Cancelled "London E.C.", Type I	£550	
B. Watermark inverted		
NB9a (containing No. N18b × 4) (2.24)	£700	£600
Pane Nos. NB9 or NB9a		

	Wmk Upright	Wmk Inverted
(1) "Stamp Auctions, Harmer, Rooke, expert advice free/Millennium Oat-Flakes"	£600	£600
(2) "Millennium Oat-Flakes/Stamp Auctions, Harmer, Rooke, expert advice free"	£600	£600

2d. Booklet Panes of Six. Harrison

NB10/a, NB11/a

6 × 2d. Orange. Die I. Watermark Simple Cypher
From Booklets BB20 (part), BB30/31 and BB32 (part)

	Perf Type	
	I	P
A. Watermark upright		
NB10 (containing No. N19×6) (7.20)	£425	£350
s. Cancelled "London E.C.", Type H	£400	
t. Cancelled "London E.C.", Type I	£275	
u. "Specimen", Type 26 and lower left stamp with punch hole	£2000	
B. Watermark inverted		
NB10a (containing No. N19b × 6) (7.20)	£425	£350
ap. With plate work	£650	
as. Cancelled "London E.C.", Type H	£400	
at. Cancelled "London E.C.", Type I	£275	
au. "Specimen", Type 26 and lower left stamp with punch hole	£2000	

Imprimatur from the National Postal Museum Archives
Booklet pane of six. Imperforate, watermark Type W14
  Two panes as No. NB10 arranged horizontally *tête-bêche* with marginal pillars at right

6 × 2d. Orange. As last but Die II. Watermark Simple Cypher
From Booklets BB20 (part) and BB32 (part)

	Perf Type	
	I	P
A. Watermark upright		
NB11 (containing No. N20 × 6) (8.21)	£500	£375
s. Cancelled "London E.C.", Type I	£325	
B. Watermark inverted		
NB11a (containing No. N20b×6) (8.21)	£500	£375
ab. Frame breaks top right (R. 1/2) and centre bottom (R. 2/1)	£525	
ap. With plate mark	£650	
as. Cancelled "London E.C.", Type I	£325	
at. Cancelled "London E.C.", Type H	£600	

6 × ½d. Green. Block Cypher   1911-24. Booklet panes in Letterpress   **KING GEORGE V**   **ND**

III. Profile Head Issue, Wmk. Block Cypher

½d. Booklet Panes of Six. Waterlow or Harrison

6 × ½d. Green. Watermark Block Cypher
From Waterlow Booklets BB12, BB24, BB33/34 and Harrison Booklets BB14, BB26 and BB35

NB11ab

Imprimatur from the National Postal Museum Archives
Booklet pane of six. Imperforate, watermark Type W14
   Two panes as No. NB11 arranged horizontally *tête-bêche* with marginal pillars at right

	Perf Type I	P
A. Watermark upright		
NB12 (containing No. N33 × 6) (2.24)	85·00	85·00†
p. With plate mark	£275	
s. "Specimen", Type 23	£1200	
sa. "Specimen", Type 29	£1000	
t. "Specimen", Type 30	£1500	
u. "Cancelled", Type 24	£3000	
v. "Cancelled", Type 28	£675	
va. "Cancelled", Type 28P	£1200	
w. "Cancelled", Type 33	£1500	
x. "Cancelled", Type 33P	£550	
y. Cancelled "London E.C.", Type I	£300	
z. Cancelled "London Chief Office", Type J, in violet	£250	
zaa. Cancelled "London Chief Office", Type J, in black	£900	
za. Cancelled "London Chief Office", Type K, in violet	£400	
B. Watermark inverted		
NB12a (containing No. N33a × 6) (2.24)	£500	85·00
ab. Watermark sideways inverted	£25000	
ap. With plate mark	£275	
as. "Specimen", Type 23	£1200	
at. "Specimen", Type 30	£1500	
av. "Cancelled", Type 28	£675	
ava. "Cancelled", Type 28P	£1200	
aw. "Cancelled", Type 33	£1500	
ax. "Cancelled", Type 33P	£550	
ay. Cancelled "London E.C.", Type I	£300	
aya. Cancelled "London E.C.", Type I/J	£800	
az. Cancelled "London Chief Office", Type J, in violet	£250	
aza. Cancelled "London Chief Office", Type K, in violet	£400	

No. NB12sa. is without selvedge, NB12ab is unique and trimmed at right and base.

† This pane has vertical rule and horizontal bars in the selvedge. The rare right feed upright watermark pane with vertical rule only (being on the opposite side of the sheet to the inverted watermark pane with imperforate selvedge) is priced £500.

Imprimatur from the National Postal Museum Archives
Booklet pane of six. Imperforate, watermark Type W15
   Two panes as No. NB12 arranged horizontally *tête-bêche* with marginal pillars at right

Specimen and Cancelled overprints from the National Postal Museum Archives
Booklet pane of six. Perf. 15 × 14, watermark Type W15 (inverted)
"Specimen", Type 32 and upper left stamp with
   punch hole £1500
"Cancelled", Type 33 and upper left stamp with
   punch hole £1500

171

1d. Booklet Panes of Six. Waterlow or Harrison

6 × 1d. Scarlet. Watermark Block Cypher
From Waterlow Booklets BB12, BB24, BB33/34 and Harrison Booklets BB14, BB26 and BB35

	Perf Type I	P
A. Watermark upright		
NB13 (containing No. N34 × 6) (2.24)	85·00	85·00†
b. Watermark sideways	£7000	
p. With plate mark	£275	
s. "Specimen", Type 23	£1200	
sa. "Specimen", Type 29	£1000	
t. "Specimen", Type 30	£1500	
u. "Cancelled", Type 28	£675	
v. "Cancelled", Type 28P	£1200	
w. "Cancelled", Type 33	£1500	
x. "Cancelled", Type 33P	£550	
y. Cancelled, "London E.C.", Type I	£300	
z. Cancelled "London Chief Office", Type J, in violet	£250	
zaa. Cancelled "London Chief Office", Type J, in black	£900	
za. Cancelled "London Chief Office", Type K, in violet	£400	
B. Watermark inverted		
NB13a (containing No. N34b × 6) (2.24)	£500	85·00
ap. With plate mark	£275	
as. "Specimen", Type 23	£1200	
at. "Specimen", Type 30	£1500	
au. "Cancelled", Type 28	£675	
av. "Cancelled", Type 28P	£1200	
aw. "Cancelled", Type 33	£1500	
ax. "Cancelled", Type 33P	£550	
ay. Cancelled "London E.C.", Type I	£300	
az. Cancelled "London Chief Office", Type J, in violet	£250	
aza. Cancelled "London Chief Office", Type K, in violet	£400	

No. NB13sa is without selvedge. NB13b is unique and is without selvedge.

† This pane has vertical rule and horizontal bars in the selvedge. The rare right feed upright watermark pane with vertical rule only (being on the opposite side of the sheet to the inverted watermark pane with imperforate selvedge) is priced £500.

Imprimatur from the National Postal Museum Archives
Booklet pane of six. Imperforate, watermark Type W15
Two panes as No. NB13 arranged horizontally *tête-bêche* with marginal pillars at right

Specimen and Cancelled overprints from the National Postal Museum Archives
Booklet pane of six. Perf. 15 × 14, watermark Type W15 (inverted)
"Specimen", Type 32 and upper left stamp with punch hole £1500
"Cancelled", Type 33 and upper left stamp with punch hole £1500

1½d. Booklet Panes of Six. Waterlow or Harrison

6 × 1½d. Red-brown. Watermark Block Cypher
From Waterlow Booklets BB12, BB24, BB33/34 and Harrison Booklets BB14, BB26 and BB35

	Perf Type I	P
A. Watermark upright		
NB14 (containing No. N35 × 6) (2.24)	50·00	50·00†
b. Frame damage (R. 2/1 — see N35m)	£600	
p. With plate mark	£200	
s. "Specimen", Type 23	£1200	
sa. "Specimen", Type 29	£1000	
t. "Specimen", Type 30	£1500	
u. "Cancelled", Type 24	£3000	
v. "Cancelled", Type 28	£675	
va. "Cancelled", Type 28P	£1200	
w. "Cancelled", Type 33	£1500	
x. "Cancelled", Type 33P	£550	
y. Cancelled "London E.C.", Type I	£300	
ya. Cancelled "London Chief Office", Type I/J	£800	
z. Cancelled "London Chief Office", Type J, in violet	£250	
za. Cancelled "London Chief Office", Type K, in violet	£400	
B. Watermark inverted		
NB14a (containing No. N35c × 6) (2.24)	£400	50·00
ap. With plate work	£200	
as. "Specimen", Type 23	£1200	
at. "Specimen", Type 30	£1500	
av. "Cancelled", Type 28	£675	
ava. "Cancelled", Type 28P	£1200	
aw. "Cancelled", Type 33	£1500	
ax. "Cancelled", Type 33P	£550	
ay. Cancelled "London E.C.", Type I	£225	
az. Cancelled "London Chief Office", Type J, in violet	£250	
aza. Cancelled "London Chief Office", Type K, in violet	£325	
azb. Cancelled "London Chief Office", Type J, in black	£900	

No. NB14sa is without selvedge.

† This pane has vertical rule and horizontal bars in the selvedge. The rare right feed upright watermark pane with vertical rule only (being on the opposite side of the sheet to the inverted watermark pane with imperforate selvedge) is priced £500.

Imprimatur from the National Postal Museum Archives
Booklet pane of six. Imperforate, watermark Type W15
Two panes as No. NB14 arranged horizontally
    tête-bêche with marginal pillars at right .... —

Specimen and Cancelled overprints from the National Postal Museum Archives
Booklet pane of six. Perf. 15×14, watermark Type W15 (inverted)
"Specimen", Type 32 and upper left stamp with punch hole. £1500
"Cancelled", Type 33 and upper left stamp with punch hole £1500

4 × 1½d. Red-brown. Block Cypher   1911-24. Booklet panes in Letterpress   **KING GEORGE V**   **ND**

1½d. Booklet Panes with Advertising Labels. Waterlow

4 × 1½d. Red-brown. with two labels printed in black or green (NB15/a (72))
From Waterlow Booklets BB12, BB33/34

	Perf Type I	Perf Type P
A. Watermark upright		
NB15 (containing No. N35 3 4) (3.24)	£225	£225†
b. Watermark sideways	£11000	
p. With plate mark	£500	
s. "Specimen", Type 23	£1500	
t. "Specimen", Type 30	£1800	
u. "Cancelled", Type 24		
v. "Cancelled", Type 28	£800	
va. "Cancelled", Type 28P	£1500	
w. "Cancelled", Type 33P	£800	
x. "Cancelled", Type 33	£1200	
y. Cancelled, "London E.C.", Type I	£300	
z. Cancelled, "London Chief Office", Type J, in violet	£250	
za. Cancelled, "London Chief Office", Type K, in violet	£400	

No. NB15b unmounted price £13000.

B. Watermark inverted		
NB15a (containing No. N35c 3 6) (3.24)	£500	£225
ab. Watermark sideways inverted	£11000	
ap. With plate work	£500	
as. "Specimen", Type 23	£1500	
at. "Specimen", Type 30	£1800	
av. "Cancelled", Type 28	£800	
ava. "Cancelled", Type 28P	£1500	
aw. "Cancelled", Type 33P	£800	
ax. "Cancelled", Type 33	£1200	
ay. Cancelled "London E.C.", Type I	£300	
az. Cancelled, "London Chief Office", Type J, in violet	£250	
aza. Cancelled, "London Chief Office", Type K, in violet	£400	

† This pane has vertical rule and horizontal bars in the selvedge. The rare right feed upright watermark pane with vertical rule only (being on the opposite side of the sheet to the inverted watermark pane with imperforate selvedge) is priced £500.

The following advertising labels exist in two settings: Nos. (7), (89); (9), (88); (17), (91); (19), (90); (78); (77), (99).

Pane Nos. NB15 or NB15a	Wmk Upright	Wmk Inverted
G.P.O. Advertising labels:		
(1) "Air Mails (enquire) / Cable via Imperial"	£250	£250
(1a) As (1), but text on both labels inverted	£300	£300
(2) "Air Mails (enquire) / Telephone Service"	£250	£250
(3) "Cable via Imperial / Air Mails (enquire)"	£250	£250
(4) "Cable via Imperial / Telephone Service"	£250	£250
(5) "via Empiradio / Cable via Imperial"	£300	£300
(6) "via Empiradio / Telephone Service"	£350	£350
(7) "Saving is Simple / Home Safe" (Setting 1: "i" of "is" over "mp" of "Simple")	£225	£225
(8) "Telephone Service / Air Mails (enquire)"	£225	£225
(9) "Telephone Service / Air Mails, letters and parcels" (Setting 1: line under "Installed free" without loops and almost straight)	£225	£225
(10) "Telephone Service / Cable via Imperial"	£250	£250

Pane Nos. NB15 or NB15a	Wmk Upright	Wmk Inverted
J. J. Cash Ltd. Advertising labels:		
(11) "Cash's names. The best method of marking personal and household linen / List of styles. J. & J. Cash"	£350	£350
(12) "Cash's washing ribbons. Ideal for shoulder straps / Book of ribbons. J. & J. Cash" (unnumbered, or numbered 144, 152, 160, 163, 167 or 175)	£375	£375
(13) "Cash's names. The best method of marking all linen / Cash's booklet, "Lose less linen", J. & J. Cash" (numbered 150)	£375	£375
(14) "Cash's lingerie ribbons. Ideal for shoulder straps / Book of ribbons. J. & J. Cash" (numbered 181)	£375	£375
(15) Do. but with "Cash's" in larger type and numbered 185	£375	£375
(16) "Cash's "Lose less linen" book / Free booklet. J. & J. Cash" (numbered 3 or 196)	£400	£400
(17) "Cash's "Safety first. Cash's names" booklet / Free booklet J. & J. Cash" (numbered 237) (Setting 1)	£375	£375
(18) "Cash's satin lingerie ribbons / Cash's ribbon booklet. J. & J. Cash" or "Book of ribbons" no. 190 (numbered 2, 190, 207, 225 or 229)	£375	£375
(19) "Cash's satin lingerie ribbons / Samples [central] of Cash's ribbons J. & J. Cash" (numbered 4, 5, 243 or 249) (Setting 1: flight of arrow small and pointed over "A" of "Attach")	£375	£375
Castell Bros. Advertising labels:		
(20) "Bodiam. Use it with pride / Bodiam. Castell Bros."	£350	£350
(21) "Castletone fashionable writing paper / Castell Bros."	£375	£375
(22) "Castletone Stationery / Castell Bros."	£375	£375
(23) "Bodiam (Six named colours) / Bodiam Castell Bros."	£375	£375
(24) "Pepys Stationery. Bodiam Castletone / Royal York. Stonehenge"	£350	£350
Cruise Departments Advertising labels:		
(25) "American Holiday £40 / ss. Minnekahda. Atlantic Transport Co."	£350	£350
(26) "Holiday Trips £40. Tourist third Cabin only [in four lines] / ss. Minnekahda and Minnesota Atlantic Transport Co. Ltd."	£350	£350
(27) "Holiday Trips £40. Tourist 3rd Cabin [in two lines] / ss. Minnekahda and Minnesota Atlantic Transport Line"	£375	£375
(28) "Holiday Trips £40. Tourist 3rd Cabin only [in three lines] / ss. Minnekahda and Minnesota Atlantic Transport Line"	£375	£375
(29) "Your holiday problem solved. £39 15s. 0d. [wording upright] / Atlantic Transport Line [wording sideways]"	£350	£350
(30) "South Africa for Sunshine / Union Castle Line"	£350	£350
(31) "Your 3 weeks holiday. A trip to New York £38 / White Star Line"	£375	£375
(32) "Your 3 weeks holiday. Why not a trip? £38 / White Star Line"	£375	£375
(33) "Your 3 weeks holiday. Take a trip. £38 / White Star Line"	£350	£350
(34) "Your Holiday. Cruise British by White Star / The Cruise Department"	£350	£350
(35) "33 Spring and Summer Cruises / White Star Line"	£350	£350

ND KING GEORGE V 1911-24. Booklet panes in Letterpress 4 × 1½d. Red-brown. Block Cypher

Pane Nos. NB15 or NB15a	Wmk Upright	Wmk Inverted
John Knight Ltd. Advertising labels:		
(36) "Have YOU tried Knight's Castile / John Knight Ltd."	£400	£400
(37) "For a limited period, Knight's Castile / Robinson and Cleaver Ltd."	£400	£400
(38) "[Soap picture] Knight's Castile / [Knight picture] Knight's Castile"	£425	£425
(39) "Try the three perfumes of Knight's Castile / Three visitors' tablets [small type]"	£400	£400
(40) "Try the three perfumes of Knight's Castile / Three visitors' tablets [large type]"	£400	£400
(41) "Knight's Castile, delicately perfumed / A British soap"	£400	£400
(42) "You ought to try 'zyxt' / John Knight Ltd."	£400	£400
(43) "What is your week-end job? 'ZYXT' / John Knight Ltd."	£400	£400
(44) "Whatever your week-end job, 'ZYXT' / John Knight Ltd."	£400	£400
(45) "[Picture of zyxt] / 'zyxt' is 4d. a tablet"	£425	£425
(46) "Knight's Castile, new artistic pack / John Knight Ltd."	£400	£400
(47) "Free to users of Family Health Soap / John Knight Ltd."	£400	£400
(48) "Royal Primrose Soap / John Knight Ltd."	£400	£400
(49) "Have you had your copy of the new list of British Gifts. Family Health Soap / John Knight Ltd."	£400	£400
(50) "Family Health and Hustler Too! / John Knight Ltd."	£400	£400
(51) "John Knight Ltd. / Family Health and Hustler Too!"	£400	£400
(52) "Have YOU tried Shavallo? / John Knight Ltd."	£400	£400
(53) "To obtain real luxury in shaving, Shavallo / 21 days for 2d. SHAVALLO"	£400	£400
(54) "Why not try Shavallo shaving cream? / John Knight Ltd."	£400	£400
(55) "John Knight's Shavallo 1/- / It's British"	£400	£400
Sundry Advertising labels:		
(56) "If interested in Billiards / The Billiard Player"	£400	£400
(57) "Bring the breath of the pine forest, etc. Cleaver's Terebene / F. S. Cleaver, Twickenham"	£400	£400
(58) "Have YOU tried Cleaver's Terebene? / F. S. Cleaver, London"	£400	£400
(59) "Desti cigarettes / Silmos Lollies"	£400	£400
(60) "Desti cigarettes / Telephone Service"	£400	£400
(61) "Dutton's shorthand / Reginald P.O. Dutton"	£375	£375
(62) "Buy Gilette blades / The blade with a shave in it"	£400	£400
(63) "Garden work for amateurs / Cable via Imperial"	£425	£425
(64) "Gaze's all weather tennis courts [sideways] / Send to Harmer, Rooke, Auctions [upright]"	£400	£400
(65) "Glastonbury's / Soft Sheepskin Shoes"	£400	£400
(66) "Gospo / Cable via Imperial"	£400	£400
(67) "Auctions, Harmer, Rooke, cash advanced, 69 Fleet Street [inverted] / Harmer Rooke, Auctions [upright]"	£400	£400
(68) "Note new address, Harmer Rooke / Stamp collectors should visit 188/189 Strand W.C.2"	£400	£400

Pane Nos. NB15 or NB15a	Wmk Upright	Wmk Inverted
(69) "Auctions, Harmer, Rooke, cash advanced, 188 Strand [inverted] / Harmer, Rooke, Auctions [upright]"	£400	£400
(70) "Best seats [sideways] / Keith Prowse [sideways]"	£400	£400
(71) "La Corona, Havana Cigars / Acknowledged the world over"	£400	£400
(72) "India Rubber Sponge [in green] / R. G. McKinlay [in green]"	£5000	£5000
(73) "Millennium Oat-Flakes / Wright's Coal Tar Soap"	£350	£350
(74) "Pitman's correspondence course / Pitman's W.C.1"	£400	£400
(75) "Pomeroy skin food. Helps the plain / Mrs. Pomeroy"	£400	£400
(76) "Pomeroy skin food. Trial size jar / Superfluous hair. Mrs. Pomeroy"	£400	£400
(77) "Poultry World. Free copy / Poultry World, 27 Stamford Street, S.E.1" (for 31 Stamford Street, see No. 99)	£400	£400
(78) "H.T. Battery / Ripaults Ltd. [known in two settings: top to bottom measuring 43 and 44 mm]"	£375	£375
(79) "Robinson and Cleaver famous for linen handkerchiefs / Hemstitched Handkerchiefs"	£400	£400
(80) "Robinson and Cleaver famous for Irish Linens / Ladies' Linen Hemstitched Handkerchiefs"	£375	£375
(81) "Scarborough's Hotels / Cable via Imperial"	£375	£375
(82) "Scarborough's Hotels / Harmer, Rooke weekly Stamp Auctions."	£400	£400
(83) "Scarborough's Hotels / Wright's Coal Tar Soap"	£400	£400
(84) "Wireless World. Free copy / Complete foreign programmes. Wireless World"	£400	£400
(85) "Save the outside wrappers. Wright's Coal Tar Soap Wright to the Proprietors, 46 Southwark Street, S.E.1"	£400	£400
(86) "Wright's Coal Tar Soap / Telephone Service"	£400	£400
(87) "Wright's Lysol / Air Mail, letters and parcels"	£400	£400
From Harrison Booklets BB14 and BB35:		
(88) "Telephone Service / Air Mails, letters and parcels" (Setting 2: bolder type; line under "Installed free" has only three loops)	£275	£275
(89) "Saving is Simple / Home Safe" (Setting 2: bolder type than Setting 1: "i" of "is" over "p" of "Simple")	£325	£325
(90) "Cash's satin lingerie ribbons / Samples [central] of Cash's ribbons, J. & J. Cash" (Setting 2: bolder type than Setting 1) (numbered 257, 275 or 285; flight of arrow large "V" shaped, and pointed over "tt" of "Attach")	£400	£400
(91) "Cash's "Safety first. Cash's names" booklet / Free booklet J. & J. Cash" (Setting 2) (numbered 7 or 263)	£425	£425
(92) "Pepys Stationery / Ruskin Linen"	£400	£400
(93) "Pepys Stationery. Castletone / Castells, London"	£400	£400
(94) "Pepys Stationery. Bodiam in white and six colours/Just added: Bodiam Grey. Castells"	£375	£375
(95) "For every woman. Bodiam in 7 colours / Pepys Stationery"	£400	£400

Pane Nos. NB15 or NB15a	Wmk Upright	Wmk Inverted
(96) "For every woman, Bodiam. For every man, Royal York / White and azure. Pepys Stationery Productions"	£400	£400
(97) "Kargo. (Card Golf) / Castell Bros. (Pepys Stationery)"	£400	£400
(98) "Cruises [picture of sailor] / White Star Line"	£625	£625
(99) "Poultry World., Free copy / Poultry World, 31 Stamford Street, S.E.1"	£400	£400
(100) "Shavallo for a swift smooth shave / Shavallo, Barbers use it"	£375	£375
(101) "corot models. 33, old bond street / corot. 33, old bond street"	£400	£400
(102) "corot models. 33, old bond street, sb. 19 / corot 33, old bond street"	£400	£400
(103) "corot models. 33, old bond street / corot (dept. s.b 20) 33, old bond street"	£400	£400

The numbers printed on the panes (i.e. on NB15(12) onwards) correspond to the edition numbers of the booklets in which they were issued. See Appendix 2.

Imprimatur from the National Postal Museum Archives
Booklet pane of four with blank advertisement label. Imperforate, watermark Type W15

Two panes as No. NB15 arranged horizontally *tête-bêche* with marginal pillars at right

Specimen and Cancelled overprints from the National Postal Museum Archives
Booklet pane of four with advertising labels. Perf. 15 × 14, watermark Type W15 (inverted)

No. NB15a (18) numbered "2" with stamps overprinted "Specimen", Type 32 and upper label with punch hole £1500

No. NB15a (88) with stamps overprinted "Cancelled", Type 33 and upper label with punch hole. £1500

Section NE

General Notes on the Photogravure Issues (1934-36)

INTRODUCTION. In 1934 Harrison & Sons regained the contract for printing the low values as well as the commemorative issues through pioneering in this country the use of the photogravure process for printing stamps. The Mackennal Head continued to be used.

The main advantages of the photogravure process were high-speed production and lower cost. As the original designs are based on photographs a new issue can reach the printing cylinder stage much more quickly than printing plates can be prepared by the letterpress process. Also double cylinders of 480 were used instead of printing plates of 240, whilst the rotary machines run very much faster. Thus it was possible to supply the greatly increased quantities of stamps required by the Post Office and at the same time effect considerable economies in production.

The following is a brief description of the terms used in connection with the photogravure process.

MULTIPOSITIVE. The prepared design is photographed in such a manner as to give a positive image on the plate. This positive is then used to make the multipositive plate. This plate contains 480 images, the equivalent of two post office sheets. The images on the plate will appear as negatives.

A photograph of the multipositive is now produced on to a carbon tissue. This has been prepared with a screen of fine lines which are insoluble, and result in the break-up of the design with numerous tiny rectangles of exactly the same area. The precise depth of these rectangles, or cells, will vary according to the amount of light which has been allowed to affect the carbon tissue.

THE CYLINDER. The carbon (with a positive impression) is now wrapped round the copper cylinder and treated with an acid resistant. The lighter portions of the design will leave shallower recesses on the cylinder. Several cylinders may be made from a single multipositive, and constant flaws existing on two or more cylinders are called multipositive flaws.

PRINTING. The cylinder is inked by means of an inking roller, and then scraped with the doctor knife. This leaves the cylinder clean but for the ink left in the recesses. The cylinder now meets the paper on the impression roller and the printing is thus accomplished.

Each revolution of the cylinder prints two panes of 240 stamps and these revolutions are continuous until the whole of the reel of paper has been printed. This is known as "web" printing.

In some cases one of the panes must have been faulty as cylinder blocks are known from only one side of the cylinder. Some cylinder numbers are unique, or perhaps only two or three examples are known. They are probably registration sheets that were put into circulation, and provide the collector of modern issues the same excitement of discovery as a Victorian "abnormal". These numbers are shown in the cylinder listings with an asterisk. Single pane cylinders have been used, however, first in the reign of King George VI and note is made of these in our listing.

DOUBLE PAPER. The high-speed printing in the roll instead of sheet-by-sheet had its down side. Occasionally the paper tore and was simply joined by overlapping and sticking together the two ends. This gave rise to the joined paper varieties, where stamps were printed on paper of double thickness.

CYLINDER MARKS. Various marginal markings were etched on the cylinders, such as perforation register squares, and small lines and crosses used as guide marks. The punched holes are to facilitate accurate perforation. They fit on to lugs at the sides of the perforating machine.

CYLINDER NUMBERS. There are records of every cylinder made, whether or not they were put to press. They were etched twice on each cylinder. The left-hand pane had the number without a full stop, and the right-hand pane had a full stop after the number. When the cylinder number was followed by the letter "R", it signified that the cylinder had to be worked in the reverse direction. This only applied in the early days, when Harrison & Sons were using German machines that only printed one sheet at a time. From these early printings came the varieties "printed on the gum" and inverted watermarks on the stamps with large format.

CONTROLS. The control was now no longer screwed into the plate, but etched on the cylinder in the margin. When it became necessary to change the control, the old control had to be filled in, and a new one etched in its place. Traces of the old control are sometimes visible.

SHEET PERFORATORS. Perforator types are described and illustrated in Appendix 1. All cylinder blocks are from the bottom left corner of the sheet. To obviate repeated reference to Appendix 1 we give the following abbreviations describing the left and bottom margins.

- (I/E) Imperf. left and one extension hole in each row, bottom margin. Perf. type 2
- (P/P) Left and bottom margins perf. through. Perf. types 2A, 4A and 6A
- (I/2E) Imperf. left and two extension holes in each row, bottom margin. Perf. type 4
- (E/I) One extension hole in left margin of each row and imperf. bottom margin. Perf. type 5
- (I/P) Imperf. left and bottom margin perf. through. Perf. type 6
- (E/P) One extension hole in left margin of each row and bottom margin perf. through. Perf. type 6B

These abbreviations appear above the cylinder block listings of the photogravure issues between 1934 and 1953.

ARRANGEMENT. The stamps are listed in order of value with the sheet stamps first followed by the sheet controls and cylinder numbers listed according to the perforators used. For booklet panes, see Section NF.

VARIETIES. To produce a perfect cylinder by the methods described was difficult, and probably many cylinders were spoiled and not used. The gaps in the numbering of the cylinders known to philatelists point to that conclusion. Even with the cylinders that were used, most show a small number of minor flaws inherent in the process. Larger and more obvious flaws are collectable items, more especially when attempts at retouching have been made after the cylinder has been put to press. Retouches can be made to the multipositive, or to the cylinder, and most of the retouches known are in the latter category. Some of these repairs are well executed, and others can be detected with the naked eye.

STAMP SIZES. After the initial printings of the 1d. and 1½d. values, the sizes of the designs were reduced slightly to allow for more accurate perforation and the ½d., 1d., 1½d. and 2d. appeared thus. Later the size was reduced again and this was adopted for all values. They are known as the Large, Intermediate and Small Format stamps respectively. Within these three groups there are further slight variations in size of the stamps from booklets and coils. In all cases the actual sizes are given. The 2½d. to 1s. were all in the small size, 17·9 × 21·7 mm.

WATERMARK AND PERFORATION. All stamps in this Section are watermarked Multiple Block Cypher, Type **W15** and perforated 15 × 14. In the listings, sideways watermarks show the top of the Crown pointing to the left when the stamp is viewed through the front or printed surface. Stamps fed into the printing press the wrong way round will show the top of the Crown pointing to the right and are described as sideways-inverted.

POSITIONS OF CONTROLS AND CYLINDER NUMBERS. For the 1½d. Large Format the controls U 34 and V 34 appeared in the bottom margin under the second stamp (as had been the practice in the letterpress stamps) and the cylinder numbers appeared in the left margin of the 20th row. (Position A.)

In later printings of the 1½d. Large Format, the 1d. Large Format and the ½d., 1d. and 1½d. Intermediate Format the control V 34 appeared as a fraction in the left margin of the 19th row, the cylinder number remaining in the 20th row. (Position B.)

A further change was made in the Intermediate Format where the ½d. and 1d. control W 35 appeared in the left margin of the 18th row, the position of the cylinder number remaining unchanged. (Position C.)

Finally the Intermediate Format 1½d. control V 34 and 2d. controls V 34 and W 35 had the control and cylinder number in the left margin of the 18th row. This became the norm and applied to all values in the Small Format. (Position D.)

On the lesser used values from 3d. upwards where new cylinders were less often needed, the practice was to add a line under the control to show a new accounting period. Subsequently another line was added at the left and so on until the whole control was "boxed in". These are listed in small type.

The control positions are illustrated below.

A

B

C

D

Boxed Control

ASTERISKS. Asterisks against cylinder numbers indicate that they are "abnormals". See under "Printing" on the first page of these notes.

Asterisks against prices for cylinder blocks indicate that they contain a listed variety.

COILS. These are listed in the same way as in the letterpress issues and the notes about coil stamps which appear under Section N also apply here. Only the 2d., 2½d. and 3d. values exist made up from sheets with coil joins.

TRIALS FOR PHOTOGRAVURE STAMPS WITH APPROVED HEAD

Trials were prepared using frames of the letterpress issues of 1912-22 in combination with the head actually used for the eventual photogravure issue but in the sizes employed in the letterpress stamps.

Trials of the 1d., 1½d. and 4d. designs were printed in various colours using a solid background to simulate the effect of photogravure.

KING GEORGE V Photogravure Issues ½d. Green, Type N11

On glazed, unwatermarked paper without gum. Imperf.
1d., 1½d. and 4d. each in red, emerald-green,
   royal blue, bright magenta and purple....... *Each from* £750
On ordinary, unwatermarked paper with gum. Imperf.
1d., 1½d. and 4d. each in red, pearl-green,
   emerald-green, royal blue, dull lilac and
   brown .... *Each from* £750
   Trial for a lighter background to the King's head. This was not approved, but the following exists on card marked "Normal" and "Suggested". The trial is affixed next to the issued stamp.
½d. green small format with lighter background,
   perforated 15 × 14 .... £3750

Die Proofs from H. A. Richardson (Royal Mint engraver) Archive
Stamp-size proofs of 1d., 1½d. and 4d. in black, optd "CANCELLED" in red (19.5×2.5 mm), all three affixed to a single piece annotated "Modifications to uniform dies" and dated "1933" £9500

1934 1½d. "Photogravure" Essays by Bradbury, Wilkinson

A
Graduated shading behind portrait from 8-12 o'clock

B
Even shading behind portrait

Perforated (15 × 14) in deep red-brown on gummed paper.
Design A £2000
Design B £2000
   Originally produced as eight blocks of six, four on unwatermarked paper supplied by De La Rue, two on unwatermarked paper supplied by Bradbury Wilkinson, and two on Block Cypher watermarked paper.
   The blocks on De La Rue supplied paper have been subsequently split.

1934 1½d. "Photogravure" Essays by Harrison & Sons

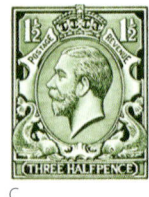

C
Profile portrait

D
"Lafayette" portrait

E
"Vandyk" portrait

F
"Downey" portrait

G
Bas-relief profile portrait

On paper watermarked with "Harrison" script. Perforated (15 × 14). With gum.
Type C In red, green or brown on ordinary paper....*Each* £2200
Type C In red or brown on coated paper....................*Each* £2200
Type C In green (imperforate) on coated paper........*Each* £2200
Type D In red, green or brown on ordinary paper....*Each* £2200
Type D In red or green on coated paper....................*Each* £2200
Type D In brown (imperforate) on coated paper......*Each* £2200
Type E In red, green or brown on ordinary paper.....*Each* £2200
Type E In red, green or brown on coated paper........*Each* £2200
Type F In red, green or brown on ordinary paper.....*Each* £2200
Type G In red, green or brown on ordinary paper....*Each* £2200
Type G In red, green or brown on coated paper.......*Each* £2200
   Originally produced as blocks of six, all of which have been subsequently split.

ESSAYS
Imperf. on paper watermarked Block Cypher. Similar to issued design, but with large head
1d. scarlet £180

Essay for the Unissued 6d. value

1935. Wmk. Block Cypher. Perf. 15 × 14
6d. purple with "Cancelled", Type 28.................................. £18000

Proof
1936 February. As illustrated but with toned background to the head. On coated paper, perforated 15 × 14.
6d. purple (doubly fugitive ink) £18000
   Production of this stamp commenced in February 1935 but Harrisons were unable to obtain satisfactory impressions from the cylinders in the doubly fugitive ink required for this denomination and no registration sheet was approved. Production was abandoned in May 1936 after 21,484 sheets of 240 had been printed and all were destroyed except for reference examples now in the Post Office. The examples with dark background in private hands have the "Cancelled" overprint.
   The 5d. value, which was issued on 17 February 1936, is also known printed in magenta. An example exists which is imperforate and overprinted "Cancelled" as Type 33 (Price £38000). In the B.P.M.A. there is an imperforate block of the 5d. which is printed from a single plate of six impressions. These stamps, which are not overprinted, are in doubly fugitive purple ink intended for the 6d. value. These were submitted to the Post Office in December 1933 by Harrison & Sons.
   Further information on the background to this value was published in *The GB Journal* for October 1979, Volume 17, no. 5 and in the Post Office *Philatelic Bulletin*, Volume 16, Nos. 7 and 8.

178

1d. Scarlet, Type N12   Photogravure Issues   **KING GEORGE V**   NE

W15    **N11**    **N12**

N13    **N14**    **N15**

½d. Green, Type N11

1934 (17 November). **Intermediate Format** (18.4×22.2 mm.)

N46

	Unmtd mint	Mtd mint	Used
(1) Green	2·00	1·00	50
(2) Bluish green	2·50	1·50	50
a. Watermark inverted	35·00	25·00	15·00
b. Imperf. three sides (single)†	£7750	£5250	
s. "Specimen", Type 32		£650	
t. "Cancelled", Type 28P		£110	
u. "Cancelled", Type 33		£135	
ua. "Cancelled", Type 33P			
v. "Specimen", Type 23		£550	
w. "Perforated double"		£175	

†This is known in a block of four in which the bottom pair is imperf. at top and sides; it came from a sheet.

Controls and Cylinder Numbers
Blocks of four (Position B)

		Perf. Type			
		2(I/E)	2A(P/P)	4(I/2E)	6(I/P)	6B(E/P)
Cyl. No.	Control	No dot	Dot	No dot	Dot
3	V 34	75·00	55·00	75·00	30·00	20·00
4	V 34	35·00	30·00	75·00	30·00	30·00

Perf. Type 2A includes Dot sheets perforated Type 4A.

Blocks of six (Position C)

		Perf. Type			
		2(I/E)	2A(P/P)	5(E/I)	5(E/I)	6(I/P)	6B(E/P)
Cyl. No.	Control	No dot	Dot	No dot	Dot	No dot	Dot
4	W 35	£175	£150	55·00	55·00	40·00	40·00

Cylinder 4 dot is known with Perforation Type 3 but with no extension hole in bottom margin. This occurs with controls V 34 (*very rare*) and W 35 (*price £500*).

Imprimatur from the National Postal Museum Archives
Imperforate, watermark Type W15. Intermediate Format
Watermark upright (pair) £8500

1935 (14 February). **Small Format** (17.9 × 21.7 mm.)

N47 (=S.G.439)

	Unmtd mint	Mtd mint	Used
(1) Green	1·00	50	50
(2) Bluish green	1·00	50	50
a. Watermark inverted	22·00	11·00	1·50
b. Watermark sideways, Crown pointing to left*	17·00	10·00	5·00
c. Watermark sideways inverted, Crown pointing to right	£600	£450	£150
d. Horn variety (Cyl. 36 No dot, R. 1/12)		£350	
s. "Cancelled", Type 28P		80·00	
t. "Cancelled", Type 33P		80·00	
u. "Cancelled", Type 33		£170	
v. "Specimen", Type 32			

*Viewed from the front of the stamp.

N47d

Controls and Cylinder Numbers
Blocks of six (Position D)

		Perf. Type			
		2(I/E)	2A(P/P)	5(E/I)	5(E/I)	6(I/P)	6B(E/P)
Cyl. No.	Control	No dot	Dot	No dot	Dot	No dot	Dot
11	W 35	85·00	85·00	20·00	30·00	25·00	25·00
12*	W 35	†	—	†	†	†	†
13	W 35	£150	£150	75·00	75·00	50·00	50·00
18	W 35	†	†	85·00	85·00	75·00	75·00
22	W 35	70·00	70·00	30·00	30·00	25·00	25·00
24*	W 35	†	£1200	†	†	†	†
25	W 35	†	£200	35·00	35·00	25·00	25·00
27	W 35	†	†	60·00	60·00	75·00	75·00
30	X 35	†	†	20·00	30·00	25·00	25·00
31	X 35	†	†	80·00	80·00	80·00	80·00
32	X 35	†	†	25·00	35·00	15·00	15·00
36	X 35	£100	85·00	15·00	15·00	25·00	25·00
39	X 35	£100	85·00	15·00	15·00	15·00	15·00
39	Y 36	†	†	15·00	15·00	20·00	20·00
40	X 35	†	†	15·00	15·00	†	†
41	X 35	£125	†	60·00	60·00	60·00	60·00
41	Y 36	†	†	75·00	75·00	†	†
42	X 35	—	†	15·00	15·00	35·00	35·00
42	Y 36	£125	£175	15·00	15·00	35·00	35·00
44	Y 36	†	†	15·00	30·00	†	†
45	Y 36	†	£200	15·00	15·00	†	†
46*	Y 36	†	†	†	—	†	†
48	Y 36	†	†	20·00	20·00	†	—
48	Z 36	†	†	20·00	20·00	†	†
49	Y 36	†	†	15·00	25·00	25·00	20·00

The only known example of cylinder 12 dot is a single specimen with attached control.
Cylinder 49 no dot has been recorded with perforator Type 2A(P/P).

*See under "Printing" in the General Notes.

179

KING GEORGE V — Photogravure Issues — 1½d. Red-brown, Type N11

Coils (Stamps 17.9 × 21.7 mm.)
Vertical delivery printed in continuous reels

Code No.	Issued	Number in roll	Face value		
D	1935	960	£2.0.0	Bottom delivery	£450
G	1935	480	£1.0.0	Bottom delivery	£450
W	1935	960	£2.0.0	Bottom delivery	£100
Y	1935	1920	£4.0.0	Bottom delivery	£125

Sideways delivery printed in continuous reels with watermark sideways (Crown to left)

P	1935	480	£1.0.0	Left side delivery	95·00

As last but watermark with Crown to right, printed on Timson Press

P	1935	480	£1.0.0	Left side delivery	£500

Imprimaturs from the National Postal Museum Archives
Imperforate, watermark Type W15. Small Format

Watermark upright (pair)	£8500
Watermark sideways (pair)	£8500

1d. Scarlet, Type N12

1934 (24 September). Large Format (18.7 × 22.5 mm.)

N48

	Unmtd mint	Mtd mint	Used
(1) Scarlet	3·00	1·60	50
(2) Bright scarlet	3·00	1·60	50
a. Watermark inverted	£175	£125	
b. Printed on the gummed side	£1000	£750	†
c. Imperf. between (pair)	£12500	£8500	

Examples of No. N48 are known used at Tamworth on 18 August at Harrow on 23 September 1934.

Controls and Cylinder Numbers
Blocks of four (Position B)

		Perf. Type			
Cyl. No.	Control	2(I/E) No dot	2A(P/P) Dot	2(I/E) Dot	4(I/2E) No dot
1	V 34	30·00	30·00	†	£100
2	V 34	40·00	40·00	£250	£100
5R	V 34	30·00	30·00	†	£100
6R	V 34	30·00	30·00	†	£100
9R*	V 34	†	†	—	†
10R	V 34	£350	£350	†	†
11R	V 34	30·00	30·00	†	60·00
14	V 34	£250	£250	†	†
15	V 34	£250	£250	†	£200

Perf. Type 2A includes Dot sheets perforated Type 4A.

Cylinder Nos. 1, 2, 5R, 11R and 15 all no dot are known with watermark inverted. These sheets with inverted watermark were not from the continuous roll, but from sheetfed German presses.

Cylinder 6R (no dot) has a small split dot which was added in error.

*See under "Printing" in the General Notes.

1934. Intermediate Format (18.4 × 22.2 mm.)

N49

	Unmtd mint	Mtd mint	Used
(1) Scarlet	8·00	5·00	1·20
(2) Bright scarlet	10·00	6·00	1·20
(3) Pale scarlet	20·00	10·00	8·00
a. Watermark inverted	35·00	25·00	15·00
s. "Specimen", Type 32		£650	
t. "Cancelled", Type 28P		£110	
u. "Cancelled", Type 33		£150	
ua. "Cancelled", Type 33P		£120	
v. "Specimen", Type 23		£650	

Controls and Cylinder Numbers
Blocks of four (Position B)

		Perf. Type				
Cyl. No.	Control	2(I/E) No dot	2A(P/P) Dot	4(I/2E) No dot	6(I/P) No Dot	6B(E/P) Dot
20	V 34	£250	£250	†	£250	—
24	V 34	£125	75·00	£100	75·00	55·00
25	V 34	75·00	50·00	75·00	55·00	55·00
28	V 34	†	£350	£350	£300	£350

Perf. Type 2A includes Dot sheets perforated Type 4A.
Variety (Reverse feed). Cylinder 25 no dot exists with Perforation Type 2A.
Cylinder 28 no dot is known with experimental use of Perforation Type 5.

Blocks of six (Position C)

		Perf. Type			
Cyl. No.	Control	5(E/I) No dot	5(E/I) Dot	6(I/P) No dot	6B(E/P) Dot
24	W 35	£200	£200	£200	£200

Coils (Stamps 18.75 × 22.25 mm.)
Vertical delivery printed in continuous reels

Code No.	Issued	Number in roll	Face value		
E	1934	480	£2.0.0	Bottom delivery	£350

Imprimatur from the National Postal Museum Archives
Imperforate, watermark Type W15. Intermediate Format

Watermark upright (pair)	£8500

1935 (8 February). Small Format (17.9 × 21.7 mm.)

N50 (=S.G.440)

	Unmtd mint	Mtd mint	Used
(1) Scarlet	1·00	50	50
(2) Bright scarlet	1·00	50	50
a. Watermark inverted	20·00	9·00	3·00
b. Watermark sideways, Crown pointing to left* (30.4.35)	40·00	20·00	12·00
c. Watermark sideways inverted, Crown pointing to right	£195	£125	
d. Imperf. (pair)	£7000	£5000	
e. Imperf. three sides (pair)	£9500	£7000	
f. Double impression	†	†	£24000
g. Printed on double paper			
s. "Cancelled", Type 28P		85·00	
t. "Cancelled", Type 33P		75·00	
u. "Cancelled", Type 33		£200	

*Viewed from the front of the stamp.

N50f

180

1½d. Red-brown, Type N11   Photogravure Issues   **KING GEORGE V**   **NE**

The stamp shown above has a light wavy line postmark and it is believed to be unique.

Controls and Cylinder Numbers
Blocks of six (Position D)

Cyl. No.	Control	Perf. Type 2(I/E) No dot	2A(P/P) Dot	5(E/I) No dot	5(E/I) Dot	6(I/P) No dot	6B(E/P) Dot
32	W 35	£250	†	—	£250	£250	£250
34	X 35	†	†	15·00	15·00	15·00	15·00
35	X 35	†	†	40·00	40·00	†	†
39	X 35	†	†	15·00	15·00	15·00	15·00
40*	X 35	†	†	—	—	†	†
41	X 35	†	†	†	†	£100	£150
42	X 35	—	†	15·00	15·00	30·00	30·00
44	X 35	†	†	£150	£150	£150	£150
45	X 35	†	†	£200	£200	†	†
46	X 35	75·00	75·00	15·00	15·00	15·00	15·00
50	X 35	60·00	50·00	15·00	15·00	25·00	25·00
50	Y 36	60·00	60·00	15·00	15·00	†	—
53	Y 36	60·00	60·00	15·00	15·00	25·00	25·00
54	Y 36	75·00	75·00	15·00	15·00	†	£750

Cylinder 53 no dot has been recorded with perforator Type 2A(P/P).

*See under "Printing" in the General Notes.

Coils
Vertical delivery printed in continuous reels (Stamps 18·15 × 21·7 mm.)

Code No.	Issued	Number in roll	Face value		
B	1935	960	£4.0.0	Bottom delivery	£300
E	1935	480	£2.0.0	Bottom delivery	£175
X	1935	960	£4.0.0	Bottom delivery	£100
Z	1935	1920	£8.0.0	Bottom delivery	£100

Sideways delivery printed in continuous reels with watermark sideways (Crown to left) (Stamps 17·9 × 21·7 mm)

| O | 1935 | 480 | £2.0.0 | Left side delivery | £125 |

As last but watermark with Crown to right, printed on Timson Press

| O | 1935 | 480 | £2.0.0 | Left side delivery | £650 |

Imprimaturs from the National Postal Museum Archives
Imperforate, watermark Type W15. Small Format
Watermark upright (pair) £8500
Watermark sideways (pair) £8500

1½d. Red-brown, Type N11

1934 (20 August). **Large Format (18.7 × 22.5 mm.)**

N51

		Unmtd mint	Mtd mint	Used
(1)	Red-brown	2·00	1·00	60
(2)	Bright red-brown	2·00	1·00	60
a.	Watermark inverted	£300	£200	
b.	Imperf. (pair)			
c.	Imperf. between stamp and bottom margin		£2500	
d.	Frame break under second E of PENCE (Cyls. 38, 42, 43, 45, 54, 55, all Dot (R. 20/3)		75·00	

No. N51b came from the bottom row of a sheet (Cyl. 97 no dot).

N51d

During the printing of cyl. 55 the line was retouched

Controls and Cylinder Numbers
Pairs (Position A)

Cyl. No.	Control	Perf. Type 2(I/E) No dot	2A(P/P) Dot
8	U 34	50·00	50·00
13	V 34	40·00	40·00
34	U 34	60·00	60·00
34	V 34	50·00	50·00
38	V 34	60·00	50·00
42	V 34	35·00	45·00
43	V 34	65·00	65·00
45	V 34	55·00	55·00

Cylinder 13 is etched over 13 inverted on no dot cylinders and cylinder numbers 69 and 94 are found printed over indecipherable figures.

Cylinder 34 no dot is known with "3" omitted in later printings with control U 34. Cylinder 34 no dot with control V34 is known with watermark inverted.

Cylinder 45 no dot is also known with Perforation Type 2A (P/P).

Blocks of four (Position B)

Cyl. No.	Control	Perf. Type 2(I)(E) No dot	2A(P/P) Dot	4(I/2E) No dot	6(I/P) No dot	6B(E/P) Dot
17	V 34	£250	£250	†	†	†
46	V 34	35·00	35·00	£250	60·00	†
47	V 34	75·00	50·00	£200	35·00	†
49*	V 34	£650	£650	†	—	†
54	V 34	30·00	75·00	†	†	†
55	V 34	55·00	65·00	†	†	†
63*	V 34	£800	†	†	†	†
68R	V 34	40·00	80·00	£100	†	†
69	V 34	30·00	45·00	£100	†	†
70*	V 34	†	£550	£550	†	†
94	V 34	75·00	40·00	£100	50·00	†
97	V 34	75·00	30·00	70·00	30·00	†
98	V 34	60·00	30·00	70·00	30·00	30·00
100	V 34	30·00	30·00	50·00	30·00	30·00
101	V 34	40·00	30·00	50·00	30·00	30·00
102	V 34	75·00	85·00	75·00	£175	£125

Perf. Type 2A includes Dot sheets perforated Type 4A or Type 6A.

Variety (Reverse feed). Cylinder 68R and cylinder 101 from the no dot panes are known with Perforation Type 2A(P/P).

Cylinder 68R dot is known with watermark inverted.

Cylinder 98 no dot is known with experimental use of Perforation Type 5(E/I).

*See under "Printing" in the General Notes.

Colour Trials
Imperf. on paper watermarked Block Cypher 1½d. in the large format
Ultramarine, deep grey-green or scarlet .... From £160
Red-brown £200
Red-brown with "Cancelled", Type 33* £800

Care should be taken not to confuse the red-brown colour trial with the issued Imperf. The colour trial exhibits all the traits of a finished proof. The highlights are noticeable when compared with the rather flat impression of the issued stamps and the paper is of better quality.

All four trials including red-brown, overprinted "Cancelled", are known with Cyl. No. 16 below R. 20/1 but no issued stamps were printed from this cylinder.
Perforated (15 ×14) on gummed paper
  watermarked Block Cypher 1½d. large format
  in ultramarine or deep grey-green .... Each £1500
  1½d. intermediate format affixed to brown parcel
  paper cancelled by an experimental red
  "London/Parcel section" handstamp dated
  "19. DEC" in grey-brown, dark brown or light
  red-brown .... Each £2250

Imprimatur from the National Postal Museum Archives
Imperforate, watermark Type W15. Large Format
Watermark upright (pair) £8500

181

KING GEORGE V
Photogravure Issues **2d. Orange, Type N13**

1934. Intermediate Format (18.4 × 22.2 mm.)

N52

	Unmtd mint	Mtd mint	Used
Red-brown	9·00	5·00	2·00
a. Watermark inverted	20·00	12·00	8·00
b. Imperf. (pair)	£1700	£1250†	
c. Imperf. three sides (lower stamp in vert. pair)	£6750	£4750	
d. Imperf. between (horiz. pair)			
t. "Cancelled", Type 28P		£110	
u. "Cancelled", Type 33			
v. "Cancelled", Type 33P			
w. "Specimen", Type 23		£700	

†No. N52b exists from NPM archive sales.

Controls and Cylinder Numbers
Blocks of four (Position B)

		Perf. Type			
		2(I/E)	2A(P/P)	4(I/E2)	6(I/P)	6B(E/P)
Cyl. No.	Control	No dot	Dot	No dot	No dot	Dot
104	V 34	80·00	60·00	£100	60·00	50·00
105	V 34	80·00	80·00	£200	80·00	80·00
106	V 34	£100	£100	80·00	60·00	60·00
107	V 34	†	£800	£700	£200	£200

Perf. Type 2A includes Dot sheets perforated Type 4A.
Cylinder 104 no dot is known with experimental use of Perforation Type 5(E/I).

Blocks of six (Position D)

		Perf. Type		
		6A(P/P)	6(I/P)	6B(E/P)
Cyl. No.	Control	Dot	No dot	Dot
113	V 34	—	£200	£200

Coils (Stamps 18.50 × 22.5 mm.)
Vertical delivery printed in continuous reels

Code No.	Issued	Number in roll	Face value	
L	1934	480	£3.0.0 Top delivery	£400

Imprimatur from the National Postal Museum Archives
Imperforate, watermark Type W15. Intermediate Format
Watermark upright (pair) £8500

1935 (7 February). Small Format (17.9 × 21.7 mm.)

N53 (=S.G.441)

	Unmtd mint	Mtd mint	Used
(1) Red-brown	1·00	50	50
(2) Bright red-brown	1·00	50	50
a. Watermark inverted	8·00	4·00	1·00
b. Watermark sideways	15·00	10·00	5·00
ba. Wmk. sideways-inverted			
c. Flaw in N.E. corner (Cyls. 116, 119 No dot, R. 19/1)		60·00	
d. Ditto retouched (Cyl. 116, No dot, R. 19/1)		60·00	
e. Printed on double paper			
s. "Cancelled", Type 28P		80·00	
t. "Cancelled", Type 33P		80·00	
u. "Cancelled", Type 33		£175	
v. "Specimen", Type 32		£650	

N53c   N53d

Controls and Cylinder Numbers
Blocks of six (Position D)

		Perf. Type				
		2(I/E)	2A(P/P)	5(E/I)	5(E/I)	6(I/P)	6B(E/P)
Cyl. No.	Control	No dot	Dot	No dot	Dot	No dot	Dot
116	W 35	£100*	40·00	60·00*		35·00	60·00*	25·00
119	W 35	80·00*	25·00	†	£850	75·00*	25·00
124	W 35	†	†	25·00	25·00	20·00	20·00
127	X 35	†	†	50·00	50·00	20·00	20·00
128	X 35	†	†	†	†	35·00	35·00
130	X 35	†	†	15·00	25·00	25·00	25·00
132	X 35	80·00	£100	15·00	15·00	15·00	15·00
133	X 35	†	†	25·00	25·00	†	†
135	X 35	£100	£100	15·00	15·00	†	†
135	Y 36	†	†	15·00	15·00	†	†
137	X 35	†	£100	15·00	20·00	†	†
137	Y 36	†	£100	15·00	15·00	†	†
139	Y 36	†	†	85·00	85·00	†	†
140	Y 36	†	†	20·00	15·00	†	†
141	X 35	†	†	15·00	15·00	†	†
141	Y 36	†	†	25·00	25·00	†	†
143 (i)	Y 36	†	£175	60·00	60·00	†	†
143 (ii)	Y 36	†	†	75·00	†	†	†
144	Y 36	75·00	75·00	15·00	15·00	80·00	80·00
144	Z 36	£100	75·00	15·00	15·00	†	†
146	Y 36	80·00	80·00	15·00	15·00	†	†
148	Y 36	£125	75·00	15·00	15·00	†	†
149	Y 36	90·00	90·00	15·00	15·00	†	†
149	Z 36	80·00	80·00	15·00	15·00	†	†
153	Y 36	†	†	†	—	†	†
153	Z 36	80·00	£100	25·00	25·00	†	†

Varieties:
Cylinder 116 known Perforation Type 5(E/I) with extension hole missing (£500).
Cylinder 139 dot (Reverse feed) Perforation Type 2(I/E) (£650).
Cylinder 149 dot (Reverse feed) Perforation Type 2(I/E) (£500).
Cylinder 143 no dot exists in two states. The second state (ii) shows a large flaw in the margin opposite the 19th row and retouching to the base of figures 36 of the control.
*These cylinder blocks include a listed variety.

Coils (Stamps 17.9 3 21.7 mm.)
Vertical delivery printed in continuous reels

Code No.	Issued	Number in roll	Face value	
K	1935	960	£6.0.0 Bottom delivery	£250
L	1935	480	£3.0.0 Top delivery	£250
L	1935	480	£3.0.0 Bottom delivery	—

Sideways delivery printed in continuous reels with watermark sideways

| N | 1935 | 480 | £3.0.0 Left side delivery | £250 |

Imprimaturs from the National Postal Museum Archives
Imperforate, watermark Type W15. Small Format
Watermark upright (pair) £8500
Watermark sideways (pair) £8500

2d. Orange, Type N13

1935. *(19 January).* **Intermediate Format (18.4 × 22.2 mm.)**

N54

	Unmtd mint	Mtd mint	Used
(1) Orange	5·00	2·50	1·50
(2) Bright orange	5·00	2·50	1·50
a. Imperf. (pair)	£7250	£5750	
b. Broken tablet (Cyl. 5 No dot, R. 20/9)		£150	
c. Ditto retouched		£125	

No. N54 is known postmarked on 19 January, two days prior to the official first day of issue.

N54b   N54c

Controls and Cylinder Numbers
Blocks of six (Position D)

		Perf. Type				
		2(I/E)	2A (P/P)	5(E/I)	5(E/I)	6(I/P) 6B(E/P)
Cyl. No.	Control	No dot	Dot	No dot	Dot	No dot Dot
5 (i)	V 34	£1000	£100	†	†	40·00 40·00
5 (i)	W 35	†	†	60·00	60·00	40·00 40·00
5 (ii)	W 35	£140	£140	†	†	35·00 35·00

Cylinder 5 exists in two states: (i) 5 very faint; (ii) the 5 has been re-etched to appear bolder and larger. Control V34 Dot was perf. 6A (P/P).

Imprimatur from the National Postal Museum Archives
Imperforate, watermark Type W15. Intermediate Format
Watermark upright (pair) £8500

1935. Small Format (18.15 × 21.7 mm.)

N55 (=S.G.442)

	Unmtd mint	Mtd mint	Used
(1) Orange	1·50	75	75
(2) Bright orange	1·50	75	75
a. Watermark sideways (17·9 3 21·7 mm.) (30.4.35)	£225	£125	90·00
c. Retouched leaves (Cyl. 13 Dot, Control A37, R. 18/1)		50·00	
d. Broken value tablet (Cyl. 8 No dot, R. 20/1)		£125	
e. Coil join (vert. pair)			
s. "Specimen", Type 30			
t. "Specimen", Type 32			
u. Wmk. sideways, "Cancelled", Type 28			

For No. N55 bisected and used on cover, see Appendix 7.

N55c   N55d

3d. Violet, Type N13

No. N55c only exists from late coil and sheet printings so not all positional examples show the retouches.

Controls and Cylinder Numbers
Blocks of six (Position D)

		Perf. Type					
		2(I/E)	2A(P/P)	5(E/I)	5(E/I)	6(I/P)	6B(E/P)
Cyl. No.	Control	No dot	Dot	No dot	Dot	No dot	Dot
8	X 35	†	†	£125*	70·00	£125*	70·00
10	X 35	†	†	12·00	20·00	12·00	20·00
10	Y 36	£1000	†	12·00	12·00	†	†
10	Z 36	£175	†	50·00	50·00	12·00	12·00
12	X 35	†	†	12·00	12·00	25·00	20·00
12	Y 36	†	†	20·00	25·00	†	—
12	Z 36	£150	†	20·00	20·00	†	†
12	A 37	†	†	20·00	12·00	†	†
13	Z 36	65·00	65·00	25·00	12·00	20·00	20·00
13	A 37	†	†	20·00	50·00*	†	†

Cylinder 10 dot perf. Type 3(P/E) has been reported with control Y 36.

*These cylinder blocks include a listed variety.

Coils
Vertical delivery made up from sheets with coil joins every 20th stamp (Stamps 18·15 × 21·7 mm.)

Code No.	Issued	Number in roll	Face value		
Q	1935	960	£8.0.0	Bottom delivery	£575
R	1935	480	£4.0.0	Top delivery	£650

Sideways delivery printed in continuous reels with watermark sideways (Stamps 17·9 × 21·7 mm.)

| T | 1935 | 480 | £4.0.0 | Left side delivery | £275 |

Imprimaturs from the National Postal Museum Archives
Imperforate, watermark Type W15. Small Format
Watermark upright (pair) £8500
Watermark sideways (pair) £8500

2½d. Blue, Type N12

1935 *(18 March)*

N56 (=S.G.443)

	Unmtd mint	Mtd mint	Used
(1) Bright blue	2·50	1·50	1·25
(2) Ultramarine	5·00	3·00	1·50
a. Retouched panel (Cyl. 8 Dot, R. 18/1)	40·00	25·00	
b. Retouched panel (Cyl. 8 No dot, R. 18/1)	40·00	25·00	
c. Coil join (vert. pair)			
d. Printed on double paper			
s. "Specimen", Type 23		£700	

No N56d came from a paper join—see Printing.

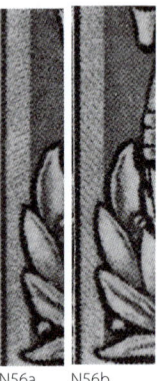

NE KING GEORGE V   Booklet Panes in Photogravure   5d. Yellow-brown, Type N14

N56a   N56b

Controls and Cylinder Numbers
Blocks of six (Position D)

Cyl. No.	Control	2(I/E) No dot	2A(P/P) Dot	5(E/I) No dot	5(E/I) Dot
6	W 35	£200	£200	35·00	35·00
7	W 35	£450	£350	35·00	35·00
8	Y 36	£250*	£250*	40·00*	40·00*
9	Y 36	£1400	†	£1400	£1400

*These cylinder blocks include a listed variety.

Coils
Vertical delivery made up from sheets with joins every 20th stamp

Code No	Issued	Number in roll	Face value		
F	1935	960	£10.0.0	Bottom delivery	£1250

Imprimatur from the National Postal Museum Archives
Imperforate, watermark Type W15
Watermark upright (pair) £8500

3d. Violet, Type N13

1935 (18 March)

N57 (=S.G.444)

	Unmtd mint	Mtd mint	Used
(1) Reddish violet	3·00	1·50	1·25
(2) Violet	3·25	1·75	1·50
a. Coil join (vert. pair)			
b. Coil join (horiz. pair)			
c. Watermark inverted	—	—	£9000
s. "Specimen", Type 30			
t. "Specimen", Type 23		£650	
u. "Cancelled", Type 33			
v. "Cancelled", Type 28		£800	

Controls and Cylinder Numbers
Blocks of six (Position D)

Cyl. No.	Control	2(I/E) No dot	2A (P/P) Dot	5(E/I) No dot	5(E/I) Dot	6(I/P) No dot	6B (E/P) Dot
1	W 35	40·00	40·00	†	†	†	†
2	W 35	75·00	£125	†	†	†	†
3*	W 35	†	£1250	†	†	†	†
6	X 35	†	†	40·00	40·00	30·00	30·00
12	Y 36	†	†	50·00	50·00	†	†
13	Y 36	†	†	30·00	30·00	†	†
14	Y 36	85·00	85·00	30·00	35·00	†	†
14	Z 36	£750	£350	25·00	25·00	†	†

Cyl. No.	Control	2(I/E) No dot	2A (P/P) Dot	5(E/I) No dot	5(E/I) Dot	6(I/P) No dot	6B (E/P) Dot
14	Z 36 bar —	†	†	40·00	25·00	£125	£125
14	Z 36 bars ⌊	†	†	25·00	25·00	†	†

Variety: Cylinder 1 dot known Perforation Type 3(P/E).
*See under "Printing" in the General Notes.

Coils
Vertical delivery made up from sheets with joins every 20th stamp

Code No	Issued	Number in roll	Face value		
C	1935	960	£12.0.0	Bottom delivery	£900

Sideways delivery made up from sheets with joins every 12th stamp

| S | 1935 | 480 | £6.0.0 | Left side delivery | — |

Imprimatur from the National Postal Museum Archives
Imperforate, watermark Type W15
Watermark upright (pair) £9000

4d. Grey-green, Type N13

1935 (2 December)

N58 (=S.G.445)

	Unmtd mint	Mtd mint	Used
(1) Deep grey-green	4·00	2·00	1·25
(2) Blackish green	18·00	10·00	4·00
a. Watermark inverted	†	†	£9000
s. "Specimen", Type 23		£700	
t. "Cancelled", Type 28		£850	
u. "Specimen", Type 30			

No. N58 is known postmarked at Portsmouth and Southsea on 30 November 1935.

Controls and Cylinder Numbers
Blocks of six (Position D)

Cyl. No.	Control	2 (I/E) No dot	2A (P/P) Dot	5 (E/I) No dot	5 (E/I) Dot	6 (I/P) No dot	6B (E/P) Dot
3	W 35	£950	40·00*	†	†	†	†
8	X 35	†	†	85·00	85·00	—	—
9	X 35	†	†	£200	£200	†	†
11	X 35	£100	£100	30·00	30·00	£100	£100
11	Y 36	†	†	30·00	30·00	†	†
11	Y 36 bar —	†	†	50·00	40·00	30·00	30·00
11	Y 36 bars ⌊	†	†	40·00	40·00	£150	£150
11	Y 36 bars ⌋	†	†	50·00	50·00	†	†
11	Y 36 bars ☐	†	†	40·00	40·00	†	†

*Cylinder 3 in Perforation Type 2A(P/P) has no dot, presumably omitted in error.

Imprimatur from the National Postal Museum Archives
Imperforate, watermark Type W15
Watermark upright (pair) £9000

5d. Yellow-brown, Type N14

1936 *(17 February)*
N59 (=S.G.446)

	Unmtd mint	Mtd mint	Used
(1) Yellow-brown	13·00	6·50	2·75
(2) Deep yellow-brown	13·00	6·50	2·75
s. "Specimen", Type 23		£650	
t. "Cancelled", Type 33			
u. Imperf "Specimen", Type 26		£5500	

For this value printed in magenta, see the note describing the unissued 6d. under Photogravure, Trials and Essays at the front of this Section.

Controls and Cylinder Numbers
Blocks of six (Position D)

		Perf. Type				
		2 (I/E)	2A (P/P)	5 (E/I)	5 (E/I)	6 (I/P)	6B (E/P)
Cyl. No.	Control	No dot		Dot	No dot	Dot	No dot	Dot
5	X 35	†		†	£300	£300	†	†
5	Y 36	£150		£150	60·00	60·00	†	†
5	Z 36	†		†	†	†	60·00	60·00
5	Z 36 bar —	†		£250	75·00	75·00	75·00	75·00
5	Z 36 bars └	†		†	†	†	75·00	75·00
5	Z 36 bars ⌴	†		†	70·00	70·00	†	†
5	Z 36 bars ☐	†		†	£125	80·00	†	†

Imprimatur from the National Postal Museum Archives
Imperforate, watermark Type W15
Watermark upright (pair) £9000

9d. Olive-green, Type N15

1935 *(2 December)*
N60 (=S.G.447)

	Unmtd mint	Mtd mint	Used
Deep olive-green	20·00	12·00	2·25
s. "Specimen", Type 23		£650	
t. "Cancelled", Type 28			
u. "Cancelled", Type 33			
v. Imperf "Specimen", Type 26		£6000	

Controls and Cylinder Numbers
Blocks of six (Position D)

		Perf. Type			
		5 (E/I)	5 (E/I)	6 (I/P)	6B (E/P)
Cyl. No.	Control	No dot	Dot	No dot	Dot
15	X 35	£140	£140	£160	£160
15	X 35 bar —	†	†	£150	£150
15	X 35 bars └	£175	£175	†	†
15	X 35 bars ⌴	£175	£175	†	†
15	X 35 bars ☐	†	†	£250	£250

Imprimatur from the National Postal Museum Archives
Imperforate, watermark Type W15
Watermark upright (pair) £9500

10d. Turquoise-blue, Type N15

1936 *(24 February)*
N61 (=S.G.448)

	Unmtd mint	Mtd mint	Used
Turquoise-blue	30·00	15·00	10·00
s. "Specimen", Type 32		£700	
t. "Cancelled", Type 33			
u. "Specimen", Type 23		£700	

Controls and Cylinder Numbers
Blocks of six (Position D)

		Perf. Type				
		2 (I/E)	2 (I/E)	5 (E/I)	5 (E/I)	6 (I/P)	6B (E/P)
Cyl. No.	Control	No dot	Dot	No dot	Dot	No dot	Dot
3	Y 36	†	—	£150	£150	†	†
3	Y 36 bar —	£600	£600	£150	£150	†	†
3	Y 36 bars └	†	†	£200	£200	†	†
3	Y 36 bars ⌴	†	†	£250	£250	†	†
3	Y 36 bars ☐	†	†	†	†	£350	£350

Imprimatur from the National Postal Museum Archives
Imperforate, watermark Type W15
Watermark upright (pair) £9500

1s. Bistre-brown, Type N15

1936 *(24 February)*
N62 (=S.G.449)

	Unmtd mint	Mtd mint	Used
Bistre-brown	40·00	15·00	1·25
a. Double impression	—	—	†
s. "Specimen", Type 32		£125	
t. "Specimen", Type 23		£700	
u. "Cancelled", Type 33		£850	

N62a

KING GEORGE V — Booklet Panes in Photogravure 1935

Controls and Cylinder Numbers
Blocks of six (Position D)

		Perf. Type			
		5(E/I)	5(E/I)	6(I/P)	6B(E/P)
Cyl. No.	Control	No dot	Dot	No dot	Dot
3	Y 36	£160	£160	†	†
4	Y 36	£160	£160	†	†
5	Z 36	£200	£200	£850	£850
5	Z 36 bar —	£160	£160	†	†
5	Z 36 bars ⌐	£300	£300	†	†
5	Z 36 bars ⊔	£300	£300	†	†
5	Z 36 bars □	†	†	£325	£325

On cylinder 5 both panes show a partially erased "1" before the "5".

Imprimatur from the National Postal Museum Archives
Imperforate, watermark Type W15
Watermark upright (pair) £9500

Section NF

1935 Booklet Panes in Photogravure

CHECKLIST OF KING GEORGE V PANES IN PHOTOGRAVURE

Spec. Cat. Nos.	Description	From Booklets Nos.	Page
Photogravure Issue			
NB20, NB20a	6 × ½d. intermediate format	BB15, BB27, BB36	188
NB21, NB21a	6 × ½d. small format	BB17, BB29, BB37	188
NB22, NB22a	6 × 1d. intermediate format	BB15, BB27, BB36	188
NB23, NB23a	6 × 1d. small format	BB17, BB29, BB37	189
NB24, NB24a	6 × 1½d. intermediate format	BB15, BB27, BB36	189
NB25, NB25a	4 × 1½d. intermediate format and two printed labels	BB15, BB36	189
NB26, NB26a	6 × 1½d. small format	BB17, BB29, BB37	190
NB27, NB27a	4 × 1½d. small format and two printed labels	BB17, BB37	190

BOOKLET PANES WITH CYLINDER NUMBERS. Booklet panes are printed from specially made double–pane cylinders (no dot and dot) and the sheet layout corresponds to that used for the typographed panes, with half the stamps having the watermark inverted.

They are in panes of six (the 1½d. values also existing incorporating two advertising labels). The cylinder number in row 18 of the cylinder appears in the binding margin on the left side of the sheet. It comprises a letter and number. E was used for the ½d., F for the 1d. and G for the 1½d. Sometimes the letter is partly trimmed off.

The prices for booklet cylinder panes are for stamps with the watermark upright, from normal printing. Rarely, sheets were printed with the watermark inverted to the direction of print, resulting in booklet cylinder panes with inverted watermarks. These are listed separately.

BOOKLET PERFORATORS. Booklet cylinder panes are listed according to the perforator type. Further information on these is given in Appendix 1. The letters in brackets above the price columns indicate the appearance of the binding margin of the cylinder pane as follows:
- (E) Extension hole in the margin in each row
- (I) Imperf. margin
- (P) Perf. margin

Booklet panes without cylinder numbers are priced according to whether the watermark is seen to be upright or inverted and by reference to the binding margin. As specimen and cancelled panes are much scarcer, no binding margin perforation distinction is made in the listing.

BOOKLET PANE PRICES. Prices quoted are for lightly mounted examples with good perforations all round and with binding margin attached. Panes showing some degree of trimming are worth less than the published prices in this Catalogue. Unmounted mint panes are worth more and the following percentage may be added to the basic panes. Nos. NB20/27a (ex NB27), + 30%. NB27, + 50%.

Booklet Pane Cylinder Number

NF KING GEORGE V Booklet Panes in Photogravure 6 × ½d. Green.

½d. Booklet Panes of Six. Harrison

NB20/a, NB21/a

6 × ½d. Green. INTERMEDIATE FORMAT
(Stamps 18.4 × 21.9 mm.)
From Booklets BB15, BB27 and BB36

	Perf Type		
	E	P	I
A. Watermark upright			
NB20 (containing No. N46 × 6) (1.35)	£300	£250	£300
t. "Cancelled", Type 28P	£750		
u. "Cancelled", Type 33	£1200		
v. "Cancelled", Type 33P	£650		
B. Watermark inverted			
NB20a (containing No. N46a × 6) (1.35)	£325	£275	£325
at. "Cancelled", Type 28P	£750		
au. "Cancelled", Type 33	£1200		
av. "Cancelled", Type 33P	£650		

Booklet Cylinder Numbers
Panes of six

	Perf. Type			
	B3(I)	B3A(P)	B4(E)	B4A(I)
Cyl. No.	No dot	Dot	No dot	Dot
E 1	£1500	£1500	£350	£350

Imprimatur from the National Postal Museum Archives
Booklet pane of six. Imperforate, watermark Type W15
Two panes as No. NB20 arranged horizontally *tête-bêche*

6 × ½d. Green. SMALL FORMAT (17.8 × 21.65 mm.)
From Booklets BB17, BB29 and BB37

	Perf Type		
	E	P	I
A. Watermark upright			
NB21 (containing No. N47 3 6) (7.35)	£125	85·00	£125
t. "Cancelled", Type 33P	£450		
u. "Cancelled", Type 33	£1100		
v. "Cancelled", Type 28P	£600		
w. "Specimen", Type 32 with punch hole on R. 1/1	£3000		
B. Watermark inverted			
NB21a (containing No. N47a 3 6) (7.35)	£140	95·00	£140
at. "Cancelled", Type 33P	£450		
au. "Cancelled", Type 33	£1100		
av. "Cancelled", Type 28P	£600		

Booklet Cylinder Numbers
Panes of six

	Perf Type				
	B3(I)	B3A(P)	B4(E)	B4A(I)	B4B(E)
Cyl. No.	No dot	Dot	No dot	Dot	Dot
E 4	£300	£300	£125	£125	†
Wmk. inverted	£1500	†	£1500	£1500	†
E 5	†	†	£150	£125	£1500
E 6	†	†	£125	£150	£150

Imprimatur from the National Postal Museum Archives
Booklet pane of six. Imperforate, watermark Type W15
Two panes as No. NB21 arranged horizontally *tête-bêche* (£48000)

1d. Booklet Panes of Six. Harrison

NB22/a, NB23/a

6 × 1d. Scarlet INTERMEDIATE FORMAT
(Stamps 18.4 × 21.9 mm.)
From Booklets BB15, BB27 and BB36

	Perf Type		
	E	P	I
A. Watermark upright			
NB22 (containing No. N49 × 6) (1.35)	£300	£250	£300
t. "Cancelled", Type 28P	£750		
v. "Cancelled", Type 33P	£650		
B. Watermark inverted			
NB22a (containing No. N49a × 6) (1.35)	£325	£275	£325
at. "Cancelled", Type 28P	£750		
au. "Cancelled", Type 33	£1200		
av. "Cancelled", Type 33P	£650		

Booklet Cylinder Numbers
Panes of six

	Perf Type		
	B4(E)	B4A(I)	B4B (E)
Cyl. No.	No dot	Dot	Dot
F 1	£350	£350	£1500

Imprimatur from the National Postal Museum Archive
Booklet pane of six. Imperforate, watermark Type W15
Two panes as No. NB22 arranged horizontally *tête-bêche* (£48000)

188

6 × 1d. Scarlet   Booklet Panes in Photogravure   **KING GEORGE V**   **NF**

6 × 1d. Scarlet SMALL FORMAT
(Stamps 17.9 × 21.65 mm.)
From Booklets BB17, BB29 and BB37

	Perf Type		
	E	P	I
A. Watermark upright			
NB23 (containing No. N50 3 6) (7.35)	£125	85·00	£125
t. "Cancelled", Type 33P	£450		
u. "Cancelled", Type 33	£1000		
v. "Cancelled", Type 28P	£600		
B. Watermark inverted			
NB23a (containing No. N50a 3 6) (7.35)	£140	95·00	£140
at. "Cancelled", Type 33P	£450		
au. "Cancelled", Type 33	£600		
av. "Cancelled", Type 28P	£500		
aw. "Specimen", Type 32 with punch hole on R. 1/1	£3250		

Booklet Cylinder Numbers
Panes of six

	Perf. Type				
Cyl. No.	B3(I) No dot	B3A(P) Dot	B4(E) No dot	B4A(I) Dot	B4B(E) Dot
F 6	£175	£175	£150	£150	†
F 7	£1200	£1200	£125	£125	£125

Imprimatur from the National Postal Museum Archives
Booklet pane of six. Imperforate, watermark Type 15
  Two panes as No. NB23 arranged horizontally *tête-bêche* (£48000)

1½d. Booklet Panes of Six. Harrison.

NB24/a, NB26/a

6 × 1½d. Red-brown. INTERMEDIATE FORMAT
(Stamps 18.4 × 21.9 mm.)
From Booklets BB15, BB27 and BB36

	Perf Type		
	E	P	I
A. Watermark upright			
NB24 (containing No. N52 × 6) (1.35)	£225	£175	£225
t. "Cancelled", Type 28P	£800		
u. "Cancelled", Type 33	£1300		
v. "Cancelled", Type 33P	£650		
B. Watermark inverted			
NB24a (containing No. N52a × 6) (1.35)	£240	£190	£240
at. "Cancelled", Type 28P	£800		
av. "Cancelled", Type 33P	£650		

1½d. Booklet Panes with Advertising Labels

NB25/a, NB27/a (various advertisements) (Cyl. G15.))

4 × 1½d. Red-brown with Advertising Labels
(Stamps 18.0 × 21.9 mm.)
Panes of six, comprising two printed labels and four stamps. The advertisements were etched on the printing cylinders, and therefore appear in the colour of the stamps
From Booklets BB15 and BB36

	Perf Type		
	E	P	I
A. Watermark upright			
NB25 (containing No. N52 × 4) (1.35)	£800	£700	£800
c. White scratch from frame through "TH" (R.1/1) advert (5)	£950		
t. "Cancelled", Type 28P	£1400		
u. "Cancelled", Type 33P	£1000		
B. Watermark inverted			
NB25a (containing No. N52a × 4)	£800	£700	£800
ab. White scratch from frame through "TH" (R. 1/1) advert (5)	£950		
at. "Cancelled", Type 28P	£1400		
au. "Specimen", Type 23	£1500		
av. "Cancelled", Type 33P	£1000		

NB25c, NB25ab

Pane Nos. NB25 or NB25a

	Wmk Upright	Wmk Inverted
(1) "Cash's satin lingerie ribbons / Samples of Cash's ribbons. J. & J. Cash Ltd." (Numbered 9)	£850	£850
(2) "For Safety of Capital / Amalgamated Fixed Trust"	£725	£725
(3) "For Safety of Capital / Commercial Fixed Trust"	£700	£700
(4) "For Safety of Capital / National Fixed Trust"	£700	£700
(5) "Saving is Simple / Home Safe"	£800	£800
(6) "Telephone Service / Air Mails, Letters & Parcels"	£800	£800

Booklet Cylinder Numbers
Panes of six

	Perf Type			
Cyl. No.	B3(I) No dot	B3A(P) Dot	B4(E) No dot	B4A(I) Dot
G4	£1500	£1500	£250	£250

NF KING GEORGE V Booklet Panes in Photogravure 6 × 1½d. Red-brown.

Panes of six including two labels

No dot cylinders

Cyl. No.	Advert.	Perf Type B3(l)	Perf Type B4(E)
G 7	NB25(5)	—	£1000
G 9	NB25(4)	†	£1000
G 10	NB25(2)	†	£1000
G 15	NB25(4)	†	£1000
G 16	NB25(4)	£1000	£1000
G 17	NB25(3)	£1000	†

Dot cylinders

Cyl. No.	Advert.	Perf Type B3A(P)	Perf Type B4A(I)
G 7.	NB25(6)	£1000	£1000
G 9.	NB25(1)	†	£1100
G 10.	NB25(3)	†	£1000
G 15.	NB25(3)	£1000	£875
G 16.	NB25(2)	£1000	£1000
G 17.	NB25(3)	£1000	†

Imprimatur from the National Postal Museum Archives
Booklet pane of four with advertisements. Imperforate, watermark Type W15
 Two panes as No. NB25(4) arranged horizontally *tête-bêche* (£48000)

6 × 1½d. Red-brown. SMALL FORMAT
(Stamps 17.8 × 21.65 mm.)
From Booklets BB17, BB29 and BB37

	Perf Type E	P	I
A. Watermark upright			
NB26 (containing No. N53 × 6) (7.35)	40·00	30·00	40·00
t. "Cancelled", Type 33P	£450		
u. "Cancelled", Type 33	£1000		
v. "Cancelled", Type 28P	£600		
B. Watermark inverted			
NB26a (containing No. N53a × 6) (7.35)	50·00	40·00	50·00
at. "Cancelled", Type 33P	£450		
au. "Cancelled", Type 33	£1000		
av. "Cancelled", Type 28P	£600		
aw. "Specimen", Type 32 with punch hole on R. 1/1	£3000		

4 × 1½d. Red-brown. Booklet Panes with Advertising Labels (Stamps 17.8 × 21.65 mm.)
 Panes of six, comprising two labels letterpress in *black* and four stamps
From Booklets BB17 and BB37

	Perf Type E	P	I
A. Watermark upright			
NB27 (containing No. N53 × 4) (7.35)	£250	£200	£250
t. "Cancelled", Type 28P	£600		
u. "Cancelled", Type 33	£1350		
v. "Cancelled", Type 33P	£500		
B. Watermark inverted			
NB27a (containing No. N53a × 4) (7.35)	£250	£200	£250
at. "Cancelled", Type 28P	£600		
au. "Cancelled", Type 33	£1350		
av. "Cancelled", Type 33P	£500		
aw. "Specimen", Type 32 with punch hole on upper label	£3000		

Pane Nos. NB27 or NB27a

	Wmk Upright	Wmk Inverted
(1) "Cash's "Lose less Linen" book / Free booklet J. & J. Cash" (numbered 318)	£300	£300
(2) "Cash's satin lingerie ribbons / Samples [central] of Cash's ribbons. J. & J. Cash" (numbered 306)	£300	£300
(3) "Cash's satin lingerie ribbons / Samples [in text] of Cash's ribbons. "Attach this to a". J. & J. Cash" (numbered 323, 331, 335, 342 or 348)	£275	£275
(4) "Cash's satin lingerie ribbons" / Samples [in text] of Cash's ribbons. "Attach this to a post-", J. & J. Cash" (numbered 312)	£300	£300
(5) "Number One Bond / Pepys Stationery"	£300	£300
(6) "Kargo 2/6 per pack / Castell Bros. (Pepys Stationery)"	£275	£275
(7) "Drages fine furniture / 50 months to pay"	£300	£300
(8) "For Safety of Capital / Amalgamated Fixed Trust"	£200	£200
(9) "For Safety of Capital / Century Fixed Trust (pointer) [in large type]"	£250	£250
(10) "For Safety of Capital / Century Fixed Trust (pointer) [in small type]"	£275	£275
(11) "For Safety of Capital / Century Fixed Trust (see last page)"	£225	£225
(12) "For Safety of Capital / Commercial Fixed Trust"	£200	£200
(13) "For Safety of Capital / National Fixed Trust"	£200	£200
(14) "For Safety of Capital / Universal Fixed Trust (pointer) [in large type]"	£250	£250
(15) "For Safety of Capital / Universal Fixed Trust (see last page)"	£250	£250
(15a) Advertisement transposed	£8000	†
(16) "Saving is Simple / Home Safe"	£300	£300
(17) "Telephone Service / Air Mails, letters and parcels ["Installed free" deleted by handstamp]	£500	£500

 The numbers on panes NB27(1)–27(4) correspond to the numbers of the booklets in which they were issued. See Appendix 2.

Booklet Cylinder Numbers
Panes of six

	Perf. Type				
Cyl. No.	B3(I) No dot	B3A(P) Dot	B4(E) No dot	B4A(I) Dot	B4B(E) Dot
G 20	£150	£125	£125	£125	†
G 24	†	†	£125	†	†
G 27	£1500	£1500	†	£1500	†
G 30	£1500	†	85·00	85·00	85·00
G 31	†	†	£200	£200	†

 Cylinder G 24 dot was used with advertisement labels and is listed below.

Panes of six including two labels

		Perf. Type				
Cyl. No.	Advert.	B3 (I) No dot	B3A (P) Dot	B4 (E) No dot	B4A (I) Dot	B4B(E) Dot
G 24	NB27(2)	†	†	†	£350	†
G 24	NB27(12)	†	†	†	£225	†
G 24	NB27(13)	†	†	†	£325	†
G 24	NB27(16)	†	†	†	£325	†
G 24	NB27(17)	†	†	†	£600	†
G 26	NB27(3) (No. 323)	†	†	£300	£325	†
G 26	NB27(4)	†	£325	†	£350	†
G 26	NB27(5)	†	†	£850	£850	†
G 26	NB27(6) Wmk. inverted	†	†	£1200	£1200	†
G 26	NB27(6)	†	†	£350	£350	†
G 26	NB27(8)	£300	£500	£225	£225	†
G 26	NB27(12)	£300	£300	£225	£225	†
G 26	NB27(12) Wmk. inverted	†	†	£1500	£1500	†
G 26	NB27(13)	£500	£300	£225	£225	†

4 × 1½d. Red-brown. Booklet Panes in Photogravure

Cyl. No.	Advert.	B3 (I) No dot	B3A (P) Dot	B4 (E) No dot	B4A (I) Dot	B4B(E) Dot
	Wmk. inverted	†	†	†	—	†
G 28	NB27(3) (No. 331)	†	†	£300	£300	†
G 28	NB27(3) (No. 335)	†	†	£300	£300	†
G 28	NB27(3) (No. 342)	†	†	£300	£300	£300
G 28	NB27(3) (No. 348)	†	†	£300	£300	†
G 28	NB27(7)	†	†	£300	†	£300
G 28	NB27(8)	†	†	£225	£225	£225
G 28	NB27(9)	†	†	£275	£275	£275
G 28	NB27(10)	†	†	£300	£300	†
G 28	NB27(11)	†	†	£250	£250	£250
G 28	NB27(12)	†	†	£225	£225	†
G 28	NB27(13)	†	†	£225	£225	£225
G 28	NB27(14)	†	†	£275	£275	†
G 28	NB27(15)	†	†	£275	£275	£275

No examples of cylinder G 26 with advertisement NB27(1) have been reported.

Imprimatur from the National Postal Museum Archives
Booklet pane of four with blank advertisement labels. Imperforate, watermark Type W15

Two panes as No. NB27 arranged horizontally *tête-bêche* without marginal markings (£48000)

Section NG

The Recess-Printed "Seahorse" High Values (1913-34)

INTRODUCTION. The high values, 2s.6d., 5s., 10s. and £1 were designed by Bertram Mackennal with lettering by George W. Eve, and were originally to have been produced from a single master die engraved by J. A. C. Harrison and then to have the original values engraved. However, the first master die produced had the Union flag in Britannia's shield heraldically incorrect and consequently each value ended up not only having the value engraved but also its own flag which differs slightly with each value.

Waterlow Bros. & Layton, who already printed the National Insurance stamps, were invited to print the new high value definitives in recess, which neither Harrison & Sons nor Somerset House could undertake at the time. In 1915, the contract was put out to tender and gained by De La Rue & Co., who were in turn replaced by Bradbury, Wilkinson & Co. in 1918. Prior to De La Rue gaining the contract, it was decided to lighten the colour of the 10s. value, to avoid lightly postmarked examples being re-used, and to discontinue the £1 value, which passed from currency in 1917 and was only printed by Waterlow Bros and Layton.

When, in 1934, Waterlow & Sons won the contract, the re-engraved dies were used. These re-engraved dies were produced from the 5s. value which was modified to form a master die and were again, engraved by J. A. C. Harrison.

RECESS-PRINTING. This term means the same as "Line-Engraved" and "Intaglio" printing. It is the opposite to letterpress (described in the General Notes to Section M) as the engraver cuts out of the die the part of the design that is to be inked. The master die is hardened and a circular steel die is softened and applied under pressure to the master die. This "Transfer Roller", as it is called, is then hardened and used to roll or rock in the individual impressions on the printing plate. This process is more fully described in the General Notes to the Line-Engraved issues in Vol. 1. In printing, the cut-out hollows of the plate are filled with ink, any surplus being wiped away. The resulting impression has a depth of ink equal to the depth of the cuts in the original die and the raised image can usually be felt with the finger.

Interestingly, that the freelance engraver, J. A. C. Harrison, who had specialised in line-engraving, was commissioned by the Royal Mint to engrave the heads and frames for the typographed issues produced by Harrison & Sons and showed that he was equally at home in this reverse process. Later he was employed by Waterlows and engraved the 1924–25 British Empire Exhibition and £1 P.U.C. designs.

PLATES. The flat plates made by the Royal Mint for Waterlow & Layton and De La Rue came in sets of 40. As Bradbury, Wilkinson used rotary presses, they made their own plates from dies supplied by the Mint. These carried 80 impressions (2×40) and were curved to fit their presses, so stretching the height of the stamps' impressions by an extra ½mm. After printing, they were separated into sheets of 40.

MARGINAL MARKINGS ON THE PLATES. Each sheet contained 40 stamps arranged in 10 rows of 4, and showed hand–engraved marginal markings. On each Waterlow and De La Rue plate, marginal crosses appear centrally on the four sides of each sheet. Plate numbers were also engraved in the top margin, although they were so far above the stamps that they rarely appear on the issued sheets.

On the Bradbury, Wilkinson plates lines were engraved on either side of the crosses—horizontally in the top and bottom margins, and vertically in the side margins. As these were engraved by hand, slight differences in the lengths are apparent, and are an aid in plating.

Bradbury's official plate numbers, located at top of the sheet in between the two panes, were removed when the sheets were trimmed. However, the identification of all plates can be established by the differences that exist in the disposition and size of their marginal markings. It is beyond the scope of this catalogue to include these, but they are recorded in *Discovering Seahorses* (Bryan Kearsley). We do record the number of plates used by the different printers, including their official plate numbers and their most significant varieties.

VARIETIES. Apart from the more important varieties we list, there are numerous stamps showing minor varieties or doubling of their frame lines. To list these is beyond the scope of this catalogue, but they are illustrated or described in *Discovering Seahorses*. These stamps include a number of examples of impressions on the plate being entered a second time, creating duplication of parts of the design. When this was done before the plate was first put to press, it is known as a "fresh entry". If it took place once the plate had been in use, it is a "re-entry". Most of these varieties described as "re-entries" are technically fresh entries since they fall into the first group.

PAPER. Various versions of stout wove paper were used up to 1927, by which time printings had started to be made on undampened paper. From then on, including the Re-engraved issue, the paper was softer and more porous. Changes to the types of paper account for some fractional differences to the height of Bradbury, Wilkinson stamps.

Apart from a few examples found on Waterlow Bros & Layton printings, a paper with a ribbed appearance, somewhat akin to laid paper, also appeared on some Bradbury, Wilkinson stamps in 1921/22. When held up to the light, faint horizontal lines are noticeable in the paper's texture. With Bradbury examples, the back of the King's head often looks 'permed', suggesting this had more to do with the paper's manufacture than the incorrect pressure applied to the gumming rollers during Waterlow Bros & Layton's contract.

HOW TO DISTINGUISH BETWEEN THE PRINTINGS
Differences between Waterlow Bros & Layton and De la Rue

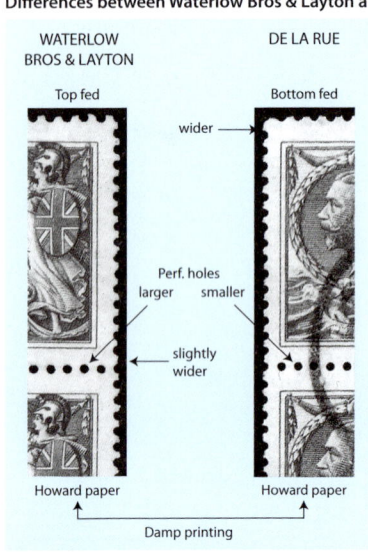

The Recess-Printed "Seahorse" High Values (1913-34) **KING GEORGE V**

Perforations of Marginal Stamps

Top Margin	Imperforate — Waterlow	Perforated—De La Rue
Bottom Margin	Imperforate — De la Rue	Perforated—Waterlow
Right Margin	Up to 12 holes — Waterlow	Single hole—De La Rue

Gum
Waterlow – Applied evenly. Colour clear to pale yellow
De La Rue – Unevenly applied/streaky. Colour yellow to brown

Worn Plates & Watermarks
Only De La Rue stamps ever showed signs of plate wear and errors to their watermarks (inverted/reversed or no watermark etc.), including their displacement.

Differences between Waterlow Bros & Layton and De La Rue and Bradbury, Wilkinson

WATERLOW BROS & LAYTON and DE LA RUE

Shorter in height
(22.1 mm)

Wider gutter
(4.9 mm)

BRADBURY, WILKINSON

Taller in height
(22.6 – 23.1 mm)

Narrower gutter
(3.9 – 4.2 mm)

The plates used by Waterlow Bros & Layton and De La Rue were flat, whereas Bradbury's were curved to fit their rotary presses, so stretching their stamps' impressions by an extra ½ mm.

Bradbury, Wilkinson Marginal Markings and Guide Dot

Bradbury's additional trim lines either side of crosses (2s.6d. Plate 3/5 left, State 1).

Marginal Markings. Note the extra horizontal (and vertical) lines either side of the four central crosses

Waterlow Bros & Layton and De La Rue feature only four central crosses

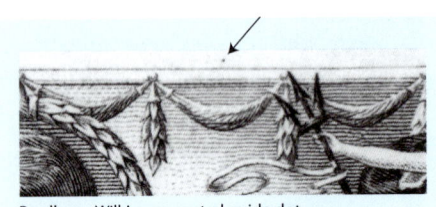

Bradbury, Wilkinson-central guide dot.

Guide Dot
Only Bradbury used guide dots when laying down its plates. If the dots had not already been burnished out, they got progressively smaller with later printings.

The 10s Bradbury stamp has a distinguishing feature of its own. It centres on its outer vertical frame lines. Each one has been crudely etched, making its appearance much thicker and more heavily inked than those produced by either De La Rue or Waterlow Bros & Layton.

Bradbury, Wilkinson
In all, Bradbury printed nearly 72 million Seahorse stamps, using some 40 plates to do so. Certain traits help to distinguish their various plates, which, conveniently, fall into three distinctive Series; each one having its own constant flaws, in addition to the variations to their stamp heights.

Notes on the identification of the three series are given under their respective values but the differences are summarised in the following table.

10s. Plates

Bradbury plates

Royal Mint plates

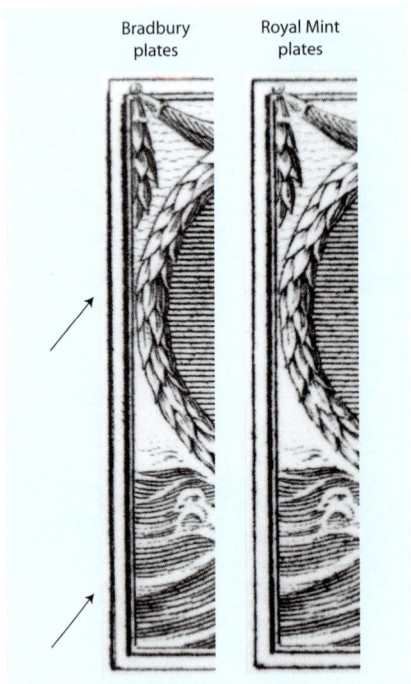

Identifying Bradbury, Wilkinson Plates (Series I to III)

2s.6d. Plates
Series I (1918-25) Damp printing	–/1 states 1&2
	–/1 re-entered state 3
	2/4 states 1 & 2
	3/5 states 1&2
	4/6 (no examples found)
Series II (1926-30) Dry printing	5/7, 6/8, 7/9, 8/10
Series III (1930-34) Dry printing	9/11, 10/12, 11/13

5s. Plates
Series I (1919-25) Damp printing	1/2 Complete visor
	3/4 Broken visor
Series II (1926-28/29) Dry printing	4/5 Broken visor
Series III (1928/29-34) Dry printing	5/6 broken visor, states 1 & 2

10s. Plates
Series I (1919-25) Damp printing	1/3 broken "S"
	2/7 Complete "S"
Series II (1926-30) Dry printing	3/8 Broken "S"
Series III (1930-34) Dry printing	4/9 Complete "S"

Average Stamp height
Series I (1918-25) Damp printing	22.6-22.75 mm. Wide top side perfs similar to De La Rue
Series II (1926-29/30) Dry printing	22.9-23.1 mm Slightly wider bottom side perfs (Top fed sheets only)
Series III (1929/30-34) Dry printing	22.9 mm. Even perfs

Colour Assessment

Shades should normally be compared using solid areas of colour. As there are none on these stamps, the best area for comparison is the lead, dark horse, or if this is obscured by a postmark, the back of the King's head or the top right-hand corner.

De La Rue "Worn Plate" Shades
Some shades were rendered paler, primarily, due to plate wear across much of the stamps' design. Yet the colour of ink used often did not vary much from the time when their plates were in prime condition, as a comparison of the lead dark horse can testify. It is for this reason, these shades no longer justify separate listing.

Very Rare Shades
During the 26 years Seahorses were in circulation, a few extremely rare shades did emerge, mainly, it is thought, from either pre-production trials or from the early stages of a print run, when colour consistency could be variable. Known individual examples of these shades include:

Waterlow Bros & Layton	2s.6d. £1	Blackish sepia (grey-sepia) Bright "electric" deep green (plate unknown, but in circulation autumn 1914)
Bradbury, Wilkinson	2s.6d.	Sepia (Plate -/1 State 1)
	5s.	Very deep carmine-red (Plate 1/2)
	10s.	Steel blue and Bright metallic blue, both Plate 1/3 with broken "S"

Note: All images in section NG, apart from the master die stages and N10 and W17. are copyright GB Philatelic Publications Ltd and Bryan Kearsley and are reproduced with their permission.

Stages of Original Master Die
Stage 1 has the Union flag in the shield more or less heraldically correct (no horizontal lines in the St. Andrew's Cross). Stages 2 to 5a have incorrect shields in that there are horizontal lines in the St. Andrew's Cross. Stage 6 is without shield and Stage 6a has a "Z" in the space for the shield. Other features of the various stages are noted below.

Stage 1
Proofed 24 August 1912. Upper garlands incomplete; no circles above top frame line; centre horse's head and Britannia's arms, dress and foot quite pale and unshaded. The only recorded example is in the H. C. V. Adams collection at the Royal Philatelic Society. However it is possible that others may exist in private hands.

Stage 2
Proofed 30 August 1912. Upper garlands completed; incomplete circles on top frame line; centre horse's head and Britannia's arms, dress and foot unshaded as before; dark horse has ring of white around the mouth and only light shading to hoof.

Stage 3
Proofed 6 September 1912. The 2nd and 3rd circles on top frame line are completed; centre horse's head shaded and some shading added to Britannia's arm and dress but foot remains unshaded; the ring of white around dark horse's mouth has been removed but hoof is unchanged.

Stage 4
Proofed 11 September 1912. All circles except the first now completed; Britannia's foot shaded and finer shading added to her dress; dark horse's head further shaded but hoof as before.

Stage 5
Proofed 18 September 1912. The first circle is still uncomplete; the dark horse's hoof is now shaded; the bottom frame line at left is missing. The die was hardened on 20 September 1912 (stage 5a).

Stages 6 and 6a were then produced from a transfer roller that was taken up from the stage 5a die but with the shield removed.

Stage 6
Proofed 23 September 1912. Blank shield. Outer frame line and all circles at top removed.

Stage 6a
Proofed late September 1912. Blank shield has a zig-zag line in it. Outer frame line restored with all circles except the first, which is still incomplete.

KING GEORGE V — The Recess-Printed "Seahorse" High Values (1913-34)

Stage 2

Stage 6

Stage 3

Stage 6a

Stage 4

Stage 5

Stages of Completed Dies with Values and Shields Inserted

Each value had its own figures, lettering and shields engraved in from dies laid out from the roller with the blank shield. They are listed under each individual value but exist in two states for each value. Those illustrated here are from the 2s.6d. value but they are the same for the other values.

State (a) Completed but first circle still unfinished. Guide lines around design still visible (not illustrated).
State (b) Fully completed with first circle finished and guide lines removed.

Die Proofs

Stage 1
In light brown on thick card ....From £50000
Stage 2
In indigo-blue or grey-blue on thick card..................From £50000
In grey-blue on laid paper...From £50000
In brown on card ....From £50000
Stage 3
In grey-brown on thick card ....From £50000
Stage 4
In carmine, green, grey-green, indigo or brown on
    thick card...From £50000
Stage 5. Before hardening
In dull green, indigo, brown or red-brown on
    thick card...From £50000
Stage 5a. After hardening, taken on 21 September 1912 and later
In green, chestnut, sepia or indigo-black on card..From £50000
Ex H. A. Richardson Archive.
In black on card, cut to stamp size, optd
    "Cancelled" in red..£18000
Stage 6
In indigo-black on wove paper ....
1973 Reprint by Bradbury Wilkinson on laid paper
    in three shades of blue..Each £17000
Stage 6a
In indigo-black on esparto paper with or without
    pale colouring around frame..£50000
In indigo-black on tick card, cut to stamp size £17500

Colour Trial
Taken on 28 January 1913 from Stage 5a die and endorsed "From Master Plate—Waterlow's Ink" in manuscript
In ultramarine on wove paper .... —

Number of Good Sheets Delivered and Plates used by Printers of Seahorse Stamps
Including Overprints for Post Office Agencies and the Irish Free State*

Printer and contact period	2s.6d. Sheets 40-set	Plates	5s. Sheets 40-set	Plates
Waterlow & Layton 26 Oct. 1912 -14 July 1915	75,479	2	28,556	2
De La Rue 15 July 1915 -31 July 1918	150,519	5‡	71,842	2§
Bradbury, Wilkinson 1 Aug. 1918 -31 Dec. 1933	1,076,443	11¶	553,536	4¶
Waterlow & Sons 1 Jan. 1934 -Jan. 1939†	220,300 est.	1¶	120,600 est.	1¶

Printer and contact period	10s. Sheets 40-set	Plates	£1 Sheets 40-set	Plates
Waterlow & Layton 26 Oct. 1912 -14 July 1915	12,157	2	5,952	2
De La Rue 15 July 1915 -31 July 1918	28,745	2§		
Bradbury, Wilkinson 1 Aug. 1918 -31 Dec. 1933	181,572	4¶		
Waterlow & Sons 1 Jan. 1934 -Jan. 1939†	31,250 est.	1		

* Best estimates indicate that fewer than 5% were overprinted, representing around 113,00 sheets
† Last Seahorse printing
‡ including two ex Waterlow
§ ex Waterlow
¶ Double-pane plates, excluding those re-entered

The number of good sheets printed excludes all waste and trials. The estimated number of re-engraved sheets is based on their Waste Records (Jan. 1935–1939) and Consumption sales figures).

Source; British Postal Museum & Archive

Notes:
All the Royal Mint plates supplied to Waterlow & Layton and De La Rue consisted of a single pane of 40 stamps. Those made by Bradbury, Wilkinson were double-pane plates holding 80 stamps, 40 to each pane. The same was true of Waterlow's Re-engraved plates, except for the 10s, which was a single-pane plate.

About 25% of sheets (30,491) printed by Waterlow & Layton were perforated by the IR Stamping Department at Somerset House. The only way of distinguishing between the two is their choice of pinning points. The IR used the top and bottom marginal crosses, while Waterlow chose those on the sides.

N10

NG KING GEORGE V The Recess-Printed "Seahorse" High Values (1913-34) **2s.6d. Brown**

W17

A   B

Type A. Background behind portrait consists of horizontal lines
Type B. Background behind portrait consists of horizontal and diagonal lines.

All stamps in this Section are Type **N10**, watermarked Single Cypher, Type **W17** and the word "POSTAGE" in each of the four margins and perforated 11 × 12.
Printed in sheets of 40 (4 × 10).

PRICES FOR STAMPS IN USED CONDITION
Many of the stamps in this Section were used on parcels and as a result were subject to heavy cancelling. The "used" prices in this catalogue are for fine used examples; inferior examples with very heavy or smudged postmarks are of less value. For well centred, lightly used examples, add the following percentages to the prices quoted.
Waterlow Bros & Layton printings — 2s.6d. (N63), 5s. (N66), 10s. (N69), £1 (N72) **+35%**
De La Rue printings — 2s.6d. (N64), 5s. (N67), 10s. (N70) **+45%**
Bradbury, Wilkinson printings — 2s.6d. (N65), 5s. (N68), 10s. (N71) **+35%**

Background Type A

1913–18. 2s.6d. Brown

N63 (=S.G.399/400)

(a) Waterlow & Layton printings (30.6.13)

	Unmtd mint	Mtd mint	Used
(1) Very deep sepia-brown (Vandyke brown)	£3750	£2750	£1750
(2) Deep sepia-brown	£850	£400	£200
(3) Sepia-brown	£600	£300	£150
a. Re-entry (Pl. HV3, R. 2/1)	£2800	£1800	£800
b. Ribbed paper (vertical ribbing)		£750	
s. "Specimen", Type 26		£650	
t. "Specimen", Type 29		£1800	
u. "Cancelled", Type 24		£850	
v. "Cancelled", Type 27		£2800	
w. "Cancelled", Type 27 Imperf.		—	

N63/64a (Plate 3, R.2/1)

Plates. Waterlow & Layton used two plates (HV1 and HV3).

Rough Plate Proofs
On buff paper in brown £225
Ditto, in carmine £325
Ditto in indigo £425

Die Proofs
The states are illustrated in General Notes, below Stage 6a.
State (a)
In blue-green on card marked "3" above design £65000
In blue-green on card £65000
State (b)
In deep green on card marked "3" above design £65000
In deep green or dull grey-blue on card £65000
In deep red-brown on thin wove paper £65000
In vermilion or brown on India paper £65000

Plate Proofs
Three impressions together from supposed trial plate arranged 17 mm. apart horizontally.
    Size 39 × 22·25 mm.
In black on soft card .... Strip of three £25000
Proofed on 19 December 1912. Impressions 5
    mm. apart horizontally and vertically.
Size 39 × 22·5 mm. Very clear impressions
In dull blue-green on glazed card £5750
Size approx. 38·8 × 22 mm. (depending on shrinkage)
Thin plate-glazed paper without gum or watermark
In red, blue, green, brown or black .... From £5500
Thicker wove paper without gum or watermark
In deep carmine, carmine, vermilion, orange-
    chrome, olive-green, bottle-green,
    blue-green, ultramarine, purple-brown or
    sepia-brown .... From £5500
Thin gummed wove paper watermarked "JAS
    WRIGLEY LD–219"
In black £5500
Thin card
In green, after plate had been cleaned £5500

Colour Trials
Imperf. on thin paper pasted on card
In green endorsed "30–4–13" in M/S and stamped
    "WATERLOW BROS. & LAYTON, LTD." £20000
Imperf. on ungummed paper watermarked "JAS
    WRIGLEY LD–219"
In 19 different colours .... From £5500
    The Royal Philatelic Collection contains a set of 19 colour trials on thin wove paper, dated 29 January 1913, in the folllowing colours: deep rose-red, deep red, pale vermilion, black, deep olive, blue-green (selected colour for £1), bottle green, light chrome-yellow, grey-blue, indigo, powder blue, deep ultramarine, very bright blue, dull brown, sepia-brown, pale brown, brownish maroon and deep brown-purple.
Perf. 11 × 12 on gummed paper. Wmk. Type **W17**
Ultramarine, indigo, green, purple, grey or
    brown .... From £15000

2s.6d. Brown — The Recess-Printed "Seahorse" High Values (1913-34) — KING GEORGE V

Perf. 11 × 12 on ungummed paper. No wmk.
  Bright brown, bright blue, magenta, sepia,
  carmine, indigo or green .... From £15000
Perf. 11 × 12 on gummed thinnish white paper.
  Wmk. Type **W17** in near to issued colour.
  Overprinted "Cancelled," Type 24 .... £2400

(b) 2s.6d. De La Rue printings (9.15)
N64 (=S.G.405/408)

	Unmtd mint	Mtd mint	Used
(1) Pale sepia-brown (from unworn plate)	£2500	£1500	£1200
(2) Chrome (very pale sepia-brown) (from unworn plate)	£7500	£4000	£3500
(3) Grey-brown (inc. worn plates)	£700	£400	£300
(4) Dark brown (inc. worn plates)	£700	£400	£300
(5) Deep yellow-brown	£675	£375	£250
(6) Yellow-brown	£550	£325	£225
(7) Pale yellow-brown	£675	£375	£275
(8) Bright yellow-brown	£675	£375	£275
(9) Cinnamon-brown	£3750	£2500	£2000
(10) Brown	£2400	£1500	£1200
(11) Very deep brown	£3250	£2250	£1800
(12) Reddish brown (chestnut)	£3250	£2250	£1800
(13) Sepia ("Seal brown")	£550	£325	£250
(14) Blackish brown	£2400	£1500	£1200
a. Re-entry (Pl. HV3, R. 2/1)	£3000	£2000	£950
c. No watermark	£10000	£6500	
f. Wmk. inverted			
Shade (3)	£1800	£1250	£1000
Shade (5)	£2400	£1500	
Shade (6)	£1800	£1250	£875
Shade (11)	£3500	£2750	
Shade (13)	£1800	£1250	£1000
Shade (14)	£2800	£1800	
g. Wmk. reversed:			
Shade (3)	£1800	£1250	£1000
Shade (5)	£1700	£850	£850
Shade (6)	£1800	£1250	£1000
Shade (13)	£1800	£1250	£1000
Shade (14)	—	—	—
h. Wmk. inverted and reversed,			
Shades (3), (4) and (6)	£4750	£4000	
s. "Specimen," Type 23		£1400	
t. "Cancelled," Type 24		£1400	

Shades (13) and (14) are often found with dark brown gum. Shade (11) is usually found with watermark low and inverted.

Shades formerly listed as Pale brown and Pale brown (worn plate) are believed to be underinked or poor impressions from worn plates of shades (3) and (4). They have now been included under those shades to avoid further confusion.

No. N64a is from the Waterlow plate, and the re-entry marks are similar, but not so pronounced, due to plate wear. It is known with watermark upright and inverted. The 're-entry' formerly listed as N64b is now known to be a "kiss"-print and has been deleted.

N64a (Pl. 3, R.2/1)

Misplaced Watermarks
ya. Single stamp showing complete letters from "POSTAGE" (no portion of watermark **W17**), inverted or reversed ....
yb. Horizontal strip of 3 or 4 sufficient to show complete "POSTAGE" watermark, inverted or reversed .... From £10000
yc. Vertical strip of four showing watermark "POSTAGE" reversed £11000

Nos. yb and yc may show a portion of **W17** and "POSTAGE" complete.

Plates. De La Rue used the two Waterlow plates and three additional plates. (HV9, 11 and 12)

Colour Trials
Size 38·7 × 22·1 mm. Imperf. on gummed paper wmk. Type **W17**
In issued shades (5), (6) and (7) .... From £1000

Imprimatur from the National Postal Museum Archives
Imperforate, watermark Type **W17**

Watermark upright
An example exists showing a reversed plate number "12" in sheet margin at top.

(c) 2s.6d. Bradbury, Wilkinson printings (12.18)
N65 (=S.G.413a/415a)

	Unmtd mint	Mtd mint	Used
(1) Olive-brown	£350	£190	£100
(2) Dull sepia-brown	£350	£190	£100
(3) Chocolate-brown	£325	£160	75·00
(4) Reddish brown	£325	£160	75·00
(5) Pale brown	£340	£175	85·00
a. Re-entry (Pl. –/1L, State 1, R. 1/1)	£850	£475	£300
b. Re-entry (Pl. –/1L, State 1, R. 2/4)	£850	£475	£300
c. Re-entry (Pl. –/1R., State 1, R. 1/4)	£850	£475	£300
d. Re-entry (Pl. –/1L, State 3, R. 10/1)	£850	£475	£300
e. Re-entry (Pl. 2/4L, State 1, R.1/1)	£850	£475	£300
f. Re-entry (Pl. 2/4L, State 1, R. 1/3)	£850	£475	£300
g. Re-entry (Pl. 2/4L, State 1, R. 1/4)	£1100	£650	£400
h. Re-entry (Pl. 2/4L, State 1, R. 2/2)	£850	£475	£300
i. Re-entry (Pl. 2/4L, State 1, R. 2/3)	£850	£475	£300
j. Re-entry (Pl. 2/4L, State 1, R. 5/2)	£850	£475	£300
k. Re-entry (Pl. 2/4L, State 1, R. 5/3)	£850	£475	£300
l. Re-entry (Pl. 2/4L, State 1, R. 7/1)	£850	£475	£300

NG KING GEORGE V   The Recess-Printed "Seahorse" High Values (1913-34) 2s.6d. Brown

	Unmtd mint	Mtd mint	Used
m. Re-entry (Pl. 2/4L, State 1, R. 10/2)	£1250	£700	£400
n. Re-entry (Pl. 2/4R, State 1, R. 1/2)	£850	£475	£300
o. Re-entry (Pl. 2/4R, State 1, R. 1/3)	£1250	£700	£400
p. Re-entry (Pl. 2/4R, State 1, R. 7/1)	£1250	£700	£400
q. Re-entry (Pl. 3/5R, State 1, R. 2/4)	£850	£475	£300
r. Re-entry (Pl. 3/5L, State 2, R. 1/2)	£1600	£1000	£500
s. Re-entry (Pl. 3/5L, State 2, R. 8/1)	£850	£475	£300
t. Re-entry (Pl. 3/5L, State 2, R. 8/2)	£850	£475	£300
u. Re-entry (Pl. 3/5R, State 2, R. 10/1)	£850	£475	£300
v. Ribbed paper (Plate 2/4 L and R only)	£600	£400	£200
w. "Specimen", Type 15		£2000	
x. "Specimen", Type 23		£900	
y. "Specimen", Type 26			
z. "Specimen", Type 31 in violet or black		£1200	
za. "Specimen", Type 32		£4000	
zb. "Cancelled", Type 24		£400	
zc. "Cancelled", Type 28		£1500	
zd. "Cancelled", Type 33		£1500	
ze. "Specimen", Type 23 and "Cancelled" Type 24		£3000	

The "ribbed paper" appeared only on printings from Plate 2/4 L (State 1).

Plates. Bradbury, Wilkinson plates came in three different types (Series I-III) displaying constant flaws to the value tablet, along with variations to the height of the stamps. They used 22 individual plates (11 double panes, Left (L) and Right (R)), some appearing in more than one state.
A table summarising the features of the three series is provided in the introduction to this section. More detailed notes are given under each value.

Identifying Series I, II and III of the Bradbury, Wilkinson 2s.6d.

Series I Weakened frame line above "AL" of "HALF".

Series II Frame line above "AL" strengthened. Broken letters in "CROWN" and "POSTAGE".

All plates: O P
Plates 5/7 L Row 7 & 6/8 L & R: R
Plate 7/9 L & R: R R
Plate 8/10 L & R: C R

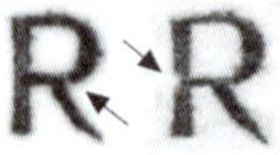

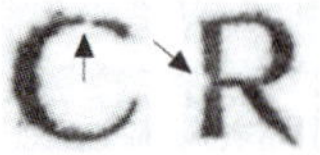

Series III
Value tablet frame-lines and letters complete. Only some faint vertical hair-lines and a dot to the right of "N" of "CROWN" are visible.

Series I (1918-25) damp printing
  Official plate Nos. -/1 (three states), 2/4* (two states)
    3/5 (two states), 4/6 (no examples found)
  Stamp height 22.6-22.75mm. Margin 4.2mm.
  Both top perfs wider, similar to De La Rue.

Series II (1926-30) dry printing
  Official plate Nos. 5/7, 6/8, 7/9, 8/10.
  Stamp height 22.9-23.1mm. Margin 3.9mm.
  Slightly wider bottom side perfs (Top–fed sheets only).

Series III (1930-34) dry printing
  Official plate Nos. 9/11, 10/12, 11/13
  Stamp height 22.9mm. Margin 3.9mm. Even perfs.

N65a (Plate -/1L, R.1/1)

2s.6d. Brown *The Recess-Printed "Seahorse" High Values (1913-34)* **KING GEORGE V** **NG**

N65b. (Plate -/1L, R.2/4)

N65f. (Plate 2/4L, R.1/3)

N65c. (Plate -/1R, R.1/4)

N65g. (Plate 2/4L, R.1/4)

N65d. (Plate -/1L, R.10/1)

N65h. (Plate 2/4L, R.2/2)

N65e. (Plate 2/4L, R.1/1)

N65i. (Plate 2/4L, R.2/3)

201

Stanley Gibbons
Great Britain Department

BY APPOINTMENT TO
HER MAJESTY THE QUEEN
PHILATELISTS
STANLEY GIBBONS LTD
LONDON

Stanley Gibbons, a name synonymous with quality.

Ever since the birth of our hobby Stanley Gibbons has been at the forefront of GB philately and we invite collectors access to one of the finest GB stocks in the world by registering for our renowned free monthly brochure. Whatever your budget or collecting interests you will find a range of the highest quality material for the discerning collector.

To receive our monthly brochures or for further enquires please email gb@stanleygibbons.com or phone 020 7557 4424.

Est 1856
STANLEY GIBBONS

Proud PTS members

Stanley Gibbons
399 Strand, London, WC2R 0LX
+44 (0)20 7836 8444
www.stanleygibbons.com

2s.6d. Brown *The Recess-Printed "Seahorse" High Values (1913-34)* **KING GEORGE V**

N65j. (Plate 2/4L, R.5/2)

N65n. (Plate 2/4R, R.1/2)

N65k. (Plate 2/4L, R.5/3)

N65o (Plate 2/4R, R.1/3)

N65l. (Plate 2/4L, R.7/1)

N65p. (Plate 2/4R, R.7/1)

N65m. (Plate 2/4L, R.10/2)

N65q. (Plate 3/5R, R.2/4)

KING GEORGE V The Recess-Printed "Seahorse" High Values (1913-34) 5s. Carmine

N65r. (Plate 3/5L, R.1/2)

N65s. (Plate 3/5L, R.8/1)

N65t. (Plate 3/5L, R.8/2)

N65u. (Plate 3/5R, R.10/1)

Experimental printing.
1921 (10 January) Wmk. Simple Cypher Type **W14** (sideways and reversed), perf. 11 × 12, 22¾ mm.
high and overprinted "Cancelled", Type 24 ....£750
Do., watermark "POSTAGE" only .... Strip of three £6500

Do., but without watermark £7500
Do. watermark "POSTAGE" only (inverted) ...*Strip of three* £9000
Vertical pair. One with wmk. **W14** and one without*Pair* £10000
Major re-entry (Pl. 2/4, State 1, R. 1/3) £2800
Major re-entry (Pl. 2/4, State 1, R. 1/7) £2800
Plate 2/4 was used for two experimental printings.
Two paper types were used;
    Type A Engine sized (opaque) stamps centred to left
    Type B Tub sized (translucent) stamps well centered or centered to right
    Only two sheets of each have survived.

Imprimatur from the National Postal Museum Archives
Imperforate, watermark Type **W17**
Watermark upright

Imprimatur from the British Postal Museum & Archive
Imperforate, watermark Type **W17**
Watermark upright

1913–18. 5s. Carmine

(a) Waterlow & Layton printings (30.6.13)
N66 (=S.G.401)

	Unmtd mint	Mtd mint	Used
(1) Rose-carmine	£1300	£625	£325
(2) Pale rose-carmine	£1400	£750	£375
(3) Carmine-red	£1500	£850	£450
s. "Specimen", Type 26		£950	
t. "Cancelled", Type 24		£1800	
u. "Cancelled", Type 27		£3250	
v. "Cancelled", Type 27 Imperf			

Plates. Waterlow used two plates (HV2 and 6).

Rough Plate Proof
on buff in carmine..£225

Die Proofs
State (a) but with first circle completed
In sepia-brown on card showing guide lines
    outside design...£50000
In deep grey-brown on card still showing guide lines £50000
State (b)
In sepia, deep grey-blue, indigo or blue-green on card..£50000
In grey-brown on card endorsed "10 October 1912"........£50000
In blue, brown, carmine or green on India paper.............£50000
In red-brown, dark brown, chestnut-brown, deep
    blue, carmine, green or blue-green on thin paper ...£50000
In red-brown on thin paper endorsed "14 October
    1912"..£50000
In indigo-blue or blue-green on esparto paper.................£50000

Colour/Paper Trials (Joynson paper)
Perf. 11 × 12 on gummed thinnish white paper, wmk. Type **W17** in near to issued colour. Overprinted
"Cancelled", Type 24 .... £3250

(b) 5s. De La Rue printings (9.15)
N67 (=S.G.409/410)

	Unmtd mint	Mtd mint	Used
(1) Bright carmine	£1100	£650	£400
(2) Carmine	£1250	£700	£475
(3) Pale carmine (worn plate)	£1400	£800	£500
a. No watermark		£18000	
b. Watermark inverted	£6750	£4750	
c. Watermark reversed	£6250	£4500	
d. Watermark inverted and reversed		£18000	†
s. "Specimen", Type 23		£1250	
t. "Cancelled", Type 24		£1250	

On shade (2) the colour shows through to the back of the stamp.

10s. Blue — The Recess-Printed "Seahorse" High Values (1913-34) — KING GEORGE V

Misplaced Watermark
ya. Single stamp showing complete letters from "POSTAGE" (no portion of watermark **W17**), inverted..
yb. Horizontal strip of 3 sufficient to show complete "POSTAGE" watermark, inverted (shade 1).... —

Plates. De La Rue used only the two Waterlow plates. Certain stamps from the first vertical rows of plates 2 and 6 show the left outer frame line doubled, these are now believed to have been caused by excessive wiping of the inked plate.

Imprimatur from the National Postal Museum Archives
Imperforate, watermark Type **W17**
Watermark upright

(c) 5s. Bradbury, Wilkinson printings (1.19)
N68 (=S.G.416)

	Unmtd mint	Mtd mint	Used
(1) Rose-carmine	£550	£325	£135
(2) Pale rose-carmine	£650	£400	£180
(3) Rose-red	£475	£325	£135
a. Ribbed paper (Pl. 1/2)		£750	
s. "Specimen", Type 15	£2400		
sa. "Specimen", Type 23	£1200		
t. "Specimen", Type 26	£1500		
u. "Specimen", Type 31 in violet or black	£1200		
v. "Specimen", Type 32	£6500		
w. "Cancelled", Type 24	£1000		
x. "Cancelled", Type 28	£2500		
v. "Cancelled", Type 33	£2500		
z. "Specimen", Type 23 and "Cancelled", Type 24	£6000		

Identifying Series I, II and III

Complete visor – Plate 1/2, State 1 only

Broken visor – All other plates

Series I (1919-25) damp printing
Official plate Nos. 1/2, 3/4
Stamp height 22.6-22.75mm. Margin 4.2mm.
Both top side perfs wider, similar to De La Rue.

Series II (1926-28/29) dry printing
Official plate No. 4/5
Stamp height 22.9-23.1mm. Margin 3.9mm.
Margin slightly wider bottom side perfs (top fed sheets only).

Series III (1928/29-34) dry printing
Official plate 5/6 (two states)
Stamp height 22.9mm. Margin 3.9mm.
Even perfs

Experimental printing.
1920 (11 February). Wmk. Simple Cypher Type **W14** perf. 11 × 12, 22¾ mm. high and overprinted "Cancelled", Type 24 .... £1300
Do. but "Cancelled", 23 mm. high* £1500
*This contains the positional dot in the upper margin normally absent from issued 23 mm. stamps.

Imprimatur from the National Postal Museum Archives
Imperforate, watermark Type **W17**
Watermark upright

Imprimatur from the British Postal Museum & Archive
Imperforate, watermark Type **W17**
Watermark upright

1913–18. 10s. Blue

(a) Waterlow Bros and Layton printings (1.8.13)
N69 (=S.G.402)

	Unmtd mint	Mtd mint	Used
(1) Indigo-blue	£2200	£1200	£475
(2) Indigo	£2400	£1300	£575
s. "Specimen", Type 23			
t. "Specimen", Type 26		£1200	
u. "Specimen", Type 29		£2200	
v. "Cancelled", Type 24		£1500	
w. "Cancelled", Type 27			
x. "Cancelled", Type 28			

Plates. Waterlow used two plates (HV4 and 7).

Die Proofs
State (a)
In blue-green on card marked "2" above design.............. £7500
In blue-green on card £75000
State (b)
In blue-green on card £75000
In deep green on card marked "2" above design.......... £75000
As last but endorsed "12 November 1912"....................£75000

Colour / Paper Trials (Joynson paper)
On paper watermarked Type **W17**, gummed, in near to issued colour
On paper watermarked Type **W17**, gummed, in near to issued colour. Overprinted "Cancelled", Type 24 .... £4250

(b) 10s. De La Rue printings (12.15?)
N70 (=S.G.411/413)

	Unmtd mint	Mtd mint	Used
(1) Blue	£4000	£3250	£875
(2) Deep blue (inc. worn plate)	£5500	£3750	£1000
(3) Bright ("Cambridge") blue	£14000	£9500	£4250
(4) Pale blue	£4250	£3500	£875
(5) Deep (intense) bright blue	£12500	£8000	£4000
(6) Deep bright blue	£6250	£4000	£1200
(7) Bright blue	£6000	£3750	£1100
c. Watermark inverted and reversed. (Shade 2)	—	—	†
s. "Specimen", Type 26		£2800	
t. "Cancelled", Type 24		£3000	

Although issue in December 1915 has long been accepted, the earliest postmark date currently on record is February 1916.

Plates. De La Rue used only the two Waterlow plates.

NG KING GEORGE V The Recess-Printed "Seahorse" High Values (1913-34) 10s. Blue

Imprimatur from the National Postal Museum Archives
Imperforate, watermark Type **W17**
Watermark upright

(c) 10s. Bradbury, Wilkinson printings (1.19)
N71 (=S.G.417)

	Unmtd mint	Mtd mint	Used
(1) Dull blue	£850	£475	£175
(2) Dull grey-blue	£850	£475	£175
(3) Blackish-blue ("Steel blue")	£1600	£1100	£400
a. Re-entry (Pl. 1/3L, R.1/1)	£2250	£1800	£1000
ab. Re-entry (Plate 1/3L, R.2/1)	£1750	£1200	£800
b. Re-entry (Plate 2/7L, R.6/1)	£2500	£2000	£1200
s. "Specimen", Type 15		£4000	
sa. "Specimen", Type 23		£1400	
t. "Specimen", Type 26			
u. "Specimen", Type 31 in violet or black		£1400	
v. "Specimen", Type 32		£6500	
w. "Cancelled", Type 24			
wa. "Cancelled", Type 24 and manuscript "Cancelled 1st Sept"	£7000	†	
x. "Cancelled", Type 28		£4000	
y. "Cancelled", Type 33		£4000	
z. "Specimen", Type 23 and "Cancelled", Type 24		£6500	

Shade (3) was previously described as "Steel blue", but this description is more appropriately ascribed to a very rare shade noted in the introduction to this section.

N71a (Plate 1/3L [Pl.5], R.1/1)

N71ab (Plate 1/3L [Pl.5], R. 2/1)

N71b (Plate 2/7? [Pl.2], R.6/1)

Identifying Series I, II and III of the Bradbury Wilkinson 10s.

Broken "S" in 'POSTAGE'
Series I, Official plate 1/3
Series II, Official plate 3/8

Complete "S" in 'POSTAGE'
Series I, Official plate 2/7
Series III, Official plate 4/9

Series I (1919-25) damp printing
Official plate Nos. 1/2 amd 3/4
Stamp height 22.6-22.75mm. Margin 4.2mm.
Both top side perfs wider similar to De La Rue

Series II (1926-30) dry printing
Official plate No. 4/5
Stamp height 22.9-23.1mm. Margin 3.9mm.
Slightly wider bottom side perfs (top fed sheets only)

Series III (1930-34) dry printing
Official plate No. 4/9
Stamp height 22.9 mm. Margin 3.9mm. Even perfs.

Imprimatur from the National Postal Museum Archives
Imperforate, watermark Type **W17**
Watermark upright

Imprimaturs from British Postal Museum & Archive
Imperforate, watermark Type **W17**
Watermark upright
As last but on Joynson paper (registered January 1923)

Experimental Royal Mint Plate Proofs
Between 1929 and 1934, the Royal Mint conducted a series of experiments and trials to improve the making of recess plates by borrowing some of the manufacturing techniques of the letterpress process.

Nov/Dec 1929. From a special curved plate comprising nine complete rolled-in impressions, plus one part impression, with outer frame lines incomplete. Imperforate.

In black on hard unwatermarked paper...... *The sheet* £85000
As last, but single example £9000

Three black proof sheets of the above are recorded. The first with two inscribed notes in pencil "Pt Nickel Sheet (from wax mould of burnished steel rolled in original). 1.11.29 2nd Pull"; and additionally, "After polishing face with white powder and cloth".

The second is inscribed and dated "Copper plate after polishing and burnishing 18/12/29".

The third with "EXPERIMENTAL PLATE" printed at right, bears no other inscription, and came from a larger plate proof. The last two sheets are thought to have been subsequently split.

A fourth sheet consisting of 36-set proof in black on thick paper, inscribed "Copper (on leads) before burnishing (as deposited) only polished 17/12/29"; now forms part of the British Postal Museum & Archive collection.

1913. £1 Green. Printed by Waterlow (1.8.13?)

N72 (=S.G.403/404)

	Ummtd mint	Mtd mint	Used
(1) Green	£4800	£3500	£1400
(2) Deep green	£6500	£4500	£2000
(3) Dull blue-green	£4800	£3500	£1600
r. Ribbed paper (horizontal ribbing)			
s. "Specimen", Type 23		£4250	
t. "Specimen", Type 26		£3250	
u. "Cancelled", Type 24 (Shade 3)		£4250	
v. "Cancelled", Type 27		£5500	
w. "Cancelled", Type 28		£5750	

Plates. Waterlow used two plates (HV5 and 8).

Die Proofs
State (a)
In blue-green on card marked "4" above design................. —
In blue-green on card .... —
State (b)
In deep green on card marked "4" above design .... —
As last but endorsed "12 November 1912"........................... —
Ex. H. A. Richardson Archive
In black on card, cut to stamp size, optd.
   "CANCELLED" in red £30000

Colour Trial on Joyson paper from the National Postal Museum Archives
Perforated 11 × 12, watermark Type **W17**
In yellowish green and "Cancelled", Type **24** £3250

WATERLOW RE-ENGRAVED ISSUE

Waterlow Re-engraved – cross-hatching behind King's head.

Other printers – single hatching behind King's head.

Background Type B. The re-engraved Die
The background to the portrait consists of horizontal and diagonal lines. There are numerous other minor differences between this and the original die.

Like Bradbury, Waterlow plates were curved and consisted of double panes of 40 stamp set in rows of four. Only the 10s. plate was made as a single pane.

The sheets were marked with horizontal and vertical trim lines in all four corners, with their dividing lines set within the printed panes – a small cross in the centre and short vertical lines between columns 2 and 3 and horizontal ones between rows 5 and 6. The Postal Services Department are known to have supplied these stamps to the Post Office on 16 October 1934.

KING GEORGE V
The Recess-Printed "Seahorse" High Values (1913-34) 2s.6d. Brown Waterlow re-engraved issue

Printed by Waterlow
1934 (October). **2s.6d. Brown**

N73 (=S.G.450)

	Unmtd mint	Mtd mint	Used
(1) Chocolate-brown	£170	£100	45·00
(2) Reddish brown	£225	£140	65·00
s. "Specimen", Type 30		£3750	
sa. "Specimen", Type 23		£3750	
sb. "Specimen", Type 32		£3750	
t. "Cancelled", Type 33	£5500	†	

Imprimatur from the National Postal Museum Archives
Imperforate, watermark Type **W17**
Watermark upright

Imprimatur from British Postal Museum & Archive
Imperforate, watermark Type **W17**
Watermark upright

1934 (October). **5s. Red**

N74 (=S.G.451)

	Unmtd mint	Mtd mint	Used
Bright rose-red	£425	£200	95·00
s. "Specimen", Type 30		£3750	
sa. "Specimen", Type 23		£3750	
sb. "Specimen", Type 32		£3750	
t. "Cancelled", Type 33	£6500	†	

No specific date of issue but it exists on cover postmarked 20.10.1934.

Imprimatur from the National Postal Museum Archives
Imperforate, watermark Type **W17**
Watermark upright

Imprimatur from British Postal Museum & Archive
Imperforate, watermark Type **W17**
Watermark upright

1934 (October). **10s. Indigo**

N75 (=S.G.452)

	Unmtd mint	Mtd mint	Used
Indigo	£525	£375	95·00
s. "Specimen", Type 30		£3750	
sa. "Specimen", Type 23		£3750	
sb. "Specimen", Type 32		£3750	
t. "Cancelled", Type 33	£6500	†	

Imprimatur from the National Postal Museum Archives
Imperforate, watermark Type **W17**
Watermark upright

Imprimatur from British Postal Museum & Archive
Imperforate, watermark Type **W17**
Watermark upright

Plates
Waterlow used three plates
2s.6d. Plate No   38549 (80-set)
5s.   38550 (80-set)
10s.   38551 (40-set)

Section NH

Commemorative Issues (1924–35)

All stamps in this section are watermarked Multiple Block G v R and Crown, Type **W15**, except No. NCom9.

N16 **N17**
(Des. Harold Nelson. Dies eng. J. A. C. Harrison)

1924 and 1925 BRITISH EMPIRE EXHIBITION

Recess-printed by Waterlow & Sons from dies and plates of their own manufacture and printed in sheets of 120 stamps in two panes of 60, the panes being separated before issue into post office sheets of 10 rows of 6. There were no Controls or plate numbers.

It is probable that there was a single plate for each of the 1924 values; the Post Office collection contains the original proofs which were submitted about 12 April 1924. It was decided to re-issue the stamps in 1925 and the original dies were changed to the new date. Waterlow returned the 1925 dies to the Royal Mint and they were later transferred to the British Postal Museum & Archive. The 1½d. bears the engraved number "10289" and the 1d. is numbered "10290". Die proofs exist which confirm that both issues were from the original dies and that the transfer rollers for 1924 and 1925 stamps were taken from them. There are many flaws which are merely transient and unrelated to plate defects.

The perforation was at first by a line machine which had very small holes. Later this was changed for a comb machine with larger holes.

The coil stamps were made by the British Stamp and Ticket Automatic Delivery Co. Ltd. for use in the vending machines they supplied and which were installed in various places inside the Exhibition.

It had been the intention of the Exhibition Board that the stamps would only be available to personal callers. However, such was the interest and demand for the stamps that it was agreed to supply the stamps by post from 1 July 1924. It is not clear from records whether all postal sales were dealt with by the Exhibition Post Offices. It is known that the London Chief Office supplied bulk orders to stamp dealers to the value of £391 18s. 11d. during the first few weeks of the 1924 Exhibition. Stamps of both issues were available from the Chief Office for a short period after the close of the Exhibition in 1925.

1924 (23 April). **Type N16,** Dated "1924". Line Perf. 14

NCom1 (=S.G.430)

	Unmtd mint	Mtd mint	Used
1d. Scarlet	12·00	10·00	11·00
a. Bottom margin imperf.		£4750	
aa. Left side margin imperf.		£4250	
b. Scratch across lion's nose (Left pane, R. 1/4)	£225	£150	75·00
c. Tail to "N" of "EXHIBITION" (Left pane, R. 1/5)	£225	£150	75·00
d. Comb perf. 14	12·00	10·00	11·00
e. Do. with var. b	£225	£150	75·00
ea. Do. with var. c	£225	£150	75·00
f. Coil join (vert. pair) (7.24)			
s. "Specimen", Type 15		£1750	
t. "Specimen", Type 23		£1100	
u. "Specimen", Type 30		£1100	
v. "Cancelled", Type 28		£1100	

NCom2 (=S.G.431)

	Unmtd mint	Mtd mint	Used
1½d. Brown	20·00	15·00	15·00
a. Comb perf. 14 (8.24)	20·00	15·00	15·00
b. Left side margin imperf.		£5250	
c. Coil join (vert. pair) (8.24)			
s. "Specimen", Type 15		£1750	
t. "Specimen", Type 23		£1100	
u. "Cancelled", Type 24		£1100	
v. "Cancelled", Type 28		£1100	
w. "Specimen", Type 30			

No. NCom2 exists printed on both sides, the one on the gummed side being partly sideways; we do not list this as a variety.

First Day Cover (NCom1/2) £450

NCom1b   NCom1c

Essays
Various designs by Harold Nelson .... From £3000
Essays were also submitted by Eric Gill, N. Rooke, J. D. Batten and E. W. Tristan.

Die Proofs
1924. Finished die proofs on wove proof paper
1d. in black £13500
1½d. in black £11500
1½d. in black endorsed "21 March 1924" £11500
1½d. in black endorsed "Mar 24/24" £11500
1½d. in brown £11500
1½d. in pale brown endorsed "21 March 1924" £12500
1½d. in deeper brown endorsed "24 March 1924" £12500
1924. On sunken card and signed "Harold Nelson 1924"
1d. and 1½d. together in issued colours with very large margins* £19500

Warning *Beware of signed cards showing issued stamps with the perforations trimmed off.

Progressive proofs of the 1½d. in black and also in the issued colour of both values exist in the J. A. C. Harrison collection at the British Library.

Coils
Vertical delivery made up from sheets with joins every tenth stamp

NH KING GEORGE V Commemorative Issues (1924–35) British Empire Exhibition, Postal Union Congress

Code No.	Value	Issued	Number in roll	Face value		
—	1d.	July 1924	1200	£5.0.0	Bottom delivery	—
—	1½d.	July 1924	1200	£7.10.0	Bottom delivery	—

The above are believed to exist with comb as well as line perforation.

1925 (9 May). **Type N17**. Dated. "1925". Comb Perf. 14

NCom3 (=S.G.432)

	Unmtd mint	Mtd mint	Used
1d. Scarlet	25·00	15·00	30·00
a. Coil join (vert. pair)			
s. "Specimen", Type 30		£1000	

NCom4 (=S.G.433)

	Unmtd mint	Mtd mint	Used
1½d. Brown	60·00	40·00	70·00
a. Coil join (vert. pair)		£150	
s. "Specimen", Type 30		£1000	

First Day Cover (NCom3/4) £1800

The Post Office registration sheet is in the Royal Philatelic Collection. One example with imperforate margins on card is from this sheet and currently in private hands.

Die Proofs
1925 Finished die proofs on wove proof paper.
1d. in red overprinted "Cancelled" (43 × 8.5mm.) £12000
1½d. in brown overprinted "Cancelled"
(43 × 8.5mm.) £12000

Die Proof from H. A. Richardson Archive
Stamp size in black on thin wove paper optd. "CANCELLED" in red (19.5×2.5mm)
1d. and 1½d. £9000

Coils
Vertical delivery made up from sheets with joins every tenth stamp

Code No.	Value	Issued	Number in roll	Face value		
—	1d.	1925	1200	£5.0.0	Bottom delivery	—
—	1½d.	1925	1200	£7.10.0	Bottom delivery	—

Withdrawn
The 1924 Exhibition closed on 1 November, but the special Exhibition post office continued to operate between the period of the two openings. During this time both stamps and stationery items dated 1924 were available. During the 1925 Exhibition sales of the 1924 issue were 1780 1d. and 1860 1½d.

The post office remained open after the official closure of the Exhibition on 31 October 1925 and finally closed on 19 December, when the stamps were withdrawn except for the 1925 1½d. which had sold out on 30 October 1925.

Quantities Sold
Coils 1924 1925
  1d. 191 rolls   1d. 161 rolls
  1½d. 58 rolls   1½d. 87 rolls

Sheets
The total printing order was for 17 million stamps. The quantities of stamps (not sets) sold at Wembley were; 1924 issue 13,214,491; 1925 issue 3,545,128.

N18 (Des. John Farleigh. Eng. C. G. Lewis at the Royal Mint)
N19 (Des. Ernest Linzell. Eng. J. A. C. Harrison at Waterlows) 
N20 (Des. John Farleigh. Eng. T. E. Storey at the Royal Mint) 

1929 (10 May). **Postal Union Congress**

A. Letterpress issues. Types N18, N19 (1d., 1½d.), N20
The intermediate-sized medal head as employed for the 5d. to 8d. definitive stamps, was used on 15 January 1929 by the Royal Mint to produce the heads employed for the low values.

Letterpress by Waterlow & Sons from plates made at the Royal Mint. The sheet layout and perforation is the same as for the concurrent letterpress set.

Perforation 15 × 14

NCom5 (=S.G.434)

	Unmtd mint	Mtd mint	Used
½d. Green	3·00	2·25	2·25
a. Watermark inverted	35·00	15·00	12·00
b. Watermark sideways	80·00	55·00	50·00
c. Varnish ink			
d. "CO" joined (Pl. 2, R. 13/9)			
s. Imperf. optd. "Specimen", Type 30		£2500	
t. "Cancelled", Type 33		£650	
u. "Cancelled", Type 33P		£240	

NCom6 (=S.G.435)

	Unmtd mint	Mtd mint	Used
1d. Scarlet	3·00	2·25	2·25
a. Watermark inverted	35·00	15·00	12·00
b. Watermark sideways	£140	95·00	90·00
c. Varnish ink		£4000	
d. Broken wreath at left (Pl. 4, R. 19/12)		£200	
e. "CO" joined (Pl. 2, R. 19/11)		£225	
f. "1829" for "1929" and closed loop on 2 (Pls. 1 or 4, R. 2/3)		£425	
g. Broken "O" in "POSTAL" (bklt. pane R. 2/2)		£500	
s. Imperf. optd. "Specimen", Type 30		£2500	
t. "Cancelled", Type 33		£650	
u. "Cancelled", Type 33P		£240	

NCom7 (=S.G.436)

	Unmtd mint	Mtd mint	Used
1½d. Purple-brown	3·00	2·25	1·75
a. Watermark inverted	15·00	5·00	6·00
b. Watermark sideways	90·00	60·00	55·00
c. "1829" for "1929" (R. 2/5)		£450	
d. "Q" for "O" in "UNION" (bklt. pane R. 2/1)		£500	
da. Ditto, watermark inverted		£500	
e. Blob on "1" of "1929" (Pl. 6, R. 16/1)		£550	
f. Blob on "ES" (sideways coil)		£475	
s. Imperf. optd. "Specimen", Type 30		£2500	
t. "Cancelled", Type 33		£500	
u. "Cancelled", Type 33P		£200	

NCom8 (=S.G.437)

(1)	2½d. Blue	28·00	10·00	10·00
(2)	Pale blue	60·00	35·00	12·00
a.	Watermark inverted			
	(Shade 1)	£3750	£2750	£1100
	(Shade 2)	£3750	£2750	£1100
s.	Imperf. optd. "Specimen", Type 30		£3750	
t.	"Specimen", Type 32		£3000	

First Day Cover (NCom5/8)	£675
Sheets of notepaper with London address of P.U.C. franked with NCom5/8 cancelled with official First Day postmark	£1500

The inverted watermarks on the ½d., 1d. and 1½d. values listed above come from booklets. Inverted watermarks from sheets command a substantial premium over the above prices but they need to have sheet margins attached or to be in a block or strip of larger size or different shape to prove that they were not from booklet panes of six (3 × 2).

The stamps with watermark sideways come from coils.

No. NCom6 is known used in Wolverhampton and Aberdeenshire on 1 May and in Scarborough on 3 May 1929. Nos. NCom5/7 are all known used in Bradford on 9 May 1929.

NCom5d

NCom6d

NCom6e

NCom6f(1d.)

NCom6g

NCom7c(1½d.)

No. NCom6f and NCom7c are best collected as positional pieces to avoid confusion with over-inked examples.

NCom7d(1½d.)

NCom7e(1½d.)

NCom7f

Variety NCom7d is on an upright watermark pane. Variety NCom7da is a very similar flaw in the same position on R. 2/1 of an inverted watermark pane.

Controls. Prices are for unused singles.

		Perf. Type
		2 (E)
½d.	K 29	10·00
	L 29	30·00
1d.	K 29	10·00
	L 29	30·00
1½d.	K 29	10·00
	L 29	30·00
2½d.	K 29	30·00
	L 29	55·00

Watermark varieties known:
Wmk inverted: ½d. K 29, L 29; 1d. K 29; 1½d. K 29, L 29; 2½d. K 29, L 29.

½d. Booklet Panes of Six

NComB1/a

Stanley Gibbons
Great Britain Department

BY APPOINTMENT TO
HER MAJESTY THE QUEEN
PHILATELISTS
STANLEY GIBBONS LTD
LONDON

Stanley Gibbons, a name synonymous with quality.

Ever since the birth of our hobby Stanley Gibbons has been at the forefront of GB philately and we invite collectors access to one of the finest GB stocks in the world by registering for our renowned free monthly brochure. Whatever your budget or collecting interests you will find a range of the highest quality material for the discerning collector.

To receive our monthly brochures or for further enquires please email gb@stanleygibbons.com or phone 020 7557 4424.

Est 1856
STANLEY GIBBONS

Proud PTS members

Stanley Gibbons
399 Strand, London, WC2R 0LX
+44 (0)20 7836 8444
www.stanleygibbons.com

From Booklets BB13 and BB25

A. Watermark upright
NComB1

	Perf Type	
	I	P
½d. (containing No. NCom5 × 6) (5.29)	£200	£200
p. With plate mark	£425	
t. "Cancelled", Type 33	£4250	
u. "Cancelled", Type 33P	£1600	

B. Watermark inverted
NComB1a

	Perf Type	
	I	P
½d. (containing No. NCom5a × 6) (5.29)	†	£225
at. "Cancelled", Type 33	£4250	
au. "Cancelled", Type 33P	£1600	

1d. Booklet Panes of Six

NComB2/a

From Booklets BB13 and BB25

A. Watermark upright

NComB2

	Perf. Type	
	I	P
1d. (containing No. NCom6 × 6) (5.29)	£200	£200
b. Broken "O" in "POSTAL" (R. 2/2 — see NCom 6g)	£625	
p. With plate mark	£425	
t. "Cancelled", Type 33	£4250	
u. "Cancelled", Type 33P	£1600	

B. Watermark inverted
NComB2a

	Perf. Type	
	I	P
1d. (containing No. NCom6a × 6) (5.29)	†	£225
at. "Cancelled", Type 33	£4250	
au. "Cancelled", Type 33P	£1600	

1½d. Booklet Panes of Six

NComB3/a

From Booklets BB13 and BB25

A. Watermark upright
NComB3

	Perf Type	
	I.	P.
1½d. (containing No. NCom7 × 6) (5.29)	75·00	60·00
b. "Q" for "O" in "UNION" (R. 2/1 — see N Com 7d.)	£650	
p. With plate mark	£225	
t. "Cancelled", Type 33	£3000	
u. "Cancelled", Type 33P	£1200	

B. Watermark inverted
NComB3a

	Perf. Type	
	I	P
1½d. (containing No. NCom7a × 6) (5.29)	†	80·00
ab. "Q" for "O" in "UNION" (R. 2/1— see NCom 7da.)	£650	
at. "Cancelled", Type 33	£3000	
au. "Cancelled", Type 33P	£1200	

KING GEORGE V — Commemorative Issues (1924–35) — Postal Union Congress

1½d. Booklet Panes with Advertising Labels

NComB4/a (various advertisements)

From Booklet BB13
Panes of six, comprising two labels printed in black and four stamps

A. Watermark upright
NComB4

	Perf. Type I	Perf. Type P
1½d. (containing No. NCom7 × 4) (5.29)	£375	£375
p. With plate mark	£700	
t. "Cancelled", Type 33	£2400	
u. "Cancelled", Type 33P	£1500	

B. Watermark inverted
NComB4a

	Perf. Type I	Perf. Type P
1½d. (containing NCom7a × 4) (5.29)	†	£375
at. "Cancelled", Type 33	£2400	
au. "Cancelled", Type 33P	£1500	

Pane Nos. NComB4 or NComB4a

	Wmk Upright	Wmk Inverted
(1) "Cash's washing Ribbons / J. & J. Cash Ltd."	£375	£375
(2) "Cleaver's Terebene / F. S. Cleaver & Sons Ltd."	£375	£375
(3) "Stamp Collectors / Desti Ltd."	£375	£375
(4) "Holiday trips £40 Tourist 3rd Cabin only [in three lines] / Atlantic Transport Line"	£375	£375
(5) "Telephone Service / Air Mails, Letters & Parcels"	£375	£375

Coils
Vertical delivery printed in continuous reels

Code No.	Denomination	Number in roll	Face value	Delivery direction	Rolls sold	
D	½d.	960	£2.0.0	Bottom	2,993	£900
G	½d.	480	£1.0.0	Top	11,811	£575
W	½d.	960	£2.0.0	Bottom	14,555	£475
Y	½d.	1920	£4.0.0	Bottom	7,628	£550
B	1d.	960	£4.0.0	Bottom	952	—
E	1d.	480	£2.0.0	Top	5,916	£900
X	1d.	960	£4.0.0	Bottom	15,373	£475
Z	1d.	1920	£8.0.0	Bottom	8,219	£550
K	1½d.	960	£6.0.0	Bottom	3,245	£900
L	1½d.	480	£3.0.0	Top	2,847	£900

Sideways to left delivery printed in continuous reels. Watermark sideways

P	½d.	480	£1.0.0	Left	43,458	£475
O	1d.	480	£2.0.0	Left	4,653	£600
N	1½d.	480	£3.0.0	Left	38,077	£500

All the coils were issued from 10 May 1929.

Coils W and X are more common but all are very scarce and coil B is unknown in private hands.

Die Proofs
Head only
In black, uncleared, on card dated "15.1.29" £10000

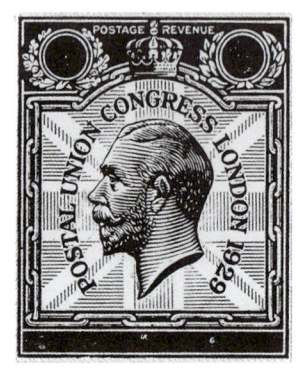

(a)

(b)

(c)
(Illustrations twice normal size)

Progressive stages of master die for Linzell's design for 1d. and 1½d. in black on proof paper
(a) Crown is black and unfinished. Frame surrounds incomplete £11000
(b) Left of Crown still uncompleted £10000
(c) Completed master die, dated "January 22 1929" £10000
(d) Completed master die in brown, undated £11000

Completed die proofs, cleared
1d. in black on proof paper £10000
1d. in red on wove paper, dated "4.2.29" £11000
1½d. in black on proof paper £10000
1½d. in pale brown on wove paper, dated "4.2.29" £11500

1½d. in brown on proof paper, undated..............£10500
1d. and 1½d. in red, *se-tenant* on single piece of
  proof paper £22000

Die Proofs from H. A. Richardson Archive
Stamp size in black orptd. "CANCELLED" in red (19.5×2.5mm)
a. Master die proof for 1d. and ½d £7000
b. ½d., 1d., 1½d. and 2½d. as issued.............Each £7000
c. ½d. with alternative crown above King's head................£8500
d. 2½d. with alternative frame and value (two
  designs) .... Each £8500

Plate Proofs
Specially prepared imperforate miniature sheet of four stamps on thin white glazed paper and mounted in sunken card frames for presentation purposes
½d. in green.. *Block of four* £20000
1d. in scarlet .... *Block of four* £20000
1½d. in purple-brown............................ *Block of four* £20000
2½d. in blue .... *Block of four* £20000

Imprimaturs from the National Postal Museum Archives
Nos. NCom5/8 imperforate, watermark Type **W15**
Watermark upright (set of 4) £20000
Nos. NCom5b/7b imperforate, watermark Type **W15**
Watermark sideways (set of 3) £20000
Booklet panes of six. Imperforate, watermark Type W15
Two panes as No. NComB1 arranged horizontally
  tête-bêche with marginal pillars at right £48000
As last but two panes as No. NComB2 ....£48000
As last but two panes as No. NComB3 ....£48000
Booklet pane of four with blank advertisement labels. Imperforate, watermark Type **W15**
Two panes as No. NComB4 arranged horizontally
  tête-bêche with marginal pillars at right £48000
1½d. Imprimatur from original registration sheet
  mounted on card £18000

Plate Markings and Control Schedule
See the General Notes on the King Edward VII issues under "Plate Markings".

Plate No.	Description	Controls	
½d. Green			
1	½ dot (base) under 1st	K 29	L 29
2	½ dot (base) under 2nd	K 29	L 29
3	½ dot (top) under 3rd	K 29	L 29
4	Dot 20th left side 7 mm.	K 29	L 29
5	Dot 19th left side 7 mm.	K 29	
6	Dot (inner) 19th left side 20 mm.	K 29	L 29
8	Large dot (breaking top) under 4th	K 29	L 29
1d. Scarlet			
1	Dot 1st left side; scoop 19th right side; dot 20th right side	K 29	L 29
2	Dot 2nd left side; minute dot 20th right side 10 mm.	K 29	L 29
3	Dot 3rd left side; vertical crack 19th left side	K 29	L 29
4	Dot 4th left side; tiny dot 2nd left side; dot 5th right side 21½ mm. (The rules 19th and 20th right side are thicker than those of plate 3)	K 29	L 29
1½d. Purple-brown			
1	Dot 1st left side	K 29	L 29
2	Dot 2nd left side; ½ cut top at right of 3rd	K 29	L 29
3	Dot 3rd left side; internal score 20th left side	K 29	L 29
4	Dot 4th left side; base of 3rd slightly ragged	K 29	L 29
5	Large dot above 1st top row; ½ cut (base) at right of 2nd	K 29	L 29
6	Large dot above 2nd top row	K 29	L 29
2½d. Blue			
1	½ dot (inner) 20th left side	K 29	L 29
2a	No marking	K 29	
2b	Added ½ dot (outer) 19th left side	K 29	L 29

It is not yet possible to correlate philatelic plate descriptions with the official plate numbers.

Quantities Sold ½d. 677,500,000; 1d. 341,000,000; 1½d. 751,250,000; 2½d. 26,750,000

N21
(Des. Harold Nelson. Eng. J. A. C. Harrison)

W18

B. 1929 (10 May). Recess-printed Issue. Type N21
Recess-printed by Bradbury, Wilkinson & Co. from a plate of their own manufacture in sheets of 20 (five rows of four). Watermark **W18**.

NCom9 (=S.G.438)

	Unmtd mint	Mtd mint	Used
£1 Black	£1100	£750	£550
s. "Specimen", Type 32 in red	£3500	£3000	

First day Cover (NCom9) £10000
First Day Cover (NCom5/9)...£14000
Sheets of notepaper with London address of
  P.U.C. franked with NCom5/9 cancelled
  with official First Day postmark..................................£14000

Most of the stamps in the sheet show traces of guide (hair) lines used when laying down the plate.
There were no sheet markings. The margins were perforated through the sheets containing 20 examples (4 × 5).
The contract for printing this stamp was given to Bradbury, Wilkinson on condition that it was engraved by J. A. C. Harrison, at that time contracted to Waterlow & Sons who gave special permission for him to do the work.

Essays
Artist's drawings by Harold Nelson............................. *From* £4250

Proof
From a specially prepared block of four stamps.
Imperf. in black on thin white card .... *Each stamp* £17500
Specially prepared imperforate miniature sheet
  of four stamps in black on thin white glazed
  paper and mounted in sunken card frame
  (125 × 110 mm. approx.) for presenting
  purposes. Overall size approx. 170 × 170 mm.
£1 in black... *Block of four* £70000
It is believed that three are in private hands.

NH KING GEORGE V — Commemorative Issues (1924–35) Silver Jubilee

Quantity Sold 66,788. This figure comes from a 1937 memo in the P.O. Archives, at which time the stamp was still on sale.

N22

N23

N24

N25
(Des. Barnett Freedman)

1935 *(7 May).* **Silver Jubilee. Types N22/25**

Printed in photogravure by Harrison & Sons in sheets of 120 stamps (20 rows of 6).

Three different multipositives were used for the ½d., 1d. and 1½d. Type I was used for sheet stamps. Types II (inverted watermark) and III (upright watermark) were used for booklet printings.

Differences between the types:—

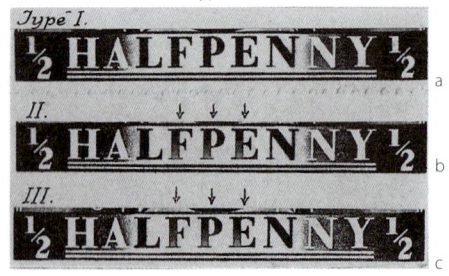

a. "FPE" with solid shading
b. "FPE" solid shading at top, lightly shaded at base
c. As Type II but frame lines below "HALFPENNY" thinner

a. Wide shading between "NN"
b. Narrow shading between "NN"
c. Wide shading between "NN", deeper shading in fleur-de-lis and surround than in Types I or II

g. Top frame lines thick
h. Top frame lines thin
i. As Type II but upper line thickened above "JU"

Perforation 15 × 14

NCom10 (=S.G.453)

	Unmtd mint	Mtd mint	Used
½d. Green (Type I)	1·00	1·00	1·00
a. Type II (inv. wmk.)	15·00	8·00	3·00
b. Type III	20·00	12·00	4·00
s. "Specimen", Type 23		£1400	
t. "Cancelled", Type 28P		£300	
u. "Cancelled", Type 33P		£300	
v. "Cancelled", Type 28			

NCom11 (=S.G.454)

	Unmtd mint	Mtd mint	Used
1d. Scarlet (Type I)	2·00	1·50	2·00
a. Type II (inv. wmk.)	15·00	8·00	4·00
b. Type III	15·00	8·00	4·00
c. Repair below "I" of "SILVER" (Cyl. 37, R. 2/2 cyl. Pane)		£175	
s. "Specimen", Type 23		£1400	
t. "Cancelled", Type 28P		£300	
u. "Cancelled", Type 33P		£300	
v. "Cancelled", Type 28			

NCom12 (=S.G.455)

	Unmtd mint	Mtd mint	Used
1½d. Red-brown (Type I)	1·25	1·00	1·00
a. Type II (inv. wmk.)	5·00	3·00	1·50
b. Type III	6·00	4·00	1·50
c. White dot after "E" (booklet pane R. 1/1)		£175	
s. "Specimen", Type 23		£1400	

Silver Jubilee Commemorative Issues (1924–35) **KING GEORGE V** NH

	Unmtd mint	Mtd mint	Used
t. "Cancelled", Type 28		£300	
u. "Cancelled", Type 28P			
v. "Cancelled", Type 33P		£300	

NCom13 (=S.G.456)

	Unmtd mint	Mtd mint	Used
2½d. Blue	8·00	5·00	6·50
a. Retouch to left panel and top of 2½ (Cyl. 34., R. 17/1)		60·00	
s. "Specimen", Type 23		£1750	

NCom14 (=S.G.456a)

	Unmtd mint	Mtd mint	Used
2½d. Prussian blue	£18500	£13500	£15000

First Day Cover* (NCom10/13) £650

*The price quoted is for the illustrated commemorative cover. Plain envelopes are worth much less than the figure quoted.

Being large format stamps, "Specimen" Type 23 and "Cancelled" Types 28 and 33 were applied twice to each stamp, whereas the P punch hole was applied once centrally.

For a long time it was thought that the 2½d. Prussian blue came from colour trials but it has now been proved that this could not be so as the issued stamps are in the normal size of 38·4 × 22 mm. whereas the colour trials were printed from a different cylinder producing stamps size 38·75 × 22·25 mm. Four of the sheets of No. NCom14, printed in the wrong shade, were issued in error by the Post Office Stores Department on 25 June 1935. It is known that three of the sheets were sold from the sub-office at 134 Fore Street, Upper Edmonton, London, between that date and 4 July.

Nos. NCom10/13 are known postmarked on 4 May 1935 at Wimbledon and NCom11 at the House of Commons on the same date.

Nos. NCom10/13 are also known postmarked on 6 May at Pembury, Tunbridge Wells, and Freshwater, Isle of Wight one day prior to the official first day of issue. No. NCom13 was also used 6 May at Theobalds Road, London W.C.1.

NCom11c (1d.)

NCom12c (1½d.)

NCom13a Normal

The panel has been considerably deepened and the retouch extends downwards at the top of the figures "2½"

Controls and Cylinder Numbers (Blocks of Six)
All the following are found only with control W 35.

Descriptions of the Perforation Types will be found in Appendix 1. Type 5A is Type 5(E/I) but with the extension hole missing from the left margin.

		Perf. Type				
		5(E/I)	5A(I/I)	5(E/I)	6(I/P)	6B(E/P)
Value	Cyl. No.	No dot	No dot	Dot	No dot	Dot
½d.	18	35·00	45·00	25·00	25·00	25·00
	20*	£850	†	†	†	†
	47	†	†	†	£150	£150
	55	35·00	35·00	25·00	50·00	35·00
	60	50·00	85·00	35·00	35·00	35·00
	61	60·00	85·00	60·00	60·00	75·00
	62	£150	£150	£150	†	†
1d.	14	30·00	40·00	30·00	30·00	30·00
	22	90·00	90·00	90·00	70·00	80·00
1½d.	2*	†	—	†	†	†
	7	30·00	£125	30·00	30·00	30·00
	21	50·00	50·00	40·00	30·00	30·00
	27	—	—	—	£200	£200
	48	25·00	50·00	50·00	30·00	50·00
2½d.	34	90·00	80·00	80·00	†	†

*Asterisks against cylinder numbers 2 and 20 indicate that they are "abnormals" (see under "printing" in the General Notes to Section NE).

The 1½d. cylinder 7 dot is known with Perforation Type 5(E/I) but with two extension holes in the left margin (2E/I).

Four controls of the 2½d. Prussian blue exist. Two with no dot cylinder from the normal position and two examples with dot cylinder. Both dot examples come from the *right* of the no dot pane, the sheets having been divided by hand leaving the full interpane margin attached to the left pane. One of these exists as a single and the other in a strip of three.

217

KING GEORGE V — Commemorative Issues (1924–35) Silver Jubilee

Booklet Panes of Four

NComB7/a

From Booklets BB16 2s. and BB28 3s.

A. Watermark upright
NComB5

½d. Type III (containing No. NCom10b × 4) (5.35)		50·00
s. "Cancelled", Type 33P		£1400
u. "Cancelled", Type 28		£1900

B. Watermark inverted
NComB5a

½d. Type II (containing No. NCom10a × 4) (5.35)		60·00
as. "Cancelled", Type 33P		£1400
at. "Cancelled", Type 28P		£1400
au. "Cancelled", Type 28		£1900

A. Watermark upright
NComB6

1d. Type III (containing No. NCom11b 3 4) (5.35)		45·00
s. "Cancelled", Type 33P		£1400
u. "Cancelled", Type 28		£1900

B. Watermark inverted
NComB6a

1d. Type II (containing No. NCom11a × 4) (5.35)		55·00
as. "Cancelled", Type 33P		£1400
at. "Cancelled", Type 28P		£1400

A. Watermark upright
NComB7

1½d. Type III (containing No. NCom12b × 4) (5.35)		18·00
b. White dot after E (R. 1/1 see NCom 12c)		£130
s. "Cancelled", Type 33P		£1300
u. "Cancelled", Type 28		£1600

B. Watermark inverted
NComB7a

1½d. Type II (containing No. NCom12a × 4) (5.35)		22·00
as. "Cancelled", Type 33P		£1300
at. "Cancelled", Type 28P		£1300
au. "Cancelled", Type 28		£1600

Previous references to panes "Cancelled" Type 33 were to panes contained in a complete 2s. booklet, which is listed as such in Appendix 2.

Booklet Cylinder Numbers
Panes of four
Perforation Type B4 (E)

Value	Cyl. No.	
½d.	33	£300
	35	£275
1d.	26	£3000
	37	£300*
1½d.	30	£160
	41	£160
	58	£350
	59	£160
	66	£140

These were printed from double pane cylinders but after the panes were separated the interpane gutter containing the dot cylinder number was removed, so that only no dot cylinder panes survive.

*Contains the listed variety No. NCom11c.

Essays

Artists' drawings in various designs............................. *From £4250*

A number of hand-painted essays by various artists were submitted.

Two designs by C. Hayden (Harrison & Sons) in vertical format were submitted on 12 October 1934. Hayden was an artist working for Harrison & Sons, one of three printers invited by the Post Office to submit designs that used the Mackennal head. "Harrison & Sons" script watermarked paper, imperf.

Card containing 1d. and 1½d. in sizes 24.5 × 30 mm and 28 × 33.5mm. inscribed "Messrs. Harrison & Sons Ltd. Oct. 1934". Imperforate in bright rose red

Imperforate, on card approx 75 × 45 mm.

As last but stamp size 24 × 29.5 mm.

1d., 1½d. in scarlet.	*Each* £6000
1d., 1½d. in pale brown	*Each* £6000

As last but stamp size larger, 27.5 × 33.5mm.

1d., 1½d. in scarlet	*Each* £6000
1d., 1½d. in pale brown	*Each* £6000

Three designs by Barnett Freedman were selected and Harrisons were asked to produce essays in photogravure of all and in different sizes for the first design. They were all submitted for the 1½d. value, each set in the colours that were accepted plus the Prussian blue colour on unwatermarked paper, imperforate and mounted on card. They were numbered 1, 2, 3 and 4. The King accepted No. 4 but rejected the Prussian blue colour.

No. 1

No. 2 in horizontal format

Vandyk head

First Design

(a) Design No. 1. As No. 1. Size 28 × 34 mm. Four examples on card 130 × 80 mm. Card containing 1½d. in yellow-green, scarlet, red-brown and Prussian blue £40000

(b) Design No. 1. As No. 1 but reduced to 25 × 30½ mm. Card 170 × 170 mm. Card containing 1½d. in yellow-green, scarlet, red-brown, Prussian blue and ultramarine £45000

(c) Design No. 1. As before size 28 × 34 mm. but with ultramarine added. Card containing 1½d. in yellow-green, scarlet, red-brown, Prussian blue and ultramarine £45000

Second Design

(d) Design No. 2 in horizontal format. Card 80 × 174 mm. Card containing 1½d. in yellow-green, scarlet, red-brown, Prussian blue and ultramarine £45000

Third Design

Design No. 3 (the accepted design with Mackennal head) Card containing 1½d. in yellow-green, scarlet, red-brown, Prussian blue and ultramarine £45000

Colour Trials

Special cylinders were used for the colour trials as they are larger than the issued stamps and show some slight differences in the shading.

19 November 1934. Proofs of the 1½d. value.

Inscribed "Proof received 19.11.34". Card containing 1½d. in yellow-green, red-brown, scarlet and Prussian blue £40000

Only the Prussian blue colour was pulled for the 2½d. at this time.

Undated card. Colour trials 28 November, 1934, of the accepted design size 39 × 22 mm. 1½d.

Two examples in brown, imperforate £22000

Do. but single example £11000

19 December 1934. 1½d. value. Imperforate with "Proof received 19.12.34" above design.

Card with the selected red-brown but size 39 × 22.5 mm. £11000

The size of the issued stamp was 38.4 × 22 mm.

31 December, 1934. 1½d. values (5). Imperforate with "Revised proof, furnished 31.12.34" above top stamp. Card containing 1½d. in red-brown and four shades of brown £45000

Additional inscription "Centre panel lightened round the oblong. Detail in wreath strengthened".

Plate Proofs

Imperforate, watermarked, each gummed on soft card about 4 in. × 3 in. and dated 15th or 18th January 1935 on the back in pencil

½d. in green size 39 × 22·5 mm. instead of 38·4 × 22 mm. ..

1d. in scarlet size as above ....

2½d. in Prussian blue size 38·75 × 22·25 mm. instead of 38·4 × 22 mm. ....

Imprimaturs from the National Postal Museum Archives

Nos. NCom10/13 imperforate, watermark Type W15

Watermark upright (set of 4) £22000

Booklet panes of four. Imperforate, watermark Type W15

Two panes as No. NComB5 arranged horizontally tête-bêche £48000

One pane as No. NComB5a (wmk. inverted) with interpane margins at sides £22000

Two panes as No. NComB6 arranged horizontally tête-bêche £48000

One pane as No. NComB6 (wmk. upright) with interpane margins at sides £22000

Two panes as No. NComB7 arranged horizontally tête-bêche £48000

One pane as No. NComB7 (wmk. upright) with interpane margins at sides £22000

Quantities Sold (including those in booklets)

½d. 353,400,000; 1d. 150,400,000; 1½d. 490,000,000; 2½d. 14,200,000

German Propaganda Forgeries

Stamps designed in the style of the 1935 Silver Jubilee exist showing Stalin in the centre and dated 1939–1944. Price £175 each unused or used.

KING GEORGE V MEMORIAL ESSAY

Block of Six with Endorsement
(Illustration reduced to ¾ actual size)

It was proposed to issue a stamp with a face value of 1½d. to be sold at 3d., the premium being devoted to King George's Jubilee Trust. After consideration the project was abandoned but a few of the essays exist. An example on a letter from King George's Jubilee Trust states that only eight of these stamps were proofed. We believe this to mean that only eight were stuck on letters.

From a plate of 6 (3 × 2) made by Harrison & Sons and proofed by Sir Donald Banks in black on gummed chalk-surfaced paper watermarked Type **W16**.

Imperforate
Single on correct letter endorsed in M/S "Donald Banks" etc. .... —
Single off letter endorsed "2 CB" £12500
Block of six, one endorsed "2 CB" £75000

Perf. 15 × 14
Single in dark grey on correct letter endorsed "2 C" in pencil on reverse £10000

Colour Trials
A series of 16 colour trial essays were also produced from the special plate of six (3×2). The blocks have been subsequently split, a block of four of each is held by the BPMA.

1st etching, on gummed watermarked Type **W16**
paper imperforate in blue-grey, dark blue-grey, dark grey or red-brown on ordinary paper .... Each £5000
Do. on chalk-surfaced (coated) paper .... Each £5000

2nd etching (deeper colours and more pronounced detailing) on gummed watermarked Type **W16** paper
Imperforate in blue-grey, dark blue-grey, dark grey or red-brown on ordinary paper .... Each £5000
Imperforate in blue-grey, dark blue-grey or red-brown on coated paper .... Each £5000
Perforated (15×14) in dark grey on coated paper £5000
Perforated (15×14) in dark grey with "d" added after "1½" £5000
Perforated (15×14) in dark grey with "d" added after "1½" and Rosemary border extended upwards to give the effect of a wreath £5000

Mourning essay

Mourning Essay

1½d. Photogravure issue (SG. 441) in black or violet (mourning colours) £18000
Originally printed from a special plate of six impressions, only two single examples of each are believed to exist in private hands.

The King Edward VIII Issue

Section P

INTRODUCTION. During the brief reign of King Edward VIII only the four most commonly used values were issued: ½d., 1d., 1½d. and 2½d. By contrast to previous definitive issues the design was kept extremely simple and was very suitable for reproduction by photogravure.

The stamps were watermarked Type **W19** and photogravure-printed by Harrison & Sons in sheets of 240 (12 × 20). They were perforated 15 × 14.

See also the information on photogravure printing in the General Notes on the King George V photogravure issues and the information on coil stamps in the General Notes on the King George V letterpress issues.

Withdrawal dates are given for the sheet stamps but the booklets and the coils were not recalled because of delays in introducing the King George VI stamps in booklet and coil formats. The King Edward VIII booklets remained on sale until December 1937 and the coils were recalled on 5 January 1938.

1936 *(May 10-12th)* **Accession Issue Essays.** (Small format)

The following essays are based on the King's portrait dressed in the uniform of the Seaforth Highlanders, photographed by Bertram Park they were printed "under running conditions" from Non-Chrome faced cylinders by Harrison & Sons.

Type A (1½d.)   **Type B** (4d.)

Design Type A (Imperforate on gummed "GvR" watermark, chalk coated paper)

a) 1½d.	red brown	£1500 *each*

Design Type A (Perf. 15x14 on gummed "GvR" watermarked, chalk coated paper)

a) 1½d.	in blue, red, brown, orange, green or blackish-olive	£1500 *each*
b) 1½d.	in purple doubly fugitive ink	£1750 *each*

Design Type B (Perf. 15x14 on gummed "GvR" watermarked, ordinary lightly coated paper)

1936 *(29 April)*

a) 4d. in red, brown, green or blackish-olive	£1500 *each*

1936 *(26 June)* **Definitive Issue Essays**

The following essays were based on H.J. Brown's suggestion that was forwarded by the Post Office to Harrison & Sons for further work, including incorporating the portrait of the King by Hugh Cecil. Unbeknown to the Post Office, Brown was an 18 year old student at Torquay Technical School.

Fig.1 H.J. Brown's Original Sketch dated 30th March 1936, submitted to the Post Office on 1st April 1936.

Fig. 2
Hand painted essay based on Brown's design.   *Price* £2500

KING EDWARD VIII *Essays* Definitive Issue Essays

Fig. 3

Bromide stamp size essays produced by Harrison & Sons based on the Brown design, the first with the hand painted portrait, the second with the Hugh Cecil photographic portrait.

Price from £375 each

Fig. 4

Bromide stamp size essays produced by Harrison & Sons using the hand painted portrait with alternative typographic designs.

Price from £375 each

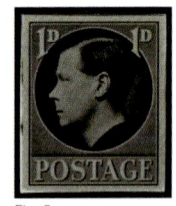

Fig. 5

Bromide stamp size essay based on a Bavarian stamp design produced by the Post Office following the King's request to consider some foreign stamp designs.

Design Type A (Value at foot "Postage" & "Revenue" at either side)

Design Type A (Perf. 15x14 on gummed "GvR" watermarked, ordinary coated paper)

½d. green	£2000
1d. red	£2000
1½d. brown	£2000
2½d. bright blue	£2000

Design Type B (Value at foot "Postage" & "Revenue" in panels at either side)

Design Type B (Perf. 15x14 on gummed "GvR" watermarked, ordinary coated paper)

½d. green	£2000
1d. red	£2000
1½d. brown	£2000
2½d. bright blue	£2000

Design Type C ("Postage" at foot, face value twice at top – No Crown Emblem)

Design Type C (Perf. 15x14 on gummed "GvR" watermarked, ordinary coated paper)

½d. green	£2000
1d. red	£2000
1½d. brown	£2000
2½d. bright blue	£2000

Design Type D (As issued stamp but on "GvR" block cypher watermarked paper.)

Design Type D (Perf. 15 x14 on gummed "GvR" watermarked, ordinary coated paper)

½d. green	£1750
1d. red	£1750
1½d . brown	£1750
2½d. bright blue	£1750

All of the above essays on "GvR" watermarked paper can be found with the watermark upright or inverted.

222

Coronation Essays *Essays* **KING EDWARD VIII**

Other Essays

Fig. 6

Unaccepted bromide essays produced by L.N. & M. Williams for 1d., 4d. and 10d. values. *From* £180 *each*

1936 *(July-Aug)* **Coronation Essays** (Large format 22 x 28 mm)

A series of five 1½d. essays were submitted by Harrison & Sons on the 7 September 1936 for consideration by the Post Office and the Fine Arts Commission, five incorporated the Henry Cecil portrait of the King in the uniform of the Welsh Guards, a sixth design (22 x 27mm) of the earlier accession essay incorporating the Bertram Park photograph of the King in the uniform of the Seaforth Highlanders.

Welsh Guards Uniform Designs

Type A Rectangular frame

Type B Double oval frame With curtain

Type C Oval wreath with emblems in all four corners

Type D Single oval frame with curtain

Type E Oval wreath with emblems in upper corners only

Seaforth Highlanders Uniform design

Type F POSTAGE only at foot.

1936 *(7 September)* **1½d. Large format** imperforate essays printed on gummed lightly coated paper, Watermarked "E8R" sideways.

Design Type A in green, red, brown or blue	£1750 *each*
Design Type B in green, red, brown or blue	£1750 *each*
Design Type C in green, red, brown or blue	£1750 *each*
Design Type D in green, red, brown or blue	£1750 *each*
Design Type E in green, red, brown or blue	£1750 *each*
Design Type F in green, red, brown or blue	£1750 *each*

Following feedback from the Post Office & Royal Fine Arts Commission further essays were produced by Harrison & Sons, these were supplied to the post Office and considered at a meeting on 23 September 1936.

Type G As Type B but With strengthened portrait

Type H Oval wreath with no emblems

Type I Double oval frame without curtain

KING EDWARD VIII Essays 1½d. Large format

Type J Seaforth design With typography from Type H

Type K Seaforth design with POSTAGE & face value unframed

Type L Oval wreath with Hugh Cecil portrait.

1936 *(23 September)* **1½d. Large format** imperforate essays printed on gummed lightly coated paper, Watermarked "E8R" sideways.

Design Type G in green, red, brown or blue	£1750 *each*
Design Type H in green, red, brown or blue	£1750 *each*
Design Type I in green, red, brown or blue	£1750 *each*
Design Type J in green, red, brown or blue	£1750 *each*
Design Type K in green, red, brown or blue	£1750 *each*
Design Type L in green, red, brown or blue	£1750 *each*

The Commission reported back to the Post Office on the 5th November, they felt the design should not feature the same Hugh Cecil portrait as the current definitives and suggested a crowned effigy be more appropriate. They were very critical of the typography and suggested that a professional typographer be called in to assist in this.

It is unclear what action the Post Office took as a direct result of the commission's findings; however it seems that many of the previous designs were subsequently abandoned at this point.

The Post Office had also received in September the artwork from Harrison & Sons for a design utilising the effigy head from the Royal Mint's official medals engraved by Humphrey Paget it is unknown if these had been shown to the commission but it became the emphasis for the next series of essays.

The Humphrey Paget Effigy

Type M Paget head design

Type N Paget Head in "Plaque" design

1936 *(23 Sept - 12 Oct)* **1½d. Large format** imperforate essays printed on gummed lightly coated paper, Watermarked "E8R" sideways.

Design type M in green, red, brown or blue	£1750 *each*
Design Type N in green, red, brown or blue	£1750 *each*

The Paget head essays were shown to the Postmaster General and the Director General who suggested that Mr. Eric Gill, a well known typographer and designer to review the designs and carry out modifications to the technical details.

Type O Modified plaque design with large head

Type P Modified plaque design with small head

Type Q Eric Gill design with large head

Type R Eric Gill design with small head

1936 *(Nov 12th)* **2½d. Large format** imperforate essays printed on gummed lightly coated paper, Watermarked "E8R" Upright.

Design Type O in green, red, brown or blue	£1750 *each*
Design Type P in green, red, brown or blue	£1750 *each*
Design Type Q in green, red, brown or blue	£1750 *each*
Design Type R in green, red, brown or blue	£1750 *each*

The Postmaster General reviewed these designs on 13 November, he decided to abandon the "Plaque" design but proceed with Eric Gill's, he requested Harrisons to produce some more essays with reduced shading on the King's head, these were delivered to the Post Office on 27th November.

2½d. Large format   Definitives   **KING EDWARD VIII**   P

Type S Gill's design with heads cut from Type Q with heavy shading

Type T Gill's design with toned background & medium shading

Type U Gill's design with uniform background & light shading

The Percy Metcalfe "Crowned" Effigy

Whilst this work was being conducted the Postmaster General approached the King to ask permission to use the Paget effigy, the King however further complicated matters by suggesting they use the "Crowned" effigy as produced by Percy Metcalfe for the forthcoming Coronation medal. Essays using the Metcalfe portrait were produced by Harrisons and also delivered on 27 November. All the latest essays were reviewed by the Postmaster General and Director General who agreed that the Fine Arts Commission should once again be consulted. They met on 30 November and were much more positive about these essays than those from September. They stated a preference for the Metcalfe effigy from the Coronation medal but made a few technical suggestions including, tilting the King's portrait backwards slightly and strengthening the "P" of "Postage". The modifications were made by Harrisons and delivered to the Post Office on 8 December, on 11 December 1936, King Edward VIII abdicated and the issue was abandoned.

Type V Metcalfe effigy with portrait upright

Type W Metcalfe effigy with portrait tilted backwards

1936 *(27th November)* **2½d. Large format** imperforate essays printed on gummed lightly coated paper, Watermarked "E8R" Upright.

Design Type S in green, red, brown or blue	£1750 *each*
Design Type T in green, red, brown or blue	£1750 *each*
Design Type U in green, red, brown or blue	£1750 *each*

1936 *(27 Nov – 8 Dec)* **2½d. Large format** imperforate essays printed on gummed lightly coated paper, Watermarked "E8R" Upright.

| Design Type V in green, red, brown or blue | £1750 *each* |
| Design Type W in green, red, brown or blue | £1750 *each* |

W19   P1

(Des. H. J. Brown after photograph by Hugh Cecil)

UNUSED PRICE QUOTATIONS
Unused prices quoted in this section are for mint unmounted examples.

1936 *(1 September).* **½d. Green, Type P1**

P1 (=S.G.457)

	Mint	Used
Green	30	30
a. Watermark inverted	10·00	5·00
b. Pearl beside Crown (Cyl. 7 Dot, 10 Dot or 12 Dot, R. 20/2)	35·00	10·00
c. White spot over T (Cyl. 25 Dot, R. 1/6)	40·00	
d. Double impression		
s. "Specimen", Type 30	£750	
t. "Cancelled", Type 33P	70·00	
u. "Cancelled", Type 33	£175	
v. "Specimen", Type 32		

No. P1 is known used at Knebworth, Herts, on 1 September 1936

225

P KING EDWARD VIII Definitives 1d. Scarlet, Type P1

Cyl. 7, 10 Dot P1b    Cyl. 12 Dot    P1c

Later states of No. P1b from re-chromed cylinders show the flaw very faintly

P2b

Controls and Cylinder Numbers (Blocks of Six)
Perforation Type 5 (E/I) on both dot and no dot cylinders

Cyl. No.	Control	No dot	Dot
2*	A 36	†	—
4	A 36	60·00	60·00
5	A 36	25·00	20·00
7	A 36	10·00	35·00*
10	A 36	10·00	35·00*
12	A 36	10·00	35·00*
13	A 36	10·00	10·00
15	A 36	15·00	15·00
16	A 36	10·00	10·00
21	A 36	—	†
21	A 37	40·00	40·00
22	A 37	10·00	10·00
24	A 37	35·00	35·00
25	A 37	35·00	20·00
26	A 37	10·00	10·00

Perforation Types 2 (no dot cylinder I/E) and 2A (dot cylinder P/P)

7	A 36	£400	£500*
10	A 36	£400	£500*

*Asterisks against cylinder numbers indicate that they are "abnormals" (see under "Printing" in the General Notes to Section NE). Asterisks against prices for cylinder blocks indicate that they contain a listed variety.

A36 21 no dot is known only on single stamps.

Coils
Vertical delivery printed in continuous reels

Code No.	Issued	Number in roll	Face value	
D	1937	960	£2.0.0 Bottom delivery	£175
G	1937	480	£1.0.0 Bottom delivery	£175
W	1937	960	£2.0.0 Bottom delivery	£100
Y	1937	1920	£4.0.0 Bottom delivery	£125

Imprimaturs from the National Postal Museum Archives
Imperforate, watermark Type **W19**

Watermark upright pair £5500
Watermark inverted pair £5500
Tête-bêche pair £13500
Tête-bêche pair with vertical gutter margin £13500
Quantity Sold 1,752,128,324
Withdrawn 29.7.37

1936 (14 September). **1d. Scarlet, Type P1**

P2 (=S.G.458)

	Mint	Used
Scarlet	60	50
a. Watermark inverted	9·00	5·00
b. Scar on cheek (Cyl. 3 No dot, R. 13/7)	75·00	
s. "Specimen", Type 30	£750	
t. "Specimen", Type 32		
u. "Cancelled", Type 33P	70·00	
v. "Cancelled", Type 33	£175	

No. P2 is known used at Knebworth, Herts, on 1 September and at Cricklewood, NW2, on 11 September 1936.

Controls and Cylinder Numbers (Blocks of Six)
Perforation Type 5 (E/I) on both dot and no dot cylinders

Cyl. No.	Control	No dot	Dot
2	A 36	10·00	10·00
3	A 36	15·00	10·00
4	A 36	10·00	10·00
5	A 36	50·00	50·00
6	A 36	10·00	10·00
13	A 37	40·00	15·00
14	A 37	£125	£125

Perforation Types 2 (no dot cylinder I/E) and 2A (dot cylinder P/P)

3	A 36	†	£1000
4	A 36	—	†
5	A 36	†	£500
6	A 36	£850	£850
7*	A 36	—	—

Two examples of cylinder 7 no dot are known.

Coils
Vertical delivery printed in continuous reels

Code No.	Issued	Number in roll	Face value	
B	1937	960	£4.0.0 Bottom delivery	£225
E	1937	480	£2.0.0 Bottom delivery	£175
X	1937	960	£4.0.0 Bottom delivery	£100
Z	1937	1920	£8.0.0 Bottom delivery	£125

Imprimaturs from the National Postal Museum Archives
Imperforate, watermark Type **W19**

Watermark upright pair £5000
Watermark inverted pair £5000
Tête-bêche pair £12000
Tête-bêche pair with vertical gutter margin £12000

Imprimaturs from the British Postal Museum & Archive
Tête-bêche pair £7000
Block of Six, Control A36, Cylinder 2 dot £10000
Quantity Sold 702,908,324
Withdrawn 29.7.37

1936 (1 September). **1½d. Red-brown, Type P1**

P3 (=S.G.459)

	Mint	Used
Red-brown	30	30
a. Watermark inverted	1·00	1·00
b. Hair flaw (Cyl. 2 No dot, R. 18/1)	75·00	
c. Ditto, retouched	50·00	
d. Imperforate (pair)†	£30000	
s. "Specimen", Type 30	£750	
t. "Cancelled", Type 33P	50·00	
u. "Cancelled", Type 33	£100	
v. "Specimen", Type 32		

† Imperforate imprimaturs as No.P3d, also exist from NPM archive sales.

No. **P3** is known used at Knebworth, Herts, on 1 September 1936

2½d. Bright blue, Type P1 *Definitives* **KING EDWARD VIII** **P**

P3b   P3c   P4a

The 1½d. in the issued colour imperforate on gummed paper with the word "PROOF" instead of "POSTAGE" is regarded as a bogus item.

Controls and Cylinder Numbers (Blocks of Six)
Perforation Type 5 (E/I) on both dot and no dot cylinders

Cyl No.	Control	No dot	Dot
2	A 36	80·00*	8·00
4	A 36	10·00	10·00
6	A 36	10·00	10·00
8	A 36	10·00	10·00
9	A 36	10·00	10·00
12	A 36	10·00	10·00
12	A 37	£100	£100
13	A 36	15·00	15·00
13	A 37	10·00	10·00
15	A 36	£175	£175
15	A 37	10·00	10·00
16	A 36	10·00	10·00
16	A 37	30·00	30·00
17	A 37	20·00	20·00
18*	A 37	—	†
20	A 37	15·00	15·00

Perforation Types 2 (no dot cylinder I/E) and 2A (dot cylinder P/P)

2	A 36	—*	£1000
4	A 36	£1000	£850
8	A 36	†	£400
9	A 36	—	†
12	A 36	£400	£400

Perforation Types 6 (no dot cylinder I/P) and 6B (dot cylinder (E/P).

4	A 36	†	—
15	A 37	—	£1000
20	A 37	20·00	20·00

Cylinder 12 dot (A 36) is known with Perforation Type 2 (I/E) (reverse feed).
A single example of cylinder 18 no dot is known.

Imprimaturs from the National Postal Museum Archives
Imperforate, watermark Type **W19**
Watermark upright pair £5500
Watermark inverted pair £5500
Tête-bêche pair £13500
Tête-bêche pair with vertical gutter margin £13500
Tête-bêche pair with wide vertical gutter margin £13500

Imprimaturs from the British Postal Museum & Archive
Tête-bêche pair £7000
Block of six, Control A36, Cylinder 2 dot £10000
Quantity Sold 1,813,067,592
Withdrawn 29.7.37

1936 *(1 September).* **2½d. Bright blue, Type P1**

P4 (=S.G.460)

	Mint	Used
Bright blue	30	85
a. Flaw in ear (Cyl. 2 Dot, R. 13/12)	50·00	
b. Coil join (vert. pair) (1937)		
c. Coil join (horiz. pair) (1937)		
s. "Specimen", Type 30	£800	
t. "Cancelled", Type 33		

No. **P1** is known used at Knebworth, Herts, on 1 September 1936

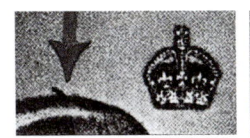

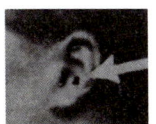

Controls and Cylinder Numbers (Blocks of Six)
Perforation Type 5 (E/I) on both dot and no dot cylinders

Cyl. No.	Control	No dot	Dot
2	A 36	20·00	20·00
2	A 36 bar—	20·00	20·00

Cylinder 2 no dot is known without control number.

Coils
Vertical delivery made up from sheets with joins every 20th stamp

Code No.	Issued	Number in roll	Face value
F	1937	960	£10.0.0 Bottom delivery £1500

Sideways delivery made up from sheets with joins every 12th stamp

| M | 1937 | 480 | £5.0.0 Left side delivery £1500 |

Imprimatur from the National Postal Museum Archives
Imperforate, watermark **W19**
Watermark upright pair £6000

Imprimatur from the British Postal Museum & Archive
Block of six, Control A36, Cylinder 2 dot £10000
Quantity Sold 31,834,800
Withdrawn 29.7.37

First Day Covers
On plain covers with operational postmarks of the first day of issue. For some values special covers also exist and these are worth more than the prices quoted.
KFD 1 (1.9.36) ½d., 1½d., 2½d. (Nos. P1, P3, P4) £150
KFD 2 (14.9.36) 1d. (No. P2) £180

Section PB

Booklet Panes in Photogravure (1936)

CHECKLIST OF KING EDWARD VIII BOOKLET PANES

Spec. Cat. Nos.	Description	From Booklet Nos.	Page
PB1, PB1a	6 × ½d.	BC2–4	228
PB2, PB2a	6 × 1d.	BC2–4	228
PB3, PB3a	6 × 1½d.	BC2–4	228
PB4, PB4a	2 × 1½d.	BC1	229
PB5, PB5a	4 × 1½d. and two printed labels	BC2, BC4	229

BOOKLET PANE PRICES. Prices quoted are for unmounted examples with good perforations all round and with binding margin attached. Panes with some degree of trimming are worth less than the published prices in this Catalogue.

½d. Booklet Panes of Six

PB1/a

6 × ½d. Watermark Block Cypher Type **W19**
From Booklets BC2/4

		Perf Type	
A. Watermark upright	E	P	I
PB1 (containing No. P1 × 6) (10.36)	40·00	30·00	40·00
s. "Cancelled", Type 33P	£425		
u. "Cancelled", Type 33	£1100		

		Perf Type	
B. Watermark inverted			
PB1a (containing No. P1a × 6) (10.36)	60·00	45·00	60·00
as. "Cancelled", Type 33P	£425		
au. "Cancelled", Type 33	£1100		

Booklet Cylinder Numbers
Panes of six

	B3(I)	B3A(P)	B4(E)	B4A(I)	B4B(E)
Cyl. No.	No dot	Dot	No dot	Dot	Dot
E 2	—	£850	75·00	75·00	95·00
E 4	†	†	95·00	95·00	†

Imprimatur from the British Postal Museum & Archive
Two panes as PB1/1a *tête-bêche*, Cylinder E4 dot at left £30000

1d. Booklet Panes of Six
6 × 1d. Watermark Block Cypher Type **W19**
From Booklets BC2/4

		Perf Type	
A. Watermark upright	E	P	I
PB2 (containing No. P2 × 6) (10.36)	35·00	25·00	35·00
s. "Cancelled", Type 33P	£425		
u. "Cancelled", Type 33	£1100		

		Perf Type	
B. Watermark inverted			
PB2a (containing No. P2a × 6) (10.36)	50·00	40·00	50·00
as. "Cancelled", Type 33P	£425		
au. "Cancelled", Type 33	£1100		

Booklet Cylinder Numbers
Panes of six

	B3(I)	B3A(P)	B4(E)	B4A(I)	B4B(E)
Cyl. No.	No dot	Dot	No dot	Dot	Dot
F 3	£125	£250	£100	£100	£120
F 6*	†	†	†	—	†

*Asterisks against cylinder numbers indicate that they are "abnormals" (see under "Printing" in the General Notes to Section NE).

Imprimatur from the British Postal Museum & Archive
Two panes as PB2/2a *tête-bêche*, Cylinder F3 dot at left £30000

1½d. Booklet Panes of Six
6 × 1½d. Watermark Block Cypher Type **W19**
From Booklets BC2/4

		Perf Type	
A. Watermark upright	E	P	I
PB3 (containing No. P3 × 6) (10.36)	20·00	15·00	20·00
s. "Cancelled", Type 33P	£300		
u. "Cancelled", Type 33	£650		

		Perf Type	
B. Watermark inverted			
PB3a (containing No. P3a × 6) (10.36)	20·00	15·00	20·00
as. "Cancelled", Type 33P	£300		
au. "Cancelled", Type 33	£650		
av. "Specimen", Type 32 and upper left stamp with punch hole	£1500		

No PB3av comes from the National Postal Museum Archive sales

Imprimatur from the British Postal Museum & Archive
Two panes as PB3/3a *tête-bêche*, Cylinder E5 dot at left £30000

Booklet Panes in Photogravure **KING EDWARD VIII** **PB**

1½d. Booklet Panes of Two
2 × 1½d. Watermark Block Cypher Type **W19**
From Booklet BC1

	Perf Type
	P
A. Watermark upright	
PB4 (containing No. P3 × 2) (1/37)	30·00
B. Watermark inverted	
PB4a (containing No. P3a × 2) (1/37)	30·00

Booklet panes of two were produced by using panes PB5/5a with blank labels (prior to printing the advertisements). Half booklet sheets were trimmed at left and right through the blank labels adjacent to the stamps thus creating a binding margin. This resulted in all the selvedges being perforated and removal of the G7 cylinder numbers.

1½d. Booklet Panes with Advertising Labels

PB5/a (2 advert labels) (imperf. margin and cyl. No. G 7 dot)

Panes of six comprising two labels printed in black and four stamps

From Booklets BC2 and BC4

	Perf Type		
	E	P	I
A. Watermark upright			
PB5 (containing No. P3 × 4) (10.36)	£120	£100	£120
s. "Cancelled", Type 33P	£225		
t. "Cancelled", Type 33	£650		
B. Watermark inverted			
PB5a (containing No. P3a × 4) (10.36)	£120	£100	£120
as. "Cancelled", Type 33P	£225		
at. "Cancelled", Type 33	£650		

Pane Nos. PB5 or PB5a		Wmk Upright	Wmk Inverted
(1)	"Cash's "Lose Less Linen" book / Free Booklet. J. & J. Cash" (numbered 364)	£185	£185
(2)	"Cash's names for marking all linen / Free booklet. J. & J. Cash" (numbered 372)	£185	£185
(3)	"Cash's satin lingerie ribbons / Samples [in text] of Cash's ribbons. "Attach this to a". J. & J. Cash" (numbered 357 or 379)	£150	£150
(4)	"Number One Bond / Castell Bros." (Edition 368)	£200	£200
(5)	"Ruskin Linen / Castell Bros." (Edition 374)	£200	£200
(6)	"Kargo. 2/6 per pack. / Castell Bros." (Edition 355)	£175	£175
(7)	"Drages 50 pay-way / Free book. Drages" (Editions 17, 367, 373, 378, 380, 381, 382 or 384)	£100	£100
(8)	"Everitt's / Everitt's" (Edition 371)	£200	£200
(9)	"For Safety of Capital / Century Fixed Trust (see last page)" (Edition 359)	£125	£125
(10)	"For Safety of Capital / Universal Fixed Trust (see last page)" (Editions 356 or 358)	£110	£110
(11)	"Spread your Capital / Century Fixed Trust" [text on both panes diagonal] (Editions 361 or 363)	£125	£125
(12)	"Spread your Capital / Universal Fixed Trust" [text on both labels diagonal] (Editions 360 or 362)	£125	£125
(13)	"Stamp Collectors / Chas. Nissen" (Edition 354)	£150	£150
(14)	"Saving is Simple / Home Safe" (Editions 365, 369, 375 or 383)	£200	£200
(15)	"Come on the telephone / Air Mails, letters and parcels" (Editions 16, 366, 376 or 385)	£100	£100
(16)	"Your friends are on the telephone / Air Mails, letters and parcels" (Editions 370 or 377)	£125	£125

Edition Nos. The numbers printed in brackets for (4) to (16) refer to the edition numbers of the booklets in which the panes were issued (16 and 17 being 5s. booklets, all others being 2s. booklets). Only pane Nos. PB5(1), (2) and (3) were actually printed with numbers on the advertising label. See Appendix 2.

Booklet Cylinder Numbers
Panes of six

	Perf. Type				
	B3(I)	B3A(P)	B4(E)	B4A(I)	B4B(E)
Cyl. No.	No dot	Dot	No dot	Dot	Dot
G 4	£1500	—	85·00	95·00	£1000
G 5 (i)	—	85·00	40·00	40·00	50·00
G 5 (ii)	£250	†	85·00	†	†

State (ii) of G 5 shows two faint horizontal lines in the margin at left of stamp No 1.

Panes of six including two labels

		Perf. Type		
		B4(E)	B4A(I)	B4B(E)
Cyl.No.	Advert No.	No dot	Dot	Dot
G 7	PB5(1)	£225	£225	†
G 7	PB5(2)	£225	£225	†
G 7	PB5(3) (No. 357)	£200	£200	†
G 7	PB5(3) (No. 379)	£225	£225	†
G 7	PB5(4)	£225	£225	†
G 7	PB5(5)	£225	£225	£350
G 7	PB5(6)	£225	£225	†
G 7	PB5(7)	£150	£150	£200
G 7	PB5(8)	£225	£225	†
G 7	PB5(9)	£200	£200	†
G 7	PB5(10)	£150	£150	†
G 7	PB5(11)	£150	£150	†
G 7	PB5(12)	£175	£175	†
G 7	PB5(13)	£225	£225	†
G 7	PB5(14)	£135	£135	£135
G 7	PB5(15)	£135	£135	£135
G 7	PB5(16)	£150	£150	£150

Specimen overprints from the British Postal Museum & Archive
Booklet pane of six. Perf. 15 × 14, watermark Type W19 (inverted)
"Specimen", Type 32 and upper left stamp with punch hole

King George VI issues

Section Q
General Notes on the Photogravure Low Values (1937–51)

Introduction. The abdication, on 10 December 1936, placed the Post Office in a difficult position as the date fixed for the Coronation of King George VI on 12 May 1937, was the date originally chosen for his predecessor. The Post Office had been told by the King that the new stamps "should follow generally the design of the recent Edwardian issue, but that he desires that they should be somewhat more ornamental". Several artists were invited to submit designs in January 1937, but on 13 February the drawing of the King's head by Edmund Dulac was shown to the Director General of the Post Office. Essays were submitted to the King on 26 February and the final choice was Eric Gill's "four emblems" design used in conjunction with Dulac's portrait. The original plan was to issue the ½d., 1d., 1½d. and 2½d. values by Coronation Day. These values were issued on 10 May, but the 1½d. value was held back until it replaced the Coronation stamp of the same value on 30 July.

The 2d. and 3d. values followed on 31 January 1938. A new problem arose when Harrison & Son found that the deep etching and additional ink required was wearing the cylinders too quickly. Solid colour rules in the bottom sheet margins were introduced to offset this. Pale backgrounds were approved for the next three values, 4d., 5d. and 6d. The unified series was completed by the third group of 7d. to 1s. values. The Dulac head on a hexagonal background was chosen for this group and final colour essays were approved on 12 September 1938 for 9d., 10d. and 1s., followed on 9 January 1939 by 7d. and 8d. Although approved earlier, the 9d., 10d. and 1s. were not issued until 1 May 1939 and the 11d. was added on 29 December 1947.

The ½d. to 3d. were issued in pale colours between 1941 and 1942 as a wartime economy measure designed to save both wear on the cylinders, for these values were those most in demand, and printing ink. By 1951 the ½d. to 2½d. and 4d. were issued in changed colours in accordance with the colour regulations of the Universal Postal Union for stamps with international use. The ½d. to 2½d. were issued to coincide with the opening of the Festival of Britain on 3 May 1951. An increase in the postage rate was made the following year on 1 May 1952 (see Appendix 6).

German Propaganda Forgeries
Propaganda forgeries of the low value ½d. to 3d. stamps in deep colours and 1937 1½d. Coronation were produced by the German authorities during the Second World War. They are of considerable interest to specialists. Printed in lithography on wavy-line watermarked paper they are easily recognised by the large gauge 11 perforation. Various design changes were made to include the Russian hammer and sickle and the "Star of David".

Printer, sheet layout and markings. All low values were printed in photogravure by Harrison & Sons in sheets of 240 (20 horizontal rows of 12). They were printed in double-pane width (no dot and dot) but were guillotined apart before being supplied to the Post Office. Further information on small lines and crosses used as guide marks are given in the General Notes, Section NE.

Watermark and perforations. All stamps in this Section are watermarked Block "GvIR" (Type **W20**) and perforated 15 × 14. See Section NE, General Notes for a list of the abbreviations following the perforator types. To that list add Perforator 3 (P/E) and 3A (I/P) and also the alternate extension variety known as Perf. 5AE (AE/I).

A broken dandy roll variety is recorded below Nos. Q5A and Q7.

Controls. Following the introduction of control numbers on later ½d. and 1d. Victorian issues, their use had been extended by 1913 to all values up to 1s. After 1947 however, these controls were no longer needed as the cylinder number fulfilled the same function.

Cylinder blocks containing varieties. These are indicated by asterisks against the prices.

Coil stamps. See the notes on these in the General Notes on the King George V letterpress issues, which also apply here. Note that, while we list coil joins where they exist, we do not price them due to the ease with which they can be faked.

CHECKLIST OF KING GEORGE VI ISSUES

Description	Spec. Cat. Nos.	S.G. Nos.	Page
1937–47 Photogravure Definitives, Original Colours			
½d. green	Q1	462	231
1d. scarlet	Q4	463	234
1½d. red-brown	Q7	464	238
2d. orange	Q10	465	240
2½d. ultramarine	Q13	466	242
3d. violet	Q16	467	245
4d. grey-green	Q19	468	247
5d.	Q21	469	248
6d.	Q22	470	248
7d.	Q23	471	249
8d.	Q24	472	249
9d.	Q25	473	250
10d.	Q26	474	250
11d.	Q27	474a	251
1s.	Q28	475	251
1937 Coronation of King George VI			
1½d.	QCom1	461	268
1939–48 Recess-Printed "Arms" High Values			
2s.6d. brown	Q29	476	263
2s.6d. yellow-green	Q30	476a	264
5s.	Q31	477	264
10s. dark blue	Q32	478	265
10s. ultramarine	Q33	478a	265
£1	Q34	478b	266
1940 Centenary of First Adhesive Postage Stamps			
½d.	QCom2	479	269
1d.	QCom3	480	269
1½d.	QCom4	481	269
2d.	QCom5	482	269
2½d.	QCom6	483	269
3d.	QCom7	484	269
1941–42 Photogravure Definitives, Lighter Colours			
½d. pale green	Q2	485	232
1d. pale scarlet	Q5	486	235
1½d. pale red-brown	Q8	487	239
2d. pale orange	Q11	488	241
2½d. light ultramarine	Q14	489	243
3d. pale violet	Q17	490	246
1946 Victory			
2½d.	QCom8	491	270
3d.	QCom9	492	270
1948 Silver Wedding			
2½d.	QCom10	493	271
£1	QCom11	494	271
1948 Channel Islands Liberation			
1d.	QCom12	C1	271
2½d.	QCom13	C2	271

½d. Green *Photogravure Low Values* **KING GEORGE VI** **QA**

Description	Spec. Cat. Nos.	S.G. Nos.	Page
1948 Olympics			
2½d.	QCom14	495	272
3d.	QCom15	496	272
6d.	QCom16	497	272
1s.	QCom17	498	272
1949 Universal Postal Union			
2½d.	QCom18	499	273
3d.	QCom19	500	273
6d.	QCom20	501	273
1s.	QCom21	502	273
1950–51 Photogravure Definitives, New Colours			
½d. pale orange	Q3	503	233
1d. light ultramarine	Q6	504	237
1½d. pale green	Q9	505	240
2d. pale red-brown	Q12	506	241
2½d. pale scarlet	Q15	507	245
4d. light ultramarine	Q20	508	247
1951 Recess-Printed "Festival" High Values			
2s.6d.	Q35	509	267
5s.	Q36	510	267
10s.	Q37	511	267
£1	Q38	512	267
1951 Festival of Britain			
2½d.	QCom22	513	274
4d.	QCom23	514	274

W20 **Q1** **Q2**

(Des. Edmund Dulac (head) and Eric Gill (frames))

Q3
(Des. Edmund Dulac)

UNUSED PRICE QUOTATIONS
Unused prices quoted in this Section are for mint unmounted examples.

½d. Type Q1

1937 (10 May). ½d. **Green**

Q1 (=S.G.462)

	Mint	Used
Green	30	25
a. Watermark inverted (8.37)	10·00	60
b. Watermark sideways (1.38)	75	60
c. Broken circle to value (Cyl. 18 No dot, R. 19/2)	75·00	
d. Spur to 2 of ½ (Cyl. 2 Dot, R. 20/6)	85·00	
s. "Cancelled", Type 33	£140	
t. "Cancelled", Type 33P	45·00	
u. "Specimen", Type 32		

No. Q1 is known used at Tonbridge Wells on 1 May 1937.

Q1c

Q1d

No. Q1d usually shows the cylinder wear along the bottom of the stamp.

Controls and Cylinder Numbers (Blocks of Six)
Without marginal rule. Perforation Type 5 (E/I)

Cyl. No.	Control	No dot	Dot
2	A 37	7·00	7·00
2	B 37	35·00	35·00
3	A 37	7·00	7·00
4	A 37	7·00	7·00
6	A 37	7·00	7·00
8	A 37	7·00	7·00
8	B 37	50·00	50·00
10	A 37	7·00	7·00
11	A 37	50·00	50·00
12	A 37	20·00	20·00
12	B 37	7·00	10·00

Perforation Type 2A (P/P)

Cyl. No.	Control	No dot	Dot
6	A 37	†	£225

Perforation Type 6 (no dot I/P) and 6B (dot E/P)

Cyl. No.	Control	No dot	Dot
2	A 37	5·00	5·00

With marginal rule. Perforation 5 (E/I)

Cyl. No.	Control	No dot	Dot
2	B 37	20·00	8·00
12	B 37	10·00	10·00
16	B 37	7·00	7·00
17	B 37	7·00	7·00
18	B 37	90·00*	7·00
19	B 37	30·00	20·00
20	B 37	£250	£250
22	B 37	7·00	7·00
24	B 37	25·00	25·00
25	B 37	7·00	7·00
31	B 37	7·00	7·00
32	B 37	30·00	8·00
35	C 38	10·00	10·00
37	C 38	15·00	15·00

QA KING GEORGE VI Photogravure Low Values ½d. Pale Green

Cyl. No.	Control	No dot	Dot
40	C 38	7·00	7·00
42	C 38	50·00	50·00
43 (i)	C 38	8·00	8·00
43 (ii)	C 38	20·00	25·00
52	C 38	10·00	8·00
53	C 38	10·00	8·00
55	C 38	7·00	7·00
56	C 38	15·00	15·00
58	C 38	50·00	50·00
58	D 38	7·00	7·00
59	C 38	8·00	8·00
61	C 38	30·00	30·00
64	D 38	7·00	7·00
67	D 38	20·00	7·00
68	D 38	7·00	7·00
68	E 39	75·00	75·00
69	D 38	7·00	10·00
70	D 38	7·00	10·00
72 (i)	D 38	80·00	80·00
72 (ii)	D 38	10·00	10·00
73	D 38	7·00	7·00
74	D 38	15·00	15·00
76	D 38	20·00	50·00
76	E 39	7·00	10·00
77	E 39	7·00	7·00
78	E 39	7·00	7·00
81	D 38	7·00	7·00
81	E 39	10·00	25·00
82	D 38	10·00	10·00
90	E 39	10·00	10·00
90	F 39	25·00	40·00
93	E 39	70·00	70·00
95	E 39	7·00	7·00
98	E 39	7·00	7·00
99	E 39	7·00	7·00
100	E 39	7·00	7·00
100	F 39	£100	£100
101	E 39	50·00	50·00
101	F 39	7·00	10·00
104	F 39	7·00	7·00
105 (i)	F 39	25·00	25·00
105 (ii)	F 39	†	£125
105 (iii)	F 39	£100	£150
106 (i)	F 39	10·00	10·00
106 (ii)	F 39	30·00	30·00
108	F 39	15·00	15·00
110	F 39	40·00	40·00
113	F 39	10·00	10·00
119	G 40	12·00	12·00
120	G 40	10·00	10·00
120	I 41	10·00	10·00

Perforation Type 6 (no dot I/P) and 6B (dot E/P)

Cyl. No.	Control	No dot	Dot
58	D 38	40·00	40·00
67	D 38	20·00	20·00
68	D 38	60·00	60·00
69	D 38	40·00	25·00
70	D 38	75·00	75·00
72 (i)	D 38	£100	£100
72 (ii)	D 38	20·00	50·00
73	D 38	60·00	60·00
74	D 38	30·00	40·00
76	D 38	10·00	10·00
76	E 39	25·00	35·00
81	E 39	30·00	50·00
82	D 38	10·00	10·00
101	F 39	£125	£125

Varieties:
Cylinder 3 dot exists in five states:
State (i) With no cutting line
State (ii) With cutting line engraved too close to the stamp
State (iii) With additional cutting line in correct place below
State (iv) With upper cutting line breaking up (various stages)
State (v) With upper cutting line removed

Cylinder 43 exists in two states:
State (i) both dot and no dot panes show "43" engraved over "23", the "2" showing clearly
State (ii) retouch on both panes, the "2" no longer visible. The base of figure "38" of control has been retouched

Cylinder 72 exists in two states:
State (i) both dot and no dot panes show a very weak control
State (ii) both controls retouched

Cylinder 98 no dot and dot exist in two states:
State (i) Numbers badly cut
State (ii) Numbers recut wider and wider apart

Cylinder 105 no dot exists in two states:
State (i) Pale control
State (iii) Control strongly retouched

Cylinder 105 dot exists in three states:
State (i) Without retouch
State (ii) "3" of control lightly retouched at base
State (iii) Control completely retouched

Cylinder 106 exists in two states:
State (i) both dot and no dot panes show trace of a previous control. The F 39 control has been lightly retouched
State (ii) The control has been further retouched, and the "shadow control" almost completely removed

Retouched controls
The following F 39 controls were retouched before the cylinders were put to press: 90, 100, 100., 101, 101., 104

"Shadow" controls
Distinct traces of a previous control are seen on the following:
E 39   Cyl. 68, 68., 76, 76., 77, 77., 81, 81. (D 38)
F 39   Cyl. 90, 90., 101, 104., 108, 110. (E 39)
G 40   Cyl. 119, 119., 120, 120. (F 39)
I 41   Cyl. 120, 120. (F 39)

Coils
Vertical delivery printed in continuous reels

Code No.	Issued	Number in roll	Face value		
D	1937	960	£2.0.0	Bottom delivery	45·00
G	1937	480	£1.0.0	Bottom delivery	45·00
W	Late 1937	960	£2.0.0	Bottom delivery	25·00
Y	1937	1920	£4.0.0	Bottom delivery	25·00

Sideways delivery printed in continuous reels with watermark sideways
P   Jan. 1938 480   £1.0.0 Left side delivery

Imprimaturs from the National Postal Museum Archive
Imperforate, watermark Type **W20**
Watermark upright (pair) £6500
Watermark inverted (pair) £6500
Watermark sideways (pair) £6500
Tête-bêche (pair) .... pair £15000
Tête-bêche (pair) with vertical gutter margin .... pair £15000

Imprimatur from the British Postal Museum & Archive
Tête-bêche (pair) with vertical gutter margin £8000

1941 *(1 September).* **½d. Pale Green**

Q2 *(=S.G.485)*

	Mint	Used
Pale green	30	30
a. Tête-bêche (horizontal pair)	£18000	
b. Watermark inverted	4·00	50
c. Imperf. (pair)	£8500	

½d. Pale Orange Photogravure Low Values KING GEORGE VI QA

	Mint	Used
e. Spur to R of REVENUE (Cyl. 153 Dot, R. 1/5)		75·00
f. Closed final E of REVENUE (Cyl. 153 No dot, R. 3/1)		£100
s. "Specimen", Type 9		
t. "Cancelled", Type 33		
u. "Cancelled", Type 34		
v. "Specimen", Type 23		
w. "Specimen", Type 30		

Code No.	Issued	Number in roll	Face value		
Y	1942	1920	£4.0.0	Bottom delivery	35·00

Imprimaturs from the National Postal Museum Archives
Imperforate, watermark Type **W20**

Watermark upright (pair)	£5000
Watermark inverted (pair)	£5000
Watermark sideways (pair)	£5000
Tête-bêche (pair)	£15000
Tête-bêche (pair) with vertical gutter margin	£15000

Imprimaturs from the British Postal Museum & Archive

Watermark upright (marginal single)	£1500
Watermark upright (marginal block of eight)	£12000

Q2/3e   Q2/3f

Controls and Cylinder Numbers (Blocks of Six)
Perforation Type 5 (E/I)

Cyl. No.	Control	No dot	Dot
124	J 41	£250	£250
124	K 42	9·00	15·00
124	L 42	20·00	10·00
125	J 41	8·00	8·00
125	K 42	12·00	12·00
128	M 43	12·00	12·00
128	N 43	10·00	10·00
128	O 44	25·00	50·00
129	M 43	20·00	50·00
129	O 44	10·00	9·00
129	P 44	£100	85·00
130	N 43	10·00	25·00
130	P 44	70·00	70·00
132	P 44	25·00	9·00
134	Q 45	25·00	10·00
134	S 46	£125	£100
135	R 45	9·00	9·00
135	S 46	75·00	75·00
137	None	75·00	40·00
141	T 46	10·00	10·00
141	U 47	20·00	20·00
142	S 46	12·00	12·00
142	T 46	9·00	9·00
143	U 47	8·00	9·00
146	None	20·00	9·00
150	None	25·00	25·00
151	None	40·00	40·00
152	None	10·00	10·00
153	None	15·00	15·00

Perforation Type 6 (I/P)

		Perf. Type		
		6 (I/P)	6B (E/P)	6 (I/P)
		No dot	Dot	Dot
124	J 41	50·00	75·00	75·00
124	L 42	25·00	75·00	15·00
125	J 41	25·00	75·00	25·00
130	P 44	60·00	25·00	†
132	P 44	30·00	40·00	†

Perforation Type 5AE (AE/I). No dot cylinder only

129	P 44	£100
130	P 44	£125
132	P 44	£125
134	Q 45	85·00

Coils
Vertical delivery printed in continuous reels

Code No.	Issued	Number in roll	Face value		
D	1942	960	£2.0.0	Bottom delivery	50·00
G	1942	480	£1.0.0	Bottom delivery	50·00
W	1942	960	£2.0.0	Bottom delivery	30·00

1951 (3 May). ½d. Pale Orange

Q3 (=S.G.503)

	Mint	Used
Pale orange	30	30
a. Tête-bêche (horizontal pair)	£20000	
b. Watermark inverted	50	50
c. Imperf. (pair)	£7000	
e. Spur to R of REVENUE (Cyl. 153 Dot, R. 1/5)		85·00
f. Closed final E of REVENUE (Cyl. 153 No dot, R. 3/1)		85·00
g. Broken middle E of REVENUE (Cyl. 154 No dot, R. 20/1)		75·00
h. White dot in crown (Cyl. 154 No dot, R. 7/3)		£100
j. Coil join (horizontal pair)		

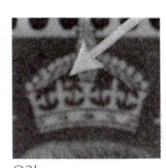

Q3g   Q3h

Cylinder Numbers (Blocks of Six)
Perforation Type 5 (E/I)

Cyl. No.	No dot	Dot
151	20·00	20·00
152	60·00	60·00
153	50·00	50·00
154	90·00*	40·00
155	30·00	30·00

Coils
Vertical delivery printed in continuous reels

Code No.	Issued	Number in roll	Face value		
D	May 1951	960	£2.0.0	Bottom delivery	50·00
G	May 1951	480	£1.0.0	Bottom delivery	30·00
W	May 1951	960	£2.0.0	Bottom delivery	25·00
Y	May 1951	1920	£4.0.0	Bottom delivery	30·00
EXP*	Feb. 1952	240	10.0	Bottom delivery	£300
AA*	July 1954	240	10.0	Bottom delivery	£175

Sideways delivery made up from sheets with joins every 12th stamp

P	May 1951	480	£1.0.0	Left side delivery

*The EXP (exposed) and AA coils were used in vending machines in exposed positions.

233

QA KING GEORGE VI — Photogravure Low Values — 1d. Scarlet

Imprimaturs from the National Postal Museum Archives
Imperforate, watermark Type **W20**

Watermark upright (pair)	£5500
Watermark inverted (pair)	£5500
Tête-bêche pair	£15000
Tête-bêche pair with vertical gutter margin	£15000

1d. Type Q1

1937 (10 May). **1d. Scarlet**

Q4 (=S.G.463)

	Mint	Used
Scarlet	30	25
a. Watermark inverted (8.37)	40·00	3·00
b. Watermark sideways (2.38)	20·00	9·00
c. Extra serif to N (Cyl. 3 Dot, R. 17/1)	85·00	
t. "Cancelled", Type 33	£125	
u. "Cancelled", Type 33P	70·00	

No. Q4 is known used at Tunbridge Wells on 1 May 1937.

Q4c

Controls and Cylinder Numbers (Blocks of Six)
Without marginal rule. Perforation Type 5 (E/I)

Cyl. No.	Control	No dot	Dot
1	A 37	£1500	†
3	A 37	7·00	7·00
4	A 37	7·00	7·00
7	A 37	7·00	7·00
8	A 37	7·00	7·00
8	B 37	7·00	7·00
9	A 37	£750	†
10	A 37	25·00	50·00
11	B 37	7·00	7·00

Perforation Type 6 (no dot I/P) and 6B (dot E/P)

Cyl. No.	Control	No dot	Dot
7	A 37	20·00	15·00

Perforation Type 2A (P/P)

Cyl. No.	Control	No dot	Dot
11	B 37	†	£500

With marginal rule. Perforation Type 5 (E/I)

Cyl. No.	Control	No dot	Dot
8	B 37	7·00	7·00
11	B 37	50·00	30·00
12	B 37	7·00	20·00
12	C 38	20·00	20·00
15	C 38	7·00	7·00
16	C 38	7·00	7·00
18	C 38	7·00	7·00
19	D 38	15·00	15·00
22	D 38	20·00	20·00
23	D 38	20·00	20·00
24	D 38	10·00	15·00
26	D 38	7·00	7·00
26	E 39	10·00	20·00
27	E 39	7·00	7·00
30	F 39	£150	£150
33	F 39	50·00	50·00
39	F 39	75·00	75·00
39	G 40	50·00	20·00
40	G 40	7·00	7·00

Cyl. No.	Control	No dot	Dot
40	H 40	50·00	50·00
41	G 40	7·00	7·00
41	H 40	15·00	15·00
42	F 39	75·00	75·00
43	H 40	60·00	75·00
44	H 40	20·00	20·00
45	G 40	75·00	75·00
45	H 40	15·00	15·00
46	H 40	7·00	7·00
47	H 40	7·00	7·00
48	H 40	75·00	75·00
48	I 41	7·00	10·00
49	H 40	£100	55·00
49	I 41	10·00	20·00
51	H 40	10·00	20·00
51	I 41	75·00	15·00
53	I 41	10·00	10·00
54	I 41	10·00	30·00
61	I 41	10·00	10·00

Perforation Type 6 (no dot I/P) and 6B (dot E/P)

Cyl. No.	Control	No dot	Dot
26	E 39	8·00	12·00
27	E 39	20·00	20·00
27	F 39	35·00	35·00
30	F 39	8·00	8·00
31	F 39	10·00	12·00
33	F 39	6·00	6·00
39	F 39	50·00	50·00
42	F 39	15·00	25·00

On cylinder 19 (both panes), the tail of the "9" was originally engraved short and close to the loop. Before being put to press, the tail was re-engraved long and wide of the loop.

"Shadow" controls
Distinct traces of the previous control are seen on the following:
C 38 Cyl. 12., 15, 15. (B 37)
E 39 Cyl. 26, 26., 27. (D 38)
G 40 Cyl. 40, 40. (F 39)
H 40 Cyl. 43. (G 40)
I 41 Cyl. 48, 48., 49, 49. (H 40)

Coils
Vertical delivery printed in continuous reels

Code No.	Issued	Number in roll	Face value		
B	1937	960	£4.0.0	Bottom delivery	60·00
E	1937	480	£2.0.0	Bottom delivery	45·00
X	1937	960	£4.0.0	Bottom delivery	20·00
Z	25.9.37	1920	£8·0·0	Bottom delivery	25·00

Sideways delivery printed in continuous reels with watermark sideways

O	Feb. 1938	480	£2.0.0	Left side delivery	40·00

Imprimaturs from the National Postal Museum Archive
Imperforate, watermark Type **W20**

Watermark upright (pair)	£6500
Watermark inverted (pair)	£6500
Watermark sideways (pair)	£6500
Tête-bêche (pair)	£15000
Tête-bêche (pair) with vertical gutter margin	£15000

Imprimaturs from the British Postal Museum & Archive

Tête-bêche (pair) with vertical gutter margin	£8000
Watermark upright (block of six), cylinder B6 no dot (sheet 26410) at left	£12500

Variations in the Multipositives
For the 1d. in pale scarlet and the later issue in light ultramarine several master negatives were employed, these being retouched prior to the preparation of the multipositives.

234

1d. Pale Scarlet *Photogravure Low Values* **KING GEORGE VI QA**

Type I

Type II

Type I, used for sheet stamps from cylinders 75 to 172, has a white spot in front of the ear, a white strand of hair behind the ear and the upper lip is straight.

Type II (cylinders 174 to 190), has the white spot and strand of hair touched out and other minor differences but upper lip is concave.

Pre Type I

Type I

On sheet stamps only for cylinders 66 to 74 there is a further type which we call Pre Type I. The white spot and strand of hair are less prominent than Type I, resembling Type II, but the upper lip is straight. However, there is a further difference between this and Type I to be found in the thistle.
Pre Type I. The thistle is made up of five inner lines with a space between the third and fourth lines.
Type I. An additional short line has been added in this space in the thistle, the third line being ill-defined.

1941 *(11 August)*. **1d. Pale Scarlet**

A. Type I
Q5 (=S.G.486)

	Mint	Used
Pale scarlet	30	30
a. Watermark sideways (10.42)	5·00	4·50
b. Ditto, thick paper	50·00	20·00
f. Flaw on cheek (Cyl. 149 No dot, R. 3/4)	£175	
g. Pre Type I	30	30

	Mint	Used
h. Curved frames (Cyl. 74 No dot, R. 20/1, 2) Pair	£200	
s. "Specimen", Type 9		
t. "Cancelled", Type 33		
u. "Cancelled", Type 34		
v. "Specimen", Type 23		
w. "Specimen", Type 30		

B. Type II.
Q5A (= 48)

	Mint	Used
Pale scarlet	30	30
b. Thick paper	15·00	5·00
c. Imperf. (pair)	£8000	
d. Imperf. three sides (horizontal pair)	£8500	

No. Q5Ad is perforated at foot only and comes from the same sheet as No. Q5Ac sold over a Post Office counter.

Q5f

Q5h

Broken Dandy Roll Variety
za. "RᵥıR" for "GᵥıR" ....
One used example has been recorded.

Controls and Cylinder Numbers (Block of Six)
Pre Type I. Perforation Type 5 (E/I)

Cyl. No.	Control	No dot	Dot
66	J 41	8·00	15·00
69	J 41	8·00	8·00
70	J 41	8·00	8·00
71	J 41	12·00	12·00
72	J 41	8·00	8·00
72	K 42	15·00	15·00
72	L 42	60·00	60·00
73	J 41	8·00	8·00
73	K 42	15·00	15·00
74	J 41	£250*	95·00
74	K 42	£250*	95·00

Type I. Perforation Type 5 (E/I)

Cyl. No.	Control	No dot	Dot
75	K 42	10·00	8·00
76	K 42	15·00	15·00
76	L 42	30·00	40·00
76	M 43	40·00	40·00
78	L 42	8·00	8·00
80	M 43	10·00	25·00
81	L 42	8·00	8·00
82	L 42	40·00	40·00
82	M 43	50·00	25·00
86	M 43	8·00	8·00
90	N 43	40·00	50·00
90	O 44	25·00	20·00
91	N 43	25·00	25·00
91	O 44	25·00	25·00
91	P 44	70·00	35·00
92	M 43	40·00	50·00
92	N 43	8·00	8·00
93	M 43	15·00	10·00
94	N 43	15·00	15·00
94	O 44	25·00	15·00
95	N 43	£120	£120
95	O 44	20·00	20·00

235

QA KING GEORGE VI *Photogravure Low Values* **1d. Pale Scarlet**

Cyl. No.	Control	No dot	Dot
96	M 43	20·00	20·00
96	N 43	20·00	20·00
97	N 43	10·00	10·00
98	O 44	10·00	8·00
99	N 43	50·00	50·00
100	N 43	£120	£120
100	O 44	10·00	10·00
101	P 44	15·00	10·00
102	O 44	15·00	15·00
102	P 44	20·00	20·00
105	O 44	40·00	40·00
105	P 44	30·00	50·00
106	P 44	50·00	25·00
106	Q 45	15·00	15·00
107	P 44	8·00	8·00
107	Q 45	50·00	20·00
112	P 44	30·00	20·00
113	P 44	10·00	10·00
113	Q 45	20·00	30·00
118	Q 45	35·00	35·00
118	R 45	12·00	12·00
120	Q 45	50·00	50·00
120	R 45	20·00	20·00
121	Q 45	40·00	20·00
122	Q 45	30·00	40·00
122	R 45	8·00	8·00
123	R 45	20·00	20·00
124	S 46	30·00	15·00
125	R 45	70·00	70·00
125	S 46	30·00	40·00
127	S 46	15·00	15·00
127	T 46	15·00	15·00
129	S 46	35·00	25·00
129	T 46	20·00	15·00
130	S 46	25·00	25·00
132	T 46	50·00	30·00
133	T 46	15·00	30·00
134	T 46	8·00	8·00
136	T 46	10·00	10·00
139	T 46	15·00	10·00
140	T 46	10·00	40·00
140	U 47	10·00	10·00
141	T 46	8·00	8·00
142	T 46	8·00	8·00
143	T 46	15·00	40·00
145	None	15·00	20·00
146	U 47	8·00	8·00
148	U 47	20·00	20·00
149	U 47	8·00	8·00
150	None	10·00	10·00
153	U 47	8·00	10·00
155	U 47	30·00	30·00
156	None	30·00	40·00
157	None	15·00	15·00
160	None	10·00	10·00
166	None	10·00	10·00
167	None	8·00	8·00
168	None	—	†
169	None	10·00	10·00
171	None	15·00	8·00
172	None	10·00	10·00

Pre Type I. Perforation Type 6 (no dot I/P) and 6B (dot E/P)

Cyl. No.	Control	No dot	Dot
72	L 42	£120	£120

Type I. Perforation Type 6 (no dot I/P) and 6B (dot E/P)

Cyl. No.	Control	No dot	Dot
76	L 42	£150	£150
121	Q 45	15·00	15·00
123	S 46	25·00	40·00
124	S 46	30·00	30·00
125	R 45	50·00	40·00
125	S 46	15·00	10·00
127	S 46	30·00	30·00
129	S 46	20·00	20·00
150	U 47	15·00	25·00
153	U 47	15·00	35·00
171	None	£200	£200
172	None	35·00	50·00

Perforation Type 5AE (no dot cylinder only AE/I)

Cyl. No.	Control	No dot	Dot
90	O 44	70·00	
91	N 43	70·00	
91	O 44	£100	
91	P 44	70·00	
94	N 43	70·00	
94	O 44	70·00	
98	O 44	50·00	
100	O 44	50·00	
101	P 44	70·00	
102	O 44	£100	
102	P 44	50·00	
105	O 44	70·00	
106	P 44	70·00	
106	Q 45	70·00	
107	P 44	50·00	
107	Q 45	£100	
112	P 44	70·00	
113	P 44	50·00	

Type II. Perforation Type 5 (E/I)

Cyl. No.	Control	No dot	Dot
174	None	25·00	25·00
175	None	15·00	15·00
178	None	15·00	15·00
179	None	25·00	40·00
180	None	15·00	15·00
181	None	15·00	15·00
182	None	15·00	15·00
183	None	35·00	35·00
186	None	20·00	20·00
189	None	15·00	15·00
190	None	35·00	35·00
192	None	—	†

Perforation Type 6 (no dot I/P) and 6B (dot E/P)

Cyl. No.	Control	No dot	Dot
174	None	90·00	90·00
179	None	90·00	90·00
180	None	90·00	90·00
181	None	90·00	90·00
185	None	30·00	30·00
190	None	90·00	70·00

Cylinder 124 sometimes shows a dot after the number. Printings from the no dot pane may always be recognised by the presence of a cut in the rule under the first stamp, bottom row.

Two sheets are known of Cyl. 192 no dot and an additional cylinder block has been reported. The arrows in the top and bottom margins are omitted.

Two examples of Cyl. 168 no dot are known, first reported in 2000.

"Shadow" control
Cylinder 156 dot shows traces of U 47 control and was only issued without control

Coils

Type I and II
Vertical delivery printed in continuous reels

Code No.	Issued	Number in roll	Face value		
B	1942	960	£4.0.0	Bottom delivery	60·00
E	1942	480	£2.0.0	Bottom delivery	45·00
X	1942	960	£4.0.0	Bottom delivery	35·00
Z	1942	1920	£8.0.0	Bottom delivery	35·00

Type I
Sideways delivery printed in continuous reels with watermark sideways

| O | Oct. 1942 | 480 | £2.0.0 | Left side delivery | 30·00 |

Imprimaturs from the National Postal Museum Archives
Imperforate, watermark Type **W20**

Watermark upright (pair) £5500
Watermark sideways (pair) £5500

1d. Light Ultramarine *Photogravure Low Values* **KING GEORGE VI** QA

Imprimaturs from the British Postal Museum & Archive

Watermark upright (marginal single).......................... £1500
Watermark sideways (pair)... £3000

Variations in the Multipositives

Type Ia derives from panes of four from Booklets BD8/10. The upper lip is straight as Type I but the Crown and large pearls are as Type II. The hair at the back of the head has been retouched but the band of dark shading at the back of the neck is narrower and more clear-cut than Type II.

Type Ib is from pane Nos. QB18/a, QB19/a and QB20/a. The upper lip is straight as Type I. The white spot in the ear and pale strand of hair are partially touched out. The Crown and rose are similar to Type II.

Type Ic derives from the ordinary panes of six Nos. QB15/a. The upper lip is straight as Type I. The white spot in the ear and the pale strand of hair have been touched out and the head blends into the background. The Crown shows as a clear impression and the lines in the rose and leaves are heavy as Type I.

Although these types normally show the upper lip straight, examples of the "concave" lip of Type II can be found in booklet panes. These are isolated instances and cannot be identified by position. They are best collected in the pane so that their variation from the normal is clearly evident.

Further information about these can be found in an article by P. C. Worsfold in the *GB Journal* Vol. 32, No. 2, May/June 1994.

1951 (3 May). **1d. Light Ultramarine**

A. Type II
Q6 (=S.G.504)

	Mint	Used
Light ultramarine	30	30
b. Imperf. (pair)	£4800	
c. Imperf. three sides (horizontal pair)	£6500	
d. "Keyhole" flaw (Cyl. 192 No dot, R. 6/12)	£275	

No. Q6c comes from a sheet printing and is perforated at bottom only.

B. Type I. Horiz. coil with sideways wmk. (5.51)
Q6A (=S.G.504a)

	Mint	Used
Light ultramarine	1·10	1·25
b. Retouched nose and forehead	75·00	

C. Type Ia. From pane Nos. QB16b or QB16c (12.52)
Q6B

	Mint	Used
Light ultramarine	2·50	
b. Watermark inverted	4·50	2·50

D. Type Ib. From pane Nos. QB18/QB20a (3.52)
Q6C

	Mint	Used
Light ultramarine	2·50	
b. Watermark inverted	4·50	2·50

For tête-bêche variety, see No. QB18b.

E. Type Ic. From pane Nos. QB15 or QB15a (1.53)
Q6D

	Mint	Used
Light ultramarine	2·50	
b. Watermark inverted	4·50	2·50

Q6d

Q6Ab

Cylinder Numbers (Blocks of Six)
Type II. Perforation Type 5 (E/I)

Cyl. No.	No dot	Dot
190	20·00	15·00
191	15·00	15·00
192	40·00	30·00

Perforation Type 6 (no dot I/P) and 6B (dot E/P)

Cyl. No.	No dot	Dot
191	50·00	50·00
192	20·00	20·00

Top and bottom rows exist with the arrows omitted from cylinder 192 dot.

Coils

Type II
Vertical delivery printed in continuous reels

Code No.	Issued	Number in roll	Face value		
B	May 1951	960	£4.0.0	Bottom delivery	70·00
E	May 1951	480	£2.0.0	Bottom delivery	40·00
X	May 1951	960	£4.0.0	Bottom delivery	30·00
Z	May 1951	1920	£8.0.0	Bottom delivery	35·00
EXP*	Feb. 1952	240	£1.0.0	Bottom delivery	£400
AB*	May 1954	240	£1.0.0	Bottom delivery	£200

Type I
Sideways delivery printed in continuous reels with watermark sideways

O	May 1951	480	£2.0.0	Left side delivery	30·00

*The EXP (exposed) and AB coils were used in vending machines in exposed positions.

237

QA KING GEORGE VI Photogravure Low Values 1½d. Red-brown

Imprimaturs from the National Postal Museum Archives
Imperforate, watermark Type **W20**

Watermark upright (pair)	£5500
Watermark inverted (pair)	£5500
Watermark sideways (pair)	£5500
Tête-bêche pair	£15000
Tête-bêche pair with vertical gutter margin	£15000

Imprimaturs from the British Postal Museum & Archive

Watermark sideways block of four, cylinder B76 in lower margin	£10000
Tête-bêche pair	£9000
Tête-bêche pair, vertical format	£9000
Tête-bêche block of four with vertical gutter margin	£18000

1½d. Type Q1

1937 (30 July). **1½d. Red-brown**

Q7 (=S.G.464)

	Mint	Used
Red-brown	30	25
a. Watermark inverted (8.37)	15·00	1·25
b. Watermark sideways (2.38)	1·25	1·25
c. Imperf. three sides (pair)	£6500	
d. Crown flaw (Cyl. 145 Dot, 150 Dot, R. 19/7)	£125	
s. "Cancelled", Type 33P	50·00	
t. "Cancelled", Type 33	80·00	
u. "Specimen", Type 26		
v. "Specimen", Type 30		

No. Q7 is known used at Cranbrook, Kent on 29 July 1937.

Q7d

Broken Dandy Roll Variety
za. G Inverted and Reversed
One used example has been recorded.

Controls and Cylinder Numbers (Blocks of Six)
Perforation Type 5 (E/I). Without marginal rule

Cyl. No.	Control	No dot	Dot
1	A 37	35·00	15·00
12	A 37	15·00	10·00
14	A 37	8·00	10·00
17	B 37	8·00	8·00
18	B 37	8·00	8·00
22	B 37	20·00	10·00
30	B 37	8·00	8·00
32	B 37	15·00	8·00
33	B 37	£200	—
35	B 37	†	£350

With marginal rule

Cyl. No.	Control	No dot	Dot
38	B 37	8·00	25·00
42	B 37	8·00	8·00
45	B 37	8·00	15·00
46	B 37	50·00	50·00
48	B 37	8·00	15·00
49	B 37	8·00	8·00
50	B 37	8·00	8·00
51	B 37	15·00	8·00
52	B 37	30·00	30·00
54	B 37	8·00	8·00
55	B 37	8·00	8·00

Cyl. No.	Control	No dot	Dot
56	B 37	15·00	25·00
59	B 37	8·00	8·00
60(i)	B 37	25·00	25·00
60(ii)	B 37	30·00	30·00
61	B 37	70·00	70·00
64	B 37	8·00	8·00
65	B 37	8·00	8·00
68	B 37	8·00	8·00
68	C 38	30·00	30·00
69	C 38	8·00	8·00
70	C 38	8·00	8·00
71	B 37	8·00	8·00
71	C 38	30·00	30·00
74	C 38	8·00	8·00
76	C 38	10·00	10·00
77	C 38	8·00	8·00
81	C 38	8·00	8·00
83	C 38	70·00	70·00
84	C 38	8·00	8·00
85	C 38	20·00	50·00
86	C 38	15·00	10·00
88	C 38	25·00	20·00
89	C 38	£150	£300
90	C 38	30·00	30·00
91	C 38	20·00	20·00
92	C 38	10·00	10·00
93	C 38	15·00	10·00
93	D 38	10·00	20·00
95	C 38	8·00	8·00
96	C 38	8·00	8·00
98	C 38	20·00	10·00
102	D 38	8·00	8·00
104	C 38	15·00	10·00
104	D 38	50·00	50·00
106	D 38	25·00	25·00
107	D 38	8·00	8·00
108	D 38	10·00	10·00
109	D 38	8·00	8·00
110	D 38	8·00	8·00
112	D 38	8·00	8·00
113	D 38	8·00	8·00
116	D 38	8·00	8·00
120	D 38	8·00	10·00
120	E 39	8·00	10·00
121	D 38	15·00	15·00
122	D 38	20·00	20·00
122	E 39	8·00	8·00
123	E 39	8·00	8·00
124	E 39	8·00	8·00
125	E 39	70·00	70·00
126	E 39	8·00	8·00
128	E 39	8·00	8·00
135	E 39	10·00	10·00
136	E 39	10·00	10·00
138	E 39	70·00	†
139	E 39	50·00	50·00
141	F 39	8·00	8·00
144	E 39	8·00	10·00
145	E 39	8·00	8·00
148	E 39	8·00	8·00
148	F 39	50·00	50·00
149	F 39	10·00	10·00
150	E 39	8·00	8·00
150	F 39	30·00	30·00
151	E 39	8·00	8·00
152	E 39	20·00	30·00
153	F 39	10·00	8·00
154	E 39	8·00	8·00
156	E 39	10·00	10·00
159	F 39	8·00	8·00
161	F 39	8·00	8·00
164	F 39	8·00	8·00
165	G 40	8·00	8·00
167	F 39	8·00	8·00
173	G 40	8·00	8·00

In cylinder 98 the figure "9" is retouched.

1½d. Pale Red-brown — Photogravure Low Values — KING GEORGE VI — QA

Perforation Type 6 (no dot I/P) and 6B (dot E/P)

Cyl. No.	Control	No dot	Dot
83	C 38	£100	£100
104	D 38	—	—
145	E 39	80·00	80·00
161	F 39	£100	£100

Perforation Type 2A (P/P)

Cyl. No.	Control	No dot	Dot
106	D 38	†	£250
135	E 39	†	£350
162	F 39	†	—

Varieties:
The left pane of cylinder 12 has a tiny dot after the "12", later erased.

Cylinder 60 exists in two states. In state (ii) the cylinder has been rechromed, and the control on both panes is weak and irregular in depth.

Control C 38 with cylinder 96 exists normal, both much weaker and lightly retouched and practically invisible with no trace of dot.

Control D 38 with cylinder 107 exists normal and in various weaker states to being practically invisible.

The right pane of cylinder 110 was without dot. It may be distinguished by the pick up bar under the first stamp, which has a nick in base at left.

In the right pane of cylinder 112 the cylinder number is engraved very close to the stamp, causing the stop sometimes to be perforated out. It can be identified if the cutting line is present.

Retouched controls
The following controls were retouched before the cylinders were put to press:
E 39   Cyl. 120.
F 39   Cyl. 141, 141. and 149

"Shadow" controls
Distinct traces of previous control are seen on the following:
C 38   Cyl. 71. (B 37)
D 38   Cyl. 106 (fraction bar of C 38) later removed
E 39   Cyl. 120, 122, 122., 124, 124., 125, 125. (D 38)
F 39   Cyl. 141, 141., 149 (E 39)
G 40   Cyl. 165, 165., 173. (F 39)

Coils
Vertical delivery printed in continuous reels

Code No.	Issued	Number in roll	Face value		
K	1937	960	£6.0.0	Top delivery	—
K	1937	960	£6.0.0	Bottom delivery	70·00
L	1937	480	£3.0.0	Top delivery	90·00

Sideways delivery printed in continuous reels with watermark sideways
N   Feb. 1938 480   £3.0.0   Left side delivery   60·00

Imprimatur from the National Postal Museum Archives
Imperforate, watermark Type **W20**

Watermark upright (pair).. £6500

1942 (28 September). **1½d. Pale Red-brown**
Q8 (=S.G.487)

	Mint	Used
Pale red-brown	60	80
a. Coil join (horizontal pair)	(6.50)	
c. Retouched forehead (Cyl. 192 No dot, R. 19/1)	85·00	
d. Spot in daffodil leaf (Cyl. 192 Dot, R. 10/10)	£100	
e. Extended serif to 1 of ½ (Cyl. 192 Dot, R. 7/11)	£100	
s. "Specimen", Type 9		
t. "Cancelled", Type 28		
u. "Cancelled", Type 33		
v. "Specimen", Type 23		

Q8/9c   Q8/9d   Q8/9e

Controls and Cylinder Numbers (Blocks of Six)
Perforation Type 5 (E/I)

Cyl. No.	Control	No dot	Dot
174	N 43	25·00	25·00
175	L 42	15·00	15·00
175	N 43	25·00	25·00
176	L 42	15·00	15·00
179	Q 45	15·00	15·00
183	N 43	15·00	15·00
183	O 44	15·00	20·00
184	S 46	15·00	15·00
185	S 46	15·00	15·00
185	U 47	15·00	15·00
185	None	40·00	30·00
186	R 45	20·00	20·00
186	S 46	15·00	20·00
187	U 47	25·00	25·00
187	None	15·00	15·00
191	None	75·00	75·00
192	None	£100*	15·00

Perforation Type 6 (I/P)

		Perf. Type		
		6 (I/P)	6B (E/P)	6 (I/P)
Cyl. No.	Control	No dot	Dot	Dot
178	O 44	35·00	25·00	50·00
178	P 44	£100	£100	
183	O 44	25·00	50·00	40·00

Perforation Type 5AE (AE/I), no dot cylinder only
179   Q 45   £150

On cylinder 183 the control O 44 has been retouched on both panes.

On cylinder 187 dot the arrow is missing in the bottom margin.

Coils
Sideways delivery made up from sheets with joins every 12th stamp

Code No.	Issued	Number in roll	Face value		
N	June 1950	480	£3.0.0	Left side delivery	75·00

Imprimatur from the National Postal Museum Archives
Imperforate, watermark Type **W20**

Watermark upright (pair).. £5000

Imprimatur from the British Postal Museum & Archive
Watermark upright (marginal single)........................ £1500

QA KING GEORGE VI — Photogravure Low Values — 1½d. Pale Green

1951 (3 May). 1½d. Pale Green

Q9 (=S.G.505)

	Mint	Used
Pale green	65	60
a. Watermark inverted	6·00	1·00
b. Watermark sideways (14.9.51)	3·25	5·00
c. Retouched forehead (Cyl. 192 No dot, R. 19/1)	60·00	
d. Spot in daffodil leaf (Cyls. 192 Dot, 195 Dot, 196 Dot, R. 10/10)	90·00	
e. Extended serif to 1 of ½ (Cyls. 192 Dot, 195 Dot, R. 7/11)	90·00	
f. Coil join (vertical pair)		
g. Coil join (horizontal pair)		
h. Malformed fleur-de-lis at right (Cyl. 194 Dot, R. 19/8)	£100	
j. Spur to rose leaf (Pane QB26a, G 4 Dot, No. 1)	45·00	

Q9h   Q9j

Cylinder Numbers (Blocks of Six)
Perforation Type 5 (E/I)

Cyl. No.	No dot	Dot
190	50·00	50·00
192	85·00*	15·00
193	25·00	50·00
194	15·00	15·00
195	15·00	20·00
196	20·00	15·00
197	60·00	40·00
199	60·00	60·00

Perforation Type 6 (no dot I/P) and 6B (dot E/P)

Cyl. No.	No dot	Dot
195	50·00	70·00
197	50·00	70·00

Coils
Vertical delivery made up from sheets with joins every 20th stamp

Code No.	Issued	Number in roll	Face value		
K	May 1951	960	£6.0.0	Bottom delivery	65·00
L	May 1951	480	£3.0.0	Top delivery	50·00

Sideways delivery made up from sheets with joins every 12th stamp

| N | May 1951 | 480 | £3.0.0 | Left side delivery | 35·00 |

Vertical delivery printed in continuous reels

| K | Sept. 1951 | 960 | £6.0.0 | Bottom delivery | 55·00 |
| L | Sept. 1951 | 480 | £3.0.0 | Top delivery | 75·00 |

Sideways delivery printed in continuous reels with watermark sideways

| N | 14.9.51 | 480 | £3.0.0 | Left side delivery | 30·00 |

Imprimatur from the National Postal Museum Archives
Imperforate, watermark **W20**

Watermark upright (pair) £5500

2d. Type Q1

1938 (31 January). 2d. Orange

Q10 (=S.G.465)

	Mint	Used
Orange	1·20	50
b. Watermark inverted (6.40)	60·00	22·00
c. Watermark sideways (2.38)	75·00	40·00
d. Coil join (vertical pair)		
s. "Specimen", Type 26	£325	
t. "Cancelled", Type 33P	95·00	
u. "Specimen", Type 26		

For No. Q10 bisected and used on cover, see Appendix 7.

Controls and Cylinder Numbers (Blocks of Six)
Perforation Type 5 (E/I)

Cyl. No.	Control	No dot	Dot
1	B 37	20·00	20·00
1	C 38	£300	£300
7	D 38	20·00	20·00
8	D 38	20·00	20·00
10	E 39	20·00	20·00
11	E 39	20·00	20·00
11	F 39	£100	£100
11	G 40	50·00	50·00
12	E 39	35·00	25·00
12	G 40	35·00	35·00
14	G 40	20·00	20·00
14	H 40	30·00	£100
15	G 40	20·00	20·00
15	H 40	70·00	£100
17	H 40	20·00	20·00
17	I 41	20·00	20·00
20	I 41	45·00	35·00

Perforation Type 6 (no dot I/P) and 6B (dot E/P)

Cyl. No.	Control	No dot	Dot
10	E 39	30·00	30·00
11	E 39	80·00	80·00
11	F 39	30·00	30·00
12	E 39	30·00	30·00
12	F 39	20·00	20·00

Retouched Controls
The following Controls were retouched before the cylinders were put to press:
F 39   Cyl. 11, 12, 12.

"Shadow" Controls
Distinct traces of the previous Control are seen on the following:
G 40   Cyl. 12. (traces of F 39)

Coils
Vertical delivery made up from sheets with joins every 20th stamp

Code No.	Issued	Number in roll	Face value		
Q	1937	960	£8.0.0	Bottom delivery	75·00
R	1937	480	£4.0.0	Top delivery	£100

Sideways delivery printed in continuous reels with watermark sideways

| T | Feb. 1938 | 480 | £4.0.0 | Left side delivery | 85·00 |

Imprimaturs from the National Postal Museum Archives
Imperforate, watermark Type **W20**

Watermark upright (pair) £5500
Watermark inverted (pair) £5500
Watermark sideways (pair) £5500
Tête-bêche (pair) £15000
Tête-bêche (pair) with vertical gutter margin £15000

Imprimatur from the British Postal Museum & Archive
Tête-bêche pair with vertical gutter margin, as above from NPM £6000

2d. Pale Orange *Photogravure Low Values* **KING GEORGE VI** **QA**

1941 *(6 October).* **2d. Pale Orange**

Q11 (=S.G.488)

	Mint	Used
Pale orange	50	50
a. Watermark inverted	4·00	1·00
b. Watermark sideways (6.42)	28·00	19·00
c. Tête-bêche (horizontal pair)	£18000	
d. Imperf. (pair)	£7500	
f. Coil join (vertical pair)		
s. "Specimen", Type 9		
t. "Cancelled", Type 33		
u. "Specimen", Type 23		
v. "Specimen", Type 30		

Controls and Cylinder Numbers (Blocks of Six)
Perforation Type 5 (E/I)

Cyl. No.	Control	No dot	Dot
23	M 43	80·00	£100
24	J 41	12·00	12·00
24	K 42	12·00	12·00
25	J 41	80·00	80·00
25	K 42	12·00	12·00
25	L 42	15·00	15·00
25	M 43	12·00	30·00
26	L 42	30·00	30·00
30	M 43	20·00	12·00
30	N 43	12·00	12·00
32	N 43	15·00	15·00
32	O 44	40·00	35·00
33	O 44	12·00	12·00
34	P 44	40·00	40·00
36	Q 45	20·00	20·00
38	P 44	80·00	80·00
39	P 44	80·00	80·00
39	Q 45	60·00	60·00
40	Q 45	30·00	20·00
40	R 45	£100	£100
41	R 45	40·00	40·00
42	S 46	12·00	40·00
42	U 47	50·00	30·00
45	R 45	20·00	20·00
45	T 46	12·00	12·00
47	T 46	12·00	12·00
47	U 47	50·00	30·00
49	U 47	30·00	50·00
50	U 47	50·00	50·00
52	None	40·00	15·00
54	None	25·00	25·00
55	None	80·00	80·00
58	None	40·00	40·00
59	None	30·00	40·00
60	None	12·00	12·00
61	None	50·00	30·00
62	None	30·00	30·00
67	None	30·00	30·00
68	None	80·00	80·00

Perforation Type 6 (no dot I/P) and 6B (dot E/P)

Cyl. No.	Control	No dot	Dot
25	J 41	35·00	†
25	L 42	35·00	£100
34	P 44	15·00	†
38	P 44	40·00	75·00
45	S 46	75·00	50·00
45	T 46	30·00	50·00
47	T 46	12·00	12·00
52	None	30·00	50·00
53	None	60·00	30·00
55	None	15·00	15·00
58	None	60·00	40·00
59	None	30·00	40·00
61	None	50·00	50·00
62	None	40·00	40·00
64	None	60·00	25·00
67	None	60·00	60·00
68	None	75·00	75·00

Perforation Type 6 (dot I/P)

Cyl. No.	Control	No dot	Dot
25	J 41		35·00
25	L 42		35·00
34	P 44		60·00
38	P 44		70·00

Perforation Type 5AE (AE/I), no dot cylinder only

Cyl. No.	Control	No dot	Dot
39	P 44		£200
40	Q 45		£160

Retouched controls
The following controls were retouched before the cylinders were put to press:
U 47 Cyl. 47, 47.

Miscut sheets show cyl. no. and L 42 control in right-hand margin. See also 5d.

Coils
Vertical delivery printed from sheets with joins every 20th stamp

Code No.	Issued	Number in roll	Face value		
Q	1942	960	£8.0.0	Bottom delivery	70·00
R	1942	480	£4.0.0	Top delivery	90·00
V	Mar. 1949	960	£8.0.0	Bottom delivery	80·00

Sideways delivery printed in continuous reels with watermark sideways

T	June 1942	480	£4.0.0	Left side delivery	70·00

Imprimaturs from the National Postal Museum Archives
Imperforate, watermark Type **W20**

Watermark upright (pair)	£5500
Watermark inverted (pair)	£5500
Watermark sideways (pair)	£5500
Tête-bêche pair	£15000
Tête-bêche pair with vertical gutter margin	£15000

Imprimaturs from the British Postal Museum & Archive
Watermark upright (marinal single)	£1500
Watermark sideways block of four with vertical gutter margin and cylinder D14 dot	£10000

●────────────────────

1951 *(3 May).* **2d. Pale Red-brown**

Q12 (=S.G.506)

	Mint	Used
(1) Pale red-brown	75	40
(2) Bright red-brown	3·00	1·00
a. Watermark inverted	6·00	6·50
b. Watermark sideways		
Shade (1)	1·75	2·00
Shade (2)	4·75	2·25
c. Tête-bêche (horizontal pair)	£18000	
d. Imperf. three sides (horizontal pair)	£8000	
e. "Swan head" to 2 (wmk. sideways, roll 10)	30·00	
f. Ditto retouched		
Shade (1)	25·00	
Shade (2)	25·00	
g. Retouches to Rose, Thistle and Cross on Crown (Cyl. 75 No dot, R. 1/3, 4 and 8)	£125	
h. Missing jewel in Crown (Cyl. 75 No dot, R. 19/1)	75·00	
j. E and N joined (sideways coil)	85·00	
k Coil join (vertical pair)		

No. Q12d comes from a sheet printing and is perforated at bottom only.

QA KING GEORGE VI Photogravure Low Values 2½d. Ultramarine

Q12e

Q12f
Tip of 2 less rounded than normal and slightly shorter

Q12g (R. 1/3)

Q12h

Q12j

Cylinder Numbers (Blocks of Six)
Perforation Type 5 (E/I)

Cyl. No.	No dot	Dot
67	£150	£100
68	25·00	15·00
69	30·00	30·00
71	30·00	30·00
72	30·00	30·00
73	30·00	30·00
75	65·00*	30·00

Perforation Type 6 (no dot I/P) and 6B (dot E/P)

Cyl. No.	No dot	Dot
69	50·00	60·00
70	£100	£100
71	40·00	40·00

Coils
Vertical delivery made up from sheets with joins every 20th stamp

Code No.	Issued	Number in roll	Face value		
Q	May 1951	960	£8.0.0	Bottom delivery	£100
R	May 1951	480	£4.0.0	Top delivery	£150
V	May 1951	960	£8.0.0	Bottom delivery	—

Sideways delivery printed in continuous reels with watermark sideways

T	May 1951	480	£4.0.0	Left side delivery	25·00

Vertical delivery printed in continuous reels

Q	Dec. 1951	960	£8.0.0	Bottom delivery	£100
R	Jan. 1952	480	£4.0.0	Top delivery	—
V	Dec. 1951	960	£8.0.0	Bottom delivery	£100

Imprimaturs from the National Postal Museum Archives
Imperforate, watermark Type **W20**

Watermark upright (pair) £5500
Watermark inverted (pair) £5500
Watermark sideways (pair) £5500
Tête-bêche pair £15000
Tête-bêche pair with vertical gutter margin £15000

Imprimaturs from the British Postal Museum & Archive
Watermark sideways block of six, cylinder D14 dot
  at left £12500
Tête-bêche pair £9000
Tête-bêche block of four £18000

2½d. Type Q1

1937 (10 May). **2½d. Ultramarine**

Q13 (=S.G.466)

	Mint	Used
Ultramarine	40	25
a. Watermark inverted (6.40)	55·00	22·00
b. Watermark sideways (6.40)	75·00	35·00
c. Tête-bêche (horizontal pair)	£22000	
d. Scratch on temple (Cyl. 2 No dot, R. 20/1)		22·00
g. Coil join (vertical pair)		
h. Coil join (horizontal pair)		
s. "Cancelled", Type 33		
t. "Cancelled", Type 33P	70·00	

No. Q13 is known used at Ripon, Yorks, on 9 May 1937.

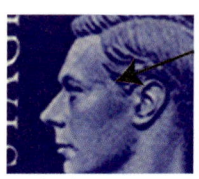

Q13d Early printing, A37, B37, A38, A39 controls, Perf. Type 5

Controls and Cylinder Numbers (Blocks of Six)
Perforation Type 5 (E/I). Without marginal rule

Cyl. No.	Control	No dot	Dot
1	A 37	£750	£750
2	A 37	25·00*	10·00
2	B 37	25·00*	10·00
2	D 38	£100*	£100

Perforation Type 6 (no dot I/P) and 6B (dot E/P)

Cyl. No.	Control	No dot	Dot
2	A 37	25·00*	10·00
2	D 38	50·00*	40·00

With marginal rule. Perforation Type 5 (E/I)

Cyl. No.	Control	No dot	Dot
3	E 39	10·00	10·00
3	G 40	80·00	80·00
6(i)	G 40	30·00	30·00
6(ii)	G 40	70·00	70·00
6	H 40	£100	£100
7	G 40	30·00	40·00
10	G 40	60·00	40·00
10	H 40	£175	£175
13(i)	G 40	75·00	—
13(ii)	G 40	75·00	75·00
15	G 40	10·00	20·00
15	H 40	20·00	30·00
20	H 40	15·00	40·00
22	H 40	10·00	10·00
23	H 40	40·00	30·00
25	H 40	30·00	50·00
28	H 40	20·00	30·00
30	H 40	60·00	60·00
34	H 40	40·00	50·00
36	H 40	£100	£100
40	H 40	70·00	70·00
41	H 40	40·00	80·00
41	I 41	20·00	30·00
43	H 40	50·00	50·00
43	I 41	30·00	20·00
44	H 40	50·00	70·00

2½d. Light ultramarine *Photogravure Low Values* **KING GEORGE VI** **QA**

Cyl. No.	Control	No dot	Dot
44	I 41	60·00	60·00
45	I 41	10·00	10·00
48	I 41	10·00	10·00
53	I 41	40·00	60·00
56	I 41	20·00	40·00
57	I 41	30·00	40·00
58	I 41	60·00	80·00
59	I 41	20·00	50·00
61	I 41	20·00	20·00
62	I 41	50·00	75·00
63	I 41	15·00	40·00
64	I 41	60·00	40·00
65	I 41	£350	£450

Perforation Type 6 (no dot I/P) and 6B (dot E/P)

Cyl. No.	Control	No dot	Dot
6(i)	G 40	30·00	30·00
6(ii)	G 40	70·00	20·00
8	G 40	70·00	70·00
10	H 40	60·00	60·00
20	H 40	60·00	40·00
22	H 40	60·00	50·00
23	H 40	80·00	80·00
25	H 40	80·00	80·00
30	H 40	80·00	80·00
41	H 40	£150	£150

Varieties:
Cylinder 6 Control G 40 exists in two states:
  (i) Control faint
  (ii) Control heavily retouched

Cylinder 13 exists in two states:
  (i) Control faint
  (ii) Control heavily retouched

Retouched controls
The following controls were retouched before the cylinders were put to press:
G 40 Cyl. 7, 7.
I 41 Cyl. 41, 41., 43, 43.

"Shadow" controls
Distinct traces of the previous control are seen on the following:
D 38 Cyl. 2 (C 38)
H 40 Cyl. 6 (G 40)
I 41 Cyl. 44 (H 40)

Coils
Vertical delivery made up from sheets with joins every 20th stamp

Code No.	Issued	Number in roll	Face value		
F	1937	960	£10.0.0	Bottom delivery	£200

Sideways delivery made up from sheets with joins every 12th stamp
| M | 1937 | 480 | £5.0.0 | Left side delivery | £100 |

Vertical delivery printed from continuous reels
| F | 1940 | 960 | £10.0.0 | Bottom delivery | £120 |

Sideways delivery printed from continuous reels with watermark sideways
| M | June 1940 | 480 | £5.0.0 | Left side delivery | 85·00 |

Imprimatur from the National Postal Museum Archives
Imperforate, watermark Type **W20**

Watermark upright (pair) £6500

1941 *(21 July)*. **2½d. Light ultramarine**

Q14 (=S.G.489)

	Mint	Used
Light ultramarine	30	30
a. Watermark inverted (3.42)	1·50	1·00
b. Watermark sideways (8.42)	15·00	12·00
c. *Tête-bêche* (horizontal pair)	£18000	
d. Imperf. (pair)	£4800	
da. Imperf. three sides (horizontal pair)	£7500	
f. b for d in value (Cyl. 239 Dot, R. 18/3)	75·00	
g. White dot by clover leaf (Cyl. 172 Dot, R. 18/2)	50·00	
s. "Specimen", Type 9		
t. "Cancelled", Type 28		
u. "Cancelled", Type 33		
v. "Specimen", Type 23		
w. "Specimen", Type 30		

No. Q14da is perforated at foot only and from the same sheet as No. Q14d sold over a Post Office counter.

Q14f   Q14g

Controls and Cylinder Numbers (Blocks of Six)
Perforation Type 5 (E/I)

Cyl. No.	Control	No dot	Dot
69	J 41	7·00	7·00
70	J 41	10·00	7·00
72	J 41	10·00	7·00
73	J 41	£200	—
75	J 41	50·00	90·00
77	J 41	50·00	75·00
80	J 41	50·00	50·00
80	K 42	70·00	70·00
81	J 41	20·00	20·00
81	K 42	75·00	75·00
82	J 41	†	£150
83	J 41	50·00	50·00
83	K 42	40·00	60·00
84	J 41	30·00	30·00
84	K 42	40·00	10·00
84	L 42	80·00	50·00
86	K 42	15·00	15·00
87	K 42	7·00	7·00
90	K 42	20·00	30·00
92	K 42	70·00	50·00
95	K 42	60·00	60·00
95	L 42	60·00	60·00
96	K 42	15·00	15·00
96	L 42	80·00	80·00
97	L 42	15·00	50·00
99	L 42	15·00	30·00
100	L 42	15·00	15·00
101	L 42	30·00	30·00
104	L 42	20·00	10·00
110	L 42	—	†
110	M 43	30·00	50·00
111	L 42	40·00	40·00
111	M 43	70·00	70·00
113	L 42	60·00	60·00
113	M 43	40·00	40·00
114	L 42	30·00	30·00
117	L 42	60·00	30·00
117	M 43	75·00	75·00
118	M 43	10·00	20·00
119	M 43	40·00	40·00
120	M 43	10·00	10·00
121	M 43	60·00	40·00
121	N 43	30·00	60·00
124	M 43	20·00	20·00

243

QA KING GEORGE VI *Photogravure Low Values* **2½d. Light ultramarine**

Cyl. No.	Control	No dot	Dot
127	M 43	75·00	75·00
130	M 43	50·00	50·00
131	M 43	60·00	60·00
131	N 43	60·00	60·00
132	M 43	40·00	40·00
132	N 43	40·00	60·00
133	M 43	60·00	60·00
133	N 43	60·00	60·00
135	M 43	60·00	60·00
135	N 43	40·00	40·00
136	N 43	15·00	15·00
138	N 43	50·00	50·00
142	N 43	40·00	30·00
142	O 44	60·00	60·00
143	N 43	60·00	60·00
144	N 43	30·00	50·00
145	N 43	30·00	15·00
145	O 44	30·00	20·00
146	N 43	80·00	60·00
146	O 44	20·00	20·00
147	O 44	30·00	30·00
148	O 44	20·00	10·00
149	O 44	15·00	7·00
150	O 44	20·00	40·00
151	P 44	60·00	60·00
152	O 44	20·00	20·00
152	P 44	30·00	40·00
153	O 44	10·00	20·00
154	O 44	7·00	7·00
155	O 44	50·00	30·00
155	P 44	50·00	50·00
156	P 44	50·00	50·00
157	P 44	50·00	30·00
159	P 44	20·00	20·00
162	P 44	40·00	60·00
164	P 44	40·00	40·00
165	P 44	50·00	50·00
166	P 44	60·00	60·00
168	P 44	60·00	60·00
172	P 44	40·00	75·00*
172	Q 45	40·00	75·00*
173	Q 45	30·00	50·00
174	P 44	15·00	30·00
174	Q 45	10·00	10·00
177	Q 45	40·00	10·00
178	Q 45	60·00	60·00
184	Q 45	—	—
186	Q 45	40·00	40·00
186	R 45	50·00	50·00
187	R 45	30·00	50·00
187	Q 45	50·00	50·00
190	Q 45	60·00	40·00
190	R 45	50·00	40·00
194	R 45	60·00	60·00
195	S 46	20·00	40·00
197	S 46	10·00	10·00
201	S 46	50·00	50·00
201	T 46	25·00	40·00
202	S 46	25·00	7·00
202	T 46	25·00	25·00
203	S 46	7·00	15·00
203	T 46	7·00	15·00
204	T 46	10·00	7·00
204	U 47	40·00	40·00
205	S 46	60·00	60·00
205	T 46	7·00	7·00
206	S 46	10·00	10·00
209	U 47	25·00	25·00
210	T 46	25·00	25·00
211	U 47	30·00	15·00
212	U 47	35·00	35·00
213	U 47	10·00	10·00
216	U 47	10·00	7·00
217	U 47	25·00	25·00
219	None	50·00	50·00
220	U 47	10·00	10·00
222	None	7·00	7·00
223	None	7·00	7·00
224	None	15·00	30·00
225	U 47	7·00	7·00
225	None	40·00	40·00
226	None	60·00	60·00
227	U 47	7·00	7·00
228	None	40·00	40·00
229	None	50·00	50·00
230	None	35·00	35·00
231	None	35·00	35·00
234	None	25·00	25·00
235	None	10·00	20·00
236	None	7·00	7·00
238	None	7·00	7·00
239	None	7·00	7·00
240	None	7·00	7·00
241	None	10·00	10·00
244	None	60·00	40·00
245	None	30·00	40·00
246	None	40·00	40·00
247	None	30·00	30·00
248	None	10·00	10·00
249	None	7·00	7·00
250	None	15·00	25·00
252	None	10·00	10·00
253	None	7·00	7·00
254	None	7·00	7·00
255	None	7·00	7·00
256	None	20·00	20·00
260	None	7·00	7·00
261	None	30·00	15·00
263	None	40·00	30·00
266	None	25·00	25·00

Perforation Type 6 (no dot I/P) and 6B (dot E/P)

Cyl. No.	Control	No dot	Dot
111	L 42	£120	£120
135	M 43	70·00	†
138	N 43	10·00	40·00
144	N 43	20·00	20·00
146	N 43	50·00	50·00
148	O 44	†	£120
151	N 43	30·00	†
151	O 44	7·00	10·00
152	O 44	60·00	60·00
156	P 44	80·00	†
161	P 44	50·00	50·00
164	P 44	50·00	50·00
165	P 44	40·00	50·00
167	P 44	50·00	50·00
172	P 44	60·00	60·00
173	Q 45	30·00	30·00
179	Q 45	60·00	60·00
184	Q 45	10·00	7·00
187	Q 45	30·00	30·00
187	R 45	50·00	50·00
190	Q 45	50·00	50·00
194	R 45	30·00	30·00
195 (i)	R 45	20·00	20·00
195 (ii)	R 45	£150	£150
196	R 45	30·00	50·00
236	None	30·00	30·00
238	None	50·00	30·00
239	None	30·00	20·00
240	None	30·00	20·00
246	None	80·00	80·00
260	None	50·00	50·00
261	None	£100	£100
263	None	50·00	30·00

Perforation Type 6 (dot I/P)

Cyl. No.	Control	No dot	Dot
135	M 43		40·00
138	N 43		40·00
144	N 43		40·00
146	N 43		40·00
151	N 43		25·00
151	O 44		40·00
152	O 44		40·00
156	P 44		40·00
161	P 44		40·00
164	P 44		60·00
165	P 44		60·00
167	P 44		40·00

2½d. Pale Scarlet Photogravure Low Values — KING GEORGE VI — QA

Cyl. No.	Control	No dot	Dot
173	Q 45		60·00
184	Q 45		£150

Perforation Type 5AE (AE/I), no dot cylinder only

Cyl. No.	Control	No dot	Dot
142	O 44	£125	
145	O 44	75·00	
146	N 43	£125	
148	O 44	£125	
149	O 44	95·00	
150	O 44	£125	
152	O 44	95·00	
154	O 44	95·00	
156	P 44	£175	
162	P 44	£125	
164	P 44	95·00	
165	P 44	95·00	
172	P 44	£125	
172	Q 45	75·00	
174	Q 45	75·00	
177	Q 45	£125	
184	Q 45	£125	
186	Q 45	75·00	
190	Q 45	—	
219	None	£150	
223	None	£125	
245	None	—	
248	None	£125	
249*	None	£125	

* Extension hole at top of rows 18 and 20 (see Perforators, Appendix 1).

Varieties:
Cylinder 100 had the L and fraction bar engraved by hand.
On cylinder 146 the control N 43 has been heavily retouched on both panes. The retouches show as an outline of heavy dots.
Cylinder 195 exists in two states. In state (ii) the control has been heavily retouched.
The U 47 controls have been retouched on cylinder 212 (dot pane) and cylinder 217 (no dot pane).

Errors of engraving
Cylinder 144 (both panes) were originally engraved "141". Cylinder 166 dot pane was originally engraved "116", and cylinder 204 (no dot pane) was originally engraved "104".

"Shadow" controls
Distinct traces of the previous control are seen on L 42 cylinder 96 dot (K 42) and on O 44 cylinder 146 (both panes N 43).

Coils
Vertical delivery printed in continuous reels

Code No.	Issued	Number in roll	Face value	
F	1942	960	£10.0.0	Bottom delivery £100
U	Nov. 1949	1920	£20.0.0	Bottom delivery —

Sideways delivery printed from continuous reels with watermark sideways
M Aug. 1942 480 £5.0.0 Left side delivery 40·00

Imprimatur from the National Postal Museum Archives
Imperforate, watermark Type **W20**

Watermark upright (pair) £5500

Imprimatur from the British Postal Museum & Archive
Watermark upright (marginal single) £1500

1951 (3 May). **2½d. Pale Scarlet**
Q15 (=S.G.507)

	Mint	Used
Pale scarlet	60	40
a. Watermark inverted	2·00	1·25
b. Watermark sideways	1·75	1·75
ba. Damaged S in POSTAGE (wmk. sideways)	40·00	
d. Tête-bêche (horizontal pair)		

Q15ba

Cylinder Numbers (Blocks of Six)
Perforation Type 5 (E/I)

Cyl. No.	No dot	Dot
259	50·00	50·00
261	50·00	50·00
264	£125	£125
266	50·00	50·00
267	30·00	50·00
268	30·00	50·00
269	15·00	15·00
270	40·00	40·00
273	30·00	30·00
274	20·00	30·00
275	50·00	30·00
276	20·00	20·00
277	30·00	30·00
279	50·00	50·00

Coils
Vertical delivery printed from continuous reels

Code No.	Issued	Number in roll	Face value	
F	May 1951	960	£10.0.0	Bottom delivery £100
U	May 1951	1920	£20.0.0	Bottom delivery —

Sideways delivery printed from continuous reels with watermark sideways
M 3.5.51 480 £5.0.0 Left side delivery 40·00

Imprimatur from the National Postal Museum Archives
Imperforate, watermark Type **W20**

Watermark upright (pair) £5500

3d. Type Q1

1938 (31 January). **3d. Violet**
Q16 (=S.G.467)

	Mint	Used
Violet	5·00	1·00
a. Top margin imperf.		
b. Dark spot below eye (Cyl. 11 No dot, R. 19/1)	85·00	
c. Dotted line into margin (Cyl. 14 No dot, R. 20/1)	85·00	
f. Coil join (vertical pair)		
g. Coil join (horizontal pair) (6.38)		
s. "Specimen", Type 26	£300	

245

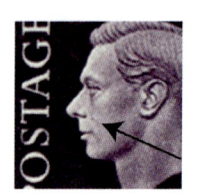

QA KING GEORGE VI *Photogravure Low Values* 3d. Pale Violet

	Mint	Used
s. "Specimen", Type 9		
t. "Cancelled", Type 33		
u. "Specimen", Type 30		

Q16b  Q16c

Q17a

Q17b

Q17c Q17d

Controls and Cylinder Numbers (Blocks of Six)
Perforation Type 5 (E/I)

Cyl. No.	Control	No dot	Dot
3	C 38	60·00	60·00
5(i)	C 38	60·00	60·00
5(ii)	C 38	†	95·00
9	C 38	60·00	75·00
9	D 38	60·00	60·00
11	E 39	£110*	60·00
12	E 39	60·00	60·00
14	G 40	£110*	60·00
17	G 40	£200	£200
18	G 40	60·00	60·00
18	H 40	60·00	60·00

Perforation Type 6 (no dot I/P) and 6B (dot E/P)

Cyl. No.	Control	No dot	Dot
11	E 39	£100*	85·00
12	E 39	75·00	85·00

Varieties:
Cylinder 5 dot exists in two states:
(i) No dot after "5".
(ii) added dot after "5".
Cylinders 3, 5 and 9 dot have a white dot in the "3" of the control with damage in the shape of two additional white dots on cylinder 9 dot.

"Shadow" controls
Distinct traces of the previous control are seen in the following:
E 39   Cyl. 11. (D 38)
H 40   Cyl. 18 (G 40)

Coils
Vertical delivery made up from sheets with joins every 20th stamp

Code No.	Issued	Number in roll	Face value	
C	1938	960	£12.0.0 Bottom delivery	£125

Sideways delivery made up from sheets with joins every 12th stamp

| S | June 1938 | 480 | £6.0.0 Left side delivery | £100 |

Imprimatur from the National Postal Museum Archives
Imperforate, watermark Type W20

Watermark upright £6500

1941 (3 November). **3d. Pale Violet**

Q17 (=S.G.490)

	Mint	Used
Pale violet	2·50	1·00
a. White patch in hair and blemish in background (Cyl. 34 Dot, R. 9/10)	£100	
b. Ditto, retouched	85·00	
c. Broken circle to value (Cyl. 27 No dot, R. 18/2)	85·00	
d. Ditto, retouched	85·00	
e. Top margin imperf.		
f. Coil join (vertical pair) (1942)		
g. Coil join (horizontal pair) (6.43)		

Controls and Cylinder Numbers (Blocks of Six)
Perforation Type 5 (E/I)

Cyl. No.	Control	No dot	Dot
21	J 41	25·00	25·00
21	K 42	22·00	22·00
21	L 42	25·00	35·00
22	L 42	50·00	60·00
22	M 43	25·00	25·00
22	N 43	60·00	50·00
25	N 43	22·00	22·00
25	O 44	25·00	25·00
26	N 43	25·00	25·00
26	O 44	45·00	35·00
27	R 45	£100*	30·00
27	None	£100*	45·00
28	Q 45	22·00	22·00
30	None	60·00	60·00
32	None	95·00	95·00
34	None	22·00	22·00

Perforation Type 6 (I/P)

Cyl. No.	Control	No dot 6 (I/P)	No dot 6B (E/P)	Dot 6 (I/P)
21	J 41	25·00	95·00	50·00
21	L 42	£200	£200	†

Cyl. No.	Control	No dot 6 (I/P)	Dot 6B (E/P)
22	L 42	£150	£150
28	P 44	25·00	30·00
29	O 44	22·00	30·00
29	P 44	50·00	75·00

Perforation Type 2A (P/P)

| 30 | None | † | — |

Perforation Type 5AE (AE/I), no dot cylinder only

| 25 | O 44 | £150 | |
| 28 | Q 45 | £200 | |

"Shadow" control
Distinct traces of the previous control are seen on K 42 cylinder 21 dot (J 41).

Error of engraving
On cylinder 27 the dividing arrow was incorrectly engraved between stamps 7 and 8 in the upper and lower margins. This was erased by lines and re-engraved in the correct position between stamps 6 and 7.

Coils
Vertical delivery made up from sheets with joins every 20th stamp

Code No.	Issued	Number in roll	Face value		
C	1942	960	£12.0.0	Bottom delivery	£100

Sideways delivery made up from sheets with joins every 12th stamp

S	June 1943	480	£6.0.0	Left side delivery	80·00

Imprimatur from the National Postal Museum Archives
Imperforate. Watermark Type **W20**
Watermark upright (pair)... £5500

Imprimatur from the British Postal Museum & Archive
Watermark upright (marginal single).. £1500

4d. Type Q2

1938 (21 November). **4d. Grey-green**

Q19 (=S.G.468)

	Mint	Used
Grey-green	60	75
a. Imperf. (horizontal pair)	£9000	
b. Imperf. three sides (horizontal pair)	£9500	
c. Heavy line (Cyl. 6 Dot, R. 1/4)	£125	
s. "Specimen", Type 9		
t. "Cancelled", Type 33		
u. "Specimen", Type 23	£200	
v. "Specimen", Type 30		

No. Q19b is perforated at foot only and came from the same sheet as No. Q19a sold over a Post Office counter.

Q19c

Controls and Cylinder Numbers (Blocks of Six)
Single Pane cylinder. Perforation Type 6B (no dot E/P)

Cyl. No.	Control	No dot	Dot
1	D 38	11·00	
1	E 39	11·00	
1	G 40	15·00	
1	I 41	11·00	
1	K 42	15·00	
1	K 42bar _	15·00	
1	K 42bars ⌊	11·00	

Perforation Type 6 (no dot I/P)
| 1 | I 41 | 25·00 | |

Double Pane cylinder. Perforation Type 6 (no dot I/P) and 6B (dot E/P)

Cyl. No.	Control	No dot	Dot
6	None	11·00	11·00
9	O 44	11·00	11·00
9	O 44bar _	30·00	11·00
9	O 44bars ⌊	11·00	25·00
9	O 44bars ⌐	11·00	11·00

"Shadow" controls
Distinct traces of the previous control are seen on the following:
I 41 Cyl. 1 (G 40)
K 42 (incl. 1 and 2 bars) Cyl. 1 (I 41)

Imprimatur from the National Postal Museum Archives
Imperforate, watermark Type **W20**
Watermark upright (pair)... £6500

1950 (2 October). **4d. Light Ultramarine**

Q20 (=S.G.508)

	Mint	Used
Light ultramarine	2·00	1·75
a. Retouched background to POS (Cyl. 13 No dot, R. 9/2)	£100	
b. Double impression	†	£7000
c. Coil join (vertical pair)		
d. Coil join (horizontal pair)		

Two used examples of No. Q20b are known. The double impression is not as clear as the King George V varieties since it is a pale stamp, but inscription and frame are doubled nevertheless. It was probably due to paper movement in the press.

No Q20 is known used at Salisbury on 30 September and Inverness and Windsor Castle on 1 October 1950.

Q20a

Cylinder Numbers (Blocks of Six)
Perforation Types

	2 (I/E)	3 (P/E)	5 (E/I)	5 (E/I)	6 (I/P)	6B (E/P)
Cyl. No.	No dot	Dot	No dot	Dot	No dot	Dot
13	£175	£175	25·00	35·00	50·00	50·00

Coils
Vertical delivery made up from sheets with joins every 20th stamp

Code No.	Issued	Number in roll	Face value		
A	2.10.50	960	£16.0.0	Bottom delivery	80·00

Sideways delivery made up from sheets with joins every 12th stamp
| H | 2.10.50 | 480 | £8.0.0 | Left side delivery | 65·00 |

Imprimatur from the National Postal Museum Archives
Imperforate, watermark Type **W20**
Watermark upright (pair)... £5500

QA KING GEORGE VI Photogravure Low Values 5d. Brown

5d. Type Q2

1938 *(21 November).* **5d. Brown**

Q21 (=S.G.469)

	Mint	Used
Brown	3·50	85
a. Imperf. (pair)	£8500	
b. Imperf. three sides (horizontal pair)	£9000	
s. "Specimen", Type 9		
t. "Specimen", Type 23	£250	
u. "Specimen", Type 30		

No. Q21b is perforated at foot only and came from the same sheet as No. Q21a sold over a Post Office counter.

Controls and Cylinder Numbers (Blocks of Six)
Single Pane cylinder. Perforation Type 6B (no dot E/P)

Cyl. No.	Control	No dot	Dot
1	D 38	25·00	
1	E 39	25·00	
1	G 40	25·00	
1	I 41	£125	
1	K 42	25·00	

Perforation Type 6 (no dot I/P)
| 1 | I 41 | 50·00 | |

Double Pane cylinder. Perforation Type 5 (E/I)
3	L 42	£350	£350
3	L 42bar	30·00	30·00
3	L 42bars ⌐	30·00	30·00
3	L 42bars ☐	50·00	35·00
3	L 42bars ☐	25·00	25·00

Perforation Type 6 (no dot I/P) and 6B (dot E/P)
| 3 | L 42bars ⌐ | 25·00 | 25·00 |
| 4 | K 42 | † | 40·00 |

Perforation Type 5AE (no dot AE/I)
| 3 | L 42bars ⌐ | £750 | |

"Shadow" control
Distinct traces of the previous control are seen on E 39 cylinder 1 no dot (D 38).

Variety:
Cylinder 1 no dot with control I 41 has a large smudge between the cylinder number and the stamp
Miscut sheets show cyl. no. and L 42 on right-hand margin. See also 2d. pale orange.

Imprimatur from the National Postal Museum Archives
Imperforate, watermark Type **W20**

Watermark upright (pair) £6500

6d. Type Q2

1939 *(30 January).* **6d. Purple**

Q22 (=S.G.470)

	Mint	Used
Purple	1·50	60
a. Coil join (vertical pair)		
b. Extra thorn on rose stem (Cyl. 41 No dot, R. 20/9)	85·00	
c. Coil join (vertical pair)		
s. "Specimen", Type 9		
t. "Cancelled", Type 33		
u. "Specimen", Type 23		
v. "Specimen", Type 30		

Q22b

Controls and Cylinder Numbers (Blocks of Six)
Letterpress control in black. Single Pane cylinders. Perforation Type 2 (no dot I/E)

Cyl. No.	Control	No dot	Dot
1	D 38	30·00	
1	E 39	22·00	
10	F 39	22·00	
10	G 40	22·00	
10	H 40	50·00	
21	H 40	£100	
25	J 41	25·00	
25	K 42	22·00	
25	L 42	22·00	
30	M 43	25·00	
32	L 42	25·00	
32	M 43	22·00	
32	N 43	22·00	
33	O 44	22·00	
33	Q 45	22·00	
33	T 46	£200	
36	T 46	22·00	
36	U 47	22·00	
36	None	30·00	
37	T 46	75·00	
37	None	30·00	
39	None	30·00	
41	None	25·00	

Perforation Type 3 (no dot P/E)
| 25 | K 42 | £225 | |
| 32 | N 43 | £175 | |

Perforation Type 6B (no dot E/P)
| 1 | D 38 | 75·00 | |
| 25 | L 42 | £100 | |

Perforation Type 6 (no dot I/P)
| 1 | D 38 | £125 | |
| 37 | None | £100 | |

Varieties:
Cylinder 25. With control J 41 in state 1 there is a coloured slightly diagonal line running through P of POSTAGE and extending through "25" which has been partly erased in state 2. This remains faint with control K 42 and is completely removed with control L 42. The pick-up bar is omitted below R. 20/10 (control K 42).
Cylinder 37. The pick-up bar under R. 20/1 is badly damaged and under R. 20/10 it is completely omitted.

7d. Emerald-green *Photogravure Low Values* **KING GEORGE VI**   **QA**

Coil
Vertical delivery made up from sheets with joins every 20th stamp

Code No.	Issued	Number in roll	Face value	
J	30.1.39	480	£12.0.0 Bottom delivery	£250

Imprimatur from the National Postal Museum Archives
Imperforate, watermark Type **W20**

Watermark upright (pair) £6500

7d. Type Q3

1939 *(27 February).* **7d. Emerald-green**

Q23 (=S.G.471)

	Mint	Used
Emerald-green	5·00	60
a. Imperf. three sides (horizontal pair)	£9000	
b. Cracked cylinder (Cyl. 10 Dot, R. 1–20/12) Each stamp	60·00	
c. Damaged N in REVENUE (Cyls. 9 and 10 No dot, R. 20/2)	75·00	
d. Mark in crown (Cyl. 9 No dot, R. 14/3)	£140	
e. Accent on second E (Cyl. 12 Dot, R. 19/11)	£140	
s. "Specimen", Type 23	£250	
t. "Cancelled", Type 33		
u. "Specimen", Type 30		

No. Q23a comes from the top row of the sheet and is perforated at bottom only.

Q23d

Q23b   Q23c   Q23e

The illustration of No. Q23b is typical of a plate crack which occurred in all stamps in the 12th vertical row of cylinder 10 dot. This cylinder was withdrawn and replaced by cylinder 9.

No. Q23c occurred in more than one state. In its second state with control S 46 the coloured line is thinner as if an attempt had been made to remove it. Without control it is as in the second state but in addition there is damage to the V of REVENUE.

Controls and Cylinder Numbers (Blocks of Six)
Single Pane cylinders. Perforation Type 6B (no dot E/P)

Cyl. No.	Control	No dot	Dot
1	E 39bar _	£100	
1	E 39bars ⌐	90·00	
2	E 39	65·00	
2	E 39bar _	85·00	
2	E 39bars ☐	65·00	
2	E 39bars ☐	75·00	
2	E 39bars ☐	75·00	
3	E 39bars ∟	65·00	
3	E 39bars ⌐	65·00	
3	E 39bars ☐	75·00	
3	E 39bars ☐	65·00	

Perforation Type 6 (no dot I/P)
1	E 39bar _	£100
2	E 39bars ☐	£100
3	E 39bars ∟	£100

Double Pane cylinders. Perforation Type 5 (E/I)
9	None	£100*	75·00
10	S 46	£100*	65·00
10	None	£100*	75·00
12	None	65·00	65·00

Perforation Type 6 (no dot I/P) and 6B (dot E/P)
9	None	£250*	£250
10	S 46	£100*	65·00
10	None	£150*	75·00
12	None	75·00	£125

Imprimatur from the National Postal Museum Archives
Imperforate, watermark Type **W20**

Watermark upright (pair) £6500

8d. Type Q3

1939 *(27 February).* **8d. Bright Carmine**

Q24 (=S.G.472)

	Mint	Used
Bright carmine	7·50	80
b. Hole in leaf (Cyl. 6 No dot, R. 20/1)	85·00	
s. "Specimen", Type 9		
t. "Cancelled", Type 33		
u. "Specimen", Type 23	£250	
v. "Specimen", Type 30		

Q24b

Controls and Cylinder Numbers (Blocks of Six)
Single Pane cylinders. Perforation Type 6B (no dot E/P)

Cyl. No.	Control	No dot	Dot
1	E 39	70·00	
1	E 39bar _	85·00	
1	E 39bars ∟	70·00	
1	E 39bars ⌐	70·00	
1	E 39bars ☐	85·00	
1	E 39bars ☐	70·00	
3(i)	O 44	£200	
3(ii)	O 44	70·00	
3	O 44bar _	70·00	

249

QA KING GEORGE VI Photogravure Low Values 9d. Deep Olive-green

Double Pane cylinders

Cyl. No.	Control	No dot	Dot
Perforation Type 5 (E/I)			
6	S 46	£100*	70·00
9	None	80·00	£100
Perforation Type 6 (no dot I/P) and 6B (dot E/P)			
6	S 46bar_	90·00*	60·00
9	None	80·00	£1000

Varieties:
The control O 44 exists in two states:
 (i) Control very faint and
 (ii) Control retouched with heavy outline

Imprimatur from the National Postal Museum Archives
Imperforate, watermark Type **W20**

Watermark upright (pair) £6500

9d. Type Q3

1939 (1 May). **9d. Deep Olive-green**

Q25 (=S.G.473)

	Mint	Used
Deep olive-green	6·50	80
a. Sloping serif to top stroke of last E of PENCE and dot to right of central cross in Crown (Cyl. 3 No dot, R. 18/1)	50·00	
b. Serif touched out but dot remains (Cyl. 2 No dot, R. 18/1)	50·00	
c. Spot between E and V (Cyl. 5 No dot, R. 1/2)	£200	
s. "Specimen", Type 9		
t. "Cancelled", Type 33		
u. "Specimen", Type 23	£250	
v. "Specimen", Type 30		

No. Q25a is a multipositive variety occurring on cylinder 3 which was replaced by cylinder 2 where it was partially corrected. A different multipositive was used for cylinder 5.

Q25a   Q25c

Controls and Cylinder Numbers (Blocks of Six)
Letterpress control, in black. Single Pane cylinders. Perforation Type 2 (no dot I/E).

Cyl. No.	Control	No dot	Dot
2	I 41	75·00*	
2	K 42	75·00*	
2	L 42	85·00*	
2	N 43	£125*	
2	O 44	75·00*	
2	P 44	85·00*	
2	R 45	75·00*	
3	E 39	75·00*	
3	G 40	95·00*	
3	H 40	85·00*	
3	N 43	£125*	

Perforation Type 3 (no dot P/E)
| 2 | R 45 | — | |

Double Pane cylinders

Cyl. No.	Control	No dot	Dot
Perforation Type 5 (E/I)			
5	None	80·00	80·00

Cyl. No.	Control	No dot	Dot
Perforation 5AE (no dot cyl. only AE/I)			
5	None	£800	
Perf. Type 6 (no dot I/P) and 6B (dot E/P)			
5	None	£100	80·00
Perf. Type 2 (no dot I/E) and 2A (dot P/P)			
5	None	£200	£200

Imprimatur from the National Postal Museum Archives
Imperforate, watermark Type **W20**

Watermark upright (pair) £6500

10d. Type Q3

1939 (1 May). **10d. Turquoise-blue**

Q26 (=S.G.474)

	Mint	Used
Turquoise-blue	7·00	80
a. Imperf. (pair)	—	
b. Broken fleur-de-lis (Cyl. 7 No dot, R. 20/7)	£125	
s. "Specimen", Type 9		
t. "Cancelled", Type 33		
u. "Specimen", Type 23	£250	
v. "Specimen", Type 30		

Q26b

Controls and Cylinder Numbers (Blocks of Six)
Letterpress control, in black. Single Pane cylinders. Perforation 2 (no dot I/E)

Cyl. No.	Control	No dot	Dot
1	E 39	70·00	
1	F 39	90·00	
1	H 40	70·00	
1	I 41	£125	
1	J 41	90·00	
1	K 42	70·00	
1	L 42	70·00	
1	M 43	90·00	
1	N 43	70·00	
1	O 44	70·00	

Double Pane cylinders.

Cyl. No.	Control	No dot	Dot
Perforation Type 6 (no dot I/P) and 6B (dot E/P)			
5	Q 45	70·00	70·00
5	T 46	70·00	70·00
5	U 47	£100	£100
5	None	80·00	£100
6	Q 45	†	£200
7	None	£200	£200

Perforation Type 5 (E/I)
| 7 | None | £600 | £600 |

Imprimatur from the National Postal Museum Archives
Imperforate, watermark Type **W20**

Watermark upright (pair) £6500

11d. Plum *Photogravure Low Values* **KING GEORGE VI** **QA**

11d. Type Q3

1947 *(29 December).* **11d. Plum**

Q27 (=S.G.474a)

	Mint	Used
Plum	3·00	2·75
b. Tail to N (Cyl. 1 No dot, R. 13/1)	£125	
c. Spot in G (Cyl. 1 No dot, R. 20/2)	45·00	
s. "Specimen", Type 26	£275	

Q27b

Q27c (Later retouched out on perf. type 6)

Cylinder Number (Blocks of Six)
Double Pane cylinder

Cyl. No.	No dot	Dot
Perforation Type 5 (E/I)		
1	55·00*	450·00

| Perf. Type 6 (no dot I/P) and 6B (dot E/P) | | |
| 1 | 60·00* | 50·00 |

Imprimatur from the National Postal Museum Archives
Imperforate, watermark Type **W20**

Watermark upright (pair) £6500

1s. Type Q3

1939 *(1 May).* **1s. Bistre-brown**

Q28 (=S.G.475)

	Mint	Used
Bistre-brown	9·00	75
a. Broken Crown (Cyl. 16 Dot, S 46, R. 18/2)	£100	
b. Missing barb on rose (Cyl. 6 Dot, R. 7/12)	£200	
c. Tail to T broken (Cyl. ?, R. 20/5)		
s. "Specimen", Type 9		
t. "Specimen", Type 23	£160	
u. "Cancelled", Type 33		
v. "Specimen", Type 30		

Q28a

Q28b

Q28c

Variety No. Q28a was corrected by retouching before control U 47 was employed with cylinder 16. It was a multipositive flaw as it first occurred on cylinder 13 but was retouched before being put to press and later retouched again by two vertical lines. It was also retouched before being put to press on cylinders 17 and 19 and on the latter there are two dots close together to the left of the central cross in the Crown.

Controls and Cylinder Numbers (Blocks of Six)
Photogravure control, in bistre-brown. Single Pane cylinder. Perforation Type 6B (no dot E/P)

Cyl. No.	Control	No dot	Dot
7	E 39	80·00	
7	G 40	90·00	

Letterpress control, in black. Single Pane cylinders. Perforation Type 6B (no dot E/P)

Cyl. No.	Control	No dot	Dot
6	H 40	£150	
6	J 41	90·00	
6	K 42	80·00	
6	M 43	90·00	
6	O 44	90·00	
7	H 40	90·00	

Perforation Type 6 (no dot I/P). Perforation Type 6 (dot I/P)

Cyl. No.	Control	No dot	Dot
6	J 41	£150	
6	M 43	£150	
13	Q 45	†	—

On cylinder 6 the number was originally engraved in reverse. This was corrected before the cylinder was put to press.

Double Pane cylinders. Perforation Type 6 (no dot I/P) and 6B (dot E/P)

Cyl. No.	Control	No dot	Dot
13	Q 45	80·00	80·00
14	None	—	†
16	S 46	90·00	£150*
16	U 47	80·00	£100
16	None	£200	£200
17	None	£200	£200
19	None	£200	£200

Perforation Type 5 (E/I)

Cyl. No.	Control	No dot	Dot
16	None	£140*	£150
17	None	£200	£200
19	None	90·00	£150

"Shadow" controls
Trace of O of unissued O 44 control is seen on U 47 cylinder 16 no dot. Shadow of complete O 44 control is clearly seen on this cylinder without control.

Imprimatur from the National Postal Museum Archives
Imperforate, watermark Type **W20**

Watermark upright (pair) £6000

First Day Covers
On plain covers with operational postmarks of the first day of issue. For some values special covers also exist and these are worth more than the prices quoted.

251

KING GEORGE VI Photogravure Low Values Emergency Postage Dies

			Plain covers
QFD 1	(10.5.37)	½d., 1d., 2½d. (Nos. Q1, Q4, Q13)	45·00
QFD 2	(30.7.37)	1½d. (No. Q7)	45·00
QFD 3	(31.1.38)	2d., 3d. (Nos. Q10, Q16)	£100
QFD 4	(21.11.38)	4d., 5d. (Nos. Q19, Q21)	65·00
QFD 5	(30.1.39)	6d. (No. Q22)	60·00
QFD 6	(27.2.39)	7d., 8d. (Nos. Q23, Q24)	85·00
QFD 7	(1.5.39)	9d., 10d., 1s. (Nos. Q25, Q26, Q28)	£500
QFD 8	(21.7.41)	2½d. (No. Q14)	45·00
QFD 9	(11.8.41)	1d. (No. Q5)	22·00
QFD 10	(1.9.41)	½d. (No. Q2)	22·00
QFD 11	(6.10.41)	2d. (No. Q11)	60·00
QFD 12	(3.11.41)	3d. (No. Q17)	£110
QFD 13	(28.9.42)	1½d. (No. Q8)	55·00
QFD 14	(29.12.47)	11d. (No. Q27)	55·00
QFD 15	(2.10.50)	4d. (No. Q20)	£120
QFD 16	(3.5.51)	½d., 1d., 1½d., 2d., 2½d. (Nos. Q3, Q6, Q9, Q12, Q15)	55·00

Emergency Postage Dies

The adoption of photogravure printing resulted in the concentration of cylinder engraving facilities and the cylinders themselves at a single location, Harrison and Sons of High Wycombe.

Concern was expressed at the risk of disruption to supplies of stamps, should Harrisons' premises be damaged by fire, and it was decided in late 1937 to prepare dies and plates for values from ½d. to 2½d. to be printed by letterpress, a process that could be used by a wide range of printers.

The design chosen was a modified version of that previously approved for use on postcards, letter cards and wrappers, comprising a head of King George VI engraved by J.A.C. Harrison, within a frame designed by Eric Gill.

In November 1938 J.A.C. Harrison began work on the ½d. die, reducing the postal stationery image from 19.25 × 23 mm. to 18 × 21.5 mm. to allow space for perforating, while keeping to the printing plate dimensions of the King George V stamps.

The design underwent modification and die proofs, bromides and plate proofs showing the development of these Emergency stamps are held by the British Postal Museum and Archive.

Eventually by the beginning of March 1942 plates were available for ½d., 1d., 2d., 2½d., 3d. and 6d. values.

Die Proofs

½d. Die Proof, uncleared surround

3d. Die Proof

All in black

½d. Original die proof uncleared surround	£1500
½d. "Second working die" proof, cleared surround	£1500
1d. Die proof, "before alteration"	£1500
1d. "Working die" proof, approved "5.7.39"	£1500
2d. Die proof, dated "6.7.39"	£1500
2½d. Die proof, dated "6.7.39"	£1500
3d. Die proof, dated "30.9.41"	£1500
6d. "Original" die proof, uncleared surround, Dated "3.2.39"	£1500
6d. "1st working die" proof, cleared surround, Endorsed "taken from roller, "16.5.39"	£1500
½d., 1d., 1½d., 2d., 2½d. and 6d. Cleared die proofs cut to stamp size, mounted on manilla paper, overprinted "CANCELLED" diagonally in red	Each £1500

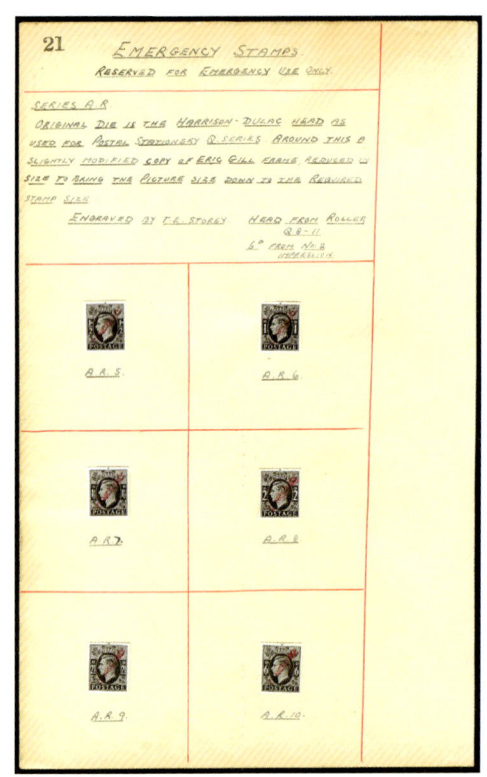

Cleared Die Proofs overprinted "CANCELLED" in red.

Note

Postal Stationery die

Similar proofs exist taken from postal stationery dies, these are outside the scope of this catalogue.

Apart from the difference in size mentioned above, the die proofs for the emergency stamps may be distinguished by the single uncoloured oval surrounding the King's head. Postal stationery dies had an additional coloured oval surround.

Section QB
Booklet Panes in Photogravure (1937–54)

General Notes

Introduction. All the panes were printed in photogravure by Harrison & Sons. Panes of six were printed, as previously, from booklet sheet double-pane cylinders (no dot and dot) and additionally, from October 1938 to January 1943, from single-pane cylinders (no dot). Panes of two were produced as previously on the 1937 issues, then from panes of six, trimmed as necessary and on subsequent issues from the first two columns of counter sheets. Panes of four of the 1937 colours were produced during 1940 from the outside two columns of coil sheets, resulting in sideways watermarks, and of the later colours in 1948 and 1951 from the top and bottom rows of counter sheets and from 1952 on the booklet sheet single-pane cylinders. For details of each booklet and its contents refer to Appendix 2.

Arrangement. The panes are listed in face value order of the stamps they include. The main listing is followed by errors and cylinder flaws with illustrations.

Booklet errors. Those listed as "Imperf. pane" show one row of perforations either at the top or bottom of the pane of six.

Booklet Perforators. Booklet panes are listed according to the perforator type. For description and illustrations see Appendix 1. The letters in brackets above the price columns indicate the appearance of the binding margin of the pane as follows:
- (E) Extension hole in the margin in each row
- (P) Perf. margin
- (I) Imperf. margin
- (BP) Perforations only extend across binding margin at bottom of cylinder panes and across top middle or bottom of ordinary
- (Ie) As (BP) except that the two perforation pins in the margin next to the stamp have been removed (leaving a single ½ hole in the margin)

CHECKLIST OF KING GEORGE VI BOOKLET PANES

Spec. Cat. Nos.	Description	From Booklets Nos.	Page
QB1, QB1a	6 × ½d. green	BD11–15, BD21–25	254
QB2, QB2a	4 × ½d. green, wmk. sideways	BD3–3a	254
QB3, QB3a	2 × ½d. green	BD2–2a	254
QB4, QB4a	6 × ½d. pale green	BD16–18, BD26–29	254
QB5, QB5a	4 × ½d. pale green	BD6–6a	255
QB6	2 × ½d. pale green	BD4	255
QB7, QB7a	6 × ½d. pale orange	BD19–20, BD30–32, F1–13, H1–5	255
QB8–8b	4 × ½d. pale orange	BD7–BD10	255
QB9	2 × ½d. pale orange	BD5	255
QB10, QB10a	6 × 1d. scarlet	BD11–12, BD21–24	255
QB11, QB11a	4 × 1d. scarlet, wmk. sideways	BD3–3a	255
QB12, QB12a	2 × 1d. scarlet	BD2–2a	256
QB13, QB13a	4 × 1d. pale scarlet Type I or II	BD6–6a	256
QB14, QB14a	2 × 1d. pale scarlet Type I or II	BD4	256
QB15, QB15a	6 × 1d. light ultramarine, Type Ic	BD32, H1–6	256
QB16, QB16a	4 × 1d. light ultramarine Type II	BD7–7a	256
QB16b, QB16c	4 × 1d. light ultramarine Type Ia	BD8–10	256
QB17	2 × 1d. light ultramarine Type II	BD5	256
QB18–20a	3 × 1d. light ultramarine and three printed labels Type Ib	BD20, BD31, F1–14	257
QB21, QB21a	6 × 1½d. red-brown	BD11–12, BD21–24	258
QB22, QB22a	2 × 1½d. red-brown	BD1–1a, BD2–2a	258
QB23, QB23a	4 × 1½d. red-brown and two printed labels	BD11–12, BD23–24	259
QB24, QB24a	4 × 1½d. pale red-brown	BD6–6a	260
QB25	2 × 1½d. pale red-brown	BD4	260
QB26, QB26a	6 × 1½d. pale green	BD20, BD31–32	260
QB27–27b	4 × 1½d. pale green	BD7–10	260
QB28	2 × 1½d. pale green	BD5	260
QB29, QB29a	6 × 2d. orange	BD13–15, BD25	260
QB30, QB30a	6 × 2d. pale orange	BD16–18, BD26–29	261
QB31, QB31a	6 × 2d. pale red-brown	BD19, BD30, BD32, H1–7	261
QB32, QB32a	6 × 2½d. ultramarine	BD13–15, BD25	261
QB33, QB33a	6 × 2½d. light ultramarine	BD16–18, BD26–29	261
QB34, QB34a	6 × 2½d. pale scarlet	BD19–20, BD30–32	262

Booklet Pane Prices. The prices quoted are for unmounted mint panes, binding margin attached, and with good perforations. Panes showing some degree of trimming will be worth less than the published prices in this Catalogue.

253

QB KING GEORGE VI Booklet Panes in Photogravure ½d. Green

½d. Green Booklet Panes of Six
From Booklets BD11/15 and BD21/25

	Perf. Type		
	E	P	I
A. Watermark upright			
QB1 (containing No. Q1 × 6) (8.37)	70·00	50·00	70·00
s. "Cancelled", Type 33P	£300		
t. "Cancelled", Type 33	£875		
B. Watermark inverted			
QB1a (containing No. Q1a × 6) (8.37)	£100	80·00	£100
as. "Cancelled", Type 33P	£300		
at. "Cancelled", Type 33	£875		
au. "Specimen", Type 32 and upper left stamp with punch hole	£3000		

Booklet Cylinder Numbers
Panes of six

	Perf. Type	
	B3(I)	B3A(P)
Cyl. No.	No dot	Dot
E 10	£125	£125
E 19 (shown as E. 19)	80·00	†
E 22 (shown as E. 22)	80·00	†
E 28	80·00	†
E 29	80·00	†
E 38	£125	†
E 39	£125	†
E 41	£110	†
E 42	£110	†
E 43	—	†
E 45	80·00	†
E 46	£125	†
E 48	80·00	†
E 49	£125	†
E 50	£125	†

	Perf. Type		
	B4(E)	B4A(I)	B4B(E)
Cyl. No.	No dot	Dot	Dot
E 2	80·00	80·00	80·00
Wmk. inverted	£500	£500	£500
E 5	90·00	90·00	100·00
E 10	80·00	90·00	100·00
E 18	80·00	80·00	100·00
E 35	80·00	125·00	125·00
E 36	125·00	125·00	†

In cylinder E 42 only the "2" shows and a small part of "4", so that it can easily be mistaken for E 2.

½d. Green Booklet Panes of Four
From Booklets BD3/a made up from coil printings intended for sideways delivery

	Perf. Type I
A. Selvedge at top. Watermark sideways	
QB2 (containing No. Q1b × 4) (6.40)	£110

	Perf. Type E
B. Selvedge at bottom. Watermark sideways	
QB2a (containing No. Q1b × 4) (6.40)	£110
s. "Specimen", Type 23 and upper left stamp with punch hole	£2400

Booklet Cylinder Numbers
Panes of four. Selvedge at bottom.

	Perf. Type E
Cyl. No.	No dot
A 40 (top row)	£200
A 40 (bottom row)	£200

½d. Green Booklet Panes of Two
From Booklets BD2/a

	Perf. Type		
	E	P	I
A. Watermark upright			
QB3 (containing No. Q1 × 2) (2.38)	£120	£120	£120
B. Watermark inverted			
QB3a (containing No. Q1a × 2) (2.38)	£120	£120	£120
ab. "Specimen", Type 30 and left stamp with punch hole	£1200		

Made up from guillotined panes of six.

Booklet Cylinder Numbers
Panes of two

	Perf. Type	
	B3(I)	
Cyl. No.	No dot	Dot	Dot
E 10	£175		
E 28	£200		

	Perf. Type		
	B4(E)	B4A(I)	B4B(E)
E 2	†	£175	£200
E 10	†	£175	†
E 18	£200	†	†

½d. Pale Green Booklet Panes of Six
From Booklets BD16/18 and BD26/29

	Perf. Type			
	I	P	BP	Ie
A. Watermark upright				
QB4 (containing No. Q2 × 6) (3.42)	30·00	£120	£175	30·00
s. "Specimen", Type 30 and upper left stamp with punch hole			£3250	
B. Watermark inverted				
QB4a (containing No. Q2b × 6) (3.42)	45·00	£120	£175	75·00

Booklet Cylinder Numbers
Panes of six

	Perf. Type	
	B3(I)	B6(Ie)
Cyl. No.	No dot	Dot
E 53	75·00	†
E 56	75·00	†
E 58	75·00	†
E 59	75·00	†
E 62	75·00	†
E 65	85·00	£450
E 66	75·00	75·00
E 67	75·00	75·00
E 68	75·00	75·00
E 70	75·00	75·00
E 71	75·00	75·00
E 72	75·00	75·00
E 73	75·00	75·00
E 75	75·00	75·00
E 76	75·00	75·00
E 77	75·00	75·00
E 78	75·00	75·00
E 79	75·00	75·00
E 80	75·00	75·00
E 81	75·00	75·00
E 82	75·00	75·00
E 83	75·00	75·00

	Perf. Type
	B5(BP)
E 65	95·00
E 66	—

254

½d. Pale Green   Booklet Panes in Photogravure   **KING GEORGE VI**   **QB**

½d. Pale Green Booklet Panes of Four
From Booklets BD6/a made up from counter sheets

	Perf. Type P
A. Selvedge at top. Watermark upright	
QB5 (containing No. Q2 × 4) (−.48)	—

	Perf. Type I
B. Selvedge at bottom. Watermark upright	
QB5a (containing No. Q2 × 4) (−.48)	—

½d. Pale Green Booklet Panes of Two
From Booklet BD4 made up from columns 1 and 2 of sheets
Watermark upright

	Perf. Type E
QB6 (containing No. Q2 × 2) (12.47)	15·00
a. ½ arrow in margin, top or bottom	25·00

Booklet Cylinder Numbers
Panes of two

	Perf. Type E	
Cyl. No.	No dot	Dot
137	75·00	75·00
143	—	†
147	£140	†
150	£100	£100

½d. Pale Orange Booklet Panes of Six
From Booklets BD19/20, BD30/32, F1/13 and H1/5

	Perf. Type	
	I	Ie
A. Watermark upright		
QB7 (containing No. Q3 × 6) (5.51)	10·00	20·00
b. Imperf. pane of 6*	£20000	

*Booklet error. See General Notes.

B. Watermark inverted		
QB7a (containing No. Q3b × 6) (5.51)	10·00	20·00

Booklet Cylinder Numbers
Panes of six

	Perf. Type	
	B3(I)	B6(Ie)
Cyl. No.	No dot	Dot
E 82	50·00	50·00
E 83	50·00	50·00
E 84	40·00	45·00
E 85	65·00	40·00

½d. Pale Orange Booklet Panes of Four
From Booklets BD7/10

	Perf. Type P
A. Selvedge at top. Watermark upright	
QB8 (containing No. Q3 × 4) (5.51)	15·00

From Booklet BD7

	Perf. Type I
B. Selvedge at bottom. Watermark upright	
QB8a (containing No. Q3 × 4) (5.51)	50·00

From Booklets BD8/10

	Perf. Type P
C. Selvedge at top. Watermark inverted	
QB8b (containing No. Q3b × 4) (12.52)	15·00

Imprimatur from the British Postal Museum & Archive
Two panes as QB8a/b tête-bêche with horizontal gutter margin,
Cylinder E8b no dot at left £30000

½d. Pale Orange Booklet Panes of Two
From Booklet BD5 made up from columns 1 and 2 of sheets
Watermark upright

	Perf. Type	
	E	E (½v)
QB9 (containing No. Q3 × 2) (5.51)	15·00	25·00

Booklet Cylinder Numbers
Panes of two

	Perf. Type E	
Cyl. No.	No dot	Dot
151	†	75·00
153	50·00	50·00
154	75·00	—
155	50·00	†

1d. Scarlet Booklet Panes of Six
From Booklets BD11/12 and BD21/24

		Perf. Type	
	E	P	I
A. Watermark upright			
QB10 (containing No. Q4 × 6) (8.37)	£100	65·00	85·00
s. "Cancelled", Type 33P	£450		
t. "Cancelled", Type 33	£825		
v. "Specimen", Type 32 and upper left stamp with punch hole	£3000		
B. Watermark inverted			
QB10a (containing No. Q4a × 6) (8.37)	£325	£275	£325
as. "Cancelled", Type 33P	£450		
at. "Cancelled", Type 33	£825		

Booklet Cylinder Numbers
Panes of six

	Perf. Type	
	B3(I)	B3A(P)
Cyl. No.	No dot	Dot
F 3	†	—
F 7	£110	†
F 9 (shown as F. 9)	80·00	†
F 14	75·00	†
F 15	75·00	†
F 16	£100	†

	Perf. Type		
	B4(E)	B4A(I)	B4B(E)
Cyl. No.	No dot	Dot	Dot
F 1	75·00	80·00	75·00
F 3	75·00	75·00	75·00
F 4	£150	£150	£150
F 5	85·00	75·00	80·00
F 10	100·00	100·00	†

1d. Scarlet Booklet Panes of Four
From Booklets BD3/a made up from coil printings intended for sideways delivery

	Perf. Type E
A. Selvedge at top. Watermark sideways	
QB11 (containing No. Q4b × 4) (6.40)	£175

	Perf. Type I
B. Selvedge at bottom. Watermark sideways	
QB11a (containing No. Q4b × 4) (6.40)	£175
as. "Specimen", Type 23 and upper left stamp with punch hole	£2400

QB KING GEORGE VI Booklet Panes in Photogravure 1d. Scarlet

Booklet Cylinder Numbers
Panes of four, selvedge at top

	Perf. Type
	B4(E)
Cyl. No.	No dot
B 17 (top row)	£275
B 17 (bottom row)	£275

1d. Scarlet Booklet Panes of Two
From Booklets BD2/a

	Perf. Type		
	E	P	I
A. Watermark upright			
QB12 (containing No. Q4 × 2) (2.38)	£125	£125	£125
b. "Specimen", Type 30 and left stamp with punch hole	£1200		
B. Watermark inverted			
QB12a (containing No. Q4a × 2) (2.38)	£125	£125	£125
Made up from guillotined panes of six.			

Booklet Cylinder Numbers
Panes of two

	Perf. Type			
	B3(I)	B4(E)	B4A(I)	B4B(E)
Cyl. No.	No dot	No dot	Dot	Dot
F 1	†	†	£200	£250
F 5	†	—	£200	—
F 15	£250	†	†	†

1d. Pale Scarlet Booklet Panes of Four
From Booklet BD6/a made up from counter sheets

	Perf. Type P
A. Selvedge at top. Watermark upright.	
QB13 (containing No. Q5 × 4) Type I (–.48)	—
b. (containing No. Q5A × 4) Type II	—

	Perf. Type I
B. Selvedge at bottom. Watermark upright.	
QB13a (containing No. Q5 × 4) Type I (–.48)	—
ab. (containing No. Q5A × 4) Type II	—

1d. Pale Scarlet Booklet Panes of Two
From Booklet BD4 made up from columns 1 and 2 of sheets

	Perf. Type	
	E	I
A. Watermark upright. Type I		
QB14 (containing No. Q5 × 2) (12.47)	75·00	75·00
b. ½ arrow in margin, top or bottom	50·00	
B. Watermark upright. Type II		
QB14a (containing No. Q5A × 2) (12.47)	£100	£100
ab. ½ arrow in margin, top or bottom	£110	£110

Booklet Cylinder Numbers
Panes of two

Type I	Perf. Type E	
Cyl. No.	No dot	Dot
157	£100	£100
159	†	£125
160	90·00	90·00
171	—	†
172	£150	£150

	Perf. Type		
Type II	E	I	E
Cyl. No.	No dot	No Dot	Dot
175	£150	†	£150
179	£150	£400	£150

1d. Light Ultramarine Booklet Panes of Six
From Booklets BD32 and H1/6

	Perf. Type	
	I	Ie
A. Watermark upright. Type Ic		
QB15 (containing No. Q6D × 6) (1.53)	40·00	50·00
B. Watermark inverted. Type Ic		
QB15a (containing No. Q6Db × 6) (1.53)	45·00	55·00

Booklet Cylinder Numbers
Panes of six

	Perf. Type	
	B3(I)	B6(Ie)
Cyl. No	No dot	Dot
F 8	65·00	65·00

1d. Light Ultramarine Booklet Panes of Four
From Booklet BD7/a made up from counter sheets

	Perf. Type P
A. Selvedge at top. Watermark upright. Type II	
QB16 (containing No. Q6 × 4) (5.51)	50·00

From Booklet BD7

	Perf. Type I
B. Selvedge at bottom. Watermark upright. Type II	
QB16a (containing No. Q6 × 4) (5.51)	50·00

From Booklets BD8/10

	Perf. Type P
C. Watermark upright. Type Ia	
QB16b (containing No. Q6B × 4) (12.52)	20·00
D. Watermark inverted. Type Ia	
QB16c (containing No. Q6Bb × 4) (12.52)	35·00

Imprimatur from the National Postal Museum Archives
Booklet pane of four. Imperforate, watermark Type **W20**

Two panes as No. QB16b/c *tête-bêche* with horizontal gutter margin

Imprimatur from the British Postal Museum & Archive
Two panes as QB16b/c *tête-bêche* with horizontal gutter margin, Cylinder F3 no dot at left.................£30000

1d. Light Ultramarine Booklet Panes of Two
From Booklet BD5 made up from columns 1 and 2 of sheets

	Perf. Type			
	E	E(½v)	I	I(½v)
Watermark upright. Type I I				
QB17 (containing No. Q6 × 2) (5.51)	15·00	30·00	30·00	75·00

Booklet Cylinder Numbers
Panes of two Perf. Type

	Perf. Type		
	E	I	E
Cyl. No.	No dot	No Dot	Dot
191	†	†	75·00
192	75·00	£400	75·00

1d. Light Ultramarine *Booklet Panes in Photogravure* **KING GEORGE VI** **QB**

1d. Light Ultramarine Booklet Panes with Printed Labels
Panes of six comprising three stamps and three labels

QB18/a (cylinder F5 dot illustrated)

From Booklets BD20, BD31, F1/5, F7, F9, F11 and F14
1st setting "MINIMUM INLAND PRINTED PAPER RATE 1½d."
17 mm. high

	Perf. Type	
	I	Ie
A. Watermark upright. Type Ib		
QB18 (containing No. Q6C × 3) (3.52)	18·00	30·00
b. Partial tête-bêche pane	£8500	
B. Watermark inverted. Type Ib		
QB18a (containing No. Q6Cb × 3) (3.52)	18·00	30·00

Imprimatur from the National Postal Museum Archives
Booklet pane with printed labels. Imperforate, watermark Type W20
Two panes as No. QB18/a arranged tête-bêche £50000

Imprimatur from the British Postal Museum & Archive
Two panes as No. QB18/a tête-bêche.......................£30000

QB19/a (dented frame variety illustrated)

From Booklets F6, F8 and F10
2nd setting "MINIMUM INLAND PRINTED PAPER RATE 1½d."
15 mm. high

	Perf. Type	
	I	Ie
A. Watermark upright. Type Ib		
QB19 (containing No. Q6C × 3) (9.53)	85·00	£100
b. Second label with 2mm. spacing error between "1½d." and "MINIMUM"	£275	
c. Dented frame, bottom right (R. 1/2)	£275	

	Perf. Type	
	I	Ie
B. Watermark inverted. Type Ib		
QB19a (containing No. Q6Cb × 3) (9.53)	85·00	£100
ab. Spur on R (No. 2)	£225	
ac. Blob on E (No. 2)	£225	
ad. Third label with 2 mm. spacing error between "RATE" and value**	£450	

Listed Varieties

QB19ab, QB20ac   QB19ac, QB20ad   QB19c

Booklet Cylinder Numbers
Panes with printed labels from Booklets BD20, BD31, F1/F11 and F14

			Perf. Type	
			B3(I)	B6(Ie)*
Advert.	Cyl. No.	Cyl. No.	No dot	Dot
"MINIMUM INLAND RATE 1½d."	(17 mm.)	F 5	75·00	50·00
Ditto	(15 mm.) Spacing error**	F 7	£575	£575
Ditto	(15 mm.) Spacing corrected†	F 7	£800	£800

For March 1954, edition F14, a scissor cut was made in the left selvedge (1½v) and the bottom selvedge torn off by hand, resulting in torn bottom perfs. Cylinder pane price £400.

*The extension hole is at the top of the pane instead of at the bottom because the panes containing three stamps and three labels had the cylinder number etched one row lower on the cylinder than the panes of six stamps (row 18 for panes of six stamps and row 19 for panes with labels).

**Unlike cylinder F 5, where the labels were included on the cylinder, cylinder F 7 contained impressions of the stamps only, the labels being printed by letterpress in a separate operation. There was an error of spacing on the third label where the vertical distance between "RATE" and "1½d." was 2 mm. instead of 1 mm, resulting in that label being 16mm high. Also, as listed, that spacing error occurred on non-cylinder panes.

†In a later printing of the cylinder panes this was corrected.

257

QB KING GEORGE VI Booklet Panes in Photogravure 1½d. Red-brown

As before, but labels changed

QB20/a

From Booklets F12/13 and F14a
"SHORTHAND IN ONE WEEK"

	Perf. Type	
	I	Ie
A. Watermark upright. Type Ib		
QB20 (containing No. Q6C × 3) (1.54)	75·00	85·00
b. Major retouch (Nos. 1 and 2)	£200	
B. Watermark inverted. Type Ib		
QB20a (containing No. Q6Cb × 3) (1.54)	65·00	85·00
ac. Spur on R (No. 2)	£180	
ad. Blob on E (No. 2)	£180	

Listed Variety

QB20b

Major retouch extends from back of head in No. 1 to front of face in No. 2 giving a mottled effect to the background.
The main differences are found in the thickening of the letters "REVEN" in No. 1 and "STAGE" in No. 2

Booklet Cylinder Number
Panes with printed labels from Booklets F12/13

		Perf. Type	
		B3(I)	B6(Ie)*
Advert.	Cyl. No.	No dot	Dot
"SHORTHAND IN ONE WEEK"	F 7	£300	£300

*As with the previous label cylinder panes, one extension hole at top instead of bottom.

1½d. Red-brown Booklet Panes of Six
From Booklets BD11/12 and BD21/24

	Perf. Type		
	E	P	I
A. Watermark upright			
QB21 (containing No. Q7 × 6) (8.37)	70·00	60·00	60·00
b. "Necklace" flaw (R. 2/2)	£350		
s. "Cancelled", Type 33P	£325		
t. "Cancelled", Type 33	£550		
u. "Specimen", Type 32 and upper left stamp with punch hole	£1500		
B. Watermark inverted			
QB21a (containing No. Q7a × 6) (8.37)	£110	£100	£110
as. "Cancelled", Type 33P	£325		
at. "Cancelled", Type 33	£550		

Listed Variety

QB21b

Booklet Cylinder Numbers
Panes of six

	Perf. Type	
	B3(I)	B3A(P)
Cyl. No.	No dot	Dot
G 8	£120	£120
G 30	85·00	†
G 34	75·00	†
G 36	75·00	†
G 40	75·00	†
G 44	95·00	†
G 45	75·00	†
G 48	85·00	†
G 57	75·00	†
G 58	75·00	†
G 61	£200	†
G 69	£125	†
G 71	£150	†

	Perf. Type		
	B4(E)	B4A(I)	B4B(E)
Cyl. No.	No dot	Dot	Dot
G 8	75·00	75·00	75·00
G 19	75·00	75·00	75·00
G 20	75·00	75·00	85·00
G 28	75·00	75·00	75·00
G 49	75·00	90·00	†
G 50	75·00	90·00	90·00

Cylinder G 28 no dot appears as G. 28. The erroneous dot was not removed and additionally appears on cylinder panes of two produced from panes of six.

1½d. Red-brown Booklet Panes of Two
From Booklets BD1/a and BD2/a

	Perf. Type		
	E	P	I
A. Watermark upright			
QB22 (containing No. Q7 × 2) (1.38)	35·00	35·00	35·00
B. Watermark inverted			
QB22a (containing No. Q7a × 2) (1.38)	50·00	50·00	50·00
ab. "Specimen", Type 30 and left stamp with punch hole	£1200		

Made up from guillotined label panes, then from guillotined panes of six.

Booklet Cylinder Numbers
Panes of two

	Perf. Type		
	B4(E)	B4A(I)	B4B(E)
Cyl. No.	No dot	Dot	Dot
G 19	†	£195	£225
G 20	†	£195	—
G 28	£225	†	†
G 50	£225	£450	†

Cylinder G 28 no dot appears as G. 28.

258

1½d. Red-brown Booklet Panes with Advertising Labels

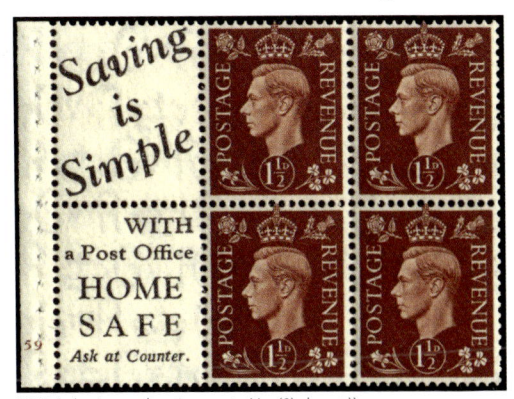

QB23/a (various advertisements, No. (9) shown)

Panes of six, comprising two labels printed in black and four stamps
From Booklets BD11/12 and BD23/24

	Perf. Type		
	E	P	I
A. Watermark upright			
QB23 (containing No. Q7 × 4) (8.37)	£175	£140	£175
s. "Cancelled", Type 33P	£300		
t. "Cancelled", Type 33	£650		
u. "Specimen", Type 32 and upper left stamp with punch hole	£3000		
B. Watermark inverted			
QB23a (containing No. Q7a × 4) (8.37)	£175	£140	£175
as. "Cancelled", Type 33P	£300		
at. "Cancelled", Type 33	£650		

		Wmk Upright	Wmk Inverted
(1)	"Cash's name tapes J. & J. Cash Ltd. / Coventry" at foot (numbered 405)	£225	£225
(2)	"Cash's satin lingerie ribbons / Samples of Cash's ribbons Coventry" at foot (numbered 21, 389, 395, 410, 416 or 424)	£225	£225
(3)	"Cash's satin lingerie ribbons / Coventry, Warwickshire" at foot (numbered 430, 441 or 448)	£225	£225
(4)	"Cash's satin lingerie ribbons / Booklet containing samples" (numbered 453)	£250	£250
(5)	"Cash's satin lingerie ribbons / Booklet containing patterns" (numbered 459, 467, 473, 482, 492 or 498)	£225	£225
(6)	"Fontana Note / Wm. Collins, Sons & Co. Ltd."	£250	£250
(7)	"Drages. 50 Pay-Way / Drages Ltd."	£200	£200
(8)	"Drages. Terms to suit YOU / Drages Ltd."	£140	£140
(9)	"Saving is Simple ["is" 3.5 mm. high] / Home Safe"	£180	£180
(10)	"Saving is Simple ["is" 4.5 mm. high] / Home Safe"	£140	£140
(11)	"Send your good wishes / by Greetings Telegram"	£140	£140
(12)	"You can reach your / friends at sea by Radio Telegram"	£140	£140
(13)	"Atlantic Holidays / Cunard White Star"	£250	£250
(14)	"Post Early / In The Day"	£160	£160
(15)	"Commander Stephen / King-Hall" (text on both labels sideways)	£250	£250
(16)	"Times Furnishing Company / London, W.C.1"	£275	£275

The numbers on panes QB23(1) to (5) correspond to the edition numbers of the booklets in which they were issued. See Appendix 2.

Booklet Cylinder Numbers
Panes of six including two labels

		Perf. Type				
		B3(I)	B3A(P)	B4(E)	B4A(I)	B4B(E)
Cyl. No.	Advert No.	No dot	Dot	No dot	Dot	Dot
G 10	QB23(2) No. 389	†	†	£250	£250	£250
	QB23(6)	†	†	£300	£300	†
	Wmk inverted	†	†	£600	£600	†
	QB23(7)	†	†	£375	†	£375
	Wmk inverted	†	†	£450	£1000	£450
	QB23(8)	†	†	£180	†	£180
	QB23(9)	†	—	£250	£250	£250
	Wmk inverted	†	—	£500	†	£500
	QB23(10)	†	—	†	†	†
	Wmk inverted	†	—	†	†	†
G 18	QB23(1) No. 405	†	†	†	£250	†
	QB23(2) No. 21	†	†	£300	£300	†
	No. 395	†	†	†	£250	†
	No. 410	†	†	£250	£250	†
	No. 416	†	†	£250	£250	†
	No. 424	†	†	£250	£250	†
	QB23(3) No. 430	†	†	£250	£250	†
	No. 448	†	†	£250	£250	†
	QB23(8)	£200	†	£185	£185	£200
	QB23(9)	†	—	£200	£200	†
	QB23(10)	†	—	£180	£180	£180
	QB23(11)	†	†	£180	£180	£180
	QB23(12)	†	†	£180	£180	£180
	QB23(13)	†	†	£300	†	£300

Single Pane cylinders (no dot)

		Perf. Type	
Cyl. No.	Advert No.	B3(I)	B3A(P)
G 29	QB23(9)‡	£375	†
	QB23(9) Re-engraved	£400	†
	QB23(11)	£180	†
	QB23(12) ‡	£375	†
	QB23(12) Re-engraved	£400	†
G 37	QB23(2) No. 441	£250	£250
	QB23(3) No. 448	£250	£250
	QB23(9)	£200	£200
	QB23(10)	£180	£180
	QB23(11)	£180	£180
	QB23(12)	£180	£180
G 41	QB23(4) No. 453	£275	†
	QB23(5) No. 459	£260	†
	QB23(11)	£180	†
	QB23(12)	£180	†
	QB23(14)	£180	†
G 46	QB23(5) No. 467	£260	†
	QB23(5) No. 473	£260	†
G 46	QB23(10)		†
	QB23(11)	£180	†
	QB23(12)	£180	†
	QB23(14)	£180	†
	QB23(15)	£300	†
	QB23(16)	£325	†
G 59	QB23(5) No. 482	£250	†
	No. 492	£250	†
	QB23(10)	£180	†
	QB23(11)	£180	†

QB KING GEORGE VI Booklet Panes in Photogravure 1½d. Pale Red-brown

Cyl. No.	Advert No.	Perf. Type B3(I)	B3A(P)
	QB23(14)	£180	†
G 67	QB23(11)	£700	†
G 70	QB23(5) No. 498	£250	†
	QB23(10)	£180	†
	QB23(11)	£180	†
	QB23(14)	£180	†

‡The cylinder number was originally engraved incorrectly on the advertisement pane. This was later erased and re-engraved in its correct position in the margin.

1½d. Pale Red-brown Booklet Panes of Four
From Booklet BD6/a made up from counter sheets

A. Selvedge at top. Watermark upright — Perf. Type P
QB24 (containing No. Q8 × 4) (–.48) —

B. Selvedge at bottom. Watermark upright — Perf. Type I
QB24a (containing No. Q8 × 4) (–.48) —

1½d. Pale Red-brown Booklet Panes of Two
From Booklet BD4 made up from columns 1 and 2 of sheets

Watermark upright — Perf. Type E
QB25 (containing No. Q8 × 2) (12.47) 15·00
a. ½ arrow in margin, top or bottom 25·00

Booklet Cylinder Numbers
Panes of two

Cyl. No.	Perf. Type E No dot	Dot
185 (without control)	—	†
185 (with control U47)	55·00	55·00
187 (without control)	55·00	55·00

1½d. Pale Green Booklet Panes of Six
From Booklets BD20 and BD31/32

	Perf. Type I	Ie
A. Watermark upright		
QB26 (containing N. Q9 × 6) (3.52)	30·00	40·00
b. Spur to rose leaf (G4 dot R. 1/1 cyl. pane)	†	95·00
B. Watermark inverted		
QB26a (containing No. Q9a ×6) (3.52)	40·00	50·00

Booklet Cylinder Numbers
Panes of six

	Perf. Type B3(I)	B6(Ie)
Cyl. No.	No dot	Dot
G 4	70·00	95·00*

1½d. Pale Green Booklet Panes of Four
From Booklets BD7/10

A. Selvedge at top. Watermark upright — Perf. Type P
QB27 (containing No. Q9 × 4) (5.51) 15·00

From Booklets BD7

B. Selvedge at bottom. Watermark upright — Perf. Type I
QB27a (containing No. Q9 × 4) (5.51) 50·00

From Booklets BD8/10

C. Selvedge at top. Watermark inverted — Perf. Type P
QB27b (containing No. Q9a × 4) (12.52) 20·00

1½d. Pale Green Booklet Panes of Two
From Booklet BD5 made up from columns 1 and 2 of sheets

	Perf. Type E	E(½v)
Watermark upright		
QB28 (containing No. Q9 × 2) (5.51)	15·00	25·00

Booklet Cylinder Numbers
Panes of two

Cyl. No.	Perf. Type E No dot	Dot
192	†	75·00
194	£100	†
195	†	£150
196	†	£150
199	†	£120

2d. Orange Booklet Panes of Six
From Booklets BD13/15 and BD25

	Perf. Type I	P
A. Watermark upright		
QB29 (containing No. Q10 × 6) (6.40)	£175	£175
s. "Cancelled", Type 33P	£700	
t. "Specimen", Type 23 and upper left stamp with punch hole	£3250	
B. Watermark inverted		
QB29a (containing No. Q10b × 6) (6.40)	†	£425
as. "Cancelled", Type 33P	†	£700

Booklet Cylinder Numbers
Panes of six from single pane cylinders (no dot)

Cyl. No.	Perf. Type B3(I)
H 1	£225
H 2	£225
H 4	£350
H 5	£250
H 6	£250
H 7	£225

Imprimatur from the British Postal Museum & Archive
Two panes as QB29/a tête-bêche, Cylinder H2 no dot at left £22000

2d. Pale Orange Booklet Panes of Six
From Booklets BD16/18 and BD26/29

A. Watermark upright

	Perf. Type				
	I	E	P	BP	Ie
QB30 (containing No. Q11 × 6) (3.42)	30·00	£300	£100	£180	45·00
b. Imperf. pane of 6*	£20000				
s. "Specimen", Type 30 and upper left stamp with punch hole	£3250				

*Booklet error. See General Notes.

B. Watermark inverted

	Perf. Type				
	I	E	P	BP	Ie
QB30a (containing No. Q11a × 6) (3.42)	30·00	£300	£100	£180	60·00

Booklet Cylinder Numbers
Panes of six
Single Pane cylinders (no dot)

	Perf. Type
Cyl. No.	B3(I)
H 10	85·00
H 11	85·00
H 14	85·00
H 15	85·00
H 16	85·00
H 17	£300
H 18	85·00

Double Pane cylinders

	Perf. Type	
	B4(E)	B4A(I)
Cyl. No.	No dot	Dot
H 20	85·00	85·00
H 22	†	—

	Perf. Type		
	B3(I)	B5(BP)	B6(Ie)
Cyl. No.	No dot	Dot	Dot
H 20	85·00	85·00	85·00
H 22	85·00	85·00	85·00

	Perf. Type	
	B3(I)	B6(Ie)
Cyl. No.	No dot	Dot
H 23	85·00	85·00
H 24	85·00	85·00
H 25	£225	£225
H 26	£200	£200
H 28	85·00	85·00
H 29	85·00	85·00
H 31	85·00	85·00
H 32	85·00	85·00
H 34	85·00	85·00
H 41	85·00	85·00
H 45	85·00	85·00
H 46	85·00	85·00
H 47	£200	£200

2d. Pale Red-brown Booklet Panes of Six
From Booklets BD19, BD30, BD32 and H1/7

A. Watermark upright

	Perf. Type	
	I	Ie
QB31 (containing No. Q12 × 6) (5.51)	40·00	40·00

B. Watermark inverted

	Perf. Type	
	I	Ie
QB31a (containing No. Q12a × 6) (5.51)	50·00	70·00

Booklet Cylinder Numbers
Panes of six

	Perf. Type	
	B3(I)	B6(Ie)
Cyl. No.	No dot	Dot
H 41	£100	£100
H 47	75·00	75·00
H 48	£225	£225

2½d. Ultramarine Booklet Panes of Six
From Booklets BD13/15 and BD25

A. Watermark upright

	Perf. Type	
	I	P
QB32 (containing No. Q13 × 6) (6.40)	£150	£150
s. "Cancelled", Type 33P	£550	

B. Watermark inverted

	Perf. Type	
	I	P
QB32a (containing No. Q13a × 6) (6.40)	†	£375
as. "Cancelled", Type 33P	†	£550

Booklet Cylinder Numbers
Panes of six from single pane cylinders (no dot)

	Perf. Type
Cyl. No.	B3(I)
J 3	£200
J 5	£200
J 7	£200
J 10	£250

Specimen overprint from the National Postal Museum Archives
Booklet pane of six. Perf. 15 × 14, watermark Type **W20**
"Specimen", Type 23 and upper left stamp with punch hole.. £1500

2½d. Light Ultramarine Booklet Panes of Six
From Booklets BD16/18 and BD26/29

A. Watermark upright

	Perf. Type				
	I	E	P	BP	Ie
QB33 (containing No. Q14 × 6) (3.42)	20·00	£250	70·00	£180	25·00
b. Imperf. pane of 6*	£15000				
s. "Specimen", Type 30	£1500				

*Booklet error. See General Notes.

B. Watermark inverted

	Perf. Type				
	I	E	P	BP	Ie
QB33a (containing No. Q14a × 6) (3.42)	20·00	£250	70·00	£180	25·00

Booklet Cylinder Numbers
Panes of six
Single Pane cylinders (no dot)

	Perf. Type
Cyl. No.	B3(I)
J 15	75·00
J 16	75·00
J 17	75·00
J 18	75·00
J 20	75·00
J 21	75·00

Double Pane cylinders

	Perf. Type	
	B3(I)	B5(BP)
Cyl. No.	No dot	Dot
J 23	75·00	£100
J 25	75·00	80·00
J 28	75·00	80·00

KING GEORGE VI — Booklet Panes in Photogravure 2½d. Pale Scarlet

	Perf. Type	
	B3(I)	B5(BP)
Cyl. No.	No dot	Dot
J 29	75·00	£300
J 30	75·00	£100

	Perf. Type	
	B4(E)	B4A(I)
Cyl. No.	No dot	Dot
J 23	75·00	75·00
J 25	£100	£100
J 28	85·00	85·00

	Perf. Type	
	B3(I)	B6(Ie)
Cyl. No.	No dot	Dot
J 29 see above	60·00	60·00
J 30 see above	60·00	60·00
J 31	60·00	60·00
J 32	60·00	60·00
J 34	60·00	60·00
J 35	60·00	60·00
J 39	60·00	60·00
J 43	£125	£125
J 45	60·00	60·00
J 48	60·00	60·00
J 49	60·00	60·00
J 50	60·00	60·00
J 51	60·00	60·00
J 52	60·00	60·00
J 53	60·00	60·00
J 54	70·00	70·00
J 58	60·00	60·00
J 59	60·00	60·00
J 60	60·00	60·00
J 61	60·00	60·00
J 62	60·00	50·00
J 65	£125	£125

Specimen overprints from the National Postal Museum Archives

Booklet pane of six, Perf. 15×14, watermark Type **W20**.
"Specimen", Type 30 ....£1500

●━━━

2½d. Pale Scarlet Booklet Panes of Six
From Booklets BD19/20 and BD30/32

	Perf. Type	
	I	Ie
A. Watermark upright		
QB34 (containing No. Q15 × 6) (5.51)	8·00	12·00
B. Watermark inverted		
QB34a (containing No. Q15a × 6) (5.51)	10·00	15·00

Booklet Cylinder Numbers
Panes of six

	Perf. Type	
	B3(I)	B6(Ie)
Cyl. No.	No dot	Dot
J 62	£100	£100
J 66	60·00	60·00
J 67	55·00	55·00
J 68	£200	£200
J 69	60·00	60·00
J 70	60·00	60·00

Section QC
Recess-Printed "Arms" High Values (1939–48)

Introduction. Waterlow, who had retained the contract for recess printing in 1936, proceeded with the printing of the King George VI high values. Edmund Dulac's design for the 2s.6d. and 5s. was accepted and George R. Bellew of the Royal College of Arms was entrusted with the 10s. design subsequently used, in 1948, for the £1. As was the case for the low values, colours were changed during the Second World War. The 2s.6d. changed from brown to green and the 10s. from dark blue to ultramarine in 1942.

Watermark. All stamps in Sections QC and QD are watermarked "GvIR" (Type **W21**).

Sheet Layout. These stamps were issued in sheets of 40 (5 rows of 8) but the 2s.6d., 5s. and £1 values were printed in two panes of 40 and then guillotined. Only the 10s. value was printed in sheets of 40. There were no plate numbers and the plates can only be distinguished by marginal markings. A detailed study of these by Major-General Sir Leonard Atkinson, K.B.E. appears in *The GB Journal* for July, September and November 1968. A series of articles by Gerry Bater, F.R.P.S.L. was published in *Gibbons Stamp Monthly* in January and February 1995 (10s. dark blue), October and November 1995 (5s.), June 1996 (£1), September 1996 (10s. ultramarine) and March 1997 (2s.6d brown).

UNUSED PRICE QUOTATIONS
Unused prices quoted in Sections QC and QD are for mint unmounted examples.

W21

Q4
(Des. Edmund Dulac)
(Eng. J. A. C. Harrison)

Q5
(Des. Hon. George R. Bellew, M.V.O.)

1939 *(4 September).* **2s.6d. Type Q4. Brown.** Perf. 14
Q29 (=S.G.476)

	Mint	Used
2s.6d. Brown	95·00	8·00
a. Mark in Shield (R. 1/7)	£190	80·00
b. Gashed Diadem (R. 2/7)	£190	80·00
c. Gashed Crown (R. 5/5)	£190	80·00
d. Mark in Crown (R. 2/3)		
e. Doubling of hoof over "A" (R. 1/8)		
f. Dot below lion's left knee (R. 2/6)		
g. Two marks in Unicorn's neck (R. 4/8)		
h. Triple "T" guide (R. 3/8)		
s. "Specimen", Type 23	£300	

Q29a

Q29b

Q29c

Q29d

Q29e, Q30e

Q29f, Q30f

KING GEORGE VI Recess-Printed "Arms" High Values (1939–48) 2s.6d. Green

Q29g, Q30g

Q29h

Plates. Four double plates were used. One plate was also used for printing in green as demonstrated by the matched varieties in both colours.

Imprimatur from the National Postal Museum Archives
Imperforate, watermark Type **W21**

Watermark upright £10000

1942 (9 March). **2s.6d. Type Q4. Green** As last but colour changed

Q30 (=S.G.476b)

		Mint	Used
2s.6d.	Yellow-green	15·00	1·50
a.	Major re-entry (R. 5/2)	£120	40·00
b.	Re-entry in shield and left frame (R. 1/7)	£120	50·00
c.	Lion's right eye re-entry (R. 4/6)		
d.	Minor re-entries From	35·00	15·00
e.	Doubling of hoof over "A" (R. 1/8)		
f.	Dot below lion's left knee (R. 2/6)		
g.	Two marks on Unicorn's neck (R. 4/8)		
s.	"Specimen", Type 9		
t.	"Specimen", Type 23	£300	
u.	"Cancelled", Type 34	£500	
v.	"Specimen", Type 30		
w.	"Specimen", Type 26	£300	
x.	"Cancelled", Type 33	£500	

For illustrations of Nos. Q30e/g, see Q29e/g.

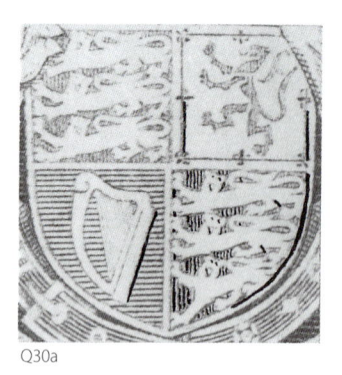

Q30a

Q30b

Q30c

Plates. Ten double plates were used.

Imprimatur from the National Postal Museum Archives
Imperforate, watermark Type **W21**
Watermark upright £10000

1939 (21 August). **5s. Type Q4. Red.** Perf. 14

Q31 (=S.G.477)

		Mint	Used
5s.	Red	20·00	2·00
a.	Major re-entry (R. 4/2)	£225	£100
b.	Re-entry in harp, etc. (R. 2/1)	£120	80·00
c.	Re-entry to right base of Crown (R. 5/2)		
d.	Diagonal scratch (R. 2/6)		
e.	Minor re-entries From	50·00	20·00
f.	Guide mark in hair (T or (⊥) R. 2/7, 5/2 etc.)	65·00	25·00
s.	"Specimen", Type 9		
t.	"Specimen", Type 23	£300	
u.	"Cancelled", Type 34	£500	
v.	"Specimen", Type 26	£300	
w.	"Cancelled", Type 33	£500	
x.	"Specimen", Type 30		

Q31a

Q31c

Q31d

Plates. Seven double plates were used.

10s. Dark blue. Recess-Printed "Arms" High Values (1939–48)   **KING GEORGE VI**   **QC**

Imprimatur from the National Postal Museum Archives
Imperforate, watermark Type **W21**
Watermark upright ....

1939 *(30 October).* **10s. Type Q5. Dark blue.** Perf. 14

Q32 (=S.G.478)

		Mint	Used
10s.	(1) Dark blue	£260	22·00
	(2) Steel blue-black	£325	35·00
a.	Major re-entry (R. 3/7)	£425	£100
b.	Minor re-entries From	£350	75·00
c.	Retouched medallion (R. 4/1)	£350	75·00
d.	Dot on scroll (R. 2/5)	£350	75·00
e.	Retouch to lower lip (R. 2/7)	£350	75·00
f.	Flaws on both sides of scroll (R. 3/6)	£350	75·00
g.	Flaw on left side of scroll (R. 4/6)	£350	£100
h.	Dark line across bottom right stem (R. 1/4)	£350	75·00
i.	Gash on chin (R. 4/8)	£350	75·00
s.	"Specimen", Type 23	£500	

No. Q32 is known used in Belfast on 3 October 1939.

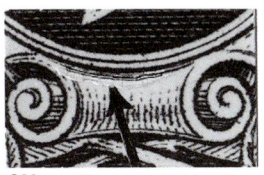

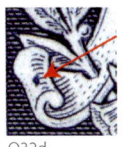

Q32a

Q32c   Q32d   Q32e

Q32f Left scroll

Q32f Right scroll

Q32g Left scroll

Q32h   Q32i

Plates. One single plate was used
Although only one plate was used it exists in three different states and in the third state every stamp was re-entered. We have therefore restricted our listing of re-entries and varieties to those we consider to be the more important ones.

Of these var. d exists in all three states; var. c in state 2 but with the lines of shading only doubled in state 3; vars. e and h exist in states 2 and 3; vars. a, f, g and i exist only in state 3.

States 2 and 3 have an oblique line in the margin opposite row 5.

All stamps in the eighth vertical row of state 3 have, amongst other things, the left frame retouched.

Imprimatur from the National Postal Museum Archives
Imperforate, watermark Type **W21**
Watermark upright £10000

1942 *(30 November).* **10s. Type Q5.** As last but colour changed

Q33 (=S.G.478b)

		Mint	Used
10s.	Ultramarine	45·00	5·00
b.	Plate crack (Pl. 2, R. 4/5)		
s.	"Specimen", Type 9		
t.	"Specimen", Type 23	£425	
u.	"Cancelled", Type 34	£550	
v.	"Cancelled", Type 33	£550	
w.	"Specimen", Type 30		

No. Q33 is known used in Beckenham, Kent, on 30 September 1948.

Q33b
The crack developed in later printings, we show the pronounced state.

Plates. Official sources record three plates, but it is likely that a fourth was used. The plates were all single pane.

Imprimatur from the National Postal Museum Archives
Imperforate, watermark Type **W21**

Watermark upright £12000

265

KING GEORGE VI — Recess-Printed "Arms" High Values (1939–48) £1. Type Q5. Brown.

1948 *(1 October).* **£1. Type Q5. Brown.** Perf. 14

Q34 (=S.G.478b)

	Mint	Used
£1 Brown	25·00	26·00
s. "Specimen", Type 30		

Plates. One double plate was used.

Imprimatur from the National Postal Museum Archives
Perf. 14, watermark Type **W21**
Watermark upright ....

First Day Covers
On plain covers with operational postmarks of the first day of issue.

			Plain covers
QFD17	(21.8.39)	5s. (No. Q31)	£850
QFD18	(4.9.39)	2s.6d. brown (No. Q29)	£1800
QFD19	(30.10.39)	10s. dark blue (No. Q32)	£3250
QFD20	(9.3.42)	2s.6d. yellow-green (No. Q30)	£1750
QFD21	(30.11.42)	10s. ultramarine (No. Q33)	£3750
QFD22	(1.10.48)	£1 (No. Q34)	£325

Section QD
Recess-Printed "Festival" High Values (1951)

Sheet Layout. All values were issued in sheets of 40 (10 horizontal rows of 4) but they were printed in two panes of 40 which were then guillotined.
Watermark and Perforation. All stamps are watermarked "GviR" (Type **W21**) and comb perforated 11×12.

Q6. H.M.S. *Victory*

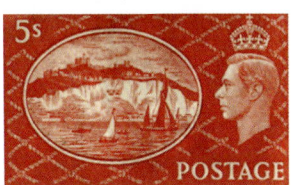

Q7. White Cliffs of Dover
(Des. Mary Adshead)

Q8. St. George and the Dragon

Q9. Royal Coat-of-Arms
(Des. Percy Metcalfe, C.V.O.)

1951 *(3 May).* **2s.6d. Type Q6. Yellow-green**

Q35 (=S.G.509)

	Mint	Used
2s.6d. Yellow-green	7·50	1·00
s. "Specimen", Type 30	£1000	
t. "Cancelled", Type 33		

Imprimatur from the National Postal Museum Archives
Imperforate, watermark Type **W21**

Watermark upright £11000
For die proofs see below No. Q38.

1951 *(3 May).* **5s. Type Q7. Red**

Q36 (=S.G.510)

	Mint	Used
5s. Red	35·00	1·00
s. "Specimen", Type 30	£1000	

Imprimatur from the National Postal Museum Archives
Imperforate, watermark Type **W21**

Watermark upright £11000

1951 *(3 May).* **10s. Type Q8. Ultramarine**

Q37 (=S.G.511)

	Mint	Used
10s. Ultramarine	15·00	7·50
s. "Specimen", Type 30	£1000	

Imprimatur from the National Postal Museum Archives
Imperforate, watermark Type **W21**

Watermark upright £11000

1951 *(3 May).* **£1. Type Q9. Brown**

Q38 (=S.G.512)

	Mint	Used
£1 Brown	45·00	18·00
a. Re-entry in "DIEU" (R. 5/1 and R. 5/4)	£150	75·00
s. "Specimen", Type 30	£1000	

Q38a

Imprimatur from the National Postal Museum Archives
Imperforate, watermark Type **W21**

Watermark upright £11000

Die Proofs
In black on thin card. No watermark
Head and crown for 2s.6d. and 5s. £3000
St. George and dragon for 10s. £3000
Head only for 10s. and £1 .... £3000

Quantities Sold 2s.6d. 40,723,192; 5s. 22,141,445; 10s. 10,122,720; £1 2,383,720

First Day Cover
On plain cover with operational postmarks of the first day of issue. Special covers exist which are worth more than the price quoted.

QFD23   (3.5.51)   2s.6d., 5s., 10s., £1   £950

Nos. Q36/9 are known used at Grimsby and No Q38 at Huddersfield on 2 May 1951.

Section QE
Commemorative Issues (1937–51)

All stamps in this Section are watermarked "GvIR" (Type **W20**) and were photogravure printed by Harrison & Sons.

Except for the Stamp Centenary issue and the Silver Wedding £1 they were in sheets of 120 (20 horizontal rows of 6).

First Day Covers. Prices for first day covers (Nos. QCom 1/21) are for complete sets used on special covers which are cancelled with ordinary operational postmarks. Plain covers are worth less than the prices quoted.

UNUSED PRICE QUOTATIONS
Unused prices quoted in this Section are for mint unmounted examples.

Q10. King George VI and Queen Elizabeth
(Des. Edmund Dulac)

1937 (13 May). **Coronation of King George VI**
Perf. 15 × 14
QCom1 (=S.G.461) **Q10**

		Mint	Used
1½d.	Maroon	30	30
a.	Ray flaw	10·00	
b.	Ray flaw corrected	10·00	
c.	Colon flaw	70·00	
d.	"Comet" flaw	60·00	
e.	Spur to A in MAY	30·00	
f.	Extra decoration	50·00	
g.	Pearl behind tiara	50·00	
h.	Spot in lacing by Orb	30·00	
ha.	White dot above Y (with var. h)	50·00	
i.	Pearl in Orb	5·00	
j.	Crack in Orb	50·00	
k.	Short foot to 2	50·00	
l.	Patch in oval	40·00	
m.	Long tail to S	50·00	
n.	Extended bar to E	50·00	
o.	Inner vertical line in 1 at left	40·00	
p.	"Beetle" on monogram	£100	
q.	Double fraction bar	85·00	
r.	White spot on E		
s.	"Cancelled", Type 33 (twice)	£300	
t.	"Specimen", Type 32	£750	
First Day Cover (QCom1)			35·00

Despite strict instructions not to issue this stamp before 13 May it is known pre-released on mail from West Ealing on 7 May, Cheadle Hulme, Cheshire on 10 May, on 11 May (High Wycombe, Bucks and Southampton) and from a number of sub-offices on 12 May, which was a Bank Holiday.

Varieties
a. Ray flaw. This was a multipositive flaw (R. 19/1) in which the right arm of the ornament in upper left corner is almost solid. It was issued on cylinders 4, 6, 7, 8, 10, 12, 16, 17, 19 and 24, all no dot.
b. Ray flaw corrected. This was corrected before issue on cylinders 2, 3, 18, 20, 23, 27 and 30 and cylinders 4, 7, 10, 16 and 19 were also reissued with the correction. Naturally there is some variation in the skill of the correction from cylinder to cylinder so it is not practical to give an illustration of this. Every stamp in position R. 19/1 no dot either has the flaw or it has been corrected.
c. Colon flaw. Two white dots between 12 and May (Cyl. 7 no dot, R. 10/1). Later corrected in the fourth printing of Cyl. 7 no dot.
d. "Comet" flaw between MAY and 1937 on East point of diamond (Cyl. 6 dot, R. 16/6).
e. Spur to foot of A in MAY (R. 18/4 on Cyls. 2, 4, 6, 7 all no dot and possibly Cyl. 3). Later corrected.
f. Extra decoration on King's uniform in the shape of a white cross (Cyl. 7 no dot, R. 1/5).
g. Pearl behind Queen's tiara (Cyl. 7 no dot, R. 6/6). Later corrected. Also short line over G which was not corrected.
h. Spot in lacing to right of Cross of Orb (R. 7/6). This is a multipositive variety which is found on cylinders 3, 4, 6 and 7 dot but was later retouched although traces of the flaw can be found on the later cylinders. This stamp also contains another variety, a small white dot above left arm of Y in MAY but it only occurs on cylinder 6 dot.
i. Pearl in Orb. A faint white spot on lower part of Orb which is visible on all dot cylinders in position R. 18/1.
j. Crack in Orb. Very marked variety (Cyl. 20 no dot, R. 4/1).
k. Short foot in 2 of date (Cyl. 2 no dot, R. 15/5).
l. Large patch in oval at bottom right (Cyl. 19 dot, R. 13/1).
m. Long tail to bottom of S of POSTAGE (Cyl. 3 dot, R. 11/1).
n. Extended middle bar to first E of REVENUE (Cyl. 23 dot, R. 10/2).
o. Faint vertical line at left in large figure 1 of value (Cyl. 23, R. 7/2). Later printing.
p. "Beetle" on "E" of monogram (Cyl. 19 no dot, R. 12/3).
q. Extra fraction bar in left value (Cyl. 10 no dot, R. 4/2).
r. White spot on "E" of monogram (Cyl. 12 no dot, R. 15/2).

Centenary of First Adhesive Postage Stamps
Commemorative Issues (1937–51) **KING GEORGE VI** **QE**

Controls and Cylinder Numbers (Blocks of Six)
All the following are found with control A 37.
An R shows the existence of the Ray flaw, and RC denotes Ray flaw corrected.

Perforation Type 5 (E/I)

Cyl. No.	No dot	Cyl. No.	Dot
2	25·00	3.	10·00
3	10·00	4.	20·00
4R	10·00		
4RC	—		
		6.	10·00
6R	10·00	7.	10·00
7R	10·00		
7RC	10·00		
8R	40·00	8.	30·00
10R	20·00	10.	20·00
10RC	£100		
12R	60·00	12.	60·00
16R	35·00	16.	15·00
16RC	35·00		
17R	35·00		
18	10·00	17.	20·00
19R	20·00	18.	10·00
19RC	40·00	19.	20·00
20	50·00		
23	10·00	20.	50·00
24R	85·00	23.	10·00
27	125·00	24.	75·00
30	10·00	27.	125·00
2.	25·00	30.	10·00

It is believed that only 3 sheets were printed from cylinder 4 no dot with the ray flaw corrected. A cylinder block and a vertical corner position strip of 3 showing the cylinder number and ray flaw corrected exist.

Imprimatur from the National Postal Museum Archives
Imperforate, watermark Type **W20**

Watermark upright £4000

Quantity Sold 388,731,000

Q11. Queen Victoria and King George VI
(Des. H. L. Palmer)

1940 (6 May). Centenary of First Adhesive Postage Stamps

QCom2 (=S.G.479) Q11
Printed in sheets of 160 arranged in 20 horizontal rows of 8
Perf. 14½×14

	Mint	Used
½d. Green	30	75
a. Hole in central cross of Crown (Cyl. 1 Dot, R. 17/3)	£150	
s. "Specimen", Type 9		
t. "Specimen", Type 23		
u. "Specimen", Type 30		

QCom3 (=S.G.480) Q11
	Mint	Used
1d. Scarlet	1·00	75
s. "Specimen", Type 9		
t. "Specimen", Type 23		
u. "Specimen", Type 30		

QCom4 (=S.G.481) Q11
	Mint	Used
1½d. Red-brown	50	1·50
s. "Specimen", Type 9		
t. "Specimen", Type 23		
u. "Specimen", Type 30		

QCom5 (=S.G.482) Q11
	Mint	Used
2d. Orange	1·00	75
s. "Specimen", Type 9		
t. "Specimen", Type 23		
u. "Specimen", Type 30		

QCom6 (=S.G.483) Q11
	Mint	Used
2½d. Ultramarine	2·25	50
a. Retouched neck (Cyl. 2 Dot, R. 20/2)	50·00	
b. Retouch to King's face and hair (Cyl. 5 No dot, R. 20/1)	50·00	
c. Loop to Crown (Cyl. 3 No dot, R. 6/6)	£150	
s. "Specimen", Type 9		
t. "Specimen", Type 23		
u. "Specimen", Type 30		

QCom7 (=S.G.484) Q11
	Mint	Used
3d. Violet	3·00	3·50
s. "Specimen", Type 9		
t. "Specimen", Type 23		
u. "Specimen", Type 30		

First Day Cover (QCom2/7) .... 55·00

For No. QCom5 bisected and used on cover see Appendix 7.

No. QCom3 was used at Willington Quay, Wallsend and Bexleyheath, Kent on 4 May and at Coulsdon, Surrey, and South Lambeth on 5 May 1940.

Nos. QCom2u/7u are from a presentation album from the 1947 Paris Postal Congress.

QCom2a (½d.)

QCom6a (2½d.)

QCom6b (2½d.)

KING GEORGE VI — Commemorative Issues (1937–51) Victory

QCom6c (2½d.)

Controls and Cylinder Numbers (Blocks of Six)
All the following are found with control G 40.
Type of Perforation: Bottom margin imperf., top margin perforated through and a single extension hole at each side.

Value	Cyl. No.	No dot	Dot
½d.	1	50·00	20·00
	3	12·00	12·00
	6	25·00	35·00
1d.	1	15·00	15·00
	2	75·00	75·00
	3	15·00	15·00
	5	15·00	15·00
1½d.	2	15·00	15·00
	3	15·00	15·00
2d.	1	20·00	20·00
	2	15·00	15·00
	3	20·00	20·00
2½d.	2	25·00	70·00*
	3	30·00	30·00
	4	£500	£500
	5	70·00*	25·00
	7	25·00	25·00
3d.	5	40·00	40·00

Imprimaturs from the National Postal Museum Archives
Nos. QCom2/7 imperforate, watermark Type **W20**

Watermark upright (set of 6) £25000

Quantities Sold
½d. 82,896,960; 1d. 232,903,680; 1½d. 40,412,800; 2d. 121,065,120; 2½d. 312,957,440; 3d. 22,128,000

Q12
(Des. H. L. Palmer)

Q13
(Des. Reynolds Stone)

Symbols of Peace and Reconstruction

1946 (11 June). **Victory**

QCom8 (=S.G.491) **Q12**

		Mint	Used
2½d.	Ultramarine	20	20
a.	Extra port-hole aft (Cyl. 11 No dot, R. 16/1)	95·00	
b.	Extra port-hole at fore (Cyl. 8 Dot, R. 5/6)	120·00	
s.	"Specimen", Type 9		
t.	"Cancelled", Type 28		
u.	"Specimen", Type 30		

QCom9 (=S.G.492) **Q13**

		Mint	Used
3d.	Violet	20	50
a.	Shiny ink	60	35
b.	Seven berries (Cyl. 4 No dot, R. 12/5)	50·00	
c.	Gash on temple (Cyls. 2 Dot, 4 Dot, 5 Dot, R. 9/6)	30·00	
s.	"Specimen", Type 9		
t.	"Cancelled", Type 28		
u.	"Specimen", Type 30		

First Day Cover (QCom8/9) .... 65·00

Nos. QCom8/9 are known used at Warrington on 10 June 1946.

Nos. QCom8u/9u are from a presentation album for the 1947 Paris Postal Congress.

The 3d. value was the subject of an article by Andrew A. Whitworth in June 1950 *Gibbons Stamp Monthly* which was reprinted in the May 1984 issue.

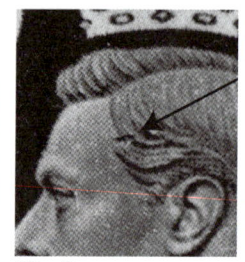

QCom8a QCom8b

QCom9b QCom9c

Controls and Cylinder Numbers (Blocks of Six)
All the following are found with control S 46.
Perforation Type 5 (E/I)

Value	Cyl. No.	No dot	Dot
2½d.	3	25·00	25·00
	4	20·00	15·00
	6	†	—
	7	10·00	15·00
	8	45·00	45·00
	9	£100	£100
	10	15·00	10·00
	11	35·00	45·00
	12	25·00	35·00
	13	£150	£150
	15	75·00	75·00
	17	30·00	20·00
3d.	2	£200	—
	4	£250	£350
	5	20·00	20·00

Cylinder 5 was printed in shiny ink.

Royal Silver Wedding *Commemorative Issues (1937–51)* **KING GEORGE VI** QE

Perforation Type 6 (no dot I/P) and 6B (dot E/P)

2½d.	9	70·00	70·00
3d.	2	10·00	10·00
	4	10·00	10·00

Cylinder 4 has a vertical line in the margin under the first stamp in the bottom row. Early printings without this line. *Price £20 each.*

Imprimaturs from the National Postal Museum Archives
Nos. QCom8/9 imperforate, watermark Type **W20**
Watermark upright (*set of* 2) £7500

Quantities Sold 2½d. 307,832,500; 3d. 43,085,700
Stamps of this issue were overprinted for use in Tangier. In the case of the 3d. value the overprint was applied to the stop panes of Cyls. 2. and 4., Perforation Type 5.

Cylinder Numbers
2½d. Perforation Type 5 (E/I). Blocks of six

Cyl. No.	No dot	Dot
1	£100	£100
4	5·00	5·00
5	20·00	20·00
6	£150	£150

£1 Blocks of four

1	£200	£200

Imprimaturs from the National Postal Museum Archives
Imperforate, watermark Type **W20**

Watermark upright (*set of* 2) £25000

Quantities Sold 2½d. 147,500,000; £1 419,628

Q14  **Q15**
King George VI and Queen Elizabeth
(Des. G. T. Knipe and Joan Hassall from photographs by Dorothy Wilding)

Q16. Gathering Vraic
(Des. J. R. R. Stobie)

Q17. Islanders gathering Vraic
(From drawing by E. Blampied)

1948 (26 April). Royal Silver Wedding

QCom10 (=S.G.493) **Q14**
The £1 value was printed in sheets of 20, arranged in 4 horizontal rows of 5
Perf. 15 × 14 (2½d.), 14 × 15 (£1)

	Mint	Used
2½d. Ultramarine	35	20
a. Spot on shoulder (Cyl. 5 No dot, R. 15/1)	42·00	
s. "Specimen", Type 30		

QCom11 (=S.G.494) **Q15**

£1 Blue	40·00	40·00
s. "Specimen", Type 30		
t. "Cancelled", Type 34P	£675	

First Day Cover (QCom10/11) £425
No. QCom11 is known used at Hornsea, Yorkshire, on 25 April 1948.

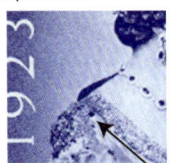

QCom10a

1948 (10 May). Channel Islands Liberation

Issued to commemorate the third anniversary of the liberation, these stamps were intended primarily for use in the Channel Islands. They were also available at the G.P.O. London and the following seven Head Post Offices, Belfast, Birmingham, Bristol, Cardiff, Edinburgh, Leeds and Manchester.

For stamps issued in the Channel Islands during the German Occupation 1940–45 see APPENDIX 7.

Perf. 15 × 14
QCom12 (=S.G.C1) **Q16**

	Mint	Used
1d. (1) Scarlet	25	30
(2) Rose-red	15·00	8·00

QCom13 (=S.G.C2) **Q17**

2½d. Ultramarine	25	30
a. Crown flaw (R. 1/1)	50·00	
b. Line across wheel (R. 6/1)	50·00	
c. Broken wheel (R. 20/5)	75·00	

First Day Cover (QCom12/13) .... 35·00

QCom13a

QE KING GEORGE VI Commemorative Issues (1937–51) Olympic Games

QCom13b

QCom13c

Cylinder Numbers (Blocks of Six)
Perforation Type 6 or 6B (both no dot)

Value	Cyl. No.	Perf. Type 6 (I/P)	Perf. Type 6B (E/P)
1d.	2	10·00	50·00
2½d.	4	20·00	60·00

Imprimaturs from the National Postal Museum Archives
Nos. QCom12/13 imperforate, watermark Type **W20**

Watermark upright (set of 2) £6500

Quantities Sold 1d. 5,934,000; 2½d. 5,398,000

Essays
Photographic essays exist in an unaccepted design and in the above designs with a different crown. (Price from £75 each).

Specimens
Both values exist in Post Office archives overprinted "SPECIMEN" by a handstamp measuring 13×1·75 mm.

1948 (29 July). **Olympic Games** Perf. 15 × 14
QCom14 (=S.G.495) **Q18**

	Mint	Used
2½d. Ultramarine	50	10
b. Ear lobe flaw (Cyl. 2 Dot, R. 17/1)	60·00	
s. "Specimen", Type 26	£450	

QCom15 (=S.G.496) **Q19**

3d. Violet	50	50
a. Crown flaw (Cyl. 1 No dot, R. 20/2)	75·00	
b. Crown flaw retouch (Cyl. 1 No dot, R. 20/2)	50·00	
c. Hooked 3 (Cyl. 1 No dot, R. 19/2)	35·00	
s. "Specimen", Type 26	£450	

QCom16 (=S.G.497) **Q20**

6d. Bright purple	3·25	75
a. Initials H.L.P. (Strip of 3)	£325	
b. Ditto, retouched (Strip of 3) From	£200	
s. "Specimen", Type 26	£450	

QCom17 (=S.G.498) **Q21**

1s. Brown	4·50	2·00
b. White blob on Lands End (Cyl. 3 R. 7/3)	95·00	
c. White spot below 9 (Cyl. 3, R. 8/4)	95·00	
s. "Specimen", Type 26	£450	

First Day Cover (QCom14/17)		45·00

No. QCom14/17 are known used at Norwich on 28 July 1948.

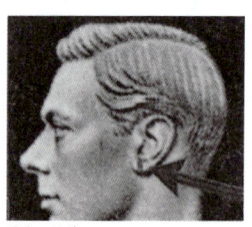

Q18. Globe and Laurel Wreath
(Des. Percy Metcalfe, C.V.O.)

Q19. "Speed"
(Des. Abram Games)

Q20. Olympic Symbol
(Des. Stanley D. Scott)

Q21. Winged Victory
(Des. Edmund Dulac)

QCom14b
A less pronounced flaw exists on R. 19/1

QCom15a

QCom15b

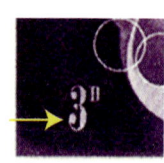

QCom15c

Part of QCom16a

In the 6d. value the initials H, L and P (H. L. Palmer) were engraved on the 4th, 5th and 6th marginal rules respectively, on the bottom row of Cylinder 9. Three attempts were made to remove these initials by retouching. In the first only the P was almost obliterated, in the second the H was removed as well and finally all three letters were touched out.

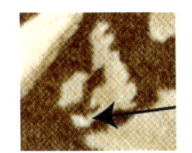

QCom17b QCom17c

Cylinder Numbers (Blocks of Six)
Perforation Type 5 (E/I)

Value	Cyl. No.	No dot	Dot
2½d.	2	10·00	50·00
	3	5·00	5·00
3d.	1 (inc. QCom15a and c)	55·00	15·00
	1 (inc. QCom15b/c)	60·00	15·00
6d.	9	20·00	20·00
1s.	3	20·00	20·00

Imprimaturs from the National Postal Museum Archives
Nos. QCom14/17 imperforate, watermark Type **W20**
Watermark upright (*set of* 4)..£15000

Quantities Sold   2½d. 155,350,980; 3d. 32,554,642; 6d. 24,397,370; 1s. 32,187,465

Q22. Two Hemispheres
(Des. Mary Adshead)

Q23. U.P.U Monument, Berne
(Des. Percy Metcalfe, C.V.O.)

Q24. Goddess Concordia, Globe and Points of Compass
(Des. H. Fleury)

Q25. Posthorn and Globe
(Des. George R. Bellew, M.V.O.)

1949 (10 October). **Universal Postal Union** Commemorating the 75th Anniversary. Perf. 15 × 14

QCom18 (=S.G.499) **Q22**

		Mint	Used
2½d.	Ultramarine	25	10
a.	Imperforate between stamp and top margin	£3750	
b.	Major retouch (Cyl. 5 No dot, R. 18/2)	£110	
c.	Lake in Asia (Cyl. 3 Dot, R. 14/1)	95·00	
d.	Lake in India (Cyl. 2 No dot, R., 8/2)	80·00	
s.	"Specimen", Type 30		

QCom19 (=S.G.500) **Q23**

3d.	Violet	25	50
s.	"Specimen", Type 30		

QCom20 (=S.G.501) **Q24**

6d.	Bright purple	50	75
s.	"Specimen", Type 30		

QCom21 (=S.G.502) **Q25**

1s.	Brown	1·00	1·25
a.	Retouched background to 1/– (R. 8/5)	75·00	
s.	"Specimen", Type 30		

First Day Cover (QCom18/21)		80·00

Many retouches are known on the 2½d. value. See article by Niall Fair in October 1953 issue of *Gibbons Stamp Monthly*. This was followed in September 1954 by an article by Andrew A. Whitworth identifying the cylinder and sheet positions of retouches previously described. These articles were reprinted in *Gibbons Stamp Monthly*, March 1983 and December 1984 respectively.

QCom18b

QCom18c   QCom18d

273

QE **KING GEORGE VI** *Commemorative Issues (1937–51)* **Festival of Britain**

QCom21a

Imprimaturs from the National Postal Museum Archives
Nos. QCom22/23 imperforate, watermark Type **W20**

Watermark upright (*set of 2*) £7000

Quantities Sold 2½d. 260,142,000; 4d. 22,197,000

Cylinder Numbers (Blocks of Six)
Perforation Type 5 (E/I)

Value	Cyl. No.	No dot	Dot
2½d.	2	5·00	5·00
	3	40·00	40·00
	5	£120*	50·00

Perforation Type 6 or 6B (both no dot)

		Perf. Type	
Value	Cyl. No.	6 (I/P)	6B (E/P)
3d.	2	20·00	50·00
6d.	2	20·00	80·00
1s.	2	80·00	30·00

Imprimaturs from the National Postal Museum Archives
Nos. QCom18/21 imperforate, watermark Type **W20**

Watermark upright (*set of 4*) £15000

Quantities Sold 2½d. 135,150,000; 3d. 16,450,000; 6d. 11,450,000; 1s. 11,400,000

Q26. "Commerce and Prosperity" (Des. Edmund Dulac)
Q27. Festival Symbol (Des. Abram Games)

1951 *(3 May)*. **Festival of Britain** Perf. 15 × 14

QCOM22 (=S.G.513) **Q26**

	Mint	Used
2½d. Scarlet	20	15
b. Deformed small 2 (Cyl. 5 Dot, R. 20/2)	35·00	

QCOM23 (=S.G.514) **Q27**

4d. Ultramarine	30	35
First Day Cover (QCom22/3)		38·00

Nos. QCom22/3 are known used at High Wycombe and Ipswich on 2 May 1951.

QCom22b

Cylinder Numbers (Blocks of Six)
Perforation Type 5 (E/I)

Value	Cyl. No.	No dot	Dot
2½d.	3	30·00	†
	5	15·00	40·00*
4d.	1	15·00	†

SECTION R
Postage Due Stamps – General Notes

Introduction. In the Post Office circular No. 5 (April 14 1914) the announcement was made of the introduction on 20 April of Postage Due Labels of the values ½d., 1d., 2d. and 5d.

Printers. Preliminary printings of the ½d., 1d., 2d. and 5d. were made at Somerset House and then by Harrison & Sons. The 1s. in the Simple Cypher watermark was printed exclusively at Somerset House, and the remaining values, which were introduced later, were printed by Harrison. The Somerset House and Harrison printings of the ½d., 1d., 2d. and 5d. can only be distinguished with certainty when they have control attached; the Somerset House controls always having a stop after the letter.

From 1924 to 1934 the contract was held by Waterlow & Sons who first printed the 1d. on thick chalk-surfaced paper with the Simple Cypher watermark and thereafter all values, with the addition of the 2s. 6d., on the Block Cypher watermarked paper.

In 1934 the contract reverted to Harrison but again these printings can only be distinguished from the Waterlow issues when they have control attached. Harrison continued to print all the Postage Due issues during the reigns of King Edward VIII and King George VI.

The stamps were letterpress in sheets of 240, arranged in 12 horizontal rows of 20, and perforated 14 × 15.

Watermarks. Except for Nos. R3a, R6a and R8a, normal stamps have the watermark sideways. Varieties exist with sideways-inverted, sideways and reversed, and sideways-inverted and reversed watermarks, and the following four illustrations show these watermark positions *as seen from the back of the stamp*:

Sideways

Sideways-inverted

Sideways and Reversed

Sideways-inverted and Reversed

The preliminary Somerset House printings almost always have the watermark sideways-inverted.

Cover Prices. These are provided for most stamps up to 1s. Values are expressed as a multiplier based on the used price quoted for each stamp. They reflect minimum values for postage dues used on cover. Exceptional and interesting covers will be worth more.

RA Postage Due Stamps — King George V

SECTION RA
The Postage Due Stamps

King George V Postage Dues (1914–31)

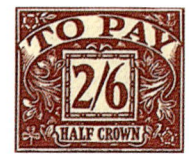

R1 "POSTAGE DUE"
R2 "TO PAY"

1914 *(20 April)–23.* **Wmk. Simple Cypher, Type W14, Sideways.**

Printed at Somerset House and by Harrison & Sons

	Unmtd mint	Mtd mint	Used
R1 (=S.G.D1) **R1**			
½d. Emerald (20.4.14)	1·50	50	25
a. Wmk. sideways-inverted	2·00	1·00	1·00
b. Wmk. sideways and reversed	30·00	18·00	20·00
c. Wmk. sideways-inverted and reversed			
d. Without watermark	£2500	£1500	
e. Varnish ink			
s. "Specimen", Type 23 (wmk. sideways, invtd.)		45·00	
t. "Cancelled", Type 24 (wmk. sideways, invtd.)		£850	
R2 (=S.G.D2/2a) **R1**			
1d. (1) Carmine (20.4.14)	1·50	50	25
(2) Pale carmine	1·50	75	50
a. Wmk. sideways-inverted	2·00	1·00	1·00
b. Wmk. sideways and reversed			20·00
c. Wmk. "POSTAGE" inverted. Strip of 3			
d. Wmk. sideways-inverted and reversed	30·00	18·00	20·00
e. Without watermark	£2750	£2000	
f. Varnish ink. Shade (1)		£2000	
s. "Specimen", Type 23 (wmk. sideways, invtd.)		45·00	
t. "Cancelled", Type 24 (wmk. sideways, invtd.)		£850	
R3 (=S.G.D3) **R1**			
1½d. Chestnut (1922)	£150	48·00	20·00
a. Wmk. sideways-inverted	£190	70·00	20·00
s. "Specimen", Type 23		75·00	
t. "Cancelled", Type 24 (wmk. sideways, invtd.)		£850	
R4 (=S.G.D4) **R1**			
2d. Agate (20.4.14)	1·50	50	25
a. Wmk. sideways-inverted	3·00	2·00	2·00
b. Wmk. sideways-inverted and reversed	25·00	15·00	18·00
ba. Wmk "POSTAGE". Strip of 3			
c. Without watermark	£2000	£1200	
s. "Specimen", Type 23 (wmk. sideways, invtd.)		45·00	
t. "Specimen", Type 26 (wmk. sideways, invtd.)		40·00	
u. "Cancelled", Type 24 (wmk. sideways, invtd.)		£850	
v. "Cancelled", Type 33		£850	
R5 (=S.G.D5/5a) **R1**			
3d. (1) Violet (1918)	28·00	5·00	75
(2) Bluish violet	28·00	6·00	2·75
a. Wmk. sideways-inverted	40·00	15·00	10·00
b. Wmk. sideways-inverted and reversed			
s. "Specimen", Type 23		45·00	
t. "Specimen", Type 26		75·00	
R6 (=S.G.D6) **R1**			
4d. Dull grey-green (12.20)	£300	£150	50·00
a. Wmk. sideways-inverted	£150	40·00	5·00
s. "Specimen", Type 23 (wmk. sideways, invtd.)		45·00	
t. "Cancelled", Type 24 (wmk. sideways, invtd.)			
R7 (=S.G.D7) **R1**			
5d. Brownish cinnamon (20.4.14)	23·00	7·00	3·50
a. Wmk. sideways-inverted	40·00	16·00	16·00
s. "Specimen", Type 23		45·00	
t. "Specimen", Type 23 (wmk. sideways, invtd.)			
u. "Specimen", Type 30		£850	
R8 (=S.G.D8/8a) **R1**			
1s. (1) Bright blue (1915)	£150	40·00	5·00
(2) Deep bright blue	£150	40·00	5·00
a. Wmk. sideways-inverted	£150	40·00	40·00
b. Wmk. sideways-inverted and reversed			
s. "Specimen", Type 23 Shade (2)		45·00	
sa. "Specimen", Type 23 Shade (1) (wmk. sideways, invtd.)			
t. "Specimen", Type 26			
u. "Cancelled", Type 24 (wmk. sideways, invtd.)			

Prices for Stamps on Cover. Nos. R1 from × 6, R2 from × 4, R3 from × 4, R4 from × 6, R5/6 from × 10, R7 from × 15.

The 1d. is known bisected used for half twice value at the following sorting offices: Barrhead (1922), Bristol (1918), Cowbridge, Glamorgan (1916), Cowes (1923), Elgin (1921), Kidlington (1922, 1923), Malvern (1915), Plaistow, London E. (1916), River, Dover (1922), Rock Ferry, Birkenhead (1915, 1918), St. Owens, Jersey (1924), Salford, Manchester (1914), South Tottenham, London N. (1921), Warminster (1922), Wavertree, Liverpool (1921), Whitchurch (1922), Winton, Bournemouth (1921), Wood Green, London N. (1921).

The 1d. is also known bisected and used to make up a 1½d. rate on understamped letters from Ceylon (1921) or Tasmania (1922, Palmers Green) and to pay ½d. on a returned printed paper matter envelope at Kilburn, London (1923).

The 2d. was bisected and used as a 1d. at Bethnal Green (1918), Anerley, London SE (1921), Didcot (1919), West Kensington (1921 and 1922), Streatham, Ealing in London, Victoria Docks & N. Woolwich (1921), also Malvern (1921 and

1923), Sheffield (1921), Shipley (1922), Kirkwall (1922) and Ledbury (1922) and Hythe, Southampton in 1923. Christchurch, Dorset in 1921 following the increase of the postage rate to 1½d. on 13 June.

The 3d. was used at Malvern (trisected and used for 1d.), and Warminster (1922).

Watermark Varieties. The following have been recorded:
- ½d. Wmk sideways: Types II, III
  Wmk sideways-inverted: Types I, II, III
- 1d. Wmk sideways: Types II, III
  Wmk sideways-inverted: Types I, II, III
  Wmk sideways and reversed: Type III
- 1½d. Wmk sideways: Type III
  Wmk sideways-inverted: Types II, III
- 2d. Wmk sideways: Types II, III
  Wmk sideways-inverted: Types I, II, III
- 3d. Wmk sideways: Types II, III
  Wmk sideways-inverted: Types II, III
- 4d. Wmk sideways: Type III
  Wmk sideways-inverted: Type III
- 5d. Wmk sideways: Type II
  Wmk sideways-inverted: Type I
- 1s. Wmk sideways: Type III
  Wmk sideways-inverted: Types II, III

Controls. Prices are for mtd mint singles.

Somerset House Printings:

		I.	P.
½d.	D. 14	†	10·00
1d.	D. 14	†	10·00
2d.	D. 14	†	12·00
5d.	D. 14	†	45·00
1s.	F. 15	†	65·00
	O. 19	†	65·00
	S. 21	†	65·00
	V. 23	£100	†

Watermark varieties known:
Wmk sideways-inverted, Type I: ½d. D. 14; 1d. D. 14; 2d. D. 14; 5d. D. 14.
Wmk sideways-inverted, Type II: 1s. F. 15.
Wmk sideways, Type III: 1s. V. 23.
Wmk sideways-inverted, Type III: 1s. O. 19, S. 21.

Harrison Printings:

		I.	P.
½d.	D 14	5·00	5·00
	I 16	5·00	5·00
	N 19	5·00	5·00
	R 21	5·00	20·00
	S 22	†	5·00
	U 22	5·00	15·00
	W 23	10·00	20·00
1d.	D 14	5·00	5·00
	E 14	5·00	5·00
	G 15	5·00	50·00
	I 16	5·00	5·00
	K 17	5·00	5·00
	N 19	5·00	5·00
	P 20	5·00	†
	Q 20	10·00	†
	Q 21	10·00	20·00
	R 21	5·00	7·00
	S 21	5·00	5·00
	S 22	5·00	5·00
	T 22	5·00	5·00
	U 23	5·00	5·00
1½d.	U 22	70·00	†
	U 23	70·00	†
	V 23	£100	£100
2d.	D 14	6·00	6·00
	H 16	6·00	6·00
	I 16	6·00	6·00
	K 17	10·00	6·00
	O 19	6·00	6·00
	P 20	6·00	6·00
	R 21	6·00	10·00
	U 23	25·00	10·00

King George V Postage Due Stamps RA

		I.	P.
3d.	L 18	8·00	20·00
	O 20	8·00	8·00
	T 22	8·00	8·00
	V 23	8·00	8·00
	W 23	8·00	40·00
4d.	Q 20	75·00	75·00
5d.	D 14	40·00	£250

Watermark varieties known:
Wmk sideways, Type II: ½d. D 14, I 16, W 23; 1d. D 14, E 14, G 15, I 16, T 22, U 23; 2d. D 14, H 16, I 16, P 20; 3d. T 22, V 23, W 23; 5d. D 14.
Wmk sideways-inverted, Type II: ½d. W 23; 1d. U 23; 1½d. V 23; 3d. V 23, W 23.
Wmk sideways, Type III: ½d. N 19, R 21, S 22, U 22; 1d. K 17, N 19, P 20, Q 20, Q 21, R 21, S 21, S 22, T 22, U 23; 1½d. U 22, U 23; 2d. K 17, O 19, P 20, R 21, U 23; 3d. L 18, O 20, T 22, V 23; 4d. Q 20.
Wmk sideways-inverted, Type III: ½d. N 19, U 22; 1d. Q 21, R 21, S 21, S 22, T 22; 1½d. U 22, U 23; 2d. R 21, U 23; 3d. T 22; 4d. Q 20.
Wmk sideways and reversed, Type III: 1d. R21.
Wmk sideways-inverted and reversed, Type III 1d. Q20; 2d. P20.

Die Proofs (uncleared)
½d. in black on white card	£5750
½d. in black on white card annotated "Proof from Soft Die Jan 1914"	£5750
1d. in black on white card	£5750
1d. in black on white card annotated "Proof from Soft Die 9 Jan 1914"	£5750
1d. in black on white card annotated "Proof from Soft Die 9.1.1914"	£5750
2d. in black on white card	£5750
2d. in black on white proof paper numbered "123" at foot	£5750
2d. in black on white card annotated "No 228" and "19.XII.13"	£5750
5d. in black on white card	£5750
5d. in black on white card annotated "Proof from Soft Die - Jan 1914"	£5750
5d. in black on white card annotated "Proof from Soft Die - Jany 1914"	£5750
5d. in black on white card annotated "No 279" and "5.1.14"	£5750
1s. in black on white card	£5750

Die proofs from the archive of Royal Mint Engraver H.A. Richardson, printed in black on white card, cut to stamp size and overprinted "CANCELLED" in red (19.5 x 2.5mm) mounted on thin card with various annotations.

½d. (Cleared or Uncleared surround)	Each £4750
1d. (Cleared or Uncleared surround)	Each £4750
2d. (Cleared or Uncleared surround)	Each £4750
3d. (Cleared or Uncleared surround)	Each £5500
4d. (Cleared surround)	£5500
5d. (Cleared or Uncleared surround)	Each £4750
1s. (Cleared surround)	£5500
2s.6d. (Uncleared)	£5750

Bromides
½d. Stamp size bromide without central numerical value tablet of Eve's design mounted on card numbered "83" and "132" in corners ... £2500
1d. Stamp size bromide without central numerical value tablet of Eve's design mounted on card numbered "85" and "134" in corners ... £2500
5d. Stamp size bromide without central numerical value tablet of Eve's design mounted on card numbered "84" and "133" in corners ... £2500

RA Postage Due Stamps — King George V

Original Sketch Artwork
Pen and ink sketches by G.W. Eve on stout white card illustrating ornamental detailing and alternate frame designs for 2d. value, card with printed address "116 Adelaide Road"...................£12000

Pen and ink sketches by G.W. Eve on large piece of white paper illustrating ornamental detailing and alternate frame designs for 2d. value £10000

Colour Trials
Wmk. Simple Cypher (sideways-inverted). Imperf. 1s. value in 14 different colours and optd. "CANCELLED", Type 28.................................From £2000

Wmk Simple Cypher (sideways-inverted). Perf 14 × 15:
2d. value in 18 different colours.........................Each £110
As above, but optd "SPECIMEN", Type 23: Colours
Nos. 1, 6, 10...Each £160

The 2d. in the trial colours were described as No. 1 Carmine, No. 2 Claret, No. 3 Magenta, No. 4 Scarlet, No. 5 Red-brown, No. 6 Bartozzi brown, No. 7 Fawn, No. 8 Umber, No. 9 Bronze-green, No. 10 Blue-green, No. 11 Faience green, No. 12 Agate (as issued), No. 13 Mauve, No. 14 Violet, No. 15 Azure blue, No. 16, Royal blue, No. 17 Orange, No. 18 Blue, No. 19 Russian green.

The 1s. in the trial colours were described as No. 20 Bronze-green, No. 21 Pearl green, No. 22 Claret, No. 23 Mauve, No. 24 Violet, No. 25 Azure blue, No. 26 Orange, No. 27 Violet (as No. 24), No. 28 Royal blue, No. 29 Japanese blue, No. 30 Gloriosa blue, No. 31 Red-brown, No. 32 Magenta, No. 33 Grey.

Imprimaturs from the National Postal Museum Archives
Imperforate, watermark Type **W14**.........................£4000
1½d. value, watermark sideways-inverted...............£4000
3d. value, watermark sideways.................................£4000
4d. value, watermark sideways-inverted...................£4000
1s. value, watermark sideways-inverted....................£4000

1924. Thick Chalk-Surfaced Paper. Wmk. Simple Cypher, Type W14, Sideways

Printed by Waterlow & Sons

R9 (=S.G.D9) **R1**

	Unmtd mint	Mtd mint	Used
1d. Carmine	10·00	6·00	6·00
a. Wmk. sideways-inverted			

Price for Stamp on Cover. No. R9 from ×15.

Controls. Prices are for mounted mint singles.

	I.	P.
B 24	15·00	†
C 25	15·00	†

1924–31. Wmk. Block Cypher, Type W15, Sideways

Printed by Waterlow & Sons, and later (from 1934) by Harrison & Sons

R10 (=S.G.D10) **R1**

	Unmtd mint	Mtd mint	Used
½d. Emerald (6.25)	2·50	1·25	75
a. Wmk sideways-inverted	6·00	3·00	1·50
s. "Specimen", Type 23		45·00	
t. "Specimen", Type 26			
u. "Specimen", Type 30			

R11 (=S.G.D11) **R1**

	Unmtd mint	Mtd mint	Used
1d. Carmine (4.25)	2·50	60	25
a. Wmk. sideways-inverted	—	—	30·00
s. "Specimen", Type 23		55·00	
t. "Specimen", Type 26			
u. "Specimen", Type 30			

R12 (=S.G.D12) **R1**

	Unmtd mint	Mtd mint	Used
1½d. Chestnut (10.24)	£160	47·00	22·00
a. Wmk. sideways-inverted	—	—	75·00
s. "Specimen", Type 23		55·00	

R13 (=S.G.D13) **R1**

	Unmtd mint	Mtd mint	Used
2d. Agate (7.24)	9·00	1·00	25
a. Wmk. sideways-inverted	—	—	30·00
s. "Specimen", Type 23		45·00	
t. "Specimen", Type 30			
u. "Cancelled", Type 33			

R14 (=S.G.D14) **R1**

	Unmtd mint	Mtd mint	Used
3d. Dull violet (10.24)	15·00	1·50	25
a. Wmk. sideways-inverted	50·00	20·00	40·00
b. Experimental paper, Wmk. W16	£175	95·00	95·00
c. Printed on the gummed side (Control L 29)	£180	£125	†
s. "Specimen", Type 23		55·00	

R15 (=S.G.D15) **R1**

	Unmtd mint	Mtd mint	Used
4d. Dull grey-green (10.24)	70·00	15·00	4·25
a. Wmk. sideways-inverted	£100	50·00	40·00
s. "Specimen", Type 23		55·00	
t. "Specimen", Type 26			

R16 (=S.G.D16) **R1**

	Unmtd mint	Mtd mint	Used
5d. Brownish cinnamon (1.31)	£175	65·00	45·00

R17 (=S.G.D17) **R1**

	Unmtd mint	Mtd mint	Used
1s. Deep blue (9.24)	60·00	8·50	50
a. Wmk. sideways-inverted	£250	£150	£100
s. "Specimen", Type 23		55·00	
t. "Cancelled", Type 33			

R18 (=S.G.D18) **R2**

	Unmtd mint	Mtd mint	Used
2s.6d. Purple/yellow (10.24)	£275	85·00	1·75
a. Wmk. sideways-inverted	£750	—	40·00
s. "Specimen", Type 23		55·00	
t. "Specimen", Type 30			
u. "Cancelled", Type 28			

Prices for Stamps on Cover. Nos. R10 from × 5, R11 from × 4, R12 from × 4, R13 from × 6, R14 from × 10, R15 from × 8, R16 from × 4, R17 from × 50.

The 1d. is known bisected and used for half the face value at the following sorting offices: Ashton under Lyne (1932), Hastings (1930), Penryn, Cornwall (1928), Shenfield (1926), Wimbledon, London SW (1925).

The 2d. is known bisected and used to make up a 2½d. rate on an understamped letter from Malta at Perranwell Station, Cornwall (1932).

Controls. Prices are for mounted mint singles.
Waterlow Printings:

		I.	P.
½d.	B 24	†	5·00
	F 26	5·00	†
	I 28	5·00	†
	K 29	†	5·00
	L 29	5·00	†
	M 30	5·00	†
	O 31	5·00	†

King George V Postage Due Stamps RA

		I.	P.
	P 31	5·00	†
	Q 32	5·00	†
	S 33	5·00	†
1d.	B 24	20·00	†
	F 26	5·00	12·00
	I 28	5·00	†
	K 29	5·00	60·00
	L 29	5·00	†
	N 30	5·00	†
	O 31	5·00	†
	Q 32	5·00	†
	S 33	5·00	£100
1½d.	B 24	90·00	†
2d.	A 24	12·00	†
	C 25	12·00	†
	E 26	12·00	†
	F 26	12·00	†
	H 27	70·00	†
	I 28	12·00	†
	K 29	12·00	†
	L 29	12·00	†
	M 30	12·00	†
	O 31	12·00	†
	P 31	12·00	†
	Q 32	12·00	†
	R 32	12·00	†
	T 33	60·00	†
3d.	B 24	10·00	†
	D 25	20·00	†
	E 26	10·00	†
	F 26	10·00	†
	G 27	10·00	†
	H 27	†	50·00
	I 28	10·00	†
	K 29	10·00	†
	L 29	10·00	†
	N 30	10·00	†
	O 31	10·00	†
	Q 32	10·00	†
	R 32	10·00	†
	T 33	10·00	†
4d.	A 24	40·00	†
	B 24	32·00	†
	E 26	32·00	†
	F 26	32·00	†
	I 28	†	£175
	K 29	32·00	†
	L 29	32·00	†
	N 30	32·00	†
	Q 32	32·00	†
	R 32	32·00	†
	T 33	£175	†
5d.	N 30	£175	†
	O 31	£175	†
	Q 32	£175	†
	S 33	£175	†
1s.	A 24	£850	†
	B 24	50·00	†
	C 25	50·00	†
	E 26	—	50·00
	F 26	25·00	†
	G 27	25·00	†
	I 28	25·00	†
	K 29	25·00	†
	M 30	45·00	†
	O 31	45·00	†
	Q 32	25·00	†
	R 32	25·00	†
	S 33	25·00	†
2s.6d.	B 24	£275	†
	H 27	£275	†
	I 28	£275	†
	K 29	£275	—
	L 29	£275	†
	N 30	£275	†
	O 31	£275	†
	Q 32	£275	†
	R 32	£275	†
	S 33	£275	†

Watermark varieties known:
Wmk sideways-inverted, ½d. B 24; 1½d. B 24.
Waterlow Printing. Experimental wmk **W16**:

		I.	P.
3d.	D 25	£225	†

Harrison Printings:

½d.	U 34	10·00	†
	U 34 [streaky gum]	6·00	†
	W 35	6·00	†
	Y 36	5·00	†
1d.	U 34	25·00	25·00
	W 35	18·00	†
	Y 36	6·00	—
2d.	V 34	30·00	†
	X 35	8·00	†
	Y 36	20·00	†
3d.	W 35	25·00	†
	Y 36	12·00	15·00
4d.	V 34	35·00	†
	X 35	35·00	†
5d.	U 34	£175	†
	W 35	£175	†
1s.	U 34	40·00	†
	W 35	40·00	†
	X 35	40·00	†
2s.6d.	U 34	£300	†
	V 34	£300	†
	X 35	£300	†
	Z 36	£300	†

The U 34 controls are generally on smooth-gummed paper but all the later controls are on paper with streaky gum.

Colour Trial for the 4d. value prepared in 1920
Imperforate on unwatermarked paper affixed to white card
3d. dull grey–green.. £3250

In 1922 a miniature plate of four impressions of the ½d. value was produced by the Royal Mint, for the production of colour trials for the proposed 1½d. value. No examples of these trials appear to have reached collectors, however the miniature plate was again used for a second series of four trials in 1923 and 1924 for the proposed 2s.6d. value.

From these trials each colour is represented by an irregular imperforate block of three on unwatermarked wove paper, mounted on white or manila card, annotated with the official colour description or a reference number. Each card is further annotated in the position of the removed fourth stamp "For HM" (His Majesty)

8 September 1923
Light Sepia, Prouts Brown, Buff Tint, Special
    Umber or Umbrian Brown .... £12,000 *per card*
Single example in light sepia (Previously listed as
    Drab) £3250

21 November 1923
No. 56 (Deep Green), No.57 (Pale Carmine), No.60
    (Orange), No.61 (Bright Orange), No.63
    (Brownish Orange), No.64 (Deep Bright
    Orange) or No.66 (Rose pink)........................ £12,000 *per card*
Single example in No.60 Orange £3250

6 December 1923
Claret Lake, Purple, Pansy Lake, Dahlia Claret,
    Royal Scarlet or Plum .... £12,000 *per card*
From this last series of colours, purple was chosen and a final set of trials on coloured papers was then produced.

21 January 1924
Purple on Lemon (SD1), Buff 93 (SD2), Chrome 57
    (SD3), Deep canary 49 (SD4) or No.7 "Bright
    Yellow" (SD6) .... £12000 *per card*
Single example in Purple on Deep canary 139
    (SD5) £3250

The chosen colour was purple on deep canary 139 (SD5), no card bearing an irregular block of three is known to exist of this colour, but a single example can be found in the Royal Philatelic Collection with a second damaged example (from the T.E. Field collection) in private hands.

Imprimaturs from the National Postal Museum Archives
Imperforate, watermark Type **W15** (sideways)
½d., 1d., 1½d., 2d., 3d., 4d., 5d., 1s., 2s. 6d.....................Each £2500

SECTION RB
King Edward VIII Postage Dues (1936–37)

UNUSED PRICE QUOTATIONS
Unused prices quoted for R19–26 are for mint unmounted examples.

1936–37. Wmk. "E 8 R", Type W19, Sideways
Printed by Harrison & Sons

		Unmtd mint	Used
R19 (=S.G.D19) **R1**			
½d.	Emerald (June 1937)	15·00	10·50
a.	Broken "2" in "½" (R. 3/14), 7/13 and 9/9	50·00	
R20 (=S.G.D20) **R1**			
1d.	Carmine (May 1937)	2·00	1·75
R21 (=S.G.D21) **R1**			
2d.	Agate (May 1937)	15·00	12·00
R22 (=S.G.D22) **R1**			
3d.	Dull violet (Mar. 1937)	2·00	2·00
s.	"Specimen", Type 30		
R23 (=S.G.D23) **R1**			
4d.	Dull grey-green (Dec. 1936)	65·00	34·00
s.	"Specimen", Type 30		
R24 (=S.G.D24/a) **R1**			
5d.	(1) Brownish cinnamon (Nov. 1936)	90·00	30·00
	(2) Yellow-brown ('37)	40·00	28·00
s.	"Specimen", Type 30		
R25 (=S.G.D25) **R1**			
1s.	Deep blue (Dec. 1936)	25·00	8·50
s.	"Specimen", Type 30		
R26 (=S.G.D26) **R2**			
2s.6d.	Purple/yellow (May 1937)	£325	12·00

Prices for Stamps on Cover. Nos. R19 *from* × 8, R20 *from* × 10, R21 *from* × 6, R22 *from* × 25, R23/4 *from* × 5.
The 1d. is known bisected (Solihull, 3 July 1937).

Listed Variety

R19a, R27a, R35a

Controls. Prices are for mint singles.

		I.	P.
½d.	A 37	25·00	†
1d.	A 37	15·00	†
2d.	A 37	20·00	†
3d.	A 37	15·00	†
4d.	A 36	55·00	†
5d.	A 36	£150	†
	A 37	£100	†
1s.	A 36	30·00	†
2s.6d.	A 37	£500	†
	C 38	£750	†

Imprimaturs from the National Postal Museum Archives
Imperforate, watermark Type **W19** (sideways)
  ½d., 1d., 2d., 3d., 4d., 5d., 1s., 2s. 6d. ....*Each* £2500

SECTION RC
King George VI Postage Dues (1937–52)

UNUSED PRICE QUOTATIONS
Unused prices quoted for R27–39 are for mint unmounted examples.

1937–38. Wmk. "GvIR", Type W20, Sideways
Printed by Harrison & Sons

	Unmtd mint	Used
R27 (=S.G.D27) **R1**		
½d. Emerald (1938)	13·00	8·75
a. Broken "2" in "½" (R. 3/14), 7/13 and 9/9	50·00	
s. "Specimen", Type 9		
t. "Specimen", Type 30		
R28 (=S.G.D28) **R1**		
1d. Carmine (1938)	3·00	50
a. Wmk. sideways-inverted	£150	
s. "Specimen", Type 9		
t. "Cancelled", Type 33		
u. "Specimen", Type 30		
R29 (=S.G.D29) **R1**		
2d. Agate (1938)	2·75	30
a. Wmk. sideways-inverted	£150	
s. "Specimen", Type 9		
t. "Cancelled", Type 33		
u. "Specimen", Type 30		
R30 (=S.G.D30) **R1**		
3d. Violet (1938)	11·00	30
a. Wmk. sideways-inverted	£150	
s. "Specimen", Type 9		
t. "Cancelled", Type 33		
u. "Specimen", Type 30		
R31 (=S.G.D31) **R1**		
4d. Dull grey-green (1937)	£110	10·00
a. Wmk. sideways-inverted	£300	
s. "Specimen", Type 9		
t. "Cancelled", Type 33		
u. "Specimen", Type 30		
R32 (=S.G.D32) **R1**		
5d. Yellow-brown (1938)	16·50	75
a. Wmk. sideways-inverted	£150	
s. "Specimen", Type 9		
t. "Cancelled", Type 33		
u. "Specimen", Type 30		
R33 (=S.G.D33) **R1**		
1s. Deep blue (1937)	80·00	75
a. Wmk. sideways-inverted	£150	
s. "Specimen", Type 9		
t. "Cancelled", Type 33		
u. "Specimen", Type 30		
R34 (=S.G.D34) **R2**		
2s. 6d. Purple/yellow (1938)	85·00	1·25

	Unmtd mint	Used
s. "Specimen", Type 9		
t. "Cancelled", Type 33		
u. "Specimen", Type 30		

Prices for Stamps on Cover. Nos. R27 from × 6, R28/9 from × 4, R30 from × 6, R31 from × 6, R32 from × 15, R33 from × 25.

The 2d. is known bisected (St. Albans, 5 June; Camberley; Boreham Wood, (all 1951) and Harpenden, 4 June 1951 and 30 October 1954).

Controls. Prices are for mounted mint singles.

		I.	P.
½d.	C 38	25·00	†
	E 39	25·00	—
	G 40	£200	£300
1d.	C 38	10·00	†
	E 39	10·00	†
1d.	G 40	10·00	—
	I 41	20·00	10·00
	K 42	†	10·00
	M 43	20·00	†
	O 44	12·00	†
	P 44	—	†
	Q 45	75·00	†
	U 47	75·00	†
2d.	C 38	10·00	†
	E 39	12·00	†
	G 40	—	12·00
	I 41	—	50·00
	K 42	—	10·00
	M 43	10·00	†
	O 44	£150	†
	Q 44	†	—
	Q 45	10·00	†
	U 47	50·00	†
3d.	B 37	30·00	†
	C 38	30·00	†
	D 38	35·00	†
	F 39	†	£250
	I 41	†	30·00
	K 42	75·00	£750
	M 43	30·00	†
	O 44	35·00	†
	R 45	35·00	†
	U 47	30·00	†
4d.	B 37	£140	†
	C 38	£140	†
	E 39	£140	†
	G 40	†	£300
	H 40	£200	†
	I 41	†	£150
	K 42	†	£150
	M 43	£150	†
	O 44	£250	†
	P 44	£150	†
	T 46	£250	†
5d.	C 38	40·00	†
	E 39	35·00	†
	G 40	40·00	†
	I 41	†	30·00
	M 43	55·00	†
	O 44	50·00	†
	P 44	35·00	†
	T 46	35·00	—

		I.	P.
1s.	B 37	£125	†
	C 38	£125	†
	E 39	£125	†
	G 40	£125	†
	J 41	£125	†
	K 42	£125	†
	M 43	£125	†
	O 44	£125	†
	P 44	£125	—
	R 45	£125	†
	S 46	£140	†
2s.6d.	C 38	£150	†
	D 38	£150	£200
	E 39	£200	†
	I 41	£275	—
	K 42	£375	£600
	L 42	£375	†
	O 44	£180	†
	P 44	£180	†
	Q 45	£600	†
	S 46	£600	†
	U 47	£1500	†

NOTE. Controls ceased after 1947.

Watermark varieties known:
Wmk sideways-inverted, 4d. K 42, T 46.

Imprimaturs from the National Postal Museum Archives
Imperforate, watermark Type **W20** (sideways)
½d., 1d., 2d., 3d., 4d., 5d., 1s...Each £2500
Perf. 14 × 15, watermark Type **W20** (sideways)
2s.6d. ....

●———

1951–54. Colours Changed and New Value. Wmk. "GvIR", Type W20, Sideways

Printed by Harrison & Sons

	Unmtd mint	Used
R35 (=S.G.D35) **R1**		
½d. (1) Yellow-Orange (18.9.51)	3·50	3·50
(2) Bright-orange (5.54)	40·00	
a. Broken "2" in "½" (R. 3/14)	£150	
R36 (=S.G.D36) **R1**		
1d. Violet-blue (6.6.51)	1·50	75
a. Wmk. sideways-inverted		
R37 (=S.G.D37) **R1**		
1½d. Green (11.2.52)	2·00	2·00
a. Wmk. sideways-inverted	£120	
b. Stop after THREE	£150	
R38 (=S.G.D38) **R1**		
4d. Blue (14.8.51)	50·00	22·00
a. Wmk. Sideways-inverted	†	£1000
R39 (=S.G.D39) **R1**		
1s. Ochre (6.12.51)	28·00	5·25
a. Wmk. Sideways-inverted	£2800	

Prices for Stamps on Cover. Nos. R35 *from* × 10, R36 *from* × 6, R37 *from* × 10, R38 *from* × 4, R39 *from* × 10.

The dates of issue given above are those on which the stamps were first issued by the Supplies Department to postmasters except No. R35(2) which was reported used in Torquay in May 1954.

The 1d. is known bisected (Dorking, 14 April and 23 June, 1952 and Camberley, 6 April, 1954).

On 6 June 1951, the post office at Bury St. Edmunds ran out of 1d. Postage Due stamps. Two unofficial handstamps were made on the instructions of the postmaster, and the overprint "POSTAGE DUE" applied to the current 1d. postage stamp (No. Q6) after they were fixed to the covers. About a hundred were said to have been used on 7 June. In addition 20 unused examples were sold over the post office counter to an individual who then sold them to dealers. *Price* £600 *used on piece.*

Similar shortages at other offices were met by the use of unoverprinted postage stamps as postage dues, sometimes endorsed "Surcharge" in manuscript, while the postmaster at Herne Bay utilised the handstamp that would normally have been struck on underpaid envelopes to "overprint" 1d. stamps.

Imprimaturs from the National Postal Museum Archives
Imperforate, watermark Type **W20** (sideways)
½d., 1d., 1½d., 4d., 1s..Each £2500

Appendices

Appendix 1

Perforators

KING EDWARD VII

The gauge of the perforators continued to be 14 × 14, until September 1911 when it was altered to 15 × 14 for some of the later printings made by Harrison & Sons. This was done to facilitate easier and equal separation.

A perforator was a standard machine that could be fitted with different "combs", the pin plate that creates the perforations. The sheet of stamps was passed through the machine from one direction only, so the visual differences in perforation of a sheet of stamps occur as a result of the direction of entry of the sheet (top, bottom, left side or right side), potentially two perforation varieties for each horizontal or vertical comb perforator.

Horizontal Comb Perforation

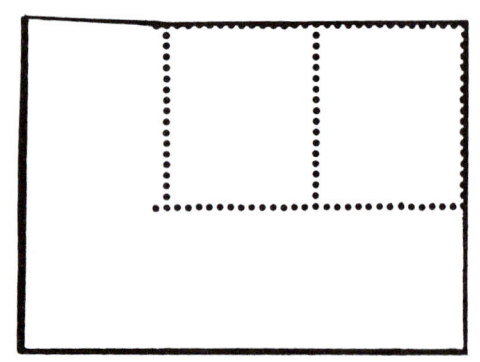

Type H1 (Bottom feed)

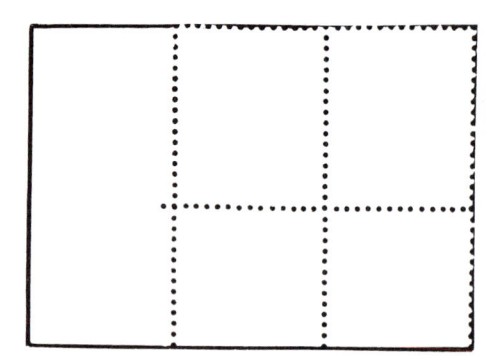

Types H1A or H2A (Top feed)

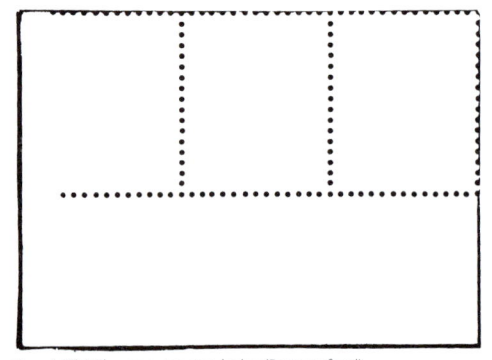

Type H2(c) Eleven extension holes (Bottom feed)

Type H2(a), (d), (e), (f) and (g) are the same, with extension holes as listed on the following page.

1. HORIZONTAL COMB PERFORATION

Set to perforate the sheet horizontally from bottom to top or top to bottom.

Perforation Type	Left Margin	Bottom Margin	Right Margin	Notes
Type H1	One extension hole	Imperforate	One extension hole	All D.L.R. values only. Bottom feed
Type H1A	One extension hole	Perf. through	One extension hole	D.L.R. ½d., 1d., 2½d., 3d., 5d. and 6d. Top feed
Type H2(a)	Nine extension holes	Imperforate	One extension hole	Harrison perf. 14 ½d., 3d., 4d. and Somerset House £1. Bottom feed
Type H2(c)	11 extension holes	Imperforate	One extension hole	
Type H2(d)	12 extension holes	Imperforate	One extension hole	
Type H2(e)	14 extension holes	Imperforate	One extension hole	
Type H2(f)	17 extension holes	Imperforate	One extension hole	
Type H2(g)	17 extension holes	Imperforate	13 extension holes	
Type H2A(b)	One extension hole	Perf. through	Ten extension holes	Harrison only. Perf. 14 ½d., 1d., 3d. and 4d. Somerset House £1. Top feed
Type H2A(c)	One extension hole	Perf. through	11 extension holes	
Type H2A(d)	One extension hole	Perf. through	12 extension holes	
Type H2A(e)	One extension hole	Perf. through	14 extension holes	

Thus, De La Rue had perforators with one type of comb only, whereas Harrisons had perforators with seven different combs over a period. However, any comb may have been amended by adding to or reducing the number of pins in the pin plate, so Harrisons would not have needed seven perforators.

Vertical Comb Perforation

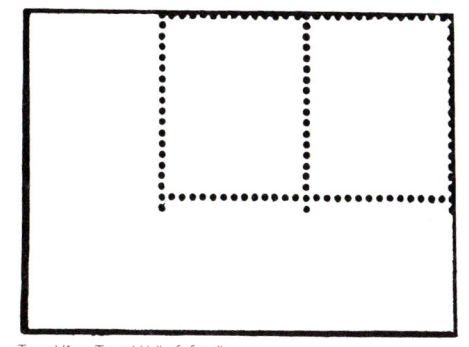

Type V1 or Type V4 (Left feed)

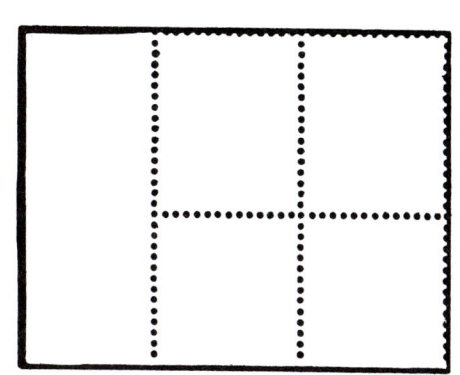

Type V2 (Left feed)

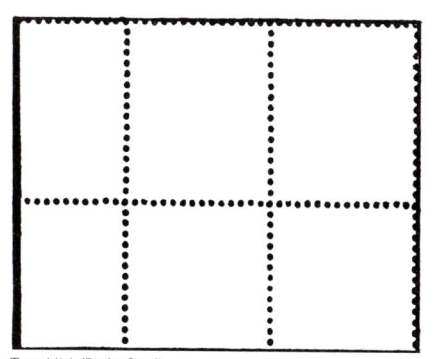

Type V1A (Right feed)
(This illustration is perf. 15 × 14 (Type V3A))

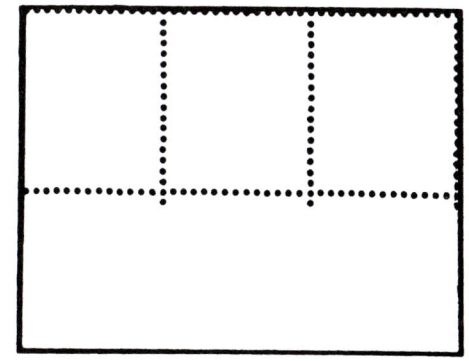

Type V2A or Type V4A (Right feed)

APPENDIX 1   Perforators King Edward VII

II. VERTICAL COMB PERFORATIONS.

Set to perforate the sheet from side to side

Perforation Type	Left Margin	Bottom Margin	Right Margin	Notes
Type V1	Imperforate	One extension hole	Perf. through	All three contractors perf. 14. Left feed.
Type V1A	Perf. through	Perf. through with 17 pins	Imperforate	Harrison perf. 14 and Somerset Hse, right feed
Type V2	Imperforate	Perf. through with 13 pins	Perf. through	D.L.R. ½d. yellow-green, 1d. and occasionally 4d. bi-colour. Left feed
Type V2(a)	Imperforate	Perf. through with 12 pins	Perf. through	D.L.R. Controls E5 and F6 only. Left feed
Type V2A	Perf. through	One extension hole	Imperforate	As for Type V2 but right feed
Type V3	Imperforate	One extension	Perf. through	Harrison perf. 15 × 14. Left feed
Type V3A	Perf. through	Perf. through with 17 pins	Imperforate	As Type V3 but right feed
Type V4	Imperforate	One extension hole at top and bottom	Perf. through	D.L.R. ½d. and 1d. see below, left feed
Type V4A	Perf. through	One extension hole at top and bottom	Imperforate	As Type V4 but right feed

Types V4 and V4A. This is a recently found type of vertical perforator yielding a single extension hole in both top and bottom margins. So far it is only known to exist for the ½d. and 1d. values perforated 14. As a control piece would be as Type V1 with left feed and V2A with right feed, the three vertical types can only be distinguished by at least a complete vertical strip of 20.

There is evidence to believe that Types V4 and V4A were employed quite extensively but were not recognised at the time. Information is needed from those who have complete vertical control strips from any of the three vertical perforators.

Letterpress Booklet Panes
The letter in brackets below the following three diagrams refers to the booklet selvedge at left.
(E)   Extension hole in the margin in each row
(P)   Perforated margin
(I)   Imperforate margin

Types B1 and B1A A horizontal comb perforator with a single extension pin at each end of the comb head (Type B1(E)) but which also perforated through the central gutter so that panes from gutter margins were Type B1A(P). Employed by De La Rue for Booklets (1) to (6).

For Booklet (7) Harrison used a different horizontal comb which also had a single pin on each side of the central gutter, hence this only occurs as Type B1(E). This continued in use for the King George V booklets until Booklet 6, BB18, issued in February 1919.

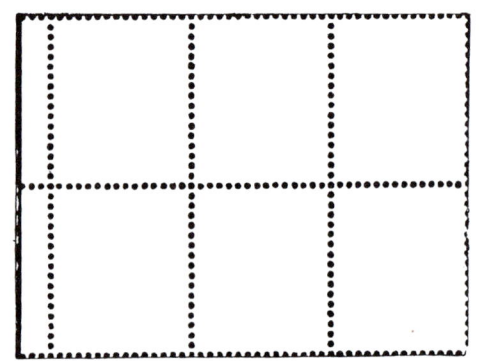

Type B1(E)

Type B1A(P)

286

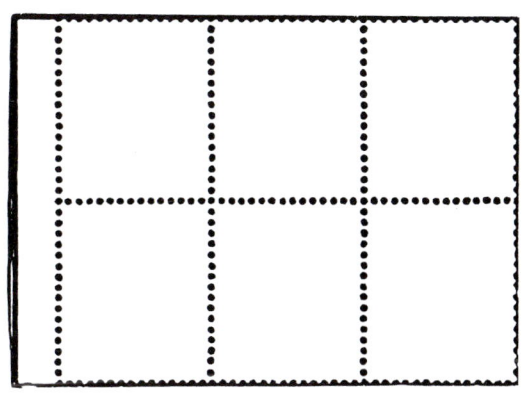

King Edward VII / King George V *Perforators* **APPENDIX 1**

KING GEORGE V

1911-24. Letterpress. ½d. to 1s.
The gauge of perforation was 14¾ or 15 horizontally by 14 vertically, the exception being the Die 1A ½d. and 1d. which have been found perf. 14, and the 6d. perf. 14 issued in 1920-21 when the 15 × 14 machine was out of action.

I. HORIZONTAL COMB PEFORATION

Type 1 As for Types H2(a), H2(d) and H2(e) (bottom feed) of King Edward VII. In the case of Type 1 the left margin has 9, 12 or 14 extension holes and bottom margin imperforate. The right margin has one extension hole. Also two perforation combs with extension holes of 15 and 16 at left respectively.

Type 1A As for H2A above, but top feed with perforated through bottom margin and one extension hole in left margin. The right margin had extension holes in the numbers listed above.

II VERTICAL COMB PERFORATION

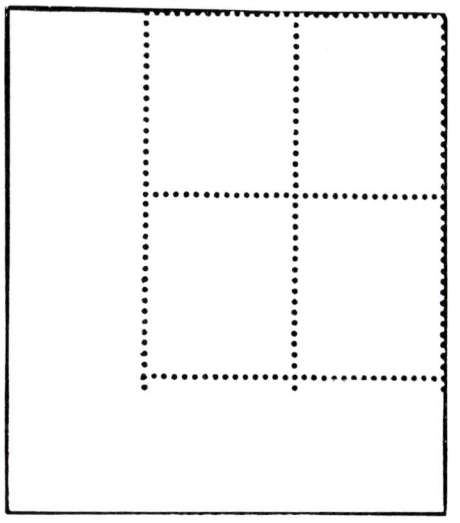

Type B3 (I)

Type 2 (Left feed)

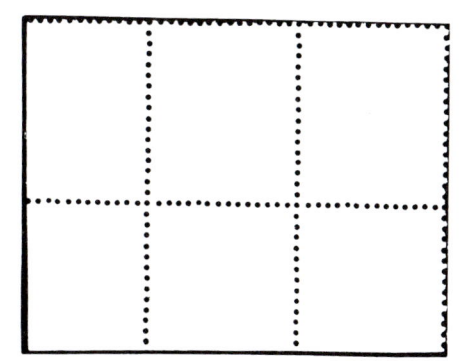

Type 2A (Right feed)

Types B3 and B3A A vertical comb perforator. With left feed the left-hand pane (without horizontal bars and watermark upright) was imperforate as shown above and all other panes were perforated through (as Type B1A(P)). With right feed the right-hand pane (without horizontal bars and watermark inverted) was imperforate and all other panes perforated through. The perforator was the same for "left" and "right" feed, the latter occurring when the operator rotated stamp sheets 180 degrees on the pile, prior to perforation. All Georgian panes have vertical marginal rules at the side and the centre panes have short horizontal bars as well.

This perforator was employed on all panes by Harrison from February 1919, by Waterlow from 1924 to 1933 and by Harrison in 1934. The use of right feed by Waterlow is rare and is known in only a single example from the Harrison provisional printing.

Type B3 was also used for the ½d. and 1d. Downey Head Die 1B watermark Crown booklet panes as a result of the urgency to issue the new Georgian stamps. In a small number of Downey Head booklets, panes from the centre of the sheet (with horizontal bars in the margin) have imperforate margin (Type B3(I)) and the outer panes (without horizontal bars) are perforated through (Type B3A(P)). This was achieved by dividing the booklet pane sheets vertically and perforating the half sheets on the vertical perforator used for counter sheets, Type 2, as no vertical booklet pane perforator existed at that time. Downey Head Crown watermark panes with this perforation are scarce.

Type 2 In general use throughout the period. Type 2A extension spur of 14 pins through bottom margin on a normal width selvedge. Up to 17 pins have been seen on wider bottom selvedges.

287

APPENDIX 1   Perforators   King George V

Left feed— Bottom margin   A single extension hole.
            Top margin   Perforated through.
            Left margin   Imperforate.
            Right margin   Perforated through.

Type 2A
Right feed— Bottom margin   Perforated through.
            Top margin   A single extension hole.
            Left margin   Perforated through.
            Right margin   Imperforate.

Right feed occurs by rotation of the sheet top to bottom.

The comb spurs each contain 14 pins and therefore give the perforation 15×14. At least two comb-heads are known. In one of them, the pins are set so that the 14 pins perforate a distance one-half millimetre in excess of the other comb-head. Stamps from this comb-head can be recognized by the fact that the outer top corner perforation is thinner than normal and the gauge is approximately 14¾.

Type 2(c) (left feed). As Type 2 but with single extension hole missing in the bottom margin. It is believed that this perforator has an extension spur as Type 2 so that right feed of the sheet would result in controls indistinguishable from Type 2A. Perforator Type 2(c) was used by Harrison in most years for Downey Head and Watermark Royal Cypher issues, particularly in 1911 and 1917; by Somerset House in 1913 and 1923/24 only and by Waterlow, particularly in 1924, 1926 and 1931. It would appear to have been a reserve perforator for all three printers.

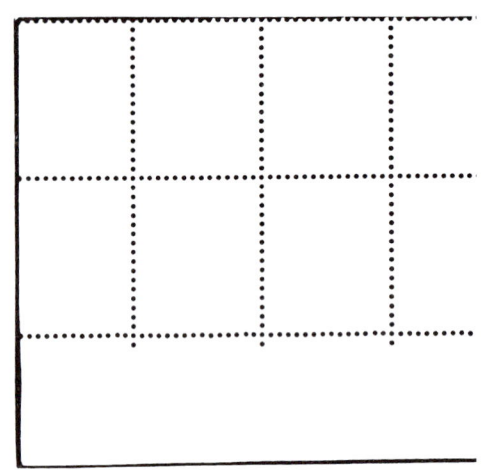

Type 3 (Right feed)

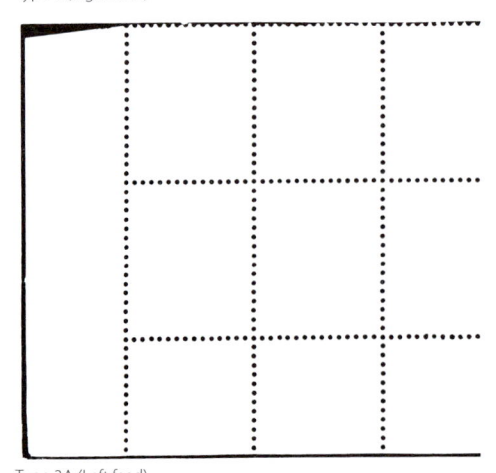

Type 3A (Left feed)

Type 3 Type 3 and Type 3A configurations of perforator pin heads were used variously by Harrison, Somerset House and Waterlow, probably as reserve perforators. Unlike Types 2 and 2A, which use the same pin plate as left and right feed on the same perforator, generally Types 3 and 3A were used on different perforators. Type 3 only was used by Harrison for earlier Downey Head issues. Conversely, Type 3A only was used by Waterlow from 1924 to 1930 and in 1934. Additionally, both Types 3 and 3A were commonly used together by Somerset House in 1913. Accordingly, it is likely that the Somerset House perforator Types 3 and 3A is on the same pin plate, which would have a single extension hole at the top and the extension spur of pins at the bottom.

Type 3 For Somerset House printings.
Right feed— Bottom margin   A single extension hole.
             Top margin   Perforated through.
             Left margin   Perforated through.
             Right margin   Imperforate.

For Harrison Downey Head printings, as above except top margin, a single extension hole (evidenced from complete sheet selvedges).

Type 3A For Somerset House printings.
Left feed—   Bottom margin   Perforated through.
             Top margin   A single extension hole.
             Left margin   Imperforate.
             Right margin   Perforated through.

Left feed occurs by rotation of the sheet top to bottom. For Waterlow printings the top margin configuration is unknown.

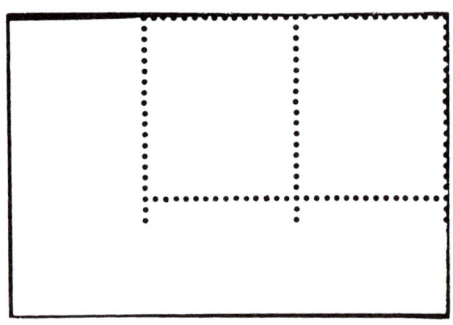

Type 4 (Left feed)

Type 4 As for Type 2, but the bottom margin shows two extension holes with left feed. It is known that this perforator was used with right feed and, as Type 4A, it is indistinguishable from Type 2A. Consequently, in the Control and Cylinder Number listings, Type 4 with right feed is listed as Type 2A. This perforator was used only by Harrison on later Profile Head and early Photogravure issues in 1934/35.

1913-30. Engraved. 2s.6d. to £1
The gauge was 11 horizontally by 12 vertically and two machines were in operation:—
(a) Used exclusively by Waterlow and Layton, gave the marginal perforation similar to Type 1 (top feed).
(b) Used by the other two contractors, gave marginal perforations similar to Type 5 (bottom feed). Bradbury, Wilkinson also used the top feed which gave marginal perforations similar to Type 6B.

Photogravure
The photogravure stamps issued prior to the Silver Jubilee issue were generally perforated on the machines in use at the end of the typographed period—Type 2— by guillotining the printed double sheets into single sheets prior to perforation from the side. Occasionally Type 4 and rarely Type 3 were also used.

Shortly afterwards, the general perforator in use was a new horizontal single comb perforator set to perforate the printed double sheets from bottom to top. At each end of the comb

King George V *Perforators* **APPENDIX 1**

head on both dot and no dot panes was a single extension pin (Type 5).

Type 5 perforator was adapted for the Silver Jubilee issue by the removal of alternate sets of vertical pins.

Later during the reign of Edward VIII, double (two-row) comb heads were introduced for Type 5 perforators and these became the norm from 1942.

At the same time as the Type 5 double-sheet perforators, a supplementary perforator in use was as Type 6. This is a continuous web perforator with a triple comb head enabling three rows of stamps to be perforated at a time. The outer ends of the comb heads were without extension pins, and the pins crossed the interpane margins.

The continuous web perforator was soon modified by the removal of the pins in the interpane margin, leaving only single extension holes. Cylinder blocks from the no dot pane show no alteration.

Type 5 Cylinder blocks from dot and no dot panes.
  Left margin   A single extension hole.
  Bottom margin   Imperforate.
Type 6 Cylinder blocks from the no dot pane.
  Left margin   Imperforate.
  Bottom margin   Perforated through.
Type 6A Cylinder blocks from the dot pane.
  Left margin   Perforated through.
  Bottom margin   Perforated through.
Type 6B Cylinder blocks from the dot pane.
  Left margin   A single extension hole.
  Bottom margin   Perforated through.

The ½d., 1½d., 2d., 2½d. and 3d. King George VI pale colours of 1941-42 were at first printed from single pane cylinders with dot but were perforated with the left-pane perforator, Type 6.

Similarly, early printings of the 4d., 5d., 6d., 7d., 8d. and 1s. King George VI were from single pane cylinders without dot but were perforated with the right-pane perforator, Type 6B.

Type 5 with the two-row comb head in normal use at the end of the reign of George VI is the same as Type A under "Perforators" in Vol. 3 of this work. Also Type 6 (no dot) and Type 6B (dot) are the same as Types B and C as described under "Perforators" in Vol. 3.

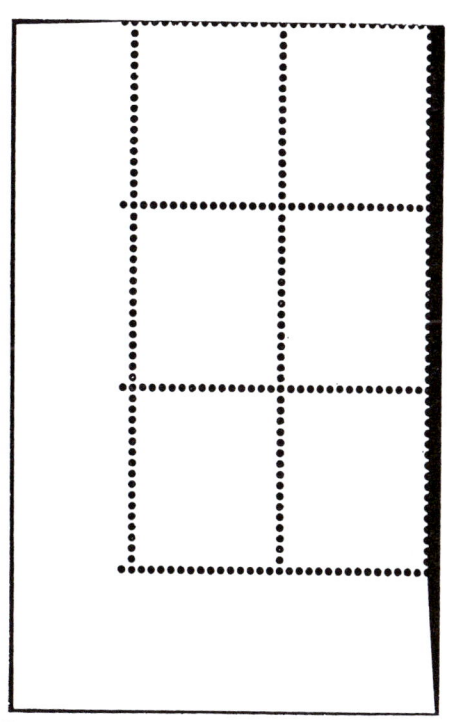

Type 5
No dot and Dot panes

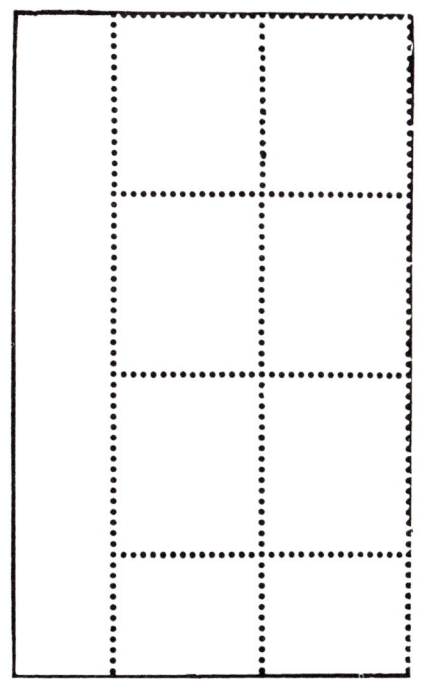

Type 6
Left or No dot pane

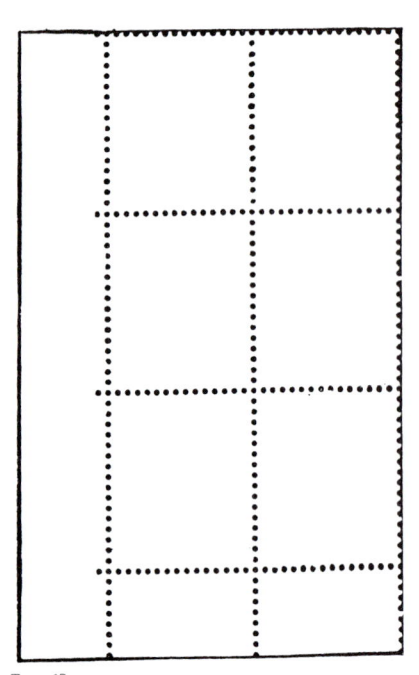

APPENDIX 1 Perforators King George V

The Type 4 perforator was adapted for the Silver Jubilee issue by removing and resetting vertical pins for the larger stamps and relocating selvedges.

The descriptions for Types B5 and B6 illustrate the cylinder panes*. On non-cylinder panes the three perforation holes (or one hole in the case of B6) can be either in the top, middle or bottom row. The watermark is either upright (panes from dot cylinder adjoining the central gutter) or inverted (panes from no dot cylinder adjoining the central gutter), so B5 and B6 perforated panes occur on only one quarter of panes and B5 is very scarce, having been replaced after only a few months.

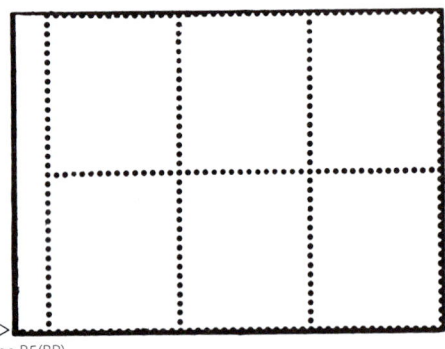

Type B5(BP)

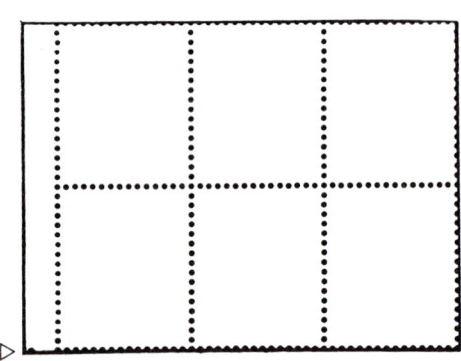

Type B6(Ie)

*Exceptionally, QB18 to QB20 label panes had the cylinder number placed beside the stamps printed on the top row of the pane, so the B6 perforation hole is at the top of the selvedge (see listing illustrations).

Type 6B
Right or Dot pane
Variety: Type 5AE has extension hole in the left-hand margin missing on alternate rows in the no dot pane. Normally, the extension hole is opposite the bottom of even number stamp rows from row 2 to row 20. Exceptionally, as noted in the listings, the extension hole is opposite the top of the even number stamp rows.

Type 6A is not illustrated but looks the same as Type 2A. Specialists can differentiate between these perforators as Type 2 is vertical single comb sheet fed whereas Type 6 is horizontal triple comb reel fed. Unless proven to be Type 6A, controls and cylinder blocks are listed as Type 2A.

Photogravure Booklet Panes
From 1935, two new single comb horizontal perforators (B4) were introduced for the booklets containing the stamps printed in photogravure, although occasional use was made of the B3 perforator of the typographed issue which was retained as a reserve machine. From 1943 perforation was done in the reel by a triple-comb perforator (B5) adapted after a few months by the extraction of two selvedge pins to Type B6. This B6 perforator was used until 1955. Booklet panes with cylinder numbers may be found with the following perforations:

Type	Cyl. No. Pane	Perforation
B3	No dot	Imperf. margin. (Known as I.)
B3A	Dot	Perf. margin. (Known as P.)
B4	No dot	Extension hole in the margin in each row. (Known as E.)
B4A	Dot	Imperf. margin. (Known as I.)
B4B	Dot	Extension hole in the margin in each row. (Known as E.)
B5	Dot	Perforations at bottom only extend across margin. (Known as BP.)
B6	Dot	As for B5 except that the two perforation pins next to the stamp margin have been removed (leaving a single ½ hole in the margin). (Known as Ie.)

For illustrations of E, P and I see B1, B1A and B3 respectively under King Edward VII.

Appendix 2

Post Office Booklets of Stamps

BOOKLET PRICES. Prices in this Appendix are for booklets containing panes with "average" perforations (i.e) full perforations on two edges of the pane only). Booklets containing panes with complete perforations are worth more.

General Notes
This Appendix is arranged for each of the four reigns in ascending order of issued booklet values, noting the seven Post Office series and five sub-series of Series 6, whose allocation was by major type of booklet. Within each series and sub-series, there is allocated a catalogue number for those booklets of precisely the same format and contents. Each issued booklet was called an edition by the Post Office and, from January 1913 to August 1943, the edition number in each series was printed on the top right corner of the booklet. From September 1943, booklets were dated only and so for those editions (and the first 14 booklets) an "edition number" has been allocated in brackets. Series 6 slot machine booklets had no edition numbers or dates and so have catalogue numbers based on dates of issue. Perhaps it is worth recording that, whilst collectors refer to "booklets", The Post Office, printers and contractors called their product "Books of Stamps" and reserved the term "booklets" for the 6d. and 1s. slot machine booklets only.

BOOKLET SHEET ARRANGEMENT AND MAKE-UP
Originally, there were two basic requirements for booklets, firstly, that the stamps should always be upright when the booklet was opened and, secondly, that there should always be a binding margin at the left of each pane so that the booklet opened in that direction.

Consequently, booklets are made up from specially printed sheets which are differently arranged from Post Office counter sheets to facilitate these requirements. Apart from panes for 6d. and 1s. slot machine booklets, all booklets had panes of six stamps printed in single sheets during the letterpress period up to 1934 and in single or double sheets thereafter in the photogravure period. Thus, by way of example in the photogravure period, the printer's double sheet of 480 stamps, consisting of two panes (with no dot and dot cylinder numbers) separated by a vertical gutter, each of 240 stamps arranged in 20 rows of 12 stamps, had additional vertical gutters provided between the sixth and seventh columns in both panes and the stamps in the fourth, fifth and sixth and the tenth, 11th and 12th columns in both panes are inverted in relation to the others (i.e. tête-bêche). Two horizontal rows of the printer's sheet (producing eight booklets) would be arranged thus:

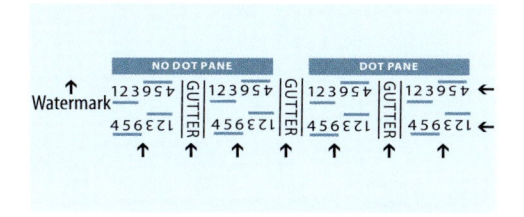

The printer's double sheet is divided through the central gutter into the pane size and the pane of stamps, interleaves and covers are stacked in the required order (equivalent to 40 booklets). Then, the mass is stitched vertically, twice with a double-headed machine in the gutter between the sixth and seventh columns of each pane and, following checking, once at the outer edges of each pane. Finally, the booklets in each pane are guillotined both horizontally and vertically as indicated by the arrows. From the diagram, it is easy to see how 50% of booklet stamps have inverted watermarks. However, booklets can have panes with upright and inverted watermarks because there was no reason to stack sheets in the same direction.

In the letterpress period, the booklet sheet format was the same, but printed on half a printer's sheet, usually 240 stamps but 264 stamps from the introduction of Series 2 in 1918. Booklets were stapled up to July 1917 and stitched thereafter. Occasionally, stitching malfunctioned and the normal procedure was to remove the thread and booklet covers and staple the panes and interleaves, saved with their holes, between new front and back covers, which do not have stitch holes. Where known, such staple repair editions are listed.

BOOKLETS USED FOR REFERENCE OR TRIALS
During the reigns of King Edward VII and King George V, many issued booklets were used by the printers or the Post Office to carry out trials for covers and interleaves or retained for the record, whilst the printers prepared other trial booklets with printed and blank covers and their own printed or blank labels. The first issued booklets used for trial or reference purposes were pen cancelled Type A (see Appendix 3) and later booklets were handstamped with "Specimen" or "Cancelled" overprints (see Appendix 4). Whilst many of these booklets have been "exploded" for their panes, which are listed in each booklet pane section, the pre-cancelled booklets are listed where it is known that examples remain complete.

ADVERTISER VOUCHER COPY BOOKS
In 1907, the Post Office was authorized to print trade advertisements in booklets and canvassed 24 potential advertisers. All declined and red Post Office notices were included on the glassine interleaves of the 1908 edition (4). The interleaves were changed to paper and six advertisers used the interleaves in the 1909 and 1910 editions (5) and (6). This necessitated provision of a booklet to each advertiser to illustrate insertion of the agreed advertisement and the Post Office concluded that the advertising activity required particular experience resulting in the appointment of the Post Office Advertising Contractor, Sells Ltd.

From the 1911 issues, Sells Ltd. solicited and organised all the advertising between the advertisers and the printers and Post Office and supplied a booklet of stamps to each of the former to evidence the advertisement. Such booklets required to be invalidated and this was done by the London Chief Office staff obliterating the stamps on each pane in a number of booklets which were supplied to Sells Ltd.

The obliterators are described in Appendix 3. Initially, the obliterator was dumb (Type E), then a regular datestamp (Type G) was adopted, rapidly changed to a range of datestamps without time slugs (Types F to K) which were used until April 1926. As all these obliterators included dates, this is the most accurate indication of the issue date of each edition. From Series 1 edition 23 (October 1914) to 48 (September 1916) most, if not all, such booklets had a punch hole at the top left through the booklet. Whilst the purpose of the punch hole is unknown, this practice was typical of Post Office departments on their material.

From May 1926, datestamp obliterators were discontinued and "cancelled" was applied to each stamp in the pane, probably using a forme of six, with overprints described in Appendix 4 and, additionally, punched Type P from March 1928. Exceptionally, probably in error, some of these booklets were cancelled Type 24 or Specimen Type 23, generally used for Post Office reference material, and some have omission of the Type P punch. From May 1926, advertiser voucher copy booklets were datestamped on the front cover, usually vertically beside the binding margin, again indicating the date of issue of each edition. This distinguishes these booklets from reference and trial booklets, which are invariably undated. Advertiser voucher copy booklets are listed under each catalogue number, where known to exist, in each case being abbreviated to AVC.

AIR MAIL LABELS

Air Mail labels were included in most booklets from May 1930 to December 1937. Two labels (three labels for the Silver Jubilee booklets) and Post Office information comprised a pane of booklet size. Initially, Air Mail label panes were introduced in 3s. booklets, Edition 191, followed by 5s. booklets in July 1933, Edition 4, and 2s. booklets in January 1935, Edition 289. Many 3s. booklets between June 1930, Edition 192, and February 1934, Edition 273, did not include an Air Mail label pane but from January 1935 they were included in all booklets towards either the front or the back until withdrawn at the end of 1937, by which time most mail to overseas destinations could be sent by air at flat rates without a label.

Initially, the design of the label was the boxed words "BY AIR MAIL / PAR AVION" printed in white on a blue background with the Post Office information printed in blue on the white background. The label design was replaced in July 1934 with the popular Lee-Elliot white and black wings design over the same words in smaller letters. Both designs were the same as the labels obtainable in sheets from Post Office counters.

Additionally, the same Air Mail labels were issued in booklets, the so called Imperial Airways booklets, from February 1931 to September 1936 (for which the stock lasted until May 1937). The panes comprised four labels printed by Waterlow (later, Harrison) and the booklets contained three Air Mail label panes, Post Office information including Air Mail rates and much advertising for Imperial Airways on the covers and interleaves including their airline routes. The covers and interleaves were printed by the Post Office contractor from Imperial Airways blocks and artwork. Being the nearest to a national British airline with a monopoly on many Empire routes, Imperial Airways was the logical choice as advertiser and, initially, paid £50 to advertise in an edition of 120,000 booklets, the cost of which was £70 from Waterlow to the Post Office.

VICTORIAN BOOKLET ESSAYS PREPARED BY DE LA RUE

Essay cover

Essay pane

1880 (23 February). Lilac Cover with Royal Coat of Arms entitled "TWENTY-FOUR PENNY RECEIPT STAMPS PRICE 2s 0½d", containing four panes of six revenue 1d. purple stamps, SG L20, Die 4, manuscript "cancelled" each row of three stamps. £10000

●

1885 (4 February). Orange-brown, deep grey or grey-blue cover with label entitled "120 PENNY STAMPS 10s 0½d", containing eight panes of 15 blank stamp-size labels, perf 14, attached sideways by a selvedge.

June "cheque book" cover reverse

June "cheque book" pane

1885 (15 June). Yellow enamelled cover with label entitled "120 PENNY STAMPS 10s 1d" containing eight panes of 15 blank stamps size labels, perf 14, attached sideways by a selvedge.... £8000

VICTORIAN COMMERCIAL BOOKLETS
(See also Edition 13 of Volume 1, page 236)

1891 *(2 May)* Red linen cover inscribed "Memoranda" containing 64 pages of advertisements and information with a slit in the back cover containing a 1d. lilac stamp, SG K8, perfin "SDS", sold by the Stamp Distribution Syndicate from vending machines, all enclosed in a cream paper envelope with punch holes and an SDS perfin tab. Editions have an S(number). .... *complete* £9000

1893 As above but inscribed "MEMO. BOOK." with a crown between the words, the 1d. lilac stamp, SG K8, perfin "SDC", sold by the Stamp Distribution Parent Company from vending machines, all enclosed in a cream paper envelope with punch holes and an SDC perfin tab.

Editions have series numbers/quantity printed........................
.... *complete* £9000

KING EDWARD VII

ESSAYS, TRIALS AND PROOFS

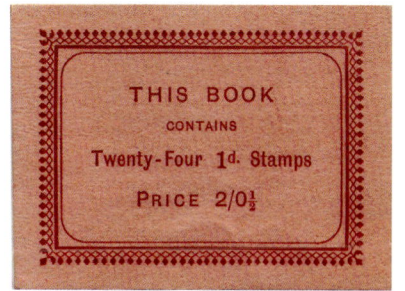

Cover, brown on pinkish brown

1903 *(26 June).* Front Cover Essays

Brown on pinkish-brown card, inscribed "THIS BOOK contains Twenty-Four 1d stamps PRICE 2/0½"	£2000
Green on light green card, inscribed "THIS BOOK contains Forty-Eight ½d stamps PRICE 2/0½"	£2000
Blue on blue-green card, inscribed "COMBINED BOOK THIS BOOK contains Twelve 1d stamps and Twenty-Four ½d stamps PRICE 2/0½"	£2000
All three above essays on De la Rue "Appendix "A" sheet	£7500
Booklet Cover Essay, front as first above, on slightly larger brown on pinkish-brown card, back cover with Royal Cypher	£4000

Pane, stapled at left

Pane, stapled at right

1903 Trial Booklets for Interleaving and Format

Blank covers containing four De la Rue panes of six perforated "Queen's Head" labels and glassine interleaves

Pink covers with green labels, stapled at right	£2500
Pink covers with brown labels, stapled at left	£3000
Blue covers with green labels, stapled at left	£3000
As above but Blue covers with ten panes of lilac labels, stapled at left	£3500

APPENDIX 2 *Post Office Booklets of Stamps* King Edward VII / Essays, Trials and Proofs

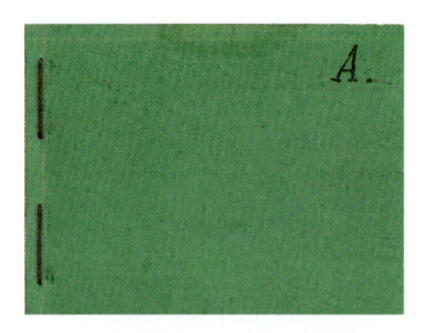

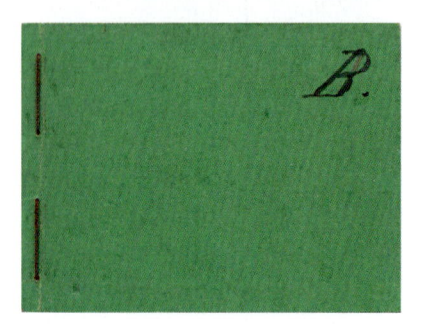

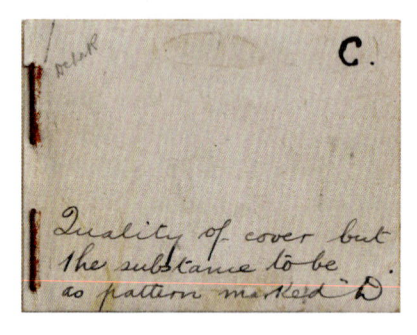

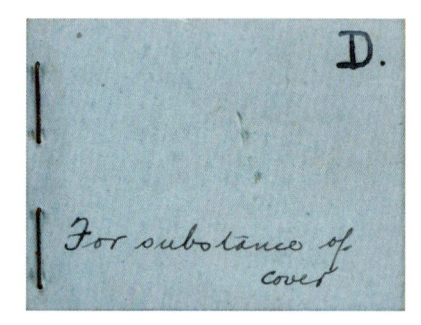

Pane representing 1d. stamps

Pane representing 1½d. stamps

1903 Trial Booklets for Substance of Cover.

Blank covers containing three De La Rue panes of six perforated "Minerva Head" labels, one red and two green, and cream paper interleaves

Green cover, marked "A" at top right	£1600
Green cover, marked "B" at top right	£1600
White cover, marked "C" at top right and manuscript "Quality of cover but the substance to be as pattern marked "D""	£1600
Blue cover, marked "D" at top right and manuscript "For substance of cover"	£1600

Type "C" is known with one red and three green panes in error

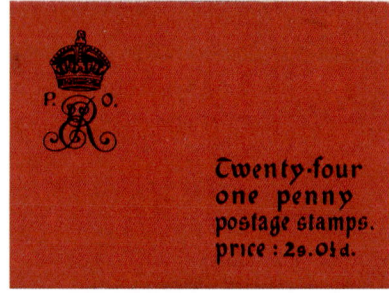

Front cover, gothic type

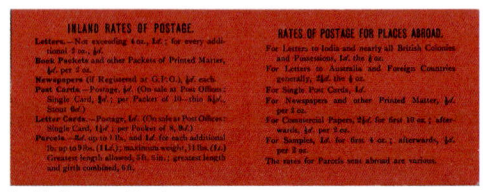

Inside front and back

294

Front cover, issued type

Inside with minor corrections

1903 (September). Trial Covers in agreed red colour for outside front and back

Double size front and back with "Twenty-four one penny postage stamps price: 2s 0½" in Kelmscott (Gothic) type, format as Type **1**	£1600
As above but amended to issued front cover type and minor text corrections	£1600
Inside front and back with Postage Rates, Inland and Abroad, original text, later minor text corrections each	£1600

1903 (October). Trial Booklet for Finish of Cover

Varnished covers as Edition No. (1) containing four panes of six perforated blank labels and glassine interleaves	£2000

1903 (November). Trial Booklet for Finish of Cover

As above but with unvarnished covers, red inside and outside (rejected)	£2500

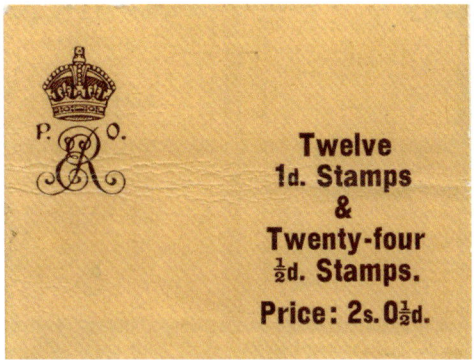

Cover trial, yellow

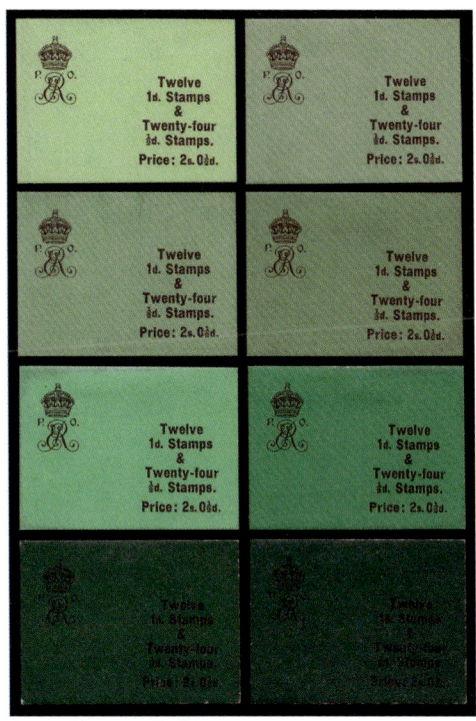

Cover trials, green shades

1904 Front Cover Trials for Colour for Edition No. (2)

All with Royal Cypher at left and inscribed "Twelve 1d. Stamps & Twenty-four ½d. Stamps Price: 2s 0½d"

30 May In yellow, light blue and dark blue (from De La Rue "Appendix A") each	£2500
29 August In eight shades of green from very light to very dark each	£1500

(1905) Booklet Essays for Edition No. (2)

Covers as Edition No. (2), except inside back as Edition No. (1), containing six De La Rue panes of six perforated "Queen's Head" labels, two red, four green, the last with a handpainted St Andrew's Cross label at top left, glassine interleaves	£6000
Blank red covers containing six panes of six blank perforated labels, six cream paper interleaves (to accommodate advertising) and 13 glassine interleaves	£3000

1906 Die Proof for Booklet Edition No. (2)

St Andrew's Cross in black on white glazed card dated "24 JAN. 06" at top right	£7500

(see also in booklet panes under MB2)

(1906) Trial Booklets for Advertising on Glassine Interleaves

Covers as Edition No. (2) containing five panes of six blank perforated labels and six glassine interleaves, all printed with parts of "The Laws of Bridge" In red, blue or black printing each	£5000

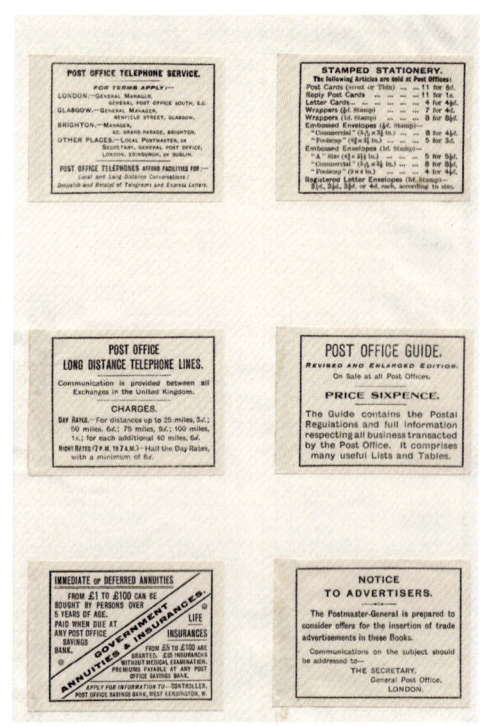

APPENDIX 2   *Post Office Booklets of Stamps*   King Edward VII / Essays, Trials and Proofs

Interleaf proofs

1908 (14 May). Interleaf Proofs for Edition No. (4).

Six paper interleaf proofs printed in black, attached to
  De La Rue Appendix sheet £7500

1909 Interleaf Proofs for Commercial Advertising in Edition No. (5).

On interleaf size paper contained between card covers, not bound. Six proof advertisements printed in green or blue .... set £6000

Interleaf trials, printed in green

Interleaf trials, printed in blue

(1909) Trial Booklets with Commercial Advertising Interleaves

Cover as Edition No. (4) containing five De La Rue panes of six perforated "Minerva Head" labels, three red and two green

Glassine interleaves printed in blue or green	each £3500
Cream paper interleaves in blue or green	each £3500

(1909) Back cover Essay for Edition No. (5)

Edition No. (4) precancelled Type A with manuscript inside back addition "Hawaii and the United States of America" and outside back "Telegrams (Inland)" replaced by "Notice to Advertisers" £1250

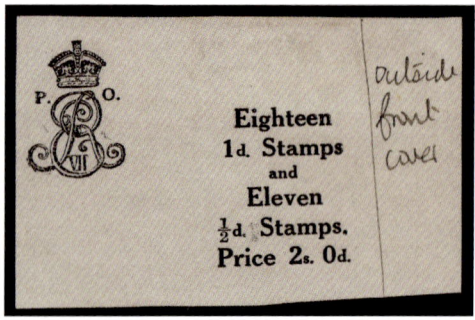

Front cover, enlarged cypher

(1910) Front Cover Proof for Edition No. (7)

On white card with enlarged Royal Cypher £1000

(1911) Booklet Essay for Edition No. (7)

Edition No. (6) precancelled Type E and with typed announcement of Sells Advertising Agency pasted inside front £2500

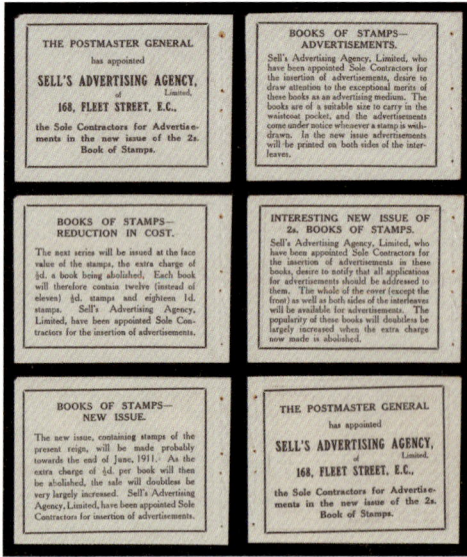

Interleaf trials, printed in black

(1911) Trial Booklet with Edition No. (7) Interleaves

Issued covers with proposed interleaves printed in black (without stamp or label panes) £3000

296

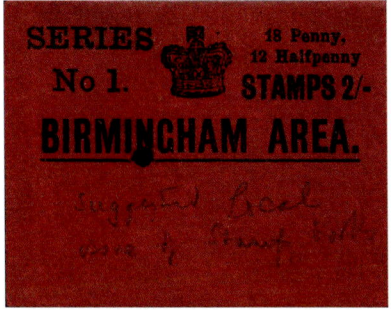

King Edward VII / Essays, Trials and Proofs Post Office Booklets of Stamps APPENDIX 2

Cover for local district

(1910) Front Cover Essay for Local District issues

Red cover with "SERIES No 1." and 2s. contents either side of a Crown, all over a (proposed city) AREA (not adopted) £1800

Booklet with multiple values

(1911) Booklet Essay for Multiple Values

Covers as Edition No. (7) containing a pane of six of all 13 Edward VII values from ½d. to 1s. with assorted interleaves used in Editions Nos. (4) to (7) (not adopted) £15000

2s. BOOKLETS

Series 1

The first 14 editions were without a number on the cover, each edition being identifiable by some feature peculiar to itself and, for the sake of convenience, these early editions are referred to by numbers in brackets, viz., No. (1) to No. (14). After this the printing contract was awarded to Harrison & Sons who instituted the numbering of the booklets on the cover, starting with No. 8.

For all the King Edward VII editions, i.e., Nos. (1) to (7) an additional ½d. was charged for the booklet itself in addition to the price of the stamps. No. (1) was sold over the counter for 2s.0½d.; Nos. (2) to (7) contained only 1s.11½d. worth of stamps, one of the stamps on one of the ½d. panes being printed with a green cross. Since that time no charge has been made for any standard-format British Post Office booklet of stamps other than the price of the stamps it contained, although a premium has been charged for "prestige" booklets since 2011.

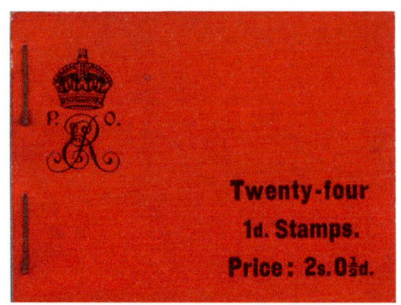

Type **1**

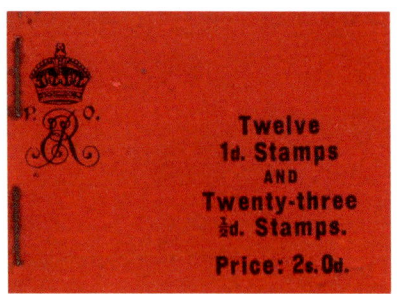

Type **2**

1904 (16 March). The first booklet issued contained four panes of six, i.e., 24 × 1d. King Edward VII stamps, printed by De La Rue, with watermark Crown, upright or inverted. It was bound with staples in a red cover bearing the Edwardian P.O. cypher and interleaved with plain greaseproof paper. Pane Nos. MB5 or 5a.

Cat. No.
BA1 Edition No. (1) (sold for 2s.0½d.). Red cover as T **1** £500
"Specimen", Type 16 (from NPM Archives) £4000

1906 (June). As before, but make-up changed to include 12 × 1d. and 23 × ½d. stamps and one green cross. Pane Nos. MB1, 1a, 2, 2a, 5 or 5a.

BA2 Edition No. (2) (contents 1s.11½d.). Red cover
as T **2** £2200
"Specimen", Type 17 £6500
Precancelled, Type A £1400

1907 (August). As before, but make-up changed to include 18 × 1d. and 11 × ½d. and one green cross. Pane Nos. MB1, 1a, 2, 2a, 5 or 5a.

BA3 Edition No. (3) (contents 1s.11½d.). Red cover
as T **2** with amended contents £3100
Precancelled, Type A £2000

This edition was issued with two different inside back covers, firstly "For letters to places abroad" and, secondly, "For letters for British Empire generally".

1908 (August). As before, but interleaves used for Post Office notices printed in red. Pane Nos. MB1, 1a, 2, 2a, 5 or 5a.

BA4 Edition No. (4) (contents 1s.11½d.). Red cover
as T **2** with amended contents £3400
Precancelled, Type A £1500
"Specimen", Type 17 £6500

1909 (August). As before, but interleaves of plain white paper printed on one side with trade advertisements in green. Edition: No. (5)—third advertisement Chas. Baker & Co.; No. (6)—third advertisement Brimsdown lamps. Pane Nos. MB1, 1a, 2, 2a, 5 or 5a.

BA5 Edition Nos. (5) and (6) (contents 1s.11½d.).
Red cover as T **2** with amended contents £2700
Edition No. (5) precancelled Type A £1300
Edition No. (5) "Specimen", Type 17 £6500
Edition No. (6) "Specimen", Type 22 (from NPM Archives) £6500
Edition No. (6) AVC precancelled Type B £1300
Edition No. (6) AVC precancelled Type D £1300
Edition No. (6) precancelled "ECE" £1800
Edition No. (6) precancelled "ECQ" (with punch hole) £1800
Edition No. (6) precancelled, Type E £2000

297

APPENDIX 2   Post Office Booklets of Stamps   King George V / Essays, Trials and Proofs

1911 *(June).* As before, but containing stamps printed by Harrison & Sons and showing a larger Post Office cypher on cover. Interleaves printed on one side with Post Office notices in green. Pane Nos. MB3, 3a, 4, 4a, 6 or 6a.

BA6 Edition No. (7) (contents 1s.11½d.). Red cover as T **2** with amended contents and enlarged cypher	£2800
Price changed in manuscript to "1/11½"	£2300
"Specimen", Type 22	£6000
Precancelled, Type E	£2000

KING GEORGE V

ESSAYS, TRIALS AND PROOFS FOR SERIES 1

(1911) Front Cover Essay

Booklet Edition No. (6) precancelled Type E with manuscript amendments to cover, deletion of "ER", replaced by script "GvR" and deletion "Eleven", replaced by "12"   £2000

1911 Trial Booklet

Cover as Edition No. (8) containing three 1d. carmine and two ½d. green Downey Head panes of six stamps, NB1 and NB3, and six blank paper interleaves   £3500

Cover and interleaf trial

1911 Trial for interleaf

Booklet Edition (10), part comprising covers and first three interleaves, the second having a varnished surface, and four 1d. carmine stamps overprinted Specimen Type 22, the front cover with manuscript "Harrison present issue. With varnish finish"   £2000

Cover and interleaf trial

1912 Trial for interleaf

Booklet with blank white card covers, pane of six ½d. green Downey Head Die 2 stamps and a gelatine interleaf, the front cover with manuscript "Interleaved Gelatine (2). Waterproofed paper for adverts. from Harrison. 1912"   £1500

298

King George V / Essays, Trials and Proofs *Post Office Booklets of Stamps*   APPENDIX 2

Cover proof, first state

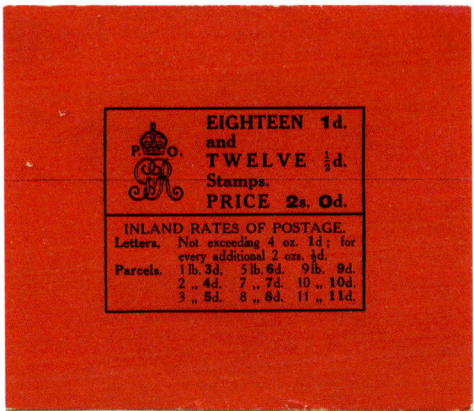

Cover proof, second state

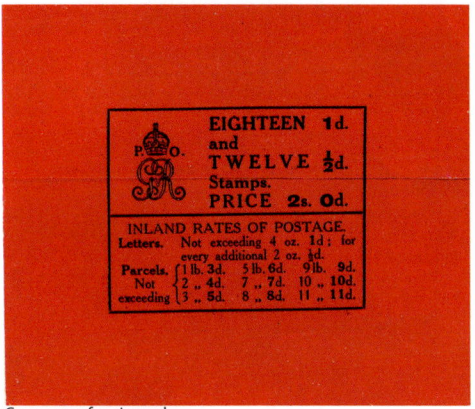

Cover proof, as issued

1911/12 Front Cover Proofs for Edition No. (11)

On issued card, red front, plain cream back, measuring approximately 10cm x 9cm

Without Royal Cypher, "not exceeding" and brackets for Parcels weights	£2500
With Royal Cypher, without "not exceeding" and brackets for Parcels weights	£4500
With Royal Cypher and all layout as Edition No. (11)	£3500

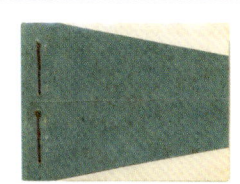

Booklet with brown "Arms" label

Booklet, interleaves only

1911/12 Booklet Essays

Covers, red outside, cream inside, containing five Harrison panes of eight brown perforated "Seated Britannia" labels and six blank paper interleaves	£6000
Covers in blue card containing two Harrison panes of six brown perforated "Arms" labels and four blank paper interleaves	£2000
Covers in blue card containing six blank paper interleaves only	£1200

1912 *(13 July).* Trial Booklet

Covers, red outside, cream inside, containing four Harrison panes of six purple perforated "Harrison Head" labels and five blank paper interleaves, the front cover with manuscript "I. H&S 13/7/12"   £5000

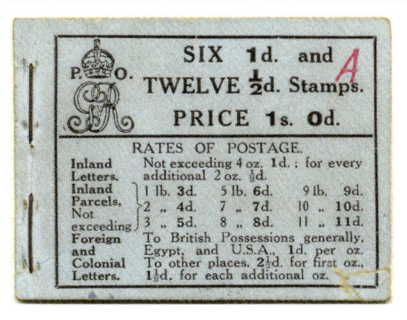

299

APPENDIX 2 Post Office Booklets of Stamps King George V / Essays, Trials and Proofs

1913 Booklet Essay for 1s. Contents

Covers, pale blue outside, cream inside, front as Type 4 but contents "SIX 1d. and TWELVE ½d. Stamps PRICE 1s.0d." containing three Harrison panes of six perforated "Arms" labels, one red and two green, and four interleaves for Art Photography/ Boots Chemist from Edition No. (14). Marked "A" at top right of front or back cover (not adopted)   £5000

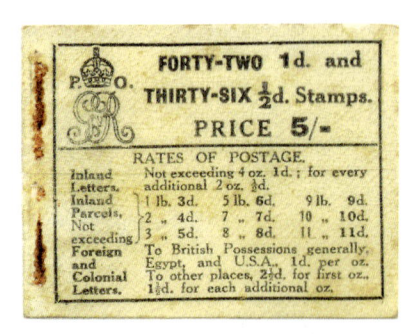

Label in 5s. booklet essay

1913 Booklet Essay for 5s. Contents

Similar to 1s. Essay but contents "FORTY-TWO 1d. and THIRTY-SIX ½d. Stamps PRICE 5/-" containing 13 Harrison panes of six buff "Harrison Head" labels, cancelled with broad diagonal green lines, and 14 interleaves for Central Translations Institute/ British Columbia from Edition No. (14). Pale blue or varnished white covers (not adopted)   £10000

1913 Booklet Essays for Front Cover Advertising

Booklet Editions Nos. 9 and 10 (April 1913) with Lipton's Tea labels pasted over lower front of covers and inside back cover reserved for rates of postage, Edition No. 10 being an advertiser voucher copy cancelled Type H(M)   each £3500

1913 Booklet for Marketing to Advertisers

Edition No. 12 covers containing five blank perforated label panes of six, watermarked "Harrison & Sons, London", and issued interleaves   £2500

1916 Booklet Essay for Charity Surcharge

Booklet Edition No. 45, advertiser voucher copy, cancelled Type I, dated 3 JY 16 with punch hole at upper left, last ½d. pane, bottom right stamp overprinted with a Red Cross and ½d. surcharge   £7500

1917 Interleaf Proof

Edition No. 55 War Loan interleaf with manuscript "Proof on chalky paper"   £500

Trial, interleaves only

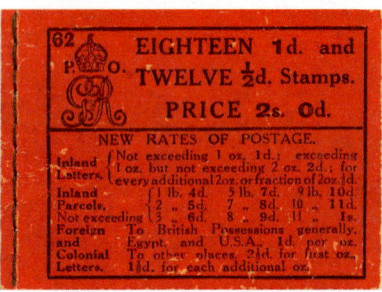

Trial, stamps cancelled Type 24

Trial, stamps cancelled Type 24

1917 Booklets used for Stitching Trials

Edition No. 56 covers stitched containing nine issued interleaves, duplicated to simulate five panes of stamps with four interleaves   £1500
Edition Nos. 57 and 62 booklet, stitched containing issued stamp panes and interleaves, the stamps cancelled Type 24   each £2500
Edition No. 67 booklet, stapled, otherwise as Edition No. 57   £3500

1918 Trial Booklet

Edition No. 76 covers containing five panes of six blank perforated labels and four interleaves, all Tidmans Sea Salt/Lockyers Hair Restorer (the fourth interleaf in Edition No. 77)   £2000

1918 Paste-up Booklet

Booklet Edition No. 80, front cover and all advertisements as issued pasted into a previous display booklet without stamps   £1500

Stanley Gibbons
Great Britain Department

BY APPOINTMENT TO
HER MAJESTY THE QUEEN
PHILATELISTS
STANLEY GIBBONS LTD
LONDON

Stanley Gibbons, a name synonymous with quality.

Ever since the birth of our hobby Stanley Gibbons has been at the forefront of GB philately and we invite collectors access to one of the finest GB stocks in the world by registering for our renowned free monthly brochure. Whatever your budget or collecting interests you will find a range of the highest quality material for the discerning collector.

To receive our monthly brochures or for further enquires please email gb@stanleygibbons.com or phone 020 7557 4424.

STANLEY GIBBONS
Est 1856

Proud PTS members

Stanley Gibbons
399 Strand, London, WC2R 0LX
+44 (0)20 7836 8444
www.stanleygibbons.com

2s. BOOKLETS

Series 1

1911 *(August).* As King Edward VII issue, but make-up changed to include 18×1d. and 12×½d. stamps of the new reign (Die 1B) with watermark Crown, upright or inverted. Interleaves printed on both sides with trade advertisements in green: No. (8)—first advertisement Aitchison & Co.; No. (9)—first advertisement Gresham Fire and Accident Insurance Society; No. (10)—first advertisement Empire Hotels. Georgian Post Office cypher on cover. Pane Nos. NB1, 1a, 3 or 3a.

BB1 Edition Nos. (8), (9) and (10). Red cover as T **2**	£1600
AVC precancelled, Type E	£800

Edition No. 8 exists without the 5th interleaf.

Type **3**

Type **4**

1912 *(April).* Cover redrawn to allow space for inland postage rates, otherwise as before. No. (11)—first advertisement Marsuma Cigarettes; No. (12)—first advertisement Palethorpes Sausages. Pane Nos. NB1, 1a, 4 or 4a.

BB2 Edition Nos. (11) and (12). Red cover as T **3**	£1900

1912 *(September).* As before, but stamps (Die 1B) with watermark Simple Cypher. Pane Nos. NB2, 2a, 5 or 5a.

BB3 Edition No. (13). Red cover as T **3**	£1300
"Specimen", Type 22	£12000

1912 *(November).* As before, but with redesigned cover showing foreign and colonial as well as inland rates of postage. Pane Nos. NB2, 2a, 5 or 5a.

BB4 Edition No. (14). Red cover as T **4**	£1600
"Specimen", Type 26	£12000
AVC precancelled, Type H	£1200

1913 *(January).* As before, but bearing booklet number on the cover. Pane Nos. NB2, 2a, 5 or 5a.

BB5 Edition Nos. 8 and 9. Red cover as T **4**	£1300
Edition No. (9) without interleaves	£1500
Edition No. (8) " Specimen", Type 26	£12000
Edition No. (9) AVC precancelled, Type H	£1200

1913 *(April).* As before, but containing stamps of the 1912–22 issue with watermark Simple Cypher, normal or inverted. Pane Nos. NB6, 6a, 7 or 7a.

BB6 Edition Nos. 10 to 35. Red cover as T **4**	£1300
Edition No. (13) AVC precancelled, Type G	£1300
AVC precancelled, Type H	£900
AVC precancelled, Type I	£600
"Specimen", Type 26	£5000

Edition No. 13 is found containing advertisements of edition No. 12. It is also known without interleaves. Edition No. 15 is also known containing interleaves of Edition No. 16.

1915 *(November).* As before, except lower panel of front cover, which was changed to show "NEW RATES OF POSTAGE". Pane Nos. NB6, 6a, 7 or 7a.

BB7 Edition Nos. 36 to 42. Red cover as T **4**	£1600
AVC precancelled, Type I	£700

1916 *(May).* As before, but advertisements on interleaves printed in black instead of green. Pane Nos. NB6, 6a, 7 or 7a.

BB8 Edition Nos. 43 to 45. Red cover as T **4**	£1750
AVC precancelled, Type I	£700

Edition No. 45 exists containing the ½d. pane of six in which the last stamp (R. 2/3) is overprinted with a red cross and surcharged ½d. This was a suggestion for a Red Cross surcharge, but the plan was never adopted.

1916 *(July).* As before, but colour of cover changed from red to orange. Pane Nos. NB6, 6a, 7 or 7a.

BB9 Edition Nos. 46 to 64. Orange cover as T **4**	£1500
"Cancelled", Type 24 (Editions 57 or 62, stitched)	£2500
AVC precancelled, Type I	£600

Edition No. 48 (without stamps) has been seen with covers printed on red card. Two examples of Edition No. 56 are known with the interleaves duplicated.

Edition Nos. 62, 63, 65 and 67 exist with covers stapled or stitched. Edition No. 64, 66 and 68 onwards were stitched, but stapling was sometimes resorted to when booklets had to be re-assembled because of mis-stitching (mainly during the King Edward VIII and early King George VI periods). In that event the re-used contents had stitching holes in the binding margin contained within new covers, all stapled. Black thread was the rule but other colours were occasionally used.

Type **5**

1917 *(September).* As before, but rates of postage transferred to an interleaf and the lower panel of the front cover used for a trade advertisement. Pane Nos. NB6, 6a, 7 or 7a.

BB10 Edition Nos. 65 to 81. Orange covers as T **5**	£1350
"Cancelled", Type 24 (Edition 67, stapled)	£3500
AVC precancelled, Type H	£850
AVC precancelled, Type I	£600

Edition Nos. 72 and 80 exist bound with staples.

These booklets were replaced by the 3s. booklets (Series 2) in October 1918, following the increase of the inland letter rate from 1d. to 1½d.

Series 4

A new series was introduced in February 1924, bound in blue covers, selling at 2s., concurrently with Series 3. A feature of this series (except the Special Jubilee booklets) and of Series 5, is the first pane of 1½d. stamps, which contained only four postage stamps. The remaining two spaces, i.e., those on the left next to the margin, were printed with trade advertisements or postal notices.

ESSAYS, TRIALS AND PROOFS FOR SERIES 4

1923 Booklet Pane Advertisement Essays

Stamp size "Millenium Oat-Flakes" advertisements	
Printed in black, fancy double lined "Millenium" and capital "OAT-FLAKES", on white imperforate glazed paper or on Simple Cypher watermarked paper *each*	£750
Printed as before on stamp-size labels adjacent to blanks, on buff paper or Block Cypher watermarked paper *each*	£750
Printed as before but in brown on glazed white paper	£750
Printed in black, fancy single line script on glazed white paper	£750

1923 Booklet Essay for Advertisement Panes

Series 3 Booklet, 3s. Edition No. 39 Advertiser Voucher Copy cancelled Type I dated 18 MY 23 with two essay labels pasted onto the two left stamps of first 1½d. pane, at top single line script, at bottom double lined on buff paper

Back Cover, Edition No. 19

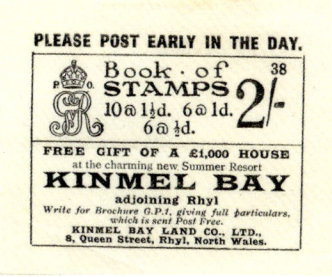

Front Cover, Edition No. 38

1925/26 Cover Proofs

Edition No. 19, back cover, final proof on cream paper	£2500
Edition No. 38, front cover, final proof on cream paper	£2500

1929 Cover Trials for Colour and Substance of Cover

Postal Union Congress covers in various shades of yellow/buff using edition No. 102 front with blue print, blank cream back, manuscript at top right "A", "B", "C" or "D"   *each* £1600

Colour and Substance of Trial "A" was adopted

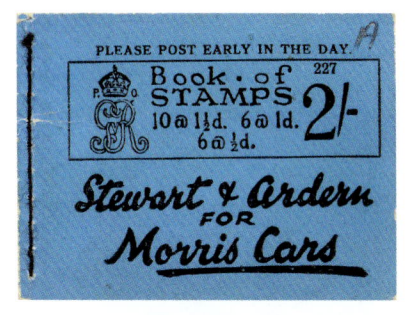

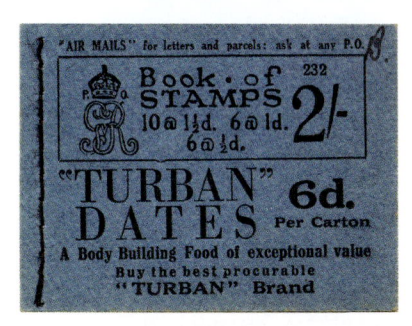

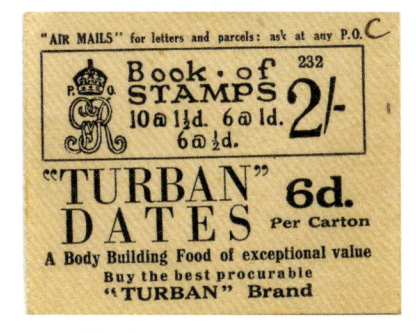

1933 Trials for Thickness of Cover

Booklet as May 1933 Edition No. 232 made up without stamps in deeper blue card, manuscript top right "B", with booklet edition No. 227, stamps torn out, manuscript top right "A" and front cover in buff card as Edition No. 232, manuscript at top right "C"   *set* £3500

This trial may have been for 2s. Booklet Edition No. 242 covers

APPENDIX 2   Post Office Booklets of Stamps   King George V / Essays, Trials and Proofs

1934 Trials for Substance of Cover

Booklet Edition No. 255 (February) covers made up with eight January postal rate interleaves, then four imperforate plain paper panes, manuscript at lower right "Harrison's No 4 alternative Cover Paper". Blue covers endorsed "4A" or Red covers endorsed "4B", punch hole at top left   each £3000

1934 Trial Booklet

Booklet Edition No. 258 (March) made up without stamps but with additional buff paper interleaf at front and back advertising a sports car, purpose unknown. Uncut tête-bêche pair   £2000

1924 Display Booklets

Produced as issued without stamp contents	
Edition Nos. I and 4	£500

2s. BOOKLETS

Series 4

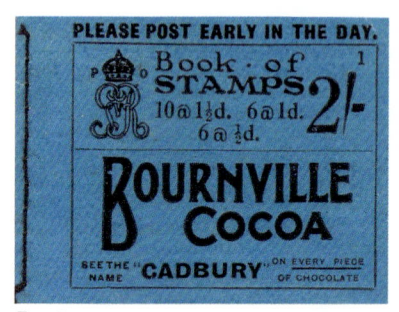

Type **6**

Type **7**

1924 (February). Containing 10 × 1½d., 6 × 1d. and 6 × ½d. stamps of the 1912–1922 issue with Simple Cypher watermark, upright or inverted. Pane Nos. NB6, 6a, 7, 7a, 8, 8a, 9 or 9a.

BB11 Edition Nos. 1 and 2. Blue cover as T **6**	£2600
AVC precancelled, Type 1	£1000

1924 (March). As before, but containing stamps with the Block Cypher watermark printed by Waterlow & Sons. Pane Nos. NB12, 12a, 13, 13a, 14, 14a, 15 or 15a.

Varieties

1924 (June). The se-tenant advertisements were accidentally inverted. Edition No. 8.

1924 (September). The upper se-tenant advertisement was deliberately inverted. Edition No. 12.

1924 (November). Some of the advertisement panes were printed on paper with watermark sideways. Edition No. 15. (Booklets containing these are very rare.)

1927 (November). The upper se-tenant advertisement was deliberately inverted. Edition No. 67.

1931 (September). The se-tenant advertisements were printed in green. Edition No. 171.

1933 (October). As a trial, 478,000 covers were printed on unglazed card of a deeper blue. The remaining production of 38,500 had normal covers. Edition No. 242.

BB12 Edition Nos. 3 to 102 and 108 to 254.	
Blue covers as T **6**	£900
"Specimen", Type 30 (Edition Nos. 16 and 53)	£4500
AVC Specimen", Type 23	£3500
AVC precancelled, Type I	£900
AVC precancelled, Type J	£650
AVC precancelled, Type K	£1200
AVC "Cancelled", Type 24 (Edition 73)	£8000
AVC "Cancelled", Type 28	£900
AVC "Cancelled", Type 28P (Edition 89)	£3500
AVC "Cancelled", Type 33	£2000
AVC "Cancelled", Type 33P	£1200

Edition Nos. 10, 11, 27, 29, 30, 31, 63, 71, 100, 129, 143 and 194 exist bound with staples. There were two types of Edition Nos. 37 and 38, the advertisement panes in each being different. Some advertisement panes in Edition No. 37 were omitted or misplaced and advertisers were given advertisement panes in Edition No. 38 to compensate.

Apart from edition No. 242, the cover colours vary substantially from light blue to deep blue with a medium gloss finish but some have a highly glazed finish, for example Edition No. 4 and part of edition No.18 which must have been experimental.

1929 (May). As before, but cover of special design printed in blue on buff and containing stamps of the P.U.C. issue. Pane Nos. NCom B1/3 or 3a.

BB13 Edition Nos. 103 to 107. Blue on buff cover as T **7**	£500
AVC "Cancelled", Type 33P	£3800
AVC "Cancelled", Type 33 (Edition 103)	£10000

Edition Nos. 104, 105 and 107 exist bound with staples.

1934 (February). As before, but containing stamps with the Block Cypher watermark printed by Harrison & Sons. Pane Nos. NB12, 12a, 13, 13a, 14, 14a, 15 or 15a.

BB14 Edition Nos. 255 to 287. Blue cover as T **6**	£1100
AVC "Cancelled", Type 33P	£1000

Edition No 286 exists bound with staples.

1935 (January). As before, but containing stamps of the photogravure issue intermediate format with the se-tenant advertisements etched on the cylinder and were printed in red-brown. From Booklet No. 289 an interleaf Air Mail label was included. Pane Nos. NB20, 20a, 22, 22a, 24, 24a, 25 or 25a.

BB15 Edition Nos. 288 to 297. Blue cover as T **6**	£2700
AVC "Cancelled", Type 28P	£2700
AVC "Cancelled", Type 33P	£2500

Edition No. 294 exists bound with staples.
Edition 294 AVC exists with the first column of stamps "Cancelled", Type 28P and the remaining columns "Cancelled", Type 33P.

304

King George V / Essays, Trials and Proofs Post Office Booklets of Stamps   APPENDIX 2

Type **8**

1935 *(May).* Silver Jubilee issue of booklets larger in size than the normal with cover of special design printed in blue on buff, containing 12 × 1½d., 4 × 1d. and 4 × ½d. and no *se-tenant* advertisements. Pane Nos. NCom B5, 5a, 6, 6a, 7 or 7a.

BB16 Edition Nos. 298 to 304. Blue on buff cover as T **8**	90·00
"Cancelled", Type 33 (Edition 302)	£10000
AVC "Cancelled", Type 33P	£3750

    Edition Nos. 298, 299/301, 302 and 304 exist bound with staples.
    Edition Nos. 298 and 304 exist with Air Mail labels omitted.

1935 *(July).* As Edition No. 297, but containing stamps of the photogravure issue small format with *se-tenant* advertisements printed in black. Pane Nos. NB21, 21a, 23, 23a, 26, 26a, 27 or 27a.

BB17 Edition Nos. 305 to 353. Blue cover as T **6**	£600
AVC "Cancelled", Type 28P	£1500
AVC "Cancelled", Type 33 (Editions 325, 341 and 349)	£3000
AVC "Cancelled", Type 33P	£1100

    Edition No. 305. Early printings of this edition contained *se-tenant* advertising labels for Telephone Service and Air Mails. The former included the words "Installed Free", which for some time had been incorrect. These words were deleted by hand-stamp. Later printings of this edition contained *se-tenant* advertising labels for Saving is Simple/Home Safe.
    Edition Nos. 309–14 were bound using purple thread.
    Edition No. 350. The *se-tenant* advertising labels exist transposed vertically with Safety of Capital (bottom) and Universal Fixed Trust (top). This was caused by a horizontal row of stamps being folded over during stacking. Four examples have been found of this variety.
    Edition No. 344 exists bound with staples.

3s. BOOKLETS

Series 2

ESSAYS, TRIALS AND PROOFS FOR SERIES 2

Essay, first brown label pane

1918 Booklet Essay for Series 2

Covers, red outside, cream inside, containing six panes of six perforated blank labels, two brown, two red and two green (to simulate stamp contents) and six blank interleaves	£5000

Cover essay, as Type **5**

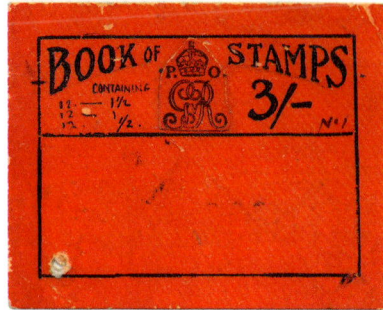

Cover essay, as Type **9**

1918 Front Cover Essays

On issued card, orange front, plain cream back	
Printed, based on Type **5** 2s. Edition No. 79 cover design for "DURO", amended with 3s. contents and "1" at top lef	£2500
As above with manuscript change to placing of contents	£2500
Hand-drawn redesigned cover, upper part with postal information as Type **9** with "No 1" at right, lower part blank	£4000

1918 Front Cover Artwork

Board with enlarged black ink essay, upper part as Edition No. 1 ("No" deleted beside "1") Type **9**, lower part blank, artwork 16.8cm×12.5cm	£3000

Cover proof, as issued

1918 Front Cover Proof

On issued card, orange front, plain cream back, as Type **9** with 3s. contents at top and "1" at right but lower part with 2s. edition "DURO" advertisement, punch hole at top left	£2500

305

APPENDIX 2   Post Office Booklets of Stamps   King George V / Essays, Trials and Proofs

Colour trial, turquoise

1921 Front Cover Trials for Colour for Edition No. 35

Booklet using front cover design for Edition No. 21, blank back, and assorted interleaves from Edition No. 33 in trial colours

Turquoise (booklet stapled)	£3500
Bright blue (booklet stitched)	£3500
Dull blue (booklet stitched), manuscript on front "A shade lighter if possible"	£3500

All with or without a punch hole

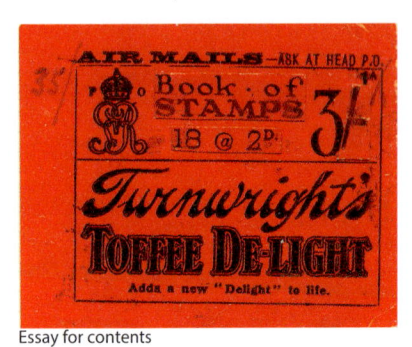

Essay for contents

1921 Front Cover Essay for Edition No. 35

| Front cover proof for Edition No. 34, orange front, cream back, contents amendments pasted on, manuscript "35/" at top left | £2500 |

Cover proof, as issued

1921 Front Cover Proofs for Edition No. 35

On issued card, blue front, plain cream back, numbered "35"

| "via Imperial" in small type, on back manuscript "2nd Proof 5.3.21" | £3000 |
| "via IMPERIAL" in block type, on back manuscript "3rd Proof", as Type **10** | £2500 |

1921 Display Booklet for Edition 35

| Produced as issued but without stamp contents | £500 |

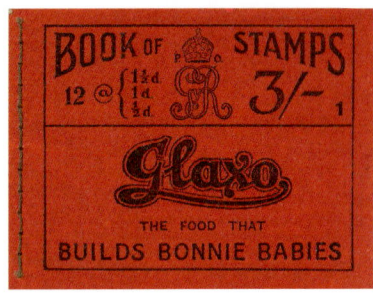

Type **9**

3s. BOOKLETS
Series 2

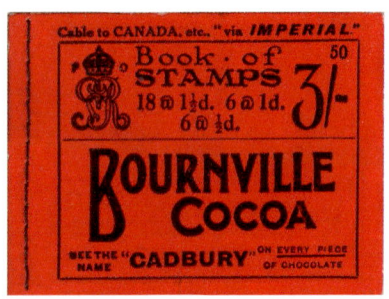

Type **10**

1918 *(October).* The minimum inland postage rate having been increased from 1d. to 1½d., a new series was introduced to replace Series 1, containing 12 × 1½d.; 12 × 1d. and 12 × ½d. stamps of the 1912–22 issue with watermark Simple Cypher, upright or inverted. Bound in orange covers and fully interleaved. Pane Nos. NB6, 6a, 7, 7a, 8 and 8a.

| BB18 Edition Nos. 1 to 11. Orange cover as T **9** | £1850 |
| AVC precancelled, Type I | £650 |

1919 *(July).* Make-up altered to contain 18 × 1½d., 6 × 1d. and 6 × ½d. Otherwise as before. Pane Nos. NB6, 6a, 7, 7a, 8 or 8a.

| BB19 Edition Nos. 12 to 26. Orange cover as T **9** | £1850 |
| AVC precancelled, Type I | £650 |

With the increase in the inland postage rate to 2d. in July 1920 Series 2 continued as 3s.6d. booklets.

1921 *(April).* An experimental booklet bound in blue covers was issued containing 18 × 2d. stamps (Die I), which sold at 3s. concurrently with the 3s.6d. booklets. Pane Nos. NB10 or 10a.

| BB20 Edition Nos. 35 and 37. Blue cover as T **10** | £2400 |
| AVC precancelled, Type I | £1000 |

Series 2 booklets were replaced by Series 3, also 3s. and 3s.6d. in August 1921.

A small number of Edition No. 37 contained Die II 2d. stamps.

306

Series 3

ESSAYS, TRIALS AND PROOFS FOR SERIES 3

Cover proof, before edition change

1927 Cover Proof

Edition No. 128, but numbered "126", front, final proof on thin cream card £2500

1929 Cover Trials for Colour and Substance of Cover

Postal Union Congress, front covers in various shades of yellow/buff using edition No. 102 front with red print, blank cream back, manuscript at top right "A", "B", "C" or "D" each £1600

Colour and Substance of trial "A" was adopted.

1933 Trials for Thickness of Cover

Booklets as May 1933 Edition No. 260, made up without stamps, in deep blue card, manuscript at top right "B", or in buff card, manuscript at top right "C" each £2500

This trial may have been for 2s. Booklet Edition No. 242 covers.

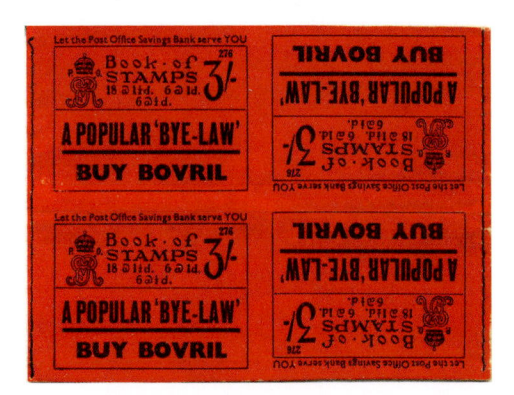

1934 Trial Booklet

Booklet Edition No. 276 (May) made up without stamps but with additional buff paper interleaf at front and back advertising a sports car, purpose unknown Uncut tête-bêche pair £1500

1922 Display Booklet

Produced as issued without stamp contents Edition No. 31 £500

1921 (December). An experimental booklet bound in blue covers, similar to Edition Nos. 35 and 37 of Series 2, was issued containing 18 × 2d. stamps (Die II), costing 3s. and sold concurrently with the 3s.6d. books. Pane Nos. NB11 or 11a.

BB21 Edition Nos. 12 and 13. Blue cover as T **10**	£2400
AVC precancelled, Type I	£1000

3s. BOOKLETS

Series 3

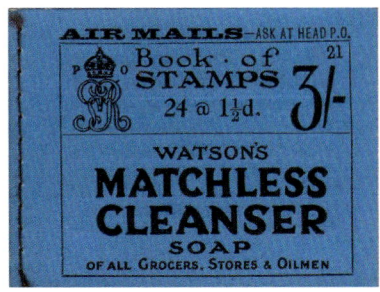

Type **11**

1922 (May). With the reduction of the minimum inland postage rate from 2d. to 1½d., the make-up was changed to include 18 × 1½d.; 6 × 1d. and 6 × ½d. Bound in scarlet covers and fully interleaved. Pane Nos. NB6, 6a, 7, 7a, 8 or 8a.

BB22 Edition Nos. 19, 20, 22, 23 and 25 to 54. Scarlet cover as T **11**	£2400
AVC precancelled", Type I	£850

Edition Nos. 22, 34 and 46 exist bound with staples.

1922 (June). An experimental booklet was issued bound in blue covers, similar to Edition Nos. 12 and 13, but containing 24×1½d. stamps. Sold concurrently with Edition Nos. 20, 22, 23 and 25. Pane Nos. NB8 or 8a.

BB23 Edition Nos. 21 and 24. Blue cover as T **11**	£2400
AVC precancelled, Type I	£1000

1924 (February). As Edition No. 54, but containing stamps with the Block Cypher watermark printed by Waterlow & Sons. Airmail label included from Edition No. 191. Pane Nos. NB12, 12a, 13, 13a, 14 or 14a.

BB24 Edition Nos. 55 to 167 and 173 to 273. Scarlet cover as T **11**	£550
"Specimen", Type 30 (Edition118)	£4500
AVC "Specimen", Type 23	£3500
AVC "Cancelled", Type 24	£8000
AVC "Cancelled", Type F (Edition 67)	£3500
AVC "Cancelled", Type I	£900
AVC "Cancelled", Type J	£600
AVC "Cancelled", Type K	£1200
AVC "Cancelled", Type 28	£850
AVC "Cancelled", Type 33P	£1200

Edition Nos. 55, 74, 106 and 219 exist bound with staples.

APPENDIX 2   Post Office Booklets of Stamps   King George V / Essays, Trials and Proofs

1929 (May). As before, but cover of special design printed in red on buff and containing stamps of the P.U.C. issue. Pane Nos. NCom B1/3 or 3a.

BB25 Edition Nos. 168 to 172. Red on buff cover as T **7**	£450
AVC "Cancelled", Type 33P	£4250

1934 (March). As Edition No. 273, but containing stamps with the Block Cypher watermark printed by Harrison & Sons. Pane Nos. NB12, 12a, 13, 13a, 14 or 14a.

BB26 Edition Nos. 274 to 288. Scarlet cover as T **11**	£650

1935 (January). As before, but containing stamps of the photogravure issue intermediate format. Pane Nos. NB20, 20a, 22, 22a, 24 or 24a.

BB27 Edition Nos. 289 to 293. Scarlet cover as T **11**	£2100
AVC "Cancelled", Type 33P	£2100

1935 (May). Silver Jubilee issue of booklets larger in size than the normal with cover of special design printed in red on buff, containing 20 × 1½d.; 4 × 1d. and 4 × ½d. Silver Jubilee stamps, watermark Block Cypher, normal or inverted. Pane Nos. NCom B5/7 or 7a.

BB28 Edition Nos. 294 to 297. Red on buff cover as T **8**	90·00
AVC "Cancelled", Type 28P	£5250
AVC "Cancelled", Type 33P	£5250

Edition Nos. 294 and 296 exist bound with staples.

1935 (July). As Edition No. 293, but containing stamps of the photogravure issue small format. Pane Nos. NB21, 21a, 23, 23a, 26 or 26a.

BB29 Edition Nos. 298 to 319. Scarlet cover as T **11**	£550
AVC "Cancelled", Type 28P	£1500
AVC "Cancelled", Type 33P	£1100

A special cover card was used to produce 4000 of edition No. 312 prior to the introduction of new cover material for edition No. 314.

Edition No. 313 was issued in June 1936 with an error on one air mail label interleaf in the sheet of 40 interleaves. The words "AIR MAIL" in the third line of the last paragraph read "AIR MAII". This label remained in use until May 1937 but the misprint was never corrected. This interleaf, with the error, was used in 2s. and 5s. booklets during the same period.

Edition Nos. 318/9 exist bound with staples.

3s.6d. BOOKLETS

Series 2

ESSAYS, TRIALS AND PROOFS FOR 3s.6d. BOOKLETS

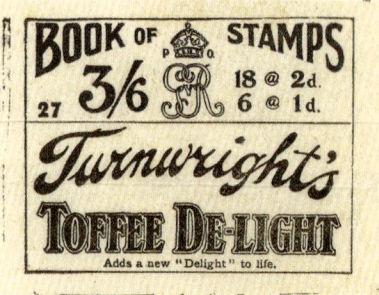

Cover proof, as issued

1920 Front Cover Proof for Edition No. 27

On unglazed paper as issued Type **12**	£3000

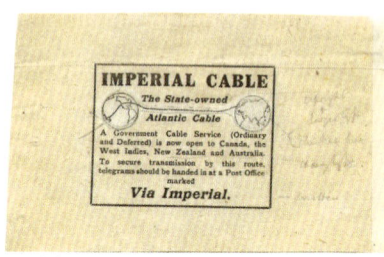

Proof, first state

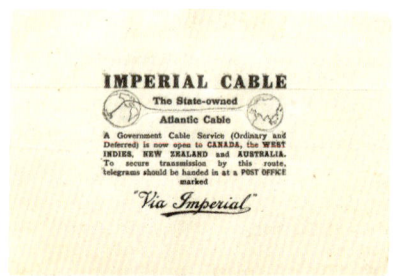

Proof, final state

1920 Imperial Cable Progressive Proofs for Edition No. 27

Artwork for globe cable route and four interleaf size progressive proofs on paper for Imperial Cable   set £1500

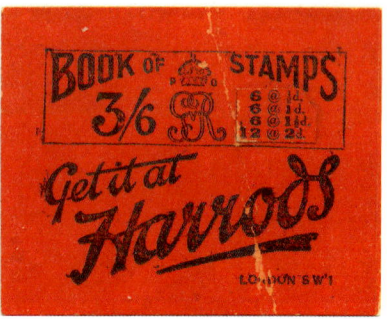

Essay, Edition No. 33

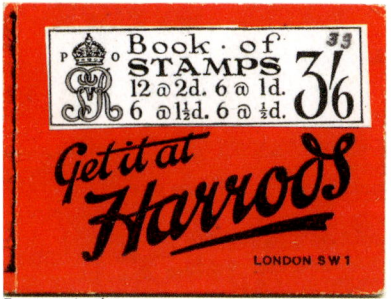

Essay, revised contents

1920 Front Cover Essays for Edition No. 33

On issued card, orange front, plain cream back, with pasted revised 3s. 6d. contents in format of previous editions as Type **12** £2500
Booklet Edition No. 31 with stamps removed and black on white contents label pasted on as Type **13** without top slogan £2500

Essay for slogan

1921 Front Cover Essay for top line Slogan for Edition No. 34

Booklet Edition No. 30 with manuscript "AIR MAILS – Ask at Head P.O." top line slogan, stamps and some interleaves removed £1500

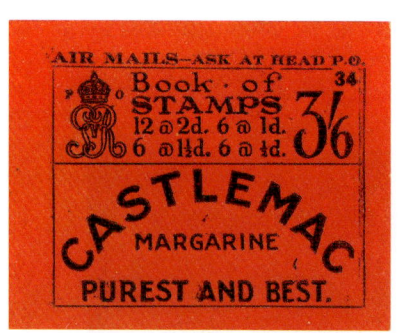

Proof, large

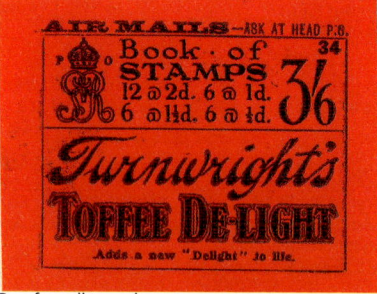

Proof, small type slogan

1921 Front Cover Proofs for top line Slogan for Edition No. 34

All on issued card, orange front, plain cream back,
As previous edition, CASTLEMAC and numbered 33, with added "AIR MAILS" at top and "ENQUIRE AT" and "HEAD POST OFFICES" at each side £2000
CASTLEMAC, numbered 34, large type "ASK AT HEAD P.O." £2000
CASTLEMAC, numbered 34, small type "ASK AT HEAD P.O." £2000
Turnwrights, numbered 34, small type "ASK AT HEAD P.O." as Type **13** £2000
Turnwrights, as above, but on white card, as Type **13** £2000

1920/21 Display Booklets

Produced as issued without stamp contents
Edition Nos. 27, 28, 29, 30, 31, 32, 33 and 34   each £500

3s.6d. BOOKLETS

Series 2

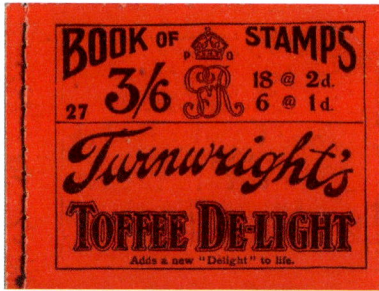

Type **12**

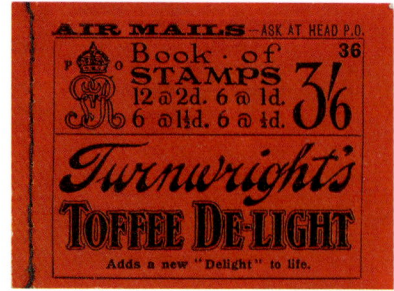

Type **13**

1920 (July). With the increase of the minimum inland postage rate from 1½d. to 2d., the make-up was changed to 18 × 2d. (Die I) and 6 × 1d., and the price was increased from 3s. to 3s.6d. Otherwise as Cat. No. BB19. Pane Nos. NB7, 7a, 10 or 10a.

309

APPENDIX 2   Post Office Booklets of Stamps   King George V / Essays, Trials and Proofs

BB30 Edition Nos. 27 to 32. Orange cover as T **12**	£2200
AVC precancelled Type I	£1000

Edition No. 32 AVC exists bound with staples.

1921 *(January)*. Make-up changed to 12 × 2d. (Die I); 6 × 1½d.; 6 × 1d. and 6 × ½d. Pane Nos. NB6, 6a, 7, 7a, 8, 8a, 10 or 10a

BB31 Edition Nos. 33, 34, 36 and 38. Orange-red cover as T **13**	£2200
AVC precancelled, Type H	£850
AVC precancelled, Type I (Edition 36)	£800

Series 2 booklets were replaced by Series 3, also 3s. and 3s.6d. in August 1921.

Series 3

1921 *(July)*. A new series was introduced to replace Series 2, containing 12×2d. (Die I or Die II, Edition No. 1, Die I Edition Nos. 2 and 4 and Die II others); 6 × 1½d., 6 × 1d. and 6 × ½d. stamps of the 1912–22 issue with watermark Simple Cypher, normal or inverted. Bound in orange-red covers, fully interleaved. Pane Nos. NB6, 6a, 7, 7a, 8, 8a, 10, 10a Die I or 11, 11a Die II.

BB32 Edition Nos. 1 to 11 and 14 to 18. Orange-red cover as T **13**	£2200
AVC precancelled Type H (Editions 4 and 5)	£1000
AVC precancelled Type I	£800

The inland postage rate was reduced from 2d. to 1½d. in May 1922 and from that date Series 3 was issued as 3s. booklets.

5s. BOOKLETS

Series 5

ESSAYS, TRIALS AND PROOFS

1913 Booklet Essay for 5s. Contents

See Series 1, proposal not adopted

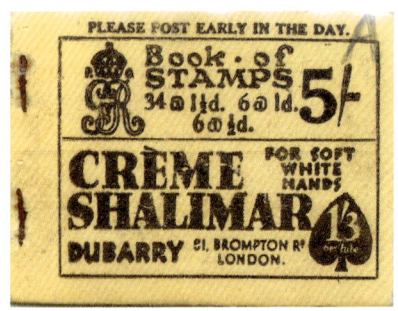

Trial, buff cover, adopted

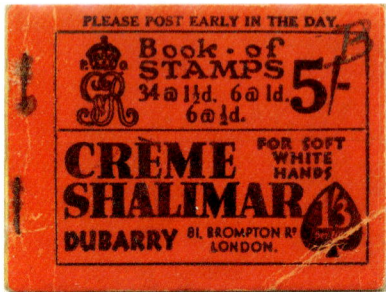

Trial, orange cover not adopted

1931 Trial Booklets for Colour of Covers

Covers as for Edition No. 1 "Crème Shalimar" Type **14**, with blank cream backs, containing eight panes of six blank gummed perforated labels, except the first printed on the two left labels with WRIGHT'S COAL TAR SOAP advertisement, and seven interleaves, all with postage rates from May 1931 2s. Edition No. 161. Various cover colours with a pencil number inside front cover

Dark Brown (1 or 1A), Orange (2) marked "B" at top right, Yellow (4), Olive (5) or Buff (6) marked "A" at top right (adopted)   each £5000

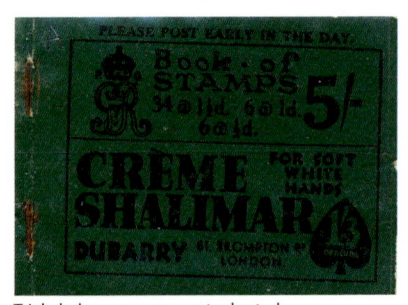

Trial, dark green cover, not adopted

As above cover design but containing eight panes of imperforate gummed paper and seven interleaves, all with postage rates from June 1931 3s. Edition No. 217 dark green   £5000

310

5s. BOOKLETS

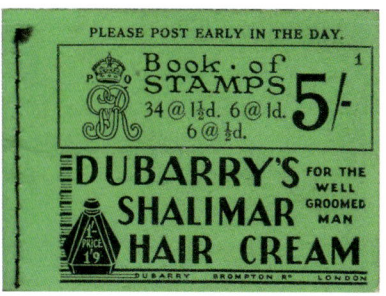

Type **14**

1931 (*August*). A new series was introduced, bound in green covers, selling at 5s. concurrently with Series 3 and 4, and containing 34 × 1½d.; 6 × 1d. and 6 × ½d. stamps with Block Cypher watermark printed by Waterlow & Son, the first 1½d. pane being similar to that in Series 4 and having four postage stamps and two *se-tenant* advertisements. Pane Nos. NB12, 12a, 13, 13a, 14, 14a, 15 or 15a.

BB33 Edition No. 1. Green cover as T **14**	£5500
AVC "Cancelled", Type 33P	£3000

This edition was issued with four different covers: "Dubarry Shalimar Shaving Stick", "Hair Cream", "Lipstick" and "Creme Shalimar."

1932 (*June*). Composition as before, but with buff covers. From Booklet No. 4 an interleaf Air Mail label was included.

BB34 Edition Nos. 2 to 6. Buff cover as T **14**	£5250
AVC "Cancelled", Type 33P	£3000

Edition No. 2 was issued with two different covers: "If you love a good joke take PUNCH" and "Take PUNCH for all the best jokes".

Edition No. 3 exists bound with staples.

1934 (*July*). As before, but containing stamps with the Block Cypher watermark printed by Harrison & Sons. Pane Nos. NB12, 12a, 13, 13a, 14, 14a, 15 or 15a.

BB35 Edition Nos. 7 and 8. Buff cover as T **14**	£2250

1935 (*February*). As before, but with stamps of the photogravure issue intermediate format and with *se-tenant* advertisements etched on the cylinder and printed in red-brown. Pane Nos. 20, 20a, 22, 22a, 24, 24a, 25 or 25a.

BB36 Edition No. 9. Buff cover as T **14**	£6200

1935 (*July*). As before, but with stamps of the photogravure issue small format and with the *se-tenant* advertisements printed in black. Pane Nos. NB21, 21a, 23, 23a, 26, 26a, 27 or 27a.

BB37 Edition Nos. 10 to 15. Buff cover as T **14**	£650
AVC "Cancelled", Type 28P	£2000
AVC "Cancelled", Type 33P	£2000

Edition No. 15 exists bound with staples.

Edition No. 10 exists with advertisement and 1½d. panes intermediate format and the 1d. and ½d. panes small format, all "Cancelled" Type 28P.

KING EDWARD VIII

6d. BOOKLETS SOLD FROM SLOT-MACHINES

TRIAL BOOKLETS

1936 Buff covers, blank both sides as issued, containing two panes of two George V 1½d. stamps with part of label for selvedge stitching, panes cut down from pane NB27(14) or similar

Upright or inverted watermark	each £2500

Series 6. Sub-series A

6d. BOOKLETS SOLD FROM SLOT MACHINES

1937 (*January*). Booklets containing 4 × 1½d. stamps, in small panes of two, were obtainable from slot-machines placed outside 40 of the larger London post offices. No interleaves and both stamp panes either watermark upright or inverted. Bound in buff unglazed covers without inscription. Pane Nos. PB4 or 4a.

BC1 No edition number. Unprinted buff cover	65·00
a. Mixed watermarks, panes upright and inverted	£150

2s. BOOKLETS

Series 4

1936 (*October*). As Cat. No. BB17, except for the King Edward VIII cypher on the cover and containing stamps of the new reign. Pane Nos. PB1, 1a, 2, 2a, 3, 3a, 5 or 5a.

BC2 Edition Nos. 354 to 385. Blue cover as T **6**	£140
AVC "Cancelled" Type 33 (Edition 359)	£2500
AVC "Cancelled" Type 33P	£800

Edition Nos. 354, 356 to 363, 367, 368, 370, 372, 375, 378, 381, 384 and 385 exist bound with staples.

3s. BOOKLETS

Series 3

1936 (*November*). As Cat. No. BB29, except for the King Edward VIII cypher on the cover and without "P" and "O" on either side of crown, and containing stamps of the new reign. Pane Nos. PB1, 1a, 2, 2a, 3 or 3a.

BC3 Edition Nos. 320 to 332. Scarlet cover as T **11**	£120
AVC "Cancelled" Type 33P	£1000

Edition Nos. 320, 321, 324, 326, 328 and 330 exist bound with staples.

5s. BOOKLETS

Series 5

1937 *(March).* As Cat. No. BB37, but with the King Edward VIII cypher on the cover and containing stamps of the new reign. Pane Nos. PB1, 1a, 2, 2a, 3, 3a, 5 or 5a.

BC4 Edition Nos. 16 and 17. Buff cover as T **14**	£275
Edition Nos. 16 and 17 exist bound with staples.	

KING GEORGE VI

6d. BOOKLETS SOLD FROM SLOT-MACHINES

Series 6. Sub-series A

1938 *(January).* As Cat. No. BC1, but containing stamps of the new reign in the original dark colours, with watermark upright or inverted. With or without interleaf. Pane Nos. QB22 or 22a.

BD1 No edition number. Unprinted buff cover	75·00
a. With interleaf	75·00

Series 6. Sub-series B

1938 *(February).* Make-up changed to contain 2 × 1½d.; 2 × 1d. and 2 × ½d. stamps in the original dark colours, with watermark upright or inverted. Bound in plain pink unglazed covers, with or without interleaves. Pane Nos. QB3, 3a, 12, 12a, 22 or 22a.

BD2 No edition number. Unprinted pink cover	£300
a. With interleaves	£300

Series 6. Sub-series C

1940 *(June).* Make-up changed to contain 4 × 1d. and 4 × ½d. stamps in the original dark colours in panes of four with watermark sideways, either with margin at top of stamps or at bottom; bound in pale green plain covers with interleaves. Booklets obtainable only from a slot-machine placed inside the G.P.O., King Edward Building, E.C.1. Pane Nos. QB2, 2a, 11 or 11a.

BD3 No edition number. Unprinted green cover. Margin at top	£150
a. Margin at bottom	£150
b. ½d. pane with margin at top, 1d. pane inverted with margin at bottom	£750
c. 1d. pane with margin at top, ½d. pane inverted with margin at bottom.	£750

1s. BOOKLETS SOLD FROM SLOT-MACHINES

Series 6. Sub-series D

1947 *(December).* Make-up changed to contain 4 × 1½d.; 4 × 1d. and 4 × ½d. stamps in the pale shades in panes of two, all with watermark upright. Bound in plain unglazed cream covers without interleaves. Pane Nos. QB6, 14, 14a or 25.

BD4 No edition number. Unprinted cream cover	28·00
a. Error. Stitched through stamps and new covers restitched	

1951 *(May).* As before, but containing stamps in the changed colours. Pane Nos. QB9, 17 or 28.

BD5 No edition number. Unprinted cream cover	28·00

Series 6. Sub-series E

1948 *(November).* Make-up changed to contain 4 × 1½d. 4 × 1d. and 4 × ½d. stamps of the pale shades in panes of four with watermark upright. Unprinted cream cover. Pane Nos. QB5, 5a, 13, 13a, 24 or 24a.

BD6 No edition number. Margin at top	£9000
a. Margin at bottom	£9000

1951 *(May).* As before, but stamps in the new colours all watermark upright and the majority have the Festival of Britain B.O datestamp applied to the front cover. Unprinted cream cover. These booklets were on sale outside the Festival of Britain post office on the South Bank. Pane Nos. QB8, 8a, 16, 16a, 27 or 27a.

BD7 No edition number. Margin at top	50·00
a. Margin at bottom	35·00
ab. Panes in wrong order, 1d., 1½d., ½d.	£300

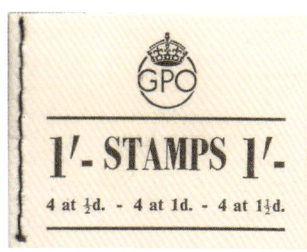

King George VI *Post Office Booklets of Stamps* **APPENDIX 2**

Type **15**

Type **16**

1952 *(December)*. As before, but with printed covers with stamps either watermark upright or inverted and with margins only at the top. At first available at Paignton head office, but later at other places. Back cover printed: "1½d. Minimum Postage Rate for Inland Printed Papers 1½d.". Pane Nos. QB8, 8b, 16b, 16c, 27 or 27b.

BD8 No edition number. Cream cover as T **15**	25·00
a. 1½d. pane reversed and stitched through stamps	£1000

1953 *(September)*. Composition as before, with Inland Letter rate on inside cover corrected in ink.

BD9 No edition number. Cream cover as T **15**	30·00

1953 *(November)*. Composition as before, with Inland Postage rates correctly printed. GPO emblem with St. Edward's crown and oval frame on the front cover and new notice on the back cover: "Minimum Foreign Letter Rate FOUR PENCE".

BD10 No edition number. Cream cover as T **16**	35·00

2s. BOOKLETS

ARTWORK AND PROOF

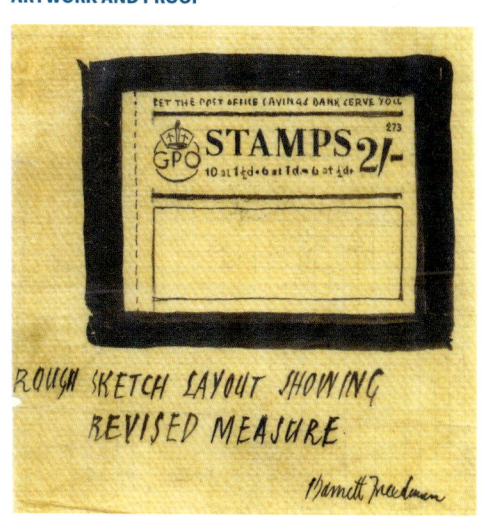

1937 Artwork for Type **17** Cover

Black pen on tracing paper of cover numbered 273, annotated "ROUGH SKETCH LAYOUT SHOWING REVISED MEASURE" signed by Barnett Freedman   £2500

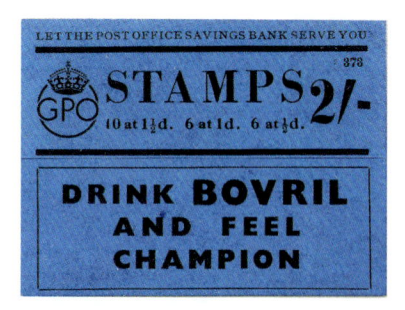

1938 Front Cover Machine Proof for Type **17**

On issued card, blue front, plain cream back, numbered "373"   £750

Series 4

1937 *(August)*. As Cat. No. BC2, except for the King George VI cypher on the cover and containing stamps of the new reign in the original dark colours. Pane Nos. QB1, 1a, 10, 10a, 21, 21a, 23 or 23a.

BD11 Edition Nos. 386 to 412. Blue cover as T **6**	£1100
AVC "Cancelled", Type 33P	£900

Edition Nos. 390, 393, 394, 396 and 405 exist bound with staples.

313

APPENDIX 2 Post Office Booklets of Stamps King George VI

Type **17**

1938 *(April)*. Composition as before, but with redesigned front cover showing GPO emblem instead of royal cypher.

BD12 Edition Nos. 413 to 508. Blue cover as T **17**	£1100
AVC "Cancelled", Type 33	£2000
AVC "Cancelled", Type 33P	£900

Edition Nos. 415, 454 and 490 exist bound with staples.
Examples of Edition No. 454 were bound in error with two front covers.

Series 2 booklets were replaced by the 2s.6d. booklets of Series 7 when the inland postage rate was increased from 1½d. to 2½d. in June 1940.

2s.6d. BOOKLETS

PROOFS

1940 Front Cover Proofs for Type **18**

On card pasted to cream paper page, seven proofs, four on red card with shades of grey to black contents panels, three on blue card, one with dark blue contents panel with manuscript "C", two with green contents panels, manuscript B above £5000

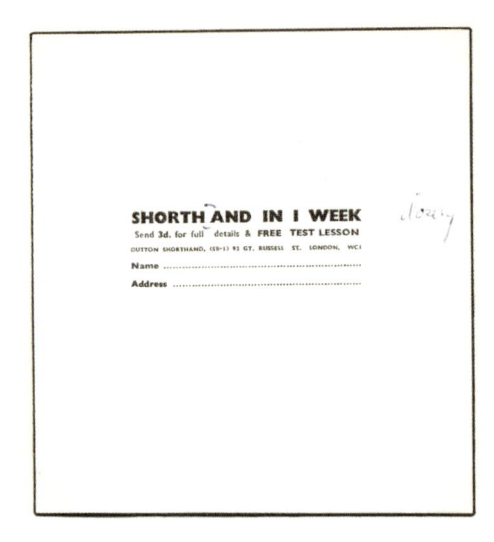

1953 Advertisement Proof for 1d. Pane QB20

On cream card, 120mm×112mm, "SHORTH AND IN 1 WEEK" and further narrative, with manuscript instruction "close up" £1000

Series 7

Type **18**

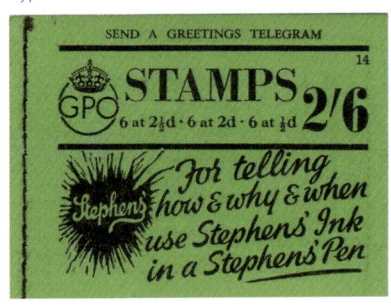

Type **19**

1940 *(June)*. The minimum inland postage rate having been increased from 1½d. to 2½d., a new series of booklets was introduced to replace Series 3 and 4, containing 6 × 2½d.; 6 × 2d. and 6 × ½d. stamps in the dark colours. Fully interleaved and bound in red covers to use up surplus card left over from Series 3. Pane Nos. QB1, 1a, 29, 29a, 32 or 32a.

BD13 Edition Nos. 1 to 8 (part). Scarlet cover as T **18**	£1700
AVC "Cancelled", Type 33p	£1100

314

1940 *(September).* Composition as before, but covers changed to blue to use up surplus card left over from Series 4.

BD14 Edition Nos. 8 (part) to 13. Blue cover as T **18**	£1700
AVC "Cancelled", Type 33p	£1100

1940 *(October).* Composition as before, but with glazed green covers of changed design.

BD15 Edition Nos. 14 to 94. Green cover as T **19**	£975

1942 *(March).* As before, but containing stamps in the pale shades. Pane Nos. QB4, 4a, 30, 30a, 33 or 33a.

BD16 Edition Nos. 95 to 146 (part). Green cover as T **19**	£975

1942 *(October).* Composition as before, but with unglazed green covers.

BD17 Edition Nos. 146 (part) to 214. Green cover as T **19**	£975
AVC, bound without the stamp panes (Edition 214)	£1000

Back cover advertisements on booklet number 176 were inverted. A later printing had the back cover bound reversed to correct the fault.

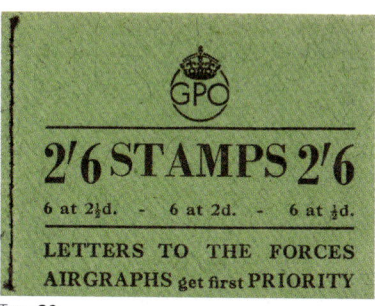

Type **20**

1943 *(August).* After Edition No. 214, the booklets were no longer numbered, but were dated with the month of issue. At the same time commercial advertising ceased, covers and interleaves being used for Post Office slogans. Changed cover design, with GPO emblem in centre. Pane Nos. QB4, 4a, 30, 30a, 33 or 33a.

Varieties:
In the August 1943 first printing, the Forces parcel rate for 3 lb. was wrongly given as 6d.; the later printing was corrected to 9d. by means of a handstamp, October 1943 to August 1944, with thinner or rougher interleaving or not interleaved; September 1944 onwards, no interleaving.

BD18 Edition dates as below. Green cover as T **20**	95·00

(1) AUG 1943	£110
a. Rate corrected	£150
(2) OCT 1943	£180
(3) NOV 1943	£170
(4) DEC 1943	£160
(5) JAN 1944	£160
(6) FEB 1944	£160
(7) MAR 1944	£160
(8) APR 1944	£160
(9) MAY 1944	£160
(10) JUNE 1944	£160
(11) JULY 1944	£160
(12) AUG 1944	£160
(13) SEPT 1944	£160
(14) OCT 1944	£160
(15) NOV 1944	£160
(16) DEC 1944	£160
a. Line above back cover printers' imprint	£225
(17) JAN 1945	£160
(18) FEB 1945	£160
(19) MAR 1945	£160
(20) APR 1945	£160
(21) MAY 1945	£160
(22) JUNE 1945	£160
(23) JULY 1945	£160
(24) AUG 1945	£160
(25) SEPT 1945	£160
(26) OCT 1945	£160
(27) NOV 1945	£160
(28) DEC 1945	£160
(29) JAN 1946	£150
(30) FEB 1946	£150
(31) MAR 1946	£150
(32) APR 1946	£150
(33) MAY 1946	£150
(34) JUNE 1946	£150
(35) JULY 1946	£150
(36) AUG 1946	£150
(37) SEPT 1946	£150
(38) OCT 1946	£400
(39) NOV 1946	£150
(40) DEC 1946	£150
(41) JAN 1947	£150
(42) FEB 1947	£150
(43) MAR 1947	£150
(44) APR 1947	£150
(45) MAY 1947	£150
(46) JUNE 1947	£150
(47) JULY 1947	£150
(48) AUG 1947	£150
(49) SEPT 1947	£150
(50) OCT 1947	£150
(51) NOV 1947	£150
(52) DEC 1947	£150
(53) JAN 1948	£180
(54) FEB 1948	£150
(55) MAR 1948	£150
(56) APR 1948	£150
(57) MAY 1948	£150
(58) JUNE 1948	£150
(59) JULY 1948	£150
(60) AUG 1948	£150
(61) OCT 1948	£140
(62) NOV 1948	£140
(63) DEC 1948	£140
(64) JAN 1949	£140
(65) FEB 1949	£150
(66) MAR 1949	£150
(67) APR 1949	£150
(68) MAY 1949	£150
(69) JUNE 1949	£150
(70) JULY 1949	£150
(71) AUG 1949	£150
(72) OCT 1949	£150
(73) NOV 1949	£150
(74) DEC 1949	£150
(75) JAN 1950	£120
(76) FEB 1950	£120
(77) MAR 1950	£120
(78) APR 1950	£120
(79) MAY 1950	£120
(80) JUNE 1950	£120
(81) JULY 1950	95·00
(82) AUG 1950	95·00
(83) SEPT 1950	95·00
(84) OCT 1950	95·00
(85) NOV 1950	95·00
(86) DEC 1950	95·00
(87) JAN 1951	95·00
(88) FEB 1951	95·00

1951 *(May).* As before, but containing stamps in the new colours. The June and some July 1951 editions were issued with a correction in red to the printed paper rate on the front cover. From July 1951 the printed paper rate reference was corrected to read "1½d." in black. The September 1951 edition was issued, firstly with all the parcel rates obliterated and secondly, "Inland Parcel Rates, enquire at any Post Office" on the inside front cover. Pane Nos. QB7, 7a, 31, 31a, 34 or 34a.

BD19 Edition dates as below. Green cover as T **20**	55·00

APPENDIX 2   Post Office Booklets of Stamps   King George VI

(1) MAY 1951	55·00
(2) JUNE 1951 (rate corrected in red)	75·00
(3) JULY 1951 (rate corrected in red)	£200
b. correct rate inside cover	£200
(4) AUG 1951	55·00
(5) SEPT 1951 (rates obliterated)	£175
b. Rates, enquire at P.O.	£175
(6) OCT 1951	55·00
(7) NOV 1951	55·00
(8) DEC 1951	55·00
(9) JAN 1952	55·00
(10) FEB 1952	55·00

1952 (March). Make-up changed to contain 6 × 2½d.; 6 × 1½d.; 3 × 1d. and 6 × ½d. The 1d. pane comprised three stamps in the top row and a Post Office notice in the lower row reading "MINIMUM INLAND PRINTED PAPER RATE 1½d." and measuring 17 mm. high. Pane Nos. QB7, 7a, 18, 18a, 26, 26a, 34 or 34a.

BD20 Edition dates as below. Green cover as T **21**	50·00
a. Panes in wrong order, 2½d., 1d. advert, 1½d., ½d.	£250
b. Extra 2½d. pane but 1½d. pane omitted	£600

(1) MAR 1952	50·00
(2) APR 1952	55·00
(3) MAY 1952	50·00
(4) JUNE 1952	50·00
(5) JULY 1952	55·00
(6) AUG 1952	50·00
(7) SEPT 1952	50·00
(8) OCT 1952	50·00
(9) NOV 1952	50·00
(10) DEC 1952	50·00
(11) JAN 1953	50·00
(12) FEB 1953	50·00
(13) MAR 1953	50·00
(14) APR 1953	50·00
(15) MAY 1953	90·00
a. Date error "May 195" for "May 1953"	£250
b. Date error "May 19" for "May 1953"	£250

The March 1952 edition has the back cover printed and bound inside out.

Type **21**

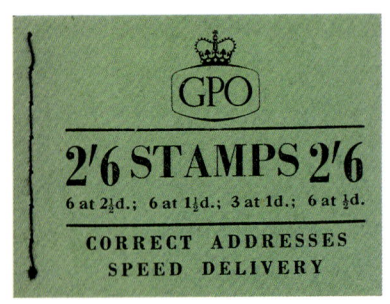

Type **22**

1953 (May). Composite booklets introduced, containing stamps of King George VI and Queen Elizabeth II. Make-up: 6 × 2½d. Q.E. II (S51), 6 × 1½d. Q.E. II (S25), 3 × 1d. K.G. VI and three labels, 6 × ½d. K.G. VI (Q3) in panes of six. Green cover as T **21** not interleaved. K.G. VI Pane Nos. QB7, 7a, 18, 18a; Q.E. II Pane Nos. SB59, 59a, SB80 or 80a.

F1	Edition date MAY 1953	35·00
	a. Date error "May 195" for "May 1953"	£150
	b. Date error " May 19" for "May 1953"	£150
F2	Edition date JUNE 1953	35·00
F3	Edition date JULY 1953	45·00
F4	Edition date AUG 1953	40·00

1953 (September). Composition as before, but with the addition of two interleaving pages, one at each end. Green cover as T **21**.

F5	Edition date SEPT 1953 (contains panes QB18 or 18a)	£250
F6	Edition date SEPT 1953 (contains panes QB19 or 19a)	£150
	a. Date error. Missing "b" in September	£175

1953 (October). Composition as before, but new style green cover as T **22**.

F7	Edition date OCT 1953 (contains panes QB18 or 18a)	60·00
F8	Edition date OCT 1953 (contains panes QB19 or 19a)	£150
F9	Edition date NOV 1953 (contains panes QB18 or 18a)	80·00
	AVC, bound without stamp panes	£100
F10	Edition date NOV 1953 (contains panes QB19 or 19a)	£250
F11	Edition date DEC 1953 (contains panes QB18 or 18a)	65·00
	AVC, bound without stamp panes	£100
F12	Edition date JAN 1954 (contains panes QB20 or 20a)	90·00
	AVC, bound without stamp panes	£100
	AVC, bound with printed label pane	£700
F13	Edition date FEB 1954 (contains panes QB20 or 20a)	£100
	AVC, bound with printed label pane	£700

1954 (March). As before, but Q.E. II Pane No. SB1 or 1a in place of 6 × ½d. K.G. VI.

F14	Edition date MAR 1954. Green cover as T **22** (contains panes QB18 or 18a)	£650
F14a	Edition date MAR 1954. Green cover as T **22** (contains panes QB20 or 20a)	

3s. BOOKLETS

PROOF

1938 Front Cover Machine Proof for Type **17**.

On issued card, red front, plain cream back, numbered "328"   £750

Series 3

1937 (August). As Cat. No. BC3, except for King George VI cypher on the cover and containing stamps of the new reign in the original dark colours. Pane Nos. QB1, 1a, 10, 10a, 21 or 21a.

BD21 Edition Nos. 333 to 343. Scarlet cover as T **11**	£1900
AVC "Cancelled", Type 33P	£1000

Edition Nos. 333 and 337 exist bound with staples.

1938 (April). Composition as before, but with redesigned front cover showing GPO emblem instead of royal cypher.

BD22 Edition Nos. 344 to 377. Scarlet cover as T **17**	£1900
AVC "Cancelled", Type 33P	£1000

Edition Nos. 360 and 370 exist bound with staples.

Series 3 booklets were replaced by the 2s.6d. booklets of Series 7 in June 1940.

5s. BOOKLETS

PROOF

1938 Front Cover Machine Proof for Type **23**.

On issued card, buff front, plain cream back, numbered "16" £750

Series 5

1937 (August). As Cat. No. BC4, but with King George VI cypher on the cover and containing stamps of the new reign in the original dark colours. Pane Nos. QB1, 1a, 10, 10a, 21, 21a, 23 or 23a.

BD23 Edition Nos. 18 to 20. Buff cover as T **14**	£2000
AVC "Cancelled", Type 33P	£1600

Edition No. 18 exists bound with staples.

Type **23**

1938 (May). Composition as before, but with redesigned front cover showing GPO emblem instead of royal cypher.

BD24 Edition Nos. 21 to 29. Buff cover as T **23**	£2000

Edition No. 22 exists bound with staples.

Series 5 was replaced by Series 8, also of 5s. booklets, in July 1940.

Series 8

1940 (July). The minimum inland postage rate having been raised from 1½d. to 2½d., a new series of 5s. booklets was introduced to replace Series 5, containing 18 × 2½d.; 6 × 2d. and 6 × ½d. stamps in the original dark colours. Bound in glazed buff covers and fully interleaved. Pane Nos. QB1, 1a, 29, 29a, 32 or 32a.

BD25 Edition Nos. 1 to 16 (part). Buff cover as T **23**	£2000
AVC "Cancelled" Type 33P	£1600

1942 (March). During the life of Edition No. 16 stamps in the pale shades were brought into use. Pane Nos. QB4, 4a, 30, 30a, 33 or 33a.

BD26 Edition Nos. 16 (part) to 29 (part). Buff cover as T **23**	£2000

1943 (February). Composition as before, but cover changed to rough unglazed buff.

BD27 Edition Nos. 29 (part) to 36. Buff cover as T **23**	£2200
AVC bound without stamp panes (Edition 36)	£1000

Type **24**

Type **25**

1943 (September). As before, but with changed cover design with GPO emblem in centre. Booklets dated and no longer numbered. Commercial advertising ceased and interleaves were used for war slogans. With or without interleaving (August 1944), later without interleaving (October 1944 onwards). Pane Nos. QB4, 4a, 30, 30a, 33 or 33a.

In the earlier printing of September 1943 an error in the Forces parcel rate—the 3 lb. rate being shown as 6d. instead of 9d.—was corrected with a handstamp, but this was later correctly printed.

BD28 Edition dates as below. Buff cover as T **24**	£130

(1)	SEPT 1943	£160
a.	Incorrect rate	£160
(2)	OCT 1943	£230
(3)	NOV 1943	£180
(4)	DEC 1943	£230
(5)	FEB 1944	£190
(6)	MAR 1944	£190
(7)	AUG 1944	£190
(8)	OCT 1944	£190
(9)	NOV 1944	£190
(10)	JAN 1945	£190
(11)	FEB 1945	£200
(12)	APR 1945	£200
(13)	JUNE 1945	£200
(14)	AUG 1945	£200
(15)	OCT 1945	£200
(16)	DEC 1945	£200
(17)	JAN 1946	£180
(18)	MAR 1946	£180
(19)	MAY 1946	£180
(20)	JUNE 1946	£180
(21)	AUG 1946	£180
(22)	OCT 1946	£180
(23)	DEC 1946	£180
(24)	FEB 1947	£180
(25)	APR 1947	£180
(26)	JUNE 1947	£180
(27)	AUG 1947	£180
(28)	OCT 1947	£180
(29)	DEC 1947	£180
(30)	FEB 1948	£180
(31)	APR 1948	£180
(32)	JUNE 1948	£180

APPENDIX 2 *Post Office Booklets of Stamps* King George VI

(33)	JULY 1948	£180
(34)	AUG 1948	£180
(35)	OCT 1948	£180
(36)	DEC 1948	£200
(37)	FEB 1949	£200
(38)	APR 1949	£200
(39)	JUNE 1949	£190
(40)	AUG 1949	£190
(41)	SEPT 1949	£190
(42)	OCT 1949	£190
(43)	DEC 1949	£190
(44)	FEB 1950	£130
(45)	APR 1950	£130
(46)	JUNE 1950	£130
(47)	AUG 1950	£130
(48)	OCT 1950	£130
(49)	DEC 1950	£130

1944 *(April)*. Composition as before, but with changed cover design. With or without interleaving.

BD29 Edition dates as below. Buff cover as T **25**	£5250
(1) APR 1944	£5250
(2) JUNE 1944	£5250

1951 *(May)*. As Cat. No. BD28, but containing stamps in the new colours. Pane Nos. QB7, 7a, 31, 31a, 34 or 34a.

BD30 Edition dates as below. Buff cover as T **24**	65·00
(1) MAY 1951	65·00
(2) JULY 1951	65·00
(3) SEPT 1951	65·00
(4) NOV 1951	65·00
(5) JAN 1952	65·00

Type **26**

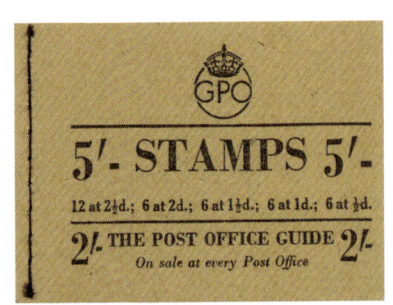

Type **27**

Type **28**

1952 *(March)*. Make-up changed to contain 18 × 2½d.; 6 × 1½d.; 3 × 1d. and 6 × ½d., the 1d. pane having three stamps in the top row and Post Office notice in the lower row reading "MINIMUM INLAND PRINTED PAPER RATE 1½d." and measuring 17 mm. high. Pane Nos. QB7, 7a, 18, 18a, 26, 26a, 34 or 34a.

BD31 Edition dates as below. Buff cover as T **26**	55·00
(1) MAR 1952	55·00
(2) MAY 1952	55·00
(3) JULY 1952	55·00
(4) SEPT 1952	55·00
(5) NOV 1952	55·00

1953 *(January)*. Make-up again altered to include the 2d. value and containing 12 × 2½d.; 6 × 2d.; 6 × 1½d., 6 × 1d. and 6 × ½d. Pane Nos. QB7, 7a, 15, 15a, 26, 26a, 31, 31a, 34 or 34a.

BD32 Edition dates as below. Buff cover as T **27**	65·00
(1) JAN 1953	65·00
(2) MAR 1953	65·00

1953 *(May)*. Composite booklets introduced, containing stamps of King George VI and Queen Elizabeth II. Make-up: 12 × 2½d. Q.E. II (S51), 6 × 2d. K.G. VI (Q12), 6 × 1½d. Q.E. II (S25), 6 × 1d. K.G. VI (Q6), 6 × ½d. K.G. VI (Q3) in panes of six. Not interleaved. Buff cover as T **27**. K.G. VI Pane Nos. QB7, 7a, 15, 15a, 31, 31a; Q.E. II Pane Nos. SB59, 59a, 80 or 80a.

H1 Edition date MAY 1953	50·00
a. Date error "May 195" for "May 1953"	£300
b. Date error "May 19" for "May 1953"	£300
H2 Edition date JULY 1953	50·00

1953 *(September)*. Composition as before, but with the addition of two interleaving pages, one at each end.

H3 Edition date SEPT 1953. Buff cover as T **27**	70·00

1953 *(November)*. Composition as before, but buff cover in new style as T **28**.

H4 Edition date NOV 1953	60·00
AVC without stamp panes	£100
H5 Edition date JAN 1954	70·00

1954 *(March)*. Composition as before, but Q.E. II (Pane No. SB1 or 1a) in place of 6 × ½d. K.G. VI.

H6 Edition date MAR 1954. Buff cover as T **28**	£500

1954 *(March)*. As before, but Q.E. II (Pane No. SB1 or 1a) in place of 6 × ½d. K.G. VI and 6 × 1d. Q.E. II (Pane No. SB20 or 20a) in place of 6 × 1d. K.G. VI.

H7 Edition date MAR 1954. Buff cover as T **28**	£275
a. Extra 1½d. pane	£800

318

Appendix 3

Booklet Pane Precancellations

Precancellations were applied to booklet panes to prevent their being used for postal purposes. The types of precancellation are illustrated and described below; precancelled booklet panes are listed and priced in the main catalogue and precancelled booklets are listed and priced in Appendix 2.

On Booklets (2) to (5) of Series 1, precancellation Type A was applied in ink by hand on make-up trials and on sample booklets distributed to sub-offices. From Booklet (5), when commercial advertisement interleaves were introduced, the primary purpose of the London Chief Office (London E.C) precancellations was for use on advertiser's voucher copies. However, some booklets were overprinted with "Specimen" or "Cancelled" for official reference purposes, trials or for use as colour standards, particularly for King Edward VII and King George V issues.

Usually, two or more strikes were applied to each pane, to ensure cancellation of each stamp, but from July 1926 a metal handstamp containing three "cancelled" impressions was used to cancel each pane with two strikes, one on each row.

Type E was employed in 1911 on the King Edward VII Harrison booklet (7) (No. BA6) and first on the King George V Downey Head issue with Crown watermark (Nos. BB1). Also it was used on the King Edward VII De La Rue. booklet (6) (No. BA5) by Harrisons for reference and trial purposes prior to the issue of the Harrison booklets. These De La Rue booklets and Type E panes are very rare.

The London Chief Office obliterators in the following Types F to I have generic types of single- or double-circle cancels. A large number were used at the Chief Office from 1912 to 1924, so there are many obliterator identification numbers or letters, typically at the bottom (but sometimes in the middle of single-circle cancels).

Type F was used on three booklets only, the Downey Head stamps with Crown watermark, booklet (12) (No. BB2) and on Profile Head stamps with Simple Cypher watermark, booklet 41 (No. BB7) and Block Cypher watermark booklet 67 (No. BB24). Each of these is very rare.

Type A St. Andrew's Cross

Type B E.C. 'A'

Type G (Double-circle with time slugs)

Type I (Double-circle without time slugs)

Type C E.C. 'U'

Type D E.C. K

Type H(L) "London, E.C." Single-circle (24–25 mm. diameter) Obliterator numbers below dates.

Type H(M) "London, E.C." Single-circle (22–23 mm. diameter)

Type A was handwritten in pen and ink across each stamp in the pane and was employed in booklets (2) to (5) (Nos. BA2/5).

Types B, C and D were used only on booklet (6) (No BA5). Additionally booklet (6) exists with "E.C.E." and "E.C.Q." cancellations in the same style.

Type H(S) "London, E.C." Single-circle (20–21 mm. diameter) Obliterator numbers below dates

Type E London Chief Office, E.C. (Double Circle)

Type F London (Chief Office) E.C. (Single Circle)

Type G was used on two booklets only, the Downey Head stamps with Crown watermark, booklet (11) (No. BB2) and with

Profile Head stamps Simple Cypher watermark booklet 13 (No. BB6). These are rare.

Type H was used on the Downey Head stamps with Simple Cypher watermark (Booklets BB3/5) and on Profile Head stamps with Simple Cypher watermark in a minority of booklets from series BB6, BB7, BB9, BB10, BB19, BB30, BB31 and BB32 up to September 1921. Type H exists in three distinct diameter sizes, as illustrated, Type H (L) (24/25mm.), Type H (M) (22/23mm.) and Type H (S) (20/21mm.), of which the large type is rare and the other types are scarce. No distinction is made between these sub-types in the listings of the panes and the booklets.

Type I is an evolution of Type G with the removal of time slugs (as these obliterations were not for a postal purpose). Type I is the most common pre-cancellation in diameter sizes from 24mm. to 26mm. and different length curved bars but no distinctions are made in the listings of panes and booklets.

Type I was used on the Downey Head stamps (Booklet BB5), the Profile Head stamps (Booklets BB6/11, BB18/23 and BB30/32) and for a short period to November 1924 with Block Cypher watermark stamps (Booklets BB12 and BB24).

Type I/J

Type I/J was used in September 1924 in the Type I period on 3s. booklet 63 (BB24) and is a steel canceller like Type I but in a similar format to Type J. ½d. and 1½d. panes from this booklet are recorded.

Type J (Curved Line) Type K (Curved and Straight Lines)

"London Chief Office" Types

Types J and K were made with rubber stamps and were applied (in violet) on Block watermark stamps (Booklets BB12 and BB24).

From April 1926 the stamps were overprinted "Cancelled", Type 28, and from March 1928 they were overprinted "Cancelled", Type 33 and additionally punched (Type P) for further security. After September 1940, it is thought that voucher copies of booklets were made up with the interleaves only (excluding the stamp panes).

Appendix 4

"Specimen" and "Cancelled" Overprints

General Notes

INTRODUCTION. Between 1847 and 1873 it was the custom for examples of major changes in design or colour and new values to be distributed with circulars to Postmasters and to be overprinted "SPECIMEN". From 1879 this was also done on stamps sent to the Universal Postal Union for distribution to member nations. However, from 1892 it was decided to overprint only the values from 2s.6d. upwards, the lower values being sent without overprint, but from 1913 onwards the 1s. values were also overprinted. The use of "SPECIMEN" overprints on stamps sent to the U.P.U. ceased completely in March 1948.

Stamps overprinted "SPECIMEN" or "CANCELLED" were made for many purposes, such as for official record copies, trial printings and on coil stamps and booklet panes. It was also the practice to preserve sheets or blocks of six of printings which varied in shade from their predecessors to serve as colour standards for matching future printings.

All the "SPECIMEN" and "CANCELLED" stamps listed are known to exist in private hands, some being very rare. Others are known to exist only in official records and are not listed.

THE OVERPRINTS. Information on "Specimen" stamps from official sources has always been very difficult to obtain. The overprints were applied by or on behalf of the authorities controlling the production of the stamps (the Postage Stamp Department of the Inland Revenue until 1915 and the Post Office Stores Department thereafter), or by the printers. There was a tendency for the overprints to remain in use in their original form, or slightly modified, for long periods, even after a change in controller or printer.

The overprints were either handstamped or printed from type settings, some by both means. Some of the type settings were of such poor quality that they cannot be distinguished from handstamps unless the stamps are in multiples. Overprints composed from the same type to fit stamps or sheets of various shapes or sizes may differ slightly in dimensions. In the interests of simplification some of the types we illustrate comprise groups of overprints of similar character but differing slightly from one another, these bearing an asterisk after the Type number.

The uses to which the various types were put at various times are indicated below:—

KING EDWARD VII. Type 16 on the De La Rue 2s.6d., 5s., 10s. and £1, were supplied to the U.P.U.; Types 15 (16 on the lower values) and 17 were used on reference copies, including booklets; Type 18 to 20 were used for colour standards and Type 22 was probably used for the same purpose on the 1911–12 issues; Type 21 was used on Harrison coil trials and Type 22 was used on De La Rue and Harrison booklets used for trials and reference copies.

When the De La Rue printing contract ended in 1910 the Inland Revenue instructed them to return all the British stamps in their possession, but they were allowed to retain items mounted in their correspondence books on condition that they were cancelled. Issued stamps were defaced by having the word "Cancelled" written across them in manuscript, while items of proof status were cancelled with pen strokes.

KING GEORGE V. The only "Specimen" overprints sent to the U.P.U. were of Type 26 on the 1s. Royal Cypher watermark and the Waterlow 2s.6d., 5s., 10s. and £1 and of Type 32 in black on the photogravure 1s. and in red on the £1 Postal Union Congress. Otherwise Types 23, 25, 26, 28, 30, 32 and 33 were generally used for colour standards. Types 23 and 28 were also used for trial printings, while Type 24 was almost exclusively used for this purpose. Type 27 is seen on Waterlow high values which were used for forensic tests. The purpose for which Type 29 was used is unknown. Type 31 (a handstamp) was used on the 1s. Royal Cypher watermark and the Bradbury, Wilkinson 2s.6d., 5s. and 10s. and it is believed that they were supplied in response to a request from a foreign administration.

Types of Overprints

SPECIMEN
9* 14¾ × 1¾ –2
(1871–1900)

SPECIMEN
15* 14½ × 2–2¼
(1891–1911)

SPECIMEN
16 15½ × 2½
(1891–1909)

SPECIMEN (curved)
17 16 × 2¾
(1904–07)

CANCELLED
18 14¼ × 1½
(1900–07)

CANCELLED
19 14 × 1½
(1906–09)

CANCELLED
20 12¼ × 1½
(1910)

CANCELLED.
21 24 × 2½
(1911)

SPECIMEN
22 14¾ × 2
(1911–12)

SPECIMEN
23* 9¾ –10 × 1¾
(1912–42)

CANCELLED
24* 14¾ × 2
(1911–28)

CANCELLED
25 12¾ × 1¼
(1912)

SPECIMEN
26* 12½ × 2
(1911–48)

CANCELLED (diagonal)
27 27 × 2¾
(1913)

CANCELLED
28* 11¾ × 1½
(1912–46)

SPECIMEN
29 11¼ × 1¼ –2
(1913)

SPECIMEN
30* 13 × 1¾
(1924–51)

SPECIMEN
31 12¼ × 1¾
(1918)

SPECIMEN
32 10½ × 2
(1924–37)

CANCELLED
33* 11–12 × 1¾
(1924–46)

CANCELLED
34* 15¼ × 1¾
(1941–48)

P (handpunch shape)

Types of Overprints referred to in the Lists. Sizes given in millimetres.

*These Types represent groups comprising several similar types differing slightly from one another within the measurements given.

Type **P** was a handpunch used on booklet panes already overprinted "CANCELLED". They come from voucher booklets sent to the advertisers. The stamps were folded in half then punched to achieve the shape as illustrated.

The dates quoted represent the main periods of usage of the overprints or groups of overprints. They do not necessarily encompass the dates of issue of all the stamps on which they are found—they may have been used on pre-issue proofs or on stamps long after their dates of issue, after new overprint types had come into use.

From 1911, types 22, 23, 24, 26, 28, 30, 32 and 33 were also used on booklet panes. Some of the stamps from sheets with the same overprints are considerably scarcer and some can be identified only if they are marginal copies or in multiples greater than blocks of six (3 × 2).

Types 23, 24 and 28 have been used to cancel specimen sheets of unprinted watermarked paper but such items are not listed.

In 1924 folders containing sets of the contemporary definitive stamps to 10s. and the British Empire Exhibition Commemorative stamps were prepared for presentation to delegates at the Stockholm U.P.U. Congress. One of these folders exists with each stamp overprinted with Type 15.

A set comprising the low values in the Block Cypher watermark overprinted with Type 32 (the 6d. with Type 26) and the Bradbury, Wilkinson high values overprinted with Type 23, all additionally overprinted with Type 24 at a much later date, is of unknown status.

KING EDWARD VIII. Types 30 and 32 have been recorded on a very small number of stamps in private hands. Type 33 was used on booklet panes and punched Type P (unless omitted in error).

KING GEORGE VI. The first issue: 1s., 2s.6d. (both colours), 5s. and 10s. (both colours) overprinted with Type 23 were for supplies sent to the U.P.U. Type 34 was used for colour standards and other overprints were used for the same purposes as during the previous reigns. Apart from those sent to the U.P.U. and booklet stamps overprinted with Type 33, very few are in private hands. Booklet panes are punched Type P (unless omitted in error). As a result of the National Postal Museum Archive sales in 1985, three booklet pane reference copies cancelled Type 23, 30 and 32 respectively, were sold, the remainder being retained in the Archive.

In 1947 folders containing sets of the contemporary definitive stamps to 10s., the 1940 Stamp Centenary and 1946 Peace Commemorative issues, Postage Due stamps to 2s.6d. and items of postal stationery, as well as stamps overprinted for use in the Morocco Agencies and Tangier, were prepared for presentation to delegates at the Paris U.P.U. Congress. One of these folders exists with each stamp overprinted with Type 9, which had not been used since Victorian times. Its purpose is unknown.

Although too late for U.P.U. distribution with "Specimen" overprint, an example of the 1948 Silver Wedding £1 is known with "CANCELLED" Type 34 and large punch holes in three corners. Its purpose is not known.

The 1937 Coronation and definitive stamps exist with a "Specimen" overprint in green applied by a Portuguese colonial postal administration. These are outside the scope of this Catalogue.

POSTAGE DUE STAMPS. Type 23 on the 1s. Royal Cypher watermark and the 2s.6d. Block Cypher watermark were used for supplies sent to the U.P.U. Otherwise the purposes of the types used on the Postage Due stamps were similar to those of the contemporary Postage stamps.

Appendix 5

Protective Underprints

In general the practice of firms underprinting their stamps to prevent theft ceased about 1881. Sloper's perforation of stamps with the initials or monogram of the firm was better and more secure, being visible from the front. These are known to philatelists as "perfins" and are outside the scope of this Catalogue. From about 1904 to 1915 two firms are known to have returned to underprinting on top of the gum. Prices are for unused but used examples are known.

Messrs. W. H. Everett & Sons Limited of London invented a hand-held roller with inking pad, six impressions of the initials being in a horizontal row, which they advertised as being with permission of the Postmaster General. Although advertised at only £1 the invention does not appear to have sold as no other firms are known using one.

Messrs. S. & J. Watts of Manchester, who used "Wattses", evidently printed from a metal plate.

The Post Office would not repurchase stamps underprinted or perforated, so there was little point in office boys stealing them.

KING EDWARD VII

1903. *W.* H. Everett & Son Limited, Bell's Buildings, Salisbury Square, London, E.C. Underprint Type **1** in purple or red

PP230	½d. blue-green (M1)	£180
PP231	1d. red (M5)	£180
PP232	1½d. purple and green (M8)	£250
PP233	2d. green and red (M11)	£250
PP234	2½d. blue (M16)	£275
PP235	6d. purple (M32)	£300

We do not distinguish between inverted or sideways varieties due to the random method of application.

1904. S. & J. Watts, Manchester. Underprint Type **2** in black (18 mm. wide).

(a) Vertical underprint, reading upwards

PP236	½d. blue-green (M1)	£180
PP237	½d. yellow-green (M2)	£180
PP238	1d. red (M5)	£180
PP239	2½d. blue (M16)	£275
PP240	3d. purple on yellow (M19)	£300
PP241	3d. purple on yellow (M20)	£300

(b) Vertical underprint, reading downwards

PP242	1d. red (M5)	£180
PP243	3d. purple on yellow (M19)	£300
PP244	3d. purple on yellow (M20)	£300
PP245	5d. purple and blue (M28)	£350

(c) As last but underprint (14 mm. wide) in black

PP246	1d. red (M5)	£180
PP247	1d. red (M6)	£180
PP248	1d. red (M7)	£180
PP249	3d. purple on yellow (M22)	£300

KING GEORGE V

1912. W. H. Everett & Son Ltd., Bell's Buildings, Salisbury Square, London, E.C. Underprint Type **1** in purple.

PP250	1d. red (N16)	£180

1912. S. & J. Watts, Manchester. Underprint Type **2** (14 mm. wide).

(a) Vertical underprint, reading upwards

PP251	1½d. red-brown (N18)	£250

(b) Vertical underprint, reading downwards

PP251a	½d. green (N5)	£180
PP252	1d. red (N16)	£180
PP253	3d. violet (N22)	£180

1924. As (b) above

PP254	1½d. red-brown	£250

Appendix 6

Postage Rates

Postage rates from 1635 have been researched from official records and the following extract is reproduced with kind permission of the Post Office. The rates given apply only to the period covered by this Catalogue.

Letter Post
The Treasury was empowered to regulate rates of postage, and subsequent changes were made by Treasury Warrant.

Date	Rates of Postage	
22 June 1897	4oz.	1d.
Then ½d. for each additional 2oz.		
1 November 1915	1oz.	1d.
	2oz.	2d.
	4oz.	2½d.
Then ½d. for each additional 2oz.		
3 June 1918	4oz.	1½d.
	6oz.	2d.
Then ½d. for each additional 2oz.		
1 June 1920	3oz.	2d.
Then ½d. for each additional 1oz.		
29 May 1922	1oz.	1½d.
	3oz.	2d.
Then ½d. for each additional oz.		
14 May 1923	2oz.	1½d.
Then ½d. for each additional 2oz.		
1 May 1940	2oz.	2½d.
Then ½d. for each additional 2oz.		
1 May 1952	2oz.	2½d.
	4oz.	3d.
Then 1d. for each additional 2oz.		

Postcards
The first postcards issued by the Post Office appeared in 1870. These bore an embossed ½d. stamp and were followed in 1882 by the Reply Postcard. Private postcards were permitted from 1894 and the maximum size allowed was 5½ x 3½in, increased in 1925 to 5⅞ x 4⅛in. The minimum size limit was 4 x 2¾in.

Date	Charge
1 January 1901	½d.
3 June 1918	1d.
13 June 1921	1½d.
29 May 1922	1d.
1 May 1940	2d.

Printed Papers
This service was introduced as "Book Post" and had been used extensively by the subscribing Lending Libraries. On 1 January 1904 the Service was renamed the Halfpenny Packet Post with revised regulations to include all types of documents.

Date	Rates of Postage	
22 June 1897	2oz. only	½d.
Because the Letter Rate was 1d. for 4oz. and ½d. for each additional 2oz. the Book Post applied only to packets up to 2oz. In weight.		
1 November 1915	2oz.	½d.
Then ½d. for each additional 2oz. up to 5lb. Book Post.		
3 June 1918	1oz.	½d.
	2oz.	1d.
After 2oz. The letter rate applied.		
1 June 1920	1oz.	½d.
	2oz.	1d.
Then ½d. for each additional 2oz. up to 2lb. Now called Printed Paper Post.		
13 June 1921	2oz.	1d.
Then ½d. for each additional 2oz. up to 2lb.		
29 May 1922	1oz.	½d.
	2oz.	1d.
Then ½d. for each additional 2oz. up to 2lb.		
14 May 1923	2oz.	½d.
Then ½d. for each additional 2oz. up to 2lb.		
1 May 1940	2oz.	1d.
Then ½d. for each additional 2oz. up to 2lb.		
1 June 1951	4oz.	1½d.
Then ½d. for each additional 2oz. up to 2lb.		

Deferment of late posted Printed Paper Matter
When minimum rate was reduced to ½d. on 29 May 1922, the 1d. rate which had previously existed was maintained for such items as Stock Exchange quotations, etc., which could not be posted before the agreed "cut-off" time. This "cut-off" time was introduced to encourage early posting and to even out peaks of work. The ½d. differential continued by custom until 1965.

Newspaper Post
From 1870 the charge had been ½d. per copy irrespective of weight, but from 1 November 1915 the maximum weight permitted was 2lb.

Date		Charge per Copy
1 November 1915	Not exceeding 6oz.	½d.
	Each additional 6oz.	½d.
1 September 1920	Not exceeding 6oz.	1d.
	Each additional 6oz.	½d.
1 July 1940	Not exceeding 40z.	1½d.
	Each additional 4oz.	½d.

Articles for the Blind
Originally introduced as Blind Literature this service was made free of charge from 17 May 1965.

Date	Rates of Postage	
1 September 1906	2oz.	½d.
	2lb.	1d.
	5lb.	1½d.
1 February 1907	2oz.	½d.
	2lb.	1d.
	5lb.	1½d.
	6lb.	2½d.
1 January 1915	2oz.	½d.
	5lb.	1d.
	6lb.	2d.
13 June 1921	1lb.	½d.
	5lb.	1d.
	6½lb.	2d.
17 February 1926	2lb.	½d.
	5lb.	1d.
	6½lb.	1½d.
3 July 1936	2lb.	½d.
	5lb.	1d.

Postage Rates APPENDIX 6

Date	Rates of Postage	
	8lb.	1½d.
	11lb.	2d.

Service renamed Articles for the Blind.

Date	Rates of Postage	
1 July 1940	2lb.	½d.
	5lb.	1d.
	8lb.	1½d.
	11lb.	2d.
	15lb.	2½d.

Express Services

Service 1. Express by Post Office messenger or, from 1934, special messenger all the way.

Date	Charges	Notes
1900	3d. per mile	Weight charge abolished
1906	3d. per mile	Weight charge of 3d. on packets exceeding 1lb. In weight imposed
1 June 1919	6d. per mile plus cost of special conveyance if used.	Charge for additional articles 1d. (additional to basic charge) per article after the first.
	Weight fee (for packets over 1lb.) 3d.	Waiting fee (after 10 mins.) 2d. for each 15 mins.
1934	As above	As above but waiting fee 2d. for each 10 mins. After the first 10 mins.

Service 2. Special Delivery at the request of the sender. Charges were the same as for **Service 1**. From 1934 the service was by the sender's request, but by Post Office messenger from the delivery office after transmission by post, see also **Service 4**.

Date	Charges	Notes
1934	Full postage plus special delivery fee of 6d.	If a special conveyance was used the advised cost was charged to the sender or if unknown at 1 shilling per mile

Service 3. Express delivery all the way at the request of the addressee. Charges were the same as for **Service 1**. Additional articles were charged at 1d. for every ten beyond the first. From 1934 the service changed to express from the office of delivery at the request of the addressee when the charge was the same as **Service 1** including charge for additional articles.

Service 4. There was a Limited Sunday Special Delivery Service, introduced in 1921, because of the withdrawal of Sunday deliveries. Charges were as for **Service 2** except the special fee was 1s.6d. per mile in 1921. From 1934 the cost was full postage plus special fee of 1s.6d.

Service 5. Express delivery of message received by telephone. Usual charge per telephone call and writing down fee (minimum charge 3d. for 30 words. 1d. for every additional 10 words). Express charges as for **Service 1**.

Official Parcel Post

This service had been first introduced on 1 August 1883.

Date	Rates of Postage	
1 June 1897	1lb.	3d.
	2lb.	4d.
	3lb.	5d.
	4lb.	6d.
	5lb.	7d.
	6lb.	8d.
	7lb.	9d.
	8lb.	10d.
	9lb.	11d.
	11lb.	1s.0d.
2 July 1906	1lb.	3d.
	2lb.	4d.
	3lb.	5d.
	5lb.	6d.
	7lb.	7d.
	8lb.	8d.
	9lb.	9d.
	10lb.	10d.
	11lb.	11d.
1 November 1915	1lb.	4d.
	2lb.	5d.
	3lb.	6d.
	7lb.	8d.
	8lb.	9d.
	9lb.	10d.
	10lb.	11d.
	11lb.	1s.0d.
3 June 1918	3lb.	6d.
	7lb.	9d.
	11lb.	1s.0d.
1 June 1920	2lb.	9d.
	5lb.	1s.0d.
	8lb.	1s.3d.
	11lb.	1s.6d.
14 May 1923	2lb.	6d.
	5lb.	9d.
	8lb.	1s.0d.
	11lb.	1s.3d.
1 July 1935	3lb.	6d.
	4lb.	7d.
	5lb.	8d.
	6lb.	9d.
	7lb.	10d.
	8lb.	11d.
	15lb.	1s.0d.
1 July 1940	3lb.	7d.
	4lb.	8d.
	5lb.	9d.
	6lb.	10d.
	7lb.	11d.
	8lb.	1s.0d.
	15lb.	1s.1d.
6 January 1947	3lb.	8d.
	4lb.	9d.
	5lb.	10d.
	6lb.	11d.
	7lb.	1s.0d.
	8lb.	1s1d.
	15lb.	1s.2d.
29 December 1947	3lb.	9d.
	4lb.	11d.
	5lb.	1s.0d.
	6lb.	1s.1d.
	7lb.	1s.3d.
	8lb.	1s.3d.
	15lb.	1s.4d.
31 July 1950	3lb.	10d.
	4lb.	1s.0d.
	5lb.	1s.2d.
	6lb.	1s.3d.
	7lb.	1s.4d.
	8lb.	1s.5d.
	15lb.	1s.6d.
1 July 1951	3lb.	11d.
	4lb.	1s.1d.
	5lb.	1s.3d.
	6lb.	1s.5d.
	7lb.	1s.6d.
	8lb.	1s. 7d.
	15lb.	1s. 8d.
31 March 1952	2lb.	11d.
	3lb.	1s.1d.
	4lb.	1s.3d.
	5lb.	1s.5d.
	6lb.	1s.7d.

APPENDIX 6   Postage Rates

Date		Rates of Postage
	7lb.	1s. 9d.
	8lb.	1s.10d.
	11lb.	1s.11d.
	15lb.	2s.0d.

Railex

This was a new service, introduced on 1 January 1934. It provided for the conveyance of a postal packet to a railway station by Post Office messenger for despatch on the first available train, and for its immediate delivery by Post Office messenger from the station of destination.

Date	Charge	Rates of Postage
1 January 1934	Not exceeding 2oz.	2s. 6d.
	Over 2oz. And up to 1lb.	3s. 0d.
1 July 1940	Not exceeding 2oz.	3s. 0d.
	Over 2oz. And up to 1lb.	3s. 6d.

Appendix 7

Post Office Savings Bank Stamps

A coupon scheme whereby deposits of small amounts could be made to Savings Bank accounts had been suggested a number of times, but the idea was not accepted by the Postmaster General until 1910. It was then hoped that the new scheme could be introduced on 16 September 1911, the 60th anniversary of the Post Office Savings Bank.

On 23 Febuary 1911, G.W. Eve was invited to prepare a design for the P.O.S.B. stamp.

Original sketch for the 'Deposit Receipt' stamp £5000

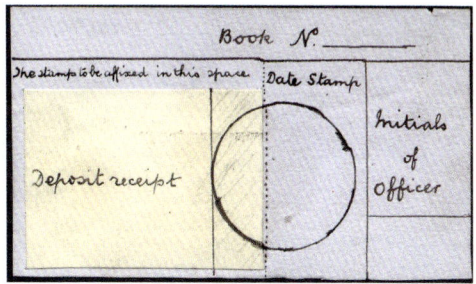

Sketch of the Savings Bank receipt sent to G.W. Eve on 23 Febuary 1911.

Die Proofs

Uncleared proof of Die 2 head

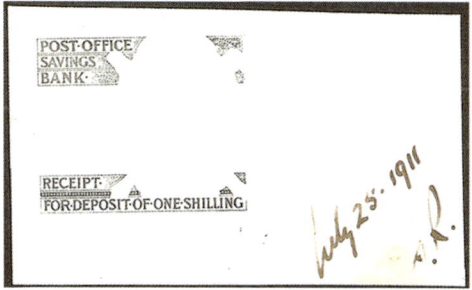

Die proof of lettering

Head and frame De La Rue Die Proof using J.A.C. Harrison Head

Post Office Savings Bank Stamp incorporating Downey Head

Although a stage 3 head was supplied to De La Rue, who were to print the Savings Bank stamps, they actually used a Die 2 Head.

Uncleared proof of Die 2 in black on proof paper, endorsed "S.B" and dated "4.7.11" (numbered "1" or "2") .... Each £2200
Cleared proof of lettering in black on white glazed card .... Each £850
Cleared proof of Head Plate in black on white glazed card (Downey Head) various stages .... Each £850
Cleared proof of Head Plate in black on white glazed card (Mackennal Head), various stages ..... Each £850

APPENDIX 7 *Post Office Savings Bank Stamps*

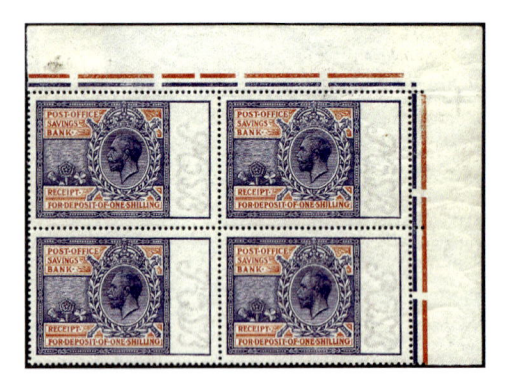

1911-20. **Post Office Savings Bank Stamps, watermark crown/POSB. Perf 15×14**

		Mint	Used
POSB1	1s. light blue and red (Downey Portrait)	£300	60·00
	a. Overprint "CANCELLED"	£325	
POSB2	1s. light blue and red (Mackennal portrait)	£250	60·00
	a. Overprinted "SPECIMEN"	£325	

*Used prices are for fine examples on original counterfoil.

Appendix 8

Channel Islands. The German Occupation 1940-1945

A. GUERNSEY

Following the German Occupation the existing supplies of current British stamps continued in use until stocks became exhausted. It had earlier been decided that locally printed stamps should be supplied, but in the event these were not ready for issue until 18 February 1941. On 24 December 1940 authority was given, by Post Office notice, that prepayment of penny postage could be effected by using half a British 2d. stamp, diagonally bisected. Such stamps were first used on 27 December 1940. The 2d. stamps available were the 1937 definitive and the 1940 Stamp Centenary commemorative. Examples of George V 2d. stamps bisected were also accepted by the Post Office, as were, in most instances, bisects of other values which had not been authorised. Bisects remained valid for postage in Guernsey until 22 February 1941, although examples are recorded two days later. The 24 February was a Monday and letters prepaid with a bisected stamp, which missed the final Saturday collection, were accepted and postmarked 24 February 1941. On Sark their use continued until 31 May 1941.

The German Commandant had a swastika overprint applied to a number of the bisected 1940 Stamp Centenary 2d. stamps and submitted these to Berlin for approval, but this scheme was turned down, as was another which involved a similar overprint on the 1937 1d. value. Examples of both exist, but are very rare.

As previously mentioned, the locally printed 1d. stamps were issued on 18 February 1941. The ½d. stamp was released on 7 April 1941 and the 2½d. on 12 April 1944. This last stamp was issued in an effort to economise on the use of paper as it was found that sealed letters were franked with two 1d. stamps and one ½d. or a larger number of ½d's, a gross waste in times of shortage. Many printings of these stamps were made, the most notable being on the French bank-note paper in 1942.

Shades of these issues abound, the more outstanding ones being the bluish green (4th) and olive-green (8th) printings of the ½d. and the vermilion (11th) printing of the 1d. These stamps continued to be used after the liberation in 1945 until 13 April 1946.

1940. Swastika overprints. Stamps of Great Britain optd.

(a) 1937 George. VI definitive optd. with a number of small swastikas
GW1 1d. scarlet (Q4) £2000

(b) 1940 Stamp Centenary commemorative, intended for bisection, optd. with a swastika on each half of the stamp
GW2 2d. orange (QCom5) £2000

Nos. GW1/2 were prepared for use, but not issued. They are, therefore, only known unused.

1940 (27 Dec). Stamps of Great Britain bisected.

(a) George V definitives   *Price on cover*
GW3   2d. orange (N20) (1912–22 issue) £400
GW4   2d. orange (N36) (1924–26 issue) £400
GW5   2d. orange (N55) (1934 issue) £450

(b) George VI 1937–39 definitives
GW6   1d. scarlet (Q4) £950
GW7   2d. orange (Q10) (Head Office c.d.s) ..... 50·00
GW7a   (Machine cancel) .... 55·00
GW7b   (Sub-office cancel) .... from 50·00

(c) 1940 Stamp Centenary commemoratives
GW8   1d. scarlet (QCom3) £950
GW9   2d. orange (QCom5) (Head Office c.d.s) .... 40·00
GW9a   (Machine cancel) .... 45·00
GW9b   (Sub-office cancel) .... from 40·00
GW10 2½d. ultramarine (QCom6) £2000
GW11 3d. violet (QCom7) .... —

GW1 Arms of Guernsey

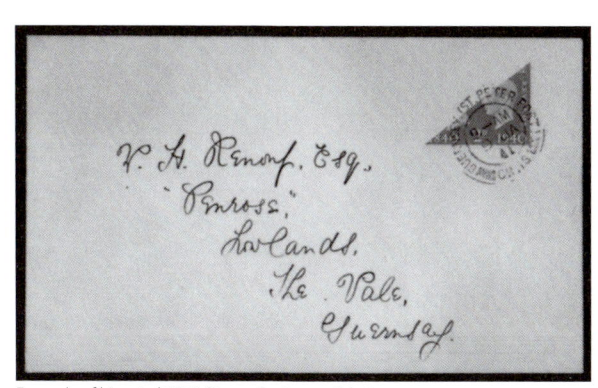

Example of bisected 1940 Stamp Centenary 2d. stamp

APPENDIX 8 Channel Islands. The German Occupation 1940-1945

"Loops" Watermark (*reduced to ½ size*)

(Designed by E. W. Vaudin)
(Printed in typography by Guernsey Press Co. Ltd.)

1941-44. Rouletted.
(a) White paper. No wmk Printing

GW12 (=S.G.1) **GW1**

½d. light green (7.4.41)	(1 (part)		6·00	3·50
a. *Emerald-green* (7.4. & 6.4.41)	(1 (part), 2, 3)		6·00	2·00
b. *Bluish green* (11.41)	(4)		35·00	13·00
c. *Bright green* (2.42)	(6)		22·00	10·00
d. *Dull green* (9.42)	(7)		4·00	2·00
e. *Olive-green* (2.43)	(8)		45·00	25·00
f. *Deep yellow-green* (7.43 & 10.43)	(9, 10)		4·00	3·00
g. *Pale yellow-green* (1.44 and later)	(11, 12, 13)		4·00	3·00
h. Imperf. (pair)			£250	
i. Imperf. between (horiz. pair)			£800	
j. Imperf. between (vert. pair)			£900	
k. Imperf. between stamp and margin			£180	
l. Printed on the gummed side			£180	

GW13 (=S.G.2)

1d. scarlet (18.2.41)	(1–10)	3·25	2·00
a. *Pale vermilion* (shades) (7.43)	(11)	5·00	2·00
b. *Carmine* (12.43 and later)	(12–16)	3·50	2·00
c. Imperf. (pair)		£200	90·00
d. Imperf. between (horiz. pair)		£800	
e. Imperf. between (vert. pair)		£950	
ea. Imperf. vert. (centre stamp of horiz. strip of 3)			
f. Imperf. between stamp and margin		£200	
g. Printed double (scarlet shade)		£150	

GW14 (=S.G.3)

2½d. ultramarine (shades) (12.4.44)	(1)	18·00	15·00
a. *Deep ultramarine* (4.44- 11.44)	(2, 3 (part), 4)	15·00	12·00
b. *Pale ultramarine* (7.44)(3 (part))		15·00	12·00
c. Imperf. (pair)		£600	
d. Imperf. between (horiz. pair)		£1250	

(b) Bluish French bank-note paper. Wmk. loops (sideways)

GW15 (=S.G.4) **GW1**

½d. bright green (11.3.42)	(5)	32·00	25·00
a. Watermark sideways-inverted		38·00	28·00
b. Watermark sideways and reversed		38·00	28·00
c. Watermark sideways-inverted and reversed		38·00	28·00

GW16 (=S.G.5)

1d. scarlet (9.4.42)	(7)	18·00	25·00
a. Watermark sideways-inverted		28·00	28·00
b. Watermark sideways and reversed		28·00	28·00
c. Watermark sideways-inverted and reversed		28·00	28·00

The dates given for the shades of Nos. 1-3 are the months in which they were printed as indicated on the printer's imprints. Others are issue dates.

Nos. GW15/6 with a watermark variety can only be identified when the word "ARMA" forms part of the watermark on the example. The reversed watermark appears to be the normal with "AMRA" reading up when viewed through the *front* of the stamp.

First Day Cover (No. GW12)	10·00
First Day Cover (No. GW13)	15·00
First Day Cover (No. GW14)	20·00
First Day Cover (No. GW15)	£325
First Day Cover (No. GW16)	£125

Commercial Covers. Covers from personal or commercial correspondence franked with Nos. GW12, GW13 or GW14 are worth from twice the value quoted for used stamps. Similar covers franked with No. GW15 or No. GW16 are valued at three times the price quoted for used stamps.

Forgeries
All three values have been forged since 1945, the colours being almost identical with one or other of the shades of the actual stamps. They are printed in sheets of 25 instead of 60, have no imprint and do not contain the varieties, neither are the "Vs" in the corners at all clear. Even so, single examples are difficult to detect and care should be exercised in buying these stamps.

Imprints and Printings (Blocks of Four)

Imprint block of ½d. 4th printing

The various printings can be identified from the sheet imprints as follows:

½d.	1st Printing 240M/3/41	30·00
	2nd Printing 2 × 120M/6/41	32·00
	(a) Large white flaw above "G" of "GUERNSEY" on bottom right stamp	35·00
	3rd Printing x × 120M/6/41	32·00
	4th Printing 4 × 120M/11/41	£200
	5th Printing 5 × 120M/2/42	90·00
	6th Printing 6 × 240M/2/42	£120
	7th Printing 7 × 120M/9/42	32·00
	8th Printing 8 × 120M/2/43	£180
	9th Printing 9 × 120M/7/43	18·00

Channel Islands. The German Occupation 1940-1945 APPENDIX 8

	10th Printing 10 × 120M/10/43	18·00
	11th Printing Guernsey Press Co., (stop and comma)	18·00
	12th Printing Guernsey Press Co. (stop only, margin at bottom 23 to 27 mm).	18·00
	13th Printing Guernsey Press Co. (stop only, margin at bottom 15 mm)	18·00
1d.	1st. Printing 120M/2/41	22·00
	2nd Printing 2 × 120M/2/41)	20·00
	3rd Printing 3 × 120M/6/41	18·00
	4th Printing 4 × 120M/6/41	20·00
	5th Printing 5 × 120M/9/41	20·00
	6th Printing 6 × 240M/11/41	18·00
	7th Printing 7 × 120M/2/42	70·00
	8th Printing 8 × 240M/4/42	18·00
	9th Printing 9 × 240M/9/42	18·00
	10th Printing 10 × 240M/1/43	18·00
	11th Printing 11 × 240M/7/43	28·00
	12th Printing Guernsey Press Co.	40·00
	13th Printing press typ.	25·00
	14th Printing "PRESS" (inverted commas unlevel)	22·00
	15th Printing "PRESS" (inverted commas level, margin at bottom 28 mm)	25·00
	16th Printing "PRESS" (inverted commas level, margin at bottom 12 mm)	22·00
2½d.	2½d. 1st Printing Guernsey Press Co.	40·00
	2nd Printing "PRESS" (inverted commas unlevel)	35·00
	3rd Printing "PRESS" (inverted commas level, margin at bottom 22 mm)	40·00
	4th Printing "PRESS" (inverted commas level, margin at bottom 15 mm)	35·00

The numbered imprints occur in the left-hand corner, bottom margin on the first printing of the 1d., and central, bottom margin on all other printings of all three values.

In the numbered imprints, for example "2 × 120M/6/41", the "2" indicates the number of the printing: "120M" denotes the number of stamps printed in thousands, in this case 120,000; and "6/41" denotes the date of the printing, June 1941.

In the first ten printings of the ½d. and the first eleven printings of the 1d. the printing details are prefixed by the name of the printer, "Guernsey Press Co.".

Varieties
½d. All printings show a break in the left outer frame line on R. 7/1 and another in the right outer frame line on R. 8/6 *(Price twice normal)*
1d. All printings from the eighth onwards show a break near the bottom of the right outer frame line which extends into the adjacent pearl on R. 4/3 and R. 9/3 *(Price twice normal)*

Sheets: 60 (6 × 10).

Quantities Printed: ½d. 1,772,160; 1d. 2,478,000; 2½d. 416,640.

Withdrawn and Invalidated: 13.4.46, but last day postmark 14.4.46. The stamps could be used in Great Britain for a short time after liberation, but were soon declared to be invalid there.

B. JERSEY
Soon after Jersey was occupied by German troops the Commandant ordered the Postmaster to forward stocks of the currently available (British) stamps to Bigwoods, the Jersey printers, to be overprinted with a swastika and "JERSEY 1940". The Bailiff of Jersey protested at this action and, after reference to Berlin, the Commandant ordered the stocks of overprinted stamps to be destroyed. Only four complete sets and a few singles are known to have survived. One of the complete sets is in the Jersey Postal Headquarters archives.

Bigwoods also prepared a local 1d. stamp depicting the Arms of Jersey and inscribed "ETATS DE JERSEY", with and without an overprint of a swastika and "1940". These also were destroyed, except for two sheets now in museums, two further sheets which were cut up for collectors and a complete (but damaged) sheet with the overprint.

(JW1)
(Overprinted by Bigwoods, States of Jersey Printers)

Two locally printed stamps followed during 1941-42, the designer, Major N.V.L. Rybot, incorporating an "A" in each corner of the 1d. design to stand for Ad Avernum Adolf Atrox (to hell with you atrocious Adolf). On the subsequent ½d. value an "A" appeared in each of the upper corners and a "B" in the lower.

These stood for "Atrocious Adolf, Bloody Benito".

This tradition of "hidden" inscriptions was continued by E. Blampied who incorporated the Royal Cypher into the design of the 3d. view.

1940. Swastika overprints. Stamps of Great Britain optd. with Type **JW1**.

(a) On 1937-39 George VI definitives

JW1	½d. green	£3500
JW2	1½d. red-brown	£3500
JW3	2d. orange	£3500
JW4	2½d. ultramarine	£3500
JW5	3d. violet	£3500
JW6	4d. grey-green	£3500
JW7	5d. brown	£3500
JW8	6d. purple	£3500
JW9	7d. emerald-green	£3500
JW10	8d. bright carmine	£3500
JW11	9d. deep olive-green	£3500
JW12	10d. turquoise-blue	£3500
JW13	1s. bistre-brown	£3500

(b) On 1940 Stamp Centenary issue

JW14	½d. green	£3500
JW15	1½d. red-brown	£3500
JW16	2d. orange	£3500
JW17	2½d. ultramarine	£3500
JW18	3d. violet	£3500

As Nos. JW1/18 were prepared but not issued, they are only known unused.

Proofs: Proof overprints made from a single block exist on the Edward VIII 1½d. and on the Stamp Centenary set (except the 1d.).

Forgeries
Forgeries of the swastika overprints were reported in circulation in 1974. They are cruder in appearance and differ from the genuine examples as follows: (1) the swastika is much thinner on the forgeries and can be at the wrong angle; (2) the ink is much thinner, many forged overprints revealing large white patches under the glass; (3) the swastika and "JERSEY 1940" have been applied separately.

APPENDIX 8 Channel Islands. The German Occupation 1940-1945

JW2
(Designed by R. W. Cutland)
(Printed in letterpress by Bigwoods)

1940. No wmk. Imperf.

(a) Type **JW2**

JW19	1d. scarlet	£3250

(b) Type **JW3**

JW20	1d. scarlet	£3250

Nos. JW19/20 were prepared but not issued. They do not exist in used condition.

Sheets: 30 (10 × 3).
A proof sheet of 6 (2 × 3) of No. JW20 exists on laid paper, ungummed and rouletted.

JW3 Arms of Jersey

(Designed by Major N. V. L. Rybot)
(Printed in letterpress by *Evening Post*, Jersey)

1941-43. White paper (thin to thick). No wmk. P11

JW21 (=S.G.1) **JW3**

½d. bright green (29.1.42)	8·00	6·00
a. Imperf. between (vert. pair)	£900	
b. Imperf. between (horiz. pair)	£800	
c. Imperf. (pair)	£300	
d. Imperf. between stamp and margin	£120	
e. On greyish paper	12·00	5·50
f. Stop before "2" (R. 1/6)	20·00	
g. Line from lion's claw (R. 6/6)	20·00	
h. Break above "T" (R. 8/1)	20·00	
i. Three breaks in P (R. 8/3)	20·00	
j. White circle flaw (R. 8/6)	20·00	

JW22 (=S.G.2)

1d. scarlet (1.4.41)	8·00	5·00
a. Imperf. between (vert. pair)	£900	
b. Imperf. between (horiz. pair)	£800	
c. Imperf. (pair)	£325	
d. On chalk-surfaced paper (10.41)	55·00	48·00
e. On greyish paper (1.43)	14·00	14·00

First Day Cover (No. JW21)	7·50
First Day Cover (No. JW22)	8·00

PLATE VARIETIES
Listed Flaws

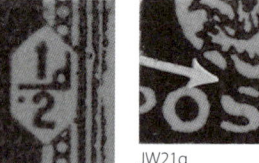

JW21f
Dark spot before "2" in tablet at right (R. 1/6)

JW21g
Heavy line from lion's claw to "S" in "POSTAGE" (R. 6/6)

JW21h
Small white break joins "T" to shield (R. 8/1)

JW21i
Three breaks in "P" (R. 8/3)

JW21j
Large white circle after "Y" of "JERSEY" (R. 8/6)

Distinctive and positioned flaws are listed but many plate flaws exist on these stamps and most are worth twice normal.

Imprints (Blocks of Six)
½d. "EVENING POST", Jersey, January 1942 .... 50·00
On greyish paper .... 80·00
1d. "EVENING POST", Jersey, 17/3/41 .... 50·00
On chalk-surfaced paper £350
On greyish paper .... 90·00

Sheets: 60 (6 × 10).

Numbers Printed: ½d., 703,500; 1d., 1,030,620.

Withdrawn and Invalidated: 13.4.46, but last day postmark 14.4.46. The stamps could be used in Great Britain for a short time after liberation, but were soon declared to be invalid there.

Forgeries
Both values exist in different colours from the originals as imperforate forgeries.

Plate Proofs (Pairs)
½d. on thin paper in black £275
1d. on thick card in black £200

JW4 Old Jersey Farm

JW5 Portelet Bay

JW6 Corbière Lighthouse

JW7 Elizabeth Castle

332

JW8 Mont Orgueil Castle **JW9** Gathering Vraic (seaweed)

(Designed by E. Blampied. Engraved by H. Cortot)

(Printed in letterpress by French Govt. Ptg. Works, Paris)

1943-44. No wmk. P13½.

JW23 (=S.G.3) **JW4**		
½d. green (1.6.43)	12·00	12·00
a. Rough grey paper (6.10.43)	15·00	14·00
JW24 (=S.G.4) **JW5**		
1d. scarlet (1.6.43)	3·00	50
a. On newsprint (28.2.44)	3·50	75
JW25 (=S.G.5) **JW6**		
1½d. brown (8.6.43)	8·00	5·75
JW26 (=S.G.6) **JW7**		
2d. orange-yellow (8.6.43)	7·50	2·00
JW27 (=S.G.7) **JW8**		
2½d. blue (29.6.43)	3·00	1·00
a. Thin paper with design showing through back (25.2.44)	£225	
b. On newsprint (25.2.44)	1·00	1·70
JW28 (=S.G.8) **JW9**		
3d. violet (29.6.43)	3·00	2·75
First Day Covers		36·00

The dates quoted for the paper varieties are those on which they were printed.
The 3d. value is known bisected from Rouge-Bouillon.

Forgeries
All values exist as imperforate forgeries in different shades.

Imprints and Printings. (Blocks of Four)

½d. 1st printing 1/5/43	50·00
2nd printing 3/5/43	50·00
3rd printing 6/10/43	65·00
1d. 1st printing 7/5/43	14·00
2nd printing 8/5/43	14·00
3rd printing 7/10/43	16·00
4th printing 28/2/44	16·00
1½d. 1st printing 17/5/43	35·00
2nd printing 18/5/43	35·00
2d. 1st printing 20/5/43	35·00
2nd printing 21/5/43	35·00
2½d. 1st printing 31/5/43	14·00
2nd printing 25/2/44	12·00
3d. 1st printing 4/6/43	14·00
2nd printing 5/6/43	14·00

Sheets: 120 (four panes 3×10), separated by interpanneau margins.

Imprint: None.

Numbers Printed: ½d., 360,000, grey paper, 120,000; 1d., 960,000, newsprint, 240,000; 1½d., 360,000; 2d., 360,000; 2½d., 360,000, newsprint, 360,000; 3d., 360,000.

Withdrawn and Invalidated: 13.4.46, but last day postmark 14.4.46. The stamps could be used in Great Britain for a short time after liberation, but were soon declared to be invalid there.

Proofs and Essays
Die proofs in black on rough paper, signed Cortot...............£225
Colour proofs, signed Cortot.. from £300
Colour proofs, unsigned .... from £225
Black presentation proofs on good quality wove paper.....£400
Epreuves-de-luxe in issued colours, with imprint
"Atelier de Fabrication des Timbres-Poste, PARIS"
and covered with tissue paper ....each £175
Mise en train proofs in black on pink paper, ½d.,
1d., 1½d. and 2d. only ....each £120
Half-size essays of ½d. and 1d. in single or two
colours on wove or India paper ....from (each) £225

OFFICIAL STAMPS

JW10 **JW11**

1940 (July). Typo. Imperf.

JWO1 **JW10** (—) black   £2200   £2500
No. JWO1 was used by Capt. Gussek, the first Jersey Commandant, on his official mail and occasionally on documents.

1940. Inscr. "HAFEN/KOMMANDANT/JERSEY" with anchor in centre. Imperf.
JWO2   **JW11** (—) black   £2200   £2500

1940. As No. JWO2, but inscr. "HAFEN/KAPITAN/etc."
JWO3   (—) black   £2200   £2500
Nos. JW02/3 were used by the Harbour Master and appear more frequently on permits or documents than on letters.

Further Reading

The list below is representative of major works relating to British postal history, stamps and postmarks of the reigns of King Edward VII to King George VI. Initially, culled from *A List of Books on the Postal History, and Adhesive Postage and Revenue Stamps of Great Britain*, compiled by Arnold M. Strange (2nd edition, Great Britain Philatelic Soc. London, 1971). Appropriate titles on the Channel Islands are also included.

POSTAL HISTORY

Dagnall, Harry. *The Mechanised Sorting of Mail*. (1976. The Author, Leicester.)

Daunton, M. J. *Royal Mail: The Post Office since 1840*. (1985. The Athlone Press, London.)

Farrugia, Jean and Gammons, Tony. *Carrying British Mails*. (1980. The National Postal Museum, London.)

Hay, Ian. *The Post Office Went to War*. (1946. H.M. Stationery Office, London.)

Jackson, G. Gibbard. *From Post Boy to Air Mail*. The Story of the British Post Office. (Sampson Low, Marston & Co., London.)

Kay, George F. *Royal Mail. The Story of the Posts in England from the Time of Edward IV to the Present Day*. (1951. Rockliffe Publishing Corporation Ltd.)

Marshall, C. F. Dendy. *The British Post Office from its Beginnings to the End of 1925*. (1926. Oxford University Press.)

Murray, Sir Evelyn, K.C.B., Secretary to the Post Office. *The Post Office*. (1927. Putnam & Co., Ltd., London.)

Robinson, Howard. *The British Post Office*. A History. (1948. Princeton University Press.)

Robinson, Howard. *Carrying British Mails Overseas*. (1964. George Allen & Unwin Ltd., London.)

Staff, Frank. *The Penny Post 1680-1918*. (1964. Paperback edn. 1992. Lutterworth Press, Cambridge.)

GENERAL

Alcock, R. C. and Meredith, C. W. *British Postage Stamp Varieties Illustrated. Queen Victoria Surface-Printed Issues to King George VI*. (1949. R. C. Alcock, Cheltenham.)

Hamilton, Patrick. *British Stamps. A Description of the Postage Stamps of the United Kingdom*. (1948. Peter Davies, London. Supplement published by Harris Publications Ltd., London, 1954.)

Lowe, Robson. *The Encyclopaedia of British Empire Postage Stamps. 1661-1951*. (1952. 2nd Edn. Robson Lowe Ltd., London.) Reprinted in Billig's Philatelic Handbook series (2 Vols.). (HJMR Co., North Miami, Florida.)

Mackay, James A. *Great Britain. The Story of Great Britain and her Stamps*. (1967. Philatelic Publishers, London.)

Mackay, James A. *Under the Gum—Background to British Stamps 1840-1940*. (1997. James Bendon Ltd., Limassol, Cyprus.)

Mackay, James A. *British Stamps*. (1985. Longman Group Ltd., London.)

Morgan, Glenn H. *British Stamp Exhibitions*. (1995. The Author, London.)

Oliver, Sidney A. R. and Vallancey, F. Hugh. *The Postage Stamps of Great Britain. 1840-1922*. (1923. Stamp Collecting, London.)

Rigo de Righi, A. G. *The Stamp of Royalty; British Commemorative Issues for Royal Occasions 1935-1972*. (1973. The National Postal Museum, London.)

Rose, Stuart. *Royal Mail Stamps - A Survey of British Stamp Design*. (1980. Phaidon Press, Oxford.)

Rowell, Reginald B. *Notes on Controls. Part II. Edwardian and Georgian Periods*. (1916. Stamp Collecting Handbook, London.)

Todd, T. *A History of British Postage Stamps*. (1949. Duckworth, London.)

Ward, W. *A Book about British Books of Stamps and Rolls*. (1925. Lytham.)

Williams, L. N. and M. *Commemorative Postage Stamps of Great Britain*. (1967. Arco Publications, London.)

Wilson, Sir John, Bart. *The Royal Philatelic Collection*. (1952. The Dropmore Press, London.)

PHILATELIC PERIODICALS DEVOTED TO GREAT BRITAIN

The British Philatelist (1908-54) (Chas. Nissen & Co., Ltd., London.)

The GB Journal (From 1956) (The Great Britain Philatelic Society, London.)

The G.B. Philatelist (1961-65) (The Regent Stamp Co., Ltd., London.)

Gibbons Stamp Monthly (*British Stamps* supplement from October 1981, January, April and July 1982, monthly since October 1982.)

British Philatelic Bulletin (From 1963) (title was *Philatelic Bulletin*, 1963-83). (The Post Office, London.)

The Philatelist/Philatelic Journal of Great Britain (1981-83) (The P.J.G.B., 1891-1980, was then merged with *The Philatelist*, after March 1966 the former was wholly devoted to Great Britain (Robson Lowe Ltd., London.)

The Philatelic Review (1977–82) (Candlish, McCleery Ltd., Bristol.)

Cross Post. Published by Friends of Postal Heritage (formerly Association of Friends of the National Postal Museum).

GBCC Chronicle. Published by Great Britain Collectors Club in USA.

Rundbrief. Published by GB collectors society in Germany, Forschungsgemeinschaft Grossbritannien e.V (FgGB).

KING EDWARD VII

Beaumont, K. M. and Adams, H. C. V. *The Postage Stamps of Great Britain. The Embossed Issues. The Surface-Printed Issues of Queen Victoria and King Edward VII*. (1954. The Royal Philatelic Society, London. Revised 1964 by K. M. Beaumont and John Easton.)

Bernstein, I. J. *The Official Stamps of Great Britain*. (1906. Philatelic Record Handbook.)

Buckley, Sam C. *The Marginal Varieties of the Edwardian Stamps of Great Britain, 1902-1912*. (1912. Oswald Marsh, London.)

Doupé, H. S. *A Study of the Cracked Units of the K. E. VII De La Rue One Penny Stamp, 1902-10*. (1962. The Great Britain Philatelic Society, London.)

Harris, Trevor I. *The King Edward VII Price List*. (2003 and subsequent editions. The Hendon Stamp Company.)

Melville, Fred J. *Great Britain: King Edward VII Stamps*. (1911. Melville Stamp Books, London.)

Phillips, Stanley. *Great Britain: The Harrison and Somerset House Printings (1911-1912) and How to Distinguish Them*. (1913. Stanley Gibbons Ltd., London.)

Pusterla, Terry. *King Edward VII One Penny Manual*. (2009. Mike Jackson Publications).

Wiseman, W. A. *Great Britain: The De La Rue-Years 1878-1910 Vol. I.* (1984. Bridger & Kay Ltd., London.)

Wiseman, W. A. *Great Britain: The De La Rue-Years 1878-1910.* (1990. Vol. 2. Stanley Gibbons Publications Ltd., London and Ringwood.)

KING GEORGE V

Beaumont, K. M. and Stanton, J. B. M. *The Postage Stamps of Great Britain, Part IV. The Issues of King George V.* (1957. The Royal Philatelic Society, London.)

Hacket, Alastair. *The 1935 Silver Jubilee Issue of Great Britain.* (1982. Edinburgh Stamp Shop.)

Jackson, Mike. *Downey Head Halfpenny Plating Reference.* (1998. Candlish McCleery Ltd.)

Kearsley, Bryan. *Discovering Seahorses.* (2005. GB Philatelic Publications Ltd.)

Muir, Douglas N. *George V and the G.P.O. Stamps, Conflict and Creativity.* (2010. The British Postal Museum & Archive).

Knight, Donald R. and Sabey, Alan D. *The Lion Roars at Wembley: British Empire Exhibition 60th Anniversary 1924-1925.* (1984. Donald R. Knight, New Barnet, Herts.)

Phillips, Stanley. *The Stamps of Great Britain (1911-1921).* (1921. Stanley Gibbons Ltd.)

Sabey, Alan. *The British Empire Exhibition Stamps of 1924-1925.* (1999. Pamphlet, No. 6 British Philatelic Bulletin. Edinburgh.)

Stanton, J. B. M. and Rushworth, K. G. *King George V. A Study of the Provisional Issues of 1934 and 1935.* (1960. Stanley Gibbons Ltd., London on behalf of the Great Britain Philatelic Society.)

Stitt-Dibden, W. G. *Selected Works. Vol. I. Wembley & Olympic Issues.* (No date. The Postal History Society and the G.B. Philatelic Society, London.)

Vallancey, Hugh. *Check List of British Photogravure and Jubilee Stamps, 1934-36.* (1936. The Vallancey Press, London.)

Vallancey, Hugh. *Check List of British Photogravure Stamps of King George V including Stamps overprinted for Morocco.* (1939. The Vallancey Press, London.)

Wilkinson, Leslie. *King George V Stamps Issued in Rolls.* (1998. The Great Britain Philatelic Society, London.)

KING EDWARD VIII

Kirk, A. J. *King Edward VIII. A Study of the Stamps of the Reign of King Edward VIII.* A revised edition of J. B. M. Stanton's book. (1974. 2nd Edn. The Great Britain Philatelic Society, London.)

Stanton, J. B. M. *King Edward VIII. A Study of the Stamps of the Reign of King Edward VIII.* (1958. The Great Britain Philatelic Society, London.)

KING GEORGE VI

Anon. *A Catalogue of Cylinder Flaws on King George VI Great Britain Commemoratives.* (1954. Crabtree Press, Brighton.)

Bater, Gerry. *Waterlow Procedures. King George VI "Arms to Festival" High Values. Design to Press.* (1992. The Author, Bridgewater, Somerset.)

Bert, A. L. *Great Britain: Check List of King George VI Controls and Cylinder Numbers, 1937-1954.* (1954. West Croydon.)

Birch, L. *Great Britain: The Coronation Stamp, 1937. Its Aberrations, Flaws and Abnormalities.* (No date. Midland Stamp Co., Birmingham.)

Langston, Colin W. and Corless, H. C. *Stamps of Great Britain issued in Rolls and the Machines which Use Them. An Historical Survey including a Check List of the Rolls issued since 1938.* (1961. The Authors, London.)

Stitt-Dibden, W. G. *Selected Works. Vol. I. Wembley & Olympic Issues.* (No date. The Postal History Society and the G.B. Philatelic Society, London.)

Worsfold, Peter. *Great Britain King George VI Low Value Definitive Stamps (2001.* The Great Britain Philatelic Society, London.)

BOOKLETS AND BOOKLET PANES

Alexander, Jean and Newbery, Leonard F. *British Stamp Booklets. Part I, Series I; Part 2, Series 1/2; Part 3, Series 3/5; Part 4, Series 6; Part 5, Series 7; Part 6, Series 8/9; Part 7, Series 10/11; Part 8, Appendix A and B; Part 9, Appendix C, Addenda & Corrigenda and Index* (1987-97 in nine parts. The Great Britain Philatelic Society, London.) Parts 4/7 contain information on booklets issued from 1951/70.

Wilson, Graham. *An Illustrated Guide to the GB Advertising Booklet Panes of George V, Edward VIII and George VI (CD).* The Author, Lancashire (2007).

POSTAGE DUES

Furfie, Michael. *British Postage Due Mail, 1914-1971.* (1993. The Author, Middx.)

"SPECIMEN" STAMPS

Samuel, Marcus and Huggins, Alan. *Specimen Stamps and Stationery of Great Britain.* (1980. The Great Britain Philatelic Society, London.)

POSTMARKS

Alcock, R. C. and Holland, F. C. *British Postmarks. A Short History and Guide.* (1978. 2nd. Edn. R. C. Alcock Ltd., Cheltenham. Combines three earlier works by the same authors.)

Bennett, J. Bruce, Parsons, Cyril, R. H. and Pearson, G. R. *Current Machine Postmarks of the United Kingdon.* (1963. British Postmark Society, London.)

Brummell, G. *British Post Office Numbers, 1884-1906.* (1946. R. C. Alcock Ltd., Cheltenham.)

Brummell, G. *Postmarks of the British Isles. A Short History with Notes on Collecting.* (1930. Bournemouth Guardian Ltd., Bournemouth.)

Cohen, Stanley, F. and Rosenblat, Daniel G. *Squared Circle Postmarks of the London Suburban District Offices.* (1983. Harry Hayes, Batley, West Yorkshire.)

Holland, F. C. *Introduction to British Postmark Collecting.* (1971.)

Langston, Colin M. *Surcharged and Explanatory Dies of Great Britain.* (1964. The Author.)

Mackay, James A. *Scottish Postmarks 1693-1978.* (1978. The Author, Dumfries.)

Mackay, James A. *English and Welsh Postmarks since 1840.* (1988. 2nd Edn. The Author, Dumfries.)

Mackay, James A. *British Post Office Numbers 1924-1969.* (1981. The Author, Dumfries.)

Mackay, James A. *Irish Postmarks since 1840.* (1982. The Author, Dumfries.)

Mackay, James A. *The Parcel Post of the British Isles.* (1982. The Author, Dumfries.)

Mackay, James A. *Registered Mail of the British Isles.* (1983. The Author, Dumfries.)

Mackay, James A. *Official Mail of the British Isles.* (1983. The Author, Dumfries.)

Mackay, James A. *Surcharged Mail of the British Isles.* (1984. The Author, Dumfries.)

Parsons, Cyril R. H., Peachey, Colin G. and Pearson, George R. *Collecting Slogan Postmarks.* (1986. The Authors, Aylesbury.) (Includes listings of slogan postmarks, 1917-69.)

Peach, Jack. *U.K. Machine Marks.* (1982. 2nd. Edn. Vera Trinder Ltd., London.)

Peachey, Colin G. and Swanborough, John. *Special Event Postmarks of the United Kingdom.* (1992. 4th. Edn. Vol. I. British Postmark Society, London.)

Pearson, George R. *Special Event Postmarks of the United Kingdom.* Vol. I "The Early Years" 1851-1962 (1991. 4th. Edn. British Postmark Society, Herts.)

APPENDIX 9 *Further Reading*

Pipe, W. (Ed). *Collect British Postmarks.* (2013. 9th Edu. Stanley Gibbons Ltd).
Reynolds, Paul. *The Machine Cancellations of Wales 1905-1985.* (1985. Welsh Philatelic Society, Swansea.)
Swan, V. *British Slogan Cancellations, 1917-1960.* (1960. The Author, Alton.)

CHANNEL ISLANDS

Backman, A. and Forrester, R. *The Postage Stamps of the Smaller Channel Islands.* (1989. Ilford.)
Cruickshank, Charles. *The German Occupation of The Channel Islands.* (1975. London.) Official history, non-philatelic.
Danan, Yves Maxime. *Emissions Locales et Affranchissements de Guerre des Iles da la Manche.* (1969. Paris.)
Danan, Yves Maxime. *Histoire Postale des Isles de la Manche, Tome 1 and Tome 2.* (1976 and 1978. Paris.)
Griggs, Ian. *The 1942 Jersey ½d. Arms; a Plating Study.* (1982. Ilford.)
Harris, R. E. *Islanders Deported Parts 1 and 2.* (1980. Chippenham.)
Mayne, Richard. *Mailships of the Channel Islands 1771-1971.* (1971. Chippenham.)
McKenzie, Donald. *The Red Cross Mail Service for Channel Island Civilians 1940-145.* (1975. Chippenham.)
Möhle, Heinz. *Die Briefmarken von den Kanel-Inseln; Guernsey und Jersey. Deutsche Besetzung 1940-45.* (1970. Frankfurt.)
Newport, William. *Stamps and Postal History of the Channel Islands.* (1972. London.)
Stanley Gibbons. *Channel Islands Postal History Catalogue* (1991).
Trotter, J. M. Y. *"Early Guernsey Postal History and Private Agents for Guernsey Letters." Transactions of the Société Guernesaise,* 1950. *Postal History Society Bulletin,* 1950.
Wieneke, M. *The German Field Post Office in the Channel Islands.* (1981. Jersey.)

CINDERELLA

Chatfield, Chris. *Great Britain Commemorative Labels Pre-1950.* (1991. Cinderella Stamp Club. Handbook No. 8.)

Why Don't You Take My RISK-FREE £55 to Spend New Client Trial Offer?

If YOU Buy at Auction this is How You Can Save £250+ EACH Year

INCLUDING "FOUR KINGS"

... I'll Give You £55 to get you started PLUS

(... some Collectors Save thousands of pounds)

ANDREW PROMOTING PHILATELY ON THE ALAN TITCHMARSH SHOW ITV

In all my 40+ years in the trade I have never seen an introductory offer to new clients like this .. so you may be wondering the reason why my company UPA can afford to make this offer to you?

In *'plain talk'* most auctions charge 'Buyers Premiums' –YES! You have to pay up to 25% (some charge more) **on top of the *winning price you paid***. That is Simply an Incredible surcharge. Apparently this significant premium is justified by charging the seller a lower fee in order to entice consignments for sale.

My company UPA does not charge any premiums which is one of the reasons why we hold the UK record of 2,031 different bidders in our last auction – an amazing 88% of whom were successful. Fortunately the average bidder spends an average of £250+ per auction...so that with 4 auctions a year offering 80,000+/- lots from £1 to £100,000 for you to choose from ....

with NO Buyer's Premium You Save up to £250+ EACH YEAR PLUS You take NO RISK with our 28 day unconditional Guarantee

So How can U P A offer Your 1st £55 Auction Winnings FREE ?

1. **Our Business Model is Different.** Fundamentally I believe that if a stamp/philatelic item is not selling then it is too expensive. Compare that with the stamp business whose stock is the same each time you see or hear from them. At the risk of boring you …

2. **Stamp Industry's BIGGEST problem.** … twenty years ago I started to ponder upon what is the biggest problem faced by the average stamp dealer? The answer came back loud and clear. The biggest problem faced by a stamp dealer is not what sells … **but what does not sell**. This is the reason why most stamp dealers have lots of unsold stock you have seen time and time again – worse still this is what prevents that dealer from buying new stock to offer you.

3. **Surface Sell.** There is an actual name for this – it is called 'surface sell' – good material 'floats' on the surface and sells. Less desirable stock sinks so that unless a dealer pays almost nothing to replace his stock then the profit in the business becomes stagnant and bound in less saleable stock. If only that dealer could move this stock he would have more money to invest in new stock to offer to you.

4. **Cover-up.** Twenty years ago almost the entire stamp industry spent its time disguising what did not sell – in those days so pernicious were 'unsolds' that it was common practice for one auction house to sell batches of 'unsolds' to another auction where the new auction could present them to (hopefully) different collectors as new lots. 'Passing the Philatelic Parcel' was common practice.

5. **E-Bay.** Today the philatelic world is almost unrecognisably different. In large part courtesy of the internet. How things have changed. Few 'pass the parcel'. Really active Dealers - these days they **also** sell on eBay - large lots, small lots, all manner of stamps, covers, down to fakes and forgeries – today's equivalent of the Wild West – there's philatelic 'gold' to be mined in those hills … but Boy – you have to work to find it and sadly 'all that glistens is not gold' – you pays your money and you takes your chance often with little support or recourse. UPA too sells surpluses on eBay backed by support and our guarantee – access eBay links via *www.upastampauctions.co.uk*

Continued overleaf 👉

NEW OFFER CLOSES NEXT JUNE

"This is My Promise to You ..

Massive Philatelic Choice in a Unique Reducing Estimate System Delivering VAL-YOU, with Absolutely NO Buyer's Premium and PLUS ALL lots Guaranteed"

Andrew McGavin, Managing Director Universal Philatelic Auctions

Our Business Model is Different ...

6. **You said that before**. **So Just How does UPA differ?** We looked for solutions to the 'unsolds' problem – if we could solve that problem we would sell more, utilise stock more efficiently and have funds available for new stock ... and so we created ...

7. **Selling Systems**. It is a 'given' you can order sets / singles in *standard condition* from dealers ... but the moment a stamp becomes used, or even mounted mint it is no longer standard. Is it heavy hinged, is the cancel parcel, wavy or CDS (circular date stamp)? Each stamp requires separate handling and unique pricing so the only way to handle such efficiently is in a selling system.

8. **Integrated Selling Systems**. Avon & Omniphil Approvals - 20 years ago our business sold in 2 different selling systems: individually priced stamps upon home **approval** and **unit priced** 'loose' stamps sent to collectors as *mixtures* (today you can still request either / both on-line from the UPA website below). A bit like 'Water-Works' and 'Electricity' in monopoly the 2 systems allowed us to buy more, sell more and pay higher prices to obtain better stock ... but we had no outlet for rarer / high value stamps so ...

9. **Universal Philatelic Auctions**. ... 15 years ago we created and added **UPA** to allow us to handle more valuable stamps not suited to Approvals, but we knew that in order to eliminate the 'unsolds' issue we needed to come up with a further unique selling proposition ...

10. **Best of Conventional Auctions**. ... so we scoured the stamp world for best practice ideas and all of the features that collectors like you love - such as lots unconditionally guaranteed or dislike such as pernicious buyer's premiums. UPA employed all of the best features and then carefully added unique features such as ...

11. **Standardised Airmail Shipping, Insurance Included.** ... so that no matter how much you win you'll know in advance exactly how much delivery will be ... (and we made it modest too) ... finally, and this is the **painful part** we had to recognise that if something was not selling it was too expensive ... so ...

12. **Unique UPA Reducing Estimate System.** ...we created the unique *UPA Reducing Estimate System*. Creating transparency we grabbed the bull by the horns telling you how many times a lot has been previously unsold at the end of each description ... and although we initially set to reduce by 10% each time unsold ... we didn't; in practice we reduce by 11%, then a further 12%, 13%, 14% each time re-offered and so on till sold or given away ...

13. **Today, almost 15 years later.** ... but would it work? ... Today almost 15 years later the *UPA reducing estimate system* **is unique to the trade** and 2,031 different collectors and some dealers bid in our last auction – 88% of whom were successful. Fusing all of the synergies of integrated selling systems combined with the most efficient use of stamps in the industry the system works thanks to loyal support from Collectors like you. Collectors tend to stay with UPA but as clients come and sadly some go ... we need to attract new clients joining to maintain the integrity of the system which is why ...

... which is Why I'll Give Your 1st £55 to get You Started!

www.upastampauctions.co.uk   **info@upastampauctions.co.uk**

– send the coupon / simply request in any way today!–

OR VIEW / BID ON-LINE NOW – we'll take your £55 off

Do it Today
£1st 55 FREE
REQUEST FREE CATALOGUE TODAY

NEW CLIENTS

Name..
Address..
....
....
Postcode.................Tel.....................
Country..
Email..

(GB 4KGS)

£1st 55 FREE

Universal Philatelic Auctions
(GB 4KGS)

4 The Old Coalyard,
West End
Northleach, Glos.
GL54 3HE UK
T: 01451 861111
F: 01451 861297

Offer open to Collectors aged 18+ in UK, USA, Canada, New Zealand, Australia and West Europe

Returning UPA client? Not purchased for 12 months: £26 deducted if you spend more than £52, mention offer when requesting catalogue

DO YOU COLLECT GREAT BRITAIN?

OUR MONTHLY RETAIL PRICE LIST...
Covers all issues from SG No. 1. Queen Victoria issues through to Queen Elizabeth II. At any one time, we expect to have in stock most of the stamps listed in this catalogue, so if you want to fill those blank spaces, we cordially invite you to ...

SEND FOR A FREE COPY OF OUR LATEST LIST!!

PRIVATE TREATY CATALOGUES...
Aimed at the more serious collector, **these profusely illustrated listings** are extremely popular and are issued twice monthly, they contain a wide selection of **better Singles, Rarities, Proofs, Colour Trials, High Values, Multiples, Pre-stamp, Cinderella and much other specialised material...**
Seldom offered elsewhere!!

FREE — MAY WE SEND YOU A COPY OF OUR LATEST CATALOGUE SO THAT YOU CAN SEE FOR YOURSELF WHAT YOU ARE MISSING. PLEASE WRITE, FAX OR PHONE US NOW! OR VISIT OUR WEBSITE : http://www.gbstamps.co.uk

INTERNET — To view our complete G.B. Listing, and our Private Treaty Catalogue visit our new **easy to use** website: http://www.gbstamps.co.uk

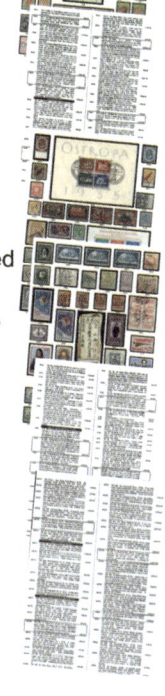

THE NO. 1 MAIL-ORDER PEOPLE!!

Arthur Ryan & Co.
OF RICHMOND

PO BOX 920 RICHMOND. SURREY. TW9 9FN
TELEPHONE: 020 8940 7777   FAX: 020 8940 7755
Email: sales@gbstamps.co.uk

CORBITTS

PUBLIC AUCTIONS
ALWAYS INCLUDE EXTENSIVE GREAT BRITAIN

Our Public Sales include interesting and unusual material, with individual collections offered intact, specialised ranges, better singles or sets and Postal History.

Visit www.corbitts.com for Great Britain Direct Sales, Private Treaty & stock items regularly updated with new material

CORBITTS

5 Mosley Street, Newcastle upon Tyne, NE1 1YE
Tel: 0191 232 7268 Fax: 0191 261 4130
Email: info@corbitts.com Website: www.corbitts.com

COMPLIMENTARY CATALOGUE AVAILABLE ON REQUEST

Members of: Philatelic Traders Society • American Stamp Dealers Association • American Philatelic Society